# Environmental Legislation

edited by
# Mary Robinson Sive

The Praeger Special Studies program—utilizing the most modern and efficient book production techniques and a selective worldwide distribution network—makes available to the academic, government, and business communities significant, timely research in U.S. and international economic, social, and political development.

# Environmental Legislation
## A Sourcebook

**PRAEGER PUBLISHERS**
**Praeger Special Studies**

New York     •     London     •     Sydney     •     Toronto

Library of Congress Cataloging in Publication Data
Main entry under title:

Environmental legislation.

    (Praeger special studies in U.S. economic, social, and
political issues)
    Bibliography: p.
    1.  Environmental law—United States.  I.  Sive, Mary
Robinson, 1928-
KF3775.E54               344'.73'046          75-61
ISBN 0-275-05470-5

PRAEGER PUBLISHERS
383 Madison Avenue, New York, N.Y. 10017, U.S.A.

Published in the United States of America in 1977
by Praeger Publishers,
A Division of Holt, Rinehart and Winston, CBS, Inc.

89   038   9876543

Printed in the United States of America

To the memory

of

Ruth Gillette Hardy

# FOREWORD:
## THE FRONTIERS
## OF THE NATIONAL
## ENVIRONMENTAL
## POLICY ACT
Irving Like

Citizens have gained the right to, and can—with the aid of the National Environmental Policy Act (NEPA) and other statutes providing substantive protection of the nation's air, water, and natural resources—use the litigation process (court suits and administrative agency proceedings) to participate more effectively in major governmental and corporate decision-making processes governing the production and consumption of much of the goods and services that are reflected in the gross national product.

NEPA declared that it is national policy to protect and enhance the environment. Its principal action-forcing provision is its requirement of preparation and publication of an environmental impact assessment of all "major Federal actions significantly affecting the human environment." This includes most private projects in which there is a significant federal fiscal or regulatory role. NEPA requires five elements to be in environmental impact statements (EIS): the positive impact of a proposed project, any adverse impact, alternatives to the project, a comparison of short-term uses of resources versus long-range productivity, and any potential irreversible commitment of resources.

Broad judicial interpretation of NEPA has made it possible for citizens, granted standing before federal courts and administrative agencies, to examine the inner workings of the market economy of the United States as it interfaces with the federal government, industry by industry, from the raw material extraction phase across the entire spectrum of fabrication, conversion of materials, transportation of materials and finished products, their end uses, and ultimate waste disposal.

NEPA gave citizens a broad new base on which to challenge administrative decisions of federal agencies. The 1946 Administrative Procedure Act (5 U.S.C. 552 et seq.) came into use by citizens in the mid-1960s as a tool for intervention in the decision-making

---

Irving Like is a partner of Reilly, Like & Schneider, Babylon, New York. He has represented Suffolk County in proceedings on application of the Long Island Lighting Company to construct atomic plants and in litigation against the U.S. Department of the Interior regarding proposed Outer Continental Shelf oil and gas drilling. He drafted New York's Conservation Bill of Rights (p. 238).

process. Under it they can participate in scientific evidentiary hearings of either a rule-making or an adjudicatory nature. A succession of cases, both before and after NEPA, culminating in Sierra Club v. Morton (405 U.S. 727 [1972]) and Aberdeen and Rockfish Railroad Company v SCRAP (412 U.S. 669 [1973]), gradually shifted the rule of the federal courts so as to grant persons with little or no economic interest but with a demonstrated public concern the standing to bring suit and to intervene in the federal courts.

The number of NEPA cases is large, and it is not easy to abstract those that are the most important in terms of defining the nature and scope of the inquiry into the decision-making process. However, some cases may be considered landmarks in delineating the standards governing the agency's decision-making processes and, thereby, the scope of the citizens' right to participate therein. Calvert Cliffs Coordinating Committee v. AEC (449 F.2d 1109 [1971]), sets forth guidelines with which the agency's decision-making process must comply. It must:

- Comply strictly with NEPA's procedural requirements.
- Assess economic and technical benefits and weigh them against environmental costs.
- Engage in a finely tuned and systematic balancing analysis at key points in the decision-making process.

Another key case is Natural Resources Defense Council v. Morton (458 F.2d 827 [1972]). It requires the "lead" agency to discuss all alternatives and their environmental effects subject to a rule of reason, including alternatives over which it has no control and that may require important actions by other agencies. In Scientists' Institute for Public Information v. AEC (481 F.2d 1079 [1973]), it was held that an environmental impact statement is required for an entire program in place of or in addition to statements for individual projects in the program, and that the AEC's breeder reactor program required such a program statement.

Committee for Nuclear Responsibility v. Schlesinger (463 F.2d 783 [1971]), ruled that responsible scientific opinion in conflict with the agency opinion must be disclosed in the impact statement.

The agency must provide an affirmative record sufficient for adequate judicial review (Environmental Defense Fund v. Froehlke, 473 F.2d 346 [1972]). The Environmental Protection Agency must fully explicate the agency's course of inquiry, its analysis, and its reasoning, and it may not be used as a promotional document in favor of the project, at the expense of a thorough and rigorous analysis of environmental risks (Brooks v. Volpe, 350 F. Supp. 269 [1972]; aff'd. 487 F.2d 1344 [1973]).

Finally there are the cases holding that NEPA creates substantive rights of action under which the agency's decision can be challenged on the merits. These cases ruled that NEPA is more than an environmental full disclosure law, that it was intended to effectuate substantive changes in decision making, and that the court has an obligation to review substantive agency decisions on the merits, under the arbitrary and capricious standard (EDF v. Corps of Engineers, 470 F.2d 289 [1972]).

We turn now to the decision-making process as it affects the relations and impacts of production and consumption. We begin with the self-evident premise that the federal government and the major corporations dominate the economic life of the United States and together are responsible for the production and consumption of most of its goods and services. Hence, if most of their activities are subject to NEPA, as we maintain they are, and if citizens have won the right to participate in the decision-making processes that govern such production and consumption, then citizens indeed can influence such decisions by making full use of NEPA.

The production, distribution, and consumption of commodities necessitate the use of space, minerals, metals, fibers, food, air, water, energy, and other resources. Ultimately all production and consumption depend on the use of energy. Energy sources include coal, oil, natural gas, and nuclear fission, as well as such emerging energy technologies as coal gasification and liquefaction, oil shale, solvent-refined coal, fluidized bed boiler combustion of coal, and solar and geothermal energy. All energy systems have impacts on the environment resulting from wastes associated with the full range of activities incident to the generation of electricity and the production and consumption of other goods and services. The oil, coal, and nuclear fuel cycles discharge noxious gaseous and liquid substances at each step from their extraction or mining to the point when the fuel is used to produce electric power. The production and consumption of electricity itself emits toxic wastes that must be safely managed or disposed of.

In addition, these fuels are used in the residential, commercial, and industrial sectors of the economy for various purposes, including transportation, heating, and as a petrochemical base for many end products that generate their own pollutants. Since energy is essential to production and consumption activities, the NEPA assessment of environmental impacts associated with energy supply and use also provides the means for NEPA analysis of the environmental and socioeconomic consequences of the modes of production and consumption. Energy systems that are governed by federal laws and federal agencies are thereby subject to NEPA. These include hydroelectric plants and nuclear plants.  They also include energy systems that depend upon uses of federal public lands.

Inquiry into such broad subjects as need, alternatives, costs, and benefits extends the reach of NEPA far beyond ecology and into the realm of the socioeconomic effects of the project.  This can be illustrated by the striking example of the nuclear power plant siting cases in which the NEPA issues include the impact of the facility on public health and safety, air and water quality, and terrestrial and aquatic ecology.  Scientific and technical evidence is received from experts representing many disciplines as to the design, construction, and operation of the proposed plant, its routine and accidental discharges of gaseous, liquid, and solid wastes, and their transport, pathways, and probable ecological and health-related effects.

Another NEPA issue is whether the proposed electric generating units are needed.  This entails an inquiry into the utility's forecase of power demand, and the historic and probable future patterns of electricity consumption in its service area.  Relevant to this investigation are demographic data and projections as to population growth, zoning, land use patterns, and industrial, commercial, and residential development.  Whether or not future power demand can be reduced by energy conservation, greater efficiency in energy utilization, or redesign of rate structure to discourage wasteful consumption of electricity is also considered in the evidentiary proceeding.

The cost/benefit balancing process required by NEPA becomes acutely important at this point.  Will measures designed to reduce future electric power consumption injure the utility financially, slow down economic growth in the area served by the utility, and decrease employment or hurt business?  On the other hand, will energy conservation, more efficient use of electricity, and more equitable rate schedules stabilize electric rates or slow their increase or reduce inflation?  Obviously the issue of need generates difficult questions dealing with socioeconomic trade-offs, future land use planning in the community, and value judgments as to life styles.

Assuming there is a need for the proposed facility, the question then to be decided is whether it should be a nuclear or fossil fuel plant (that is, coal-fired or oil-fired).  This opens the litigation process to determination of the comparative environmental and socioeconomic impacts of each of these methods of generating electric power.  It thus becomes necessary also to evaluate the environmental effects of construction and operation of coal-fired and oil-fired plants; and data must be presented as to their water pollution, air pollution, solid waste, land use, and health effects.

Even more difficult is the problem of determining which means of generating electricity is the most advantageous economically, for this requires an analysis of the economics of the alternative energy systems that embraces their entire trajectories from extraction to ultimate waste disposal or management. Since the construction of each type of plant will take a considerable period of time (coal plant, six years; nuclear plant, eight years), predictions of future capital costs of construction and fuel costs require assumptions as to the annual escalation rate applicable to the cost of money, labor, equipment, and materials, and educated guesses as to the probable inflation rate to be experienced by the economy. In order to predict the probable future cost of nuclear fuel, it is necessary to analyze the economic costs incident to each step of the nuclear fuel cycle, beginning with the mining of uranium and continuing through milling, conversion, enrichment, fuel fabrication, transportation of nuclear materials, transportation of spent fuel, fuel reprocessing, and radioactive waste management.

In arriving at such predictions, assumptions must be made as to availability and future cost of uranium, uranium enrichment, and reprocessing and waste management capacity. A complex computer model of the nuclear fuel industry may be employed to make such projections, and to permit modifications of imput variables that may affect such costs.

To predict the cost of coal, the cost components of its fuel cycle must also be analyzed; those components will reflect costs of production associated with surface and underground mining, mine safety, reclamation, processing, transportation of coal products, and disposal of coal wastes. In the case of oil, the costs of production (reflecting costs of exploration, extraction, refining, transportation, distribution, and waste disposal) cannot be used to predict future oil prices because the prices are cartel-fixed, and a substantial quantity of crude oil comes from foreign imports that are cartel-controlled. If the structure of the coal and uranium industries becomes anticompetitive in the future, projection of the future prices of coal and uranium may become as difficult and uncertain as that of oil.

The scope of NEPA permits inquiry into the market structure of a particular industry to determine whether anticompetitive concentrations or practices exist that affect costs or economic considerations relevant to the NEPA inquiry into alternatives. The extent to which NEPA will allow investigation into antitrust matters significantly affecting the cost/benefit balancing process required by NEPA remains to be charted in future litigation.

NEPA provides a tool for assessing the accelerated Outer Continental Shelf oil and gas leasing program proposed by the Secretary of the Interior, a program that would enter such frontier areas (areas never before drilled for oil and gas) as Atlantic and Alaskan waters.

The potential impacts, both offshore and onshore, are enormous. They begin with exploration and drilling (requiring giant rigs and pro-

duction platforms installed offshore) and proceed through the phases
of transportation of crude oil by tankers or pipeline to shoreline installations, refinery processing and subsequent transportation by
sea, pipeline, truck, or rail to wholesale and retail markets. Their
end uses also generate various pollutants that are injurious to air,
water, and land.

The NEPA issues raised here are on a macro scale that dwarfs
those described in the case of the nuclear power plants. The offshore
oil program is proposed as a means of helping solve national energy
problems by reducing dependence on foreign imported oil. Thus the
NEPA inquiry focuses on the environmental and socioeconomic impacts
associated with national energy supply and national energy demands,
as well as everything relevant to the supply, demand, production, and
consumption of energy. The issues are cosmic. Is there an energy
crisis? What are the domestic reserves of oil and gas, both onshore
and offshore? What will our energy needs be? How much energy can
be saved, or energy demand reduced, through energy conservation
measures, increased gasoline mileage efficiencies in automobiles,
increases in the price of oil, and so forth? What alternative energy
sources are feasible—coal, nuclear fission, solar, geothermal, oil
shale, coal gasification, coal liquefaction, nuclear fusion? Where
shall pipelines, terminals, refineries, petrochemical industries,
and other land-based facilities and infrastructure be built that support
or are related to the offshore production operations? What effect
will the accelerated Outer Continental Shelf (OCS) leasing program
have on our balance of payments, foreign relations, and national
security?

Clearly, this fragmentary listing of NEPA issues, which are
touched on in the draft and final Environmental OCS Programmatic
Statements issued by the Secretary of the Interior, shows dramatically
how the scope of NEPA has expanded to include consideration of political, economic, and social problems on a national and international
level.

The courts have held that NEPA must be read together with other
statutes under which the federal agencies authorize, regulate, build,
finance, or aid various projects and programs, such as highways,
airports, power plants, housing, agriculture, shipping and water resource improvement, and other activities involving public lands and
waterways subject to federal jurisdiction. The reach of NEPA thus
is potentially far beyond what we have thus far seen.

Already NRDC v. SEC (389 F. Supp. 689 [1974]), has forced
the SEC to move toward the adoption of rules obligating corporations
to disclose the environmental effects of their activities. The NEPA
cases already litigated have barely begun to assess the vast bulk of

federal programs and policies from the environmental standpoint. NEPA has yet to be applied in a systematic way to evaluate the environmental impact of the federal exercise of the monetary, credit, fiscal, and taxing powers that promote or create a need for, or a bias in favor of, particular programs or policies. For example, the historical evidence indicates that federal economic policies have favored the use of the automobile and truck over rail transportation, and have contributed to the growth of suburbia while neglecting certain problems of the city.

Whether these were sound policies is still being debated. The fact is that the federal economic decisions resulting in the bias that promoted the automobile, suburbia, and their associated land use patterns were not subjected to a prior NEPA assessment that would have considered and weighed, as part of a litigation process, the environmental and economic data relied upon in favor of the particular policies being sponsored by the federal government. Such a NEPA review could also have considered policies favoring mass transit and rehabilitation of urban areas as alternative priorities.

This is not to suggest that the NEPA litigation process will provide solutions to urban, suburban, and transportation problems. However, the NEPA case does provide an evidentiary forum for presenting the scientific-social-economic issues generated by major federal policies, programs, and projects and their data base.

Furthermore, if fiscal, monetary, credit, and taxing powers of the federal government are being used to stimulate economic growth and increase the gross national product (GNP) without concern for the nature and quality of such growth and the composition of the GNP, such exercise of federal economic powers will contribute substantially to the gross amount of pollution. It is yet to be determined whether NEPA can be applied to assess the environmental effects of the exercise of federal economic power that can be shown to be proximate contributions to the gross amount of pollution.

It should be possible to devise rule-making procedures and, with the aid of computer systems analysis, to model the economic system and its flows of materials, energy, and pollution. The econometricians have developed comprehensive and sophisticated models to forecast economic trends. They employ data input processing and reduction techniques that handle many variables. The art of modeling can be similarly applied to predict the environmental impacts of the totality of production and consumption decisions that constitute our economic system.

Other frontiers of NEPA are equally challenging. Federal agency action impinges on agriculture through regulation and subsidy programs at various stages of food production, processing, distribution, and marketing. It also affects housing through its regulations and policies regarding resource management (such as timber cutting) on public lands and housing construction assistance through federal loans, insurance, and guarantees.

NEPA may be used to assess the environmental and socioeconomic impact of agricultural and housing programs and production at the points of government involvement in their respective raw material/finished product spectra.

For example, through NEPA the federal government may be compelled to disclose the deleterious effects of the use of agricultural chemicals and pesticides in government-subsidized farming operations, or the adverse effects of particular land use patterns created by large government-aided housing projects. In fact, the entire range of federal subsidy programs may be subject to NEPA assessment. This includes maritime subsidies, which provide federal insurance of privately financed ship construction loans and mortgages as well as direct mortgage insurance. A NEPA analysis of these subsidies could expose the extent to which the shipping interests that are benefited by subsidies are complying with federal and state environmental laws regarding design and construction, and the award of a subsidy can be conditioned on the ship owner's demonstrating such compliance or on his agreement to use the best available commercial technology in the design and construction of his vessel in order to prevent environmental pollution, such as that caused by the discharge of oil.

The Internal Revenue Code is a subsidy-laden statute that may also merit NEPA assessment. Its subsidy apparatus takes the form of a system of tax expenditures under which governmental financial assistance programs are carried out through special tax provisions allowing exclusions from income, exemptions, deductions, tax credits, preferential tax rates, and tax deferrals. To what extent is this subsidy structure biased in favor of economic growth and development? Does it contribute to premature obsolescence and scrapping of usable commodities, thereby adding to the waste problem? A NEPA rule-making proceeding could be designed to expose the hidden biases of the subsidy scheme that cause adverse environmental impacts.

The NEPA case may not end in victory for any of its parties. Victory for any particular party may not even be desirable. It may be preferable that a particular policy or project be permitted to proceed, but with certain conditions incorporated in the permit that will avoid or mitigate certain safety or environmental hazards.

Or litigation may be beneficial if it delays the project until further environmental or economic studies are completed, if they are necessary to resolve important uncertainties. NEPA litigation may, if nothing else, heighten public ecological consciousness and set in motion political forces that later gain a legislative remedy.

The NEPA litigation process is unique in that it can be simultaneously a university without walls, disseminating scientific and technical information and applying interdisciplinary cooperation in analyzing environmental and socioeconomic problems and in weighing risks, advantages, costs, and benefits. Thus, the strategy of the NEPA litigation process must always seek not only the environmental objective but also a contribution to public awareness regarding the environmental values to be protected, and the available alternatives and options. The steady accumulation of such public knowledge will inevitably catalyze into appropriate political action not only to gain better protection of the environment but also to focus on the ultimate issues of the compatibility of our market economy institutions with our finite physical resource base, and the need for modes of production and consumption that use the best available state of the art and technology and strive for total recycling and maximum benign energy sources.

The history of environmental legislation appears to reveal a transition from dealing with the effects of pollution to exercising controls over its causes and sources.

It is our theme that the roots of pollution lie in the way goods and services are produced and consumed, and that the NEPA litigation process is a desirable means of spotlighting and reforming the methods of production and consumption.

# ACKNOWLEDGMENTS

In preparing the pages that follow I was fortunate to be able to call on a number of persons with outstanding expertise: Ruth Fleischer, formerly attorney in the General Enforcement Branch, EPA Region II; Anne Donaldson, Executive Director, Federated Conservationists of Westchester County; Professor Stephen O. Wilson, Empire State College, State University of New York; and Paul Bray, Assistant Counsel, Legislative Bill Drafting Commission, New York State Legislature, reviewed the manuscript and it benefited from their critical readings. Dr. Beatrice E. Willard, Member of the President's Council on Environmental Quality, and Donald M. Maclay, Assistant Director of the American Law Institute, extended many courtesies that made research easy. David made it all possible. None of the persons mentioned are, of course, in any way responsible for the book's shortcomings, which are mine.

# CONTENTS

# LIST OF ABBREVIATIONS

| | |
|---|---|
| AEC | Atomic Energy Commission |
| aff'd | affirmed |
| Ann. | annotated |
| APA | Administrative Procedure Act |
| Art. | article |
| CEQ | (President's) Council on Environmental Quality |
| cert. den. | certiorari denied (in effect, affirmed) |
| CFR | Code of Federal Regulations |
| Ch. | chapter |
| Comp. | compiled |
| EDF | Environmental Defense Fund |
| EIS | environmental impact statement |
| EPA | Environmental Protection Agency |
| et seq. | and following |
| FPC | Federal Power Commission |
| F. Reg. | Federal Register (daily publication printing all federal administrative rules and regulations, presidential proclamations, executive orders, and so on; updates the Code of Federal Regulations) |
| F. 2d. | Federal Reporter, second series; reports of decisions of U.S. circuit courts |
| F. Supp. | Federal Supplement; reports of decisions of U.S. district courts |
| FWPCA | Federal Water Pollution Control Act |
| Gen. | general |
| NEPA | National Environmental Policy Act |
| NPDES | National Pollutant Discharge Elimination System |
| NRDC | National Resources Defense Council |
| o.p. | out of print |
| OCS | Outer Continental Shelf |
| ORV | off-road vehicle |
| OSHA | Occupational Safety and Health Administration |
| P. L. | public laws; acts of Congress, numbered consecutively, the first two digits signifying the session |
| Rev. | revised |
| SEC | Securities and Exchange Commission |
| Sec. | section |
| Stat. | statute, statutes |
| SIPI | Scientists' Institute for Public Information |
| Ti. | title |
| U.S. | United States Reports |
| U.S.C. | U.S. Code |
| U.S.C.A. | U.S. Code Annotated |

# GLOSSARY

| | |
|---|---|
| act | a written law, formally passed by Congress or legislature |
| administrative regulation | a rule adopted by an executive or administrative agency pursuant to statute and having the force of law |
| bill | a proposed law |
| Code | a collection of laws, usually arranged according to subject matter |
| Federal Register | daily publication printing all federal administrative rules and regulations, presidential proclamations, executive orders, and so on; update the Code of Federal Regulations |
| Federal Reporter | reports of decisions of U.S. Circuit Courts |
| Federal Supplement | reports of decisions of U.S. District Courts |
| law | a legally enforceable rule |
| session laws | laws enacted by a legislative body at one of its sessions |
| statute | an act of a legislative body |
| United States Reports | reports of decisions of the U.S. Supreme Court |

"There ought to be a law!" is a cry frequently heard from people outraged at some real or imagined misconduct. It was a cry that went up loud and clear as environmental deterioration and mishaps came to public notice in the mid- and late 1960s. The evidence that it has been heard and heeded by our representatives in Congress and the state legislatures is in this book: 150 laws from nearly every state that seek to repair or prevent various types of environmental damage. These laws represent but a tiny fraction of the many thousands of such acts passed, most of them since 1970, by Congress and the state legislatures. They do not even touch the equally large or larger number of ordinances passed by counties, towns, and cities toward the same end, or the numerous treaties promulgated by international bodies and ratified by the U.S. Senate.

Laws, of course, are only the beginning. Putting a law on the books does not necessarily put it into effect. And environmental law, like any other body of law, is a mix of legislative enactments, case law, and administrative regulations. Environmental law originated with case law. But legislation is the beginning. It provides the starting point for action by the executive branch and interpretation by the judiciary. It provides the tools for political action.

This volume gives a sampling of environmental laws at the federal and state levels, plus some state constitutional provisions, presidential executive orders, and administrative regulations. Since it only deals with statutory law, it is not a text or treatise on environmental law.

In a democratic society law must be assumed to embody the values that society holds dear. The concepts in some of the legislative findings and declarations quoted here may come as a surprise to many. Statements must of course be measured against the extent to which they are put into practice. Contrasting officially adopted values and actual operating procedures can be a valuable lesson and educators wishing to expose their students to such lessons will find source material here.

Energy emergencies and construction industry slumps of recent years brought on premature predictions of the death of the environmental movement. There are enough 1974 and 1975 enactments quoted in the pages to follow to make it clear that such is hardly the case. Much of the important legislation, however, was passed in the early 1970s. The present seems a good time to look back and take stock.

That this book tries to do.  It gives nonlawyers and those concerned
with public affairs or involved in the political process some idea of
the scope of environmental problems addressed by legislation and the
solutions attempted.  Environmental law courses offered at under-
graduate and continuing education institutions will find it a reference
guide to the subject matter covered in such courses and a finding tool
for further information.  Citations throughout the text and appendixes
will enable the reader to extend research as needed.


## LAWS AND THEIR ADMINISTRATION

That laws are subject to interpretation by the courts is well-
known.  We are perhaps less aware of how much laws are subject to
interpretation by administrative agencies.  Citizens are often urged
to "write your Congressman."  They would do well to maintain contact
with enforcing agencies as well.  The opportunity for citizen participation by use of the federal Administrative Procedure Act is better-
known to regulated industries than to the average voter.  It has been
used to further suburban environmental interests more than those of
the cities.
Judicial interpretation and refinement of major congressional
acts have been of the utmost importance in the development of environmental law.  Now that there is a massive body of environmental
statutes on the books, the scene of the action is shifting from the
courts to the administrative agencies where factual questions are determined.  These determinations often make the real impact.


## HOW EFFECTIVE ARE ENVIRONMENTAL LAWS?

Estimates of the effectiveness of environmental legislation vary,
depending on who is doing the estimating.  Activists may feel that
more potent laws are needed, while those subject to their requirements
may consider existing laws confiscatory.
The effectiveness of any law is to an extent determined by public
demands, pressures, and opinions.  Enforcing agencies do not operate in a political vacuum.  They are responsive to election results,
to editorial opinion, and to release of information through the mass
media.  They are governed by judicial interpretations.  The Atomic
Energy Commission, for instance, long maintained a competent environmental analysis section in its organization, but gave that section
little input into decision making until forced to do so by the court decision in Calvert Cliffs.

Agencies may not command the range of skills, or the funding, needed to assemble all data pertinent to the decisions they must make. The private sector is thus frequently in a position to supply valid data. Agencies interact with the public in their day-to-day processes. In addition to requirements of the federal Administrative Procedure Act, many of the federal laws cited below have specific provisions for hearings and consultations with interested parties before action may be taken.

So do many state laws. The federal Freedom of Information Act, as amended in 1975, and comparable state "sunshine laws" offer additional avenues, underused by the general public.

Citizen suits are a part of the enforcement scenario of several of the laws cited in the pages that follow. Absent such provisions, the right of persons without a financial interest to sue for governmental enforcement is established in the federal courts and in several states.


## FACTORS DETERMINING A LAW'S EFFECTIVENESS

Whether a law is to be administered by an existing agency or by a new one, perhaps created expressly for its purpose, can be quite significant. The old-line agency may have little determination to be aggressive.

Laws cannot be fully effective if insufficient money is appropriated for their enforcement. The level of funding by Congress or state legislature may tell the real story, not the high-sounding language of the preamble.

The true significance of a statute may turn on an innocuous-seeming word or phrase, such as "healthful," "reasonable," "public interest," "feasible," or "prudent." The Safe Drinking Water Act refers to contaminants that "may" be dangerous to health. "No person 'shall' . . . " indicates a law with teeth, if that provision is coupled with fairly prohibitive penalties.

But a law may also be so harsh as not to be enforced at all. And a poorly worded statute may be as ineffective as one that attempts an unworkable regulatory scheme.


## DEVELOPMENT OF ENVIRONMENTAL LAW

The Storm King Mountain case (Scenic Hudson Preservation Conference v. FPC, 354 F.2d 608 [1965], cert. den. 384 U.S. 941 [1966]), is generally considered to mark the beginnings of environmental law as a separate branch of law. In that case the Second Circuit Court of Appeals recognized the right of conservation groups to intervene, and instructed the Federal Power Commission to take into account environmental impacts of a proposed power plant and its alternatives before granting a license to construct.

At approximately the same time, citizen groups began looking at older laws governing navigable waters, national forests, national parks, and other areas, and developing new interpretations. An outstanding example was a law that had been in existence for more than 60 years and required Army Corps of Engineers permits for discharges of refuse into navigable waters (33 U.S.C. 407). Few, if any, such permits had ever been requested or issued. The law offered reward moneys to anyone bringing violators to justice. (The Federal Water Pollution Control Act [FWPCA] has since partially superseded these provisions).

A landmark year was 1970. The National Environmental Policy Act (NEPA) went into effect January 1. Two new federal agencies, the Environmental Protection Agency and the President's Council on Environmental Quality, began operations.

The National Environmental Policy Act is the most important and the most basic environmental statute. The effects of such a broad law are developed through court cases. The introductory essay by Irving Like explores NEPA's interpretation by the courts, focusing on the procedural requirements for statement preparation, potential scope of matters covered, and the balancing of issues necessary for the plan process to be considered completed.

The year 1970, too, saw the passage of the Clean Air Amendments to "clean air" legislation of 1963, 1965, and 1967. In 1972 Congress passed, over a presidential veto, the Federal Water Pollution Control Act, amending "clean waters" laws dating back to 1948. The earlier federal laws since the 1950s had aimed at achieving pure air and water but had proved relatively ineffectual. The Clean Air Act of 1970 and the FWPCA of 1972 established clear federal dominance of those fields. These two laws, together with NEPA, overshadow all other environmental legislation in importance.

A large body of case law—with public interest law firms responsible for much of it—has extended the reach of those laws into every aspect of the nation's economic life. (A few cases are mentioned in context, in the pages that follow, but a full discussion is outside the scope of this book. Reference is made to Federal Environmental Law or any one of the several treatises mentioned in Appendix D.)

These three pioneering statutes were followed by other congressional action. The states also acted, both pursuant to federal mandates in the air and water laws and in recognition of their own needs. Much state legislation deals with land use, a concern essentially beyond Congress' power. It is this large body of statutory law that is sampled in the pages below.

## SCOPE AND ORGANIZATION OF THE WORK

The main body of this book consists of legislative excerpts grouped in 14 chapters and various subchapters. Interpretive text is intentionally held to a minimum. Each chapter's brief introduction notes the essence of the environmental problem that is its subject, briefly examines the policies employed in attacks on it, and summarizes the regulatory schemes exemplified by the acts then quoted. Topical analyses by the Council on Environmental Quality and other sources serve to introduce the subject matter in some instances. Comments about each legislative excerpt aim to point out its salient features and language. There are also references to laws quoted in other chapters of this book and to others not quoted here at all.

There is no attempt here at assessing the relative successes and failures of environmental legislation. Obviously, some laws are but words on paper while others have far-reaching consequences. The time has come to attempt to gain some perspective on what the environmental effort of the early 1970s has accomplished, failed to accomplish, and possibly even accomplished inadvertently. The Sixth Annual Report (1976) of the Council on Environmental Quality contains a sophisticated examination of whether environmental regulations have cost jobs, as is sometimes alleged. Such an unintended side-effect must certainly go into the equation of what the total effect has been. A comprehensive assessment remains the task of a separate study.

Most of the laws quoted here were passed in the past ten years but some older ones are also significant and are therefore included: portions of the Federal Power Act, because it was the basis for the landmark Scenic Hudson decision; the Refuse Act, because its language opened an avenue for court action to clean up our rivers; the Antiquities Act and other early federal laws demonstrating concern for historic preservation; acts establishing national parks and forests, our foremost national open space resources; the Food, Drug and Cosmetic and Soil Conservation Acts of the 1930s, and others.

The term "environment" is used broadly. The individual topics of the chapters and their subsections do not necessarily comprise all that may be subsumed under this rubric, but they seem to comprise the aspects that have received substantial legislative attention at federal and state levels.

### Method of Selection

In selecting laws for excerpting we have chosen from those in force in late 1975 some that

1. are historically significant:

- NEPA, Executive Order 11514 and CEQ Guidelines, because they form the heart of the all-pervasive federal environmental impact assessment process
- the California Air Resources Act, because it is one of the earliest seeking to control emissions at their source and recognizing the automobile as a major source of air pollution
- the environmental rights section of the Pennsylvania constitution, because it gave rise to litigation involving constitutional interpretation (it did not prevent erection of an observation tower at Gettysburg)
- the Michigan Environmental Protection Act, because it pioneered the concept of the citizen suit as an enforcement tool
- the Hawaii Land Use Act, the first statewide land use controls
- the Vermont Land Use and Development Act, the first such on the mainland
- the Adirondack Park Agency Act (New York), effecting zoning by a regional agency over an area previously largely unzoned
- the Wisconsin Shoreland Zoning Act, the basis for the landmark Just v. Marinette County case
- "forever wild" clauses from the New York Constitution and Baxter State Park legislation in Maine, first official statements, by states, of wilderness values
- the Illinois Act for Preservation of Historical and Other Special Areas, the first transfer of development rights enactment.

2. have fairly stringent requirements and sanctions:

- the Clean Air and Clean Water Acts, because they replaced earlier laws that relied on quasi-voluntary conference and other procedures
- the Flood Disaster Protection Act, because it uses the power of the purse to force local action
- the Consumer Product Safety Act, because of its citizen enforcement section
- the Federal Environmental Pesticide Control Act, because it regulates pesticides at the point of sale
- the Alaska Environmental Conservation Act, because it imposes heavy penalties, including seizure of an offending vessel
- Massachusetts wetland protection laws, because they are coupled with citizen enforcement provisions
- Idaho and Montana mining and geothermal extraction laws, because they require permit and bonding before mining operations may commence
- the Minnesota Metropolitan Council Act, because it mandates review of certain local zoning decisions by a regional body
- the Florida Environmental Land and Water Management Act, because the state government initiates and determines "critical area" designations

• Oregon's Bottle Bill, because it regulates beverage containers at the point of sale.

    3. regulate rather than simply promote study.

Laws that set up commissions to draw up regional plans, to promote recycling, to study areas of environmental concern, to plan transportation systems, and the like abound. Such laws are mentioned in various places in the text. Those chosen for excerpting, with few exceptions, promise to be most effective because they specify required actions. They insure that these actions take place by imposing penalties for noncompliance or provide incentives for compliance. Among exceptions to this are the 1974 energy laws found on pp. 35 ff. and the Resource Recovery Act of 1970.

A "pro-environment" bias is readily admitted.

    Many equally significant state laws are omitted or incorporated only by reference. Some that are quoted do not meet the criteria stated above. The sampling here presented does not attempt to be either comprehensive or rigidly selected but it does strive for geographical balance. To assemble examples of effective environmental legislation, with the possible exception of comprehensive land use legislation, one need hardly go beyond the borders of the three West Coast states. We chose to include some laws from almost every state and from various regions of the United States in order to highlight some perhaps less well-known accomplishments. There is no attempt at comparison of states' efforts. To provide references to all comparable enactments would have added needless length and complexity. The suggestions in Appendix B should enable anyone interested in checking out a particular state's laws to do so.

    With a few exceptions, a given act is excerpted in one chapter only. Sections of it may be relevant to the subjects of other chapters as well and, if so, are mentioned there, generally with page references. Thus, the FWPCA, quoted in Chapter 13, is also relevant to the discussion of land use, of citizen suits, of toxic materials, among others. Commentaries about each excerpted law appear in the general introduction to the chapter where the excerpt appears. The Energy Policy and Conservation Act of 1975 passed Congress just before the end of the year, too late to be available for inclusion. Its provisions are summarized on p. 31.

## Method of Excerpting

    This volume supplies only excerpts, not complete texts. To interpret a law or regulation one must, of course, know its full text. Even the full text is not enough without interpretive materials, however. Since this book is not intended for legal research, excerpting seemed a suitable way of emphasizing significant provisions of an act by deleting some of its more technical portions. This also enabled us to accommodate a larger number of statutes than would otherwise have been possible.

The number of pages devoted to a particular statute bears no relation to its significance. If such a principle had been followed, no more than 10 percent of the pages could in good conscience have been devoted to laws other than the Clean Air Act, NEPA, and FWPCA.

In choosing portions of a statute to excerpt, we have attempted to include

1. Legislative findings and declarations of policy. These are not necessarily the most significant sections, from a lawyer's point of view, but they do express the legislative body's intent and are of-ficial policy.

2. Major substantive provisions indicating the basic regulatory scheme of the act. This includes what is prohibited, what is ordered done, for what actions permits are required, what the penalties for violations are.

3. Language held significant by courts and authoritative com-mentators, including "sleepers," that is, phrases or clauses whose full potential import may not have been fully realized or intended at the time of passage:

- Section 803 of the Federal Power Act, because of its significance in the Scenic Hudson case;
- Section 102 of NEPA (42 U.S.C. 4332), the environmental impact statement requirement and the basis for an extensive body of case law partially alluded to in the introductory essay;
- Section 301 of the Federal Water Pollution Control Act (33 U.S.C. 1311), requiring application of "best practicable" and "best avail-able" technology for water pollution control;
- "best available technology" requirements of the Noise Control and Deepwater Port Acts (42 U.S.C. 4905[c] and 33 U.S.C. 1503[c][5], respectively);
- the Lead-Based Paint Poisoning Prevention Act, because a court held up housing construction that did not comply;
- Section 208 (of the Federal Water Pollution Control Act (33 U.S.C. 1288), with its potential for an important federal role in state land use decisions;
- Section 4(f) of the Department of Transportation Act (49 U.S.C. 1653[f]), which has profoundly affected federal highway programs;
- Section 7 of the Endangered Species Act of 1973 (16 U.S.C. 1536), whose reach is as yet untested.

4. Especially significant definitions:
- "navigable waters" in the FWPCA (Sec. 1362);
- "take" in the Endangered Species Act (Sec. 1532);
- "primary drinking water regulation" in the Safe Drinking Water Act (Sec. 300f);
- "known geothermal resources area" in the Geothermal Steam Act (Sec. 1001);
- "coastal environment," "marine environment," "adjacent coastal state," in the Deepwater Port Act (Sec. 1502);
- "development" in the Florida and Vermont land use acts;
- "project" in the California Environmental Quality Act (Sec. 21065).

We have attempted to exclude
- definitions of "person," "state," and the like.
- enumerations of powers to make contracts, appoint staff, and so on.
- exceptions, exemptions.
- technical and procedural provisions: how to obtain a permit, how to apply for a grant, appeals procedures, funding formulas, time-tables.
- enforcement procedures, except for citizen suit and citizen partici-pation provisos and liability statements that invoke marketplace controls.
- occasional entire sections of statutes, as in the case of the Clean Air Act, where focus is on the operative provisions rather than on those promoting research.
- compiler's notes and comments establishing effective dates and legislative history.
- session laws and other alternate citations.

It should be noted that portions of statutes not chosen for inclu-sion here may be those of paramount importance in determining poli-tical and court strategy. The sections found here are not intended for use in making such determinations.

The full text of all enactments chosen for excerpting may be found easily. Citations to the U.S. Code and to state codes are sup-plied at the head of the excerpted text (see List of Abbreviations). We have chosen to supply those whenever possible rather than cita-tions to annual compilations of enactments, simply because of the readier availability of code publications in general libraries. This results in the well-known (to the environmental professions) Section 102 of NEPA appearing as Section 4332 (and Section 208 of the FWPCA as Section 1288), but should pose no hardship to the intended lay audience.

Excerpts in most cases follow a uniform format: official title of the act, year of adoption, code citation (consistent with legal practice, number of title appears before the name of the code, "et seq." is used in place of "ff."), listing of the act's sections with their headings (comparable with a table of contents). The excerpted matter follows, with ellipses showing omissions except where this is self-evident.

While every effort has been made to supply correct text with amendments through September 1975, there is no claim here to absolute accuracy. The information in this volume does not in any case purport to state the law on any of the subjects encompassed. To find that, standard legal research sources must be consulted.

The publisher has corrected obvious typing errors in the texts of laws and regularized punctuation and capitalization for titles and headings of laws.

# Environmental Legislation

Air pollution is as old as industrialization. In recent years we have come to know that unseen pollution by chemical agents may be as dangerous as and more invidious than the visible pollution by particles contained in smoke. The history of efforts to deal with air pollution is summarized in the following excerpt from the Third Annual Report of the Council on Environmental Quality (pp. 202-03):

Early efforts to combat air pollution represented local response to citizen clamor over what today is recognized as only one aspect of air pollution—smoke emissions from fossil fuels, primarily coal. Chicago and Cincinnati led the way with smoke control laws in 1881. By 1912, 23 of the 28 cities with populations over 200,000 had similar laws. Although specific State enabling legislation sometimes was needed and a few States involved themselves directly in control programs, regulation for the most part remained a local concern until the mid-fifties. Even on the local level, however, air pollution control up to the middle of this century continued to be primarily a matter of controlling smoke through local ordinances.

The Federal Government entered the field after California discovered in the early fifties that automobiles were the chief source of Los Angeles smog. Smog itself was not recognized as a serious air pollution problem until the late 1940's. It took years of research to pinpoint the source of photochemical smog and to demonstrate that the problem was not unique to Los Angeles. The resulting new emphasis on gaseous pollutants, coupled with the realization that the problem should no longer be thought of as essentially

local in character, moved pollution control efforts away
from local smoke ordinances.  Soon all three levels of
government were engaged in a variety of broad programs.
The Federal Clean Air Act, originally passed in 1963,
was broadened in 1965, 1967, and particularly in 1970
to shore up State and Federal control over air pollution.

The effects of oxides in the air are of particular concern.
"Acid rain," attributed to excess oxides in the air, and sulfur dioxide,
a product of the burning of coal, both are suspected health hazards.
Carbon monoxide, a byproduct of the internal combustion engine, is
an agent of automobile-caused air pollution.  The relation between
heavy smog and high death rates is well established.
The Clean Air Act (p. 4) makes efforts to reduce air pollution
a joint federal-state responsibility.  Its goal was the achievement of
primary ambient air quality standards ("requisite to protect the public health") by the mid-1970s.  Attainment of secondary ambient air
quality standards ("requisite to protect the public welfare") would be
the eventual goal.
The act directed the Environmental Protection Agency (EPA) to
establish air quality standards for six major pollutants—hydrocarbons,
carbon monoxide, sulfur oxides, particulates, oxides of nitrogen, and
photochemical oxidants.
The Clean Air Act's original timetable was pushed back in some
of its aspects by the 1974 Energy Supply and Coordination Act (p. 33),
which extended statutory deadlines for certain stationary sources
(such as coal-burning power plants) and automobile emissions.  Its
essential operative scheme remains unchanged.  However, states must
develop implementation plans acceptable to EPA for achieving and enforcing the standards set by the agency.  Such implementation plans
consist of both state laws and administrative regulations, and provide
penalties for noncompliance.  EPA sets standards for pollutant emissions from mobile and stationary sources.
The private automobile is considered the prime offender among
mobile sources and the 1970 act constructed an elaborate scheme for
reducing automobile emissions.  EPA is directed to test prototypes of
new motor vehicles and engines, certify them as conforming to its
emission standards or to deny such certification; to inspect automobile
plants, their records, and processes; and to test vehicles and engines
coming off the production line.  Manufacturers must warrant compliance
with all applicable requirements.
EPA was also to establish standards for fuel and fuel additives
so as to minimize endangerment of public health and ensure compliance
with emission control standards.  A 90 percent reduction in per vehicle
emissions by 1975 was the original goal.  As a result, cars produced

in 1975 were equipped with catalytic converters. It was found that in
many cases these increased gasoline consumption and themselves
caused unanticipated and undesirable chemical reactions. As a result of these experiences deadlines for compliance with automobile
emission standards have experienced postponements. Standards for
new mobile sources are to be followed in design of new cars and trucks.

Stationary sources include chemical and other industrial plants,
incinerators, power plants, refineries, and others. All new construction must comply with EPA standards.

To reduce the nation's reliance on the private automobile with
its attendant ill effects on air quality, EPA concluded that certain
metropolitan areas could not achieve either primary or secondary
ambient standards by the dates specified in the act unless travel by
private automobile was curtailed. The agency required states to submit transportation plans that would effect this by designating or building
special lanes for buses and carpools and paths for bicycles, restricting parking facilities, imposing strict motor vehicle inspection and
maintenance schedules, and possible rationing gasoline sales. These
were regarded as Draconian measures by many. EPA transportation
plans remain in litigation and none have been fully implemented.

The Clean Air Act's broad language has been interpreted in a
number of cases to mandate procedures not specifically spelled out in
it. Important among these is the concept of "nondegradation" established in Sierra Club v. Ruckelshaus (344 F.Supp. 253 [1972], aff'd
Fri v. Sierra Club, 412 U.S. 541 [1973]), and the concept of indirect
or complex sources established by NRDC v. EPA (475 F.2d 968 [1973]).
The first would prohibit activities that would permit significant air
quality deterioration where the air is cleaner than ambient standards
require. A complex or indirect source may be any development that
attracts large amounts of traffic and thus causes increased air pollution from mobile sources. Clearly, the enforcement of these two concepts has potentially powerful effects on land use decisions (see pp.
131-41 below).

The 94th Congress has before it proposed amendments to the
Clean Air Act that would set allowable increments and ceilings of deterioration of different degrees in three classes of areas, as identified by the respective states. The amendments would also severely
limit the EPA administrator's authority to require indirect source
review by state and local governments.

Federal highway, airport, and mass transportation statutes
that specifically require compliance with Clean Air Act standards are
23 U.S.C. 109(j), 49 U.S.C. 1716(e), and 49 U.S.C. 1604.

California, where recognition of the health hazards of automobile-
caused smog originated and which has a strong Air Resources Act
(p. 14) antedating the 1970 federal enactments, retains authority to

set emission standards for automotive sources. Regional Boards enforce policy and standards set by its Air Resources Board.

The states may expand air pollution controls to sources not
reached by the federal law. Thus, Arizona covers agricultural
sources in its definition of air pollution (p. 19). Idaho's air pollution
controls have similar scope, but California's otherwise strong air
pollution laws exclude agriculture from their purview. Arizona also
requires motor vehicles registered there to be inspected annually for
compliance with emission standards (p. 19).

Wyoming, in authorizing the setting of ambient air standards or
emission control requirements, requires that "the social and economic
value of the source of pollution" be among the factors considered (Environmental Quality Act, Sec. 35-502.17).


## WEATHER MODIFICATION

Emissions into the air that are intended to cause changes in the
weather, such as local rainfall, and others that are suspected of
causing permanent atmospheric or geophysical changes are of a special nature. The United States merely requires persons attempting
weather modification activities to report them to the Secretary of
Commerce (p. 22). Several states are far more demanding in their
requirements. Applicants for weather modification permits in Kansas
must demonstrate competence before receiving licenses and permits
(p. 25). Illinois, Oklahoma, Pennsylvania, South Dakota, Texas,
and West Virginia are among other states regulating attempts at weather modification.

Quite recently concern has been expressed over the fate of the
ozone layer enclosing the earth and the possible effects on climate and
human health should it be depleted. Freon-type gases used in aerosol
spray cans are thought by some authorities to have the potential of de-
pleting the ozone layer. At least one state legislature (Oregon) already
has moved to ban aerosol sprays (p. 27).


## FEDERAL

### CLEAN AIR ACT (1970, as amended)
### 42 U.S.C. 1857 et seq.

Subchapter I—Air Pollution Prevention and Control
    Section 1857.        Congressional findings; purposes
            1857a.       Cooperative activities

§ 1857.  Congressional findings; purposes of subchapter.

(a) The Congress finds—
(1) that the predominant part of the Nation's population is located in its rapidly expanding metropolitan and other urban areas, which generally cross the boundary lines of local jurisdictions and often extend into two or more States;
(2) that the growth in the amount and complexity of air pollution brought about by urbanization, industrial development, and the increasing use of motor vehicles, has resulted in mounting dangers to the public health and welfare, including injury to agricultural crops and livestock, damage to and the deterioration of property, and hazards to air and ground transportation;
(3) that the prevention and control of air pollution at its source is the primary responsibility of States and local governments; and
(4) that Federal financial assistance and leadership is essential for the development of cooperative Federal, State, regional, and local programs to prevent and control air pollution.

(b) The purposes of this subchapter are—
(1) to protect and enhance the quality of the Nation's air resources so as to promote the public health and welfare and the productive capacity of its population;
(2) to initiate and accelerate a national research and development program to achieve the prevention and control of air pollution;
(3) to provide technical and financial assistance to State and local governments in connection with the development and execution of their air pollution prevention and control programs; and
(4) to encourage and assist the development and operation of regional air pollution control programs.

§ 1857c–2.  Air quality control regions.

(a) Responsibility of State for air quality; submission of implementation plan.

Each State shall have the primary responsibility for assuring air quality within the entire geographic area comprising such State by submitting an implementation plan for such State which will specify the manner in which national primary and secondary ambient air quality standards will be achieved and maintained within each air quality control region in such State. . . .

§ 1857c-3. Air quality criteria and control techniques.

(a) Air pollutant list; publication and revision by Administrator; issuance of air quality criteria for air pollutants.

(1) For the purpose of establishing national primary and secondary ambient air quality standards, the Administrator shall within 30 days after December 31, 1970, publish, and shall from time to time thereafter revise, a list which includes each air pollutant—

(A) which in his judgment has an adverse affect on public health or welfare;

(B) the presence of which in the ambient air results from numerous or diverse mobile or stationary sources; . . .

§ 1857c-4. National primary and secondary ambient air quality standards; promulgation; procedure.

(a) (1) The Administrator—

(A) within 30 days after December 31, 1970, shall publish proposed regulations prescribing a national primary ambient air quality standard and a national secondary ambient air quality standard for each air pollutant for which air quality criteria have been issued prior to such date; and

(B) after a reasonable time for interested persons to submit written comments thereon (but no later than 90 days after the initial publication of such proposed standards) shall by regulation promulgate such proposed national primary and secondary ambient air quality standards with such modifications as he deems appropriate.

§ 1857c-5. State implementation plans for national primary and secondary ambient air quality standards.

(a) Submission to Administrator; time for submission; State procedures; required contents of plans for approval by Administrator; approval of revised plan by Administrator.

(1) Each State shall, after reasonable notice and public hearings, adopt and submit to the Administrator, within nine months after the promulgation of a national primary ambient air quality standard (or any revision thereof) under section 1857c-4 of this title for any air pollutant, a plan which provides for implementation, maintenance, and enforcement of such primary standard in each air quality control region (or portion thereof) within such State. . . .

(2) The Administrator shall, within four months after the date required for submission of a plan under paragraph (1), approve or disapprove such plan, or any portion thereof.  The Administrator shall approve such plan, or any portion thereof, if he determines that it was adopted after reasonable notice and hearing and that—

(A) (i) in the case of a plan implementing a national primary ambient air quality standard, it provides for the attainment of such primary standard as expeditiously as practicable but (subject to subsection (e) of this section) in no case later than three years from the date of approval of such plan (or any revision thereof to take account of a revised primary standard); and (ii) in the case of a plan implementing a national secondary ambient air quality standard, it specifies a reasonable time at which such secondary standard will be attained; . . .

(G) it provides, to the extent necessary and practicable, for periodic inspection and testing of motor vehicles to enforce compliance with applicable emission standards; . . .

§ 1857c-6.  Standards of performance for new stationary sources.

(a) For purposes of this section:

(1) The term "standard of performance" means a standard for emissions of air pollutants which reflects the degree of emission limitation achievable through the application of the best system of emission reduction which (taking into account the cost of achieving such reduction) the Administrator determines has been adequately demonstrated. . . .

(b)(1)(A) The Administrator shall . . . publish (and from time to time thereafter shall revise) a list of categories of stationary sources. . . .

(B) Within 120 days after the inclusion of a category of stationary sources in a list under subparagraph

(A) the Administrator shall propose regulations, establishing Federal standards of performance for new sources within such category.  The Administrator shall afford interested persons an opportunity for written comment on such proposed regulations. . . .

(3) The Administrator shall, from time to time, issue information on pollution control techniques for categories of new sources and air pollutants subject to the provisions of this section. . . .

(c)(1) Each State may develop and submit to the Administrator a procedure for implementing and enforcing standards of performance for new sources located in such State.  If the Administrator finds the State procedure is adequate, he shall delegate to such State any authority he has under this Act to implement and enforce such standards. . . .

§ 1857c-7.  National emission standards for hazardous air pollutants.

(a) Definitions

For purposes of this section—

(1) The term "hazardous air pollutant" means an air pollutant to which no ambient air quality standard is applicable and which in the judgment of the Administrator may cause, or contribute to, an increase in mortality or an increase in serious irreversible, or incapacitating reversible, illness.

(b) Publication and revision by Administrator of list of hazardous air pollutants; inclusion of air pollutant in list; proposal of regulations by Administrator establishing standards for pollutant; establishment of standards; standards effective upon promulgation; issuance of information on pollution control techniques.

(1)(A) The Administrator shall, within 90 days after December 31, 1970, publish (and shall from time to time thereafter revise) a list which includes each hazardous air pollutant for which he intends to establish an emission standard under this section.

(B) Within 180 days after the inclusion of any air pollutant in such list, the Administrator shall publish proposed regulations establishing emission standards for such pollutant together with a notice of a public hearing within thirty days.  Not later than 180 days after such publication, the Administrator shall prescribe an emission standard for such pollutant, unless he finds, on the basis of information presented at such hearings, that such pollutant clearly is not a hazardous air pollutant.  The Administrator shall establish any such standard at the level which in his judgment provides an ample margin of safety to protect the public health from such hazardous air pollutant. . . .

§ 1857c-8.  Federal enforcement.

(a)(1) Whenever, on the basis of any information available to him, the Administrator finds that any person is in violation of any requirement of an applicable implementation plan, the Administrator shall notify the person in violation of the plan and the State in which the plan applies of such findings.  If such violation extends beyond the 30th day after the date of the Administrator's notification, the Administrator may issue an order requiring such person to comply with the requirements of such plan or he may bring a civil action. . . .

(2) Whenever, on the basis of information available to him, the Administrator finds that violations of an applicable implementation plan are so widespread that such violations appear to result from a failure of the State in which the plan applies to enforce the plan effectively, he shall so notify the State.  If the Administrator finds such

failure extends beyond the 30th day after such notice, he shall give
public notice of such finding.   During the period beginning with such
public notice and ending when such State satisfies the Administrator
that it will enforce such plan . . . the Administrator may enforce
any requirement of such plan with respect to any person—
>    (A) by issuing an order to comply with such requirement, or
>    (B) by bringing a civil action. . . .

§ 1857c-9.  Recordkeeping, inspections, monitoring, and entry. . . .

(c) Availability of records, reports, and information to public; disclosure of trade secrets.

Any records, reports or information obtained under subsection (a)
of this section shall be available to the public, except that upon a
showing satisfactory to the Administrator by any person that records,
reports, or information, or particular part thereof (other than emission data), to which the Administrator has access under this section
if made public, would divulge methods or processes entitled to protection as trade secrets of such person, the Administrator shall consider
such record, report, or information or particular portion thereof confidential in accordance with the purposes of section 1905 of Title 18,
except that such record, report, or information may be disclosed to
other officers, employees, or authorized representatives of the United
States concerned with carrying out this chapter or when relevant in
any proceeding under this chapter.

§ 1857d-1.  Retention of State authority.

Except as otherwise provided in sections 1857f-6a, 1857f-6c(c) (4)
and 1857f-11 of this title (preempting certain State regulation of moving sources) nothing in this chapter shall preclude or deny the right
of any State or political subdivision thereof to adopt or enforce (1) any
standard or limitation respecting emissions of air pollutants or (2)
any requirement respecting control or abatement of air pollution; except that if an emission standard or limitation is in effect under an applicable implementation plan or under section 1857c-6 or section
1857c-7 of this title, such State or political subdivision may not adopt
or enforce any emission standard or limitation which is less stringent
than the standard or limitation under such plan or section. . . .

§ 1857f-1.  Establishment of standards.

(a) Air pollutant emissions.

Except as otherwise provided in subsection (b) of this section—

(1) The Administrator shall by regulation prescribe (and from time to time revise) in accordance with the provisions of this section, standards applicable to the emission of any air pollutant from any class or classes of new motor vehicles or new motor vehicle engines, which in his judgment causes or contributes to, or is likely to cause or to contribute to, air pollution which endangers the public health or welfare. Such standards shall be applicable to such vehicles and engines for their useful life (as determined under subsection (d) of this section), whether such vehicles and engines are designed as complete systems or incorporated devices to prevent or control such pollution.

(2) Any regulation prescribed under this subsection (and any revision thereof) shall take effect after such period as the Administrator finds necessary to permit the development and application of the requisite technology, giving appropriate consideration to the cost of compliance within such period. . . .

§ 1857f-4. Penalties for violations; separate offenses.

Any person who violates paragraph (1), (2), (3), or (4) of section 1857f-2(a) of this title shall be subject to a civil penalty of not more than $10,000. Any such violation with respect to paragraph (1), (2), or (4) of section 1857f-2(a) of this title shall constitute a separate offense with respect to each motor vehicle or motor vehicle engine.

§ 1857f-5a. Compliance by vehicles and engines in actual use.

(a) Warranty.

Effective with respect to vehicles and engines manufactured in model years beginning more than 60 days after December 31, 1970, the manufacturer of each new motor vehicle and new motor vehicle engine shall warrant to the ultimate purchaser and each subsequent purchaser that such vehicle or engine is (1) designed, built, and equipped so as to conform at the time of sale with applicable regulations under section 1857f-1 of this title, and (2) free from defects in materials and workmanship which cause such vehicle or engine to fail to conform with applicable regulations for its useful life. . . .

§ 1857f-6a. State standards.

(a) No State or any political subdivision thereof shall adopt or attempt to enforce any standard relating to the control of emissions from new motor vehicles or new motor vehicle engines subject to this part. No State shall require certification, inspection, or any other approval relating to the control of emissions from any new motor vehicle or new motor vehicle engine as condition precedent to the initial retail sale, titling (if any), or registration of such motor vehicle, motor vehicle engine, or equipment.

(b) The Administrator shall, after notice and opportunity for public hearing, waive application of this section to any State which has adopted standards (other than crankcase emission standards) for the control of emissions from new motor vehicles or new motor vehicle engines prior to March 30, 1966, unless he finds that such State does not require standards more stringent than applicable Federal standards to meet compelling and extraordinary conditions. . . .

§ 1857f-6c.  Regulation of fuels.

(a) Authority of Administrator to regulate.

The Administrator may by regulation designate any fuel or fuel additive and, after such date or dates as may be prescribed by him, no manufacturer or processor of any such fuel or additive may sell, offer for sale, or introduce into commerce such fuel or additive unless the Administrator has registered such fuel or additive in accordance with subsection (b) of this section. . . .

§ 1857f-6e.  Low-emission vehicles. . . .

(e) Acquisition by Federal government by purchase or lease; procurement costs; contract provisions.
    (1) Certified low-emission vehicles shall be acquired by purchase or lease by the Federal Government for use by the Federal Government in lieu of other vehicles if the Administrator of General Services determines that such certified vehicles have procurement costs which are no more than 150 per centum of the retail price of the least expensive class or model of motor vehicle for which they are certified substitutes. . . .

§ 1857f-9.  Establishment of standards.

(a) Study; report; hearings; issuance of regulations.
    (1) Within 90 days after December 31, 1970, the Administrator shall commence a study and investigation of emissions of air pollutants from aircraft in order to determine—
        (A) the extent to which such emissions affect air quality in air quality control regions throughout the United States, and
        (B) the technological feasibility of controlling such emissions.
    (2) Within 180 days after commencing such study and investigation, the Administrator shall publish a report of such study and investigation and shall issue proposed emission standards applicable to emissions of any air pollutant from any class or classes of aircraft or aircraft engines which in his judgment cause or contribute to or are likely to cause or contribute to air pollution which endangers the public health or welfare. . . .

§ 1857h.  Definitions. . . .

(h) All language referring to effects on welfare includes, but is not
limited to, effects on soils, water, crops, vegetation, manmade materials, animals, wildlife, weather, visibility, and climate, damage
to and deterioration of property, and hazards to transportation, as
well as effects on economic values and on personal comfort and well-
being.

§ 1857h-2.  Citizen suits.

(a) Establishment of right to bring suit.

Except as provided in subsection (b) of this section, any person may
commence a civil action on his own behalf—
   (1) against any person (including (i) the United States, and (ii) any
other governmental instrumentality or agency to the extent permitted
by the Eleventh Amendment to the Constitution) who is alleged to be in
violation of (A) an emission standard or limitation under this chapter
or (B) an order issued by the Administrator or a State with respect
to such a standard or limitation, or
   (2) against the Administrator where there is alleged a failure of
the Administrator to perform any act or duty under this chapter which
is not discretionary with the Administrator.

The district courts hall have jurisdiction, without regard to the
amount in controversy or the citizenship of the parties, to enforce
such an emission standard or limitation, or such an order, or to order the Administrator to perform such act or duty, as the case may
be. . . .

(d) Award of costs; security.

The court, in issuing any final order in any action brought pursuant
to subsection (a) of this section, may award costs of litigation (including reasonable attorney and expert witness fees) to any party, whenever the court determines such award is appropriate.  The court may,
if a temporary restraining order or preliminary injunction is sought,
require the filing of a bond or equivalent security in accordance with
the Federal Rules of Civil Procedure.

§ 1857h-4.  Federal procurement.

(a) Contracts with violators prohibited.

No Federal agency may enter into any contract with any person who
is convicted of any offense under section 1857c-8(c) (1) of this title
for the procurement of goods, materials, and services to perform
such contract at any facility at which the violation which gave rise to

such conviction occurred if such facility is owned, leased, or supervised by such person. The prohibition in the preceding sentence shall continue until the Administrator certifies that the condition giving rise to such a conviction has been corrected. . . .

§ 1857h-7. Policy review.

(a) The Administrator shall review and comment in writing on the environmental impact of any matter relating to duties and responsibilities granted pursuant to this chapter or other provisions of the authority of the Administrator, contained in any (1) legislation proposed by any Federal department or agency, (2) newly authorized Federal projects for construction and any major Federal agency action (other than a project for construction) to which section 4332(2) (C) of this title applies, and (3) proposed regulations published by any department or agency of the Federal Government. Such written comment shall be made public at the conclusion of any such review.

(b) In the event the Administrator determines that any such legislation, action, or regulation is unsatisfactory from the standpoint of public health or welfare or environmental quality, he shall publish his determination and the matter shall be referred to the Council on Environmental Quality.

STATES

CALIFORNIA AIR RESOURCES ACT (1968, as amended)
Cal. Health & Safety Code Sec. 39001 et seq.

Part 1 Air Resources Board

Part 2 Regional Air Pollution Control

Chapter 1.  General provisions
        2.  District air pollution control boards
        3.  Regional air pollution control districts

§ 39008.5.  "Ambient air quality standards" means specified concentrations and durations of pollutants which reflect the relationship between the intensity and composition of pollution to undesirable effects.

§ 39009.  "Emission standards" means specified limitations on the
discharge of pollutants into the atmosphere.

§ 39009.3.  "Low emission standard." As used in this part and in
Section 14808.1 of the Government Code, the low emission standard
is an emission standard more stringent than the approved test standard.
In establishing the low emission standard the board shall attempt to
insure that no more than 50 percent of the new motor vehicles sold
and registered in California that year would be able to comply with
low emission standard.

Article 2.  Declaration of Policy

§ 39010.  The Legislature finds and declares that the people of the
State of California have a primary interest in the quality of the physical
environment in which they live, and that this physical environment is
being degraded by the waste and refuse of civilization polluting the
atmosphere, thereby creating a situation which is detrimental to the
health, safety, welfare, and sense of well-being of the people of California.

§ 39011.  It is necessary to provide a means for an intensive coordinated state, regional, and local effort to combat the problems of air
pollution within the various air basins in the state by dividing the state
into basins based upon similar meteorological and geographical conditions and with consideration for political boundary lines wherever
practicable, and to provide for state authority to establish ambient
air quality standards that could vary from basin to basin as well as
statewide motor vehicle emission standards, and to provide for control of emissions from nonvehicular sources.

§ 39012.  Local and regional authorities have the primary responsibility for the control of air pollution except for the emissions from motor
vehicles.  These authorities may control emissions from nonvehicular

sources. In addition these authorities are empowered to establish standards more restrictive than those set by the state board. The state authority shall undertake enforcement activities only after it has determined that the local or regional authorities have failed to meet their responsibilities pursuant to the provisions of this division. Such determination shall only be made after a public hearing has been held for that purpose.

§ 39020. There is in state government in the Resources Agency, the State Air Resources Board. . . .

§ 39051. The board shall after holding public hearings

(a) Divide the state into basins to fulfill the purposes of this division not later than January 1, 1969.

(b) Adopt standards of ambient air quality for each basin in consideration of the public health, safety and welfare, including but not limited to health, illness, irritation to the senses, aesthetic value, interference with visibility, and effects on the economy. These standards may vary from one basin to another. Standards relating to health effects shall be based upon the recommendations of the State Department of Public Health. . . .

(d) Adopt emission standards for all nonvehicular air pollution sources for application for each basin as found necessary as provided in Section 39054.

(e) Adopt test procedures to measure compliance with its nonvehicular emission standards and those of local and regional authorities. . . .

§ 39052. The board shall:

(a) Conduct studies and evaluate the effects of air pollution upon human, plant, and animal life and the factors responsible for air pollution. The board may call upon the state department, Department of Agriculture, the University of California, and such other state agencies it may deem necessary.

(b) Encourage a cooperative state effort in combating air pollution.

(c) Inventory sources of air pollution within the basins of the state and determine the kinds and quantity of air pollutants. The board shall use, to the fullest extent, the data of local agencies in fulfilling this purpose.

(d) Monitor air pollutants in cooperation with other agencies to fulfill the purpose of this division.

(e) Coordinate and collect research data on air pollution.

(f) Review rules and regulations of local or regional authorities filed with it pursuant to Sections 39314 and 39461 to assure that reasonable provision is made to control emissions from nonvehicular sources and to achieve the air quality standards established by the board. If the board finds, after public hearing, that any rule or regulation of a local or regional authority submitted to it will not achieve applicable air quality standards, it may repeal such rule or regulation and pro-mulgate a rule or regulation which it finds would achieve such stan-dards. Such rule or regulation shall have the same force and effect as a rule or regulation adopted by the local or regional authority, and shall be enforced by the local or regional authority.

(g) Adopt formal procedures, after consultation with the Department of Motor Vehicles, for making timely and decisive mutual agreements on vehicle air pollution matters with which both agencies are con-cerned. . . .

(k) Adopt test procedures specifying the manner in which new motor vehicles shall be approved based upon the emission standards contained in Article 2 (commencing with Section 39100) of Chapter 4 of this part. The board shall base its test procedures on driving patterns typical in the urban areas of California, and shall weight approval standards appropriately to reflect normal engine deposit accumulation. The board shall administer the test for new motor vehicles in accordance with such procedures. . . .

§ 39052.2. The board shall adopt for used motor vehicles such ex-haust emission standards as are necessary and technically feasible to carry out the purposes of this part.

§ 39052.5. The board may adopt motor vehicle emission standards more stringent than those specified in Article 2 (commencing with Section 39100) of Chapter 4 of this part, which the board has found to be necessary and technologically feasible to carry out the purposes of this part.

§ 39052.6. The board may adopt and implement motor vehicle emis-sion standards for the control of other contaminants and sources of air pollution which are not included within Article 2 (commencing with Section 39100) of Chapter 4 of this part, which the board has found to be necessary and technologically feasible to carry out the purposes of this part.

§ 39052.7. (a) The board shall establish criteria for the evaluation of the effectiveness of motor vehicle pollution control devices and of fuel additives. After the establishment of such criteria, the board shall evaluate motor vehicle pollution control devices and fuel additives which have been submitted to it for testing. . . .

§ 39081. The Legislature finds and declares:

(a) That the emission of pollutants from motor vehicles is the primary cause of air pollution in many portions of the state.

(b) That the control and elimination of such pollutants is of prime importance for the protection and preservation of the public health and well-being and for the prevention of irritation to the senses, interference with visibility, and damage to vegetation and property.

(c) That the state has a responsibility to establish uniform procedures for compliance with standards which control or eliminate such pollutants.

(d) That the California goal for pure air quality is the achievement of an atmosphere with no significant detectable adverse effect from motor vehicle air pollution on health, welfare and the quality of life and property by 1975.

(e) That vehicle emission standards applied to new motor vehicles and to used motor vehicles equipped with emission control devices are standards with which all such vehicles shall comply subject to the approval, accreditation, and certification of provisions of this part.

§ 39083.5. The provisions of this chapter shall not apply to any motorcycle as defined in Section 39084.

§ 39100. Approval of new motor vehicles for sale and registration and accreditation of devices for used motor vehicles shall be contingent upon compliance with the standards established in this part or pursuant thereto, under the test procedures established by the board pursuant to Section 39052. Motor vehicles which do not so comply with the applicable standards shall not be sold and registered in California.

§ 391003.3. No manufacturer who pays a penalty pursuant to subdivision (m) of Section 39052 shall add the amount of such penalty to the cost of any motor vehicles sold by such manufacturer and any provision of any contract of sale including such penalty as part of the cost of a motor vehicle shall be void and unenforceable.

It is the intent of the Legislature that the Air Resources Board shall determine the total number of vehicles to be tested on the assembly line and the date that this testing shall be initiated. . . .

§ 39100.5. The standards in this article have been found to be technologically feasible and capable of implementation with reasonable economic cost by a technical advisory panel of nine California engineers, scientists, and air pollution experts. In making these determinations, the board must give consideration to the economic and technological feasibility of the assembly line test procedure.

§ 39101. (Details permissible exhaust emissions for various model years.)

ARIZONA AIR POLLUTION CONTROL (1967, as amended)
36 Ariz. Rev. Stat. Sec. 1700 et seq.

§ 36-1701. Definitions.

In this article, unless the context otherwise requires:

1. "Air contaminants" includes smoke, vapors, charred paper, dust, soot, grime, carbon, fumes, gases, sulfuric acid, mist aerosols, aerosol droplets, odors, particulate matter, windborne matter, radioactive materials, or noxious chemicals, or any other material in the outdoor atmosphere.

2. "Air pollution" means the presence in the outdoor atmosphere of one or more air contaminants or combinations thereof in sufficient quantities, which either alone or in connection with other substances, by reason of their concentration and duration are or tend to be injurious to human, plant or animal life, or cause damage to property, or unreasonably interferes with the comfortable enjoyment of life or property of a substantial part of a community, or obscures visibility, or which in any way degrades the quality of the ambient air below the standards established by the director.

ARIZONA ANNUAL EMISSIONS INSPECTION
OF MOTOR VEHICLES (1975)
36 Ariz. Rev. Stat. Art. 3

§ 36-1772.  Annual emissions inspection program; powers and duties of the director; administration; periodic inspection; minimum standards, rules and regulations.

A.  The director shall administer a comprehensive annual emissions inspection program which shall require the inspection of vehicles in this state in accordance with the provisions of law and administrative regulations pursuant to this article.  Such inspection shall commence in counties with a population in excess of three hundred fifty thousand by January 1, 1976.  Inspection in other counties of the state shall commence when required by the director to meet air pollution control standards or upon application by a county board of supervisors for participation in such inspection program, subject to approval by the director.

B.  The state's annual emissions inspection program shall provide for vehicle inspections at official emissions inspection stations or at fleet emissions inspection stations.  An official or fleet emissions inspection station permit shall not be sold, assigned, transferred, conveyed or removed to another location except on such terms and conditions as the director may prescribe.

C.  Vehicles required to be inspected and registered in this state, except those provided for in § 36-1776, shall be inspected in accordance with the provisions of this article at only the following times:
     1.  No more than thirty days prior to each reregistration, or
     2.  For vehicles under § 36-1776, at least once within each twelve-month period following any original registration or reregistration.

D.  Prior to January 1, 1977 a vehicle shall not be registered or reregistered until such vehicle has been inspected.  After January 1, 1977 a vehicle shall not be registered or reregistered until such vehicle has passed inspection and if such vehicle to be registered or reregistered is being sold by a dealer licensed to sell used motor vehicles pursuant to title 28, the cost of the inspection and any repairs necessary to pass such inspection shall be borne by the dealer.

E.  The director shall adopt minimum emissions standards pursuant to § 36-1717 with which the various classes of vehicles shall be required to comply after January 1, 1977.

F.  The director is empowered to adopt such rules and regulations for purposes of implementation, administration, regulation and enforcement of the provisions of this article including:
     1.  The submission of records relating to the emissions inspection of vehicles inspected by another jurisdiction in accordance with another inspection law and the acceptance of such inspection for compliance with the provisions of this article.

2.  The exemption from inspection of:

(a) Vehicles which are temporarily or permanently immobilized and placed on privately owned lands.

(b) A motor vehicle over fifteen years old.

(c) New vehicles originally registered at time of initial retail sale and titling in this state pursuant to § 28-302.

(d) The sale of vehicles between private individuals.

(e) The sale of vehicles at private or public auctions.

(f) The sale of derelict vehicles.

3.  Governmental entity's vehicles for inspection in accordance with the standards adopted by the director although such vehicles may not be required to be registered in this state.

4.  The reinspection and recertification of any vehicle registered or operated in this state, following its involvement in an accident, mishap or collision.

5.  Compiling and maintaining records of emissions test results after servicing.

6.  Any other rule or regulation which may be required to accomplish the provisions of this article.

G.  Notwithstanding any other provisions of this article, the director may promulgate rules and regulations allowing exemptions from the requirement that all vehicles must meet the minimum standards for registration or reregistration.

§ 36-1776.  Fleet emissions inspection stations; certificates of inspection; dealer's inventory; investigations; revocation of permit.

A.  Any registered owner or lessee of a fleet of at least twenty-five vehicles may apply to the director for a permit to establish a fleet emissions inspection station.  The director shall not issue any fleet emissions inspection station permit until he has found that the applicant:

1.  Maintains an established place of business for the repair and maintenance of applicant's fleet of vehicles.

2.  Has obtained approved machinery, tools and equipment to adequately conduct the required emissions inspections, except that notwithstanding any other provisions of this article, or rules or regulations promulgated hereunder, fleet emission inspection stations shall be permitted to inspect vehicles owned or leased by the fleet emission inspection stations, by using either an idle test condition or a loaded test condition.

3.  Employs properly trained and licensed personnel with which to perform the necessary labor.

4.  Agrees to provide data as may be prescribed by the director. . . .

F.  The director shall investigate the operation of each fleet emissions
inspection station as the conditions and circumstances of such operation
may indicate.  He may require the holder of any fleet permit to submit
such documentation required concerning the operation of such inspection station.  The director may revoke and require the surrender and
forfeiture of any fleet emissions inspection station permit and certificates of inspection of such permittee if he finds that such station is
not operated in accordance with this article and the lawful rules and
regulations adopted by the director or the holder of such permit has
failed or refused to submit records or documentation required.  As
amended Laws 1975, Ch. 85, § 5.

§ 36-1777.  Authority of director to acquire enforcement equipment;
random vehicle tests.

A.  The director may acquire in the name of the state by purchase,
donation, dedication or other lawful means any special equipment,
tools, materials or facilities needed to adequately administer or enforce the provisions of this article.

B.  Any highway patrolman, any police officer or any peace officer
may use any equipment, tools, materials or facilities, approved by
the director, available to him for the purpose of conducting random
investigative tests to check the compliance of any vehicle with the inspection standards.  To facilitate such random investigative tests,
any highway patrolman, any police officer or any peace officer may
require the driver of any vehicle to stop and submit such vehicle to a
test to check its compliance with any of the standards adopted pursuant to § 36-1717.

FEDERAL

Weather Modification

WEATHER MODIFICATION (1971)<br>15 U.S.C. 330 et seq.

§ 330a.  Report requirement:  form; information; time of submission.

No person may engage, or attempt to engage, in any weather modification activity in the United States unless he submits to the Secretary
such reports with respect thereto, in such form and containing such
information, as the Secretary may by rule prescribe.  The Secretary
may require that such reports be submitted to him before, during, and
after any such activity or attempt.

§ 330b.  Duties of Secretary.

(a) Records, maintenance; summaries, publication.

The Secretary shall maintain a record of weather modification activities, including attempts, which take place in the United States and shall publish summaries thereof from time to time as he determines.

(b) Public availability of reports, documents, and other information.

All reports, documents, and other information received by the Secretary under the provisions of this chapter shall be made available to the public to the fullest practicable extent.

(c) Disclosure of confidential information; prohibition; exceptions.

In carrying out the provisions of this section, the Secretary shall not disclose any information referred to in section 1905 of Title 18 and is otherwise unavailable to the public, except that such information shall be disclosed—

(1) to other Federal Government departments, agencies, and officials for official use upon request;

(2) in any judicial proceeding under court order formulated to preserve the confidentiality of such information without impairing the proceeding; and

(3) to the public if necessary to protect their health and safety.


STATES

Weather Modification

KANSAS WEATHER MODIFICATION ACT (1974)
Gen. Stat. Kans. Sec. 82a-1401 et seq.

§ 82a–1402.  Definitions. . . .

(e) "Weather modification activity" means any operation or experimental process which has as its objective inducing change, by artificial means, in the composition, behavior, or dynamics of the atmosphere.

§ 82a–1405.  Same; licenses, issuance and limitations; permits, issuance and conditions; studies, hearings and investigations, research
and development programs; expenditure of funds; representation of
state in matters relating to weather modification.

(a) At the direction of the board, the director may issue licenses for
weather modification activities, as hereinafter provided for in this act
but any licensee shall be limited in the exercise of activities under his
license to the specified method or methods of weather modification
activity within his area of expertise.

(b) At the direction of the board, the director may issue a permit for
each specific weather modification project, which may be comprised
of one or more weather modification activities.  Every such permit
shall describe
     (1) the geographic area within which such activities are to be car-
ried out
     (2) the geographic area to be affected, and
     (3) duration of the weather modification activities of the project
which period may be non-continuous but which may not have a total
duration exceeding one calendar year from the day of its issuance.

The director shall issue a permit only after it has been established
that the project, as conceived, will provide substantial benefits or
that it will advance scientific knowledge.  The director may ask the
advisory committee to review each request for a permit and to advise
him thereon.

(c) The director shall make any studies or investigations, obtain any information, and hold any hearings that he considers necessary or proper to assist him in exercising his powers or administering or enforcing the provisions of this act. . . .

§ 82a-1406. Same; engaging in weather modification without, or in violation of license or permit; exemption from payment of fees.

(a) No person may engage in any activity for weather modification or control without a weather modification license and a weather modification permit issued by the director. No person may engage in any activity in violation of any term or condition of a license or permit issued under this act.

(b) The board, to the extent it considers exemptions appropriate and desirable, may exempt the following weather modification activities from the fee requirements of this act. . . .

§ 82a-1407. Same; license; application; requirements. The director shall issue a weather modification license to each person who:

(a) Applies in writing to the board in such form as the board shall require;

(b) Pays the license fee, if applicable; and

(c) Meets at least one of the following requirements:
    (1) The applicant shall demonstrate that he (or his official representative) has had at least eight years of professional experience in weather modification field research or activities, and has served for at least three years as a project director of weather modification activities;
    (2) The applicant shall demonstrate that he has obtained a baccalaureate degree from a recognized institution of higher learning in engineering, mathematics, or the physical sciences and has had at least three years of experience in weather modification field research or activities; or
    (3) The applicant shall demonstrate that he has obtained a baccalaureate degree from a recognized institution of higher learning in engineering, mathematics, or the physical sciences and has satisfactorily completed the equivalent of at least twenty-five (25) semester hours of meteorological studies at a recognized institution of higher learning and has had at least two years of practical experience in weather modification research or activities; and

(d) Demonstrates that he possesses the knowledge, skill, and experience necessary to conduct weather modification activities without unreasonable risk of injury to persons or property.

§ 82a-1408. Same; license fee; license year; renewal, fee; deposit of fees in general fund.  A license shall be issued under this act only upon payment to the board of a fee of one hundred dollars ($100).  Each license shall expire at the end of the calendar year for which it is issued. . . .

§ 82a-1411. Same; permit; application; requirements; financial responsibility.

(a) The director shall issue a weather modification permit to each person who:

(1) Applies in writing to the director for a permit in such form as the director shall require;

(2) Holds a valid weather modification license issued under this act;

(3) Pays the permit fee, if applicable;

(4) Files with the director proof of ability to respond in damages for liability on account of accidents arising out of any weather modification activities to be conducted by him in an amount of not less than fifty thousand dollars ($50,000) because of bodily injury to or death of one person resulting from any one accident, and, subject to said limit for one person, in an amount of not less than one hundred thousand dollars ($100,000) because of bodily injury to or death of two or more persons resulting from any one accident, and in an amount of not less than one hundred thousand dollars ($100,000) because of injury to or destruction of the property of others resulting from any one accident. . . .

(5) Submits a complete and satisfactory operational plan for the proposed weather modification project which includes a map of the proposed operating area which specifies the primary target area and shows the area reasonably expected to be affected, the name and address of the licensee, the nature and object of the intended weather modification activities, the person or organization on whose behalf it is to be conducted, a statement showing any expected effect upon the environment, the methods that will be used in determining and evaluating the proposed weather modification project, and such other information as may be required by the director;

(6) Meets the preceding requirements for a permit and before beginning operations under the proposed weather modification project, publishes a notice of intent to engage in weather modification activities. . . .

(b) Before a permit is issued, the director, or a hearing officer appointed by him, shall hold the public hearing on the proposed weather modification project in a place or places within a reasonable proximity of the area expected to be affected by the proposed weather modification activities.

(c) No permit may be issued unless the director determines, based on the information provided in the operational plan for the proposed weather modification project and on the testimony and information provided at the public hearing, that:

(1) If the project is one for profit, the proposed weather modification activities are designed to provide, and are reasonably expected to provide, an economic benefit to the people of the area in which the operation will be conducted, or will benefit the people of the state of Kansas, and is scientifically and technically feasible;

(2) If the project is a scientific or research project, the proposed weather modification activities offer promise of expanding the knowledge and the technology of weather modification;

(3) The project includes adequate safeguards for the protection of property, health, safety and welfare; and

(4) The project is designed to minimize risk and maximize scientific gains or economic benefits to the people of the state.

(d) The operational plan for the proposed project shall be placed on file with the director and will be available for public inspection during regular office hours.


OREGON AEROSOL SPRAY CONTROL (1975)
Ore. 1975 Laws, Ch. 366; Senate Bill 771

§ 1. The Legislative Assembly finds that:

(1) Scientific studies have revealed that certain chlorofluorocarbon compounds used in aerosol sprays may be destroying the ozone layer in the earth's stratosphere;

(2) The ozone layer is vital to life on earth, preventing approximately 99 percent of the sun's mid-ultraviolet radiation from reaching the earth's surface;

(3) Increased intensity of ultraviolet radiation poses a serious threat to life on earth including increased occurrences of skin cancer, damage to food crops, damage to phytoplankton which is vital to the production of oxygen and to the food chain, and unpredictable and irreversible global climatic changes;

(4) It has been estimated that production of ozone destroying chemicals is increasing at a rate of 10 percent per year, at which rate the ozone layer will be reduced 13 percent by the year 2014;

(5) It has been estimated that there has already been one-half to one percent depletion of the ozone layer;

(6) It has been estimated that an immediate halt to production of ozone destroying chemicals would still result in an approximate three and one-half percent reduction in ozone by 1990; and

(7) There is substantial evidence to believe that inhalation of aerosol sprays is a significant hazard to human health.

§. 2.   After March 1, 1977, no person shall sell or offer to sell in this state any aerosol spray which contains as a propellant trichloro-monofluoromethane, difluorodichloromethane or any other saturated chlorofluorocarbon compound not containing hydrogen.

§. 3.   Violation of the provisions of section 2 of this Act is a Class A misdemeanor.

CHAPTER

# 2

## ENERGY

Consumption of all forms of energy in the United States has been rising at rapid rates. That supply could not keep up with the ever-increasing demand was clear to many long before the Arab oil embargo of the winter of 1973-74. Alaskan oil reserves cannot make up more than a small share of the deficit and the building of the Alaska pipeline at best only offers a temporary respite. Oil deposits are found at various locations on the Outer Continental Shelf (OCS). Drilling in such locations is by permit from the United States under the Mineral Leasing Act (p. 323) and other laws (see pp. 272 ff.). Critics of the OCS oil recovery program assert that it does not exact sufficient environmental safeguards and does not take into account all the consequences on the marine environment. Indeed, not all of them are known.

The United States is rich in coal, with deposits in the western states calculated as sufficient for several hundred years. Yet, how to extract coal in a dry climate, where scars on the landscape may not heal for generations and where the water needed for mining must by necessity reduce the supply available for other purposes, say, agriculture, is an as yet unsolved problem.

Conventional hydroelectric power generation and pumped-storage facilities increasingly demand environmental sacrifices the public seems unwilling to make. Plans for several major projects have been abandoned.

One of the most thorough studies of the country's energy problem was the Ford Foundation's Energy Policy Project, concluded in 1974 (see Appendix D for citations of its report: A Time to Choose and Energy: The New Era). The Ford project postulated three possible scenarios for the nation's future course in energy consumption: (1) historical growth (continuing to increase consumption at the rate of the

29

recent past); (2) technical fix (approximately half the historical growth rate, achieved by using all now technically feasible energy-saving techniques without changing the existing standards of living); and (3) zero energy growth (requiring economic adjustments).

Neither Congress nor the American public has so far faced up to making a choice of this nature or even the need to make a choice. Nuclear energy is seen as the answer to all our energy problems by some, as invitation to doomsday by others. Certainly, the feasibility of storing radioactive wastes safely remains doubtful and the incidence and consequences of accidents in nuclear plants remain unknown. Because the safety aspect is the overriding one in the consideration of nuclear energy alternatives, legislation dealing with it is considered in Chapter 11, "Toxic and Hazardous Substances." This includes, foremost, the portion of the Energy Reorganization Act of 1974 that amended the Atomic Energy Act of 1954.

The beginning of a true national energy policy may be found in the Energy Policy and Conservation Act of December 1975, which stresses energy efficiency. But aspects of an older philosophy remain, such as the Mining Law of 1872, passed when encouraging exploration and exploitation of the seemingly limitless resources of the West was the indicated policy. This and other laws, both state and federal, dealing with mining of energy-producing resources such as coal, gas, oil, and geothermal steam are found in Chapter 9, "Resource Conservation."

Some of the states have been more forthright in facing the current energy and attendant problems than has Congress. This is demonstrated in the mining laws quoted in Chapter 9, and in those dealing with siting of energy-producing plants and transmission lines quoted in Chapter 5, "Land Use." Minnesota's Energy Act (p. 60) is another example. The problem of reconciling increasing electric power demands and environmental concerns is well stated in the legislative findings of New York's Major Steam Generating Facilities Act (p. 204).

In the present chapter are found laws aimed at increasing and managing the nation's energy supplies and encouraging the development and use of new energy sources. While the nuclear energy alternative may be receiving the greatest share of attention, there are several other alternate energy sources.

Solar energy applications so far only have been attempted on a small scale. As wind results from the heating of the earth's surface by the sun, wind energy may be considered a secondary form of solar energy.

Thermal differences of ocean waters at the surface and several thousand feet below it may also be converted to energy in usable form.

Bioconversion, the process of producing energy from crops and organic wastes, offers partial solutions to both energy and solid waste problems.

Geothermal heat, the heat of the earth's core, causes geysers, but it is also close enough to the surface in places where there are no surface manifestations. Not all such locations are known. New Zealand and Italy, among other countries, have tapped geothermal sources for electricity generation.

Most of the federal laws quoted below were passed in response to the energy crisis of the 1970s. They seek primarily to promote increased use of coal and research and development of nonconventional energy sources. The Energy Policy and Conservation Act of 1975 (42 U.S.C. 6201 et seq.) is the first to aim at reducing energy demands and conserving supplies. It mandates fuel economy labeling for automobiles and average mileages of 18.5 mpg in 1978 and 28 mpg in 1985. For major industrial energy consumers it seeks conservation measures aiming at 20 percent energy efficiency improvement by 1981, against a base year of 1972. Major energy-consuming appliances must be labeled as to energy efficiency and show 25 percent improvement of such efficiency by 1980. Gasoline allocation by voluntary agreement is to keep consumption at 1973-74 levels and, if possible, reduce it below that. The act imposes controls on domestic crude oil prices and gives the president authority to ration gasoline. It also seeks to increase domestic coal production by assisting small producers.

A federal law of the 1930s, the Federal Power Act, contained general language that proved to be a vehicle for some important and far-reaching judicial decisions 30 years later. It grants the Federal Power Commission authority to license hydroelectric projects that must be "best adapted to a comprehensive plan" for waterway improvement and also serve "other beneficial public uses, including recreational" and protect fishery resources. No power projects are permitted on wild and scenic rivers, however, by subsequent legislation (Sec. 1278(a), p. 227).

Among the energy bills passed by Congress in 1974 the Energy Supply and Environmental Coordination Act (p. 33) had as its main thrust increased use of coal. It amended portions of the Clean Air Act. The Energy Reorganization Act of 1974 separated the developmental and regulatory functions of the Atomic Energy Commission and replaced it with two new agencies: the Nuclear Regulatory Commission (p. 411) and the Federal Energy Research and Development Administration (p. 35). It is to carry out research and development functions of the former Atomic Energy Commission and to administer similar functions under more recent legislation, including 1974 acts cited below.

Several other (somewhat overlapping) 1974 enactments promote nontraditional energy sources. The Geothermal Energy Research, Development, and Demonstration Act (p. 40) provides for federally guaranteed loans to industry for research and development, exploration, extraction, and construction and operation of energy-producing

facilities. The Solar Energy Act (p. 43) calls for construction by the
federal government of demonstration facilities and the establishment
of a Solar Energy Information Data Bank. Under the Solar Heating
and Cooling Demonstration Act (p. 48), federal performance standards are to be developed, as well as demonstration projects and a
data bank to be set up. The Non-Nuclear Energy Research and Development Act (p. 53) mandates a comprehensive plan and environmental and water resource assessment. It projects federal and joint
federal-industry experiment and demonstration enterprises.

The Alaska Pipeline Act was passed by Congress in 1973 to permit construction of the pipeline after a court injunction (Wilderness
Society v. Morton, 479 F.2d 842 [1973]). It is noted for its forthright
liability provision assessing "full clean-up costs" (43 U.S.C. 1653).

Minnesota addresses itself to the need for planning against
future energy shortages and for energy conservation, particularly in
building and in transportation. Its Energy Act of 1974 (p. 60) recognizes the role of promotional activities by energy producers in creating
demand. Florida's State Minimum Building Code (p. 64) requires new
single-family residences to be planned for future conversion to solar
water heating. Indiana offers a property tax reduction for solar energy
installations (6 Ind. Stat. Ann., Sec. 1-9.5-1). Arizona has a similar
provision, and Tennessee authorizes state loans for facilities for the
recovery of energy from solid waste processing (Sec. 53-4322(2),
p.357 ). California mandates the replacement of pilot lights on gas
appliances sold in the state with less wasteful devices.


FEDERAL


FEDERAL POWER ACT (1935, as amended)
16 U.S.C. 791 et seq.

§ 797. General powers of Commission.

The Commission is authorized and empowered—

(c) To issue licenses to citizens of the United States, or to any association of such citizens, or to any corporation organized under the
laws of the United States or any State thereof, or to any State or municipality for the purpose of constructing, operating, and maintaining
dams, water conduits, reservoirs, power houses, transmission lines,
or other project works necessary or convenient for the development
and improvement of navigation and for the development, transmission,
and utilization of power across, along, from, or in any of the streams
or other bodies of water over which Congress has jurisdiction under

its authority to regulate commerce with foreign nations and among the
several States, or upon any part of the public lands and reservations
of the United States (including the Territories), or for the purpose of
utilizing the surplus water or water power from any Government dam,
except as herein provided: . . .

§ 803. Conditions of license generally.

All licenses issued under this subchapter shall be on the following
conditions:

(a) Modification of plans, etc., to secure adaptability of project.

That the project adopted, including the maps, plans, and specifications,
shall be such as in the judgment of the Commission will be best adapted
to a comprehensive plan for improving or developing a waterway or
waterways for the use or benefit of interstate or foreign commerce,
for the improvement and utilization of water-power development, and
for other utilization of water-power development, and for other beneficial public uses, including recreational purposes; and if necessary in
order to secure such plan the Commission shall have authority to require the modification of any project and of the plans and specifications
of the project works before approval. . . .

§ 811. Operation of navigation facilities; rules and regulations; penalties.

The Commission shall require the construction, maintenance, and
operation by a licensee at its own expense of such lights and signals
as may be directed by the Secretary of the Department in which the
Coast Guard is operating, and such fishways as may be prescribed by
the Secretary of the Interior. . . .

ENERGY SUPPLY AND ENVIRONMENTAL
COORDINATION ACT (1974)
15 U.S.C. 791 et seq.

§ 791.  Congressional declaration of purpose.

The purposes of this chapter are (1) to provide for a means to assist in meeting the essential needs of the United States for fuels, in a manner which is consistent, to the fullest extent practicable, with existing national commitments to protect and improve the environment, and (2) to provide requirements for reports respecting energy resources.

§ 792.  Coal conversion and allocation—Powerplant and fuel burning installations.

(a) The Federal Energy Administrator—
    (1) shall, by order, prohibit any powerplant, and
    (2) may, by order, prohibit any major fuel burning installation,
other than a powerplant,
from burning natural gas or petroleum products as its primary energy source, if the Federal Energy Administrator determines such powerplant or installation on June 22, 1974, has the capability and necessary plant equipment to burn coal, and if the requirements of subsection (b) of this section are met. . . .

§ 794.  Energy conservation study.

(a) The Federal Energy Administrator shall conduct a study on potential methods of energy conservation and, not later than six months after the date of enactment of this Act, shall submit to Congress a report on the results of such study.  The study shall include, but not be limited to, the following:
    (1) the energy conservation potential of restricting exports of fuels or energy-intensive products or goods, including an analysis of balance-of-payments and foreign relations implications of any such restrictions;
    (2) alternative requirements, incentives, or disincentives for increasing industrial recycling and resource recovery in order to reduce energy demand, including the economic costs and fuel consumption tradeoff which may be associated with such recycling and resource recovery in lieu of transportation and use of virgin materials; and
    (3) means for incentives or disincentives to increase efficiency of industrial use of energy.

(b) Within ninety days of the date of enactment of this Act, the Secretary of Transportation, after consultation with the Federal Energy Administrator, shall submit to the Congress for appropriate action an "Emergency Mass Transportation Assistance Plan" for the purpose of conserving energy by expanding and improving public mass transportation systems and encouraging increased ridership as alternatives to automobile travel.

(c) Such plan shall include, but shall not be limited to—

(1) recommendations for emergency temporary grants to assist States and local public bodies and agencies thereof in the payment of operating expenses incurred in connection with the provision of expanded mass transportation service in urban areas;

(2) recommendations for additional emergency assistance for the purchase of buses and rolling stock for fixed rail, including the feasibility of accelerating the timetable for such assistance under section 142(a)(2) of title 23. United States Code (the "Federal Aid Highway Act of 1973"), for the purpose of providing additional capacity for and encouraging increased use of public mass transportation systems;

(3) recommendations for a program of demonstration projects to determine the feasibility of fare-free and low-fare urban mass transportation systems, including reduced rates for elderly and handicapped persons during nonpeak hours of transportation;

(4) recommendations for additional emergency assistance for the construction of fringe and transportation corridor parking facilities to serve bus and other mass transportation passengers;

(5) recommendations on the feasibility of providing tax incentives for persons who use public mass transportation systems.

ENERGY RESEARCH AND DEVELOPMENT
ADMINISTRATION (1974)
42 U.S.C. 5801 et seq.

§ 5801. Congressional declaration of policy and purpose—Development and utilization of energy sources.

(a) The Congress hereby declares that the general welfare and the common defense and security require effective action to develop, and increase the efficiency and reliability of use of, all energy sources to meet the needs of present and future generations, to increase the productivity of the national economy and strengthen its position in regard

to international trade, to make the Nation self-sufficient in energy,
to advance the goals of restoring, protecting, and enhancing environmental quality, and to assure public health and safety.

(b) The Congress finds that, to best achieve these objectives, improve
Government operations, and assure the coordinated and effective development of all energy sources, it is necessary to establish an Energy
Research and Development Administration to bring together and direct
Federal activities relating to research and development on the various
sources of energy, to increase the efficiency and reliability in the use
of energy, and to carry out the performance of other functions, including but not limited to the Atomic Energy Commission's military and
production activities and its general basic research activities. In establishing an Energy Research and Development Administration to
achieve these objectives, the Congress intends that all possible sources
of energy be developed consistent with warranted priorities.

(c) The Congress finds that it is in the public interest that the licensing
and related regulatory functions of the Atomic Energy Commission
be separated from the performance of the other functions of the Commission, and that this separation be effected in an orderly manner,
pursuant to this chapter, assuring adequacy of technical and other resources necessary for the performance of each.

(d) The Congress declares that it is in the public interest and the policy of Congress that small business concerns be given a reasonable
opportunity to participate, insofar as is possible, fairly and equitably
in grants, contracts, purchases, and other Federal activities relating
to research, development, and demonstration of sources of energy
efficiency, and utilization and conservation of energy. In carrying
out this policy, to the extent practicable, the Administrator shall consult with the Administrator of the Small Business Administration.

(e) Determination of priorities which are warranted should be based
on such considerations as power-related values of an energy source,
preservation of material resources, reduction of pollutants, export
market potential (including reduction of imports), among others. On
such a basis, energy sources warranting priority might include, but
not be limited to, the various methods of utilizing solar energy.

§ 5813.  Responsibilities of the Administrator.

The responsibilities of the Administrator shall include, but not be
limited to—

(1) exercising central responsibility for policy planning, coordination,
support, and management of research and development programs respecting all energy sources, including assessing the requirements for

research and development in regard to various energy sources in relation to near-term and long-range needs, policy planning in regard
to meeting those requirements, undertaking programs for the optimal
development of the various forms of energy sources, managing such
programs, and disseminating information resulting therefrom;

(2) encouraging and conducting research and development, including
demonstration of commercial feasibility and practical applications of
the extraction, conversion, storage, transmission, and utilization
phases related to the development and use of energy from fossil,
nuclear, solar, geothermal, and other energy sources;

(3) engaging in and supporting environmental, biomedical, physical,
and safety research related to the development of energy sources and
utilization technologies;

(4) taking into account the existence, progress, and results of other
public and private research and development activities, including those
activities of the Federal Energy Administration relating to the development of energy resources using currently available technology in promoting increased utilization of energy resources, relevant to the Administration's mission in formulating its own research and development programs;

(5) participating in and supporting cooperative research and development projects which may involve contributions by public or private
persons or agencies, of financial or other resources to the performance of the work;

(6) developing, collecting, distributing, and making available for distribution, scientific and technical information concerning the manufacture or development of energy and its efficient extraction, conversion,
transmission, and utilization;

(7) creating and encouraging the development of general information
to the public on all energy conservation technologies and energy sources
as they become available for general use, and the Administrator, in
conjunction with the Administrator of the Federal Energy Administration shall, to the extent practicable, disseminate such information
through the use of mass communications;

(8) encouraging and conducting research and development in energy
conservation, which shall be directed toward the goals of reducing
total energy consumption to the maximum extent practicable, and toward maximum possible improvement in the efficiency of energy use.
Development of new and improved conservation measures shall be
conducted with the goal of the most expeditious possible application of
these measures;

(9) encouraging and participating in international cooperation in energy
and related environmental research and development;

(10) helping to assure an adequate supply of manpower for the accomplishment of energy research and development programs, by sponsoring and assisting in education and training activities in institutions of higher education, vocational schools, and other institutions, and by assuring the collection, analysis, and dissemination of necessary manpower supply and demand data;

(11) encouraging and conducting research and development in clean
and renewable energy sources.

§ 5814.  Abolition and transfers.

(a) The Atomic Energy Commission is hereby abolished.

(b) All other functions of the Commission, the Chairman and members of the Commission, and the officers and components of the Commission are hereby transferred or allowed to lapse pursuant to the provisions of this chapter.

(c) There are hereby transferred to and vested in the Administrator all functions of the Atomic Energy Commission, the Chairman and members of the Commission, and the officers and components of the Commission, except as otherwise provided in this chapter. . . .

(e) There are hereby transferred to and vested in the Administrator such functions of the Secretary of the Interior, the Department of the Interior, and officers and components of such department—
  (1) as relate to or are utilized by the Office of Coal Research established pursuant to sections 661 to 668 of Title 30;
  (2) as relate to or are utilized in connection with fossil fuel energy research and development programs and related activities conducted by the Bureau of Mines "energy centers" and synthane plant to provide greater efficiency in the extraction, processing, and utilization of energy resources for the purpose of conserving those resources, developing alternative energy resources, such as oil and gas secondary and tertiary recovery, oil shale and synthetic fuels, improving methods of managing energy-related wastes and pollutants, and providing technical guidance needed to establish and administer national energy policies; and
  (3) as relate to or are utilized for underground electric power transmission research.
The Administrator shall conduct a study of the potential energy applications of helium and, within six months from October 11, 1974, report to the President and Congress his recommendations concerning the management of the Federal helium programs, as they relate to energy.

(f) There are hereby transferred to and vested in the Administrator
such functions of the National Science Foundation as relate to or are
utilized in connection with—
    (1) solar heating and cooling development; and
    (2) geothermal power development.

(g) There are hereby transferred to and vested in the Administrator
such functions of the Environmental Protection Agency and the officers
and components thereof as related to or are utilized in connection
with research, development, and demonstration, but not assessment
or monitoring for regulatory purposes, of alternative automotive power
systems.

(h) To the extent necessary or appropriate to perform functions and
carry out programs transferred by this chapter the Administrator and
Commission may exercise, in relation to the functions so transferred,
any authority or part thereof available by law, including appropriation
Acts, to the official or agency from which such functions were transferred.

(i) In the exercise of his responsibilities under section 5813 of this
title, the Administrator shall utilize, with their consent, to the fullest
extent he determines advisable the technical and management capabilities of other executive agencies having facilities, personnel, or other
resources which can assist or advantageously be expanded to assist in
carrying out such responsibilities. The Administrator shall consult
with the head of each agency with respect to such facilities, personnel,
or other resources, and may assign, with their consent, specific
programs or projects in energy research and development as appropriate. In making such assignments under this subsection, the head
of each such agency shall insure that—
    (1) such assignments shall be in addition to and not detract from
the basic mission responsibilities of the agency, and
    (2) such assignments shall be carried out under such guidance as
the Administrator deems appropriate.

§ 5818. Energy Resources Council—Establishment; composition.

(a) There is established in the Executive Office of the President an
Energy Resources Council. The Council shall be composed of the
Secretary of the Interior, the Administrator of the Federal Energy
Administration, the Administrator of the Energy Research and Devel-
opment Administration, the Secretary of State, the Director, Office
of Management and Budget, and such other officials of the Federal
Government as the President may designate. The President shall
designate one of the members of the Council to serve as Chairman.

(b) It shall be the duty and function of the Council to—

(1) insure communication and coordination among the agencies of the Federal Government which have responsibilities for the development and implementation of energy policy or for the management of energy resources;

(2) make recommendations to the President and to the Congress for measures to improve the implementation of Federal energy policies or the management of energy resources with particul emphasis upon policies and activities involving two or more Departments or independent agencies; and

(3) advise the President in the preparation of the reorganization recommendations required by section 5820 of this title.

(c) The Chairman of the Council may not refuse to testify before the Congress or any duly authorized committee thereof regarding the duties of the Council or other matters concerning interagency coordination of energy policy and activities.

(d) This section shall be effective no later than sixty days after October 11, 1974, or such earlier date as the President shall prescribe and publish in the Federal Register, and shall terminate upon enactment of a permanent department responsible for energy and natural resources or two years after such effective date, whichever shall occur first.

GEOTHERMAL ENERGY RESEARCH, DEVELOPMENT, AND
DEMONSTRATION ACT (1974)
30 U.S.C. 1101 et seq.

§ 1101.  Congressional findings.

The Congress hereby finds that—

(1) the Nation is currently suffering a critical shortage of environmentally acceptable forms of energy;

(2) the inadequate organizational structures and levels of funding for energy research have limited the Nation's current and future options for meeting energy needs;

(3) electric energy is a clean and convenient form of energy at the location of its use and is the only practicable form of energy in some modern applications, but the demand for electric energy in every region of the United States is taxing all of the alternative energy sources presently available and is projected to increase; some of the sources available for electric power generation are already in short supply, and the development and use of other sources presently involve undesirable environmental impacts;

(4) the Nation's critical energy problems can be solved only if a national commitment is made to dedicate the necessary financial resources, and enlist the cooperation of the private and public sectors, in developing geothermal resources and other nonconventional sources of energy;

(5) the conventional geothermal resources which are presently being used have limited total potential; but geothermal resources which are different from those presently being used, and which have extremely large energy content, are known to exist;

(6) some geothermal resources contain energy in forms other than heat; examples are methane and extremely high pressures available upon release as kinetic energy;

(7) some geothermal resources contain valuable by-products such as potable water and mineral compounds which should be processed and recovered as national resources;

(8) technologies are not presently available for the development of most of these geothermal resources, but technologies for the generation of electric energy from geothermal resources are potentially economical and environmentally desirable, and the development of geothermal resources offers possibilities of process energy and other nonelectric applications;

(9) much of the known geothermal resources exist on the public lands;

(10) Federal financial assistance is necessary to encourage the extensive exploration, research, and development in geothermal resources which will bring these technologies to the point of commercial application;

(11) the advancement of technology with the cooperation of private industry for the production of useful forms of energy from geothermal resources is important with respect to the Federal responsibility for the general welfare, to facilitate commerce, to encourage productive harmony between man and his environment, and to protect the public interest; and

(12) the Federal Government should encourage and assist private industry through Federal assistance for the development and demonstration of practicable means to produce useful energy from geothermal resources with environmentally acceptable processes.

§ 1121.  Formation of Project—Establishment.

(a) There is hereby established the Geothermal Energy Coordination and Management Project. . . .

(c) The Project shall have overall responsibility for the provision of effective management and coordination with respect to a national geothermal energy research, development, and demonstration program. Such program shall include—
    (1) the determination and evaluation of the resource base;
    (2) research and development with respect to exploration, extraction, and utilization technologies;
    (3) the demonstration of appropriate technologies; and
    (4) the loan guaranty program under subchapter II of this chapter.

§ 1124.  Research and Development.

(a) The Chairman, acting through the appropriate Federal agencies and in cooperation with non-Federal entities, shall initiate a research and development program for the purpose of resolving all major technical problems inhibiting the fullest possible commercial utilization of geothermal resources in the United States. . . .

§ 1125.  Geothermal demonstration plants and projects—Design and construction.

(a) The Chairman, acting through the appropriate Federal agencies and in cooperation with non-Federal entities, shall initiate a progam to design and construct geothermal demonstration plans. The specific goals of such program shall include—
    (1) the development of economical geothermal resources production systems and components which meet environmental standards; . . .

§ 1141. Establishment of loan guaranty program—Congressional declaration of policy.

(a) It is the policy of the Congress to encourage and assist in the commercial development of practicable means to produce useful energy from geothermal resources with environmentally acceptable processes. Accordingly, it is the policy of the Congress to facilitate such commercial development by authorizing the Chairman of the Project to designate an appropriate Federal agency to guarantee loans for such purposes.

(b) In order to encourage the commercial production of energy from geothermal resources, the head of the designated agency is authorized to, in consultation with the Secretary of the Treasury, guarantee, and to enter into commitments to guarantee, lenders against loss of principal or interest on loans made by such lenders to qualified borrowers for the purposes of—

(1) the determination and evaluation of the resource base;

(2) research and development with respect to extraction and utilization technologies;

(3) acquiring rights in geothermal resources; or

(4) development, construction, and operation of facilities for the demonstration or commercial production of energy from geothermal resources. . . .

§ 1161. Protection of environment.

In the conduct of its activities, the Project and any participating public or private persons or agencies shall place particular emphasis upon the objective of assuring that the environment and the safety of persons or property are effectively protected; and the program under subchapter I of this chapter shall include such special research and development as may be necessary for the achievement of that objective.

SOLAR ENERGY ACT (1974)
42 U.S.C. 5551 et seq.

Subchapter II—Research, Development, and Demonstration

§ 5551.  Congressional declaration of findings and policy.

(a) The Congress hereby finds that—

(1) the needs of a viable society depend on an ample supply of energy;

(2) the current imbalance between domestic supply and demand for fuels and energy is likely to persist for some time;

(3) dependence on nonrenewable energy resources cannot be continued indefinitely, particularly at current rates of consumption;

(4) it is in the Nation's interest to expedite the long-term development of renewable and nonpolluting energy resources, such as solar energy;

(5) the various solar energy technologies are today at widely differing stages of development, with some already near the stage of commercial application and others still requiring basic research;

(6) the early development and export of viable equipment utilizing solar energy, consistent with the established preeminence of the United States in the field of high technology products, can make a valuable contribution to our balance of trade;

(7) the mass production and use of equipment utilizing solar energy will help to eliminate the dependence of the United States upon foreign energy sources and promote the national defense;

(8) to date, the national effort in research, development, and demonstration activities relating to the utilization of solar energy has been extremely limited; therefore

(9) the urgency of the Nation's critical energy shortages and the need to make clean and renewable energy alternatives commercially viable require that the Nation undertake an intensive research, development, and demonstration program with an estimated Federal investment which may reach or exceed $1,000,000,000.

(b) The Congress declares that it is the policy of the Federal Government to—

(1) pursue a vigorous and viable program of research and resource assessment of solar energy as a major source of energy for our national needs; and

(2) provide for the development and demonstration of practicable means to employ solar energy on a commercial scale.

§ 5552.  Definitions.

For the purposes of this subchapter—

(1) the term "solar energy" means energy which has recently originated in the Sun, including direct and indirect solar radiation and intermediate solar energy forms such as wind, sea thermal gradients, products of photosynthetic processes, organic wastes, and others;

(2) the term "byproducts" includes with respect to any solar energy technology or process, any solar energy products (including energy forms) other than those associated with or constituting the primary product of such technology or process;

(3) the term "insolation" means the rate at which solar energy is received at the surface of the Earth. . . .

§ 5554.  Solar energy resource determination and assessment program; objectives; implementation.

(a) The Chairman shall initiate a solar energy resource determination and assessment program with the objective of making a regional and national appraisal of all solar energy resources, including data on insolation, wind, sea thermal gradients, and potentials for photosynthetic conversion.  The program shall emphasize identification of promising areas for commercial exploitation and development.  The specific goals shall include—

(1) the development of better methods for predicting the availability of all solar energy resources, over long time periods and by geographic location;

(2) the development of advanced meteorological, oceanographic, and other instruments, methodology, and procedures necessary to measure the quality and quantity of all solar resources on periodic bases;

(3) the development of activities, arrangements, and procedures for the collection, evaluation, and dissemination of information and data relating to solar energy resource assessment. . . .

§ 5555.  Research and development program—Purpose.

(a) The Chairman shall initiate a research and development program
for the purpose of resolving the major technical problems inhibiting
commercial utilization of solar energy in the United States. . . .

(c) The specific solar energy technologies to be addressed or dealt
with in the  program shall include—
    (1) direct solar heat as a source for industrial processes, including
the utilization of low-level heat for process and other industrial purposes;
    (2) thermal energy conversion, and other methods, for the genera-
tion of electricity and the production of chemical fuels;
    (3) the conversion of cellulose and other organic materials (includ-
ing wastes) to useful energy or fuels;
    (4) photovoltaic and other direct conversion processes;
    (5) sea thermal gradient conversion;
    (6) windpower conversion;
    (7) solar heating and cooling of housing and of commercial and pub-
lic buildings; and
    (8) energy storage.

§ 5556.  Solar energy demonstration facilities program—Authorization
for design and construction of facilities; objectives.

(a) The Chairman is authorized to initiate a program to design and construct, in specific solar energy technologies (including, but not limited
to, those listed in section 5555(c) of this title, facilities or power-
plants of sufficient size to demonstrate the technical and economic feasibility of utilizing the various forms of solar energy.  The specific goals
of such programs  shall include—
    (1) production of electricity from a number of powerplants, on the
order of one to ten megawatts each;
    (2) production of synthetic fuels in commercial quantities;
    (3) large-scale utilization of solar energy in the form of direct heat;
    (4) utilization of thermal and all other byproducts of the solar facili-
ties;
    (5) design and development of hybrid systems involving the concomi-
tant utilization of solar and other energy sources; and
    (6) the continuous operation of such plants and facilities for a period
of time.

(c) In carrying out his responsibilities under this section, the Chairman, acting through the appropriate Federal agencies, may provide for
the establishment of one or more demonstration projects utilizing each
form of solar energy, which shall include, as appropriate, the specific
research, development, pilot plant construction and operation, demon-

stration plant construction and operation, and other facilities and activities which may be necessary to show commercial viability of the
specific solar technology.

§ 5557. Solar Energy Information Data Bank—Establishment; utilization of other Federal agencies; information and data to be compiled;
retrieval and dissemination services; utilization of existing scientific
and technical information.

(a) (1) In carrying out his functions under this subchapter the Chairman, utilizing the capabilities of the National Science Foundation, the
National Aeronautics and Space Administration, the Department of
Commerce, the Atomic Energy Commission, and other appropriate
Federal agencies to the maximum extent possible, shall establish and
operate a Solar Energy Information Data Bank (hereinafter in this subsection referred to as the "bank") for the purpose of collecting, reviewing, processing, and disseminating information and data in all of
the solar energy technologies referred to in section 5556(c) of this title
in a timely and accurate manner in support of the objectives of this
subchapter.
    (2) Information and data compiled in the bank shall include—
        (A) technical information (including reports, journal articles,
    dissertations, monographs, and project descriptions) on solar en-
    ergy research, development, and applications;
        (B) similar technical information on the design, construction, and
    maintenance of equipment utilizing solar energy;
        (C) general information on solar energy applications to be dis-
    seminated for popular consumption;
        (D) physical and chemical properties of materials required for
    solar energy activities and equipment; and
        (E) engineering performance data on equipment and devices
    utilizing solar energy.
    (3) In accordance with regulations prescribed under section 5561 of
this title, the Chairman shall provide retrieval and dissemination services with respect to the information described under paragraph (2)
for—
        (A) Federal, State, and local government organizations that are
    active in the area of energy resources (and their contractors);
        (B) universities and colleges in their related research and con-
    sulting activities; and
        (C) the private sector upon request in appropriate cases. . . .

§ 5565. Transfer of functions.

    Within sixty days after the effective date of the law creating a per-
manent Federal organization or agency having jurisdiction over the

energy research and development functions of the United States (or within sixty days after October 26, 1974, if the effective date of such law occurs prior to October 26, 1974) all of the authorities of the Project and all of the research and development functions (and other functions except those related to scientific and technical education) vested in Federal agencies under this subchapter along with related records, documents, personnel, obligations, and other items, to the extent necessary or appropriate, shall, in accordance with regulations prescribed by the Office of Management and Budget, be transferred to and vested in such organization or agency.

## SOLAR HEATING AND COOLING DEMONSTRATION ACT (1974)
### 42 U.S.C. 5501 et seq.

§ 5501. Congressional findings and declaration of policy.

(a) The Congress hereby finds that—

(1) the current imbalance between supply and demand for fuels and energy is likely to persist for some time;

(2) the early demonstration of the feasibility of using solar energy for the heating and cooling of buildings could help to relieve the demand upon present fuel and energy supplies;

(3) the technologies for solar heating are close to the point of commercial application in the United States;

(4) the technologies for combined solar heating and cooling still require research, development, testing and demonstration, but no insoluble technical problem is now foreseen in achieving commercial use of such technologies;

(5) the early development and export of viable solar heating equipment and combined solar heating and cooling equipment, consistent with the established preeminence of the United States in the field of high technology products, can make a valuable contribution to our balance of trade;

(6) the widespread use of solar energy in place of conventional methods for the heating and cooling of buildings would have a significantly beneficial effect upon the environment;

(7) the mass production and use of solar heating and cooling equipment will help to eliminate the dependence of the United States upon foreign energy sources and promote the national defense;

(8) the widespread introduction of low-cost solar energy will be beneficial to consumers in a period of rapidly rising fuel cost;

(9) innovation and creativity in the development of solar heating and combined solar heating and cooling components and systems can be fostered through encouraging direct contact between the manufacturers of such systems and the architects, engineers, developers, contractors, and other persons interested in installing such systems in buildings;

(10) evaluation of the performance and reliability of solar heating and combined solar heating and cooling technologies can be expedited by testing under carefully controlled conditions; and

(11) commercial application of solar heating and combined solar heating and cooling technologies can be expedited by early commercial demonstration under practical conditions.

(b) It is therefore declared to be the policy of the United States and the purpose of this subchapter to provide for the demonstration within a three-year period of the practical use of solar heating technology, and to provide for the development and demonstration within a five-year period of the practical use of combined heating and cooling technology.

§ 5503. Development and demonstration of solar heating systems for use in residential dwellings—Functions of Administrator and Secretary.

(a) The Administrator and the Secretary shall promptly initiate and carry out a program, as provided in this section, for the development and demonstration of solar heating systems (including collectors, controls, and thermal storage) for use in residential dwellings.

(b) (1) Within 120 days after September 3, 1974, the Secretary, utilizing the services of the Director of the National Bureau of Standards and in consultation with the Administrator and the Director, shall determine, prescribe, and publish—

(A) interim performance criteria for solar heating components and systems to be used in residential dwellings, and

(B) interim performance criteria (relating to suitability for solar heating) for such dwellings themselves,

taking into account in each instance climatic variations existing between different geographic areas. . . .

(c) The Administrator, in accordance with the applicable provisions of title II of the National Aeronautics and Space Act of 1958 and under program guidelines established jointly by the Administrator and the Secretary, shall, after consultation with the Secretary—

(1) enter into such contracts and grants as may be necessary or appropriate for the development (for commercial production and residential use) of solar heating systems meeting the performance criteria prescribed under subsection (b)(1)(A) of this section (including any further planning and design which may be required to conform with the specifications set forth in such criteria); and

(2) enter into contracts with a number of persons or firms for the procurement of solar heating components and systems meeting such performance criteria (including adequate numbers of spare and replacement parts for such systems).

(d) The Secretary shall (1) arrange for the installation of solar heating systems procured by the Administrator under subsection (c)(2) of this section in a substantial number of residential dwellings and (2) provide for the satisfactory operation of such installations during the demonstration period. Title to and ownership of any dwellings constructed hereunder and of solar heating systems installed hereunder may be conveyed to purchasers or owners of such dwellings under terms and conditions prescribed by the Secretary, including an express agreement that any such purchaser or owner shall, in such manner and form and on such terms and conditions as the Secretary may prescribe, observe and monitor (or permit the Secretary to observe and monitor) the performance and operation of such system for a period of five years, and that such purchaser or owner (including any subsequent owner and occupant of the property who also makes such an agreement) shall regularly furnish the Secretary with such reports thereon as the agreement may require. . . .

§ 5504. Development and demonstration of combined solar heating and cooling systems for use in residential dwellings—Functions of Administrator and Secretary.

(a) The Administrator and the Secretary shall promptly initiate and carry out a program, as provided in this section, for the development and demonstration of combined solar heating and cooling systems and suitable dwellings; determination, consultation and publication in Federal Register.

As soon as feasible, and utilizing data available from the demonstration programs under sections 5503 and 5504 of this title, the Secretary, utilizing the services of the Director of the National Bureau of Standards and in consultation with the Administrator and the Director shall determine, prescribe, and publish in the Federal Register in accordance with the applicable provisions regarding rulemaking prescribed by section 553 of Title 5—

(1) definitive performance criteria for solar heating and combined solar heating and cooling components and systems to be used in residential dwellings, taking into account climatic variations existing between different geographic areas;

(2) definitive performance criteria (relating to suitability for solar heating and for combined solar heating and cooling) for such dwellings, taking into account climatic variations existing between different geographic areas; and

(3) procedures whereby manufacturers of solar heating and combined solar heating and cooling components and systems shall have their products tested in order to provide certification that such products conform to the performance criteria established under paragraph (1).

§ 5507. Arrangements with Federal agencies for development and demonstration of solar heating and combined heating and cooling systems for commercial buildings.

The Administrator, in consultation with the Secretary, the Director, the Administrator of General Services, and the Director of the National Bureau of Standards and concurrently with the conduct of the programs under sections 5503 and 5504 of this title, shall enter into arrangements with appropriate Federal agencies to carry out such projects and activities (including demonstration projects) with respect to apartment buildings, office buildings, factories, crop-drying facilities and other agricultural structures, public buildings (including schools and

colleges), and other non-residential, commercial, or industrial buildings, taking into account the special needs of and individual differences
in such buildings based upon size, function, and other relevant factors,
as may be appropriate for the early development and demonstration of
solar heating and combined solar heating and cooling systems suitable
and effective for use in such buildings.

§ 5510. Dissemination of information to promote practical use of
solar heating and cooling technologies—Coordination by Secretary
with other Federal agencies in dissemination to Federal, State, and
local authorities, etc.

(a) The Secretary shall take all possible steps to assure that full and
complete information with respect to the demonstrations and other
activities conducted under this subchapter is made available to Federal,
State, and local authorities, the building industry and related segments
of the economy, the scientific and technical community, and the public
at large. . . .

(b) In addition, the Secretary shall—
    (1) study and investigate the effect of building codes, zoning ordi-
nances, tax regulations, and other laws, codes, ordinances, and
practices upon the practical use of solar energy for the heating and
cooling of buildings. . . .

(c) (1) In carrying out his functions under subsections (a) and (b) of
this section the Secretary, utilizing the capabilities of the National
Aeronautics and Space Administration, the Department of Commerce,
and the National Science Foundation to the maximum extent possible,
shall establish and operate a Solar Heating and Cooling Information
Data Bank. . . .

§ 5511. Federally assisted or federally constructed housing—Maximum dollar amount of federally assisted mortgage loan or maximum
per unit or other cost or floor area limitation of federally constructed
housing.

(a) (1) In determining the maximum dollar amount of any federally assisted mortgage loan (as defined in subsection (b) of this section) or
the maximum per unit or other cost or floor area limitation of any
federally constructed housing (as defined in subsection (c) of this section), where the law establishing the program under which the loan is
made or the housing is constructed specifies such maximum per unit
or other cost on floor area limitation and the structure involved is
furnished with solar heating or combined solar heating and cooling
equipment under the demonstration program established by section
5503, 5504, or 5507 of this title, the maximum amount or cost or

floor area limitation so specified which is applicable to such structure shall be deemed to be increased by the amount by which (as determined by the Secretary or the Secretary of Defense, as appropriate) the price or cost or floor area limitation of the structure including such solar heating or combined solar heating and cooling equipment exceeds the price or cost or floor area limitation of the structure with such equipment replaced by conventional heating equipment or conventional heating and cooling equipment (as the case may be). . . .

NON-NUCLEAR ENERGY RESEARCH AND DEVELOPMENT
ACT (1974)
42 U.S.C. 5901 et seq.

§ 5901.  Congressional statement of findings.

The Congress hereby finds that—

(a) The Nation is suffering from a shortage of environmentally acceptable forms of energy.

(b) Compounding this energy shortage is our past and present failure to formulate a comprehensive and aggressive research and development program designed to make available to American consumers our large domestic energy reserves including fossil fuels, nuclear fuels, geothermal resources, solar energy, and other forms of energy. This

failure is partially because the unconventional energy technologies
have not been judged to be economically competitive with traditional
energy technologies.

(c) The urgency of the Nation's energy challenge will require commitments similar to those undertaken in the Manhattan and Apollo projects; it will require that the Nation undertake a research, development,
and demonstration program in nonnuclear energy technologies with a
total Federal investment which may reach or exceed $20,000,000,000
over the next decade.

(d) In undertaking such program, full advantage must be taken of the
existing technical and managerial expertise in the various energy
fields within Federal agencies and particularly in the private sector.
. . .

§ 5902.  Congressional declaration of policy and purpose; implementation and administration of program by Administrator of Energy Research and Development Administration.

(a) It is the policy of the Congress to develop on an urgent basis the
technological capabilities to support the broadest range of energy policy
options through conservation and use of domestic resources by socially
and environmentally acceptable means.

(b) (1) The Congress declares the purpose of this chapter to be to establish and vigorously conduct a comprehensive, national program of
basic and applied research and development, including but not limited
to demonstrations of practical applications, of all potentially beneficial
energy sources and utilization technologies, within the Energy Research
and Development Administration.

(2) In carrying out this program, the Administrator of the Energy
Research and Development Administration (hereinafter in this chapter
referred to as the "Administrator") shall be governed by the terms of
this chapter and other applicable provisions of law with respect to all
nonnuclear aspects of the research, development, and demonstration
program; and the policies and provisions of the Atomic Energy Act of
1954, and other provisions of law shall continue to apply to the nuclear
research, development, and demonstration program.

(3) In implementing and conducting the research, development, and
demonstration programs pursuant to this chapter, the Administrator
shall incorporate programs in specific nonnuclear technologies previously enacted into law, including those established by the Solar Heating and Cooling Act of 1974, the Geothermal Energy Research, Development, and Demonstration Act of 1974, and the Solar Energy Research,
Development, and Demonstration Act of 1974.

§ 5904. Research, development, and demonstration program governing principles.

(a) The Congress authorizes and directs that the comprehensive program in research, development, and demonstration required by this
chapter shall be designed and executed according to the following
principles:

(1) Energy conservation shall be a primary consideration in the
design and implementation of the Federal nonnuclear energy program.
For the purposes of this chapter, energy conservation means both improvement in efficiency of energy production and use, and reduction in
energy waste.

(2) The environmental and social consequences of a proposed program shall be analyzed and considered in evaluating its potential.

(3) Any program for the development of a technology which may require significant consumptive use of water after the technology has
reached the stage of commercial application shall include thorough consideration of the impacts of such technology and use on water resouces
pursuant to the provisions of section 5912 of this title.

(4) Heavy emphasis shall be given to those technologies which utilize renewable or essentially inexhaustible energy sources.

(5) The potential for production of net energy by the proposed technology at the stage of commercial application shall be analyzed and
considered in evaluating proposals.

(b) The Congress further directs that the execution of the comprehensive research, development, and demonstration program shall conform to the following principles:

(1) Research and development of nonnuclear energy sources shall
be pursued in such a way as to facilitate the commercial availability
of adequate supplies of energy to all regions of the United States. . . .

§ 5905. Comprehensive plan and implementing program for energy
research, development, and demonstration; transmission to Congress;
purposes; scope of program.

(a) Pursuant to the authority and directions of this chapter and the Energy Reorganization Act of 1974, the Administrator shall transmit to
the Congress, on or before June 30, 1975, a comprehensive plan for
energy research, development, and demonstration. This plan shall be
appropriately revised annually as provided in section 5914(a) of this
title. Such plan shall be designed to achieve—

(1) solutions to immediate and short-term (to the early 1980's) energy supply system and associated environmental problems;

(2) solutions to middle-term (the early 1980's to 2000) energy supply system and associated environmental problems; and

(3) solutions to long-term (beyond 2000) energy supply system and associated environmental problems.

(b) (1) Based on the comprehensive energy research, development, and demonstration plan developed under subsection (a) of this section, the Administrator shall develop and transmit to the Congress, on or before June 30, 1975, a comprehensive nonnuclear energy research, development, and demonstration program to implement the nonnuclear research, development, and demonstration aspects of the comprehensive plan.

(2) This program shall be designed to achieve solutions to the energy supply and associated environmental problems in the immediate and short-term (to the early 1980's), middle-term (the early 1980's to 2000), and long-term (beyond 2000) time intervals. In formulating the nonnuclear aspects of this program, the Administrator shall evaluate the economic, environmental, and technological merits of each aspect of the program.

(3) The Administrator shall assign program elements and activities in specific nonnuclear energy technologies to the short-term, middle-term, and long-term time intervals, and shall present full and complete justification for these assignments and the degree of emphasis for each. These program elements and activities shall include, but not be limited to, research, development, and demonstrations designed—

(A) to advance energy conservation technologies, including but not limited to—

(i) productive use of waste, including garbage, sewage, agricultural wastes, and industrial waste heat;

(ii) reuse and recycling of materials and consumer products;

(iii) improvements in automobile design for increased efficiency and lowered emissions, including investigation of the full range of alternatives to the internal combustion engine and systems of efficient public transportation; and

(iv) advanced urban and architectural design to promote efficient energy use in the residential and commercial sectors, improvements in home design and insulation technologies, small thermal storage units and increased efficiency in electrical appliances and lighting fixtures;

(B) to accelerate the commercial demonstration of technologies for producing low-sulfur fuels suitable for boiler use;

(C) to demonstrate improved methods for the generation, storage, and transmission of electrical energy through (i) advances in gas turbine technologies, combined power cycles, the use of low British thermal unit gas and, if practicable, magnetohydrodynamics; (ii) storage systems to allow more efficient load following, including the use of inertial energy storage systems; and (iii) improvement in cryogenic transmission methods;

(D) to accelerate the commercial demonstration of technologies for producing substitutes for natural gas, including coal gasification: Provided, That the Administrator shall invite and consider proposals from potential participants based upon Federal assistance and participation in the form of a joint Federal-industry corporation, and recommendations pursuant to this clause shall be accompanied by a report on the viability of using this form of Federal assistance or participation;

(E) to accelerate the commercial demonstration of technologies for producing syncrude and liquid petroleum products from coal: Provided, That the Administrator shall invite and consider proposals from potential participants based upon Federal assistance and participation through guaranteed prices or purchase of the products, and recommendations pursuant to this clause shall be accompanied by a report on the viability of using this form of Federal assistance or participation;

(F) in accordance with the program authorized by the Geothermal Energy Research, Development, and Demonstration Act of 1974, to accelerate the commercial demonstration of geothermal energy technologies;

(G) to demonstrate the production of syncrude from oil shale by all promising technologies including in situ technologies;

(H) to demonstrate new and improved methods for the extraction of petroleum resources, including secondary and tertiary recovery of crude oil;

(I) to demonstrate the economics and commercial viability of solar energy for residential and commercial energy supply applications in accordance with the program authorized by the Solar Heating and Cooling Act of 1974;

(J) to accelerate the commercial demonstration of environmental control systems for energy technologies developed pursuant to this chapter;

(K) to investigate the technical and economic feasibility of tidal power for supplying electrical energy;

(L) to commercially demonstrate advanced solar energy technologies in accordance with the Solar Research, Development, and Demonstration Act of 1974;

(M) to determine the economics and commercial viability of the production of synthetic fuels such as hydrogen and methanol;

(N) to commercially demonstrate the use of fuel cells for central station electric power generation;

(O) to determine the economics and commercial viability of in situ coal gasification;

(P) to improve techniques for the management of existing energy systems by means of quality control; application of systems analysis, communications, and computer techniques; and public information with the objective of improving the reliability and efficiency of energy supplies and encourage the conservation of energy resources; and

(Q) to improve methods for the prevention and cleanup of marine oil spills.

§ 5906.  Federal assistance and participation in programs—Forms of activities authorized.

(a) In carrying out the objectives of this chapter, the Administrator may utilize various forms of Federal assistance and participation which may include but are not limited to—

(1) joint Federal-industry experimental, demonstration, or commercial corporations consistent with the provisions of subsection (b) of this section;

(2) contractual arrangements with non-Federal participants including corporations, consortia, universities, governmental entities and nonprofit institutions;

(3) contracts for the construction and operation of federally owned facilities;

(4) Federal purchases or guaranteed price of the products of demonstration plants or activities consistent with the provisions of subsection (c) of the section;

(5) Federal loans to non-Federal entities conducting demonstrations of new technologies; and

(6) incentives, including financial awards, to individual inventors, such incentives to be designed to encourage the participation of a large number of such inventors. . . .

§ 5907.  Demonstration projects—Scope of authority of Administrator.

(a) The Administrator is authorized to—

(1) identify opportunities to accelerate the commercial applications of new energy technologies, and provide Federal assistance for or participation in demonstration projects (including pilot plants demonstrating technological advances and field demonstrations of new methods and procedures, and demonstrations of prototype commercial applications for the exploration, development, production, transportation, conversion, and utilization of energy resources); and

(2) enter into cooperative agreements with non-Federal entities to demonstrate the technical feasibility and economic potential of energy technologies on a prototype or full-scale basis.

§ 5910.  Environmental evaluations by Council on Environmental
Quality—Continuing analysis of effect of nonnuclear energy technologies.

(a) The Council on Environmental Quality is authorized and directed
to carry out a continuing analysis of the effect of application of nonnuclear energy technologies to evaluate—
    (1) the adequacy of attention to energy conservation methods; and
    (2) the adequacy of attention to environmental protection and the en-
vironmental consequences of the application of energy technologies. . . .

§ 5912.  Water resource assessments—Request by Administrator for
assessment by Water Resources Council of water resource requirements and water supply availability for nonnuclear energy technologies;
preparation requirement.

(a) At the request of the Administrator, the Water Resources Council
shall undertake assessments of water resource requirements and water
supply availability for any nonnuclear energy technology and any probable combinations of technologies which are the subject of Federal
research and development efforts authorized by this chapter, and the
commercial development of which could have significant impacts on
water resources.  In the preparation of its assessment, the Council
shall—
    (1) utilize to the maximum extent practicable data on water supply
and demand available in the files of member agencies of the Council;
    (2) collect and compile any additional data it deems necessary for
complete and accurate assessments;
    (3) give full consideration to the constraints upon availability im-
posed by treaty, compact, court decree, State water laws, and water
rights granted pursuant to State and Federal law;
    (4) assess the effects of development of such technology on water
quality;
    (5) include estimates of cost associated with production and manage-
ment of the required water supply, and the cost of disposal of waste
water generated by the proposed facility or process;
    (6) assess the environmental, social, and economic impact of any
change in use of currently utilized water resource that may be required
by the proposed facility or process; and
    (7) consult with the Council on Environmental Quality. . . .

STATES

MINNESOTA ENERGY ACT (1974)
Minn. Stat., Ch. 116H

§ 116H.01.  Findings and purpose.

The legislature finds and declares that the present rapid growth in demand for energy is in part due to unnecessary energy use; that a continuation of this trend will result in serious depletion of finite quantities of fuels, land and water resources, and threats to the state's environmental quality; that the state must insure consideration of urban expansion, transit systems, economic development, energy conservation and environmental protection in planning for large energy facilities, that there is a need to carry out energy conservation measures; and that energy planning, protection of environmental values, development of Minnesota energy sources, and conservation of energy require expanded authority and technical capability and a unified, coordinated response within state government.

The legislature seeks to encourage thrift in the use of energy, and to maximize use of energy-efficient systems, thereby reducing the rate of growth of energy consumption, prudently conserving energy resources, and assuring statewide environmental protection consistent with an adequate, reliable source of energy.

§ 116H.09.  Energy emergency allocation plan.

Subdivision 1.  Within nine months after March 29, 1974, the director shall prepare and issue an emergency conservation and allocation plan

in the manner set forth in Subdivision 2. Such plan shall provide a
variety of strategies and staged conservation measures to reduce
energy use and, in the event of an energy supply emergency, shall
establish guidelines and criteria for allocation of fuels to priority
users. The plan shall contain alternative conservation actions and
allocation plans to reasonably meet various foreseeable shortage circumstances and allow a choice of appropriate responses. The plan
shall be consistent with requirements of federal emergency energy
conservation and allocation laws and regulations and shall:

(a) Give priority to individuals, institutions, agriculture and businesses which demonstrate they have engaged in energy-saving measures
and shall include provisions to insure that:

(1) Immediate allocations to individuals, institutions, agriculture and businesses be based on needs at energy conservation levels;

(2) Successive allocations to individuals, institutions, agriculture
and businesses be based on needs after implementation of required
action to increase energy conservation;

(3) Needs of individuals and institutions are adjusted to insure
the health and welfare of the young, old and infirm;

(b) Insure maintenance of reasonable job safety conditions and avoid
environmental sacrifices;

(c) Establish procedures for fair and equitable review of complaints
and requests for special exemptions regarding emergency conservation
measures or allocations.

Subdivision 2. Within four months after March 29, 1974, the director
shall circulate, in a manner designed to assure widespread public
notice, a tentative plan of energy conservation measures and allocation priorities and criteria, and shall solicit, in a time, form and manner prescribed by him, public comments thereon. Further, the director may require all utilities, coal suppliers and petroleum suppliers
to comment thereon, as prescribed by him, and to submit suggested
emergency conservation measures and allocation criteria. . . .

Subdivision 3. In the process of soliciting public comments on the
tentative plan, the director shall hold at least five public meetings in
various geographical areas of the state to insure public comment.
The final plan shall be based on comments received from the public
and utilities, coal suppliers and petroleum suppliers, the independent
evaluation and analysis of the director and the guidelines set forth in
subdivision 1.

Subdivision 4. At least once every five years and whenever construction of a new large energy facility is completed which affects the supply of energy in Minnesota, the director shall review and if necessary
revise the emergency conservation and allocation plan. . . .

§ 116H.10.  Forecasts, statistics and information.

Subdivision 1.  In order to further the purposes of sections 116H.01 to
116H.15, the director shall develop and maintain an effective program
of collection, compilation, and analysis of energy statistics.  The sta-
tistical program shall be developed to insure a central state repository
of energy data and so that the state may coordinate and cooperate with
other governmental data collection and record keeping programs. . . .

§ 116H.11.  State energy policy and conservation report.

Subdivision 1.  Beginning January 1, 1976, and at least every two
years thereafter, the director shall transmit to the governor and the
legislature a comprehensive report designed to identify emerging
trends related to energy supply, demand, conservation, public health
and safety factors, and to specify the level of statewide and service
area energy need.  The report shall include, but not be limited to, all
of the following:
    (a) A final report on the accuracy and acceptability of the energy
forecasts received under section 116H.10 and the alternatives to meeting that demand;
    (b) An estimate of statewide and geographical area energy need for
the forthcoming five- and ten-year period which, in the judgment of
the director, will reasonably balance requirements of state and service area growth and development, protection of public health and
safety, preservation of environmental quality, and conservation of
energy resources.  Such forecasts established by the director shall
serve as the basis for certification of large energy facilities in section
116H.13;
    (c) The anticipated level of statewide and geographical area energy
demand for 20 years, which shall serve as the basis for long-range
action;
    (d) The identification of potential adverse social, economic, or en-
vironmental effects caused by a continuation of the present energy demand trends;
    (e) An assessment of the state's energy resources, including exam-
ination of the availability of commercially developable and imported
fuels;
    (f) The estimated reduction in annual energy consumption resulting
from various energy conservation measures. . . .

§ 116H.12.  Energy conservation.

Subdivision 1.  After consultation with the director and the commissioner of public safety, the commissioner of highways shall . . .
promulgate regulations establishing maximum energy use standards
for street, highway and parking lot lighting.  Such standards shall be

consistent with overall protection of the public health, safety and welfare. No new highway, street or parking lot lighting shall be installed in violation of these regulations and existing lighting levels shall be reduced consistent with the regulations as soon as feasible and practical, consistent with overall energy conservation.

Subdivision 2. The director may investigate promotional practices by energy suppliers and . . . may promulgate regulations to limit such practices in order to reduce the rate of growth of energy demand.

Subdivision 3. After July 1, 1974, no new natural gas outdoor lighting shall be installed in the state.

Subdivision 4. In recognition of the compelling need for energy conservation in order to safeguard the public health, safety and welfare, it is necessary to provide building design and construction standards consistent with the most efficient use of energy. Therefore, the commissioner of administration, in consultation with the director, shall, no later than April 1, 1975, . . . promulgate building design and construction standards regarding heat loss control, illumination and climate control. Such standards shall apply to all new buildings and remodeling affecting heat loss control, illumination and climate control. Such standards shall be economically feasible in that the resultant savings in energy procurement shall exceed the cost of the energy conserving requirements amortized over the life of the building. The standards shall become part of the state building code and be effective six months after promulgation.

Subdivision 5. The director, in conjunction with the commissioner of administration, shall conduct studies of the state's purchase and use of supplies, automobiles and equipment having a significant impact on energy use in order to determine the potential for energy conservation. The director may promulgate regulations to insure that energy use and conservation will be considered in state purchasing and, where appropriate, to require certain minimum energy efficiency standards in purchased products and equipment. No state purchasing of equipment or material use shall occur that is not in conformity with these regulations.

Subdivision 6. In consultation with the director, the commissioner of highways shall begin an efficiency study of the present traffic flow system within the state. The study shall consider the feasibility of a computer-coordinated traffic system and other measures for increasing the efficiency of present traffic loads.

Subdivision 7. The commissioner of administration shall begin a study of expanding the state telecommunication system to reduce travel between all state departments and agencies.

Subdivision 8. The tax study commission shall study the feasibility of encouraging car pools and private busing through the use of tax incentives.

Subdivision 9. In conjunction with the motor vehicle services division, the director shall study the feasibility of modifying motor vehicle license fees to reflect energy consumption.

§ 116H.13. Certificate of need.

Subdivision 1. Within six months after the submission of the first biennial report the director shall . . . promulgate assessment of need criteria to be used in the determination of need for large energy facilities pursuant to this section.

Subdivision 2. After promulgation of the assessment of need criteria, no large energy facility shall be sited or constructed in Minnesota without the issuance of a certificate of need by the director pursuant to sections 116H.01 to 116H.15 and consistent with the criteria for assessment of need.

Subdivision 3. No proposed large energy facility shall be certified for construction unless the applicant has justified its need. In assessing need, the director shall evaluate:

(1) The accuracy of the long-range energy demand forecasts on which the necessity for the facility is based;

(2) The effect of existing or possible energy conservation programs under section 116H.01 to 116H.15 or other federal or state legislation on long-term energy demand;

(3) The relationship of the proposed facility to overall state energy needs;

(4) Promotional activities which may have given rise to the demand for this facility;

(5) Socially beneficial uses of the output of this facility, including its uses to protect or enhance environmental quality;

(6) The effects of the facility in inducing future development;

(7) Possible alternatives for satisfying the energy demand including but not limited to potential for increased efficiency of existing energy generation facilities. . . .


FLORIDA STATE MINIMUM BUILDING CODE (1974)
Fla. Stat. 553.70 et seq.

§ 553.87. Single-family residences; solar water heating requirement.

Notwithstanding the provisions of §§ 553.12 and 553.13, no single-family residence shall be constructed within the state unless the plumbing therein is designed to facilitate the future installation of solar water-heating equipment. The words "facilitate the future installation" as used in this section shall mean the provision of readily accessible piping to allow for pipe fittings that will allow easy future connection into the system of solar water-heating equipment. It is the intent of the legislature to minimize cost of rearranging plumbing should solar water heaters be added to buildings.

# 3

## ENVIRONMENTAL POLICY

Legislative findings and declarations of purpose in various acts cited throughout this volume provide statements of environmental policies. Those specifying broad environmental goals and environmental rights declarations of state constitutions are referenced here. This chapter, in addition, cites procedural provisions for public participation in environmental decision making and for intervention via the judicial process.

The nation's foremost environmental statute is the National Environmental Policy Act. Its origins are detailed in the Third Annual Report of the Council on Environmental Quality (pp. 222-24):

NEPA's enactment.

The two bills that became NEPA were largely modeled after the Employment Act of 1946. That Act, which grew out of the concern about economic dislocations after World War II, declared a responsibility in the Federal Government to maintain a prosperous and stable national economy. The Act also created the three-man Council of Economic Advisers to advise the President in carrying out that responsibility and in preparing an annual report on the economy. The Employment Act was a watershed in the Federal Government's relationship to national economic problems. By following both aspects of that Act—declaring a Federal responsibility for action and providing for a council and an annual report—the sponsors of the 1969 bills hoped to create a similar watershed in the Government's relationship to environmental problems.

Instead of being an inadvertent contributor to environmental degradation, the Federal Government was to be
made a central participant in environmental renewal.
The bills directed the President to submit an annual report to Congress on the state of the environment. Similar
to the President's annual Economic Report, it would serve
over the years as an indicator of environmental conditions,
a record of governmental and private actions to enhance environmental quality, and a forum for raising important environmental issues.

During consideration of the bills which led to NEPA,
some supporters of the proposed law feared that the declaration of a national environmental policy might be an
empty utterance unless the statute embodied some means
of guaranteeing that Federal agencies would heed the new
policy. Witnesses repeatedly referred to the disastrous
oil blowout in early 1969 from offshore wells operating under Interior Department leases in the Santa Barbara Channel. Prior to the blowout, they said, the Federal Government had assured that environmental factors had been considered and that precautions had been taken to prevent oil
spillage. Events showed that the Government's assurances
had been more thorough than its precautions. Witnesses
supporting the proposed legislation produced many other
examples of what the Senate report later termed "the manner in which Federal policies and activities have contributed
to environmental decay and degradation." They called for
an "action-forcing" mechanism that would guarantee that
in the future the Government would follow through in its
pledge to protect the environment.

Congress' response to this need was the provision that
became section 102 of NEPA, a provision without a close
statutory precedent. The section directs all Federal agencies to interpret and administer their authorities in concert
with the new environmental policy. Subsection 102(2)(C)
requires agencies to prepare, for all "major Federal actions
significantly affecting the quality of the human environment,"
a detailed statement of what the environmental impacts will
be. In preparing the statement, agencies must consider alternative actions and consult with other agencies having environmental expertise.

Precursors of section 102.

Although the "action-forcing" provision of section 102
[42 U.S.C. 4332], requiring environmental impact consid-

eration, had no direct legislative model, it had foundations
in a number of earlier legislative and judicial developments
relating to enrivonmental protection.  The importance of
section 102 is that it brings these separate strands together
and confirms them in a statute applicable across the entire
Federal Government.

Individual agencies previously had mandates to consider
particular environmental concerns in planning their activities.  One of the earliest such mandates is section 10(a)
of the Federal Power Act [16 U.S.C. 803(a)].  As amended
in 1935, that law requires the Federal Power Commission
(FPC), in licensing any dam or related project, to consider
the interests of commerce, water power and "other beneficial public uses, including recreational purposes."  Two
landmark court decisions interpreted this requirement as
imposing an affirmative duty on the FPC to investigate and
consider less environmentally damaging alternatives to any
proposal.  In Scenic Hudson Preservation Conference v.
FPC, decided in 1965, the U.S. Court of Appeals for the
Second Circuit ruled that section 10(a) requires the FPC
to consider "[t]he totality of a project's immediate and
long-range effects."  It said the FPC cannot fulfill this
responsibility by sitting "as an umpire blandly calling
balls and strikes for adversaries appearing before it; the
right of the public must receive active and affirmative
protection at the hands of the Commission."  Two years
later, in Udall v. FPC, the U.S. Supreme Court gave its
sanction to this reading of the Act.

In 1966 the Congress enacted section 4(f) of the Department of Transportation Act [49 U.S.C. 1653(f)], which
requires the Department of Transportation (DOT) to consider alternatives to proposed transportation projects that
affect the environment.  Section 4(f) provides that before
the Department may approve a transportation project that
encroaches on a public park, wildlife refuge, or historic
site, the Secretary of Transportation must find that there
is no feasible and prudent alternative and that the project
has been planned to minimize the encroachment.  Together
with section 10(a) of the Federal Power Act, this requirement presaged the broad duty imposed by NEPA to explore less environmentally damaging alternative actions.

NEPA's provision that agencies preparing impact
statements must consult with agencies having environmental
expertise also had precursors.  The Fish and Wildlife Coordination Act [16 U.S.C. 661 et seq.], as amended in

1958, was intended to bring concern for wildlife into the
planning of Federal water resource projects. To help
guarantee that wildlife values are fully considered, it requires Federal agencies to consult with the Federal Fish
and Wildlife Service and State wildlife authorities in planning water resource projects. The National Historic
Preservation Act of 1966 [16 U.S.C. 470 et seq.] creates
a similar consultation mechanism to protect historic buildings and sites from encroachment by federally funded projects. Each of these consultation requirements is designed
to assure that the governmental bodies charged with protecting environmental values pay close attention to the
environmental effects of particular projects. Agencies can
combine their consultations under these statutes and under
NEPA's broader requirement and thus avoid any duplication
of effort.

The "action-forcing" provisions in section 102 of NEPA
build upon the foundations of the four earlier laws and apply
to all types of Government activities. Teamed with NEPA's
establishment of a national environmental policy and its
creation of the Council on Environmental Quality, section
102 provides a mechanism for significant reform in Government decisionmaking.

NEPA's requirement of environmental impact statements for
all "major Federal actions significantly affecting the qualify of the
human environment" has turned out to be the heart of the act and the
vehicle for significant court interpretations (see Irving Like's introductory essay, which also explores NEPA's future potential, pp. vi-xiv).
An assessment of the effect of Section 102 (42 U.S.C. 4332) on federal
agency operations appears in the Sixth Annual Report of the Council on
Environmental Quality (1976).

The council, established by the act, was given its key role in
the environmental impact assessment process by Presidential Executive Order 11514 of 1970 (p. 79). Subsequently, the council issued
guidelines (pp. 81-86) that spell out in detail when environmental impact
statements are to be filed, how they are to be prepared, and what information they are to contain. Federal administrative agencies, in
turn, have adopted regulations for implementing the environmental
assessment process. Those of the Department of Transportation are
quoted in part as an example (p. 86-90). They serve to insure the department's compliance with its obligations under NEPA and other acts
of Congress.

Under the Housing and Community Development Act of 1974 (p.
90) the responsibility for environmental review rests on recipients of

federal grants. Several other acts of Congress state the national environmental commitment: Congress' own Office of Technology Assessment (p. 91) is designed to provide the lawmakers with information on
potential effects of technology on the environment. The Intergovernmental Coordination Act of 1968 (p. 92) called for "review of Federal
programs and projects having a significant impact on area and community development." The machinery for coordinated federal-state-
local planning set in motion by Circular A-95 of the Office of Management and Budget under the mandate of this act has proved an important
tool in the environmental planning process.

Finally, the Endangered Species Act of 1973 makes the continued
existence of endangered and threatened species and the ecosystems
that support them an overriding national concern (Sec. 1536, p. 508).

The Environmental Protection Agency is the enforcing arm for
most of the federal legislation referenced throughout this volume. Established in 1970, it combined portions of existing departments with
new bureaus and offices as needed.

"Little NEPA's," state statutes patterned after but not necessarily
identical with the National Environmental Policy Act, are in force in
a number of states while others have instituted environmental assessment procedures through administrative or executive action. A complete listing appears each year in the CEQ's Report. California,
Hawaii, Indiana, Maryland, Massachusetts, Michigan, Minnesota,
Montana, New York, North Carolina, South Dakota, Virginia, Washington, and Wisconsin are among the states having passed laws requiring
environmental impact assessment for specified public actions, while
Delaware, Georgia, Mississippi, Nevada, North Dakota, and others
have instituted more limited review processes. Puerto Rico was one
of the first U.S. jurisdictions to pass a Public Policy Environmental
Act. It follows NEPA almost word for word. California's (p. 94) extends to all "projects" with "significant effect on the environment" and
applies to local as well as state agencies (court interpretation extends
it to certain private projects as well). Massachusetts' constitutional
environmental rights provision (p. 97) is made effective by citizen
suit (p. 107) and environmental impact legislation (p. 98).

Portions of several state constitutions assert environmental
rights, variously stated. Pennsylvania's (p. 100) lacks legislative
follow-up and was deemed not self-executing in Commonwealth v.
National Gettysburg Battlefield Tower (311 A.2d 588 [1973]). The
Pennsylvania Supreme Court in that case refused to enjoin construction
of an observation tower near the battlefield. Illinois, Rhode Island,
and Texas are other states recognizing a constitutional right to a de-
cent environment. The environmental article of New York's constitution is found below on p. 238.

Several states followed the national lead and consolidated health, conservation, and other natural resource functions exercised by different departments into Departments of Environmental Conservation or similarly named agencies. Alaska's comprehensive conservation statute (p. 100) does this. It details the powers of the new department and, significantly, imposes heavy penalties including detention of a vessel to secure payment for oil spill clean-up.

## PUBLIC PARTICIPATION IN DECISION MAKING

"Until the conservation movement began to flourish and citizen groups started demanding a right to participate in policy formation, the average specialized body seldom got a consumer reaction," states former Federal Power Commission member Charles R. Ross, who was involved in the Scenic Hudson case. With public participation the administrative decision-making process may be expected to arrive at a result that represents a fair balancing of competing interests and commands credibility:

> The impact of decisions about water could determine the long-run future of the nation, not simply the future of the paper industry, nor the future of a national park, nor the future of conservation or recreation, but the future of man himself.
>
> In recent years, therefore, beginning with initial attempts by such special interest groups as the conservationists, the decisionmaking process has undergone a dramatic change. No longer could the nation be casual about the methods used to reach water development decisions. All interested parties (removed as they might be from the direct consequences of a decision), including those expressing a concern for future generations, demanded not only the right to be heard, but also that the decision-making process itself be the one best adapted to arrive at a result which would balance fairly the competing interests of all groups. The developers and the environmentalists alike need a forum where they can express their positions, confident that the final decision will be one which has been arrived at as a result of an adequate presentation by all sides, including staff and decision-makers who are expert and independent. Such decisions will have the credibility necessary to command the respect of all, which is vital to the preservation of all our private and governmental institutions. . . .

The most neglected aspect (and the most important) of
decision-making is feedback on the impact of a particular
decision upon the general public.  Until the conservation
movement began to flourish and citizen groups started demanding a right to participate in policy formation, the
average specialized body seldom got a consumer reaction.
Industry groups who follow FPC actions closely understand
the subtleties of each decision, and most decisions are made
in light of the dire consequences predicted for the industry.
. . . Fortunately the intimacy which has characterized the
relationship of the regulator and the regulated is dissolving
under the glare of citizen scrutiny.  Beneficial as this is,
we must be careful that these citizen groups remain independent and not become a part of the system, and we must
encourage greater reverse flow from the man on the street.
. . . Seldom does government get enough citizen input. . . .

Today's decisions are now profiting by the increased
participation of citizen groups, although some people claim
that this participation has effectively prevented timely decisions.  One of the landmarks in the history of citizen participation is the Scenic Hudson case in which I was involved.
. . . The usual contemptuous remark about "little ol' ladies
in tennis shoes" holding up progress raised my hackles
since it appeared to me that a decision—quite presump-
tuously—had already been made to grant the license.  However, the Second Circuit Court of Appeals not only recognized the rights of conservation groups to intervene, but
also reminded the FPC in very forceful language that the
purpose of the Commission was not simply to umpire, but
to act affirmatively to develop a fair record of the case.
Ever since this decision, government agencies have had
their feet held to the fire, and legitimately so.  [Charles
R. Ross, Environmental Quality and Water Development,
ed. Charles R. Goldman (Freeman, 1973), pp. 398-99,
401-03.  Reprinted by permission of the publisher.]

Leading federal environmental statutes and administrative regulations mandate that the public be heard.  A partial list of statutes
quoted in this volume includes:

Clean Air Act (Sec. 1857c-4[a] [1] [B], 1857c-5)
Executive Order 11514 (Sec. 2[b])
CEQ Guidelines (Sec. 1500.9 [d])
Coastal Zone Management Act (Sec. 1455[c])
Wilderness Act (Sec. 1132[d])

Noise Control Act (Sec. 4905[c][2])
Deepwater Port Act (Sec. 1504[g])
Resource Recovery Act (Sec. 3254c[a])
Consumer Product Safety Act (Sec. 2064)
Nuclear Regulatory Commission (Sec. 5817)
Federal-Aid Highway Act (Sec. 128)
Airport and Airway Development Act (Sec. 1716[d])
Urban Mass Transportation Act (Sec. 1602[d], 1604[i], 1610[c])
Executive Order 11644 (Sec. 4[b])
FWPCA (Sec. 1314[a], 1342[a])

Federal agencies are, in addition, governed by the Administrative Procedure Act of 1946, which covers decision-making procedures and regulatory acts of agencies. Pursuant to these mandates all agencies have adopted regulations governing citizen input, as exemplified by those quoted on pp. 86-90 below.

Montana's 1972 Constitution provides for citizen participation and the 1975 legislature passed legislation to make this operative (p. 104). Much state legislation cited in various chapters of this book mandates public hearings. New York's Power Plant Siting Act and Wyoming's Industrial Siting and Development Act should be particularly noted.

CITIZEN SUITS

Public participation is carried a step further when citizens have recourse to the courts to compel public officials to enforce laws on the books. Much of the body of environmental law in fact grew out of such litigation, which forced judicial review of administrative determinations and expanded "standing" rules of the federal courts.

Federal statutes making citizen suits a part of their enforcement machinery include the Clean Air Act (Sec. 1857h-2a), the Ocean Dumping Act (Sec. 1415[g]), the Safe Drinking Water Act (Sec. 300j-8), the Consumer Product Safety Act (Sec. 2073), and the FWPCA (Sec. 1365). Over and above these specific provisions, organizations whose members would be affected by proposed projects or programs may sue in federal court to have them reviewed (see pp. vii, xxvii).

Michigan's Environmental Protection Act of 1970 (p. 105) relies in part on the state's political subdivisions and its citizens to act to protect the environment. Massachusetts carries out its consitutional mandate by spelling out what actions may be brought for the purpose of protecting natural resources (p. 107). Other states afford citizens access to the courts under specified statutes such as Montana's mining legislation (Sec. 50-1055, 50-1612). New York's power plant siting

act (Public Service Law, Sec. 144) and Wyoming's Industrial Siting
and Development Act (Sec. 35.502.85) permit citizen organizations to
be parties to licensing proceedings. New York's Constitution, in addition, offers a qualified citizen suit possibility to enforce its environmental article (Art. XIV:5). Connecticut has citizen suit legislation
modeled on that of Michigan.


FEDERAL


NATIONAL ENVIRONMENTAL POLICY ACT (1969, as amended)
42 U.S.C. 4331 et seq.

Subchapter I—Policies and Goals
  Section 4331.  Congressional declaration of national environmental
                 policy
         4332.  Cooperation of agencies; reports; availability of infor-
                 mation; recommendations; international and national
                 coordination of efforts
         4333.  Conformity of administrative procedures to national
                 environmental policy
         4334.  Other statutory obligations of agencies
         4335.  Efforts supplemental to existing authorizations

Subchapter II—Council on Environmental Quality
  Section 4341.  Reports to Congress; recommendations for legislation
         4342.  Establishment; membership; chairman; appointments
         4343.  Employment of personnel, experts and consultants
         4344.  Duties and functions
         4345.  Consultation with the Citizen's Advisory Committee
                 on Environmental Quality and other representatives
         4346.  Tenure and compensation of members
         4347.  Authorization of appropriations

§ 4331.  Congressional declaration of national environmental policy.

(a) The Congress, recognizing the profound impact of man's activity
on the interrelations of all components of the natural environment,
particularly the profound influences of population growth, high-density
urbanization, industrial expansion, resource exploitation, and new
and expanding technological advances and recognizing further the
critical importance of restoring and maintaining environmental quality
to the overall welfare and development of man, declares that it is the
continuing policy of the Federal Government, in cooperation with State
and local governments, and other concerned public and private organi-

zations, to use all practicable means and measures, including financial and technical assistance, in a manner calculated to foster and promote the general welfare, to create and maintain conditions under which man and nature can exist in productive harmony, and fulfill the social, economic, and other requirements of present and future generations of Americans.

(b) In order to carry out the policy set forth in this chapter, it is the continuing responsibility of the Federal Government to use all practicable means, consistent with other essential considerations of national policy, to improve and coordinate Federal plans, functions, programs, and resources to the end that the Nation may—

(1) fulfill the responsibilities of each generation as trustee of the environment for succeeding generations;

(2) assure for all Americans safe, healthful, productive, and esthetically and culturally pleasing surroundings;

(3) attain the widest range of beneficial uses of the environment without degradation, risk to health or safety, or other undesirable and unintended consequences;

(4) preserve important historic, cultural, and natural aspects of our national heritage, and maintain, wherever possible, an environment which supports diversity and variety of individual choice;

(5) achieve a balance between population and resource use which will permit high standards of living and a wide sharing of life's amenities; and

(6) enhance the quality of renewable resources and approach the maximum attainable recycling of depletable resources.

(c) The Congress recognizes that each person should enjoy a healthful environment and that each person has a responsibility to contribute to the preservation and enhancement of the environment.

§ 4332. Cooperation of agencies; reports; availability of information; recommendations; international and national coordination of efforts.

The Congress authorizes and directs that, to the fullest extent possible:

(1) the policies, regulations, and public laws of the United States shall be interpreted and administered in accordance with the policies set forth in this chapter, and

(2) all agencies of the Federal Government shall—

(A) utilize a systematic, interdisciplinary approach which will insure the integrated use of the natural and social sciences and the environmental design arts in planning and in decisionmaking which may have an impact on man's environment;

(B) identify and develop methods and procedures, in consultation with the Council on Environmental Quality established by subchapter II of this chapter, which will insure that presently unquantified environmental amenities and values may be given appropriate consideration in decisionmaking along with economic and technical considerations;

(C) include in every recommendation or report on proposals for legislation and other major Federal actions significantly affecting the quality of the human environment, a detailed statement by the responsible official on—

(i) the environmental impact of the proposed action,

(ii) any adverse environmental effects which cannot be avoided should the proposal be implemented,

(iii) alternatives to the proposed action,

(iv) the relationship between local short-term uses of man's environment and the maintenance and enhancement of long-term productivity, and

(v) any irreversible and irretrievable commitments of resources which would be involved in the proposed action should it be implemented.

Prior to making any detailed statement, the responsible Federal official shall consult with and obtain the comments of any Federal agency which has jurisdiction by law or special expertise with respect to any environmental impact involved. Copies of such statement and the comments and views of the appropriate Federal, State, and local agencies, which are authorized to develop and enforce environmental standards, shall be made available to the President, the Council on Environmental Quality and to the public as provided by section 552 of Title 5, and shall accompany the proposal through the existing agency review processes;

(D) Any detailed statement required under subparagraph (C) after January 1, 1970, for any major Federal action funded under a program of grants to States shall not be deemed to be legally insufficient solely by reason of having been prepared by a State agency or official, if:

(i) the State agency or official has statewide jurisdiction and has the responsibility for such action,

(ii) the responsible Federal official furnishes guidance and participates in such preparation,

(iii) the responsible Federal official independently evaluates such statement prior to its approval and adoption, and

(iv) after January 1, 1976, the responsible Federal official provides early notification to, and solicits the views of, any other State or any Federal land management entity of any actions or any alternative thereto which may have significant impacts upon such State or affected Federal land management entity and, if there is any disagreement on such impacts, prepares a written assessment of such impacts and views for incorporation into such detailed statement.

The procedures in this subparagraph shall not relieve the Federal official of his responsibilities for the scope, objectivity, and content of the entire statement or of any other responsibility under this chapter; and further, this subparagraph does not affect the legal sufficiency of statements prepared by State agencies with less than statewide jurisdiction.

(E) study, develop, and describe appropriate alternatives to recommended courses of action in any proposal which involves unresolved conflicts concerning alternative uses of available resources;

(F) recognize the worldwide and long-range character of environmental problems and, where consistent with the foreign policy of the United States, lend appropriate support to initiatives, resolutions, and programs designed to maximize international cooperation in anticipating and preventing a decline in the quality of mankind's world environment;

(G) make available to States, counties, municipalities, institutions, and individuals, advice and information useful in restoring, maintaining, and enhancing the quality of the environment;

(H) initiate and utilize ecological information in the planning and development of resource-oriented projects; and

(I) assist the Council on Environmental Quality established by subchapter II of this chapter.

§ 4333. Conformity of administrative procedures to national environmental policy.

All agencies of the Federal Government shall review their present statutory authority, administrative regulations, and current policies and procedures for the purpose of determining whether there are any deficiencies or inconsistencies therein which prohibit full compliance with the purposes and provisions of this chapter and shall propose to the President not later than July 1, 1971, such measures as may be necessary to bring their authority and policies into conformity with the intent, purposes, and procedures set forth in this chapter.

§ 4341. Reports to Congress; recommendations for legislation.

The President shall transmit to the Congress annually beginning July 1, 1970, an Environmental Quality Report (hereinafter referred to as the "report") which shall set forth

(1) the status and condition of the major natural, manmade, or altered environmental classes of the Nation, including, but not limited to, the air, the aquatic, including marine, estuarine, and fresh water, and the terrestrial environment, including, but not limited to, the forest, dryland, wetland, range, urban, suburban, and rural environment;

(2) current and foreseeable trends in the quality, management and utilization of such environments and the effects of those trends on the social, economic, and other requirements of the Nation;

(3) the adequacy of available natural resources for fulfilling human and economic requirements of the Nation in the light of expected population pressures;

(4) a review of the programs and activities (including regulatory activities) of the Federal Government, the State and local governments, and nongovernmental entities or individuals, with particular reference to their effect on the environment and on the conservation, development and utilization of natural resources; and

(5) a program for remedying the deficiencies of existing programs and activities, together with recommendations for legislation.

§ 4342.  Establishment; membership; Chairman; appointments.

There is created in the Executive Office of the President a Council on Environmental Quality (hereinafter referred to as the "Council"). The Council shall be composed of three members who shall be appointed by the President to serve at his pleasure, by and with the advice and consent of the Senate.  The President shall designate one of the members of the Council to serve as Chairman.  Each member shall be a person who, as a result of his training, experience, and attainments, is exceptionally well qualified to analyze and interpret environmental trends and information of all kinds; to appraise programs and activities of the Federal Government in the light of the policy set forth in subchapter I of this chapter; to be conscious of and responsive to the scientific, economic, social, esthetic, and cultural needs and interests of the Nation; and to formulate and recommend national policies to promote the improvement of the quality of the environment.

§ 4344.  Duties and functions.

It shall be the duty and function of the Council—

(1) to assist and advise the President in the preparation of the Environmental Quality Report required by section 4341 of this title;

(2) to gather timely and authoritative information concerning the conditions and trends in the quality of the environment both current and prospective, to analyze and interpret such information for the purpose of determining whether such conditions and trends are interfering, or are likely to interfere, with the achievement of the policy set forth in subchapter I of this chapter, and to compile and submit to the President studies relating to such conditions and trends;

(3) to review and appraise the various programs and activities of the Federal Government in the light of the policy set forth in subchapter I of this chapter for the purpose of determining the extent to which such programs and activities are contributing to the achievement of such policy, and to make recommendations to the President with respect thereto;

(4) to develop and recommend to the President national policies to foster and promote the improvement of environmental quality to meet the conservation, social, economic, health, and other requirements and goals of the Nation;

(5) to conduct investigations, studies, surveys, research, and analyses relating to ecological systems and environmental quality;

(6) to document and define changes in the natural environment, including the plant and animal systems, and to accumulate necessary data and other information for a continuing analysis of these changes or trends and an interpretation of their underlying causes;

(7) to report at least once each year to the President on the state and condition of the environment; and

(8) to make and furnish such studies, reports thereon, and recommendations with respect to matters of policy and legislation as the President may request.

PROTECTION AND ENHANCEMENT OF ENVIRONMENTAL
QUALITY (1970)
Exec. Order 11514, 35 F. Reg. 4247

§ 3.  Responsibilities of Council on Environmental Quality.

The Council on Environmental Quality shall:

(a) Evaluate existing and proposed policies and activities of the Federal Government directed to the control of pollution and the enhancement of the environment and to the accomplishment of other objectives which affect the quality of the environment.  This shall include continuing review of procedures employed in the development and enforcement of Federal standards affecting environmental quality.  Based upon such evaluations the Council shall, where appropriate, recommend to the President policies and programs to achieve more effective protection and enhancement of environmental quality and shall, where appropriate, seek resolution of significant environmental issues.

(b) Recommend to the President and to the agencies priorities among programs designed for the control of pollution and for enhancement of the environment.

(c) Determine the need for new policies and programs for dealing with environmental problems not being adequately addressed.

(d) Conduct, as it determines to be appropriate, public hearings or conferences on issues of environmental significance.

(e) Promote the development and use of indices and monitoring systems
    (1) to assess environmental conditions and trends,
    (2) to predict the environmental impact of proposed public and private actions, and
    (3) to determine the effectiveness of programs for protecting and enhancing environmental quality.

(f) Coordinate Federal programs related to environmental quality.

(g) Advise and assist the President and the agencies in achieving international cooperation for dealing with environmental problems, under the foreign policy guidance of the Secretary of State.

(h) Issue guidelines to Federal agencies for the preparation of detailed statements on proposals for legislation and other Federal actions affecting the environment, as required by section 102(2)(C) of the Act [section 4332(2)(C) of this title].

(i) Issue such other instructions to agencies, and request such reports and other information from them, as may be required to carry out the Council's responsibilities under the Act.

(j) Assist the President in preparing the annual Environmental Quality Report provided for in section 201 of the Act [section 4341 of this title].

(i) Issue such other instructions to agencies, and request such reports and other information from them, as may be required to carry out the Council's responsibilities under the Act.

(j) Assist the President in preparing the annual Environmental Quality Report provided for in section 201 of the Act [section 4341 of this title].

(k) Foster investigations, studies, surveys, research, and analysis relating to
    (1) ecological systems and environmental quality,
    (2) the impact of new and changing technologies thereon, and
    (3) means of preventing or reducing adverse effects from such technologies.

PREPARATION OF ENVIRONMENTAL IMPACT
STATEMENTS: GUIDELINES (1973)
38 F. Reg. 20550 et seq.

§ 1500.2.  Policy.

(a) As early as possible and in all cases prior to agency decision concerning recommendations or favorable reports on proposals for

(1) legislation significantly affecting the quality of the human environment (see §§ 1500.5(i) and 1500.12) (hereafter "legislative actions") and

(2) all other major Federal actions significantly affecting the quality of the human environment (hereafter "administrative actions"), Federal agencies will, in consultation with other appropriate Federal, State and local agencies and the public assess in detail the potential environmental impact.

(b) Initial assessments of the environmental impacts of proposed action should be undertaken concurrently with initial technical and economic studies and, where required, a draft environmental impact

statement prepared and circulated for comment in time to accompany
the proposal through the existing agency review processes for such
action. In this process, Federal agencies shall:

(1) Provide for circulation of draft environmental statements to
other Federal, State, and local agencies and for their availability to
the public in accordance with the provisions of these guidelines;

(2) consider the comments of the agencies and the public; and

(3) issue final environmental impact statements responsive to the
comments received.

The purpose of this assessment and consultation process is to provide
agencies and other decision-makers as well as members of the public
with an understanding of the potential environmental effects of proposed
actions, to avoid or minimize adverse effects wherever possible, and
to restore or enhance environmental quality to the fullest extent practicable. In particular, agencies should use the environmental impact
statement process to explore alternative actions that will avoid or
minimize adverse impacts and to evaluate both the long- and short-
range implications of proposed actions to man, his physical and social
surroundings, and to nature. Agencies should consider the results
of their environmental assessments along with their assessments of
the net economic, technical and other benefit of proposed actions and
use all practicable means, consistent with other essential considerations of national policy, to restore environmental quality as well as
to avoid or minimize undesirable consequences for the environment.

§ 1500.5. Types of actions covered by the Act.

(a) "Actions" include but are not limited to:

(1) Recommendations or favorable reports relating to legislation
including requests for appropriations. The requirement for following
the section 102(2)(C) procedure as elaborated in these guidelines applies to both

(i) agency recommendations on their own proposals for legislation (see § 1500.12); and

(ii) agency reports on legislation initiated elsewhere. In the
latter case only the agency which has primary responsibility for
the subject matter involved will prepare an environmental statement.

(2) New and continuing projects and program activities: directly
undertaken by Federal agencies; or supported in whole or in part
through Federal contracts, grants, subsidies, loans, or other forms
of funding assistance (except where such assistance is solely in the
form of general revenue sharing funds, distributed under the State
and Local Fiscal Assistance Act of 1972, 31 U.S.C. 1221 et seq. with
no Federal agency control over the subsequent use of such funds); or
involving a Federal lease, permit, license, certificate, or other entitlement for use.

(3) The making, modification, or establishment of regulations, rules, procedures, and policy.

§ 1500.6. Identifying major actions significantly affecting the environment.

(a) The statutory clause "major Federal actions significantly affecting the quality of the human environment" is to be construed by agencies with a view to the overall, cumulative impact of the action proposed, related Federal actions and projects in the area, and further actions contemplated. Such actions may be localized in their impact, but if there is potential that the environment may be significantly affected, the statement is to be prepared. Proposed major actions, the environmental impact of which is likely to be highly controversial, should be covered in all cases. In considering what constitutes major action significantly affecting the environment, agencies should bear in mind that the effect of many Federal decisions about a project or complex of projects can be individually limited but cumulatively considerable. . . .

(b) Section 101(b) of the Act indicates the broad range of aspects of the environment to be surveyed in any assessment of significant effect. . . .

(d) (1) Agencies should give careful attention to identifying and defining the purpose and scope of the action which would most appropriately serve as the subject of the statement. In many cases, broad program statements will be required in order to assess the environmental effects of a number of individual actions on a given geographical area (e.g., coal leases), or environmental impacts that are generic or common to a series of agency actions (e.g., maintenance or waste handling practices), or the overall impact of a large-scale program or chain of contemplated projects (e.g., major lengths of highway as opposed to small segments). Subsequent statements on major individual actions will be necessary where such actions have significant environmental impacts not adequately evaluated in the program statement.

(2) Agencies engaging in major technology research and development programs should develop procedures for periodic evaluation to determine when a program statement is required for such programs. . . .

(e) In accordance with the policy of the Act and Executive Order 11514 agencies have a responsibility to develop procedures to insure the fullest practicable provision of timely public information and understanding of Federal plans and programs with environmental impact in order to obtain the views of interested parties. In furtherance of this policy, agency procedures should include an appropriate early notice system for informing the public of the decision to prepare a draft environmental statement on proposed administrative actions (and for

soliciting comments that may be helpful in preparing the statement)
as soon as is practicable after the decision to prepare the statement
is made. . . .

§ 1500.8.  Content of environmental statements.

(a) The following points are to be covered:

(1) A description of the proposed action, a statement of its purposes,
and a description of the environment affected, including information,
summary technical data, and maps and diagrams where relevant, adequate to permit an assessment of potential environmental impact by
commenting agencies and the public. . . .

(2) The relationship of the proposed action to land use plans, policies, and controls for the affected area.  This requires a discussion of
how the proposed action may conform or conflict with the objectives
and specific terms of approved or proposed Federal, State, and local
land use plans, policies and controls, if any, for the area affected including those developed in response to the Clean Air Act or the Federal
Water Pollution Control Act Amendments of 1972.  Where a conflict
or inconsistency exists, the statement should describe the extent to
which the agency has reconciled its proposed action with the plan,
policy or control, and the reasons why the agency has decided to proceed notwithstanding the absence of full reconciliation.

(3) The probable impact of the proposed action on the environment.

(i) This requires agencies to assess the positive and negative
effects of the proposed action as it affects both the national and international environment. . . .

(ii) Secondary or indirect, as well as primary or direct, consequences for the environment should be included in the analysis.
Many major Federal actions, in particular those that involve the
construction or licensing of infrastructure investments (e.g., highways, airports, sewer systems, water resource projects, etc.),
stimulate or induce secondary effects in the form of associated investments and changed patterns of social and economic activities.
Such secondary effects, through their impacts on existing community facilities and activities, through inducing new facilities and
activities, or through changes in natural conditions, may often be
even more substantial than the primary effects of the original action itself. . . .

(4) Alternatives to the proposed action, including, where relevant,
those not within the existing authority of the responsible agency. . . .
Examples of such alternatives include: the alternative of taking no
action or of postponing action pending further study; alternatives requiring actions of a significantly different nature which would provide
similar benefits with different environmental impacts (e.g., nonstruc-
tural alternatives to flood control programs, or mass transit alterna-

tives to highway construction); alternatives related to different designs
or details of the proposed action which would present different environmental impacts (e.g., cooling ponds vs. cooling towers for a power
plant or alternatives that will significantly conserve energy); alternative measures to provide for compensation of fish and wildlife losses,
including the acquisition of land, waters, and interests therein. . . .

(5) Any probable adverse environmental effects which cannot be
avoided (such as water or air pollution, undesirable land use patterns,
damage to life systems, urban congestion, threats to health or other
consequences adverse to the environmental goals set out in section
101(b) of the Act). . . .

(6) The relationship between local short-term uses of man's environment and the maintenance and enhancement of long-term productivity.
This section should contain a brief discussion of the extent to which the
proposed action involves tradeoffs between short-term environmental
gains at the expense of long-term losses, or vice versa, and a discussion of the extent to which the proposed action forecloses future options. . . .

(7) Any irreversible and irretrievable commitments of resources
that would be involved in the proposed action should it be implemented.
. . .

(8) An indication of what other interests and considerations of Federal policy are thought to offset the adverse environmental effects of
the proposed action identified pursuant to paragraphs (a)(3) and (5) of
this section. The statement should also indicate the extent to which
these stated countervailing benefits could be realized by following reasonable alternatives to the proposed action (as identified in paragraph
(a)(4) of this section) that would avoid some or all of the adverse environmental effects. . . .

(b) In developing the above points agencies should make every effort
to convey the required information succinctly in a form easily understood, both by members of the public and by public decisionmakers,
giving attention to the substance of the information conveyed rather
than to the particular form, or length, or detail of the statement. . . .
In the case of documents not likely to be easily accessible (such as
internal studies or reports), the agency should indicate how such information may be obtained. If such information is attached to the
statement, care should be taken to ensure that the statement remains
an essentially self-contained instrument, capable of being understood
by the reader without the need for undue cross reference. . . .

§ 1500.9. Review of draft environmental statements by Federal,
Federal-State, and local agencies and by the public. . . .

(d) Public review. The procedures established by these guidelines
are designed to encourage public participation in the impact statement

process at the earliest possible time. Agency procedures should make provision for facilitating the comment of public and private organizations and individuals by announcing the availability of draft environmental statements and by making copies available to organizations and individuals that request an opportunity to comment. Agencies should devise methods for publicizing the existence of draft statements, for example, by publication of notices in local newspapers or by maintaining a list of groups, including relevant conservation commissions, known to be interested in the agency's activities and directly notifying such groups of the existence of a draft statement, or sending them a copy, as soon as it has been prepared. A copy of the draft statement should in all cases be sent to any applicant whose project is the subject of the statement. Materials to be made available to the public shall be provided without charge to the extent practicable, or at a fee which is not more than the actual cost of reproducing copies required to be sent to other Federal agencies, including the Council. . . .

## DEPARTMENT OF TRANSPORTATION ENVIRONMENTAL IMPACT AND RELATED STATEMENTS (1974)
### 23 C.F.R. 771 et seq.

§ 771.9.  Major and non-major actions.

(d) Major actions are those of superior, large and considerable importance involving substantial planning, time, resources or expenditures.
Any action that is likely to precipitate significant foreseeable alterations in land use; planned growth; development patterns; traffic volumes; travel patterns; transportation services, including public transportation; and natural and manmade resources would be considered a
major action.  The following are examples . . .
    (7) A project that warrants a "major action" classification because
it has been given national recognition by Congress even though it is
not included in the above list.  Such a project would be one that falls
under section 4(f) of the DOT Act or section 106 of the National Historic
Preservation Act.

(f) There will be highway sections which are not readily classified as
major or non-major actions.  There will also be those highway sections which may normally be classified as non-major actions, but
for which the FHWA Division Engineer may feel special consideration
is appropriate.  For such highway sections, the FHWA Division Engineer may, when deemed appropriate, classify them as major actions
or use the following procedure to assist in the major or non-major
determination.

§ 771.10.  Significant effect determination.

(e) The following are examples of types of actions which ordinarily
have a significant effect on the quality of the human environment.
    (1) An action that has more than minimal effect on properties pro-
tected under section 4(f) of the DOT Act or section 106 of the Historic
Preservation Act.
    (2) An action that is likely to be highly controversial on environmen-
tal grounds or with respect to the availability of adequate relocation
housing.
    (3) An action that is likely to have a significantly adverse impact
on natural, ecological, cultural or scenic resources of national, State
or local significance.
    (4) An action that
        (i) causes significant division or disruption of an established
community or disrupts orderly, planned development, or is determined to be significantly inconsistent with plans or goals that have
been adopted by the community in which the project is located, as
determined by a responsible official(s); or
        (ii) causes a significant increase in traffic congestion.
    (5) An action which
        (i) is determined to be inconsistent with any Federal, State or
local law or regulation relating to the environment; or

(ii) has a significant detrimental impact on air or water quality
or on ambient noise levels for adjoining areas; or
(iii) may contaminate a public water supply system.

§ 771.11.  Negative declarations.

(a) A draft negative declaration shall be prepared by the HA in consultation with FHWA for each major action which is a Federal action when
the studies and coordination demonstrate that implementing the proposed
action will not have a significant impact upon the quality of the human
environment of a magnitude to require the processing of an EIS.

§ 771.18.  Content of the environmental impact statement.

(i) Natural, ecological or scenic resources impacts.  This section
will summarize the significant effects on natural, ecological and scenic
resources anticipated to be associated with the implementation of the
proposed action, including a summary of consultations with the appropriate public and governmental agencies.  One example of a natural resource impact would be the effect an action would have on the consumption of energy resources.

(ii) Relocation of individuals and families impacts.

(iii) Social impacts.  This section will include a discussion of the significant social impacts anticipated to be caused by the proposed action.
The following are examples of groups that may have special problems
and require special consideration with respect to access to jobs,
schools, churches, parks, hospitals, shopping, and community services:
    (A) elderly
    (B) school-age children
    (C) those dependent upon public transportation
    (D) handicapped
    (E) illiterate
    (F) nondrivers
    (G) pedestrians
    (H) bicyclists
    (I) low income
    (J) racial, ethnic, or religious groups
(iv) Air quality.
    (A) This section shall include:  an identification of the air quality
impact of the highway section; an identification of the analysis methodology utilized; a brief summary of the early consultation with the air
pollution control agency and, where applicable, a brief summary of
any consultation with the indirect source review agency; any comments
received from the air pollution control agency, and, where applicable,

any comments received from the indirect source review agency; and
the Highway Agency's determination on the consistency of each alternative under consideration with the approved State implementation
plan. . . .

(v) Noise impacts.

(vi) Water quality impacts. Include in this section a discussion on
significant water quality impacts, including summaries of analyses
and consultations with the agency responsible for the State water quality standards. Possible water quality impacts related to highways include: erosion and subsequent sedimentation problems; use of deicing,
weed, rodent and insect control products; waste water disposal at
safety roadside rest areas; spillage of poisons or chemicals by trucks
into a water supply system; and contamination of surface and ground
water supplies and of recharge areas by polluted fill material.

(vii) Wetlands and coastal zones impacts.

(viii) Stream modification or impoundment impacts.

(ix) Flood hazard evaluation.
    (j) Alternatives.
       (1) This section shall include a discussion, with maps and
other visual aids, as appropriate, of the reasonable alternatives
studied in detail, including those that might enhance environmental quality or avoid some or all of the adverse enrivonmental effects. Examples of such alternatives include alternate locations
and designs, not implementing the proposed action, postponing
the action, providing a lower level of service, providing a reduced
facility (lanes/design), and an increase or decrease in public
transportation. . . .
    (n) The impact on properties and sites of historic and cultural
significance.
       (1) To determine whether the project will have an effect on
properties of State or local historical, architectural, archaeological, or cultural significance, the HA should consult with the
State Historic Preservation Officer (SHPO), with the local official
having jurisdiction of the property, and where appropriate, with
historical societies, museums, or academic institutions having
expertise with regard to the property.
       (2) This section of the draft EIS should contain an identification
of properties included in or eligible for inclusion in the National
Register and an evaluation of the effect the proposed action would
have on such properties. It should also contain a record of the
coordination with the DHPO concerning the identification of such
properties and the evaluation of effect.

(3) This section of the final EIS should also contain (a) documentation supporting a finding of no adverse effect and a record of coordination with the Executive Director, Advisory Council on Historic Preservation (ACHP), or (b) an executed Memorandum of Agreement when an adverse effect has been established, or comments from the Council after consideration of the project at a meeting of the ACHP and an account of actions to be taken in response to the comments of the ACHP.

## § 771.19.  Section 4(f) statements.

(a) The purpose of a section 4(f) statement is to document the consideration, consultations and alternative studies for a determination that there are no feasible and prudent alternatives to the use of land from a publicly owned park, recreation area, or wildlife and waterfowl refuge of national, State or local significance, as determined by the Federal, State or local official having jurisdiction thereof; or any land from a historic site of national, State or local significance as so determined by such official.  The purpose of the section 4(f) statement is also to support a determination that the proposed action includes all possible planning to minimize harm. . . .

## § 771.20.  Historic and cultural preservation procedures.

(a) The Advisory Council on Historic Preservation promulgated Procedures for the Protection of Historic and Cultural Properties, 36 CFR Part 800, pursuant to the National Historic Preservation Act of 1966 and Executive Order 11593.  These procedures apply to all FHWA actions which could affect a property which is included or eligible for inclusion in the National Register of Historic Places. . . .

## HOUSING AND COMMUNITY DEVELOPMENT ACT (1974)
### 42 U.S.C. 5301 et seq.

## § 5304.  Application and review requirements.

(h)(1) In order to assure that the policies of the National Environmental Policy Act of 1969 are most effectively implemented in connection with the expenditure of funds under this chapter, and to assure to the public undiminished protection of the environment, the Secretary, in lieu of the environmental protection procedures otherwise applicable, may under regulations provide for the release of funds for particular projects to applicants who assume all of the responsibilities for environmental review, decisionmaking, and action pursuant to such Act that would apply to the Secretary were he to undertake such projects as Federal projects.  The Secretary shall issue regulations to carry out this subsection only after consultation with the Council on Environmental Quality. . . .

OFFICE OF TECHNOLOGY ASSESSMENT (1972)
2 U.S.C. 471 et seq.

§ 471.  Congressional findings and declaration of purpose.

The Congress hereby finds and declares that:

(a) As technology continues to change and expand rapidly, its applications are—
(1) large and growing in scale; and
(2) increasingly extensive, pervasive, and critical in their impact, beneficial and adverse, on the natural and social environment.

(b) Therefore, it is essential that, to the fullest extent possible, the consequences of technological applications be anticipated, understood, and considered in determination of public policy on existing and emerging national problems.

(c) The Congress further finds that:
(1) the Federal agencies presently responsible directly to the Congress are not designed to provide the legislative branch with adequate and timely information, independently developed, relating to the potential impact of technological applications, and
(2) the present mechanisms of the Congress do not and are not designed to provide the legislative branch with such information.

(d) Accordingly, it is necessary for the Congress to—
(1) equip itself with new and effective means for securing competent, unbiased information concerning the physical, biological, economic, social, and political effects of such applications; and
(2) utilize this information, whenever appropriate, as one factor in the legislative assessment of matters pending before the Congress, particularly in those instances where the Federal Government may be called upon to consider support for, or management or regulation of, technological applications.

§ 472.  Office of Technology Assessment.

(a) Creation.

In accordance with the findings and declaration of purpose in section 471 of this title, there is hereby created the Office of Technology Assessment (hereinafter referred to as the "Office") which shall be within and responsible to the legislative branch of the Government.

(b) Composition.

The Office shall consist of a Technology Assessment Board (hereinafter referred to as the "Board") which shall formulate and promulgate the policies of the Office, and a Director who shall carry out such policies and administer the operations of the Office.

(c) Functions and duties.

The basic function of the Office shall be to provide early indications
of the probable beneficial and adverse impacts of the applications of
technology and to develop other coordinate information which may assist the Congress. In carrying out such function, the Office shall:

(1) identify existing or probable impacts of technology or technological programs;

(2) where possible, ascertain cause-and-effect relationships;

(3) identify alternative technological methods of implementing specific programs;

(4) identify alternative programs for achieving requisite goals;

(5) make estimates and comparisons of the impacts of alternative
methods and programs;

(6) present findings of completed analyses to the appropriate legislative authorities;

(7) identify areas where additional research or data collection is
required to provide adequate support for the assessments and estimates described in paragraph (1) through (5) of this subsection; and

(8) undertake such additional associated activities as the appropriate
authorities specified under subsection (d) of this section may direct.

INTERGOVERNMENTAL COORDINATION ACT (1968, as amended)
42 U.S.C. 4201 et seq.

## § 4221. Statement of purpose.

It is the purpose of this subchapter to encourage intergovernmental cooperation in the conduct of specialized or technical services and provision of facilities essential to the administration of State or local governmental activities, many of which are nationwide in scope and financed in part by Federal funds; to enable State or local governments to avoid unnecessary duplication of special service functions; and to authorize all departments and agencies of the executive branch of the Federal Government which do not have such authority to provide reimbursable specialized or technical services to State and local governments.

## § 4222. Authority to provide service.

The head of any Federal department of agency is authorized within his discretion, upon written request from a State or political subdivision thereof, to provide specialized or technical services, upon payment, to the department or agency by the unit of government making the request, of salaries and all other identifiable direct or indirect costs of performing such services: Provided, however, That such services shall include only those which the Director of the Office of Management and Budget through rules and regulations determines Federal departments and agencies have special competence to provide. Such rules and regulations shall be consistent with and in furtherance of the Government's policy of relying on the private enterprise system to provide those services which are reasonably and expeditiously available through ordinary business channels.

## §. 4231. Declaration of development assistance policy.

(a) The economic and social development of the Nation and the achievement of satisfactory levels of living depend upon the sound and orderly development of all areas, both urban and rural. Moreover, in a time of rapid urbanization, the sound and orderly development of urban communities depends to a large degree upon the social and economic health and the sound development of smaller communities and rural areas. The President shall, therefore, establish rules and regulations governing the formulation, evaluation, and review of Federal programs and projects having a significant impact on area and community development, including programs providing Federal assistance to the States and localities, to the end that they shall most effectively serve these basic objectives. Such rules and regulations shall provide for full consideration of the concurrent achievement of the following specific objectives and, to the extent authorized by law, reasoned choices shall be made between such objectives when they conflict:

(1) Appropriate land uses for housing, commercial, industrial, governmental, institutional, and other purposes;

(2) Wise development and conservation of natural resources, including land, water, minerals, wildlife, and others;

(3) Balanced transportation systems, including highway, air, water, pedestrian, mass transit, and other modes for the movement of people and goods;

(4) Adequate outdoor recreation and open space;

(5) Protection of areas of unique natural beauty, historical and scientific interest;

(6) Properly planned community facilities, including utilities for the supply of power, water, and communications, for the safe disposal of wastes, and for other purposes; and

(7) Concern for high standards of design.

(b) All viewpoints—national, regional, State, and local—shall, to the extent possible, be fully considered and taken into account in planning Federal or federally assisted development programs and projects. State and local government objectives, together with the objectives of regional organizations shall be considered and evaluated within a framework of national public objectives, as expressed in Federal law, and available projections of future national conditions and needs of regions, States, and localities shall be considered in plan formulation, evaluation, and review.

(c) To the maximum extent possible, consistent with national objectives, all Federal aid for development purposes shall be consistent with and further the objectives of State, regional, and local comprehensive planning. Consideration shall be given to all developmental aspects of our total national community, including but not limited to housing, transportation, economic development, natural and human resources development, community facilities, and the general improvement of living environments.


STATES


CALIFORNIA ENVIRONMENTAL QUALITY ACT
(1970, as amended)
Calif. Public Resources Code Sec. 21000 et seq.

§ 21000. The Legislature finds and declares as follows:

(a) The maintenance of a quality environment for the people of this state now and in the future is a matter of statewide concern.

(b) It is necessary to provide a high-quality environment that at all times is healthful and pleasing to the senses and intellect of man.

(c) There is a need to understand the relationship between the maintenance of high-quality ecological systems and the general welfare of the people of the state, including their enjoyment of the natural resources of the state.

(d) The capacity of the environment is limited, and it is the intent of the Legislature that the government of the state take immediate steps to identify any critical thresholds for the health and safety of the people of the state and take all coordinated actions necessary to prevent such thresholds being reached.

(e) Every citizen has a responsibility to contribute to the preservation and enhancement of the environment.

(f) The interrelationship of policies and practices in the management of natural resources and waste disposal requires systematic and concerted efforts by public and private interests to enhance environmental quality and to control environmental pollution.

(g) It is the intent of the Legislature that all agencies of the state government which regulate activities of private individuals, corporations, and public agencies which are found to affect the quality of the environment, shall regulate such activities so that major consideration is given to preventing environmental damage.

§ 21001. The Legislature further finds and declares that it is the policy of the state to:

(a) Develop and maintain a high-quality environment now and in the future, and take all action necessary to protect, rehabilitate, and enhance the environmental quality of the state.

(b) Take all action necessary to provide the people of this state with clean air and water, enjoyment of aesthetic, natural, scenic, and historic environmental qualities, and freedom from excessive noise.

(c) Prevent the elimination of fish or wildlife species due to man's activities, insure that fish and wildlife populations do not drop below self-perpetrating levels, and preserve for future generations representations of all plant and animal communities and examples of the major periods of California history.

(d) Ensure that the long-term protection of the environment shall be the guiding criterion in public decisions.

(e) Create and maintain conditions under which man and nature can exist in productive harmony to fulfill the social and economic requirements of present and future generations.

(f) Require governmental agencies at all levels to develop standards and procedures necessary to protect environmental quality.

(g) Require governmental agencies at all levels to consider qualitative factors as well as economic and technical factors and long-term benefits and costs, in addition to short-term benefits and costs, and to consider alternatives to proposed actions affecting the environment.

§ 21065.  "Project" means the following:

(a) Activities directly undertaken by any public agency.

(b) Activities undertaken by a person which are supported in whole or in part through contracts, grants, subsidies, loans, or other forms of assistance from one or more public agencies.

(c) Activities involving the issuance to a person of a lease, permit, license, certificate, or other entitlement for use by one or more public agencies.

§ 21083.  The Office of Planning and Research shall prepare and develop proposed guidelines for the implementation of this division by public agencies. . . . Such criteria shall require a finding of "significant effect on the environment" if any of the following conditions exist:

(a) A proposed project has the potential to degrade the quality of the environment, curtail the range of the environment, or to achieve short-term, to the disadvantage of long-term, environmental goals;

(b) The possible effects of a project are individually limited but cumulatively considerable;

(c) The environmental effects of a project will cause substantial adverse effects on human beings, either directly or indirectly. . . .

§ 21089.  A public agency may charge and collect a reasonable fee from any person proposing a project subject to the provisions of this division in order to recover the estimated costs incurred by the public agency in preparing an environmental impact report for such project.

§ 21100.  All state agencies, boards, and commissions shall prepare, or cause to be prepared by contract, and certify the completion of an environmental impact report on any project they propose to carry out or approve which may have a significant effect on the environment. Such a report shall include a detailed statement setting forth the following:

(a) The environmental impact of the proposed action.

(b) Any adverse environmental effects which cannot be avoided if the proposal is implemented.

(c) Mitigation measures proposed to minimize the impact, including, but not limited to, measures to reduce wasteful, inefficient, and unnecessary consumption of energy.

(d) Alternatives to the proposed action.

(e) The relationship between local short-term uses of man's environment and the maintenance and enhancement of long-term productivity.

(f) Any irreversible environmental changes which would be involved in the proposed action should it be implemented.

(g) The growth-inducing impact of the proposed action.

§ 21151. All local agencies shall prepare, or cause to be prepared by contract, and certify the completion of an environmental impact report on any project they intend to carry out or approve which may have a significant effect on the environment. . . .

§ 21152. Whenever a local agency approves or determines to carry out a project which is subject to the provisions of this division, it shall file notice of such approval or such determination with the county clerk of the county, or counties, in which the project will be located. Such notice shall indicate the determination of the local agency whether the project will, or will not, have a significant effect on the environment and shall indicate whether an environmental impact report has been prepared pursuant to the provisions of this division.

§ 21160. Whenever any person applies to any public agency for a lease, permit, license, certificate, or other entitlement for use, the public agency may require that person to submit data and information which may be necessary to enable the public agency to determine whether the proposed project may have a significant effect on the environment or to prepare an environmental impact report. . . .

MASSACHUSETTS CONSTITUTION
Art. XLIV (1972)

§ 179. Art. XLIV. Environmental protection; peoples' right to clean air and water.

The people shall have the right to clean air and water, freedom from excessive and unnecessary noise, and the natural, scenic, historic, and esthetic qualities of their environment; and the protection of the people in their right to the conservation, development and utilization of the agricultural, mineral, forest, water, air and other natural resources is hereby declared to be a public purpose.

The general court shall have the power to enact legislation necessary or expedient to protect such rights.

In the furtherance of the foregoing powers, the general court shall have the power to provide for the taking, upon payment of just compensation therefor, or for the acquisition by purchase or otherwise, of lands and easements or such other interests therein as may be deemed necessary to accomplish these purposes.

Lands and easements taken or acquired for such purposes shall not be used for other purposes or otherwise disposed of except by laws enacted by a two thirds vote, taken by yeas and nays, of each branch of the general court.

MASSACHUSETTS ENVIRONMENTAL IMPACT REPORT
(1972, as amended)
30 Mass. Stat. Ann. Sec. 61 et seq.

§ 61. Determination of environmental impact.

All agencies, departments, boards, commissions and authorities of the commonwealth shall review, evaluate, and determine the impact on the natural environment of all works, projects or activities conducted by them and shall use all practicable means and measures to minimize damage to the environment. Unless a clear contrary intent is manifested, all statutes shall be interpreted and administered so as to minimize and prevent damage to the environment. Any determination made by an agency of the commonwealth shall include a finding describing the environmental impact, if any, of the project and a finding that all feasible measures have been taken to avoid or minimize said impact.

As used in this section and section sixty-two, "damage to the environment" shall mean any destruction, damage or impairment, actual or probable, to any of the natural resources of the commonwealth and shall include but not be limited to air pollution, water pollution, improper sewage disposal, pesticide pollution, excessive noise, improper operation of dumping grounds, impairment and eutrophication of rivers, streams, flood plains, lakes, ponds, or other surface or subsurface water resources; destruction of seashores, dunes, marine resources, underwater archaeological resources, wetlands, open spaces, natural areas, parks, or historic districts or sites. Damage to the environment shall not be construed to include any insignificant damage to or impairment of such resources.

§ 62. Publication of final report; public hearing, etc.; rules and regulations; funding.

No agency, department, board, commission, or authority of the commonwealth or any authority of any political subdivision thereof shall

commence any work, project, or activity which may cause damage to
the environment until sixty days after it has published a final environmental impact report in accordance with the provision of this section
or until sixty days after a public hearing on said report. . . .

Any such agency, department, board, commission, authority, or
authority of any political subdivision which grants permit determination
orders or other actions shall prepare an environmental impact report
on any work, project or activity of any private person, firm or corporation which may cause damage to the environment and for which
no funds of the commonwealth are to be expended, provided that such
report shall be limited in scope to the subject matter jurisdiction of
such agency, department, board, commission, authority or authority
of a political subdivision by which said report is prepared. No action
shall be brought to compel such agency, department, board, commission, authority or authority of any political subdivision or any such
private person, firm or corporation to make, cause to be made or
have made on its behalf any environmental impact report other than
the report required by this section.

Environmental impact reports for any work, project or activity of
private persons, firms or corporations shall be submitted to the
secretary of environmental affairs for comment, and such comment, if
any, shall be submitted to the agency, department, board, commission, authority or authority of any political subdivision by which said
report is prepared within thirty days from its receipt. The approval
or disapproval of such secretary of any such report shall not be required. . . .

An environmental impact report shall contain detailed statements describing the nature and extent of the proposed work and its environmental impact; all measures being utilized to minimize environmental
damage, any adverse short-term and long-term environmental consequences which cannot be avoided should the work be performed; and
alternatives to the proposed action and their environmental consequences.
The preparation of said report shall be commenced during the initial
planning and design phase of any work, project, or activity subject to
this section and the report shall be so prepared and disseminated as
to inform the originating agency, reviewing agencies, the appropriate
regional planning commission, the attorney general and the public of
the environmental consequences of state actions and the alternatives
thereto prior to any commitment of state funds and prior to the commencement of the work, project, or activity. . . .

The secretaries of the executive offices shall each promulgate rules
and regulations approved by the secretary of environmental affairs to
carry out the purposes of this section which shall be applicable to all
agencies, departments, boards, commissions, authorities or instrumentalities within each of such executive offices and which shall con-

form with the requirements of the National Environmental Policy Act Pub. Law 91-190, and amendments thereto. Any draft report, final report, and all written comments required by said regulations shall be public documents. Said reports shall be submitted to the secretary of environmental affairs who shall issue a written statement indicating whether or not in his judgment said reports adequately and properly comply with the provisions of this section.

For the purposes of carrying out the provisions of this section, funds made available for the purpose of design of or planning or performing said work, project, or activity shall be available and may be expended for the research, preparation, and publication of the reports required by this section and expenses incidental thereto, and said funds may be transferred or otherwise may be made available to other state departments and resource agencies designated by the secretary of environmental affairs for the purpose of meeting the expenses incurred in evaluating the draft or final impact report. . . .

PENNSYLVANIA CONSTITUTION
Art. I, Sec. 27 (1971)

§ 27. Natural resources and the public estate.

The people have a right to clean air, pure water, and to the preservation of the natural, scenic, historic and esthetic values of the environment. Pennsylvania's public natural resources are the common property of all the people, including generations yet to come. As trustee of these resources, the Commonwealth shall conserve and maintain them for the benefit of all the people.

ALASKA ENVIRONMENTAL CONSERVATION (1971)
46 Alaska Stat. Chapter 03

Article 1. Declaration of policy (46.03.010)
      2. Department of Environmental Conservation (46.03.020-040)
      3. Water Pollution Control (46.03.050-130)
      4. Air Pollution Control (46.03.140-240)
      5. Radiation Protection (46.03.250-310)
      6. Pesticide Control (46.03.320-330)
      7. Prohibited Acts and Penalties (46.03.710-840)
      8. General Provisions (46.03.860-900)

§ 46.03.020. Powers of the department.

The department may:

(1) enter into contracts necessary or convenient to carry out the functions, powers and duties of the department;

(2) review and appraise programs and activities of state departments and agencies in light of the policy set out in § 10 of this chapter for the purpose of determining the extent to which the programs and activities are contributing to the achievement of that policy and to make recommendations to the departments and agencies, including but not limited to, environmental guidelines;

(3) consult with and cooperate with

(A) officials and representatives of any nonprofit corporation or organizationin the state;

(B) persons, organizations and groups, public and private, using, served by, interested in or concerned with the environment of the state;

(4) appear and participate in proceedings before any state or federal regulatory agency involving or affecting the purposes of the department;

(5) undertake studies, inquiries, surveys or analyses it may consider essential to the accomplishment of the purposes of the department, these activities may be carried out by the personnel of the department or in cooperation with public or private agencies, including educational, civic and research organizations, colleges, universities, institutes and foundations;

(6) at reasonable times enter and inspect with the consent of the actual owner or occupier any property or premises to investigate either of the actual or suspected sources of pollution or contamination or to ascertain compliance or noncompliance with a regulation which may be promulgated under §§ 20-40 of this chapter; information relating to secret processes or methods of manufacture discovered during investigation is confidential;

(7) conduct investigations and hold hearings and compel the attendance of witnesses and the production of accounts, books and documents by the issuance of a subpoena;

(8) advise and cooperate with municipal, regional and other local agencies and officials in the state, to carry out the purposes of this chapter;

(9) act as the official agency of the state in all matters affecting the purpose of the department under federal laws now or hereafter enacted;

(10) adopt regulations necessary to effectuate the purposes of this chapter including, by way of example and not limitation, regulations providing for

(A) control, prevention and abatement of air, water, or land or subsurface land pollution;

(B) safeguard standards for petroleum and natural gas pipeline construction, operation, modification or alteration;

(C) protection of public water supplies by setting standards for the construction, improvement and maintenance of public water supply

(D) collection and disposal of sewage and industrial waste;

(E) collection and disposal of garbage, refuse, and other discarded solid materials from industrial, commercial, agricultural and community activities or operations;

(F) control of radiation sources to prohibit and prevent unnecessary radiation;

(G) control of pesticides;

(H) such other purposes as may be required for the implementation of the policy declared in Sec. 10 of this chapter.

§ 46.03.030.  Grants and loans for water supply and sewerage systems.

§ 46.03.040.  Alaska environmental plan.

(a) The department shall formulate and annually review and revise a statewide environmental plan for the management and protection of the quality of the environment and the natural resources of the state, in furtherance of the legislative policy and purposes expressed in this chapter.

(b) The department shall submit the first plan to the governor on or before January 1, 1972, and thereafter submit periodic revisions of the plan to the governor.  The plan is effective upon approval by the governor and shall serve thereafter as a guide to the state government and the political subdivisions of the state in the development of the environment and natural resources of the state;

(c) In formulating the plan and any revisions, the department may consult with persons, organizations and groups, public or private, interested in or concerned with the environment of the state and with a department, division, board, commission or other agency of the state, with a political subdivision, or with any public authority as may be necessary to enable the department to carry out its responsibility under this section.

§ 46.03.760.  Pollution penalties.

(a) A person who violates §§ 710, 730, 740, or 750 of this chapter is guilty of a misdemeanor and upon conviction is punishable by a fine of not more than $25,000, or by imprisonment for not more than one year, or by both.  Each unlawful act constitutes a separate offense.

(b) In addition to the penalties provided in (a) of this section a person who violates §§ 740–750 of this chapter is liable, in a civil action, to the state for liquidated damages to be assessed by the court for an amount not less than $5,000 nor more than $100,000, depending on the severity of the violation.

(c) In addition to the penalties provided in (a) of this section, a person who violates a provision of § 750 of this chapter is liable to the state, in a civil action, in the case of a vessel, for damages in an amount not to exceed $100 per gross ton of the violating vessel or $14 million, whichever is less, and, in the case of an onshore or offshore facility, $100 for every $500 evaluation of the violating facility or $14 million, whichever is less. However, if the state shows that a violation of § 750 of this chapter was the result of willful negligence or willful misconduct on the part of the person charged with the violation, the person is liable to the state for the full amount of damages caused. In the case of willful negligence or willful misconduct, "damages," in this subsection, means costs associated with the abatement, containment or removal of a pollutant and reasonable restoration of the environment to its former state.

§ 46.03.770. Detention of vessel without warrant as security for damages.

A vessel which is used in or in aid of a violation of §§ 740-750 of this chapter may be detained after a valid search by the department, an agent of the department, a peace officer of the state or an authorized protection officer of the Department of Fish and Game. Upon judgment of the court having jurisdiction that the vessel was used in or the cause of a violation of §§ 740-750 of this chapter with knowledge of its owner or under circumstances indicating that the owner should reasonably have had this knowledge, the vessel may be held as security for payment to the state of the amount of damages assessed by the court under § 760(b) of this chapter, and if the damages so assessed are not paid within 30 days after judgment or final determination of an appeal, the vessel shall be sold at public auction as otherwise directed by the court, and the damages paid from the proceeds. The balance, if any, shall be paid by the court to the owner of the vessel. The court shall permit the release of the vessel upon posting of a bond set by the court in an amount not to exceed $100,000. The damages received under this section shall be transmitted to the proper state officer for deposit in the general fund. A vessel seized under this section shall be returned or the bond exonerated if no damages are assessed under § 760(b) of this chapter.

§ 46.03.780. Liability for restoration.

(a) A person who violates a provision of this chapter, or who fails to perform a duty imposed by this chapter, or violates or disregards an order, permit, or other determination of the department made under the provisions of this chapter, and thereby causes the death of fish, animals, or vegetation or otherwise injures or degrades the environment of the state is liable to the state for damages.

(b) Liability for damages under (a) of this section includes an amount equal to the sum of money required to restock injured land or waters, to replenish a damaged or degraded resource, or to otherwise restore the environment of the state to its conditions before the injury. . . .

## MONTANA CONSTITUTION (1972)
### Article II, Sec. 8

§ 8.  Right of participation.

The public has the right to expect governmental agencies to afford such reasonable opportunity for citizen participation in the operation of the agencies prior to the final decision as may be provided by law.

## MONTANA ADMINISTRATIVE PROCEDURE ACT
### (1971, as amended)
### 82 Rev. Code Mont. Ch. 42

§ 82-4226.  Legislative intent.

The legislature finds and declares pursuant to the mandate of article II, section 8, of the 1972 Montana constitution that legislative guidelines should be established to secure to the people of Montana their constitutional right to be afforded reasonable opportunity to participate in the operation of governmental agencies prior to the final decision of the agency.

§ 82-4227.  Definitions.

As used in this act:

(1) "Agency" means any board, bureau, commission, department, authority, or officer of the state or local government authorized by law to make rules except:

(a) the legislature and any branch, committee, or officer thereof;

(b) the judicial branches and any committee or officer thereof;

(c) the governor, except that an agency is not exempt because the governor has been designated as a member thereof; or

(d) the state military establishment and agencies concerned with civil defense and recovery from hostile attack.

(2) "Rule" means any agency regulation, standard, or statement of general applicability that implements, interprets, or prescribes law or policy or describes the organization, procedures, or practice requirements of any agency.  The term includes the amendment or repeal of a prior rule, but does not include:

(a) statements concerning only the internal management of an agency and not affecting private rights or procedures available to the public;

(b) declaratory rulings as to the applicability of any statutory provision or of any rule;

(c) intra-agency memoranda.

§ 82-4228. Agency requirements.

(1) Each agency shall develop procedures for permitting and encouraging the public to participate in agency decisions that are of significant interest to the public. The procedures shall assure adequate notice and assist public participation before a final decision is made on the adoption of a rule or policy, awarding a contract, granting or denying a permit, license or change of rate that is of significant interest to the public.

(2) An agency shall be deemed to have complied with the notice provisions of this act if:

(a) an environmental impact statement is prepared and distributed as required by the Montana Environmental Policy Act, Title 69, chapter 65. . . .

(3) Procedures for assisting public participation shall include a method for affording interested persons reasonable opportunity to submit data, views or arguments, orally or in written form, prior to making a final decision that is of significant interest to the public. . . .

§ 82-4229. Enforcement.

The district courts of the state have jurisdiction to set aside an agency decision under this act upon petition of any person whose rights have been prejudiced made within thirty (30) days of the date of the decision.

MICHIGAN ENVIRONMENTAL PROTECTION ACT (1970)
Mich. Comp. Laws Ann. Sec. 691.1201 et seq.

Section 1201.    Short title
    1202.    Actions for declaratory and equitable relief; standards for pollution or anti-pollution devices or procedure
    1202a.   Surety bonds or cash; posting to secure costs or judgments
    1203.    Prima facie showing of pollution; rebuttal
    1204.    Granting equitable relief; imposition or conditions
    1205.    Intervention; determination as to pollution
    1206.    Supplementary to existing administrative and regulatory procedures provided by law
    1207.    Effective date

§ 1202.

(1) The attorney general, any political subdivision of the state, any instrumentality or agency of the state or of a political subdivision thereof, any person, partnership, corporation, association, organization or other legal entity may maintain an action in the circuit court having jurisdiction where the alleged violation occurred or is likely to occur for declaratory and equitable relief against the state, any political subdivision thereof, any instrumentality or agency of the state or of a political subdivision thereof, any person, partnership, corporation, association, organization or other legal entity for the protection of the air, water and other natural resources and the public trust therein from pollution, impairment or destruction.

(2) In granting relief provided by subsection (1) where there is involved a standard for pollution or for an anti-pollution device or procedure, fixed by rule or otherwise, by an instrumentality or agency of the state or a political subdivision thereof, the court may:

(a) Determine the validity, applicability and reasonableness of the standard.

(b) When a court finds a standard to be deficient, direct the adoption of a standard approved and specified by the court. . . .

§ 1203.

(1) When the plaintiff in the action has made a prima facie showing that the conduct of the defendant has, or is likely to pollute, impair or destroy the air, water or other natural resources or the public trust therein, the defendant may rebut the prima facie showing by the submission of evidence to the contrary. The defendant may also show, by way of an affirmative defense, that there is no feasible and prudent alternative to defendant's conduct and that such conduct is consistent with the promotion of the public health, safety and welfare in light of the state's paramount concern for the protection of its natural resources from pollution, impairment or destruction. . . .

§ 1204.

(1) The court may grant temporary and permanent equitable relief, or may impose conditions on the defendant that are required to protect the air, water and other natural resources or the public trust therein from pollution, impairment or destruction.

(2) If administrative, licensing or other proceedings are required or available to determine the legality of the defendant's conduct, the court may remit the parties to such proceedings. . . .

(3) Upon completion of such proceedings, the court shall adjudicate
the impact of the defendant's conduct on the air, water or other natural resources and on the public trust therein in accordance with this
act. In such adjudication the court may order that additional evidence
be taken to the extent necessary to protect the rights recognized in this
act. . . .

§ 1205.

(1) Whenever administrative, licensing or other proceedings, and judicial review thereof are available by law, the agency or the court may
permit the attorney general, any political subdivision of the state,
any instrumentality or agency of the state or of a political subdivision
thereof, any person, partnership, corporation, association, organization or other legal entity to intervene as a party on the filing of a plead-
ing asserting that the proceeding or action for judicial review involves
conduct which has, or which is likely to have, the effect of polluting,
impairing or destroying the air, water or other natural resources or
the public trust therein.

(2) In any such administrative, licensing or other proceedings, and in
any judicial review thereof, any alleged pollution, impairment or
destruction of the air, water or other natural resources or the public
trust therein, shall be determined, and no conduct shall be authorized
or approved which does, or is likely to have such effect so long as there
is a feasible and prudent alternative consistent with the reasonable
requirements of the public health, safety and welfare. . . .

MASSACHUSETTS ACTIONS FOR PURPOSE OF PROTECTING
NATURAL RESOURCES AND ENVIRONMENT (1973)
214 Mass. Stat. Ann. Sec. 7A

§ 7A. Actions for purpose of protecting natural resources and environment; definitions.

As used in this section, "damage to the environment" shall mean any
destruction, damage or impairment, actual or probable, to any of the
natural resources of the commonwealth, whether caused by the defendant alone or by the defendant and others acting jointly or severally.
Damage to the environment shall include, but not be limited to, air
pollution, water pollution, improper sewage disposal, pesticide pollution, excessive noise, improper operation of dumping grounds, impairment and eutrophication of rivers, streams, flood plains, lakes,
ponds or other water resources, destruction of seashores, dunes,
wetlands, open spaces, natural areas, parks or historic districts or
sites. Damage to the environment shall not include any insignificant
destruction, damage or impairment to such natural resources.

As used in this section "person" shall mean any individual, association, partnership, corporation, company, business organization, trust, estate, the commonwealth or any political subdivision thereof, any administrative agency, public or quasi-public corporation or body, or any other legal entity or its legal representatives, agents or assigns.

The superior court for the county in which damage to the environment is occurring or is about to occur may, upon a civil action in which equitable or declaratory relief is sought in which not less than ten persons domiciled within the commonwealth are joined as plaintiffs, or upon such an action by any political subdivision of the commonwealth, determine whether such damage is occurring or is about to occur and may, before the final determination of the action, restrain the person causing or about to cause such damage; provided, however, that the damage caused or about to be caused by such person constitutes a violation of a statute, ordinance, by-law or regulation the major purpose of which is to prevent or minimize damage to the environment.

No such action shall be taken unless the plaintiffs at least twenty-one days prior to the commencement of such action direct a written notice of such violation or imminent violation by certified mail, to the agency responsible for enforcing said statute, ordinance, by-law or regulation, to the attorney general, and to the person violating or about to violate the same; provided, however, that if the plaintiffs can show that irreparable damage will result unless immediate action is taken the court may waive the foregoing requirement of notice and issue a temporary restraining order forthwith. . . .

If there is a finding by the court in favor of the plaintiffs it may assess their costs, including reasonable fees of expert witnesses but not attorney's fees; provided, however, that no such finding shall include damages.

The court may require the plaintiffs to post a surety or cash bond in a sum not to exceed five hundred dollars to secure the payment of any costs which may be assessed against the plaintiffs in the event they do not prevail. . . .

CHAPTER

# 4

## HISTORIC PRESERVATION;
## DESIGN RESTRICTIONS

The preservation of historic structures has been the object of legislation since shortly after the Civil War. Despite this long history and the numerous instances in federal and state statutes demanding attention to historic values such structures are falling victim to the wrecker's ball at a rapid rate. It is estimated that one-third of all buildings listed in the Historic American Buildings Survey in the 1930s were gone 40 years later. Illinois' pioneer statute (p. 122) permitting transfer of development rights is the first to recognize the market-place pressures that make for the destruction of landmarks and to provide economic incentives for their protection.

Protection of historic assets is primarily the task of local ordinances and New York City's is considered one of the more significant. Federal and state laws designate historic sites or districts, permit historic site acquisition by public bodies, and provide public funds for preservation, restoration, or salvage. State laws in addition may make property tax concessions.

Thus, the Antiquities Act of 1906 (p. 112) permitted the creation of national monuments out of existing federal lands and instituted permit procedures for archaeological exploration. Authority to acquire historic sites was added by the Historic Sites Act of 1935 (p. 113). The National Historic Preservation Act of 1966 (p. 114) created a National Register of Historic Places and a program of federal grants for historic surveys, preservation, acquisition, and development of National Register properties. In 1960 and again in 1974 Congress extended protection to historic and archaeologic properties threatened by federal dam or other construction activity (p. 117). Presidential Executive Order 11593 of 1971 (p. 118) assigns responsibility for historic preservation to all federal agencies.

Federal land suitable for a historic monument may be conveyed
to state or local governments under an Act of 1966 and the Surplus
Property Act (p. 120). The Housing and Community Development Act
of 1974 (p. 120) again calls for grants to states and communities to
further, among other objectives, "the restoration and preservation
of properties of special value for historic, architectural, or esthetic
reasons" (42 U.S.C. 5301[c] [7]). It specifies grants for historic
surveys by municipalities. Funds for historic projects were also
available under earlier urban renewal legislation.

One of the purposes of the Open Space Act is the preservation,
restoration, and acquisition of historic properties (Sec. 1500 [c]- [d],
155a[d], 1500c-1, pp. 230-32). National scenic trails are to provide
"for the conservation and enjoyment of the nationally significant scenic,
historic . . . qualities of the areas through which such trails may
pass" (Sec. 1242[b], p. 248). Historic significance plays a role in
the designation of national parks and wild and scenic rivers. The Intergovernmental Coordination Act's purpose, in part, is to protect
areas of historic significance (Sec. 4231[5], p. 94).

The National Environmental Policy Act seeks to "preserve important historic, cultural . . . aspects of our national heritage" (Sec.
4331[b][4], p. 75). A "special effort . . . to preserve . . . historic
sites" must be made in the construction of federal highways and transportation projects (23 U.S.C. 138, 49 U.S.C. 1651[b][2], 49 U.S.C.
1653 [f], chap. 12). This is extended to "important historical and cultural assets" in the case of urban mass transportation projects (49
U.S.C. 1610[a], p. 441 ). The Department of Transportation has incorporated these considerations into its regulations governing road
design hearings and environmental impact statement preparations.

Hawaii restricts public construction projects from encroaching
on registered historic sites and sets aside salvage funds (p. 121).
Other states impose similar prohibitions without providing the necessary dollars.

Since 1971 Illinois permits reimbursement of owners for the right
to develop historic properties and the transfer of such rights to a development rights bank (p. 122). Traditionally, owners of such properties merely receive tax concessions of one kind or another. Thus,
New Mexico grants a tax exemption in the amount of restoration expenses (p. 125). North Carolina defers a portion of the property tax,
and in Connecticut the state reimburses local government for tax
losses from historic landmarks given preferred tax status. In the
District of Columbia owners of designated historic landmarks may
apply for tax relief in return for signing agreements assuring continued
maintenance. The laws of many states permit the formation of historic districts for zoning and other purposes. In Virginia properties
located in such districts receive reduced assessments (p. 127).

Several coastal states have moved to protect underwater historic assets, including Rhode Island (p. 129) and Mississippi.

Among state constitutional language dealing with historic preservation is that of Missouri (p. 130), which empowers the legislature to act to preserve historic sites. The constitutions of Louisiana and Texas, among others, call attention to historic values, and that of New York authorizes state acquisition of historically significant properties (Art. XIV: 4, p. 238). The Massachusetts and Pennsylvania "environmental rights" articles recognize a right to the enjoyment of historical qualities (p. 97, 100).

A great many state laws whose main purpose places them in other chapters of this volume also make reference to historic preservation. "Damage to the environment," under Massachusetts' environmental impact legislation, means damage to "underwater archaeological resources . . . historic districts or sites" (Sec. 30-61). Citizens may sue to prevent same (Sec. 214-7A). Pennsylvania's Department of Transportation must show that there is "no feasible and prudent alternative" to a transportation plan affecting a historic landmark (Sec. 71-512). In Montana, mining activities may be prohibited on lands significant to Plains Indian history (Sec. 50-1042[2][d]). Washington's Shoreline Management Act demands the inclusion of a "historic . . . element for the restoration of buildings, sites" in required local master plans (Sec. 90.58.100[g]). Historic and archaeological resources "of statewide importance" are singled out for state protection in Colorado (Sec. 106-7-104[6], 201[c], 202[3]) and Florida (Sec. 380.05[2][a]). Historic values enter into conservation district designation in Hawaii (Sec. 205-2). Potential impact on historic values is a factor in granting power plant construction permits in New York (Public Service Law, Sec. 146.2[b]) and development permits in Vermont (Sec. 10-6086[8]).

Preservation statutes (see Chapter 6) employ historic factors in their definitions: Michigan "wilderness areas . . . contain features of historical value" (Sec. 322.752[iv][d]), a Kansas "natural and scientific area . . . has historical or archaeological features" (Sec. 74-6603[b]), the Minnesota wild and scenic river system may include "any river and its adjacent lands . . . that possesses outstanding . . . historical values" (Sec. 104.33). State scenic trails in Kentucky are "so located as to provide . . . enjoyment of the significant . . . historic . . . qualities of the areas through which such trails pass" (Sec. 148.630[1], and the Oklahoma trail system is to include heritage trails (Sec. 4[A][4]). Massachusetts provides for preservation restrictions "appropriate to preservation of a structure or site historically significant" (Sec. 184-31).

## AESTHETICS

Architectural preservation frequently is postulated along with historic preservation, as in the following enactments previously cited: National Historic Preservation Act, Executive Order 11593, Housing and Community Development Act, and Illinois, New Mexico, and Virginia statutes. Similarly, both the federal Open Space Act (Sec. 1500[c] [d], 1500c-1) and Massachusetts preservation restrictions (Sec. 184-31) serve architectural as well as historic objectives.

One of the aims of NEPA is to provide for all Americans "aesthetically and culturally pleasing surroundings" (Sec. 4331[b] [2]). "The natural beauty of the countryside" is a required consideration in the building of interstate highways (23 U.S.C. 136, 138) and other federal transportation projects (49 U.S.C. 1651[b] [2], 1653[f]; see also 23 U.S.C. 109, 49 U.S.C. 1602[h] [2] [B]). Billboards and junkyards are prohibited within given distances of interstate highways by federal law; Vermont restricts billboards on all its roads.

Aesthetic values are a consideration in the granting of federal ocean dumping permits (33 U.S.C. 1412[a] [B]) and of industrial building permits in Delaware's coastal zone (Sec. 7-7004[b] [3]).

Also, Massachusetts and Pennsylvania citizens have a constitutional right to "aesthetic values of the environment" (see Chapter 4).


## FEDERAL

### ANTIQUITIES ACT (1906)
### 16 U.S.C. 431 et seq.

§ 431. National monuments; reservation of land; relinquishment of private claims.

The President of the United States is authorized, in his discretion, to declare by public proclamation historic landmarks, historic and prehistoric structures, and other objects of historic or scientific interest that are situated upon the lands owned or controlled by the Government of the United States to be national monuments, and may reserve as a part thereof parcels of land, the limits of which in all cases shall be confined to the smallest area compatible with the proper care and management of the objects to be protected. . . .

§ 432. Permits to examine ruins, excavations, and gathering of objects; regulations.

Permits for the examination of ruins, the excavation of archaeological sites, and the gathering of objects of antiquity upon the lands under

their respective jurisdictions may be granted by the Secretaries of
the Interior, Agriculture, and Army to institutions which they may
deem properly qualified to conduct such examination, excavation, or
gathering, subject to such rules and regulations as they may prescribe.
. . .

§ 433.  American antiquities.

Any person who shall appropriate, excavate, injure, or destroy any
historic or prehistoric ruin or monument, or any object of antiquity,
situate on lands owned or controlled by the Government of the United
States, without the permission of the Secretary of the Department of
the Government having jurisdiction over the lands on which said antiquities are situated, shall, upon conviction, be fined in a sum of not
more than $500 or be imprisoned for a period of not more than ninety
days, or shall suffer both fine and imprisonment, in the discretion
of the court.

HISTORIC SITES ACT (1935)
16 U.S.C.  461 et seq.

Section 461.  Declaration of national policy
        462.  Administration by Secretary of Interior; powers and
              duties enumerated
        463.  Advisory Board on National Parks, Historic Sites,
              Buildings, and Monuments; creation, powers and duties
        464.  Cooperation with governmental and private agencies;
              employment of technical assistance
        465.  Jurisdiction of States in lands acquired
        466.  Authorization of appropriations
        467.  Conflict of laws

§ 461.  Declaration of national policy.

It is declared that it is a national policy to preserve for public use
historic sites, buildings, and objects of national significance for the
inspiration and benefit of the people of the United States.

§ 462.  Administration by Secretary of Interior; powers and duties
enumerated.

The Secretary of the Interior (hereinafter in sections 461 to 467 of this
title referred to as the Secretary), through the National Park Service,
for the purpose of effectuating the policy expressed in section 461 of
this title, shall have the following powers and perform the following
duties and functions:

(a) Secure, collate, and preserve drawings, plans, photographs, and other data of historic and archaeologic sites, buildings, and objects.

(b) Make a survey of historic and archaeologic sites, buildings, and objects for the purpose of determining which possess exceptional value as commemorating or illustrating the history of the United States.

(c) Make necessary investigations and researches in the United States relating to particular sites, buildings, or objects to obtain true and accurate historical and archaeological facts and information concerning the same.

(d) For the purpose of sections 461 to 467 of this title, acquire in the name of the United States by gift, purchase, or otherwise any property, personal or real, or any interest or estate therein, title to any real property to be satisfactory to the Secretary. . . .

(e) Contract and make cooperative agreements with States, municipal subdivisions, corporations, associations, or individuals, with proper bond where deemed advisable, to protect, preserve, maintain, or operate any historic or archaeologic building, site, object, or property used in connection therewith for public use, regardless as to whether the title thereto is in the United States. . . .

(f) Restore, reconstruct, rehabilitate, preserve, and maintain historic or prehistoric sites, buildings, objects, and properties of national historical or archaeological significance and where deemed desirable establish and maintain museums in connection therewith.

(g) Erect and maintain tablets to mark or commemorate historic or prehistoric places and events of national historical or archaeological significance.

(h) Operate and manage historic and archaeologic sites, buildings, and properties acquired under the provisions of sections 461 to 467 of this title together with lands and subordinate buildings for the benefit of the public, such authority to include the power to charge reasonable visitation fees and grant concessions, leases, or permits for the use of land, building space, roads, or trails when necessary or desirable either to accommodate the public or to facilitate administration: Provided, That the Secretary may grant such concessions, leases, or permits and enter into contracts relating to the same with responsible persons, firms, or corporations without advertising and without securing competitive bids. . . .

NATIONAL HISTORIC PRESERVATION ACT (1966)
16 U.S.C. 470 et seq.

Section 470.      Congressional finding and declaration of policy
        470a.      National Register; grants for comprehensive surveys;

§ 470.  Congressional finding and declaration of policy.

The Congress finds and declares—

(a) that the spirit and direction of the Nation are founded upon and reflected in its historic past;

(b) that the historical and cultural foundations of the Nation should be
preserved as a living part of our community life and development in order to give a sense of orientation to the American people;

(c) that, in the face of ever-increasing extensions of urban centers, highways, and residential, commercial, and industrial developments, the present governmental and nongovernmental historic preservation programs and activities are inadequate to insure future generations a genuine opportunity to appreciate and enjoy the rich heritage of our Nation; and

(d) that, although the major burdens of historic preservation have been borne and major efforts initiated by private agencies and individuals, and both should continue to play a vital role, it is nevertheless necessary and appropriate for the Federal Government to accelerate its historic preservation programs and activities, to give maximum encouragement to agencies and individuals undertaking preservation by private means, and to assist State and local governments and the National Trust for Historic Preservation in the United States to expand and accelerate their historic preservation programs and activities.

§ 470a.  National Register; grants for comprehensive surveys; matching grants-in-aid to National Trust for Historic Preservation in the United States; definitions.

(a) The Secretary of the Interior is authorized—
    (1) to expand and maintain a national register of districts, sites, buildings, structures, and objects significant in American history, architecture, archeology, and culture, hereinafter referred to as the National Register, and to grant funds to States for the purpose of preparing comprehensive statewide historic surveys and plans, in accordance with criteria established by the Secretary, for the preservation, acquisition, and development of such properties;
    (2) to establish a program of matching grants-in-aid to States for projects having as their purpose the preservation for public benefit of properties that are significant in American history, architecture, archeology, and culture; and
    (3) to establish a program of matching grant-in-aid to the National Trust for Historic Preservation in the United States.

§ 470b.  Requirements for awarding of grant funds.

(a) No grant may be made under sections 470 to 470b and 470c to 470n of this title—
    (1) unless application therefor is submitted to the Secretary in accordance with regulations and procedures prescribed by him;
    (2) unless the application is in accordance with the comprehensive statewide historic preservation plan which has been approved by the Secretary after considering its relationship to the comprehensive statewide outdoor recreation plan prepared pursuant to the Land and Water Conservation Fund Act of 1965 (78 Stat. 897). . . .

PRESERVATION OF HISTORICAL AND ARCHEOLOGICAL
DATA (1960, as amended)
16 U.S.C. 469 et seq.

§ 469. Preservation of historical and archeological data threatened by dam construction or alterations of terrain.

It is the purpose of sections 469 to 469c of this title to further the policy set forth in sections 461 to 467 of this title, by specifically providing for the preservation of historical and archeological data (including relics and specimens) which might otherwise be irreparably lost or destroyed as the result of

(1) flooding, the building of access roads, the erection of workmen's communities, the relocation of railroads and highways, and other alterations of the terrain caused by the construction of a dam by any agency of the United States, or by any private person or corporation holding a license issued by any such agency or

(2) any alteration of the terrain caused as a result of any Federal construction project or federally licensed activity or program.

§ 469a-2.  Same; survey by Secretary of Interior; recovery and preservation of data; compensation for delays in construction and for
temporary loss of use of land.

(a) The Secretary, upon notification, in writing, by any Federal or
State agency or appropriate historical or archeological authority that
scientific, prehistorical, historical, or archeological data is being
or may be irrevocably lost or destroyed by any Federal or federally
assisted or licensed project, activity, or program, shall, if he determines that such data is significant and is being or may be irrevocably
lost or destroyed and after reasonable notice to the agency responsible
for funding or licensing such project, activity, or program, conduct
or cause to be conducted a survey and other investigation of the areas
which are or may be affected and recover and preserve such data (including analysis and publication) which, in his opinion, are not being,
but should be, recovered and preserved in the public interest.

PROTECTION AND ENHANCEMENT OF THE CULTURAL
ENVIRONMENT (1971)
Exec. Order 11593, 36 F. Reg. 8921

§ 1.  Policy.

The Federal Government shall provide leadership in preserving, restoring and maintaining the historic and cultural environment of the
Nation.  Agencies of the executive branch of the Government (hereinafter referred to as "Federal agencies") shall
    (1) administer the cultural properties under their control in a
spirit of stewardship and trusteeship for future generations,
    (2) initiate measures necessary to direct their policies, plans and
programs in such a way that federally owned sites, structures, and
objects of historical, architectural or archaeological significance are
preserved, restored and maintained for the inspiration and benefit of
the people, and
    (3) in consultation with the Advisory Council on Historic Preserva-
tion (16 U.S.C. 470i), institute procedures to assure that Federal plans
and programs contribute to the preservation and enhancement of non-
federally owned sites, structures and objects of historical, architectural
or archaeological significance.

§ 2.  Responsibilities of Federal agencies.

Consonant with the provisions of the acts cited in the first paragraph
of this order, the heads of Federal agencies shall:

(a) no later than July 1, 1973, with the advice of the Secretary of the
Interior, and in cooperation with the liaison officer for historic preser-

vation for the State or territory involved, locate, inventory, and nominate to the Secretary of the Interior all sites, buildings, districts, and objects under their jurisdiction or control that appear to qualify for listing on the National Register of Historic Places.

(b) exercise caution during the interim period until inventories and evaluations required by subsection (a) are completed to assure that any federally owned property that might qualify for nomination is not inadvertently transferred, sold, demolished or substantially altered. The agency head shall refer any questionable actions to the Secretary of the Interior for an opinion respecting the property's eligibility for inclusion on the National Register of Historic Places. The Secretary shall consult with the liaison officer for historic preservation for the State or territory involved in arriving at his opinion. Where, after a reasonable period in which to review and evaluate the property, the Secretary determines that the property is likely to meet the criteria prescribed for listing on the National Register of Historic Places, the Federal agency head shall reconsider the proposal in light of national environmental and preservation policy. Where, after such reconsideration, the Federal agency head proposes to transfer, sell, demolish or substantially alter the property he shall not act with respect to the property until the Advisory Council on Historic Preservation shall have been provided an opportunity to comment on the proposal.

(c) initiate measures to assure that where as a result of Federal action or assistance a property listed on the National Register of Historic Places is to be substantially altered or demolished, timely steps be taken to make or have made records, including measured drawings, photographs and maps, of the property, and that copy of such records then be deposited in the Library of Congress as part of the Historic American Buildings Survey or Historic American Engineering Record for future use and reference. Agencies may call on the Department of the Interior for advice and technical assistance in the completion of the above records.

(d) initiate measures and procedures to provide for the maintenance, through preservation, rehabilitation, or restoration, of federally owned and registered sites at professional standards prescribed by the Secretary of the Interior.

(e) submit procedures required pursuant to subsection (d) to the Secretary of the Interior and to the Advisory Council on Historic Preservation no later than January 1, 1972, and annually thereafter, for review and comment.

(f) cooperate with purchasers and transferees of a property listed on the National Register of Historic Places in the development of viable plans to use such property in a manner compatible with preservation objectives and which does not result in an unreasonable economic burden to public or private interests.

## DISPOSAL OF LANDS FOR PUBLIC OR RECREATIONAL PURPOSES (1966)
### 43 U.S.C. 869 et seq.

§ 869-1. Same; sale or lease; reservation of mineral deposits; termination of lease for nonuse.

The Secretary of the Interior may after due consideration as to the power value of the land, whether or not withdrawn therefor,

(a) sell such land to the State, Territory, county, or other State, Territorial, or Federal instrumentality or political subdivision in which the lands are situated, or to a nearby municipal corporation in the same State or Territory, for the purpose for which the land has been classified, and conveyances of such land for historic-monument purposes under this section shall be made without monetary consideration, while conveyances for any other purpose under this section shall be made at a price to be fixed by the Secretary of the Interior. . . .

## SURPLUS PROPERTY ACT (1944, as amended)
### 50 U.S.C. 1622 et seq.

§ 1622. Disposal to local governments and nonprofit institutions. . . .

(h) (1) Notwithstanding any other provision of this Act [former sections 1611-1614 and 1615-1622, 1623-1632, 1633-1646 of this Appendix], any disposal agency designated pursuant to this Act [said sections] may, with the approval of the Administrator, convey to any State, political subdivision, instrumentalities thereof, or municipality, all of the right, title, and interest of the United States in and to any surplus land, including improvements and equipment located thereon, which, in the determination of the Secretary of the Interior, is suitable and desirable for use as a public park, public recreational area, or historic monument, for the benefit of the public. . . .

## HOUSING AND COMMUNITY DEVELOPMENT ACT (1974)
### 40 U.S.C. 461

§ 461. Comprehensive planning—Grants by Secretary. . . .

(i) In addition to the other grants authorized by this section, the Secretary is authorized to make grants to assist any city, other municipality, or county in making a survey of the structures and sites in the locality which are determined by its appropriate authorities to be of historic or architectural value. Any such survey shall be designed to identify the historic structures and sites in the locality, determine the cost of their rehabilitation or restoration, and provide such other information as may be necessary or appropriate to serve as a foundation for a balanced and effective program of historic preservation in such locality. The aspects of any such survey which relate to the identification of historic and architectural values shall be conducted in accordance with criteria found by the Secretary to be comparable to those used in establishing the national register maintained by the Secretary of the Interior under other provisions of law; and the results of each such survey shall be made available to the Secretary of the Interior. A grant under this subsection shall be made to the appropriate agency or entity specified in paragraphs (1) through (6) of subsection (a) of this section or, if there is no such agency or entity which is qualified and willing to receive the grant and provide for its utilization in accordance with this subsection, directly to the city, other municipality, or county involved.

STATES

HAWAII HISTORICAL OBJECTS AND SITES (1969)
1 Hawaii Rev. Stat. 6-1 et seq.

§ 6-10. Archeological investigation, recording and salvage; appropriations.

Whenever any public construction or improvement of any nature whatsoever undertaken by any government agency on lands which are controlled or owned by the State or by any county and which are sites of historic or prehistoric interest and value, or locations of prehistoric or historic remains, one per cent of the appropriations for such public construction or improvement, or so much thereof as may be necessary, shall be expended by the department of land and natural resources for the archeological investigation, recording and salvage of such site or remains when it is deemed necessary by the department.

§ 6-11. Prehistoric and historic sites and remains.

(a) The department of land and natural resources shall locate, identify, and preserve in suitable records information regarding prehistoric and historic sites, locations, and remains. The information shall be submitted to the director of taxation who shall clearly designate on all tax maps of the State, the location of all prehistoric or historic sites or locations and remains. The department shall cooperate with other state agencies and owners of private prehistoric or historic sites.

(b) Before any public construction or improvement of any nature whatsoever is undertaken by the State, the city and county of Honolulu, or
any of the counties, or any governmental agency or officer, the head of
such agency or such officer shall first examine the current tax map of
the area to be affected by such public construction or improvement to
determine whether any heiaus, ancient burial places, or sites, or remains of prehistorical or historical interest are designated on such map
If so designated, the proposed public construction or improvement
shall not be commenced, or, in the event it has already begun, continued, until the head of such agency or such other officer shall have
advised the department of the proposed public construction or improvement and shall have secured the concurrence of the department or,
as hereafter provided, shall have secured the written approval of the
governor.

If the concurrence of the department is not obtained after ninety days
after the filing of a request therefor with the department by, or after
the filing of a notice of objections by the department with, the agency
or officer seeking to proceed with any project, such agency or officer
may apply to the governor for permission to proceed notwithstanding
the nonconcurrence of the department and the governor may take such
action as he deems best in overruling or sustaining the department.

(c) Before any construction, alteration, or improvement of any nature
whatsoever is undertaken or commenced on a designated private prehistoric or historic site by any person, he shall give to the department
three months notice of intention to construct, alter, or improve the
site.

After the expiration of the three-month notification period, the department shall either commence condemnation proceedings for the purchase of the site or remains, permit the owner to proceed with his
construction, alteration or improvement, or undertake or permit the
recording and salvaging of any historical information deemed necessary
to preserve Hawaiian history, by any qualified agency for this purpose.

ILLINOIS PRESERVATION OF HISTORICAL AND OTHER
SPECIAL AREAS (1963, as amended)
24 Ill. Ann. Stat. 11-48.2 et seq.

§ 11-48.2-1. Declaration of policy.

It is hereby found and declared that in all municipalities the move-
ments and shifts of population and the changes in residential, commercial and industrial use and customs threaten with disappearance areas,
places, buildings, structures, works of art and other objects having
special historical, community, or aesthetic interest or value and whose
preservation and continued utilization are necessary and desirable
to sound community planning for such municipalities and to the welfare
of the residents thereof.  The granting to such municipalities of the
powers herein provided is directed to such ends, and the use of such
rights and powers for the preservation and continued utilization of such
property is hereby declared to be a public use essential to the public
interest.

§ 11-48.2-1A. Definitions.

(1) The development rights of a landmark site are the rights granted
under applicable local law respecting the permissible bulk and size of
improvements erected thereon.  Development rights may be calculated
in accordance with such factors as lot area, floor area, floor area
ratios, height limitations, or any other criteria set forth under local
law for this purpose.

(2) A preservation restriction is a right, whether or not stated in the
form of a restriction, easement, covenant or condition, in any deed,
will or other instrument executed by or on behalf of the owner of the
land or in any order of taking, appropriate to the preservation of areas,
places, buildings or structures to forbid or limit acts of demolition,
alteration, use or other acts detrimental to the preservation of the
areas, places, buildings or structures in accordance with the purposes
of the Division. . . .

(3) A transfer of development rights is the transfer from a landmark
site of all or a portion of the development rights applicable thereto,
subject to such controls as are necessary to secure the purposes of
this Division.  The transfer of development rights pursuant to sound
community planning standards and the other requirements of this Division is hereby declared to be in accordance with municipal health,
safety and welfare because it furthers the more efficient utilization of
urban space at a time when this objective is made urgent by the shrink-
ing land base of urban areas, the increasing incidence of large-scale,
comprehensive development in such areas, the evolution of building
technology and similar factors.

(4) A development rights bank is a reserve into which may be deposited development rights associated with publicly and privately-owned landmark sites. Corporate authorities or their designees shall be authorized to accept for deposit within the bank gifts, donations, bequests or other transfers of development rights from the owners of said sites, and shall be authorized to deposit therein development rights associated with

(i) the sites of municipally-owned landmarks and

(ii) the sites of privately-owned landmarks in respect of which the municipality has acquired a preservation restriction through eminent domain or purchase.

§ 11-48.2-2. Powers of corporate authorities.

The corporate authorities in all municipalities shall have the power to provide for official landmark designation by ordinance of areas, places, buildings, structures, works of art and other objects having a special historical, community, or aesthetic interest or value; and in connection with such areas, places, buildings, structures, works of art or other objects so designated by ordinance, whether owned or controlled privately or by any public body, to provide special conditions, to impose regulations governing construction, alteration, demolition and use, and to adopt other additional measures appropriate for their preservation, protection, enhancement, rehabilitation, reconstruction, perpetuation, or use, which additional measures may include, but are not limited to,

(a) the making of leases and subleases (either as lessee or lessor of any such property) for such periods and upon such terms as the municipality shall deem appropriate;

(b) inducing, by contract or other consideration, the creation of covenants or restrictions binding the land;

(c) the acquisition by purchase or eminent domain of a fee or lesser interest, including a preservation restriction, in property so designated; the deposit, as appropriate, in a development rights bank of the development rights associated with said property; and the reconstruction, operation or transfer by the municipality of any such property so acquired or the transfer of any development rights so acquired, all in accordance with such procedures and subject to such conditions as are reasonable and appropriate to carrying out the purposes of this Division;

(d) appropriate and reasonable control of the use or appearance of adjacent and immediately surrounding private property within public view;

(e) acquisition by eminent domain or by other contract or conveyance of immediately surrounding private property, or any part thereof or interest therein, the alteration or clearance of which is important for the proper preservation, reconstruction or use of the designated property;

(f) cooperative relations, including gifts, contracts and conveyances appropriate to the purposes of this Division, by and between the municipality and any other governmental body or agency and by and between the municipality and not-for-profit organizations which have as one of their objects the preservation or enhancement of areas, places, buildings, structures, works of art or other objects of special historical, community or aesthetic interest or value;

(g) acceptance and administration by the municipality of funds or property transferred on trust to the municipality by an individual, corporation or other governmental or private entity for the purpose of aiding, either in general or in connection with some specific designated property, the preservation or enhancement of areas, places, buildings, structures, works of art or other objects designed by law under the provisions hereof;

(h) issuance of interest bearing revenue bonds. . . .

(i) establishment of procedures authorizing owners of designated property to transfer development rights in such amount and subject to such conditions as are appropriate to secure the purposes of this Division. . . .

NEW MEXICO CULTURAL PROPERTIES ACT (1969)
New Mex. Stat. Sec. 4-27-4 et seq.

§ 4-27-5.  Purpose of act.

The legislature hereby declares that the historical and cultural heritage of the state is one of the state's most valued and important assets; that the public has an interest in the preservation of all antiquities, historic and prehistoric ruins, sites, structures, objects and similar places and things for their scientific and historical information and value; that the neglect, desecration and destruction of historical and cultural sites, structures, places and objects results in an irreplaceable loss to the public; and that therefore it is the purpose of the Cultural Properties Act (4-27-4 to 4-27-16) to provide for the preservation, protection and enhancement of structures, sites and objects of historical significance within the state, in a manner conforming with, but not limited by, the provisions of the National Historic Preservation Act of 1966.

§ 4-27-6.  Definitions.

As used in the Cultural Properties Act (4-27-4 to 4-27-16):

A.  "Committee" means the cultural properties review committee;

B.  "Cultural property" means a structure, place, site or object having historic, archeological, scientific, architectural, or other cultural significance;

C.  "Registered cultural property" means a cultural property which has been placed on the official register on either a permanent or temporary basis by the committee. . . .

§ 4-27-14.  Tax exemption.

To encourage the restoration and preservation of cultural properties which are under private ownership, all cultural properties listed on the official register with the written consent of the owner and which are available for educational purposes under conditions approved by the committee and in conformance with the meaning of Article 8, section 3 of the Constitution of New Mexico shall be exempt from that portion of local city, county and school property taxes which is offset by a properly documented showing of committee approved restoration, preservation and maintenance expenses.  Local city, county and school property taxes assessed against the property where the registered cultural property is located shall be reduced by the amount expended for restoration, preservation and maintenance each year. . . .

VIRGINIA HISTORIC LANDMARKS COMMISSION (1966)
11 Code of Va. 10-135 et seq.

§ 10-138.  Powers and duties of Commission.

The Commission shall

(a) Make a survey of, and designate as an historic landmark, the buildings, structures and sites which constitute the principal historical, architectural and archaeological sites which are of statewide or national significance. No structure or site shall be deemed to be an historic one unless it has been prominently identified with, or best represents, some major aspect of the cultural, political, economic, military, or social history of the State or nation, or has had a major relationship with the life of an historic personage or event representing some major aspect of, or ideals related to, the history of the State or nation. In the case of structures which are to be so designated, they shall embody the principal or unique features of an architectural type or demonstrate the style of a period of our history or method of construction, or serve as an illustration of the work of a master builder, designer or architect whose genius influenced the period in which he worked or has significance in current times. In order for a site to qualify as an archaeological site, it shall be an area from which it is reasonable to expect that artifacts, materials and other specimens may be found which give insight to an understanding of aboriginal man or the Colonial and early history and architecture of the State or nation.

(b) Prepare a register of buildings and sites which meet the requirements of the preceding paragraph, publish lists of such properties and inspect such properties from time to time; publish a register thereof from time to time setting forth appropriate information concerning the registered buildings and sites.

(c) With the consent of the landowners, certify and mark, with appropriately designed markers, buildings and sites which it has registered.

(d) Establish standards for the care and management of certified landmarks and withdraw such certification for failure to maintain the standards so prescribed.

(e) Acquire by purchase, gift, or lease and administer registered landmarks, sites and easements and interests therein; such acquisition may be made from funds provided by law or otherwise.

(f) Lease or sell property so acquired under terms and conditions designed to ensure the proper preservation of the landmark or site in question.

(g) Establish historic districts for registered landmarks and designate the area thereof by appropriate markers provided the county or city in which the district or registered landmark is located fails or refuses to take such action as is necessary to establish and maintain such districts.

(h) Identify historical districts for registered landmarks and aid and encourage the county or city in which the district or landmark is located to adopt such rules and regulations as the Commission may develop and recommend for the preservation of historical, architectural, or archaeological values. . . .

§ 10-139.  Notice to local tax-assessing official that structure or site has been designated a certified landmark.

In any case in which the Commission designates a structure or site as a certified landmark, it shall notify the official having the power to make assessments of properties for purposes of taxation within the county or city in which the structure or site is located and such designation and notification shall be, prima facie, evidence that the value of such property for commercial, residential or other purposes is reduced by reason of its designation.

§ 10-140.  Notice to local tax-assessing official of establishment of historic district.

When the Commission establishes an historic district, it shall notify the official of the county or city whose duty it is to assess property for the purpose of taxation by the county or city in which such area is located of the fact of such establishment and the boundaries of the district, together with the restrictions which are applicable to properties located in such district and of the fact that commercial, industrial and certain other uses within such district are restricted.  The tax-assessing official shall take such factors into consideration in assessing the properties therein and, based on the restrictions upon the uses of such property, place a lower valuation upon the same.

VIRGINIA PRESERVATION OF HISTORICAL SITES IN COUNTIES
AND MUNICIPALITIES (1973, as amended)
15.1 Code of Va. 503.2

§ 503.2.  Preservation of historical sites in counties and municipalities.

(a) The governing body of any county or municipality may adopt an ordinance setting forth the historic landmarks within the county or municipality as established by the Virginia Historic Landmarks Commission, and any other buildings or structures within the county or municipality having an important historic interest, amending the existing zoning ordinance and delineating one or more historic districts adjacent to such landmarks, buildings and structures; provided, that such amendment of the zoning ordinance and the establishment of such district or districts shall be in accordance with the provisions

of article 8 (§ 15.1-486 et seq.), chapter 11, of Title 15.1 of the Code
of Virginia. Such ordinance may include a provision that no building
or structure, including signs, shall be erected, reconstructed, substantially altered or restored within any such historic district unless
the same is approved by the governing body of such county or municipality as being architecturally compatible with the historic landmark,
building or structure therein. The governing body may provide for
an architectural review board to assist it in its determination. No
such historic district shall extend further than one-quarter mile from
the property line of the land pertaining to any such historic landmark,
building or structure. . . .

ANTIQUITIES ACT OF RHODE ISLAND (1974)
42 R.I. Gen. Laws 45.1 et seq.

§ 42-45.1-2. Purpose of chapter.

The general assembly of the state of Rhode Island and Providence
Plantations hereby declares that the public has an interest in the identification, interpretation, preservation, and protection of the state's
archaeological resources including underwater historic properties
situated under the navigable waters and territorial seas of the state;
that the public has a right to the knowledge to be derived and gained
from a scientific study of these resources; and that therefore it is
the purpose of this chapter to provide that activities for the identification, preservation, excavation, study, and exhibition of the state's
archaeological resources be undertaken in a coordinated and organized
manner, with due consideration given to other significant natural and
man-made environmental assets, for the general welfare of the public
as a whole.

§ 42-45.1-4.  Control of historic property.

The State of Rhode Island and Providence Plantations reserves to itself the exclusive right and privilege of field investigation on sites owned or controlled by the state, its agencies, departments or institutions in order to protect and preserve archaeological and scientific information, matter, and objects.  All such information and objects derived from state lands shall remain the property of the state and be utilized for scientific or public educational purposes.

Furthermore, subject to any local, state or federal statute, the title to all bottoms of navigable waters within the state's jurisdiction in the territorial sea and the title to any underwater historic properties lying on or under said bottoms of any other navigable waters of the state, is hereby declared to be in the state, and such bottoms and underwater historic properties shall be subject to the exclusive dominion and control of the state.

MISSOURI CONSTITUTION
Art. III, Sec. 48 (1945)

§ 48.  Historical memorials and monuments—acquisition of property.

The general assembly may enact laws and make appropriations to preserve and perpetuate memorials of the history of the state by parks, buildings, monuments, statues, paintings, documents of historical value or by other means, and to preserve places of historic or archaeological interest or scenic beauty, and for such purposes private property or the use thereof may be acquired by gift, purchase, or eminent domain or be subjected to reasonable regulation or control.

To what uses land is put may be the single most important decision affecting the quality of the environment. The concept of "carrying capacity" postulates that objective factors such as topography, climate, soil, water table, and the like determine how much population a given area can support and what economic uses are feasible without adverse health effects. Somewhat at odds with this proposition—though both are put forward by environmental advocates—is that of "nondegradation." That argument holds that areas now in a relatively natural and unspoiled state should remain thus and not be brought down to a lesser, though otherwise acceptable, level. (To what extent "significant deterioration" of air quality is permissible under the Clean Air Act is discussed below on pp. 132 ff.)

Control of private land historically has been and remains lodged in municipalities operating under state enabling acts. A few local governments have to some extent incorporated the carrying capacity principle in their zoning ordinances, notably Medford Township, New Jersey. These are outside the scope of this work. Legislation protecting parks, nature preserves, wilderness areas, wild rivers, and the like may be said to carry out the principle of nondegradation, while "critical area" designations (see pp. 138 ff.) may embody either concept.

Many states have begun to identify particular regions or particular uses of land and to subject those to controls by state or regional agencies. Such controls decree uses, densities, and types of development in specified districts. This chapter considers such laws under four headings: (1) general, (2) regional planning and zoning, (3) wetlands and shorelands, and (4) power plant and industry siting. Chapter 6 deals with lands permanently preserved; Chapter 9, with land and its agricultural, forestry, and mineral resources. The bulk of public lands fit into the latter two classifications.

Land use control laws give rise to the question of when such controls constitute taking of private property for public use, requiring just compensation under the Fifth and Fourteenth Amendments to the United States Constitution and analogous portions of state constitutions. The "taking" concept ultimately derives from the Magna Carta, though ideas of private property and private ownership of land antedate it. Had these ideas not been so firmly embedded in the minds of the colonial settlers, Indian points of view about the good earth might have had a chance of acceptance, as the following excerpt suggests:

> Magna Carta was adopted while this country was peopled by Indians. Indians had their own land use concepts, concepts to which we may yet come in our concern for the preservation of land. Indians didn't record deeds; there were no deeds. Nobody owned land. Land was the common share of the tribe. . . . The concept of private ownership of land comes from our Anglo-Saxon and Norman sources and forms part of our tradition of private property. In England, prior to Magna Carta, all land was held by the Crown. The King was the owner of all the land and anyone who claimed a right to it must claim through him by grant or recognition. Nobles and their subordinate orders of nobles and gentry owned portions of land where the owner's word was law, subject to fealty to the king. The king exercised these rights to land rather ruthlessly at times and dispossessed the nobles of their fiefdoms. The nobles revolted and forced the Magna Carta from King John. [Alfred S. Forsyth, "Land Use," lecture presented to the Federated Conservationists of Westchester County, N.Y., 1973.]

Direct federal regulation of private land use is found in the Coastal Zone Management and Flood Disaster Protection Acts, affecting specified low-lying areas only (see pp. 146 ff.). Proposals for broader federal land use involvement, through grants in support of state planning actions, have been introduced in at least two Congresses but failed of enactment. Federal air and water pollution legislation, however, has considerable impact on land use decisions everywhere, as the Council on Environmental Quality outlined in its Fifth Annual Report (pp. 31-36):

> Air Pollution Regulations—Several facets of the Clean Air Act of 1970 are likely to have significant land use impacts. Although some may be minor in terms of their land use effects, others appear to be potentially very important.

The major legislative provisions are those which establish ambient air quality standards.  Important regulations include:  (1) those formulating transportation control plans for selected metropolitan areas to meet ambient standards; (2) those providing for the approval of "indirect sources," facilities which, although not pollution sources themselves, attract large amounts of traffic; (3) those attempting to define the meaning of "significant deterioration" of air quality in areas which presently have relatively pure air; (4) those defining new source performance standards, which determine the amount of pollution that new facilities such as factories or power plants can emit; and (5) those establishing the process and requirements for air quality maintenance through 10-year air quality maintenance plans in metropolitan areas.  Each of these regulatory powers needs to be examined with respect to the way in which it affects development.

The ambient air quality standards, operating alone, would tend to induce polluting industries to locate in areas with relatively clean air, in order to reduce the costs of pollution abatement.  This incentive to locate away from existing industrial areas, however, is at least partially offset by both the "new source" performance standards and the non-degradation regulations.  The first requires all new plants, regardless of location, to employ a very high level of pollution control.  This means that, in most cases, the cost of pollution abatement will not be affected by the location of a new facility.  Although there is still some uncertainty about their final form, the nondegradation regulations may require more stringent abatement measures in relatively unpolluted regions than in regions presently attempting to meet primary and secondary air quality standards.

Although state and local planning agencies are expected to have the major role in defining what entails "significant deterioration" in any location, the regulations could interfere with what otherwise might have been a normal and often desirable relocation of manufacturing activity into new communities or small towns in rural areas.  This may become a serious problem in the development of new western energy sources.  Growing energy needs have made more attractive the large deposits of coal and oil shale which lie in Montana, Colorado, and other western states.  Those areas have relatively high quality air which will almost certainly be degraded if the energy development takes place.

Of the other air quality regulations likely to affect land use within metropolitan areas, transportation control plans have received the greatest attention. These plans are aimed at reducing the amount of automobile traffic in order to meet ambient air quality standards. They involve, most commonly, implementation of some combination of the following strategies: (1) improved transportation control; (2) diversion of through traffic around central cities; (3) improved mass transit facilities; (4) special bus and car pool lanes; (5) elimination of on-street parking in the central business district; and (6) at local option, a parking tax on off-street parking in the central business district.

The first two measures are aimed at reducing congestion and improving traffic flow to the central business district. Although, on a short-term basis, this should reduce the amount of air pollution generated by automobiles commuting to downtown, over the longer run improved access to the central city might well encourage people to live farther from their jobs and commute longer distances in their cars. This in turn could actually increase the generation of air pollutants.

The third and fourth measures are directed toward attracting more travelers to use public transit. They will tend to encourage increased development in areas served by mass transit facilities and to discourage sprawl development at the urban fringe.

The fifth and sixth measures are designed to make automobile commuting relatively more expensive and thus encourage more commuters to ride public transit. If these regulations are not vigorously enforced throughout the metropolitan area, they might also have the effect of encouraging the dispersal of employment centers out of the central city. Such dispersal could in turn affect the economic viability of the central city, as well as make it more difficult for lower-income central city residents to get to their jobs. It would also adversely affect the viability of the public transit systems that are supposed to be encouraged by other measures and would tend to encourage more development at the urban fringe. However, if the regulations are applied with the same force in the suburbs as in the central city, as EPA encourages, the effect could be just the opposite. Locations near the mass transit facilities would become more attractive, and development would tend to concentrate along public transit routes.

All of these transportation control measures, therefore, could have land use impacts. In some instances—for ex-

ample if parking controls cause residential and industrial
location patterns that discourage mass transit use—the incentives may work against each other and result in land
use patterns that actually increase the amount of air pollution generated.

Another air quality provision relates to the control of
indirect sources—facilities which, while they do not generate large amounts of pollution themselves, attract traffic
which may create air pollution problems. They include
major roads, shopping centers, stadiums, and other large
public facilities.

In most instances the indirect source review will focus
on ways to mitigate traffic congestion and reduce air pollution levels (particularly for carbon monoxide). However,
the review agency has authority to require the developer
to undertake remedial action such as the provision of public
transportation to his facility as a condition of the permit.

The indirect source regulations may have a significant
impact on development decisions. They will tend to provide
some incentive to the developer simply to avoid building the
specific types and sizes of facilities covered by the regulations. The resulting impact on land use is uncertain, but it
could be perverse in terms of the goals of the act. For instance, prospective shopping center developers might turn
to strip commercial development along highways as an alternative to uncertain project review procedures. Such a
shift could avoid the permit process if it resulted in each
store's parking lot being small enough. But this might
mean more use of automobiles if shoppers drive from one
store to another, simultaneously increasing congestion and
air pollution.

Another set of regulations with possible direct impact
on land use in metropolitan areas relates to air quality
maintenance. These regulations require air quality agencies to prepare plans for metropolitan areas to ensure
that the air quality, once it satisfies the ambient standards,
is not degraded by future development. These plans may
limit certain types of development in parts of the metropolitan area. In developing the guidelines for these plans, EPA
is recognizing the importance of their being integrated with
other planning efforts for environmental, economic and social goals.

In sum, most of these air quality regulations appear to
have the potential to affect land use patterns. In some
cases it is not clear what the ultimate effect will be. Fur-

ther analyses are obviously needed to ensure that the en-
suing regulations as a whole will work together to meet the
air quality purpose of the act, will affect land use in a desirable or at least neutral way and, further, will be consistent with the water pollution regulations described below.
The recent decision by EPA to prepare and circulate environmental impact statements on major regulatory actions
is a step in the right direction.

Water Pollution Regulations—The 1972 Amendments to the
Federal Water Pollution Control Act placed increased emphasis on the control of the effluents from point sources.
This shift in emphasis from ambient to effluent standards
tended to remove the incentive to disperse new facilities
which was similar to that associated with the ambient air
standards described above.

   However, there are at least three requirements of the
amendments which will still affect industrial location decisions: the effluent standards requiring the use of the best
practicable or the best available technology; the requirement that industries pay the full cost of treating wastes discharged to municipal plants; and the requirement that industries pretreat their wastes before discharging them into
municipal systems.

   Because it is generally less expensive to build pollution
abatement technology into a new plant than to add it to an
old one, and because abatement devices require space
which may not be available at older congested industrial
sites, the effluent standards may induce firms to abandon
old plants, particularly those located in high density urban
areas, sooner than they otherwise might have. Usually a
new plant will be located outside the central city where
more land is available at a lower price. However, new
plants may be required to satisfy stricter standards than
old plants, thus providing a countervailing incentive.

   The combination of cost sharing and pretreatment
requirements for industrial use of municipal treatment
plants could also lead firms to conclude that they can more
cheaply treat and dispose of their wastes themselves. If
so, new industrial siting decisions would be influenced less
by the availability of public sewers than they are currently,
and this would be likely to result in wider dispersal of new
industrial sites. If this stimulates industry to locate in
small towns and new communities, it could be beneficial.
If it leads industry to spread into undeveloped areas near

cities, it could counteract desirable planning and regulatory efforts. Among other problems, the dispersal could
promote inefficient development patterns from an air pollution and energy consumption point of view, development
which would eventually come in conflict with the goals of
the Clean Air Act.

Another regulation which may stimulate dispersed development is the requirement that every point source of
pollution obtain a discharge permit. If water quality at a
particular location presents a severe problem, as may occur in heavily built-up areas, the guidelines would suggest
that permits not be issued unless the industry adopts very
stringent pollution abatement techniques, perhaps even
exceeding best available control technology. This again
may tend to stimulate the dispersal of industrial and manufacturing activity. Again, it could be beneficial if it encourages industry to locate in smaller towns or new communities which need jobs, but detrimental if it simply contributes to metropolitan sprawl.

One opportunity to evaluate (and rectify if necessary)
the location incentives created by these provisions is the
requirement in Sections 1288 and 1313(e) of the Act for
wastewater management planning. These plans are intended to provide overall coordination of the many provisions of the Act as they apply to a given metropolitan
area. They will also provide the mechanism for implementing Section 1314(e) of the Act, which deals with the
control of pollution from "nonpoint" sources. One major
category of nonpoint pollution is stormwater runoff from
land rendered impervious to water by streets, highways,
parking lots, and commercial and residential development. Regulating this form of nonpoint pollution could have
significant impacts on development patterns.

Full implementation of the Noise Control Act may well affect
the location of future airports and other transportation facilities and
thus help determine the fate of surrounding areas.

The Open Space Act permits federal aid to communities seeking
to acquire lands to guide future growth (Sec. 1500c-2, p. 232), and
federal transportation laws aim at integrating transportation planning
with total urban planning.

In the past states have substantially delegated regulation of the
use of private lands to local government. As previously noted, a
number of states are recapturing some of those powers. Hawaii has
statewide districting with local controls over urban districts only (p.

141). It also levies a statewide real property tax. Vermont created
a state board to oversee developments over a certain size and to prepare a long-range plan (p. 147). Maine's Site Location Act (38 Maine
Rev. Stat. Ann. 481 et seq.) requires a state permit for "developments substantially affecting the environment," that is, generally over
20 acres in size.

The American Law Institute began work in 1964 on a Model Land
Development Code. Long before publication of the final draft in 1975,
this effort provided the impetus for the imposition of state or regional
controls for "areas of critical state concern" and "developments of
regional impact"—two concepts identified by the institute's draft codes.
Florida mandates state review of local regulations for areas of critical
state concern as designated by the governor and his cabinet (p. 150).
Colorado provides for local government designation of areas and activities "of state interest" and sets criteria for their administration (p.
155). North Carolina mandates the classification of all the state's
lands on the basis of natural characteristics and availability of public
services, the identification of areas of environmental concern, presence of key facilities, potential new communities, and large-scale
development in its 1973 Land Policy Act (Gen. Stat. N. Car. Sec.
113A-150 et seq.). "Land disturbing activity," including construction,
is restricted by the state's Sedimentation Pollution Control Act (p.
489).

Many other states have at least initiated steps to identify areas
variously termed "vital areas," areas of critical environmental concern," "areas in imminent danger of potential degradation," and to
develop proposals for legislative action. Maine and Minnesota have
instituted state review over such areas, as has Oregon over "activities
of statewide significance." Maine maintains a state register of critical areas, with plans for state acquisition.

Zoning and planning by local government are carried on pursuant
to state enabling acts. That of Connecticut (p. 163) typically requires
that "regulations prevent the overcrowding of land . . . avoid undue
concentration of population and . . . facilitate the adequate provision
for transportation, water, sewerage, schools, parks and other public
requirements." Similar language in New York permitted the suburban
Town of Ramapo to enact a local law limiting and channeling growth,
which was tested and upheld in Golden v. Planning Board of Town of
Ramapo (285 N.E.2d 291, appeal dismissed 402 U.S. 1003[1972]).
Planned United Developments, which cluster buildings and so create
common open space, are permitted by Connecticut's (p. 165) law as
well as those of many other states, including Arkansas, Hawaii, Indiana, New Jersey, and New York. California directs each city and
county to adopt an open space plan (p. 246), and in Maryland zoning
maps must show permissible sound levels under its Noise Control Act
(p. 268).

## REGIONAL PLANNING AND ZONING

Specified areas in many parts of the country are placed under regional planning and zoning controls. In Minnesota some 300 municipal units in the Minneapolis-St. Paul area share in the total tax base increase of the region on a per capita basis. This method distributes property tax revenue over an entire region impacted by development and relieves each individual community from the overpowering need to promote growth to fund increased governmental costs. Review of projects of "metropolitan" significance was added in 1974 (p. 168). The Minnesota Metropolitan Airport Zoning Act (p. 446) is a related measure. New Jersey's Hackensack Meadows Sports and Exposition Authority (p. 170) has authority to override local land use rules in its construction of a sports complex. New York's Adirondack Park Agency Act (p. 172) zoned private lands in the resort area adjoining portions of the state's constitutionally protected (p. 238) forest preserve. The act is the subject of litigation at the time of this writing.

Regional planning commissions with advisory powers only commonly are found in many states.


## WETLANDS AND SHORELANDS

The major federal land use laws operate with respect to such lands: the Coastal Zone Management Act of 1972 (p. 176) provides for federal grants to coastal states for the development and implementation of management programs for land and water resources of their coastal zones (defined in the act); the Flood Disaster Protection Act, as amended in 1973 (p. 181), denies federally subsidized flood insurance and other assistance to flood-prone localities, as designated by federal agencies, unless they adopt flood plan controls.

Environmental review criteria under the Deepwater Port Act include effects of proposed ports on land-based development (Sec. 1505) and a requirement that adjacent states be "making reasonable progress" toward compliance with the Coastal Zone Management Act (Sec. 1508[c]).

Coastal states, spurred on by the Coastal Zone Management Act, have taken steps to protect their tidal resources. Additional state efforts impose controls over inland shorelines, wetlands, and floodplains. Washington's Shoreline Management Act of 1971 (p. 188) applies to all of these and calls for state intervention if local government fails to adopt required plans. It requires permits for construction. Delaware's Coastal Zone Act of 1971 (p. 197), prohibiting heavy industry, has withstood attempts to repeal it. California's Coastal Zone

Conservation Act of 1972 (Public Resources Code, Sec. 27001 et seq.),
adopted by referendum just two weeks after passage of the federal law,
sets up permit procedures pending adoption of a long-range plan.
Such a plan has been submitted and was under discussion at the time
of this writing.

Maine's Coastal Wetlands and Zoning Law (12 Maine Rev. Stat.
Ann. 4701) was one of the first on the east coast and survived challenge in court. Wisconsin's wetlands law (p. 199) was sustained in
Just v. Marinette County (201 N.W. 2d 761 [1972]). Massachusetts'
wetlands legislation restricts construction activity in both tidal and
fresh waters and has withstood court tests. It is noted for identifying
types of wetlands by the vegetation found on them (p. 200). Massachusetts citizens may also sue to protect "flood plains . . . seashores,
dunes, wetlands" under Sec. 214-7A (p. 107). Inland wetlands and
shorelands protection is afforded by statutes in California, Maryland,
Michigan, Minnesota, and New York, among other states.

Comprehensive land use laws of Florida (Sec. 380.04[c]) and
Colorado (Sec. 106-7-104[12]) extend particular protection to shorelands, and that of Colorado also does so for floodplains (Sec. 106-7-
202[2][a]). New Hampshire's Current Use Tax extends deferred
taxation benefits to wetlands and floodplains, among other open space
lands (Sec. 79A). State scenic rivers legislation typically restricts
uses of lands bordering rivers thus designated.

Definitions of where the shoreline lies vary among states and
affect the public's effective access to ocean beaches (see Hawaii's
definition in Sec. 205-31, p. 147, and that of Washington in Sec.
90.58.030, p. 190). California's constitution recognizes a public
right to beach access (p. 203), and Texas' Open Beaches Act (p.
203) has been upheld by the courts.


POWER PLANT AND INDUSTRY SITING


Over a third of the states have acted to control the location of
major power plants and transmission lines, generally providing "one-
stop" regulation for such utilities at the state level.

New York's Major Steam Electric Generating Facilities Siting
Act of 1972 (p. 204) requires consideration of alternatives and a finding of "minimum adverse environmental impact considering the state
of available technology" before a permit is granted. A 1970 statute
regulates the siting of major utility transmission facilities (Public
Service Law, Sec. 120 et seq.). Wyoming's Industrial Development
and Siting Act of 1975 (p. 210) requires detailed studies and a finding
of "acceptable impact upon the environment, social and economic
well being" before major industrial and energy generating plants may
be built. Montana passed a Major Facility Siting Act in 1975.

Colorado's Land Use Act includes major power plants in its definition of "key facility," potentially subject to state control (Sec. 106-7-104). Delaware prohibits heavy industry and has instituted permit procedures for other industrial development in its coastal zone (p. 197). In Minnesota power plant siting is a portion of a total energy conservation effort (Sec. 116H.13).


STATES


HAWAII LAND USE COMMISSION (1961, as amended)
13 Hawaii Rev. Stat. Ch. 205

Part I  Generally

Part II  Shoreline setbacks

*Section numbers of Act 193, passed June 2, 1975, are not codified at time of writing.

§ (1).  Findings and purpose.

   The legislature finds that although the purposes of Hawaii's land use
law remain as valid today as they were at the time of its enactment
in 1961, the procedures through which these purposes must be realized have proved inadequate and unworkable.  Under existing procedures the land use commission has been unable to reconcile in an orderly and rational manner the increasingly hostile and conflicting points
of view which surround land use decisions.  This Act sets forth reforms intended to insure the effective application for an established
land use policy through an adversary process in which all interests
will have the opportunity to compete in an open and orderly manner.
The commission is constituted as a quasi-judicial body and mandated
to make impartial decisions based on proven facts and established
policies.

§ 205-2.  Districting and classification of lands.

   There shall be four major land use districts in which all lands in the
State shall be placed: urban, rural, agricultural, and conservation.
The land use commission shall group contiguous land areas suitable
for inclusion in one of these four major districts.

   (1) In the establishment of boundaries of urban districts those lands
that are now in urban use and a sufficient reserve area for foreseeable
urban growth shall be included;

   (2) In the establishment of boundaries for rural districts, areas of
land composed primarily of small farms mixed with very low density
residential lots, which may be shown by a minimum density of not
more than one house per one-half acre and a minimum lot size of not
less than one-half acre shall be included;

   (3) In the establishment of the boundaries of agricultural districts the
greatest possible protection shall be given to those lands with a high
capacity for intensive cultivation; and

   (4) In the establishment of the boundaries of conservation districts,
the "forest and water reserve zones" provided in section 183-41 are
renamed "conservation districts" and, effective as of July 11, 1961,
the boundaries of the forest and water reserve zones theretofore established pursuant to section 183-41, shall constitute the boundaires of

the conservation districts; provided that thereafter the power to determine the boundaries of the conservation districts shall be in the commission.

In establishing the boundaries of the districts in each country, the
commission shall give consideration to the general plan of the county.

Urban districts shall include activities or uses as provided by ordinances or regulations of the county within which the urban district
is situated.

Rural districts shall include activities or uses as characterized by
low density residential lots of not more than one dwelling house per
one-half acre in areas where "city-like" concentration of people,
structures, streets, and urban level of services are absent, and where
small farms are intermixed with the low density residential lots.
These districts may include contiguous areas which are not suited to
low density residential lots or small farms by reason of topography,
soils, and other related characteristics.

Agricultural districts shall include activities or uses as characterized by the cultivation of crops, orchards, forage, and forestry;
farming activities or uses related to animal husbandry, and game and
fish propagation; services and uses accessory to the above activities
including but not limited to living quarters or dwellings, mills, storage facilities, processing facilities, and roadside stands for the sale
of products grown on the premises; agricultural parks and open area
recreational facilities.

These districts may include areas which are not used for, or which
are not suited to, agricultural and ancillary activities by reason of
topography, soils, and other related characteristics.

Conservation districts shall include areas necessary for protecting
watersheds and water sources; preserving scenic and historic areas;
providing park lands, wilderness, and beach; conserving endemic
plants, fish, and wildlife; preventing floods and soil erosion, forestry;
open space areas whose existing openness, natural condition, or present state of use, if retained, would enhance the present or potential
value of abutting or surrounding communities, or would maintain or
enhance the conservation of natural or scenic resources; areas of
value for recreational purposes; and other related activities; and other
permitted uses not detrimental to a multiple use conservation concept.

§ 205-4. Amendments to district boundaries.

(a) Any department or agency of the State including the land use commission, any department or agency of the county in which the land is
situated, or any person with a property interest in the land sought to
be reclassified, may petition the land use commission for a change in
the boundary of a district. . . .

(d) Any other provisions of law to the contrary notwithstanding, agencies and persons may intervene in the proceedings in accordance with this subsection.

(1) The petitioner, the department of planning and economic development and the county planning department shall in every case appear as parties and make recommendations relative to the proposed boundary change.

(2) All departments and agencies of the State and of the county in which the land is situated shall be admitted as parties upon timely application for intervention.

(3) All persons who have some property interest in the land, who lawfully reside on the land, or who otherwise can demonstrate that they will be so directly and immediately affected by the proposed change that their interest in the proceedings is clearly distinguishable from that of the general public shall be admitted as parties upon timely application for intervention.

(4) All other persons may apply to the commission for leave to intervene as parties.  Leave to intervene shall be freely granted. . . .

(e) Together with other witnesses that the commission may desire to hear at the hearing, it shall allow a representative of a citizen or a community group to testify who indicates a desire to express the views of such citizen or community group concerning the proposed boundary change. . . .

§ 205-5.  Zoning.

(a) Except as herein provided, the powers granted to counties under section 46-4 shall govern the zoning within the districts, other than in conservation districts.  Conservation districts shall be governed by the department of land and natural resources pursuant to section 183-41. . . .

§ 205-6.  Special permit.

The county planning commission may permit certain unusual and reasonable uses within agricultural and rural districts other than those for which the district is classified.  Any person who desires to use his land within an agricultural or rural district other than for an agricultural or rural use, as the case may be, may petition the planning commission of the county within which his land is located for permission to use his land in the manner desired. . . .

§ (10).  Adoption of interim statewide land use guidance policy.

The legislature hereby adopts the following as interim statewide land use guidance policy set forth in this section.  Except when the land use commission finds that an injustice or inequity will result, the commission shall observe and comply with these interim statewide land use guidance policies during the period commencing from the effective date of this Act until the effective date of the enactment of the State plan. The State plan shall be a long-range, comprehensive plan and policies which shall serve as a guide for the future long-range development of the State. . . .

Interim Statewide Land Use Guidance Policy

The interim policies are:

(1) Land use amendments shall be approved only as reasonably necessary to accommodate growth and development, provided there are no significant adverse effects upon agricultural, natural, environmental, recreational, scenic, historic, or other resources of the area.

(2) Lands to be reclassified as an urban district shall have adequate public services and facilities or as can be so provided at reasonable costs to the petitioner.

(3) Maximum use shall be made of existing services and facilities, and scattered urban development shall be avoided.

(4) Urban districts shall be contiguous to an existing urban district or shall constitute all or a part of a self-contained urban center.

(5) Preference shall be given to amendment petitions which will provide permanent employment, or needed housing accessible to existing or proposed employment centers, or assist in providing a balanced housing supply for all economic and social groups.

(6) In establishing the boundaries of the districts in each county, the commission shall give consideration to the general plan of the county.

(7) Insofar as practicable conservation lands shall not be reclassified as urban lands.

(8) The commission is encouraged to reclassify urban lands which are incompatible with the interim statewide land use guidance policy or are not developed in a timely manner.

§ (12). Compliance with State plan.

Upon enactment of the State plan, no amendment to any land use district boundary nor any other action by the land use commission shall be adopted unless such amendment or other action conforms to the State plan.

§ 183-41.  Forest and water reserve zones.

There are hereby established forest and water reserve zones in each of the counties.  These zones shall initially encompass all of those areas in the various counties, either government or privately owned, contained within the forest reserve boundaries as established on January 21, 1957.  No use, except a nonconforming use as defined in this section, shall be made of such areas unless such use is in accord with a zoning regulation adopted pursuant to this section or unless such use is allowed under a temporary variance granted by the department of land and natural resources; . . .

To effectuate the provisions of this section, the department of land and natural resources shall have the following powers and duties, in addition to all other powers and duties:

(1) General powers.  The department shall, after notice and hearing as herein provided, review and redefine the boundaries of forest and water reserve zones as established by or under the authority of this part.  The department may allow temporary variances from zoned use where good cause is shown and where the proposed variance is for a use determined by the department to be in accordance with good conservation practices.  The department may establish subzones within the forest and water reserve zones, which subzones shall be restricted to certain uses.  In establishing permitted uses in the subzones, the d epartment shall give full consideration to all available data as to soil classification and physical use capabilities of the land so as to allow and encourage the highest economic use thereof consonant with requirements for the conservation and maintenance of the purity of the water supplies arising in or running or percolating through the land. . . .

(4) Scope of zoning regulations.  The department shall, after notice and hearing as provided herein, adopt such regulations governing the use of land within the boundaries of the forest and water reserve zones as will not be detrimental to the conservation of necessary forest growth and the conservation and development of water resources adequate for present and future needs and the conservation and preservation of open space areas for public use and enjoyment.

The department by means of the regulations may establish subzones within any forest and water reserve zone and specify the land uses permitted therein which may include, but are not limited to, farming, flower gardening, operation of nurseries or orchards, growth of commercial timber, grazing, recreational or hunting pursuits, or residential use.  The regulations may also control the extent, manner, and times of the permitted uses, and may specifically prohibit unlimited cutting of forest growth, soil mining, or other activities detrimental to good conservation practices.

§ 205-31. Definitions.

(2) "Shoreline" means the upper reaches of the wash of waves, other than storm or tidal waves, usually evidenced by the edge of vegetation growth, or the upper line of debris left by the wash of waves. . . .

VERMONT LAND USE AND DEVELOPMENT ACT (1969)
10 Vt. Stat. Ann. Sec 6001 et seq.

§ 6001. Definitions.

(3) "Development" means the construction of improvements on a tract or tracts of land, owned or controlled by a person, involving more than 10 acres of land within a radius of five miles of any point on any involved land, for commercial, or industrial purposes. "Development"

shall also mean the construction of improvements for commercial or industrial purposes on more than one acre of land within a municipality which has not adopted permanent zoning and subdivision bylaws. The word "development" shall mean the construction of housing projects such as cooperatives, condominiums, or dwellings, or construction or maintenance of mobile homes or trailer parks, with 10 or more units, constructed or maintained on a tract or tracts of land, owned or controlled by a person, within a radius of five miles of any point on any involved land. The word "development" shall not include construction for farming, logging or forestry purposes below the elevation of 2500 feet. The word "development" also means the construction of improvements on a tract of land involving more than 10 acres which is to be used for municipal or state purposes. In computing the amount of land involved, land shall be included which is incident to the uses such as lawns, parking areas, roadways, leaching fields and accessory buildings. The word "development" shall not include an electric generation or transmission facility which requires a certificate of public good under section 248 of Title 30. The word "development" shall also mean the construction of improvements for commercial, industrial or residential use above the elevation of 2500 feet. . . .

### § 6041.  Interim capability plan.

Prior to the adoption of the capability and development plan, the board shall adopt an interim land capability and development plan which will describe the present use of the land and define in broad categories the capability of the land for development and use based on ecological considerations and which plan shall be in effect until the adoption of the land use plan, or until July 1, 1972, whichever first occurs.

### § 6042.  Capability and development plan.

The board shall adopt a capability and development plan consistent with the interim land capability plan which shall be made with the general purpose of guiding and accomplishing a coordinated, efficient and economic development of the state, which will, in accordance with present and future needs and resources, best promote the health, safety, order, convenience, prosperity and welfare of the inhabitants, as well as efficiency and economy in the process of development, including but not limited to, such distribution of population and of the uses of the land for urbanization, trade, industry, habitation, recreation, agriculture, forestry and other uses as will tend to create conditions favorable to transportation, health, safety, civic activities and educational and cultural opportunities, reduce the wastes of financial and human resources which result from either excessive conges-

tion or excessive scattering of population and tend toward an efficient
and economic utilization of drainage, sanitary and other facilities and
resources and the conservation and production of the supply of food,
water and minerals. In addition, the plan may accomplish the purposes
set forth in section 4302 of Title 24.

§ 6043.  Land use plan.

After the adoption of a capability and development plan, the board
shall adopt a land use plan based on the capability and development
plan which shall consist of a map and statements of present and prospective land uses based on the capability and development plan, which
determine in broad categories the proper use of the lands in the state
whether for forestry, recreation, agriculture or urban purposes, the
plans to be further implemented at the local level by authorized land
use controls such as subdivision regulations and zoning.

§ 6044.  Public hearings.

(a) The board shall hold public hearings for the purpose of collecting
information to be used in establishing the capability and development
plan, land use plan, and interim land capability plan. . . .

§ 6081.  Permits required; exemptions.

(a) No person shall sell or offer for sale any interest in any subdivision
located in this state, or commence construction on a subdivision or
development, or commence development without a permit. This section shall not prohibit the sale, mortgage or transfer of all, or an un-
divided interest in all, of a subdivision unless the sale, mortgage or
transfer is accomplished to circumvent the purposes of this chapter.
. . .

§ 6086.  Issuance of permit; conditions.

(a) Before granting a permit the board of district commission shall
find that the subdivision or development:
    (1) Will not result in undue water or air pollution. In making this
determination it shall at least consider: the elevation of land above
sea level; and in relation to the flood plains, the nature of soils and
subsoils and their ability to adequately support waste disposal; the slope
of the land and its effect on effluents; the availability of streams for
disposal of effluents; and the applicable health and water resources department regulations.
    (2) Does have sufficient water available for the reasonably foresee-
able needs of the subdivision or development.
    (3) Will not cause an unreasonable burden on an existing water sup-
ply, if one is to be utilized.

(4) Will not cause unreasonable soil erosion or reduction in the capacity of the land to hold water so that a dangerous or unhealthy condition may result.

(5) Will not cause unreasonable highway congestion or unsafe conditions with respect to use of the highways existing or proposed.

(6) Will not cause an unreasonable burden on the ability of a municipality to provide educational services.

(7) Will not place an unreasonable burden on the ability of the local governments to provide municipal or governmental services.

(8) Will not have an undue adverse effect on the scenic or natural beauty of the area, aesthetics, historic sites or rare and irreplaceable natural areas.

(9) Is in conformance with a duly adopted development plan, land use plan or land capability plan.

(10) Is in conformance with any duly adopted local or regional plan under chapter 91 of Title 24. . . .

(c) A permit may contain such requirements and conditions as are allowable within the proper exercise of the police power and which are appropriate with respect to (1) through (10) of subsection (a). . . .

§ 6087.  Denial of application.

(a) No application shall be denied by the board or district commission unless it finds the proposed subdivision or development detrimental to the public health, safety or general welfare.

(b) A permit may not be denied solely for the reasons set forth in (5), (6) and (7) of section 6086(a) of this title.  However, reasonable conditions and requirements allowable in section 6086(c) of this title may be attached to alleviate the burdens created.

(c) A denial of a permit shall contain the specific  reasons for denial. A person may, within 6 months, apply for reconsideration of his permit which application shall include an affidavit to the district commission and all parties of record that the deficiencies have been corrected. The district commission shall hold a new hearing upon 25 days notice to the parties.  The hearing shall be held within 40 days of receipt of the request for reconsideration.

FLORIDA ENVIRONMENTAL LAND AND WATER
MANAGEMENT ACT (1972, as amended)
Fla. Stats. Ch. 380

Section 380.012.    Short title
        380.021.    Purpose
        380.031.    Definitions

## § 380.021. Purpose.

It is the legislative intent that, in order to protect the natural resources and environment of this state as provided in § 7, Art. II of the
state constitution, insure a water management system that will reverse
the deterioration of water quality and provide optimum utilization of
our limited water resources, facilitate orderly and well-planned development, and protect the health, welfare, safety, and quality of
life of the residents of this state, it is necessary adequately to plan
for and guide growth and development within this state.  In order to
accomplish these purposes, it is necessary that the state establish
land and water management policies to guide and coordinate local decisions relating to growth and development; that such state land and
water management policies should, to the maximum possible extent,
be implemented by local governments through existing processes for
the guidance of growth and development; and that all the existing rights
of private property be preserved in accord with the constitutions of
this state and of the United States.

## § 380.031. Definitions.

As used in this chapter:

(1) "Administration commission" or "commission" means the governor
and the cabinet, and for purposes of this chapter the commission shall
act on a simple majority.

(2) "Development order "means any order granting, denying, or granting with conditions an application for a development permit.

(3) A "development permit" includes any building permit, zoning permit, plat approval, or rezoning, certification, variance, or other
action having the effect of permitting development as defined in this
chapter.

(4) "Developer" means any person, including a governmental agency,
undertaking any development as defined in this chapter.

(6) "Land" means the earth, water, and air, above, below, or on the
surface, and includes any improvements or structures customarily regarded as land. . . .

(10) "Major public facility" means any publicly owned facility of more than local significance. . . .

## § 380.04. Definition of development.

(1) "Development" means the carrying out of any building or mining operation or the making of any material change in the use or appearance of any structure or land and the dividing of land into three or more parcels.

(2) The following activities or uses shall be taken for the purposes of this chapter to involve development, as defined in this section:

(a) A reconstruction, alteration of the size, or material change in the external appearance, of a structure on land.

(b) A change in the intensity of use of land, such as an increase in the number of dwelling units in a structure or on land or a material increase in the number of businesses, manufacturing establishments, offices, or dwelling units in a structure or on land.

(c) Alteration of a shore or bank of a seacoast, river, stream, lake, pond, or canal, including any coastal construction as defined in § 161.021.

(d) Commencement of drilling, except to obtain soil samples, mining, or excavation on a parcel of land.

(e) Demolition of a structure.

(f) Clearing of land as an adjunct of construction.

(g) Deposit of refuse, solid or liquid waste, or fill on a parcel of land.

## § 380.05. Areas of critical state concern.

(1) (a) The state land planning agency may from time to time recommend to the administration commission specific areas of critical state concern. In its recommendation the agency shall specify the boundaries of the proposed areas and state the reasons why the particular area proposed is of critical concern to the state or region, the dangers that would result from uncontrolled or inadequate development of the area, and the advantages that would be achieved from the development of the area in a coordinated manner and recommend specific principles for guiding the development of the area. However, prior to the designation of any area of critical state concern by the administration commission, an inventory of lands owned by the state shall be filed with the state land planning agency. The state land planning agency shall request all political subdivisions and other public agencies of the state and the federal government to submit an inventory of lands owned within the State of Florida. . . .

(b) Within forty-five (45) days following receipt of a recommendation from the agency, the administration commission shall either reject the recommendation as tendered or adopt the same with or without modification and by rule designate the area of critical state concern and the principles for guiding the development of the area. The rule may specify that such principles for guiding development shall apply to development undertaken subsequent to the designation of the area of critical state concern but prior to the adoption of land development regulations for the critical area pursuant to subsection (6) and (8). In adopting such rule, the administration commission shall consider the economic impact of the principles on development in process within the area. The commission is not authorized to adopt any rule that would provide for a moratorium on development in any area of critical state concern.

(2) An area of critical state concern may be designated only for:

(a) An area containing, or having a significant impact upon, environmental, historical, natural, or archaeological resources of regional or statewide importance.

(b) An area significantly affected by, or having a significant effect upon, an existing or proposed major public facility or other area of major public investment.

(c) A proposed area of major development potential, which may include a proposed site of a new community, designated in a state land development plan. . . .

(5) After the adoption of a rule designating an area of critical state concern the local government having jurisdiction may submit to the state land planning agency its existing land development regulations for the area, if any, or shall prepare, adopt and submit new or modified regulations, taking into consideration the principles set forth in the rule designating the area as well as the factors that it would normally consider.

(6) If the state land planning agency finds that the land development regulations submitted by a local government comply with the principles for guiding the development of the area specified under the rule designating the area, the state land planning agency shall by rule approve the land development regulations. . . .

(8) If any local government fails to transmit land development regulations within six months after the adoption of a rule designating an area of critical state concern, or if the regulations transmitted do not comply with the principles for guiding development set out in the rule designating the area of critical state concern, in either case, within one hundred twenty days, the state land planning agency shall submit to the administration commission recommended land development regulations

applicable to that local government's portion of the area of critical state concern unless it determines that the area is no longer of critical state concern. . . .

(13) No person shall undertake any development within any area of critical state concern except in accordance with this chapter. . . .

(17) Within the twelve-month period following July 1, 1972, the administration commission shall not designate more than five hundred thousand acres as areas of critical state concern. At no time shall the administration commission designate a land area to be an area of critical state concern if the effect of such designation would be to subject more than 5 percent of the land of the state to supervision under this section, except that if any supervision by the state is retained, the area shall be considered to be included within the limitations of this subsection. . . .

§ 380.06. Developments of regional impact.

(1) "Development of regional impact," as used in this section, means any development which, because of its character, magnitude, or location, would have a substantial effect upon the health, safety, or welfare of citizens of more than one county. . . . In adopting its guidelines and standards, the administration commission shall consider and be guided by:
    (a) The extent to which the development would create or alleviate environmental problems such as air or water pollution or noise;
    (b) The amount of pedestrian or vehicular traffic likely to be generated;
    (c) The number of persons likely to be residents, employees, or otherwise present;
    (d) The size of the site to be occupied;
    (e) The likelihood that additional or subsidiary development will be generated; and
    (f) The unique qualities of particular areas of the state.

(5) A developer may undertake development of regional impact if:
    (a) The land on which the development is proposed is within the jurisdiction of a local government that has adopted a zoning ordinance under chapter 163 or chapter 176 or under appropriate special or local laws and the development has been approved under the requirements of this section; or
    (b) The land on which the development is proposed is within an area of critical state concern and the development has been approved under the requirements of § 380.05; or
    (c) The developer has given written notice to the state land planning agency and to any local government having jurisdiction to adopt zoning

or subdivision regulations for the area in which the development is proposed, and after ninety days have passed no zoning or subdivision regulations have been adopted or designation of area of critical state concern issued. . . .

(11) If the development is not located in an area of critical state concern, in considering whether the development shall be approved, denied, or approved subject to conditions, restrictions, or limitations, the local government shall consider whether, and the extent in which:

(a) The development unreasonably interferes with the achievement of the objectives of an adopted state land development plan applicable to the area;

(b) The development is consistent with the local land development regulations; . . .

COLORADO LAND USE ACT (1974)
106 Colo. Rev. Stat. Art. 7

§ 106-7-101.  Legislative declaration.

(1) In addition to the legislative declaration contained in section 106-4-1(1), the general assembly further finds and declares that:

(a) The protection of the utility, value, and future of all lands within the state, including the public domain as well as privately owned land, is a matter of the public interest;

(b) Adequate information on land use and systematic methods of definition, classification, and utilization thereof are either lacking or not readily available to land use decision makers;

(c) It is the intent of the general assembly that land use, land use planning, and quality of development are matters in which the state has responsibility for the health, welfare, and safety of the people of the state and for the protection of the environment of the state.

(2) It is the purpose of this article that:

(a) The general assembly shall describe areas which may be of state interest and activities which may be of state interest and establish criteria for the administration of such areas and activities;

(b) Local governments shall be encouraged to designate areas and activities of state interest and, after such designation, shall administer such areas and activities of state interest and promulgate guidelines for the administration thereof; and

(c) Appropriate state agencies shall assist local governments to identify, designate, and adopt guidelines for administration of matters of state interest.

§ 106-7-102.  General definitions.

As used in this article, unless the context otherwise requires:

(1) "Development" means any construction or activity which changes the basic character or the use of the land on which the construction or activity occurs. . . .

(4) "Matter of state interest" means an area of state interest or an activity of state interest or both.

§ 106-7-103. Definitions pertaining to natural hazards.

As used in this article, unless the context otherwise requires:

(1) "Aspect" means the cardinal direction the land surface faces, characterized by north-facing slopes generally having heavier vegetation cover. . . .

(3) "Corrosive soil" means soil which contains soluble salts which may produce serious detrimental effects in concrete, metal, or other substances that are in contact with such soil. . . .

(6) "Expansive soil and rock" means soil and rock which contains clay and which expands to a significant degree upon wetting and shrinks upon drying.

(7) "Floodplain" means an area adjacent to a stream, which area is subject to flooding as the result of the occurrence of an intermediate regional flood and which area thus is so adverse to past, current, or foreseeable construction or land use as to constitute a significant hazard to public health and safety or to property. The term includes but is not limited to:
    (a) Mainstream floodplains;
    (b) Debris-fan floodplains; and
    (c) Dry wash channels and dry wash floodplains.

(8) "Geologic hazard" means a geologic phenomenon which is so adverse to past, current, or foreseeable construction or land use as to constitute a significant hazard to public health and safety or to property. The term includes but is not limited to:
    (a) Avalanches, landslides, rock falls, mudflows, and unstable or potentially unstable slopes;
    (b) Seismic effects;
    (c) Radioactivity; and
    (d) Ground subsidence. . . .

(10) "Ground subsidence" means a process characterized by the downward displacement of surface material caused by natural phenomena such as removal of underground fluids, natural consolidation, or dissolution of underground minerals or by man-made phenomena such as underground mining. . . .

(13) "Natural hazard" means a geologic hazard, a wildfire hazard, or a flood. . . .

(19) "Unstable or potentially unstable slope" means an area susceptible to a landslide, a mudflow, a rock fall, or accelerated creep of slope-forming materials. . . .

(21) "Wildfire hazard" means a wildfire phenomenon which is so adverse to past, current, or foreseeable construction or land use as to constitute a significant hazard to public health and safety or to property. . . .

§ 106-7-104. Definitions pertaining to other areas and activities of state interest. . . .

(6) "Historical or archaeological resources of statewide importance" means resources which have been officially included in the national register of historic places, designated by statute, or included in an established list of places compiled by the state historical society.

(7) "Key facilities" means:
    (a) Airports;
    (b) Major facilities of a public utility;
    (c) Interchanges involving arterial highways;
    (d) Rapid or mass transit terminals, stations, and fixed guideways.
. . .

(12) "Natural resources of statewide importance" is limited to shorelands of major publicly-owned reservoirs and significant wildlife habitats in which the wildlife species, as identified by the division of wildlife of the department of natural resources, in a proposed area could be endangered.

§ 106-7-201. Areas of state interest—as determined by local governments.

(1) Subject to the procedures set forth in part 4 of this article, a local government may designate certain areas of state interest from among the following:
    (a) Mineral resource areas;
    (b) Natural hazard areas;
    (c) Areas containing, or having a significant impact upon, historical, natural, or archaeological resources of statewide importance; and
    (d) Areas around key facilities in which development may have a material effect upon the facility or the surrounding community.

§ 106-7-202. Criteria for administration of areas of state interest.

(1) (a) Mineral resource areas designated as areas of state interest shall be protected and administered in such a manner as to permit the extraction and exploration of minerals therefrom, unless extraction and exploration would cause significant danger to public health and safety. If the local government having jurisdiction, after weighing sufficient technical or other evidence, finds that the economic value of the minerals present therein is less than the value of another exist-

ing or requested use, such other use should be given preference; however, other uses which would not interfere with the extraction and exploration of minerals may be permitted in such areas of state interest.
. . .

(d) Unless an activity of state interest has been designated or identified or unless it includes part or all of another area of state interest, an area of oil and gas or geothermal resource development shall not be designated as an area of state interest unless the state oil and gas conservation commission identifies such area for designation.

(2) (a) Natural hazard areas shall be administered as follows:

(I) Floodplains shall be administered so as to minimize significant hazards to public health and safety or to property. The Colorado water conservation board shall promulgate a model floodplain regulation no later than September 30, 1974. Open space activities such as agriculture, recreation, and mineral extraction shall be encouraged in the floodplains. Any combination of these activities shall be conducted in a mutually compatible manner. . . .

(II) Wildfire hazard areas in which residential activity is to take place shall be administered so as to minimize significant hazards to public health and safety or to property. The Colorado state forest service shall promulgate a model wildfire hazard area control regulation no later than September 30, 1974. . . .

(III) In geologic hazard areas all developments shall be engineered and administered in a manner that will minimize significant hazards to public health and safety or to property due to a geologic hazard. The Colorado geological survey shall promulgate a model geologic hazard area control regulation no later than September 30, 1974.

(b) After promulgation of guidelines for land use in natural hazard areas by the Colorado water conservation board, the Colorado soil conservation board through the soil conservation districts, the Colorado state forest service, and the Colorado geological survey, natural hazard areas shall be administered by local government in a manner which is consistent with the guidelines for land use in each of the natural hazard areas.

(3) Areas containing, or having a significant impact upon, historical, natural, or archaeological resources of statewide importance, as determined by the state historical society, the department of natural resources, and the appropriate local government, shall be administered by the appropriate state agency in conjunction with the appropriate local government in a manner that will allow man to function in harmony with, rather than be destructive to, these resources. Consideration is to be given to the protection of those areas essential for wildlife habitat. Development in areas containing historical, archaeological, or natural resources shall be conducted in a manner which will minimize damage to those resouces for future use.

(4) The following criteria shall be applicable to areas around key facilities:

(a) If the operation of a key facility may cause a danger to public health and safety or to property, as determined by local government, the area around the key facility shall be designated and administered so as to minimize such danger; and

(b) Areas around key facilities shall be developed in a manner that will discourage traffic congestion, incompatible uses, and expansion of the demand for government services beyond the reasonable capacity of the community or region to provide such services as determined by local government. Compatibility with nonmotorized traffic shall be encouraged. A development that imposes burdens or deprivation on the communities of a region cannot be justified on the basis of local benefit alone.

(5) In addition to the criteria described in subsection (4) of this section, the following criteria shall be applicable to areas around particular key facilities. . . .

§ 106-7-203. Activities of state interest as determined by local governments.

(1) Subject to the procedures set forth in part 4 of this article, a local government may designate certain activities of state interest from among the following:

(a) Site selection and construction of major new domestic water and sewage treatment systems and major extension of existing domestic water and sewage treatment systems;

(b) Site selection and development of solid waste disposal sites;

(c) Site selection of airports;

(d) Site selection of rapid or mass transit terminals, stations, and fixed guideways;

(e) Site selection of arterial highways and interchanges and collector highways;

(f) Site selection and construction of major facilities of a public utility;

(g) Site selection and development of new communities;

(h) Efficient utilization of municipal and industrial water projects; and

(i) Conduct of nuclear detonations.

§ 106-7-204. Criteria for administration of activities of state interest.

(1) (b) Major extensions of domestic water and sewage treatment systems shall be permitted in those areas in which the anticipated growth and development that may occur as a result of such extension can be

accommodated within the financial and environmental capacity of the area to sustain such growth and development.

(2) Major solid waste disposal sites shall be developed in accordance with sound conservation practices and shall emphasize, where feasible, the recycling of waste materials. Consideration shall be given to longevity and subsequent use of waste disposal sites, soil and wind conditions, the potential problems of pollution inherent in the proposed site, and the impact on adjacent property owners, compared with alternate locations.

(3) Airports shall be located or expanded in a manner which will minimize disruption to the environment of existing communities, will minimize the impact on existing community services, and will complement the economic and transportation needs of the state and the area.

(4) (a) Rapid or mass transit terminals, stations, or guideways shall be located in conformance with the applicable municipal master plan.
. . .

(b) Proposed locations of rapid or mass transit terminals, stations, and fixed guideways which will not require the demolition of residences or businesses shall be given preferred consideration over competing alternatives.

(c) A proposed location of a rapid or mass transit terminal, station, or fixed guideway that imposes a burden or deprivation on a local government cannot be justified on the basis of local benefit alone, nor shall a permit for such a location be denied solely because the location places a burden or deprivation on one local government.

(5) Arterial highways and interchanges and collector highways shall be located so that:
(a) Community traffic needs are met;
(b) Desirable community patterns are not disrupted; and
(c) Direct conflicts with adopted local government, regional, and state master plans are avoided.

(6) Where feasible, major facilities of public utilities shall be located so as to avoid direct conflict with adopted local government, regional, and state master plans.

(7) When applicable, or as may otherwise be provided by law, a new community design shall, at a minimum, provide for transportation, waste disposal, schools, and other governmental services in a manner that will not overload facilities of existing communities of the region. Priority shall be given to the development of total communities which provide for commercial and industrial activity, as well as residences, and for internal transportation and circulation patterns.

(8) Municipal and industrial water projects shall emphasize the most efficient use of water, including, to the extent permissible under existing law, the recycling and reuse of water. Urban development, population densities, and site layout and design of storm water and sanitation systems shall be accomplished in a manner that will prevent the pollution of aquifer recharge areas.

(9) Nuclear detonations shall be conducted so as to present no material danger to public health and safety. Any danger to property shall not be disproporationate to the benefits to be derived from a detonation.

§ 106-7-406.  Colorado land use commission review of local government order containing designation and guidelines.

(2) If the Colorado land use commission decides that modification of the designation or guidelines is required, the Colorado land use commission shall, within said thirty-day period, submit to the local government written notification of its recommendations and shall specify in writing the modifications which the Colorado land use commission deems necessary for compliance with the relevant provisions of part 2 of this article.

(3) Not later than thirty days after receipt of the modifications recommended by the Colorado land use commission, a local government shall:

(a) Modify the original order in a manner consistent with the recommendations of the Colorado land use commission and resubmit the order to the Colorado land use commission; or

(b) Notify the Colorado land use commission that the Colorado land use commission's recommendations are rejected.

§ 106-7-407.  Colorado land use commission may initiate identification, designation, and promulgation of guidelines for matters of state interest.

§ 106-7-501.  Permit for development in area of state interest or for conduct of an activity of state interest required.

(3) The local government may approve an application for a permit to engage in development in an area of state interest if the proposed development complies with the local government's guidelines and regulations governing such area. If the proposed development does not comply with the guidelines and regulations, the permit shall be denied.

(4) The local government may approve an application for a permit for conduct of an activity of state interest if the proposed activity complies with the local government's regulations and guidelines for conduct of such activity. If the proposed activity does not comply with the guidelines and regulations, the permit shall be denied.

§ 106-4-3. Duties of the commission—temporary emergency power.

(2) (a) Whenever in the normal course of its duties as set forth in this article the commission determines that there is in progress or proposed a land development activity which constitutes a danger of injury, loss, or damage of serious and major proportions to the public health, welfare, or safety, the commission shall immediately give written notice to the board of county commissioners of each county involved of the pertinent facts and dangers with respect to such activity. If the said board of county commissioners does not remedy the situation within a reasonable time, the commission may request the governor to review such facts and dangers with respect to such activity. If the governor grants such request, such review shall be conducted by the governor at a meeting with the commission and the boards of county commissioners of the counties involved. If, after such review, the governor shall determine that such activity does constitute such a danger, the governor may direct the commission to issue its written cease and desist order to the person in control of such activity. Such order shall require that such person immediately discontinue such activity. If such activity, notwithstanding such order, is continued, the commission may apply to any district court of this state in which such activity is located for a temporary restraining order, preliminary injunction, or permanent injunction, as provided for in the Colorado rules of civil procedure. Any such action shall be given precedence over all other matters pending in such district court. The institution of such action shall confer upon said district court exclusive jurisdiction to determine finally the subject matter thereof.

CONNECTICUT ZONING ENABLING ACT (1949, as amended)
8 Conn. Gen. Stat. Ch. 124

§ 8-2. Regulations.

The zoning commission of each city, town or borough is authorized
to regulate, within the limits of such municipality, the height, number
of stories and size of buildings and other structures; the percentage
of the area of the lot that may be occupied; the size of yards, courts
and other open spaces; the density of population and the location and
use of buildings, structures and land for trade, industry, residence
or other purposes, and the height, size and location of advertising
signs and billboards. Such zoning commission may divide the municipality into districts of such number, shape and area as may be best
suited to carry out the purposes of this chapter; and, within such districts, it may regulate the erection, construction, reconstruction,
alteration or use of buildings or structures and the use of land. All
such regulations shall be uniform for each class or kind of buildings,
structures or use of land throughout each district, but the regulations
in one district may differ from those in another district and may provide
that certain classes or kinds of buildings, structures or use of land
are permitted only after obtaining a special permit or special exception from a zoning commission, planning commission, combined planning and zoning commission or zoning board of appeals, whichever
commission or board the regulations may, notwithstanding any special
act to the contrary, designate, subject to standards set forth in the
regulations and to conditions necessary to protect the public health,
safety, convenience and property values. Such regulations shall be
made in accordance with a comprehensive plan and shall be designed
to lessen congestion in the streets; to secure safety from fire, panic,
flood and other dangers; to promote health and the general welfare;
to provide adequate light and air; to prevent the overcrowding of land;
to avoid undue concentration of population and to facilitate the adequate
provision for transportation, water, sewerage, schools, parks and
other requirements. Such regulations shall be made with reasonable
consideration as to the character of the district and its peculiar suitability for particular uses and with a view to conserving the value of
buildings and encouraging the most appropriate use of land throughout such municipality. Such regulations shall not prohibit the continuance of any nonconforming use, building or structure existing at the
time of the adoption of such regulations. Any city, town or borough
which adopts the provisions of this chapter may, by vote of its legislative body, exempt municipal property from the regulations prescribed
by the zoning commission of such city, town or borough; but unless it
is so voted municipal property shall be subject to such regulations.

CONNECTICUT PLANNED UNIT DEVELOPMENT ACT (1969)
8 Conn. Gen. Stat. Ch. 124a

§ 8-13b. Definitions.

"Common open space" means a parcel or parcels of land, or an area
of water, or a combination of land and water, within the site designated
for a planned unit development, and designed and intended for the use
and enjoyment of residents of the planned unit development and may
contain such complementary structures and improvements as are necessary and appropriate for the benefit and enjoyment of such residents;
. . .

"Plan" means the provisions for development of a planned unit development, including but not limited to, a plat of subdivision, covenants
relating to use, location and bulk of buildings and other structures,
intensity of use or density of development, private streets, ways and
parking facilities, and common open space and public facilities;
"planned unit development" means an area of land controlled by an
owner, to be developed as a single entity for not less than twenty-five
dwelling units, the plan for which does not correspond in lot size,
bulk, type of dwelling, density, lot coverage and required open space
to the regulations established in any zoning district created, from
time to time, under the provisions of the zoning ordinances or regulations of the municipality; "statement of objectives for planned unit development" means a written statement of the goals of the municipality
with respect to land use for residential purposes, density of population,
direction of growth, location and function of streets and other public
facilities, and common open space for recreation or visual benefit,
or both, and such other factors as the planning commission, or planning and zoning commission, of such municipality may find relevant
in determining whether a planned unit development shall be authorized.

§ 8-13c. Adoption of chapter.

Planned unit development regulations

(a) Any municipality may, by vote of its legislative body, adopt the provisions of this chapter by ordinance and include in its zoning regulations, regulations exercising the powers granted hereunder which shall be known as planned unit development regulations. . . .

§ 8-13d.  Regulations: Standards and conditions.

Such planned unit development regulations shall set forth the standards and conditions by which a proposed planned unit development shall be evaluated. . . . Such regulations and amendments thereto shall not be inconsistent with the following provisions:

(a) Such regulations adopted shall set forth the uses permitted in a planned unit development, which uses shall be limited to

(1) dwelling units in detached, semi-detached or multi-storied structures, or any combination thereof; and

(2) any nonresidential use, to the extent such nonresidential use is designed to serve the residents of such development. Such regulations may establish provisions setting forth the timing of development among the various types of dwellings.

(b) Such regulations shall establish standards governing the density, or intensity of land use, in a planned unit development. Such standards shall

(1) take into account that the density, or intensity of land use, otherwise allowable on the site under existing zoning regulations enacted pursuant to chapter 124, may not be appropriate for a planned unit development;

(2) may vary the density, or intensity of land use, otherwise applicable to the land within the planned unit development in consideration of

(A) the amount, location and proposed use of common open space;

(B) the location and physical characteristics of the site of the proposed planned development and

(C) the location, design and type of dwelling units; and

(3) may, in the case of a planned unit development proposed to be developed over a period of years, authorize a deviation in each section to be developed from the density, or intensity of use, established for the entire planned unit development.

(c) Such standards shall require that any common open space resulting from the application of standards for density, or intensity of land use, be set aside for the use and benefit of the residents of such development and such standards shall include provisions for determining the amount and location of any common open space and the improvement and maintenance of such common open space use subject to the following:

(1) Such regulations may provide that the municipality may accept the dedication of land or any interest therein for public use and maintenance, but such regulations shall not require, as a condition of the approval of a planned unit development, that land proposed to be set aside for common open space be dedicated or made available to public use. Such regulations may require that the owner provide for and establish an organization for the ownership and maintenance of any common open space, and that such organization shall not be dissolved nor shall it dispose of such common open space, by sale or otherwise, except to an organization established for the purpose of owning and maintaining such space, without first offering to dedicate such space to the municipality; and

(2) in the event that the organization established to own and maintain common open space, or any successor organization, shall at any time after establishment of the planned unit development fail to maintain such common open space in reasonable order and condition in accordance with the plan, the commission. . . .

Regional Planning and Zoning

MINNESOTA METROPOLITAN COUNCIL (1967, as amended 1974)
Minn. Stat. 473B.01 et seq.

Section 473B.21.    Legislative policy
       473B.22.    Definitions
       473B.23.    Standards and criteria
       473B.24.    Local ordinances
       473B.25.    Cooperation
       473B.26.    Metropolitan council assistance

§ 473B.011.  Definitions.

Subdivision 3.  "Metropolitan commission or commission" means the
metropolitan waste control commission, the metropolitan transit commission, and other such commissions as the legislature may hereafter designate.

Subdivision 4.  "Independent commission, board or agency" means
governmental entities with jurisdiction lying wholly or in part within
the metropolitan area but not including the metropolitan commissions
referred to herein. . . .

§ 473B.06.  Administration of metropolitan council.

Subdivision 5.  Development guide.

   The metropolitan council shall prepare and adopt, after appropriate
study and such public hearings as may be necessary, a comprehensive
development guide for the metropolitan area.  It shall consist of a
compilation of policy statements, goals, standards, programs, and
maps prescribing guides for an orderly and economic development,
public and private, of the metropolitan area.  The comprehensive development guide shall recognize and encompass physical, social, or
economic needs of the metropolitan area and those future developments
which will have an impact on the entire area including but not limited
to such matters as land use, parks and open space land needs, the
necessity for and location of airports, highways, transit facilities,
public hospitals, libraries, schools, and other public buildings.

§ 473B.061.  Review by council.

Subdivision 1.  Metropolitan significance.

   Within 12 months following April 12, 1974 the council shall adopt
regulations pursuant to the administrative procedures act, chapter
15, establishing standards and guidelines for determining whether
any proposed matter is of metropolitan significance, and establishing
a procedure for the review of all proposed matters required to be considered and reviewed by the council. . . .

Subdivision 2.  Regulations

(a) In developing the above regulations establishing standards and guidelines for determining metropolitan significance the council and the committee shall give consideration to all factors deemed relevant to that determination including the following:

(1) The impact a proposed matter will have on the orderly, economic development, public and private, of the metropolitan area and its consistency with the development guide;

(2) The relationship a proposed matter will have to the policy statement goals, standards, programs and other applicable provisions of the development guide;

(3) The impact a proposed matter will have on policy plans adopted by the council and on the development programs and functions performed and to be performed by the commission;

(4) Functions of municipal governments in respect to control of land use as provided for under the municipal planning act;

(5) Such other factors as are deemed relevant.

(b) The regulations establishing a procedure for the review of proposed matters shall include among other provisions. . . .

(c) Once the development of all of the regulations has been completed by the council and the committee, and no later than 30 days prior to the date specified for their adoption, the council shall hold a public hearing for the purpose of considering the developed regulations and receiving comments and recommendations thereon. . . .

Subdivision 3.  Council review; metropolitan significance; applications for federal and state aid.

The council shall review the following matters, applications, and plans proposed for or with respect to the metropolitan area in accordance with the regulations to be adopted and the provisions of any other relevant statute.

(a) All proposed matters of metropolitan significance to be undertaken by any private organization, independent commission, board or agency, local governmental unit, or any state agency.

(b) All applications of a metropolitan commission, independent commission, board or agency, and local governmental units for funds, grants, loans or loan guarantees from the United States of America or agencies thereof submitted in connection with proposed matters of metropolitan significance, all other applications by commissions and local governmental units for grants, loans, or loan guarantees from the United States of America or any agency thereof if review by a regional agency is required by federal law or the federal agency, and all applications of the commissions, for grants, loans, or alloca-

tions from funds made available by the United States of America to
the metropolitan area for regional facilities pursuant to a federal
revenue sharing or similar program requiring that the funds be received and granted or allocated or that the grants and allocations be
approved by a regional agency.

(c) All applications or requests of a metropolitan commission, independent commission, board or agency, and local governmental units
for state funds allocated or granted for proposed matters of metropolitan significance, and all other applications by metropolitan commissions, independent commissions, boards, agencies, and local governmental units for state funds if review by a regional agency is required
by state law or the granting state agency.

Subdivision 4.   Council review; comprehensive plans, land use plans.

Each city, town, and county all or part of which lies within the metropolitan area, shall submit to the metropolitan council for written
comment and recommendation thereon its proposed long-term comprehensive plans, including but not limited to plans for land use. . . .

NEW JERSEY SPORTS AND EXPOSITION
AUTHORITY LAW (1971)
5 N.J. Rev. Stat. Ch. 10

## § 5:10-2.  Declaration of policy.

The Legislature has determined that to provide for the establishment and operation of the needed stadiums and other facilities for the holding of . . . spectator sports, expositions and other public events and uses, a corporate agency of the State shall be created with the necessary powers to accomplish these purposes. . . .

## § 5:10-5.  Powers.

x.  To determine the location, type and character of the project or any part thereof and all other matters in connection with all or any part of the project, notwithstanding any land use plan, zoning regulation, building code or similar regulation heretofore or hereafter adopted by the state, any municipality, county, public body politic and corporate. . . .

## § 5:10-8.  Relocation of public highways; entry on lands, waters, or premises; regulations for public utility facilities.

a.  If the authority shall find it necessary in connection with the undertaking of the project to change the location of any portion of any public highway or road, it may contract with any government agency, public or private corporation which may have jurisdiction over said public highway or road to cause said public highway or road to be constructed at such location as the authority in consultation with the Meadowlands Commission shall deem most favorable. . . .

b.  In addition to the foregoing powers the authority and its authorized agents and employees may enter upon any lands, waters and premises for the purpose of making surveys, soundings, drillings and examinations as it may deem necessary or convenient for the purposes of the act, all in accordance with due process of law, and such entry shall not be deemed a trespass. . . .

NEW YORK ADIRONDACK PARK AGENCY ACT (1973)
N.Y. Exec. Law 801 et seq.

§ 805. Adirondack park land use and development plan.

1. Adoption; status report.
     a. The Adirondack park land use and development plan is hereby
adopted and shall hereafter serve to guide land use planning and development throughout the entire area of the Adirondack park, except for
those lands owned by the state. . . .

2. Official Adirondack park land use and development plan map.
     a. The official Adirondack park land use and development plan
map shall have the land use planning and regulatory effect authorized
under this article. . . .

3. Land use areas. . . .
     c. Hamlet areas. . . .
        (2) Purposes, policies and objectives. Hamlet areas will serve
as the service and growth centers in the park. They are intended
to accommodate a large portion of the necessary and natural expansion of the park's housing, commercial and industrial activities. . . .
        (3) All land uses and development are considered compatible
with the character, purposes and objectives of hamlet areas.
        (4) No overall intensity guideline is applicable to hamlet areas.
     d. Moderate intensity use areas. . . .
        (2) Purposes, policies and objectives. Moderate intensity use
areas will provide for development opportunities in areas where
development will not significantly harm the relatively tolerant phy-

sical and biological resources. These areas are designed to provide for residential expansion and growth. . . .

(3) Guidelines for overall intensity of development. The overall intensity of development for land located in any moderate intensity use area should not exceed approximately five hundred principal buildings per square mile.

(4) Classification of compatible uses: . . .

e.  Low intensity use areas.

(2) Purposes, policies and objectives. The purpose of low intensity use areas is to provide for development opportunities at levels that will protect the physical and biological resources, while still providing for orderly growth and development of the park. It is anticipated that these areas will primarily be used to provide housing development opportunities not only for park residents but also for the growing seasonal home market. In addition, services and uses related to residential uses may be located at a lower intensity than in hamlets or moderate intensity use areas.

(3) Guidelines for overall intensity of development. The overall intensity of development for land located in any low intensity use area should not exceed approximately two hundred principal buildings per square mile.

(4) Classification of compatible uses: . . .

f.  Rural use areas.

(1) Character description. Rural use areas, delineated in yellow on the plan map, are those areas where natural resource limitations and public considerations necessitate fairly stringent development constraints. These areas are characterized by substantial acreages of one or more of the following: fairly shallow soils, relatively severe slopes, significant ecotones, critical wildlife habitats, proximity to scenic vistas or key public lands. . . .

(2) Purposes, policies and objectives. . . . Residential development and related development and uses should occur on large lots or in relatively small clusters on carefully selected and well designed sites. This will provide for further diversity in residential and related development opportunities in the park.

(3) Guideline for overall intensity of development. The overall intensity of development for land located in any rural use area should not exceed approximately seventy-five principal buildings per square mile.

(4) Classification of compatible uses: . . .

g.  Resource management areas.

(1) Character description. Resource management areas, delineated in green on the plan map, are those lands where the need to protect, manage and enhance forest, agricultural, recreational and open space resources is of paramount importance because of over-

riding natural resource and public considerations.  Open space
uses, including forest management, agriculture and recreational
activities, are found throughout these areas.

Many resource management areas are characterized by substantial acreages of one or more of the following:  shallow soils, severe
slopes, elevations of over twenty-five hundred feet, flood plains,
proximity to designated or proposed wild or scenic rivers, wetlands, critical wildlife habitats or habitats of rare and endangered
plant and animal species.

Other resource management areas are included in resource management areas, with many farms exhibiting a high level of capital
investment for agricultural buildings and equipment.  These agricultural areas are of considerable economic importance to segments
of the park and provide for a type of open space which is compatible
with the park's character. . . .

(3) Guidelines for overall intensity of development.  The overall
intensity of development for land located in any resource management
area should not exceed approximately fifteen principal buildings per
square mile.

(4) Classification of compatible uses: . . .

h.  Industrial use areas. . . .

(3) Classification and compatible uses. . . .

4.  Development considerations.  The following are those factors
which relate to potential for adverse impact upon the park's natural,
scenic, aesthetic, ecological, wildlife, historic, recreational or
open space resources and which shall be considered, as provided in
this article, before any significant new land use or development or
subdivision of land is undertaken in the park.  Any burden on the public in providing facilities and services made necessary by such land
use and development or subdivision of land shall also be taken into
account, as well as any commercial, industrial, residential, recreational or other benefits which might be derived therefrom:

a.  Natural resource considerations.

(1) Water. . . .

(2) Land. . . .

(i) the quality and availability of land for outdoor recreational
purposes

(3) Air. . . .

(4) Noise. . . .

(5) Critical resource areas

(6) Wildlife. . . .

(7) Aesthetics. . . .

b.  Historic site considerations. . . .

c.  Site development considerations. . . .

d.  Governmental considerations. . . .

e.  Governmental review considerations. . . .

§ 806. Shoreline restrictions.

1. In order to provide adequate protection of the quality of the lakes, ponds, rivers and streams of the park and the visual qualities of their shorelines, no person shall undertake any new land use or development or subdivision of land that involves any shoreline within the park, except in compliance, at a minimum, with the following restrictions. In addition, compliance with these restrictions shall be required by the agency in its review of any project under section eight hundred nine and, at a minimum, by any local government in the adoption and enforcement of a local land use program. All distances contained in these restrictions shall be measured horizontally. . . .

§ 807. Local land use programs.

1. The agency is authorized to review and approve any local land use program proposed by a local government and formally submitted by the legislative body of the local government to the agency for approval. . . .

e. It incorporates at a minimum the shoreline restrictions as they relate to any shoreline within the local government. . . .

f. It requires review of class B regional projects and provides that any such project shall not be approved unless the local government body or officer having jurisdiction under the program determines that the undertaking or continuance of such project will not have an undue adverse impact upon the natural, scenic, aesthetic, ecological, wildlife, historic, recreational or open space resources of the park or upon the ability of the public to provide supporting facilities and services made necessary by the project, taking into account the commercial, industrial, residential, recreational or other benefits that might be derived from the project. . . .

§ 809. Agency administration and enforcement of the land use and development plan.

1. The agency shall have jurisdiction to review and approve all class A regional projects, including those proposed to be located in a land use area governed by an approved local land use program. In addition, the agency shall have authority to review and approve class B regional projects in any land use area not governed by an approved and validly enacted or adopted local land use program. . . .

10. The agency shall not approve any project proposed to be located in any land use area not governed by an approved local land use program, or grant a permit therefor, unless it first determines that such project meets the following criteria:

a. The project would be consistent with the land use and development plan.

b.  The project would be compatible with the character description and purposes, policies and objectives of the land use area wherein it is proposed to be located. . . .

c.  The project would be consistent with the overall intensity guideline for the land use area involved. . . .

d.  The project would comply with the shoreline restrictions if applicable. . . .

e.  The project would not have an undue adverse impact upon the natural, scenic, aesthetic, ecological, wildlife, historic, recreational or open space resources of the park or upon the ability of the public to provide supporting facilities and services made necessary by the project, taking into account the commercial, industrial, residential, recreational or other benefits that might be derived from the project. . . .

FEDERAL

Wetlands and Shorelands

COASTAL ZONE MANAGEMENT ACT (1972)
16 U.S.C. 1451 et seq.

§ 1451.  Congressional findings.

The Congress finds that—

(a) There is a national interest in the effective management, beneficial use, protection, and development of the coastal zone;

(b) The coastal zone is rich in a variety of natural, commercial, recreational, industrial, and esthetic resources of immediate and potential value to the present and future well-being of the Nation;

(c) The increasing and competing demands upon the lands and waters of our coastal zone occasioned by population growth and economic development, including requirements for industry, commerce, residential development, recreation, extraction of mineral resources and fossil fuels, transportation and navigation, waste disposal, and harvesting of fish, shellfish, and other living marine resources, have resulted in the loss of living marine resources, wildlife, nutrient-rich areas, permanent and adverse changes to ecological systems, decreasing open space for public use, and shoreline erosion;

(d) The coastal zone, and the fish, shellfish, other living marine resources, and wildlife therein, are ecologically fragile and consequently extremely vulnerable to destruction by man's alterations;

(e) Important ecological, cultural, historic, and esthetic values in the coastal zone which are essential to the well-being of all citizens are being irretrievably damaged or lost;

(f) Special natural and scenic characteristics are being damaged by ill-planned development that threatens these values;

(g) In light of competing demands and the urgent need to protect and to give high priority to natural systems in the coastal zone, present state and local institutional arrangements for planning and regulating land and water uses in such areas are inadequate; and

(h) The key to more effective protection and use of the land and water resources of the coastal zone is to encourage the states to exercise their full authority over the lands and waters in the coastal zone by assisting the states, in cooperation with Federal and local governments and other vitally affected interests, in developing land and water use programs for the coastal zone, including unified policies, criteria, standards, methods, and processes for dealing with land and water use decisions of more than local significance.

§ 1452. Congressional declaration of policy.

The Congress finds and declares that it is the national policy

(a) to preserve, protect, develop, and where possible, to restore or enhance, the resources of the Nation's coastal zone for this and succeeding generations,

(b) to encourage and assist the states to exercise effectively their responsibilities in the coastal zone through the development and implementation of management programs to achieve wise use of the land and
water resources of the coastal zone giving full consideration to ecological, cultural, historic, and esthetic values as well as to needs for
economic development.

(c) for all Federal agencies engaged in programs affecting the coastal
zone to cooperate and participate with state and local governments and
regional agencies in effectuating the purposes of this chapter, and

(d) to encourage the participation of the public, of Federal, state, and
local governments and of regional agencies in the development of
coastal zone management programs. With respect to implementation
of such management programs, it is the national policy to encourage
cooperation among the various state and regional agencies including
establishment of interstate and regional agreements, cooperative procedures, and joint action particularly regarding environmental problems.

§ 1453. Definitions.

For the purposes of this title—

(a) "Coastal zone" means the coastal waters (including the lands therein
and thereunder) and the adjacent shorelands (including the land waters
therein and thereunder) strongly influenced by each other and in proximity to the shorelines of the several coastal states, and includes
transitional and intertidal areas, salt marshes, wetlands, and beaches.
The zone extends, in Great Lakes waters, to the international boundary
between the United States and Canada and, in other areas, seaward
to the outer limit of the United States territorial sea. The zone extends inland from the shorelines only to the extent necessary to control
shorelands, the uses of which have a direct and significant impact on
the coastal waters. Excluded from the coastal zone are lands the use
of which is by law subject solely to the discretion of or which is held
in trust by the Federal Government, its officers or agents.

(b) "Coastal waters" means
    (1) in the Great Lakes area, the waters within the territorial juris-
diction of the United States consisting of the Great Lakes, their connecting waters, harbors, roadsteads, and estuary-type areas such
as bays, shallows, and marshes and
    (2) in other areas, those waters, adjacent to the shorelines, which
contain a measurable quantity or percentage of seawater including, but
not limited to, sounds, bays, lagoons, bayous, ponds, and estuaries.
    . . .

§ 1454. Management development program grants.

(a) Authorization.

The Secretary is authorized to make annual grants to any coastal state for the purpose of assisting in the development of a management program for the land and water resources of its coastal zone.

(b) Program requirements.

Such management program shall include:
(1) an identification of the boundaries of the coastal zone subject to the management program;
(2) a definition of what shall constitute permissible land and water uses within the coastal zone which have a direct and significant impact on the coastal waters;
(3) an inventory and designation of areas of particular concern within the coastal zone;
(4) an identification of the means by which the state proposes to exert control over the land and water uses referred to in paragraph (2) of this subsection, including a listing of relevant constitutional provisions, legislative enactments, regulations, and judicial decision;
(5) broad guidelines on priority of uses in particular areas, including specifically those uses of lowest priority;
(6) a description of the organizational structure proposed to implement the management program, including the responsibilities and interrelationships of local, areawide, state, regional, and interstate agencies in the management process.

§ 1455. Administrative grants.

(a) Authorization.

The Secretary is authorized to make annual grants to any coastal state for not more than 66 2/3 per centum of the costs of administering the state's management program, if he approves such program in accordance with subsection (c) of this section. Federal funds received from other sources shall not be used to pay the states' share of costs. . . .

(c) Program requirements.

Prior to granting approval of a management program submitted by a coastal state, the Secretary shall find that:
(1) The state has developed and adopted a management program for its coastal zone in accordance with rules and regulations promulgated by the Secretary, after notice, and with the opportunity of full participation by relevant Federal agencies, state agencies, local governments, regional organizations, port authorities, and other interested parties, public and private, which is adequate to carry out the purposes

of this chapter and is consistent with the policy declared in section
1452 of this title.

(2) The state has:

(A) coordinated its program with local, areawide, and interstate
plans applicable to areas within the coastal zone existing on January
1 of the year in which the state's management program is submitted
to the Secretary, which plans have been developed by a local government, an areawide agency designated pursuant to regulations established under section 3334 of Title 42, a regional agency, or an interstate agency; and

(B) established an effective mechanism for continuing consultation and coordination between the management agency designated
pursuant to paragraph (5) of this subsection and with local governments, interstate agencies, regional agencies, and areawide agencies within the coastal zone to assure the full participation of such
local governments and agencies in carrying out the purposes of this
chapter. . . .

(8) The management program provides for adequate consideration
of the national interest involved in the siting of facilities necessary
to meet requirements which are other than local in nature.

(9) The management program makes provisions for procedures
whereby specific areas may be designated for the purpose of preserving or restoring them for their conservation, recreational, ecological,
or esthetic values.

§ 1456.  Interagency coordination and cooperation—Federal agencies.
. . .

(c) (1) Each Federal agency conducting or supporting activities directly affecting the coastal zone shall conduct or support those activities in a manner which is, to the maximum extent practicable, consistent with approved state management programs.

(2) Any Federal agency which shall undertake any development
project in the coastal zone of a state shall insure that the project is,
to the maximum extent practicable, consistent with approved state
management programs.

§ 1461.  Estuarine sanctuaries.

The Secretary, in accordance with rules and regulations promulgated
by him, is authorized to make available to a coastal state grants of
up to 50 per centum of the costs of acquisition, development, and
operation of estuarine sanctuaries for the purpose of creating natural
field laboratories to gather data and make studies of the natural and
human processes occurring within the estuaries of the coastal zone.
The Federal share of the cost for each such sanctuary shall not ex-

ceed \$2,000,000.  No Federal funds received pursuant to section 1454
or 1455 of this title shall be used for the purpose of this section.

FLOOD DISASTER PROTECTION ACT (1968, as amended)
42 U.S.C. 4001 et seq.

§ 4001. Congressional findings and declaration of purpose.

(a) The Congress finds that

(1) from time to time flood disasters have created personal hardships and economic distress which have required unforeseen disaster relief measures and have placed an increasing burden on the Nation's resources;

(2) despite the installation of preventive and protective works and the adoption of other public programs designed to reduce losses caused by flood damage, these methods have not been sufficient to protect adequately against growing exposure to future flood losses;

(3) as a matter of national policy, a reasonable method of sharing the risk of flood losses is through a program of flood insurance which can complement and encourage preventive and protective measures;

. . .

(c) The Congress further finds that . . .

(2) the objectives of a flood insurance program should be integrally related to a unified national program for floodplain management and, to this end, it is the sense of Congress that within two years following the effective date of this chapter the President should transmit to the Congress for its consideration any further proposals necessary for such a unified program, including proposals for the allocation of costs among beneficiaries of flood protection. . . .

(e) It is the further purpose of this chapter to

(1) encourage State and local governments to make appropriate land use adjustments to constrict the development of land which is exposed to flood damage and minimize damage caused by flood losses,

(2) guide the development of proposed future construction, where practicable, away from locations which are threatened by flood hazards,

(3) encourage lending and credit institutions, as a matter of national policy, to assist in furthering the objectives of the flood insurance program,

(4) assure that any Federal assistance provided under the program will be related closely to all flood-related programs and activities of the Federal Government, and

(5) authorize continuing studies of flood hazards in order to provide for a constant reappraisal of the flood insurance program and its effect on land use requirements.

(g) The Congress also finds that

(1) the damage and loss which may result from the erosion and undermining of shorelines by waves or currents in lakes and other bodies of water exceeding anticipated cyclical levels is related in cause and similar in effect to that which results directly from storms, deluges, overflowing waters, and other forms of flooding, and

(2) the problems involved in providing protection against this damage and loss, and the possibilities for making such protection available through a Federal or federally sponsored program, are similar to those which exist in connection with efforts to provide protection against damage and loss caused by such other forms of flooding.

It is therefore the further purpose of this chapter to make available, by means of the methods, procedures, and instrumentalities which are otherwise established or available under this chapter for purposes of the flood insurance program, protection against damage and loss resulting from the erosion and undermining of shorelines by waves or currents in lakes and other bodies of water exceeding anticipated cyclical levels.

§ 4002. Additional Congressional findings and declaration of purpose.

(a) The Congress finds that—

(1) annual losses throughout the Nation from floods and mudslides are increasing at an alarming rate, largely as a result of the accelerating development of, and concentration of population in, areas of flood and mudslide hazards;

(2) the availability of Federal loans, grants, guaranties, insurance, and other forms of financial assistance are often determining factors in the utilization of land and the location and construction of public and of private industrial, commercial, and residential facilities;

(3) property acquired or constructed with grants or other Federal assistance may be exposed to risk of loss through floods, thus frustrating the purpose for which such assistance was extended;

(4) Federal instrumentalities insure or otherwise provide financial protection to banking and credit institutions whose assets include a substantial number of mortgage loans and other indebtedness secured by property exposed to loss and damage from floods and mudslides;

(5) the Nation cannot afford the tragic losses of life caused annually by flood occurrences, nor the increasing losses of property suffered

by flood victims, most of whom are still inadequately compensated despite the provision of costly disaster relief benefits; and

(6) it is in the public interest for persons already living in flood-prone areas to have both an opportunity to purchase flood insurance and access to more adequate limits of coverage, so that they will be indemnified for their losses in the event of future flood disasters.

(b) The purpose of this Act, therefore, is to—

(1) substantially increase the limits of coverage authorized under the national flood insurance program;

(2) provide for the expeditious identification of, and the dissemination of information concerning, flood-prone areas;

(3) require States or local communities, as a condition of future Federal financial assistance, to participate in the flood insurance program and to adopt adequate flood plain ordinances with effective enforcement provisions consistent with Federal standards to reduce or avoid future flood losses; and

(4) require the purchase of flood insurance by property owners who are being assisted by Federal programs or by federally supervised, regulated, or insured agencies or institutions in the acquisition or improvement of land or facilities located or to be located in identified areas having special flood hazards.

§ 4012. Scope of program and priorities. . . .

(c) The Secretary shall make flood insurance available in only those States or areas (or subdivisions thereof) which he has determined have—

(1) evidenced a positive interest in securing flood insurance coverage under the flood insurance program, and

(2) given satisfactory assurance that by December 31, 1971, adequate land use and control measures will have been adopted for the State or area (or subdivision) which are consistent with the comprehensive criteria for land management and use developed under section 4102 of this title, and that the application and enforcement of such measures will commence as soon as technical information on floodways and on controlling flood elevations is available.

§ 4022. State and local land use controls.

After December 31, 1971, no new flood insurance coverage shall be provided under this chapter in any area (or subdivision thereof) unless an appropriate public body shall have adopted adequate land use and control measures (with effective enforcement provisions) which the Secretary finds are consistent with the comprehensive criteria for land management and use under section 4102 of this title.

§ 4023. Properties in violation of State and local law.

No new flood insurance coverage shall be provided under this chapter for any property which the Secretary finds has been declared by a duly constituted State or local zoning authority, or other authorized public body, to be in violation of State or local laws, regulations, or ordinances which are intended to discourage or otherwise restrict land development or occupancy in flood-prone areas.

§ 4101. Identification of flood-prone areas—publication of information; establishment of flood-risk zones; estimates of flood-caused loss.

(a) The Secretary is authorized to consult with, receive information from, and enter into any agreements or other arrangements with the Secretaries of the Army, the Interior, Agriculture, and Commerce, the Tennessee Valley Authority, and the heads of other Federal departments or agencies, on a reimbursement basis, or with the head of any State or local agency, or enter into contracts with any persons or private firms, in order that he may—

(1) identify and publish information with respect to all floodplain areas, including coastal areas located in the United States, which have special flood hazards, within five years following August 1, 1968, and

(2) establish flood-risk zones in all such areas, and make estimates with respect to the rates of probable flood-caused loss for the various flood-risk zones for each of these areas, within fifteen years following such date.

§ 4102. Criteria for land management and use—studies and investigations.

(a) The Secretary is authorized to carry out studies and investigations. . . . with respect to the adequacy of State and local measures in flood-prone areas as to land management and use, flood control, flood zoning, and flood damage prevention. . . .

(c) On the basis of such studies and investigations, and such other information as he deems necessary, the Secretary shall from time to time develop comprehensive criteria designed to encourage, where necessary, the adoption of adequate State and local measures which, to the maximum extent feasible, will—

(1) constrict the development of land which is exposed to flood damage where appropriate,

(2) guide the development of proposed construction away from locations which are threatened by flood hazards,

(3) assist in reducing damage caused by floods, and

(4) otherwise improve the long-range land management and use of flood-prone areas,

and he shall work closely with and provide any necessary technical assistance to State, interstate, and local governmental agencies, to encourage the application of such criteria and the adoption and enforcement of such measures.

§ 4105.  Disaster mitigation requirements; notification to flood-prone areas—initial notification.

(a) Not later than six months following December 31, 1973, the Secretary shall publish information in accordance with section 4101(1) of this title, and shall notify the chief executive officer of each known flood-prone community not already participating in the national flood insurance program of its tentative identification as a community containing one or more areas having special flood hazards.

(b) After such notification, each tentatively identified community shall either
    (1) promptly make proper application to participate in the national flood insurance program or
    (2) within six months submit technical data sufficient to establish to the satisfaction of the Secretary that the community either is not seriously flood prone or that such flood hazards as may have existed have been corrected by floodworks or other flood control methods.

The Secretary may, in his discretion, grant a public hearing to any community with respect to which conflicting data exist as to the nature and extent of a flood hazard.  If the Secretary decides not to hold a hearing, the community shall be given an opportunity to submit written and documentary evidence.  Whether or not such hearing is granted, the Secretary's final determination as to the existence or extent of a flood hazard area in a particular community shall be deemed conclusive for the purposes of this Act if supported by substantial evidence in the record considered as a whole.

(c) As information becomes available to the Secretary concerning the existence of flood hazards in communities not known to be flood-prone at the time of the initial notification provided for by subsection (a) of this section he shall provide similar notifications to the chief executive officers of such additional communities, which shall then be subject to the requirements of subsection (b) of this section.

(d) Formally identified flood-prone communities that do not qualify for the national flood insurance program within one year after such notification or by the date specified in section 4106 of this title, whichever is later, shall thereafter be subject to the provisions of that section relating to flood-prone communities which are not participating in the program.

§ 4106. Same; nonparticipation in flood insurance program—prohibition against Federal approval of financial assistance.

(a) No Federal officer or agency shall approve any financial assistance for acquisition or construction purposes on and after July 1, 1975, for use in any area that has been identified by the Secretary as an area having special flood hazards unless the community in which such area is situated is then participating in the national flood insurance program.

(b) Each Federal instrumentality responsible for the supervision, approval, regulation, or insuring of banks, savings and loan associations, or similar institutions shall by regulation prohibit such institutions on and after July 1, 1975, from making, increasing, extending, or renewing any loan secured by improved real estate or a mobile home located or to be located in an area that has been identified by the Secretary as an area having special flood hazards, unless the community in which such area is situated is then participating in the national flood insurance program.

§ 4107. Same; consultation with local officials; scope.

In carrying out his responsibilities under the provisions of this title and this chapter which relate to notification to and identification of flood-prone areas and the application of criteria for land management and use, including criteria derived from data reflecting new developments that may indicate the desirability of modifying elevations based on previous flood studies, the Secretary shall establish procedures assuring adequate consultation with the appropriate elected officials of general purpose local governments, including but not limited to those local governments whose prior eligibility under the program has been suspended. Such consultation shall include, but not be limited to, fully informing local officials at the commencement of any flood elevation study or investigation undertaken by any agency on behalf of the Secretary concerning the nature and purpose of the study, the areas involved, the manner in which the study is to be undertaken, the general principles to be applied, and the use to be made of the data obtained. The Secretary shall encourage local officials to disseminate information concerning such study widely within the community, so that interested persons will have an opportunity to bring all relevant facts and technical data concerning the local flood hazard to the attention of the agency during the course of the study.

STATES

Wetlands and Shorelands

WASHINGTON SHORELINE MANAGEMENT
ACT (1971, as amended)
Rev. Code Wash. Ch. 90.58

§ 90.58.020. Legislative findings—state policy enunciated—use preference.

The legislature finds that the shorelines of the state are among the most valuable and fragile of its natural resources and that there is great concern throughout the state relating to their utilization, protection, restoration, and preservation. In addition it finds that ever increasing pressures of additional uses are being placed on the shorelines necessitating increased coordination in the management and development of the shorelines of the state. The legislature further finds that much of the shorelines of the state and the uplands adjacent thereto are in private ownership; that unrestricted construction on the privately owned or publicly owned shorelines of the state is not in the best public interest; and therefore, coordinated planning is necessary in order to protect the public interest associated with the shorelines of the state while, at the same time, recognizing and protecting private property rights consistent with the public interest. There is, therefore, a clear and urgent demand for a planned, rational, and concerted effort, jointly performed by federal, state, and local governments, to prevent the inherent harm in an uncoordinated and piecemeal development of the state's shorelines.

It is the policy of the state to provide for the management of the shorelines of the state by planning for and fostering all reasonable and appropriate uses. This policy is designed to insure the development of these shorelines in a manner which, while allowing for limited reduction of rights of the public in the navigable waters, will promote and enhance the public interest. This policy contemplates protecting against adverse effects to the public health, the land and its vegetation and wildlife, and the waters of the state and their aquatic life, while protecting generally public rights of navigation and corollary rights incidental thereto.

The legislature declares that the interest of all of the people shall be paramount in the management of shorelines of state-wide significance. The department, in adopting guidelines for shorelines of state-wide significance, and local government, in developing master programs for shorelines of state-wide significance, shall give preference to uses in the following order of preference which:

(1) Recognize and protect the state-wide interest over local interest;

(2) Preserve the natural character of the shoreline;

(3) Result in long term over short term benefit;

(4) Protect the resources and ecology of the shoreline;

(5) Increase public access to publicly owned areas of the shorelines;

(6) Increase recreational opportunities for the public in the shoreline;

(7) Provide for any other element as defined in RCW 90.58.100 deemed appropriate or necessary.

In the implementation of this policy the public's opportunity to enjoy the physical and aesthetic qualities of natural shorelines of the state shall be preserved to the greatest extent feasible consistent with the overall best interest of the state and the people generally. To this end uses shall be preferred which are consistent with control of pollution and prevention of damage to the natural environment or are unique to or dependent upon use of the state's shoreline. Alterations of the natural condition of the shorelines of the state, in those limited instances when authorized, shall be given priority for single family residences, ports, shoreline recreational uses including but not limited to parks, marinas, piers, and other improvements facilitating public access to shorelines of the state, industrial and commercial developments which are particularly dependent on their location on or use of the shorelines of the state and other development that will provide an opportunity for substantial numbers of the people to enjoy the shorelines of the state.

Permitted uses in the shorelines of the state shall be designed and conducted in a manner to minimize, insofar as practical, any resultant damage to the ecology and environment of the shoreline area and any interference with the public's use of the water.

§ 90.58.030. Definitions and concepts.

As used in this chapter, unless the context otherwise requires, the following definitions and concepts apply: . . .

(2) Geographical:

(a) "Extreme low tide" means the lowest line on the land reached by a receding tide;

(b) "Ordinary high water mark" on all lakes, streams, and tidal water is that mark that will be found by examining the bed and banks and ascertaining where the presence and action of waters are so common and usual, and so long continued in all ordinary years, as to mark upon the soil a character distinct from that of the abutting upland, in respect to vegetation as that condition exists on June 1, 1971 or as it may naturally change thereafter: Provided, That in any area where the ordinary high water mark cannot be found, the ordinary high water mark adjoining salt water shall be the line of mean higher high tide and the ordinary high water mark adjoining fresh water shall be the line of mean high water;

(c) "Shorelines of the state" are the total of all "shorelines" and "shorelines of state-wide significance" within the state;

(d) "shorelines" means all of the water areas of the state, including reservoirs, and their associated wetlands, together with the lands underlying them; except

(i) shorelines of state-wide significance;

(ii) shorelines on segments of streams upstream of a point where the mean annual flow is twenty cubic feet per second or less and the wetlands associated with such upstream segments; and

(iii) shorelines on lakes less than twenty acres in size and wetlands associated with such small lakes;

(e) "Shorelines of state-wide significance" means the following shorelines of the state: . . .

(f) "Wetlands" or "wetland areas" means those lands extending landward for two hundred feet in all directions as measured on a horizontal plane from the ordinary high water mark; and all marshes, bogs, swamps, floodways, river deltas, and flood plains associated with the streams, lakes and tidal waters which are subject to the provisions of this chapter; the same to be designated as to location by the department of ecology.

§ 90.58.050. Program as cooperative between local government and state—responsibilities differentiated.

This chapter establishes a cooperative program of shoreline management between local government and the state. Local government shall have the primary responsibility for initiating and administering the regulatory program of this chapter. The department shall act primarily in a supportive and review capacity with primary emphasis on insuring compliance with the policy and provisions of this chapter.

**§ 90.58.060.** Timetable for adoption of initial guidelines—public hearings, notice of.

(1) Within one hundred twenty days from June 1, 1971, the department shall submit to all local governments proposed guidelines consistent with RCW 90.58.020:

(a) Development of master programs for regulation of the uses of shorelines; and

(b) Development of master programs for regulation of the uses of shorelines of state-wide significance.

(2) Within sixty days from receipt of such proposed guidelines, local governments shall submit to the department in writing proposed changes, if any, and comments upon the proposed guidelines.

(3) Thereafter and within one hundred twenty days from the submission of such proposal guidelines to local governments, the department, after review and consideration of the comments and suggestions submitted to it, shall resubmit final proposed guidelines.

(4) Within sixty days thereafter public hearings shall be held by the department. . . .

**§ 90.58.070.** Local governments to submit letters of intent—department to act upon failure of local government.

(1) Local governments are directed with regard to shorelines of the state in their various jurisdictions to submit to the director of the department, within six months from June 1, 1971, letters stating that they propose to complete an inventory and develop master programs for these shorelines as provided for in RCW 90.58.080.

(2) If any local government fails to submit a letter as provided in subsection (1) of this section, or fails to adopt a master program for the shorelines of the state within its jurisdiction in accordance with the time schedule provided in this chapter, the department shall carry out the requirements of RCW 90.58.080 and adopt a master program for the shorelines of the state within the jurisdiction of the local government.

**§ 90.58.080.** Timetable for local governments to complete shoreline inventories and master programs.

Local governments are directed with regard to shorelines of the state within their various jurisdictions as follows:

(1) To complete within eighteen months after June 1, 1971, a comprehensive inventory of such shorelines. Such inventory shall include but not be limited to the general ownership patterns of the lands located

therein in terms of public and private ownership, a survey of the general natural characteristics thereof, present uses conducted therein and initial projected uses thereof:

(2) To develop, within twenty-four months after the adoption of guidelines as provided in RCW 90.58.060, a master program for regulation of uses of the shorelines of the state consistent with the guidelines adopted.

§ 90.58.090. Approval of master program or segments thereof, when—departmental alternatives when shorelines of statewide significance—later adoption of master program supersedes departmental program.

Master programs or segments thereof shall become effective when adopted or approved by the department as appropriate. Within the time period provided in RCW 90.58.080, each local government shall have submitted a master program, either totally or by segments, for all shorelines of the state within its jurisdiction to the department for review and approval.

(1) As to those segments of the master program relating to shorelines, they shall be approved by the department unless it determines that the submitted segments are not consistent with the policy of RCW 90.58.020 and the applicable guidelines. . . .

(2) As to those segments of the master program relating to shorelines of state-wide significance the department shall have full authority following review and evaluation of the submission by local government to develop and adopt an alternative to the local government's proposal if in the department's opinion the program submitted does not provide the optimum implementation of the policy of this chapter to satisfy the state-wide interest. . . .

§ 90.58.100. Programs as constituting use regulations—duties when preparing programs and amendments thereto—program contents.

(1) The master programs provided for in this chapter, when adopted and approved by the department, as appropriate, shall constitute use regulations for the various shorelines of the state. In preparing the master programs, and any amendments thereto, the department and local governments shall to the extent feasible:
    (a) Utilize a systematic interdisciplinary approach which will insure the integrated use of the natural and social sciences and the environmental design arts;
    (b) Consult with and obtain the comments of any federal, state, regional, or local agency having any special expertise with respect to any environmental impact;

(c) Consider all plans, studies, surveys, inventories, and systems of classification made or being made by federal, state, regional, or local agencies, by private individuals, or by organizations dealing with pertinent shorelines of the state;

(d) Conduct or support such further research, studies, surveys, and interviews as are deemed necessary;

(e) Utilize all available information regarding hydrology, geography, topography, ecology, economics, and other pertinent data;

(f) Employ, when feasible, all appropriate, modern scientific data processing and computer techniques to store, index, analyze, and manage the information gathered.

(2) The master programs shall include, when appropriate, the following:

(a) An economic development element for the location and design of industries, transportation facilities, port facilities, tourist facilities, commerce and other developments that are particularly dependent on their location on or use of the shorelines of the state;

(b) A public access element making provision for public access to publicly owned areas;

(c) A recreational element for the preservation and enlargement of recreational opportunities, including but not limited to parks, tidelands, beaches, and recreational areas;

(d) A circulation element consisting of the general location and extent of existing and proposed major thoroughfares, transportation routes, terminals, and other public utilities and facilities, all correlated with the shoreline use element;

(e) A use element which considers the proposed general distribution and general location and extent of the use on shorelines and adjacent land areas for housing, business, industry, transportation, agriculture, natural resources, recreation, education, public buildings and grounds, and other categories of public and private uses of the land;

(f) A conservation element for the preservation of natural resources, including but not limited to scenic vistas, aesthetics, and vital estuarine areas for fisheries and wildlife protection;

(g) An historic, cultural, scientific, and educational element for the protection and restoration of buildings, sites, and areas having historic, cultural, scientific, or educational values; . . .

(4) Master programs will reflect that state-owned shorelines of the state are particularly adapted to providing wilderness beaches, ecological study areas, and other recreational activities for the public and will give appropriate special consideration to same. . . .

§ 90.58.140. Development permits—grounds for granting—departmental appeal on issuance—administration by local government, conditions—rescission—when permits not required—approval when permit for variance or conditional use.

(1) No development shall be undertaken on the shorelines of the state except those which are consistent with the policy of this chapter and, after adoption or approval, as appropriate, the applicable guidelines, regulations or master program.

(2) No substantial development shall be undertaken on shorelines of the state without first obtaining a permit from the government entity having administrative jurisdiction under this chapter. . . .

§ 90.58.150. Selective commercial timber cutting, when.

With respect to timber situated within two hundred feet abutting landward of the ordinary high water mark within shorelines of state-wide significance, the department or local government shall allow only selective commercial timber cutting, so that no more than thirty percent of the merchantable trees may be harvested in any ten year period of time: Provided, That other timber harvesting methods may be permitted in those limited instances where the topography, soil conditions or silviculture practices necessary for regeneration render selective logging ecologically detrimental: Provided further, That clear cutting of timber which is solely incidental to the preparation of land for other uses authorized by this chapter may be permitted.

§ 90.58.230. Violators liable for damages resulting from violation—attorney's fees and costs.

Any person subject to the regulatory program of this chapter who violates any provision of this chapter or permit issued pursuant thereto shall be liable for all damage to public or private property arising from such violation, including the cost of restoring the affected area to its condition prior to violation. The attorney general or local government attorney shall bring suit for damages under this section on behalf of the state or local governments. Private persons shall have the right to bring suit for damages under this section on their own behalf and on the behalf of all persons similarly situated. If liability has been established for the cost of restoring an area affected by a violation the court shall make provision to assure that restoration will be accomplished within a reasonable time at the expense of the violator. In addition to such relief, including money damages, the court in its discretion may award attorney's fees and costs of the suit to the prevailing party.

§ 90.58.290. Restrictions as affecting fair market value of property.

The restrictions imposed by this act shall be considered by the county assessor in establishing the fair market value of the property.

§ 90.58.310. Designation of shorelines of state-wide significance by legislature—recommendation by director, procedure.

Additional shorelines of the state shall be designated shorelines of state-wide significance only by affirmative action of the legislature.

The director of the department may, however, from time to time, recommend to the legislature areas of the shorelines of the state which have state-wide significance relating to special economic, ecological, educational, developmental, recreational, or aesthetic values to be designated as shorelines of state-wide significance.

Prior to making any such recommendation the director shall hold a public hearing in the county or counties where the shoreline under consideration is located. . . .

§ 90.58.320. Height limitation respecting permits.

No permit shall be issued pursuant to this chapter for any new or expanded building or structure of more than thirty-five feet above average grade level on shorelines of the state that will obstruct the view of a substantial number of residences on areas adjoining such shorelines except where a master program does not prohibit the same and then only when overriding considerations of the public interest will be served.

§ 90.58.340. Use policies for land adjacent to shorelines, development of.

All state agencies, counties, and public and municipal corporations shall review administrative and management policies, regulations, plans, and ordinances relative to lands under their respective jurisdictions adjacent to the shorelines of the state so as the [to] achieve a use policy on said land consistent with the policy of this chapter, the guidelines, and the master programs for the shorelines of the state. The department may develop recommendations for land use control for such lands. Local governments shall, in developing use regulations for such areas, take into consideration any recommendations developed by the department as well as any other state agencies or units of local government.

DELAWARE COASTAL ZONE ACT (1971)
7 Dela. Code Ch. 70

§ 7001. Purpose.

It is hereby determined that the coastal areas of Delaware are the most critical areas for the future of the State in terms of the quality of life in the State. It is, therefore, the declared public policy of the State of Delaware to control the location, extent and type of industrial development in Delaware's coastal areas. In so doing, the State can better protect the natural environment of its bay and coastal areas and safeguard their use primarily for recreation and tourism. Specifically, this chapter seeks to prohibit entirely the construction of new heavy industry in its coastal areas, which industry is determined to be incompatible with the protection of that natural environment in those areas. While it is the declared public policy of the State to encourage the introduction of new industry into Delaware, the protection of the environment, natural beauty and recreation potential of the State is also of great concern. In order to strike the correct balance between these two policies, careful planning based on a thorough understanding of Delaware's potential and her needs is required. Therefore, control of industrial development other than that of heavy industry in the Coastal Zone of Delaware through a permit system at the State level is called for. It is further determined that off-shore bulk product transfer facilities represent a significant danger of pollution to the Coastal Zone and generate pressure for the construction of industrial plants in the Coastal Zone, which construction is declared to be against public policy. For these reasons, prohibition against bulk product transfer facilities in the Coastal Zone is deemed imperative.

§ 7002.  Definitions.

(e) "Heavy industry use" means a use characteristically involving
more than 20 acres, and characteristically employing some but not
necessarily all of such equipment such as, but not limited to, smoke-
stacks, tanks, distillation or reaction columns, chemical processing
equipment, scribbing towers, pickling equipment, and waste-treat-
ment lagoons. . . .

§ 7003.  Uses absolutely prohibited in the Coastal Zone.

   Heavy industry uses of any kind not in operation on the date of enactment of this chapter are prohibited in the Coastal Zone and no permits
may be issued therefor.  In addition, off-shore gas, liquid, or solid
bulk product transfer facilities which are not in operation on the date
of enactment of this chapter are prohibited in the Coastal Zone, and no
permit may be issued therefor.  Provided that this section shall not
apply to public sewage treatment or recycling plants.

§ 7004.  Uses allowed by permit only; non-conforming uses.

(a) Except for heavy industry uses, as defined in section 7002 of this
chapter, manufacturing uses not in existence and in active use on the
date of enactment of this chapter are allowed in the Coastal Zone by
permit only, as provided for under this section. . . .

(b) In passing on permit requests, the State Planner and the State
Coastal Zone Industrial Control Board shall consider the following
factors:
   (1) Environmental impact, including but not limited to, probable
air and water pollution likely to be generated by the proposed use under normal operating conditions as well as during mechanical malfunc-
tion and human error; likely destruction of wetlands and flora and
fauna; impact of site preparation on drainage of the area in question,
especially as it relates to flood control; impact of site preparation and
facility operations on land erosion; effect of site preparation and
facility operations on the quality and quantity of surface ground and
sub-surface water resources, such as the use of water for processing,
cooling, effluent removal, and other purposes; in addition, but not
limited to, likelihood of generation of glare, heat, noise, vibration,
radiation, electromagnetic interference and obnoxious odors.
   (2) Economic effect, including the number of jobs created and the
income which will be generated by the wages and salaries of these
jobs in relation to the amount of land required, and the amount of tax
revenues potentially accruing to State and local government.
   (3) Aesthetic effect, such as impact on scenic beauty of the surrounding area.

(4) Number and type of supporting facilities required and the impact of such facilities on all factors listed in this subsection.

(5) Effect on neighboring land uses including, but not limited to, effect on public access to tidal waters, effect on recreational areas, and effect on adjacent residential and agricultural areas.

(6) County and municipal comprehensive plans for the development and/or conservation of their areas of jurisdiction.

WISCONSIN ZONING OF SHORELANDS ON NAVIGABLE
WATERS (1965, as amended)
Wis. Stat. 59.971

§ 59.971. Zoning of shorelands on navigable waters.

(1) To effect the purposes of § 144.26 and to promote the public health, safety and general welfare, counties may, by ordinance enacted separately from ordinances pursuant to § 59.97, zone all lands (referred to herein as shorelands) in their unincorporated areas within the following distances from the normal high-water elevation of navigable waters as defined in § 144.26(2)(d): 1,000 feet from a lake, pond, or flowage; 300 feet from a river or stream or to the landward side of the flood plain, whichever distance is greater. If the navigable water is a glacial pothole lake, the distance shall be measured from the high watermark thereof.

(2) (a) Except as otherwise specified, all provisions of § 59.97 apply to ordinances and their amendments enacted under this section, but they shall not require approval or be subject to disapproval by any town or town board.

(b) If an existing town ordinance relating to shorelands is more restrictive than an ordinance later enacted under this section affecting the same shorelands, it continues as a town ordinance in all respects to the extent of the greater restrictions, but not otherwise.

(c) Ordinances enacted under this section shall accord and be consistent with any comprehensive zoning plan or general zoning ordinance applicable to the enacting counties, so far as practicable. . . .

(6) If any county does not adopt an ordinance by January 1, 1968, or if the department of natural resources, after notice and hearing, determines that a county has adopted an ordinance which fails to meet reasonable minimum standards in accomplishing the shoreland protection objectives of § 144.26(1), the department shall adopt such an ordinance.
. . .

MASSACHUSETTS PROTECTION OF FLOOD PLAINS,
SEACOASTS, AND OTHER WETLANDS
(1967, as amended)
131 Mass. Stat. Ann. Ch. 40 et seq.

§ 40.

No person shall remove, fill, dredge or alter any bank, freshwater
wetland, coastal wetland, beach, dune, flat, marsh, meadow or swamp
bordering on the ocean or on any estuary, creek, river, stream, pond,
or lake, or any land under said waters or any land subject to tidal
action, coastal storm flowage, or flooding, other than in the course
of maintaining, repairing or replacing, but not substantially changing
or enlarging, an existing and lawfully located structure or facility
used in the service of the public and used to provide electric, gas,
water, telephone, telegraph and other telecommunication services,
without filing written notice of his intention to so remove, fill, dredge
or alter, including such plans as may be necessary to describe such
proposed activity and its effect on the environment and without receiving and complying with an order of conditions and provided all appeal
periods have elapsed.  Said notice shall be sent by certified mail to
the conservation commssion or, if none to the board of selectmen in
a town or the mayor of a city in which the land upon which such activity
is proposed is located.  Each such notice shall be accompanied by a
filing fee of twenty-five dollars payable to the city or town. . . .
    The term "bogs" as used in this section, shall mean areas where
standing or slowly running water is near or at the surface during a
normal growing season and where a vegetational community has a significant portion of the ground or water surface covered with sphagnum
moss (Sphagnum) and where the vegetational community is made up of
a significant portion of one or more of, but not limited to nor necessarily including all, of the following plants or groups of plants: . . .
    The term "swamps", as used in this section, shall mean areas where
ground water is at or near the surface of the ground for a significant
part of the growing season or where runoff water from surface drainage frequently collects above the soil surface, and where a significant
part of the vegetational community is made up of, but not limited to
nor necessarily include all of the following plants or groups of plants:
. . .
    The term "wet meadows", as used in this section where ground water
is at the surface for the significant part of the growing season and near
the surface throughout the year and where a significant part of the
vegetational community is composed of various grasses, sedges and
rushes; made up of, but not limited to nor necessarily including all,
of the following plants or groups of plants: . . .

The term "marshes", as used in this section, shall mean areas
where a vegetational community exists in standing or running water
during the growing season and where a significant part of the vegetational community is composed of, but not limited to nor necessarily
including all, of the following plants or groups of plants: . . .

The conservation commission, selectmen or mayor receiving notice
under this section shall hold a public hearing on the proposed activities
within twenty-one days of the receipt of said notice. . . .

If after said hearing the conservation commission, selectmen or mayor,
as the case may be, determine that the area on which the proposed
work is to be done is significant to public or private water supply, to
the ground water supply, to flood control, to storm damage prevention,
to prevention of pollution, to protection of land containing shellfish,
or to the protection of fisheries, such conservation commission, board
of selectmen or mayor shall by written order within twenty-one days
of such hearing impose such conditions as will contribute to the protection of the interests described herein, and all work shall be done in
accordance wtherewith. If the conservation commission, selectmen
or mayor, as the case may be, make a determination that the proposed
activity does not require the imposition of such conditions, the applicant shall be notified of such determination within twenty-one days after said hearing. . . .

If a conservation commission has failed to hold a hearing within the
twenty-one day period as required, or if a commission, after holding
such hearing, has failed within twenty-one days therefrom to issue an
order, or if a commission, upon a written request by any person to
determine whether this section is applicable to any work, fails within
ten days to make said determination, or where an order does issue
from said commission, the applicant, any person aggrieved by said
commission's order or failure to act, or any owner of land abutting
the land upon which the proposed work is to be done, or any ten residents of the city or town in which such land is located, may, by certified mail and within ten days from said commission's order or
failure to act, request the department of natural resources to determine whether the area on which the proposed work is to be done is significant to public or private water supply, to the ground water supply,
to flood control, to storm damage prevention, to prevention of pollution, to protection of land containing shellfish or to the protection of
fisheries. The commissioner of natural resources also may request
such a determination within said ten days. . . .

No work proposed in any notice of intention shall be undertaken until
the final order, determination or notification with respect to such work
has been recorded in the registry of deeds for the district in which the
land is located. . . .

§ 40A.  Protection of inland wetlands.

The commissioner of natural resources, with the approval of the
board of natural resources shall from time to time, for the purposes
of preserving and promoting the public safety, private property, wildlife, fisheries, water resources, flood plain areas and agriculture,
adopt, amend or repeal orders regulating, restricting or prohibiting
dredging, filling, removing or otherwise altering or polluting inland
wetlands.  In this section, the term "inland wetlands" shall include
the definition of "freshwater wetlands" as set forth in section forty,
and it shall further include that portion of any bank which touches any
inland waters or any freshwater wetland, and any freshwater wetland
subject to flooding.

The commissioner shall protect flood plain areas by establishing by
order that, along any waterway or flood-prone area lines beyond which
in the direction of the waterway or flood-prone area, no obstruction
or encroachment shall be placed by any person, firm or corporation,
public or private, unless authorized by the commissioner.  The commissioner, in establishing such encroachment lines shall base their
location on the boundaries of the area which have been mapped, designated and recorded as inland wetlands in accordance with the provisions of this section. . . .

No order shall be adopted until it is approved by the selectmen or
city council of the town or city in which said wetlands or flood plains
are located; . . .

Any person having an interest in land affected by any such order,
may within ninety days after receiving notice thereof, petition the
superior court in equity to determine whether such order so restricts
the use of his property as to deprive him of the practical uses thereof
and is therefore an unreasonable exercise of the police power because
the order constitutes the equivalent of a taking without compensation.
If the court finds the order to be an unreasonable exercise of the
police power, as aforesaid, the court shall enter a finding that such
order shall not apply to the land of the petitioner; provided, however
that such finding shall not affect any other land than that of the petitioner.  The commissioner shall cause a copy of such finding to be
recorded forthwith in the proper registry of deeds or, if the land is
registered, in the registry district of the land court.  The method provided in this paragraph for the determination of the issue of whether
any such order constitutes a taking without compensation shall be exclusive, and such issue shall not be determined in any other proceeding, nor shall any person have a right to petition for the assessment
of damages under chapter seventy-nine by reason of the adoption of
any such order. . . .

CALIFORNIA CONSTITUTION
Art. XV, Sec. 2 (1879)

§ 2. Access to navigable waters.

No individual, partnership, or corporation, claiming or possessing
the frontage or tidal lands of a harbor, bay, inlet, estuary, or other
navigable water in this State, shall be permitted to exclude the right
of way to such water whenever it is required for any public purpose,
nor to destroy or obstruct the free navigation of such water; and the
Legislature shall enact such laws as will give the most liberal construction to this provision, so that access to the navigable waters of this
State shall be always attainable for the people thereof.

TEXAS OPEN BEACHES ACT (1959, as amended)
86 Vernon's Tex. Stat. Art. 5415d

ART. 5415d.  State beaches; right of public to free and unrestricted
             use and enjoyment.

§. 1.  Declaration of policy.

It is hereby declared and affirmed to be the public policy of this
state that the public, individually and collectively, shall have the free
and unrestricted right of ingress and egress to and from the state-
owned beaches bordering on the seaward shore of the Gulf of Mexico,
or such larger area extending from the line of mean low tide to the
line of vegetation bordering on the Gulf of Mexico, in the event the public has acquired a right of use or easement to or over such area by
prescription, dedication, or has retained a right by virtue of continuous
right in the public.

It shall be an offense against the public policy of this state for any
person, firm, corporation, association or other legal entity to create,
erect or construct any obstruction, barrier, or restraint of any nature
whatsoever which would interfere with the free and unrestricted right
of the public, individually and collectively, to enter or to leave any
state-owned beach bordering on the seaward shore of the Gulf of Mexico,

or such larger area, extending from the line of mean low tide to the
line of vegetation bordering on the Gulf of Mexico, in the event the
public has acquired a right of use or easement to or over such area
by prescription, dedication, or has retained a right by virtue of continuous right in the public.

It shall be an offense against the public policy of this state for any
person, firm, corporation, association, or other legal entity to create,
erect, or construct any obstruction, barrier or restraint which would
interfere with the free and unrestricted right of the public, individually
and collectively to the lawful and legal use of, any property abutting
upon or contiguous to the state-owned beach bordering on the seaward
shore of the Gulf of Mexico upon which the public has acquired a
prescriptive right.

Power Plant and Industry Siting

NEW YORK SITING OF MAJOR STEAM ELECTRIC
GENERATING FACILITIES (1972, as amended)
N.Y. Public Service Law Sec. 140 et seq.

Legislative findings. Section 1 of L.1972, c. 385, eff. July 1,
1972, provided:

The legislature hereby finds and declares that there is
at present and may continue to be a growing need for electric power and for the construction of new major steam
electric generating facilities. At the same time it is recognized that such facilities cannot be built without in some
way affecting the physical environment where such facilities are located, and in some cases the adverse effects

may be serious. The legislature further finds that it is
essential to the public interest that meeting power demands
and protecting the environment be regarded as equally important and that neither be subordinated to the other in any
evaluation of the proposed construction of major steam
electric generating facilities. Without limiting the general-
ity of the foregoing, the legislature finds and declares that
under certain circumstances power demands may be regarded as controlling even though the adverse environmental impact may be substantial, but that under other circumstances, given the nature of the resource involved and the
public interest in preserving and enhancing the quality of
life, the protection of the environment may be regarded
as controlling even though this might result in restrictions
on the availability of public utility services.

The legislature further finds that the present practices,
proceedings and laws relating to the location of major
steam electric generating facilities are inadequate to protect the environmental values and to take into account the
total cost of society of such facilities and result in delays
in new construction and increases in cost which are eventually passed on to the people of the state in the form of
higher utility rates. Furthermore, the legislature finds
that existing provisions of law do not provide adequate opportunity for individuals, groups interested in conservation and the protection of the environment, municipalities
and other public bodies to participate in a timely and meaningful fashion in the decision whether or not to locate a specific major steam electric generating facility at a specific
site. The legislature therefore hereby declares that it
shall be the purpose of this Act [adding this article and
amending section 4 of the Condemnation Law, sections
1014, 1870 of the Public Authorities Law, and sections
1230, 1277 of the Public Health Law] to provide for the expeditious resolution of all matters concerning the location
of major steam electric generating facilities presently under the jurisdiction of multiple state and local agencies, including all matters of state and local law, in a single proceeding in which the policies heretofore described shall apply and to which access will be open to citizens, groups,
municipalities and other public agencies to enable them to
participate in these decisions.

The legislature further finds that there is a need for the
state to control determinations regarding the proposed siting
of major steam electric generating facilities within the state

and to cooperate with other states, regions and countries in order to serve the public interest in creating and preserving a proper environment and in having an adequate supply of electric power, all within the context of the policy objectives heretofore set forth towards which objectives the provisions of this legislation are directed.

### § 140. Definitions.

2. "Major steam electric generating facility" means a steam electric generating facility with a generating capacity of fifty thousand kilowatts or more. . . .

4. "Board" means the New York state board on electric generation siting and the environment, which shall be in the department of public service. . . .

### § 141. Certificate of environmental compatibility and public need.

1. No persons shall, after July first, nineteen hundred seventy-two, commence the preparation of a site for, or begin the construction of, a major steam electric generating facility in the state without having first obtained a certificate of environmental compatibility and public need.

### § 142. Application for a certificate.

1. An applicant for a certificate shall file with the chairman of the board an application, in such form as the commission may prescribe, containing the following information and materials:

(a) a description of the site and a description of the facility to be built thereon, including available site information, including maps and description, present and proposed development, source and volume of water required for plant operation and cooling, and, as appropriate, geological, aesthetic, ecological, tsunami, seismic, biological, water supply, population and loan center data;

(b) studies, identifying the author and date thereof, which have been made of the expected environmental impact and safety of the project, both during its construction and its operation, including a description of

(i) the gaseous, liquid and solid wastes to be produced by the facility, including their source, anticipated volumes, composition and temperature, and such other attributes as the commission may specify, and the probable level of noise during construction and operation of the facility; and

(ii) the treatment processes to reduce wastes to be released to the environment, the manner of disposal for wastes retained and measures for noise abatement;

(iii) the concentration of wastes to be released to the environment under any operating conditions of the facility, including such meteorological, hydrological and other information needed to support such estimates;

(iv) architectural and engineering plans indicating compatibility of the facility with the environment; and

(v) how the construction and operation of the facility, including transportation and disposal of wastes, would comply with environmental, health and safety standards, requirements, regulations and rules under state and municipal laws;

(c) estimated cost information, including plant costs by account, all expenses by categories, including fuel costs, location plant service life and capacity factor, and total generating cost per kilowatt-hour, both at plant and including related transmission, and comparative costs of alternatives considered;

(d) a statement explaining the need for the facility including

(i) reasons that the facility is necessary or desirable for the public welfare and is not incompatible with health and safety;

(ii) the load demands which the facility is designed to meet;

(iii) how the facility will contribute to system reliability and safety;

(iv) how the facility conforms to a long-range plan for the development of an integrated statewide power system;

(e) a description of any reasonable alternate location or locations for, and alternate practical sources of power to, the proposed facility; a description of the comparative advantages and disadvantages of each such location and source; and a statement of the reasons why the primary proposed location and source is best suited to promote the public health and welfare, including the recreational, and other concurrent uses which the site may serve; and

(f) such other information as the applicant may consider relevant or as may be required by the commission or the board. Copies of the application, including the required information, shall be filed with the commission and shall be available for public inspection. . . .

6. a. Each application shall be accompanied by a fee of twenty-five thousand dollars to be used to establish a fund (hereafter in this section referred to as the "fund") to defray expenses incurred by municipal parties to the proceeding (except a municipality which is the applicant) for expert witness and consultant fees. . . .

§ 144. Parties to a certification proceeding.

1. The parties to the certification proceedings shall include: . . .

(i) a municipality entitled to receive a copy of the application under paragraph (a) of subdivision two of section one hundred forty-two, if

it has filed with the commission a notice of intent to be a party, within
ninety days after the date given in the published notice as the date for
filing of the application;

(j) any individual resident in a municipality entitled to receive a
copy of the application under paragraph (a) of subdivision two of section one hundred forty-two, if he has filed with the commission a notice
of intent to be a party, within ninety days after the date given in the
published notice as the date for filing of the application;

(k) any non-profit corporation or association, formed in whole or
in part to promote conservation or natural beauty, to protect the environment, personal health or other biological values, to preserve
historical sites, to promote consumer interests, to represent commercial and industrial groups or to promote the orderly development
of any area in which the facility may be located, . . .

(l) any other municipality or resident of such municipality located
within a five mile radius of such proposed facility. . . .

(m) any other municipality or resident of such municipality which
the commission or board in its discretion finds to have an interest in
the proceeding because of the potential environmental effects on such
municipality or person, . . .

(n) such other persons or entities as the commission or board may
at any time deem appropriate, who may participate in all subsequent
stages of the proceeding. . . .

§ 146.  The decision.

The board may not grant a certificate for the construction or operation of a major steam electric generating facility, either as proposed
or as modified by the board, unless it shall find and determine:

(a) the public need for the facility and the basis thereof;

(b) the nature of the probable environmental impact, including a specification of the predictable adverse effect on the normal environment
and ecology, public health and safety, aesthetics, scenic, historic
and recreational value, forest and parks, air and water quality, fish
and other marine life, and wildlife;

(c) that the facility
    (i) represents the minimum adverse environmental impact, con-
sidering the state of available technology, the nature and economics
of the various alternatives, the interests of the state with respect to
aesthetics, preservation of historic sites, forest and parks, fish
and wildlife, and other pertinent considerations;
    (ii) is compatible with the public health and safety; and
    (iii) will not discharge any effluent that will be in contravention of
the standards adopted by the department of environmental conserva-

tion or, in case no classification has been made of the receiving waters associated with the facility, will not discharge any effluent that will be unduly injurious to the propagation and protection of fish and wildlife, the industrial development of the state, and public health and public enjoyment of the receiving waters.

(d) that the facility is designed to operate in compliance with applicable state and local laws and regulations issued thereunder concerning, among other matters, the environment, public health and safety, all of which shall be binding upon the applicant, except that the board may refuse to apply any local ordinance, law, resolution or other action or any regulation issued thereunder or any local standard or requirement which would be otherwise applicable if it finds that as applied to the proposed facility such is unreasonably restrictive in view of the existing technology or the needs of or costs to consumers whether located inside or outside of such municipality. . . .

(e) that the facility is consistent with long-range planning objectives for electric power supply in the state, including an economic and reliable electric system, and for protection of the environment.

(f) that the facility will serve the public interest, convenience, and necessity, . . .

(g) that the facility is in the public interest, considering the environmental impact of the facility, the total cost to society as a whole, the possible alternative sites or alternative available methods of power generation, or alternative available sources of energy as the case may be, both within the state and elsewhere, and the immediacy and totality of the needs of the people of the state for the facility within the context of the need for public utility services and for protection of the environment. . . .

§ 149-a.  Powers of municipalities and state agencies.

1. Notwithstanding any other provision of law, no state agency, municipality or any agency thereof may, except as expressly authorized by this article or the board, require any approval, consent, permit, certificate or other condition for the construction or operation of a major steam electric generating facility with respect to which an application for a certificate hereunder has been filed, other than those provided by otherwise applicable state law for the protection of employees engaged in the construction and operation of such facility, and provided that in the case of a municipality or an agency thereof, such municipality has received notice of the filing of the application therefor. . . .

§ 149-b.  Long-range electric system planning.

Each electric corporation shall prepare and submit annually to the department, at a public hearing upon such notice and at such time and place as the department shall determine, its long-range plan for future operations drawn pursuant to regulations issued by the commission.
. . .

WYOMING INDUSTRIAL DEVELOPMENT AND
SITING ACT (1975)
W.C.S. Sec. 35-502.75 et seq.

§ 35-502.76.  Definitions.

(c) "Industrial facility" or "facility" means:
    (1) Any energy generation and conversion plant:
    (A) Designed for, or capable of, generating one hundred (100) megawatts of electricity or more or any addition thereto (except pollution control facilities approved by the department of environmental quality added to an existing plant) increasing the initial design capacity of the facility by at least one hundred (100) megawatts of electricity;

(B) Designed for, or capable of, producing one 100 million (100,000,000) cubic feet of synthetic gas per day or more. . . .

(C) Designed for, or capable of, producing fifty thousand (50,000) barrels of liquid hydrocarbon products per day or more by any extraction process. . . .

(D) Designed for, or capable of, enriching uranium minerals from U308 (yellow cake) in quantities exceeding five hundred (500) pounds of U308 per day.

(ii) Any industrial facility with an estimated construction cost of at least fifty million dollars ($50,000,000.00). The council shall adjust this amount, up or down each year using recognized construction cost indices as determined by the council. . . .

(g) "Impacted area means an area of Wyoming in which sudden or prolonged population growth may occur or may cause environmental, social or economic stresses of such nature that the total local, state and federal resources available are not sufficient to resolve them properly and effectively as determined by the council;

(h) "Commence to construct" means:

(i) Any clearing of land, excavation, construction or other action that would affect the environment of the site of any facility. . . .

(ii) The nuclear fracturing of underground formation, if any such activity is related to the possible future development of a facility subject to this act, but does not include the gathering of geological data by boring of test holes or other underground exploration, investigation or experimentation. . . .

§ 35-502.80. Permit from council required prior to commencing construction of facility; amendments; exceptions.

(a) No person shall commence to construct a facility, as defined in this act [§§ 35-502.75 to 35-502.94], in the state without first having obtained a permit issued with respect to such facility by the council. . . .

(e) If after the applicant has submitted his application in compliance with W.S. 35-502.80 (a) and has furnished the council clear and convincing proof that the proposed facility is in compliance with all local ordinances and land use plans, and there is evidence that the facility would alleviate environmental, social and economic impact in the county of the proposed facility, the council may waive all further provisions of this act.

§ 35-502.81. Application for permit; form; initial fee.

(a) An application for a permit shall be filed with the office, in such form as prescribed by rules and regulations, and shall contain the following information: . . .

(vi) A statement of why the proposed location was judged superior;

(vii) A copy of any studies which may have been made of the environmental impact of the facility;

(viii) Inventory of estimated discharges including physical, chemical, biological and radiological characteristics;

(ix) Inventory of estimated emissions and proposed methods of control;

(x) Inventory of estimated solid wastes and proposed disposal program;

(xi) The procedures proposed to avoid constituting a public nuisance, endangering the public health and safety, human or animal life, property, wildlife or plant life, or recreational facilities which may be adversely affected by the estimated emissions or discharges;

(xii) Preliminary evaluations of or plans and proposals for alleviating social, economic or environmental impacts upon local government or any special districts which may result from the proposed facility, which evaluations, plans and proposals shall cover the following:

(A) Scenic resources;

(B) Recreational resources;

(C) Archeological and historical resources;

(D) Land use patterns;

(E) Economic base;

(F) Housing;

(G) Transportation;

(H) Anticipated growth of satellite industries;

(J) Sewer and water facilities;

(K) Solid waste facilities;

(M) Police and fire facilities;

(N) Educational facilities;

(O) Health and hospital facilities;

(P) Water supply;

(Q) Other relevant areas; . . .

(b) At the time of filing an application, or as subsequently required by the director, an applicant shall pay an initial fee to be determined by the director based upon the estimated cost of investigating, reviewing, processing and serving notice of an application. The fee shall be credited to an account within the earmarked revenue fund and shall be used by the office as required to investigate, review, process and serve notice of the application. Unused fees shall be refunded to the applicant. The maximum initial fee chargeable shall not exceed one half of one percent (0.5%) of the estimated construction cost of the facility or one hundred thousand dollars ($100,000.00), whichever is less.

(c) The director shall provide the applicant with a full financial accounting, including but not limited to all materials, labor and over-

head costs relating to the expenditures of the initial fee at the time of
the council's initial decision as provided in W.S. 35-502.82 (e).

§ 35-502.83.  Fees for additional study.

(a) If additional study is required by the council, the applicant shall
pay an additional fee to be determined by the director, after consultation with the applicant and approved by the council based upon the estimated cost of an intensive study and evaluation of the proposed facility as hereafter provided. . . .

§ 35-502.84.  Studies; evaluation and report on proposed facility.

(a) Before commencing the study the director shall prepare and review, with the applicant, a study design within thirty (30) days after
the initial decision. . . . The following is a list of topics which the
council may designate as necessary for further study:
  (i) The purpose of the facility;
    (A) Consumer demand and future energy needs;
    (B) Tax base, including the potential short- and long-range de-
mands on any tax revenues generated by the facility for the extension or expansion of public services within the impacted area;
    (C) Efficient use of energy form;
    (D) Diversification of employment and job availability
  (ii) Land use impacts;
    (A) Area of land required and ultimate use;
    (B) Consistency with state, intrastate regional, county and local
land use plans if any;
    (C) Compatibility with existing and projected nearby land utiliza-
tion;
    (D) Alternative uses of the site;
    (E) Impact on population already in the area; population attracted
by construction or operation of the facility itself; impact of availability of energy from this facility on growth patterns and population
dispersal;
    (F) Geologic suitability of the site or route;
    (G) Construction practices;
    (H) Extent of erosion, scouring, wasting of land at the site;
    (J) Corridor design and construction precautions for transmis-
sion lines or aqueducts;
    (K) Scenic impacts;
    (M) Effects on natural systems, wildlife, plant life;
    (N) Impacts on important historic architectural, archeological
and cultural areas and features;
    (O) Extent of recreation opportunities and related compatible uses;
    (P) Public recreation plan for the project if any;

(Q) Public facilities and accommodation.

(iii) Water resources impacts:

(A) Hydrologic studies of adequacy of water supply and impact of facility on stream flow, lakes, reservoirs and underground waters;

(B) Hydrologic studies of impact of facilities on ground waters and underground waters;

(C) Cooling system evaluation including consideration of alternatives;

(D) Inventory of effluents including physical, chemical, biological and radiological characteristics;

(E) Hydrologic studies of effects of effluents on receiving waters, including mixing characteristics of receiving waters, changed evaporation due to temperature differentials and effect of discharge on bottom sediments;

(F) Relationship to water quality standards;

(G) Effects of changes in quantity and quality on water use by others, including both withdrawal and in situ uses; relationship to projected uses; relationship to water rights;

(H) Effects on plant and animal life, including algae, microinvertebrates and fish population;

(J) Monitoring programs.

(iv) Air quality impacts:

(A) Meteorology, wind direction and velocity, ambient temperature ranges, precipitation values, inversion occurrence, other effects on dispersion;

(B) Topography and factors affecting dispersion;

(C) Standards in effect and projected for emissions, design capability to meet standards;

(D) Emissions and controls:

(1) Stack design;

(2) Particulates;

(3) Sulfur oxides;

(4) Oxides of nitrogen;

(5) Heavy metals, trace elements, radioactive materials and other toxic substances;

(E) Relationship to present and projected air quality of the area;

(F) Monitoring program.

(v) Solid wastes impact:

(A) Solid waste inventory;

(B) Disposal program;

(C) Relationship of disposal practices to environmental quality criteria;

(D) Capacity of disposal sites to accept projected waste loadings.

(vi) Radiation impacts:

(A) Land use controls over development and population;

(B) Wastes and associated disposal program for solid, liquid, radioactive and gaseous wastes;

(C) Analysis and studies of the adequacy of engineering safeguards and operating procedures;

(D) Monitoring, adequacy of devices and sampling techniques.

(vii) Noise impacts:

(A) Construction period levels;

(B) Operational levels;

(C) Relationship of present and projected noise levels to existing noise standards;

(D) Monitoring, adequacy of devices and methods.

(viii) Social and economic impacts:

(A) Economic base;

(B) Housing;

(C) Transportation;

(D) Anticipated growth of satellite industries;

(E) Sewer and water facilities;

(F) Solid waste facilities;

(G) Police and fire facilities;

(H) Educational facilities;

(J) Health and hospital facilities;

(K) Rate of population growth. . . .

§ 35-502.85.  Parties to permit proceeding; waiver by failure to participate.

(a) The parties to a permit proceeding include:

(i) The applicant;

(ii) Each local government entitled to receive service of a copy of the application under W.S. 35-502.82(a)(i);

(iii) Any person residing in a local government entitled to receive service of a copy of the application under W.S. 35-502.82(a)(i) and any nonprofit organization with a Wyoming chapter, concerned in whole or in part to promote conservation or natural beauty, to protect the environment, personal health or other biological values, to preserve historical sites, to promote consumer interests, to represent commercial and industrial groups, or to promote the orderly development of the areas in which the facility is to be located. In order to be a party the person or organization must file with the office a notice of intent to be a party not less than ten (10) days before the date set for the hearing. . . .

§ 35-502.87. Decision of council; findings necessary for permit conditions imposed; service of decision on parties.

(a) The council shall grant a permit either as proposed or as modified by the council if it finds and determines:

(i) The nature of the probably environmental impact is acceptable, including a specification of the predictable adverse effect on the normal environment, public health and safety, aesthetics, scenic, historic and recreational value, forest and parks, air quality, water supply and quality, fish, wildlife and agricultural resources;

(ii) That by the design and location of the facility, any adverse environmental impact is reduced to the extent deemed acceptable considering:

(A) The state of available technology;

(B) The nature and economics of the various alternatives;

(C) Preservation of historic sites, forest and parks, fish and wildlife, air quality, water supply and quality, agriculture resources and land areas possessing sensitive ecological conditions; and

(D) Other pertinent considerations.

(iii) That the facility is compatible with the public health and safety;

(iv) That the facility is compatible with the state, intrastate, regional, county and local land use plans, if any, and with existing and projected nearby land utilization;

(v) That the facility is designed in compliance with applicable state and local laws and regulations issued thereunder, except that the council may refuse to apply any local law or regulation if it finds that, as applied to the proposed facility, such law or regulation is unreasonably restrictive in view of the existing technology, or of factors of cost or economics;

(vi) That the department of environmental quality has determined that the proposed facility or cumulative effects intensified by the facility will not violate state and federally established standards and implementation plans. The judgments of the department are conclusive on all questions related to the satisfaction of state and federal standards;

(vii) That the facility represents an acceptable impact upon the environmental, social and economic well-being of the municipality and people in the area where the facility is proposed to be located, considering the factors enumerated in W.S. 35-502.81(a)(xii). . . .

(d) If the council decides to grant a permit for the facility it shall issue the permit embodying the terms and conditions in detail, including the time specified to commence construction, which time shall be determined by the council's decision as to the reasonable capability of the local government, most substantially affected by the proposed facility, to implement the necessary procedures to alleviate the impact. . . .

§ 35.502.92. Penalties for violation of act; civil action by attorney general.

(a) No person shall:

(i) Commence to construct a facility after the effective date of this act without first obtaining a permit required under this act [§§ 35-502.75 to 35-502.94];

(ii) Construct, operate or maintain a facility, after having first obtained a permit, other than in specific compliance with the permit; or

(iii) Cause any of the aforementioned acts to occur.

(b) Any person violating the provisions of subsection (a) of this section is liable to a civil penalty of not more than ten thousand dollars ($10,000.00) for each violation. Each day of a continuing violation constitutes a separate offense. The penalty shall be recoverable in a civil suit brought by the attorney general on behalf of the state in the district court in and for the county of Laramie.

(c) Whoever knowingly and wilfully violates subsection (a) of this section shall be fined not more than ten thousand dollars ($10,000.00) for each violation or imprisoned for not more than one (1) year, or both. Each day of a continuing violation shall constitute a separate offense. . . .

# 6

## NATURAL AREAS,
## PARKS, RECREATION

To withdraw land from development or to dedicate it solely or chiefly to recreational purposes is one form of land use. It may be the only form that can prevent degradation of areas containing outstanding scenic or natural features or fragile environments and maintain green and open spaces near centers of population. Keeping air quality in national and state parks and similar preserves from deteriorating is an object of proposed amendments to the Clean Air Act, before Congress at the time of this writing.

This chapter considers laws that prevent or postpone development of land by direct acquisition, by severe building restrictions along the banks to protect rivers in their natural state, or by easements and preferential taxation arrangements. There is a separate section on recreational trails. This chapter focuses on preservation of resources rather than their conservation for continued production, which is the focus of Chapter 9. General land use is considered in Chapter 5. "Open space" is a term used for both natural and agricultural and forest crop lands. Acts furthering open space preservation are found here and in Chapter 9, depending on their emphasis.

The first National Park, Yellowstone, dates back to 1872. In 1916, the National Park Service was established (p. 221) to administer it and subsequently created national parks. The service also manages national monuments, authorized by the Antiquities Act of 1906 and later legislation (see Chapter 4), and national recreation areas. These are generally not wilderness, although portions of them may be. The Wilderness Act of 1964 (p. 223) provides for setting aside relatively untouched areas within national parks and national forests and keeping them in roadless, undeveloped condition.

The Wild and Scenic Rivers Act of 1968 (p. 225) looks to preserving certain water courses "in free-flowing condition" and author-

izes land acquisition for such purposes.  Additional dedicated federal
lands are contained in the National Wildlife Refuge System (p. 228).
Wildlife conservation lands may be created out of federal surplus real
property and administered by either the Fish and Wildlife Service or
transferred to a state for such purposes (p. 229).  The Migratory Bird
Treat Act also provides for the acquisition of sanctuaries (Sec. 715d,
p. 520), as does the Endangered Species Act (Sec. 1534, p. 508) and
Title III of the Ocean Dumping Act.

The Open Space Act of 1970 (p. 230) authorizes federal grants
to states and local government for acquisition of urban open lands.
Other federal laws that have among their objects the preservation of
parks and scenic or recreation areas include those governing surplus
property disposal (50 U.S.C. 1622), federal-aid highways (23 U.S.C.
138, 319), urban mass transportation (49 U.S.C. 1610), airports
(49 U.S.C. 1716) and the Department of Transportation (49 U.S.C.
1651, 1653).  The Multiple-Use Sustained Yield Act acknowledges
recreation as one of the objectives of the National Forest Service
(Sec. 528, p. 222).  Executive Order 11644 excludes off-road vehicles
from federal wilderness and primitive areas and restricts their use
in others (Sec. 4(4), p. 452).  Recreational values are a factor in
granting ocean dumping permits (33 U.S.C. 1412), and the Coastal
Zone Management Act looks to the preservation of areas for their
"conservation, recreation, ecological values" (Sec. 1455).

States and local governments have power to acquire natural
areas, ranging from wild to actively farmed.  Thus, Michigan's Wilderness and Natural Areas Act of 1972 (p. 233) distinguishes among
wilderness, wild, and natural areas for state acquisition according
to size and inherent characteristics.  The state's snowmobile registration law excludes such vehicles from all protected areas (Sec.
257.1515[d], p. 457).  In Kansas "natural and scientific preserves"
may be formally dedicated and maintained "as nearly as possible in
(their) natural condition. . . without impairment, disturbance, or
artificial development."  In addition to these, there is to be a registry
of "natural and scientific areas" of special interest that "need not be
completely natural and undisturbed" (74 Gen. Stat. Kans. 74–6601 et
seq.).  Endangered natural areas may be acquired by the state in
both Florida and Maine to prevent development if appropriate agencies
determine that such areas best be left undisturbed.

New York since 1894 has given constitutional protection to its
extensive "forever wild" forest preserve (p. 238).  Maine's Baxter
State Park "shall forever be kept . . . in the natural wild state"
(p. 239).  Some of California's state lands also are in protected wilderness status.  California directs its cities and counties to include
open space preservation in their local planning (p. 246).  New York
permits expenditures by municipalities for the acquisition of open
space (p. 246), and Arizona has similar permissive legislation.

Over 20 states have adopted wild and scenic rivers laws to supplement the protection afforded by the federal act. Minnesota's Wild and Scenic Rivers Act (p. 235) imposes state land use controls along the shores of designated rivers. How far inland such controls extend is variously defined in the laws of such states as California, Massachusetts, Michigan, New York, North Carolina, Ohio, Oregon, Virginia, West Virginia, and others.

Easements are a legal tool for maintaining privately owned land in an open or natural condition without direct acquisition by a public agency. Massachusetts permits governmental agencies and charitable organizations to acquire such conservation restrictions for 30-year periods (p. 241). New Hampshire combines easements with deferred taxation to achieve open space preservation (p. 243). Preferential taxations for productive lands, discussed in Chapter 9, help keep them open and undeveloped.

Natural area protection afforded under general land use statutes is found in many states. Habitats of endangered species are to be classified "natural resources of statewide importance" and suitably protected in Colorado (Sec. 106-7-104[12]). Conservation districts in Hawaii include "parklands, wilderness, and beach [areas]; conserving endemic plants, fish, and wildlife . . . open space areas . . . areas of value for recreational purposes" (Sec. 205-2). Scenic values and natural systems are to be protected as areas of environmental concern in North Carolina (Sec. 113A-152[1]). Vermont will grant a development permit if no undue adverse effect on "rare and irreplaceable natural areas" is shown (Sec. 10-6086[8]). Washington's Shoreline Management Act requires master plans with provision for conservation and recreation and special consideration for wilderness beaches (Sec. 90.58.100).

In Massachusetts citizens may sue to prevent damage to "open spaces, natural areas, parks" (Sec. 214-7A). Montana may refuse a mining permit in locations of "special, exceptional, critical or unique characteristics" (Sec. 50-1042[2]).


## RECREATIONAL TRAILS

Foot trails, especially in the East, traverse private lands by the owners' permission. Such permission is almost always temporary and may be lost when ownership changes or an owner wishes to develop his land. With increasing interest in hiking and bicycling in recent years has come the desire to provide for permanent trails.

Recreational trails legislation at the federal level is in the nature of a statement of national purpose rather than a forceful mandate. The National Trails System Act of 1968 (p. 247) authorizes designation

of national recreational and scenic trails.  It was intended to encourage complementary state action, and several states have, indeed,
gone considerably further in actually constructing and acquiring rights-
of-way for such trails.  Thus Kentucky may build separate recreational
trails for hiking, biking, riding, and motorized off-road vehicles on
public lands or on private lands by easement (p. 249).  Oklahoma
classifies nature, hiking, special-use, and heritage trails and may
acquire needed lands by lease, deed, or right-of-way.  Railroad
rights-of-way slated to be abandoned shall be examined for potential
trail use (p. 252).

Oregon and Washington statutes excerpted in Chapter 12 mandate that bicycle, pedestrian, and equestrian trails must be part of
certain new highway construction.  Michigan authorizes public expenditures for nonmotorized transportation lanes and paths (Sec. 247.660k),
while Oregon allocates one percent of highway construction funds to
such expenditures (Sec. 366.514).

## FEDERAL

### NATIONAL PARK SERVICE (1916, as amended)
### 16 U.S.C. 1 et seq.

§ 1.  Service created; director; other employees.

There is created in the Department of the Interior a service to be
called the National Park Service, which shall be under the charge of
a director.  The Secretary of the Interior shall appoint the director,
and there shall also be in said service such subordinate officers,
clerks, and employees as may be appropriated for by Congress.  The
service thus established shall promote and regulate the use of the
Federal areas known as national parks, monuments, and reservations
hereinafter specified, except such as are under the jurisdiction of the
Secretary of the Army, as provided by law, by such means and measures as conform to the fundamental purpose of the said parks, monuments, and reservations, which purpose is to conserve the scenery
and the natural and historic objects and the wild life therein and to
provide for the enjoyment of the same in such manner and by such
means as will leave them unimpaired for the enjoyment of future generations.

## Yellowstone National Park

§ 21. Establishment.

The tract of land in the States of Montana and Wyoming, lying near
the headwaters of the Yellowstone River and described as follows,
. . . is reserved and withdrawn from settlement, occupancy, or sale
under the laws of the United States, and dedicated and set apart as a
public park or pleasuring ground for the benefit and enjoyment of the
people; and all persons who locate, or settle upon, or occupy any part
of the land thus set apart as a public park, except as provided in section 22 of this title, shall be considered trespassers and removed
therefrom.

## North Cascades National Park

§ 90. Establishment; statement of purposes; description of area.

In order to preserve for the benefit, use, and inspiration of present
and future generations certain majestic mountain scenery, snow fields,
glaciers, alpine meadows, and other unique natural features in the North
Cascade Mountains of the State of Washington, there is hereby established, subject to valid existing rights, the North Cascades National
Park. . . .

## Virgin Islands National Park

§ 398. Establishment; administration.

A portion of the Virgin Islands of the United States, containing outstanding scenic and other features of national significance, shall be
established, as prescribed in section 398a of this title, as the "Virgin
Islands National Park".

The national park shall be administered and preserved by the Secretary of the Interior in its natural condition for the public benefit and
inspiration, in accordance with the laws governing the administration
of the national parks.

§ 398c. Addition of lands.

In furtherance of the purposes of sections 398 and 398a of this title,
providing for the establishment of the Virgin Islands National Park,
and in order to preserve for the benefit of the public significant coral
gardens, marine life, and seascapes in the vicinity thereof, the
boundaries of such park, subject to valid existing rights, are revised

to include the adjoining lands, submerged lands, and waters described
as follows: . . .

NATIONAL WILDERNESS ACT (1964, as amended)
16 U.S.C. 1131 et seq.

Section 1131.  National Wilderness Preservation System
        1132.  Extent of system
        1133.  Use of wilderness areas
        1134.  State and private lands within wilderness areas
        1135.  Gifts, bequests, and contributions
        1136.  Annual reports to Congress

§ 1131.  National Wilderness Preservation System—establishment;
Congressional declaration of policy; wilderness areas; administration
for public use and enjoyment, protection, preservation, and gathering
and dissemination of information; provisions for designation as wilderness areas.

(a) In order to assure that an increasing population, accompanied by
expanding settlement and growing mechanization, does not occupy and
modify all areas within the United States and its possessions, leaving
no lands designated for preservation and protection in their natural
condition, it is hereby declared to be the policy of the Congress to
secure for the American people of present and future generations the
benefits of an enduring resource of wilderness.  For this purpose there
is hereby established a National Wilderness Preservation System to
be composed of federally owned areas designated by Congress as "wilderness areas, " and these shall be administered for the use and enjoyment of the American people in such manner as will leave them unimpaired for future use and enjoyment as wilderness, and so as to provide for the protection of these areas, the preservation of their wilderness character, and for the gathering and dissemination of information
regarding their use and enjoyment as wilderness; and no Federal lands
shall be designated as "wilderness areas" except as provided for in
this chapter on by a subsequent Act. . . .

(c) A wilderness, in contrast with those areas where man and his own
works dominate the landscape, is hereby recognized as an area where
the earth and its community of life are untrammeled by man, where
man himself is a visitor who does not remain.  An area of wilderness
is further defined to mean in this chapter an area of undeveloped Federal land retaining its primeval character and influence, without permanent improvements or human habitation, which is protected and
managed so as to preserve its natural conditions and which
    (1) generally appears to have been affected primarily by the forces
of nature, with the imprint of man's work substantially unnoticeable;

(2) has outstanding opportunities for solitude or a primitive and unconfined type of recreation;

(3) has at least five thousand acres of land or is of sufficient size as to make practicable its preservation and use in an unimpaired condition; and

(4) may also contain ecological, geological, or other features of scientific, educational, scenic, or historical value.

§ 1132.  Extent of system—designation of wilderness areas; filing of maps and descriptions with Congressional committees; correction of errors; public records; availability of records in regional offices.

(a) All areas within the national forests classified at least 30 days before September 3, 1964 by the Secretary of Agriculture or the Chief of the Forest Service as "wilderness", "wild", or "canoe" are hereby designated as wilderness areas. . . .

(b) The Secretary of Agriculture shall, within ten years after September 3, 1964, review, as to its suitability or nonsuitability for preservation as wilderness, each area in the national forests classified on September 3, 1964 by the Secretary of Agriculture of the Chief of the Forest Service as "primitive" and report his findings to the President. The President shall advise the United States Senate and House of Representatives of his recommendations with respect to the designation as "wilderness" or other reclassification of each area on which review has been completed. . . .

(c) Within ten years after September 3, 1964, the Secretary of the Interior shall review every roadless area of five thousand contiguous acres or more in the national parks, monuments and other units of the national park system and every such area of, and every roadless island within, the national wildlife refuges and game ranges, under his jurisdiction on September 3, 1964, and shall report to the President his recommendation as to the suitability or nonsuitability of each such area or island for preservation as wilderness.  The President shall advise the President of the Senate and the Speaker of the House of Representatives of his recommendation with respect to the designation as wilderness of each such area or island on which review has been completed. . . .  A recommendation of the President for designation as wilderness shall become effective only if so provided by an Act of Congress. . . .

§ 1133.  Use of wilderness areas—purposes of national forests, national park system, and national wildlife refuge system; other provisions applicable to national forests, Superior National Forest, and national park system. . . .

(c) Except as specifically provided for in this chapter, and subject to existing private rights, there shall be no commercial enterprise and no permanent road within any wilderness area designated by this chapter and, except as necessary to meet minimum requirements for the administration of the area for the purpose of this chapter (including measures required in emergencies involving the health and safety of persons within the area), there shall be no temporary road, no use of motor vehicles, motorized equipment or motorboats, no landing of aircraft, no other form of mechanical transport, and no structure or installation within any such area. . . .

## WILD AND SCENIC RIVERS ACT (1968, as amended)
## 16 U.S.C. 1271 et seq.

Section 1271. Congressional declaration of policy
      1272. Congressional declaration of purpose
      1273. National wild and scenic rivers system; Congressional authorization for inclusion; designation by State legislatures; permanent administration by States; application for inclusion by Governors; satisfaction of criteria; eligibility for inclusion
      1274. Component rivers and adjacent lands; establishment of boundaries; classification; development plans
      1275. Additions to national wild and scenic rivers system
      1276. Rivers constituting potential additions to national wild and scenic rivers system
      1277. Land acquisition
      1278. Restrictions on water resources projects
      1279. Withdrawal of public lands from entry, sale, or other disposition under public land laws
      1280. Federal mining and mineral leasing laws
      1281. Administration
      1282. Assistance in financing State and local projects
      1283. Administration and management policies
      1284. Existing state jurisdiction and responsibilities
      1285. Claim and allowance of charitable deduction for contribution or gift of easement
      1286. Definitions
      1287. Authorization of appropriations

## § 1271. Congressional declaration of policy.

It is hereby declared to be the policy of the United States that certain selected rivers of the Nation which, with their immediate environments, possess outstandingly remarkable scenic, recreational, geologic, fish and wildlife, historic, cultural, or other similar values,

shall be preserved in free-flowing condition, and that they and their
immediate environments shall be protected for the benefit and enjoyment of present and future generations.  The Congress declares that
the established national policy of dam and other construction at appropriate sections of the rivers of the United States needs to be comple-
mented by a policy that would preserve other selected rivers or sections thereof in their free-flowing condition to protect the water
quality of such rivers and to fulfill other vital national conservation
purposes.

§ 1273.  National wild and scenic rivers system; Congressional authorization for inclusion; designation by State legislatures; permanent administration by States; application for inclusion by Governors; satisfaction of criteria; eligibility for inclusion.

(a) The national wild and scenic rivers system shall comprise rivers
(i) that are authorized for inclusion therein by Act of Congress, or (ii)
that are designated as wild, scenic or recreational rivers by or pursuant to an act of the legislature of the State or States through which
they flow, that are to be permanently administered as wild, scenic
or recreational rivers by an agency or political subdivision of the State
or States concerned without expense to the United States, that are found
by the Secretary of the Interior, upon application of the Governor of
the State or the Governors of the States concerned, or a person or persons thereunto duly appointed by him or them, to meet the criteria established in this chapter and such criteria supplementary thereto as he
may prescribe, and that are approved by him for inclusion in the system, . . .

(b) A wild, scenic or recreational river area eligible to be included
in the system is a free-flowing stream and the related adjacent land
area that possesses one or more of the values referred to in section
1271 of this title.  Every wild, scenic or recreational river in its free-
flowing condition, or upon restoration to this condition, shall be considered eligible for inclusion in the national wild and scenic rivers
system and, if included, shall be classified, designated, and administered as one of the following:
     (1) Wild river areas—Those rivers or sections of rivers that are
free of impoundments and generally inaccessible except by trail, with
watersheds or shorelines essentially primitive and waters unpolluted.
These represent vestiges of primitive America.
     (2) Scenic river areas—Those rivers or sections of rivers that are
free of impoundments, with shorelines or watersheds still largely primitive and shorelines largely undeveloped, but accessible in places by
roads.
     (3) Recreational river areas—Those rivers or sections of rivers
that are readily accessible by road or railroad, that may have some

development along their shorelines, and that may have undergone some impoundment or diversion in the past.

## § 1277. Land acquisition.

(a) Grant of authority to acquire; State and Indian lands; use of appropriated funds.

The Secretary of the Interior and the Secretary of Agriculture are each authorized to acquire lands and interests in land within the authorized boundaries of any component of the national wild and scenic rivers system designated in section 1274 of this title, or hereafter designated for inclusion in the system by Act of Congress, which is administered by him, but he shall not acquire fee title to an average of more than 100 acres per mile on both sides of the river. . . .

## § 1278. Restrictions on water resources projects.

(a) Construction projects licensed by Federal Power Commission.

The Federal Power Commission shall not license the construction of any dam, water conduit, reservoir, powerhouse, transmission line, or other project works under the Federal Power Act, as amended, on or directly affecting any river which is designated in section 1274 of this title as a component of the national wild and scenic rivers system or which is hereafter designated for inclusion in that system, and no department or agency of the United States shall assist by loan, grant, license, or otherwise in the construction of any water resources project that would have a direct and adverse effect on the values for which such river was established, as determined by the Secretary charged with its administration. Nothing contained in the foregoing sentence, however, shall preclude licensing of, or assistance to, developments below or above a wild, scenic or recreational river area or on any stream tributary thereto which will not invade the area or unreasonably diminish the scenic, recreational, and fish and wildlife values present in the area on October 2, 1968. . . .

## § 1281. Administration.

(a) Public use and enjoyment of components; protection of features; management plans.

Each component of the national wild and scenic rivers system shall be administered in such manner as to protect and enhance the values which caused it to be included in said system without, insofar as is consistent therewith, limiting other uses that do not substantially interfere with public use and enjoyment of these values. In such administration primary emphasis shall be given to protecting its esthetic,

scenic, historic, archeologic, and scientific features. Management
plans for any such component may establish varying degrees of intensity
for its protection and development, based on the special attributes of
the area.

## NATIONAL WILDLIFE REFUGE SYSTEM
### (1966, as amended)
### 16 U.S.C. 668dd et seq.

§ 668dd.   National Wildlife Refuge System—designation; public land
withdrawals; disposal of acquired lands; proceeds.

(a) For the purpose of consolidating the authorities relating to the
various categories of areas that are administered by the Secretary of
the Interior for the conservation of fish and wildlife, including species
that are threatened with extinction, all lands, waters, and interests
therein administered by the Secretary as wildlife refuges, areas for
the protection and conservation of fish and wildlife that are threatened
with extinction, wildlife ranges, game ranges, wildlife management
areas, or waterfowl production areas are hereby designated as the
"National Wildlife Refuge System" (referred to herein as the "System"),
which shall be subject to the provisions of this section. Nothing contained in this Act shall restrict the authority of the Secretary to modify
or revoke public land withdrawals affecting lands in the System as
presently constituted, or as it may be constituted, whenever he determines that such action is consistent with the public interest. No acquired lands which are or become a part of the System may be transferred or otherwise disposed of under any provision of law. . . .

(c) No person shall knowingly disturb, injure, cut, burn, remove,
destroy, or possess any real or personal property of the United States
including natural growth, in any area of the System; or take or possess any fish, bird, mammal, or other wild vertebrate or invertebrate
animals or part or nest or egg thereof within any such area; or enter

use, or otherwise occupy any such area for any purpose; unless such activities are performed by persons authorized to manage such area, or unless such activities are permitted either under subsection (d) of this section or by express provision of the law, proclamation, Executive order, or public land order establishing the area, or amendment thereof: Provided, That the United States mining and mineral leasing laws shall continue to apply to any lands within the System to the same extent they apply prior to October 15, 1966, unless subsequently withdrawn under other authority of law. With the exception of endangered species and threatened species listed by the Secretary pursuant to section 1533 of this title in States wherein a cooperative agreement does not exist pursuant to section 1535(c) of this title, nothing in this Act shall be construed to authorize the Secretary to control or regulate hunting or fishing of resident fish and wildlife on lands not within the system. . . .

(d) The Secretary is authorized, under such regulations as he may prescribe, to—

(1) permit the use of any area within the System for any purpose, including but not limited to hunting, fishing, public recreation and accommodations, and access whenever he determines that such uses are compatible with the major purposes for which such areas were established   Provided, That not to exceed 40 per centum at any one time of any area that has been, or hereafter may be acquired, reserved, or set apart as an inviolate sanctuary for migratory birds, under any law, proclamation, Executive order, or public land order may be administered by the Secretary as an area within which the taking of migratory game birds may be permitted under such regulations as he may prescribe; . . .

USE OF FEDERAL SURPLUS LANDS FOR WILDLIFE
CONSERVATION (1948, as amended)
16 U.S.C. 667b

§ 667b.  Transfer of certain real property for wildlife conservation purposes; reservation of rights.

Upon request, real property which is under the jurisdiction or control of a Federal agency and no longer required by such agency,

(1) can be utilized for wildlife conservation purposes by the agency of the State exercising administration over the wildlife resources of the State wherein the real property lies or by the Secretary of the Interior; and

(2) is valuable for use for any such purpose, and which, in the determination of the Administrator of General Services, is available for

such use may, notwithstanding any other provisions of law, be transferred without reimbursement or transfer of funds (with or without improvements as determined by said Administrator) by the Federal agency having jurisdiction or control of the property to

(a) such State agency if the management thereof for the conservation of wildlife relates to other than migratory birds, or

(b) to the Secretary of the Interior if the real property has particular value in carrying out the national migratory bird management program. . . .

OPEN SPACE ACT (1970)
42 U.S.C. 1500 et seq.

§ 1500. Congressional declaration of findings and purpose.

(a) The Congress finds that the rapid expansion of the Nation's urban areas and the rapid growth of population within such areas has resulted in severe problems of urban and suburban living for the preponderant majority of the Nation's present and future population, including the lack of valuable open-space land for recreational and other purposes.

(b) The Congress further finds that there is a need for the additional provision of parks and other open space in the built-up portions of urban areas especially in low income neighborhoods and communities and a need for greater and better coordinated State and local efforts to make available and improve open-space land throughout entire urban areas.

(c) The Congress further finds that there is a need for timely action to preserve and restore areas, sites, and structures of historic or architectural value in order that these remaining evidences of our history and heritage shall not be lost or destroyed through the expansion and development of the Nation's urban areas.

(d) It is the purpose of this chapter to help curb urban sprawl and prevent the spread of urban blight and deterioration, to encourage more
economic and desirable urban development, to assist in preserving
areas and properties of historic or architectural value, and to help
provide necessary recreational, conservation, and scenic areas by
assisting State and local public bodies in taking prompt action to

(1) provide, preserve, and develop open-space land in a manner
consistent with the planned long-range development of the Nation's urban areas,

(2) acquire, improve, and restore areas, sites, and structures of
historic or architectural value, and

(3) develop and improve open space and other public urban land, in
accordance with programs to encourage and coordinate local public and
private efforts toward this end.

§ 1500a. Grants to States and local public bodies for acquisition and
for development of open-space land—authorization; limitation on
amount of grant; limitation on donations for non-Federal share.

(a) The Secretary is authorized to make grants to States and local
public bodies to help finance

(1) the acquisition of title to, or other interest in, open-space land
in urban areas and

(2) the development of open-space or other land in urban areas for
open-space uses. . . .

(b) No grants under this chapter shall be made to

(1) defray ordinary State or local governmental expenses,

(2) help finance the acquisition by a public body of land located
outside the urban area for which it exercises (or participates in the
exercise of) responsibilities consistent with the purpose of this chapter,

(3) acquire and clear developed land in built-up urban areas unless
the local governing body determines that adequate open-space land cannot be effectively provided through the use of existing undeveloped
land, or

(4) provide assistance for historic and architectural preservation
purposes, except for districts, sites, buildings, structures, and objects which the Secretary of the Interior determines meet the criteria
used in establishing the National Register. . . .

§ 1500b. Planning requirements.

The Secretary shall make grants under section 1500a of this title
only if he finds that such assistance is needed for carrying out a unified or officially coordinated program, meeting criteria established

by him, for the provision and development of open-space land which is
a part of, or is consistent with, the comprehensively planned development of the urban area.

## § 1500c.  Conversions to other uses.

No open-space land for the acquisition of which a grant has been made
under section 1500a of this title shall be converted to uses not originally
approved by the Secretary without his prior approval.  Prior approval
will be granted only upon satisfactory compliance with regulations established by the Secretary.  Such regulations shall require findings
that

(1) there is adequate assurance of the substitution of other open-
space land of as nearly as feasible equivalent usefulness, location,
and fair market value at the time of the conversion;

(2) the conversion and substitution are needed for orderly growth
and development; and

(3) the proposed uses of the converted and substituted land are in
accord with the then applicable comprehensive plan for the urban area,
meeting criteria established by the Secretary.

## § 1500c-1.  Conversions of land involving historic or architectural purposes.

No open-space land involving historic or architectural purposes for
which assistance has been granted under this chapter shall be converted to use for any other purpose without the prior approval of the
Secretary of the Interior.

## § 1500c-2.  Acquisition of interests to guide urban development.

In order to encourage the acquisition of interests in undeveloped or
predominantly undeveloped land which, if withheld from commercial,
industrial, and residential development, would have special significance in helping to shape economic and desirable patterns of urban
growth (including growth outside of existing urban areas which is directly related to the development of new communities or the expansion
and revitalization of existing communities), the Secretary may make
grants to State and local public bodies for the acquisition of such interests in an amount not to exceed 75 per centum of the cost of such acquisition.  In the case of any interests acquired pursuant to this section, the Secretary may approve the subsequent conversion or disposition of the land involved without regard to other requirements of this
chapter but subject to such terms and conditions as he determines
equitable and appropriate with respect to the control of future use and
the application or sharing of the proceeds or value realized upon sale
or disposition.

STATES

MICHIGAN WILDERNESS AND NATURAL AREAS
ACT (1972)
Mich. Comp. Laws Ann. 322.751 et seq.

§ 322.752.  Definitions. . . .

(d) "Wilderness area" means a tract of undeveloped state land or
water under control of the department and dedicated and regulated by
the commission pursuant to this act which:

(i) Has 3,000 or more acres of state land or is an island of any
size.

(ii) Generally appears to have been affected primarily by forces
of nature with the imprint of man's work substantially unnoticeable.

(iii) Has outstanding opportunities for solitude or a primitive and
unconfined type of recreation.

(iv) Contains ecological, geological or other features of scientific,
scenic or historical value.

(e) "Wild area" means a tract of undeveloped state land or water under control of the department and dedicated and regulated by the commission pursuant to this act which:

(i) Is less than 3,000 acres of state land.

(ii) Has outstanding opportunities for personal exploration, challenge
or contact with natural features of the landscape and its biological community.

(iii) Possesses 1 or more of the characteristics of a wilderness area.

(f) "Natural area" means a tract of state land or water under control of the department and dedicated and regulated by the commission pursuant to this act which:

(i) Has retained or reestablished its natural character, or has unusual flora and fauna or biotic, geologic, scenic or other similar features of educational or scientific value, but it need not be undisturbed.

(ii) Has been identified and verified through research and study by qualified observers.

(iii) May be coextensive with or part of a wilderness area or wild area.

§ 322.754. Wilderness, wild, and natural areas.

(1) Within 6 months after the effective date of this act, and each year thereafter, the department shall review all state land under its control and shall identify those tracts which in its judgment best exhibit the characteristics of a wilderness area, wild area or natural area. The department shall propose to the commission land which in its judgment is most suitable for dedication by the commission as wilderness areas, wild areas or natural areas. The department shall administer the proposed land so as to protect its natural values.

(2) The board or a citizen may propose to the commission land which in its judgment exhibits the characteristics of a wilderness area, wild area or natural area and is suitable for dedication by the commission as such or may propose the alteration or withdrawal of previously dedicated areas. . . .

(4) The commission may exchange dedicated land for the purpose of acquiring other land which, in its judgment, are more suitable for the purposes of this act.

§ 322.755. Wild and natural areas in relative proximity to urban centers.

(1) The commission shall attempt to provide insofar as possible, wild areas and natural areas in relative proximity to urban centers of more than 100,000 population.

(2) Private land or land under the control of other governmental units may be designated in the same way as a wilderness area, wild area or natural area by the commission and administered by the department under a cooperative agreement between the owner and the commission.

§ 322.756. Acts prohibited on state land in wilderness, wild, or natural areas or proposed areas.

The following are prohibited on state land in a wilderness area, wild area or natural area or on state land proposed by the department for dedication in 1 of these categories during the 90 days a dedication is pending pursuant to section 4:

(a) Removing, cutting, picking or otherwise altering vegetation except as necessary for appropriate public access, the preservation or restoration of a plant or wildlife species, or the documentation of scientific values and with written consent of the department.

(b) Granting an easement for any purpose.

(c) Exploration for or extraction of minerals.

(d) A commercial enterprise, utility or permanent road.

(e) A temporary road, landing of aircraft, use of motor vehicles, motorboats, or other form of mechanical transport, or any structure or installation, except as necessary to meet minimum emergency requirements for administration as a wilderness area, wild area or natural area by the department.

(f) Trapping and hunting when recommended by the department.

§ 322.757. Landing aircraft or operating mechanical transportation in wilderness, wild, or natural areas, offense.

A person who lands an aircraft or operates a motor vehicle, motorboat or other form of mechanical transport in a wilderness area, wild area or natural area without the express written consent of the department is guilty of a misdemeanor.

§ 322.761. Taxation of wilderness, wild, or natural areas.

The local taxing authority shall be entitled to collect from the state a tax on a wilderness, wild or natural area within its jurisdiction at its ad valorem tax rate or $2.00 per acre, whichever is less. The department shall audit the assessments of wilderness, wild or natural areas regularly to insure that such properties are assessed in the same ratio as similar properties in private ownership. The legislature shall appropriate from the general fund for payments under this section.

MINNESOTA WILD AND SCENIC RIVERS ACT (1973)
Minn. Stat. Sec. 104.31 et seq.

Section 104.31.    Wild and scenic rivers act
        104.32.    Policy

§ 104.32.  Policy.

The legislature finds that certain of Minnesota's rivers and their adjacent lands possess outstanding scenic, recreational, natural, historical, scientific and similar values.  Because it is in the interest of present and future generations to retain these values, it is hereby declared to be a policy of Minnesota and an authorized public purpose to preserve and protect these rivers.

§ 104.33.  System; criteria for Inclusion.

Subdivision 1.  The whole or a segment of any river and its adjacent lands in this state that possesses outstanding scenic, recreational, natural, historical, scientific, or similar values shall be eligible for inclusion within the Minnesota wild and scenic rivers system.  "River" means a flowing body of water such as a stream or a segment or tributary thereof, and may include lakes through which the river or stream flows.

Subdivision 2.  Rivers or segments thereof included within the system shall be classified as wild, scenic, or recreational.

(a) "Wild" rivers are those rivers that exist in a free-flowing state, with excellent water quality, and with adjacent lands that are essentially primitive.  "Free-flowing" means existing in natural condition without significant artificial modification such as impoundment, diversion, or straightening.  The existence, however, of low dams, diversion works or other minor structures at the time any river is proposed for inclusion shall not automatically bar its inclusion as a wild, scenic, or recreational river.

(b) "Scenic" rivers are those rivers that exist in a free-flowing state and with adjacent lands that are largely undeveloped.

(c) "Recreational" rivers are those rivers that may have undergone some impoundment or diversion in the past and may have adjacent lands that are considerably developed, but that are still capable of being managed so as to further the purposes of sections 104.31 to 104.40.

§ 104.35. Management plans; hearing; establishment.

Subdivision 1. For each river proposed to be included in the wild and scenic rivers system, the commissioner shall prepare a management plan, with no unreasonable restrictions upon compatible, pre-existing, economic uses of particular tracts of land to preserve and enhance the values that cause the river to be proposed for inclusion in the system. The plan shall give primary emphasis to the area's scenic, recreational, natural, historical, scientific and similar values. The plan shall set forth the proposed classification of the river and segments thereof, and the boundaries of the area along the river to be included within the system. The boundaries shall include not more than 320 acres per mile on both sides of the river. The plan shall include proposed regulations governing the use of public lands and waters within the area, which may differ from any such statewide regulations to the extent necessary to take account of the particular attributes of the area. The plan may include proposed standards and criteria adopted pursuant to section 104.34 for local land use controls that differ from the statewide standards and criteria to the extent necessary to take account of the particular attributes of the area.

§ 104.37. Acquisition of interests in land.

To further the purposes of sections 104.31 to 104.40, the commissioner of administration, for the commissioner of natural resources, may acquire the title, scenic easements or other interests in land, by purchase, grant, gift, devise, exchange, lease, or other lawful means. "Scenic easement" means an interest in land, less than the fee title, which limits the use of such land for the purpose of protecting the scenic, recreational, or natural characteristics of a wild, scenic or recreational river area. Unless otherwise expressly and specifically provided by the parties, such easement shall be

(a) perpetually held for the benefit of the people of Minnesota;

(b) specifically enforceable by its holder or any beneficiary; and

(c) binding upon the holder of the servient estate, his heirs, successors and assigns. Unless specifically provided by the parties, no such easement shall give the holder or any beneficiary the right to enter on the land except for enforcement of the easement.

Subdivision 4. The legislature may at any time designate additional rivers to be included within the system, delete rivers previously included in the system, or change the classification of rivers theretofore classified by the commissioner.

§ 104.36.  Local land use ordinances.

Subdivision 1.  Within six months after establishment of a wild, scenic, or recreational river area, each local government containing any portion thereof shall adopt or amend its local ordinances and land use district maps to the extent necessary to comply with the standards and criteria of the commissioner and the management plan.  If a local government fails to adopt adequate ordinances, maps, or amendments thereto within six months, the commissioner shall adopt such ordinances, maps, or amendments in the manner and with the effect specified in section 105.485, subdivision 4 and 5.

Subdivision 2.  The commissioner shall assist local governments in the preparation, implementation and enforcement of the ordinances required herein, within the limits of available appropriations and personnel.

NEW YORK CONSTITUTION (1894, as amended)<br/>Art. XIV

§ 1.  Forest preserve to be forever kept wild; certain uses and exceptions authorized.

The lands of the state, now owned or hereafter acquired, constituting the forest preserve as now fixed by law, shall be forever kept as wild forest lands.  They shall not be leased, sold or exchanged, or be taken by any corporation, public or private, nor shall the timber thereon be sold, removed or destroyed. . . .

§ 4.  Conservation of natural resources and scenic beauty; pollution abatement; acquisition and preservation of lands as state nature and historical preserve.

The policy of the state shall be to conserve and protect its natural resources and scenic beauty and encourage the development and improvement of its agricultural lands for the production of food and other agricultural products.  The legislature, in implementing this policy, shall include adequate provision for the abatement of air and water pollution and of excessive and unnecessary noise, the protection of agricultural lands, wetlands and shorelines, and the development and regulation of water resources.  The legislature shall further provide for the acquisition of lands and waters, including improvements thereon and any interest therein, outside the forest preserve counties, and the dedication of properties so acquired or now owned, which because of their natural beauty, wilderness character, or geological, ecological or historical significance, shall be preserved and administered for the use and enjoyment of the people.  Properties so dedicated

shall constitute the state nature and historical preserve and they shall
not be taken or otherwise disposed of except by law enacted by two
successive regular sessions of the legislature.

§ 5.  Violations of article; how restrained.

A violation of any of the provisions of this article may be restrained
at the suit of the people or, with the consent of the supreme court
appellate division, on notice to the attorney general at the suit of any
citizen.

MAINE BAXTER STATE PARK (1927, as amended)
12 Rev. State Maine Sec. 900 et seq.

§ 900.  Purpose.

Seldom has a more generous gift been presented to a people than
has been given by Percival Proctor Baxter to the people of the State
of Maine.  It is incumbent upon them, the recipients, to preserve the
trust impressed upon them, to ensure for themselves and for future
generations the fullest use of Baxter State Park consistent with the
desires of the donor.

Governor Baxter's expressed desires were that this park "shall forever be retained and used for state forest, public park and public recreational purposes . . . shall forever be kept and remain in the natural
wild state . . . shall forever be kept and remain as a sanctuary for
beasts and birds."

Lest those that follow, uncertain of Governor Baxter's wishes, seek
to define his desires in ways inharmonious with their original intent,
this section is enacted.

It shall be the object of the Baxter State Park Authority to preserve
the grandeur and beauty of Maine's highest peak, Mount Katahdin, as
well as the 45 other mountains, the numerous lakes, ponds and
streams; to subordinate its own wishes to the intent of Governor Baxter; to recognize his wish that, in this era of change, one thing of
natural beauty remain constant.

This intent must be interpreted so as not to separate this park from
the people to whom it was given; but rather seek to have it enjoyed and
"used to the fullest extent but in the right unspoiled manner."

As a public forest it shall remain in its natural wild state and when
"the Forests of our State have been cut off and disappeared, when
civilization has encroached upon the land we now refer to as 'Wild
Land,' this park will give the people of succeeding generations a living
example of what the State of Maine was 'in the good old days' before
the song of the woodsman's axe and the whine of the power saw was
heard in the land."

As a public park and a place of recreation, it is apparent that it is
intended for "those persons who enjoy the wilderness" and that the
repeated use of the word "recreation" refers to the use of this park
compatible with its natural state as a wilderness area and an expanse
"for those who love nature and who are willing to walk and make an
effort to get close to nature . . . with pleasant foot-trails built and
attractive camp-sites laid out in the valleys, by the brooks, and on the
shores of the water."

As a tract kept in its "natural wild state," it is intended that "everything in connection with the park must be left simple and natural and
must remain as nearly as possible as it was when only the Indians
and the animals roamed at will through these areas. . . . " Access
to the park shall be provided only "as may be necessary to accommodate those persons who wish to enjoy the great unspoiled area that
now is the property of our State. . . . "

As a "sanctuary for beasts and birds" it shall be forever a "sanctuary
and home for the creatures of the wild," and as refuge "against hunting, trapping and killing" where "hunting with cameras will take the
place of hunting with guns."

While this area bears the name park, it is not to be confused with
the existing state park system and is to "be separately administered
free from any connection with the larger State Park Commission."
(Bureau of Parks and Recreation). That system, purchased with the
funds of the people, must change from time to time to accommodate
changing circumstances and the varying desires of its proprietors;
not so, Baxter State Park, purchased by the generosity of one man,
richly endowed, and presented to the people with specific stipulations.

"While I am living I fear no encroachments on the park, but as time
passes and new men appear upon the scene, there may be a tendency
to overlook these restrictions and thus break the spirit of these gifts."

Solemnly cognizant of the responsibility, it shall always be the purpose of the authority to satisfy the terms of the Trust.

MASSACHUSETTS CONSERVATION AND PRESERVATION
RESTRICTIONS (1969, as amended)
184 Ann. Laws Mass. 31 et seq.

§ 31.  Conservation and preservation restrictions; defined.

A conservation restriction means a right, whether or not stated in
the form of a restriction, easement, covenant or condition, in any
deed, will or other instrument executed by or on behalf of the owner
of the land or in any order of taking, appropriate to retaining land or
water areas predominantly in their natural, scenic or open condition
or in agricultural, farming or forest use, to forbid or limit any or
all (a) construction or placing of buildings, roads, signs, billboards
or other advertising, utilities or other structures on or above the
ground, (b) dumping or placing of soil or other substance or material
as landfill, or dumping or placing of trash, waste or unsightly or offensive materials, (c) removal or destruction of trees, shrubs or other
vegetation, (d) excavation, dredging or removal of loam, peat, gravel,
soil, rock or other mineral substance in such manner as to affect the
surface, (e) surface use except for agricultural, farming, forest or
outdoor recreational purposes or purposes permitting the land or
water area to remain predominantly in its natural condition, (f) activities detrimental to drainage, flood control, water conservation, erosion control or soil conservation, or (g) other acts or uses detrimental to such retention of land or water areas.

A preservation restriction means a right, whether or not stated in
the form of a restriction, easement, covenant or condition, in any
deed, will or other instrument executed by or on behalf of the owner
of the land or in any order of taking, appropriate to preservation of
a structure or site historically significant for its architecture, arch-
eology or associations, to forbid or limit any or all (a) alterations in
exterior or interior features of the structure, (b) changes in appearance or condition of the site (c) uses not historically appropriate, (d)
field investigation, as defined in section twenty-six A of chapter nine,
without a permit as provided by section twenty-seven C of said chapter, or (e) other acts or uses detrimental to appropriate preservation
of the structure or site.

§ 32.  Conservation and preservation restrictions; acquisition and effect of restrictions; approvals and releases, etc.

Such conservation and preservation restrictions are interests in
land and may be acquired by any governmental body or such charitable
corporation or trust which has power to acquire interest in land, in
the same manner as it may acquire other interests in land. . . .
Such a restriction may be released, in whole or in part, by the holder

for such consideration, if any, as the holder may determine, in the
same manner as the holder may dispose of land or other interests in
land, but only after a public hearing upon reasonable public notice,
by the governmental body holding the restriction or if held by a charitable corporation or trust, by the mayor, or in cities having a city
manager the city manager, and city council of the city or the selectmen of the town, whose approval shall be required, and in case of a
restriction requiring approval by the commissioner of natural resources or the Massachusetts historical commission, only with like approval of the release. . . .

In determining whether the restriction or its continuance is in the
public interest, the governmental body acquiring, releasing or approving shall take into consideration the public interest in such conservation or preservation, and any national, state, regional and local program in furtherance thereof, and also any public state, regional or
local comprehensive land use or development plan affecting the land,
and any known proposal by a governmental body for use of the land.
. . .

§ 33.  Conservation and preservation restrictions; establishment,
form, etc. of public restriction tract indexes; filing of subsequent or
successive notices, etc.

Any city or town may file with the register of deeds for the county
or district in which it is situated a map or set of maps of the city or
town, to be known as the public restriction tract index, on which may
be indexed conservation and preservation restrictions and restrictions
held by any governmental body. . . .

Except in the case of a restriction noted on the certificate of title
of registered land subject thereto, or where the general location of
the restricted land is indicated on a zoning map published by a city
or town with a reference to a marginal note or list indicating the original or then holder of the restriction and the place of record in the public records of the instrument imposing the restriction, no conservation
or preservation restriction having the benefit of section thirty-two,
and no other restriction held by any governmental body, which is not
so indexed in the public restriction tract index shall be enforceable after thirty years from the recording of the instrument imposing it unless before the expiration of such thirty years there is similarly recorded a notice of restriction identifying the instrument and its place
of record in the public records and naming one or more of the owners
of record of each parcel of land to be affected by the notice, nor enforceable after twenty years from the recording of any such notice unless
before the expiration of twenty years another such notice is so recorded, and in each case the notice is indexed in the grantor index under
the owner or owners named.  Such notices may be given by any official

of a governmental body holding the restriction, by the commissioner of natural resources in case of a restriction approved by him, by the chairman or acting chairman of the Massachusetts historical commission in case of a restriction approved by it, or by any official of any charitable corporation or trust holding the restriction or whose purposes include, in case of a conservation restriction, the conservation of land or water areas, or, in case of a preservation restriction, the preservation of buildings or sites of historical significance.

NEW HAMPSHIRE CURRENT USE TAXATION (1973)
N.H. Rev. State Ann. Ch. 79-A

Section 79-A:25. Disposition of revenues
       79-A:26. Location of contiguous land in more than one taxing
               district

§ 79-A:1. Declaration of public interest.

It is hereby declared to be in the public interest to encourage the
preservation of open space in the state by providing a healthful and
attractive outdoor environment for work and recreation of the state's
citizens, by maintaining the character of the state's landscape, and
by conserving the land, water, forest, and wildlife resources. It is
further declared to be in public interest to prevent the conversion of
open space to more intensive use by the pressure of property taxation
at values incompatible with open space usage, with a minimum disturbance of the concept of ad valorem taxation. The means for encouraging preservation of open space authorized by this chapter are the
assessment of land value for property taxation on the basis of current
use and the acquisition of discretionary easements of development
rights by town or city governments.

§ 79-A:2. Definitions.

When appearing in this chapter:

VII. "Open space land" means any or all farm land, forest land, wetland, recreation land, flood plain, or wild land, as defined by this
section, and any currently undeveloped or unoccupied land that is so
designated by action of a town or city for a period of ten years or
more.

X. "Recreation land" means any undeveloped land open to the public
recreational use without entrance fee as determined and classified by
criteria developed by the state director of parks and the director of
fish and game and adopted by the board.

XI. "Use value" means in the case of open space land the valuation
per acre which the land would command if it were required to remain
henceforth in an open space qualifying use. This valuation will be determined by the assessor in accordance with the recommendations of
the board for the class, type, grade and location of land under consideration and its income-producing capability.

XII. "Wetland" shall mean any marsh, swamp or bog subject to permanent or periodic flooding, including the surrounding shore and including any soil designated as very poorly drained by the National Cooperative Soil Survey or as determined by criteria developed by the
board.

XIII. "Wild land" means any unimproved land upon which there are no detrimental structures and on which the owner is not substantially interfering with the natural ecological processes as determined and classified by criteria developed by the board.

§ 79-A:4. Powers and duties of board.

The board shall have the following powers and duties:

I. It shall meet at least annually, prior to February first, to review all past current use land values for open space land recommended by past boards, to review the open space land use criteria previously established, to establish such new criteria and values as legislation and land management practice may indicate, to establish a schedule of criteria and values to be recommended for the current tax year, and to recommend such changes and improvement in the administration of this chapter as experience and public reaction may recommend. . . .

§ 79-A:5. Assessment of open space land.

I. Notwithstanding the provisions of RSA 75:1, the selectmen or assessing officials shall appraise open space land, as classified under the provisions of this chapter, excluding any building, appurtenance or other improvement thereon, at valuations based upon the current use values established by the board.

II. No owner of land shall be entitled to have a particular parcel of his land classified for any tax year under the provisions of this chapter unless he shall have applied to the assessing officials on or before April fifteenth of said year, on a form approved by the board and provided by the commissioner to have his parcel of land so classified. . . .

IV. Prior to July first each year, the assessing officials shall determine if previously classified lands have been reapplied or have undergone a change in use so that the land use change tax may be levied against lands changed in use, according to RSA 79-A:7. . . .

§ 79-A:7. Land use change tax.

I. Land which has been classified as open space land on or after April 1, 1974 pursuant to this chapter shall be subject to a land use change tax when it is changed to a use which does not qualify for open space assessment. Said tax shall be at the rate of ten percent of the RSA 75:1 assessed value of the land changed to other than open space use. This tax shall be in addition to the annual real estate tax imposed upon such property. Nothing in this paragraph shall be construed to require payment of an additional land use change tax when the use is changed from one non-qualifying use to another non-qualifying use. . . .

CALIFORNIA ADMINISTRATION OF OPEN SPACE
PLANS (1970, as amended)
Cal. Government Code Sec. 65550 et seq.

§ 65563. Local open-space plans: Preparation, adoption, and submission.

On or before December 31, 1973, every city and county shall prepare, adopt and submit to the Secretary of the Resources Agency a local open-space plan for the comprehensive and long-range preservation and conservation of open-space land within its jurisdiction. Every city and county shall by August 31, 1972, prepare, adopt and submit to the Secretary of the Resources Agency, an interim open-space plan. . . .

§ 65564. Action program.

Every local open-space plan shall contain an action program consisting of specific programs which the legislative body intends to pursue in implementing its open-space plan.

§ 65567. Requirements as to building permits, subdivision maps, and zoning ordinances.

No building permit may be issued, no subdivision map approved, and no open-space zoning ordinance adopted, unless the proposed construction, subdivision or ordinance is consistent with the local open-space plan.

NEW YORK ACQUISITION OF OPEN SPACES
AND AREAS (1960, as amended)
N.Y. General Municipal Law Sec. 247

§ 247. Acquisition of open spaces and areas.

1. Definitions. For the purposes of this chapter an "open space" or "open area" is any space or area characterized by
　　(1) natural scenic beauty or,
　　(2) whose existing openness, natural condition, or present state of use, if retained, would enhance the present or potential value of abutting or surrounding urban development, or would maintain or enhance the conservation of natural or scenic resources. For purposes of this section natural resources shall include but not be limited to agricultural lands defined as open lands actually used in bona fide agricultural production.

2. The acquisition of interests or rights in real property for the preservation of open spaces and areas shall constitute a public purpose for which public funds may be expended or advanced, and any county,

city, town or village after due notice and a public hearing may acquire, by purchase, gift, grant, bequest, devise, lease or otherwise, the fee or any lesser interest, development right, easement, covenant, or other contractual right necessary to achieve the purposes of this chapter, to land within such municipality. . . .

3.  After acquisition of any such interest pursuant to this act the valuation placed on such an open space or area for purposes of real estate taxation shall take into account and be limited by the limitation on future use of the land.

FEDERAL

Recreational Trails

U.S. NATIONAL TRAILS SYSTEM (1968)
16 U.S.C. 1241 et seq.

§ 1241.  National trails system; establishment; Congressional declaration of policy; initial components.

(a) In order to provide for the ever-increasing outdoor recreation needs of an expanding population and in order to promote public access to, travel within, and enjoyment and appreciation of the open-air, outdoor areas of the Nation, trails should be established

(i) primarily, near the urban areas of the Nation, and

(ii) secondarily, within established scenic areas more remotely located.

(b) The purpose of this chapter is to provide the means for attaining these objectives by instituting a national system of recreation and scenic trails, by designating the Appalachian Trail and the Pacific Crest Trail as the initial components of that system, and by prescribing the methods by which, and standards according to which, additional components may be added to the system.

§ 1242. Composition of national trails system; recreation trails; scenic trails; connecting or side trails; uniform marker.

The national system of trails shall be composed of—

(a) National recreation trails, established as provided in section 1243 of this title, which will provide a variety of outdoor recreation uses in or reasonably accessible to urban areas.

(b) National scenic trails, established as provided in section 1244 of this title, which will be extended trails so located as to provide for maximum outdoor recreation potential and for the conservation and enjoyment of the nationally significant scenic, historic, natural, or cultural qualities of the areas through which such trails may pass.

(c) Connecting or side trails, established as provided in section 1245 of this title, which will provide additional points of public access to national recreation or national scenic trails or which will provide connections between such trails.

The Secretary of the Interior and the Secretary of Agriculture, in consultation with appropriate governmental agencies and public and private organizations, shall establish a uniform marker for the national trails system.

§ 1244. National scenic trails.

(a) Establishment and designation; Appalachian Trail, administration; Pacific Crest Trail; administration; advisory councils; composition.

National scenic trails shall be authorized and designated only by Act of Congress. There are hereby established as the initial National Scenic Trails:

(1) The Appalachian Trail. . . .

(2) The Pacific Crest Trail . . . shall be administered by the Secretary of Agriculture, in consultation with the Secretary of the Interior.

(b) Additional national scenic trails; feasibility studies; consultations; submission of proposals to the President and Congress; accompanying report.

The Secretary of the Interior, and the Secretary of Agriculture where lands administered by him are involved, shall make such additional studies as are herein or may hereafter be authorized by the Congress for the purpose of determining the feasibility and desirability of designating other trails as national scenic trails. . . .

(c) Routes subject to consideration for designation as national scenic trails.

The following routes shall be studied in accordance with the objectives outlined in subsection (b) of this section:
(1) Continental Divide Trail.
(2) Potomac Heritage Trail.
(3) Old Cattle Trail of the Southwest.
(4) Lewis and Clark Trail.
(5) Natchez Trace.
(6) North Country Trail.
(7) Kittanning Trail.
(8) Oregon Trail.
(9) Santa Fe Trail.
(10) Long Trail.
(11) Mormon Trail.
(12) Gold Rush Trails in Alaska.
(13) Mormon Battalion Trail.


STATES


Recreational Trails

KENTUCKY TRAILS SYSTEM (1974)
Ky. Rev. Stat. Sec. 148.610 et seq.

Section 148.610.    Purpose of trails system
        148.620.    Definitions
        148.630.    Classes of trails established
        148.640.    Criteria for various classes of trails
        148.650.    Establishment and designation of trails
        148.660.    Proposals for additions to system
        148.670.    Procedure for locating routes of trails
        148.680.    Information forwarded by state agencies
        148.690.    Determination of boundaries of rights-of-way
        148.700.    Acquisition of land or interest in land
        148.710.    Preservation of natural vegetation
        148.720.    Limitation on use of motorized vehicles

§ 148.610. Purpose of trails system.

(1) In order to provide for the ever-increasing outdoor recreation needs
of an expanding population and in order to promote public access to,
travel within, and enjoyment and appreciation of the outdoor, natural
and remote areas of the state, trails should be established in natural,
scenic areas of the state, and in and near urban areas.

§ 148.630. Classes of trails established.

The state system of trails shall be composed of:

(1) State scenic trails which will be extended trails so located as to
provide maximum potential for the appreciation of natural areas and
for the conservation and enjoyment of the significant scenic, historic,
natural, ecological, geological, and cultural qualities of the areas
through which such trails pass.  Each of these trails will be limited
exclusively to foot use, except that the use of horses or off-road motorized vehicles or nonmotorized bicycles may also be permitted on
segments of scenic trails where specifically designated by the department. . . .

(2) State recreation trails, which will provide a variety of outdoor
recreation uses in or reasonably accessible to urban areas.  These
trails may be of the following types: foot, horse, off-road motorized
vehicles or nonmotorized bicycles as specifically designated by the
department.

(3) Connecting or side trails, which will provide additional points of
public access to state recreation trails, state scenic trails, or which
will provide connections between such trails.  They shall be of the
nature of the trails they serve.

§ 148.650. Establishment and designation of trails.

(1) State scenic trails shall be established and designated by the department on lands administered by the department and on lands under the

jurisdiction of a state department, political subdivision, or private
lands providing:

(a) Such trails are not located in nor traverse any state-owned wildlife management area; and

(b) Such trails meet the criteria established in KRS 148.610 to
148.780 and supplementary criteria as may be prescribed by the department.

(2) The department may establish and designate state recreation trails
on lands administered by the department and on lands under the jurisdiction of a state department, political subdivision, or private lands
providing:

(a) Such trails are not located in nor traverse any state-owned wildlife management area;

(b) Such trails are reasonably accessible to urban areas;

(c) Such trails meet the criteria established in KRS 148.610 to
148.780 and supplementary criteria as may be prescribed by the department; and

(d) Fee simple, scenic easements, or other rights are obtained
from private landowners through which a state recreation trail may
pass. The department may establish and designate state recreation
trails on lands under the jurisdiction of a federal agency, when in the
opinion of the federal agency and the commissioner such lands may
be so developed under the provisions of federal law and the provisions
of paragraphs (b) and (c) of this subsection.

(3) As provided in this section, trails within park, forest, recreation
areas, state natural areas, or any other public area excluding state-
owned wildlife management areas may be established and designated
state recreation trails by the department.

(4) Connecting or side trails within park, forest, recreation areas,
or natural areas may be established, designated, and marked as components of a state recreation or state scenic trail.

§ 148.710. Preservation of natural vegetation, etc.

Within the exterior boundaries of the right of way, the natural vegetation shall be kept undisturbed except for any clearing required for
construction of the trail, occasional vistas, or trail-use facilities
described in KRS 148.750. The department shall make every effort
to avoid any use of the right of way that is incompatible with the purposes for which the trails were established. Development and management of each segment of the state trails system shall be designed
to harmonize with and complement any established multiple-use plans
for that specific area in order to insure continual maximum benefits
from the land. Other uses along the trail which will not substantially

interfere with the nature and purposes of the trail may be permitted
by the department; Provided, That the owner of real property adjacent
to any part of the system may hunt on that portion of the system which
is adjacent to his property.

§ 148.720.  Limitation on use of motorized vehicles.

The use of motorized vehicles by the general public within the right
of way of any state scenic or recreation trail shall be prohibited and
nothing in KRS 148.610 to 148.780 shall be construed as authorizing
the use of motorized vehicles in these rights of way; Provided, That
the department shall establish regulations which shall authorize the
use of motorized vehicles when such vehicles are required to meet
emergencies where life or health is at risk for the maintenance of established trails, or to enable present or adjacent landowners or land
users to have access to their lands or timber rights where no reasonable alternative method of access exists or could be constructed. . . .

OKLAHOMA TRAILS SYSTEM ACT (1974, as amended)
74 Okla. Stat. Ann. 3451 et seq.

Section 3451.  Short title
        3452.  Definitions
        3453.  Purpose
        3454.  State trails system created—type of trails—planning
        3455.  Commission to supervise planning, construction, oper-
               ation, and maintenance of trails system
        3456.  Trails on federal lands—coordination with National
               Trails System
        3457.  Violations—penalties
        3458.  Limitation of liability of owners of land used for recrea-
               tional purposes.

§ 3453.  Purpose.

The purpose of the Oklahoma Trails System Act is to provide public
access to, and enjoyment and appreciation of, the Oklahoma outdoors
in order to foster the conservation, development and wise use of the
natural and historic resources of the state.  It is the intent and purpose
of the Oklahoma Trail System Act to encourage hiking, bicycling,
horseback riding and other recreational activities and, because trail
use by motorized vehicles is incompatible with some other trail uses,
it is intended to provide separate trails and facilities for motorized
vehicles whenever necessary and feasible.

§ 3454. State trails system created; type of trails; planning.

A. There is hereby created a state trails system composed of:

1. State nature trails, which will be trails designed to deepen the public's awareness and understanding of various ecological, geological or cultural qualities within the state by means of an interpretive service program;

2. State hiking trails, which will be extensive trails and will serve to connect parks, scenic areas, historical points and neighboring communities;

3. State special-use trails, which will be trails designed to provide for those trail activities which require special trail definition and will include trails for bicycling, public riding and motorcycle and minibike activities, as well as trails designed to meet the needs of the handicapped, the blind and the elderly; and

4. State heritage trails, which will be trails designed to promote the identification and interpretation of significant cultural and historic sites throughout the state.

B. The Commission, in accordance with appropriate federal, state and local governmental organizations, shall establish a uniform marker for the trails system.

C. In the planning and designation of trails, the Commission shall give due regard to the interest of federal or state agencies, all political subdivisions, private land owners, interested individuals and citizen groups. Furthermore, the Commission encourages citizen participation in trail acquisition, construction, development and maintenance where such activities will not conflict with the purposes of this act.

§ 3455. Commission to supervise planning, construction, operation and maintenance of trails system—powers and duties.

A. The Commission shall be vested with the responsibility and authority to: . . .

2. Acquire, by lease, deed or contract, rights-of-way or easements of trails across private, municipal, county, state or federal lands. In selecting the rights-of-way, every effort will be made to minimize any adverse effects on the adjacent landowner or user and his operations. . . .

B. The Commission may abandon any portion or all of a trail or easement acquired for trail purposes; or it may transfer any trail or easement to a local government having jurisdiction over the area in which the trail or easement is located, provided that such local government agrees to maintain and operate the trail. . . .

D.  The Commission shall review all formal declarations of railroad
rights-of-way abandonment for possible inclusion into the state trails
system. . . .

F.  1.  The Commission shall encourage the provision of bicycle
routes within the rights-of-way of federal aid system highways and
on or along . . . city roadways.  These bicycle routes will be composed of three (3) types of pathways:  bicycle trails, bicycle lanes and
bicycle routes. . . .

2.  Prior to the designation and construction of the bicycle pathway
system, the Commission will authorize the development of a bicycle
master plan.  This plan will be comprised of a set of clearly defined
goals, a statement of current and projected demands, a proposed layout of routes, construction specifications, cost projections and the
scheduling of implementation.  This plan will likewise devote serious
consideration to those design criteria which will help to insure the
safety of bicyclist, pedestrian and motorist alike.

Noise as a form of pollution is a relatively new concern. It is now known that excessive noise, besides being unpleasant, may also have severe ill-effects on human health. The problem lies in the definition of "excessive." Municipal noise ordinances and state laws set decibel limits but these are not always easy to enforce. A more promising avenue may be to control sources of noise in the same way that the air and water pollution laws control sources of air and water pollution. This the Noise Control Act of 1972 (p. 258) attempts to do. A selection from the Council on Environmental Quality's Fourth Annual Report (pp. 195-200) explicates the provisions of that act:

Noise

Noise affects all urban residents—in factories, in offices, near construction sites, at places of recreation, and even at home. In the past, noise was almost exclusively a local problem. Early municipal ordinances prohibited noise considered excessively or unreasonably loud. They focused on auto horns, steamboat whistles, radio loudspeakers, and sound trucks. In more recent years, the number and character of sources of noise have changed. As instruments for quantitative measurement of noise have been developed, precise numerical limits have replaced general restrictions in noise control regulations.

Noise was long accepted as a necessary though sometimes unpleasant part of living. Now it is regarded as a controllable pollutant which should be regulated. This new attitude is reflected in the Noise Control Act of 1972. The Act calls for extensive Federal regulation of major noise sources,

preempting to some extent state and local controls. The
resulting interplay among the levels of government will be
an important feature in the success of noise control efforts
in future years.

The Noise Control Act of 1972 gives the Federal Government a major new role in controlling noise problems. Regulation over new products is made a Federal responsibility.
But there is still room—and need—for vigorous local action.
Federal controls, except those for aircraft, trucks, and
railroad operations, apply only to the noise emissions of
products, not to the time, place, or manner of their use.
For example, although Federal regulation will cut the noise
generated by new construction equipment, local regulation
and enforcement will still govern its maintenance and set
the hours for its use. Communities may also wish to restrict
traffic and other noise-generating activities at times.

The most significant source of noise is transportation—
airplanes, automobiles, trucks, buses, and railroads. . . .

The Noise Control Act of 1972 directs the Environmental Protection Agency to conduct a thorough study and report
to the Congress by July 27, 1973, on the aircraft and airport noise problem, including assessment of current FAA
flight and operational noise controls, noise emission controls
and possibilities for retrofitting or phasing out existing aircraft, possibilities for establishing cumulative noise level
limits around airports, and control measures available to
airport operators and local governments. Following completion of the report, EPA is directed to propose for adoption
by the FAA any regulations on aircraft noise and sonic boom
that are necessary to protect public health and welfare. . . .

Noise from other modes of transportation—autos, trucks,
and buses—until recently has been regulated, if at all, at
the state and local levels. . . .

The Noise Control Act of 1972 preempts state and local
governments from establishing noise emission standards
applicable to the sale of new vehicles. It follows the precedent of the Clean Air Act by requiring EPA to set national
standards.

The Act also contains special provisions requiring EPA
to establish noise emission limits for the operation of railroads and motor carriers engaged in interstate commerce
and directing the Department of Transportation to issue regulations ensuring compliance. The EPA regulations will
supplement those which may be adopted for new trucks,
buses, and railroad equipment. The Act prohibits state and

local regulation of noise from these sources unless it is identical to Federal standards. State and local regulation is permitted, however, if required by special local conditions and if determined by EPA not to conflict with its regulations.

The EPA-DOT/FAA authorities for regulating transportation noise sources are part of a broader mandate under the Noise Control Act to set emission standards for new products which are major noise sources and for which standards are feasible—construction equipment; transportation equipment, including any in which an engine or motor is an integral part; and electric or electronic equipment. The Administrator of EPA must promulgate initial noise limits for products in these categories by October 1974. He has discretionary authority to regulate any other product whose noise may endanger public health or welfare.

The Noise Control Act empowers EPA to require that manufacturers label any product that emits noise capable of adversely affecting public health or welfare. EPA may also require labeling of products effective in reducing noise. . . .

Besides requiring the setting of emission standards for products that are major sources of noise pollution—construction equipment, transportation equipment, motor vehicles and engines, electrical and electronic equipment—the act also amends earlier provisions for control and abatement of aircraft noise (p. 265). Aircraft noise regulation remains a knotty problem as evidenced by disputes between the states of New York and New Jersey and the federal Department of Transportation over permitting landings of the Concorde supersonic airplane.

The Federal Aid Highway Act directs the setting of highway noise levels (23 U.S.C. 109[i]) and requires consideration of the costs of minimizing noise pollution in determining highway projects (Sec. 109[h][1], p. 423). Similar requirements must be observed in the planning of mass transportation projects (49 U.S.C. 1604[h][2], p. 440).

States may only act in areas not preempted by the federal government. Thus, the ambient noise level on highways is a proper subject for state action and Connecticut's law is quoted as an example (p. 266). California has similar legislation for its roads and, additionally, sets noise limits for motor vehicles registered in the state, including snowmobiles (Vehicle Code Sec. 27160 et seq.). Florida prohibits the sale or lease of motor vehicles, including motor-driven cycles, producing noise levels in excess of stated limits (Fla. Stats. Sec. 403.415). Mufflers and other potentially noise-producing portions of automobiles (exhaust pipe, horn) are regulated by the laws of most states.

Maryland mandates comprehensive environmental noise standards (p. 267). Washington seeks the setting of maximum noise levels and performance standards "to insure that the maximum noise levels are not exceeded and that application of the best practicable noise control technology and practice is provided." Maximum noise levels "shall take into account the economic and practical benefits . . . whether the source of the noise . . . is permanent or temporary in nature, and the state of technology relative to the control of noise generated by all such sources of the noise or the products" (Rev. Code Wash. Sec. 70.107.030). North Dakota regulates noise from farm machinery, construction equipment, motor vehicles, musical instruments, and so on as part of its Health and Safety Code (Sec. 23-01-17).

Constitutional articles in Massachusetts and New York aim at protection from "excessive and unnecessary noise." The Massachusetts legislature also includes "excessive noise" in its definition of "damage to the environment" for the purposes of environmental impact reports and citizen suits (Sec. 30-61 and 214-7A). In New York, noise abatement is a factor in granting power plant construction permits (Public Service Law Sec. 142).

Minnesota has moved to contain airport noise through its Airport Zoning Act (see Chapter 13).

## FEDERAL

### NOISE CONTROL ACT (1972)
### 42 U.S.C. 4901 et seq.

Section 4901. Congressional findings and statement of policy
 4902. Definitions
 4903. Federal programs
 4904. Identification of major noise sources
 4905. Noise emission standards for products distributed in commerce
 4906. Aircraft noise standards
 4907. Labeling
 4908. Imports
 4909. Prohibited acts
 4910. Enforcement
 4911. Citizen suits
 4912. Records, reports, and information
 4913. Research, technical assistance, and public information
 4914. Development of low-noise-emission products
 4915. Judicial review

§ 4901.   Congressional findings and statement of policy.

(a) The Congress finds—

(1) that inadequately controlled noise presents a growing danger to the health and welfare of the Nation's population, particularly in urban areas;

(2) that the major sources of noise include transportation vehicles and equipment, machinery, appliances, and other products in commerce; and

(3) that, while primary responsibility for control of noise rests with State and local governments, Federal action is essential to deal with major noise sources in commerce control of which require national uniformity of treatment.

(b) The Congress declares that it is the policy of the United States to promote an environment for all Americans free from noise that jeopardizes their health or welfare.  To that end, it is the purpose of this chapter to establish a means for effective coordination of Federal research and activities in noise control, to authorize the establishment of Federal noise emission standards for products distributed in commerce, and to provide information to the public respecting the noise emission and noise reduction characteristics of such products.

§ 4903.   Federal programs.

(b) Presidential authority to exempt activities or facilities from compliance requirements.

Each department, agency, or instrumentality of the executive, legislative, and judicial branches of the Federal Government—

(1) having jurisdiction over any property or facility, or

(2) engaged in any activity resulting, or which may result, in the emission of noise,

shall comply with Federal, State, interstate, and local requirements respecting control and abatement of environmental noise to the same extent that any person is subject to such requirements.  The President may exempt any single activity or facility, including noise emission sources or classes thereof, of any department, agency, or instrumentality in the executive branch from compliance with any such requirement if he determines it to be in the paramount interest of the United States to do so; . . .

§ 4904.  Identification of major noise sources.

(a) Development and publication of criteria.

(1) The Administrator shall, after consultation with appropriate Federal agencies and within nine months of October 27, 1972, develop and publish criteria with respect to noise.  Such criteria shall reflect the scientific knowledge most useful in indicating the kind and extent of all identifiable effects on the public health or welfare which may be expected from differing quantities and qualities of noise.

(2) The Administrator shall, after consultation with appropriate Federal agencies and within twelve months of October 27, 1972, publish information on the levels of environmental noise the attainment and maintenance of which in defined areas under various conditions are requisite to protect the public health and welfare with an adequate margin of safety.

(b) Compilation and publication of reports on noise sources and control technology.

The Administrator shall, after consultation with appropriate Federal agencies, compile and publish a report or series of reports

(1) identifying products (or classes of products) which in his judgment are major sources of noise, and

(2) giving information on techniques for control of noise from such products, including available data on the technology, costs, and alternative methods of noise control.
The first such report shall be published not later than eighteen months after October 27, 1972. . . .

§ 4905.  Noise emission standards for products distributed in commerce.

(a) Proposed regulations.

(1) The Administrator shall publish proposed regulations, meeting the requirements of subsection (c) of this section, for each product—

(A) which is identified (or is part of a class identified) in any report published under section 4904(b)(1) of this title as a major source of noise,

(B) for which, in his judgment, noise emission standards are feasible, and

(C) which falls in one of the following categories:

(i) Construction equipment.

(ii) Transportation equipment (including recreational vehicles and related equipment).

(iii) Any motor or engine (including any equipment of which an engine or motor is an integral part).

(iv) Electrical or electronic equipment.

(b) Authority to publish regulations not otherwise required.

The Administrator may publish proposed regulations, meeting the
requirements of subsection (c) of this section, for any product for
which he is not required by subsection (a) of this section to prescribe
regulations but for which, in his judgment, noise emission standards
are feasible and are requisite to protect the public health and welfare.
Not earlier than six months after the date of publication of such proposed regulations respecting such product, he may prescribe regulations, meeting the requirements of subsection (c) of this section, for
such product.

(c) Contents of regulations; appropriate consideration of other standards; participation by interested persons; revision.
(1) Any regulation prescribed under subsection (a) or (b) of this
section (and any revision thereof) respecting a product shall include
a noise emission standard which shall set limits on noise emissions
from such product and shall be a standard which in the Administrator's
judgment, based on criteria published under section 4904 of this title,
is requisite to protect the public health and welfare, taking into account
the magnitude and conditions of use of such product (alone or in combination with other noise sources), the degree of noise reduction
achievable through the application of the best available technology,
and the cost of compliance. . . .
(2) After publication of any proposed regulations under this section,
the Administrator shall allow interested persons an opportunity to
participate in rulemaking. . . .

(d) Warranty by manufacturer of conformity of product with regulations; transfer of cost obligation from manufacturer to dealer prohibited.
(1) On and after the effective date of any regulation prescribed under
subsection (a) or (b) of this section, the manufacturer of each new product to which such regulation applies shall warrant to the ultimate purchaser and each subsequent purchaser that such product is designed,
built, and equipped so as to conform at the time of sale with such regulation.

(e) State and local regulations.
(1) No State or political subdivision thereof may adopt or enforce—
(A) with respect to any new product for which a regulation has
been prescribed by the Administrator under this section, any law
or regulation which sets a limit on noise emissions from such new
product and which is not identical to such regulation of the Administrator; or
(B) with respect to any component incorporated into such new
product by the manufacturer of such product , any law or regulation

setting a limit on noise emissions from such component when so incorporated.

(2) Subject to sections 4916 and 4917 of this title, nothing in this section precludes or denies the right of any State or political subdivision thereof to establish and enforce controls on environmental noise (or one or more sources thereof) through the licensing, regulation, or restriction of the use, operation, or movement of any product or combination of products.

§ 4906. Aircraft noise standards.

The Administrator, after consultation with appropriate Federal, State, and local agencies and interested persons, shall conduct a study of the

(1) adequacy of Federal Aviation Administration flight and operational noise controls;

(2) adequacy of noise emission standards on new and existing aircraft, together with recommendations on the retrofitting and phaseout of existing aircraft;

(3) implications of identifying and achieving levels of cumulative noise exposure around airports; and

(4) additional measures available to airport operators and local governments to control aircraft noise. He shall report on such study to the Committee on Interstate and Foreign Commerce of the House of Representatives and the Committees on Commerce and Public Works of the Senate within nine months after October 27, 1972.

§ 4907. Labeling.

(a) Regulations.

The Administrator shall by regulation designate any product (or class thereof)—

(1) which emits noise capable of adversely affecting the public health or welfare; or

(2) which is sold wholly or in part on the basis of its effectiveness in reducing noise.

(b) Manner of notice; form; methods and units of measurement.

For each product (or class thereof) designated under subsection (a) of this section the Administrator shall by regulation require that notice be given to the prospective user of the level of the noise the product emits, or of its effectiveness in reducing noise, as the case may be.

. . .

§ 4908. Imports.

The Secretary of the Treasury shall, in consultation with the Administrator, issue regulations to carry out the provisions of this chapter with respect to new products imported or offered for importation.

§ 4910. Enforcement.

(a) Criminal penalties.

Any person who willfully or knowingly violates paragraph (1), (3), (5), or (6) of subsection (a) of section 4909 of this title shall be punished by a fine of not more than $25,000 per day of violation, or by imprisonment for not more than one year, or by both. If the conviction is for a violation committed after a first conviction of such person under this subsection, punishment shall be by a fine of not more than $50,000 per day of violation, or by imprisonment for not more than two years, or by both.

§ 4913. Research, technical assistance, and public information.

In furtherance of his responsibilities under this chapter and to complement, as necessary, the noise-research programs of other Federal agencies, the Administrator is authorized to:

(1) Conduct research, and finance research by contract with any person, on the effects, measurement, and control of noise, including but not limited to—

(A) investigation of the psychological and physiological effects of noise on humans and the effects of noise on domestic animals, wildlife, and property, and determination of acceptable levels of noise on the basis of such effects;

(B) development of improved methods and standards for measurement and monitoring of noise, in cooperation with the National Bureau of Standards, Department of Commerce; and

(C) determination of the most effective and practicable means of controlling noise emission.

(2) Provide technical assistance to State and local governments to facilitate their development and enforcement of ambient noise standards, including but not limited to—

(A) advice on training of noise-control personnel and on selection and operation of noise-abatement equipment; and

(B) preparation of model State or local legislation for noise control.

(3) Disseminate to the public information on the effects of noise, acceptable noise levels, and techniques for noise measurement and control.

§ 4914.  Development of low-noise-emission products.

(a) Definitions

   For the purpose of this section:
   (3) The term "low-noise-emission product" means any product which
emits noise in amounts significantly below the levels specified in noise
emission standards under regulations applicable under section 4905 of
this title at the time of procurement to that type of product.

(b) Certification of products; Low-Noise-Emission Product Advisory
Committee.
   (1) The Administrator shall determine which products qualify as
low-noise-emission products in accordance with the provisions of this
section.
   (2) The Administrator shall certify any product. . . .
       (C) which he determines is suitable for use as a substitute for a
   type of product at that time in use by agencies of the Federal Government. . . .

(c) Federal procurement of low-noise-emission products.
   (1) Certified low-noise-emission products shall be acquired by purchase or lease by the Federal Government for use by the Federal
Government in lieu of other products if the Administrator of General
Services determines that such certified products have procurement
costs which are no more than 125 per centum of the retail price of the
least expensive type of product for which they are certified substitutes.

§ 4916.  Railroad noise emission standards.

(a) Regulations; standards; consultation with Secretary of Transportation.
   (1) Within nine months after October 27, 1972, the Administrator
shall publish proposed noise emission regulations for surface carriers
engaged in interstate commerce by railroad.  Such proposed regulations shall include noise emission standards setting such limits on
noise emissions resulting from operation of the equipment and facilities of surface carriers engaged in interstate commerce by railroad
which reflect the degree of noise reduction achievable through the application of the best available technology, taking into account the cost
of compliance.  These regulations shall be in addition to any regulations that may be proposed under section 4905 of this title. . . .
   (4) Any regulation or revision thereof promulgated under this subsection shall take effect after such period as the Administrator finds
necessary, after consultation with the Secretary of Transportation,
to permit the development and application of the requisite technology,
giving appropriate consideration to the cost of compliance within such
period.

§ 4917. Motor carrier noise emission standards.

(a) Regulations; standards; consultation with Secretary of Transportation.

(1) Within nine months after October 27, 1972, the Administrator shall publish proposed noise emission regulations for motor carriers engaged in interstate commerce. Such proposed regulations shall include noise emission standards setting such limits on noise emissions resulting from operation of motor carriers engaged in interstate commerce which reflect the degree of noise reduction achievable through the application of the best available technology, taking into account the cost of compliance. These regulations shall be in addition to any regulations that may be proposed under section 4905 of this title.

(4) Any regulation or revision thereof promulgated under this subsection shall take effect after such period as the Administrator finds necessary, after consultation with the Secretary of Transportation, to permit the development and application of the requisite technology, giving appropriate consideration to the cost of compliance within such period.

CONTROL AND ABATEMENT OF AIRCRAFT
NOISE (1968, as amended)
49 U.S.C. 1431

§ 1431. Control and abatement of aircraft noise and sonic boom—definitions.

(a) For purposes of this section:

(1) The term "FAA" means Administrator of the Federal Aviation Administration.

(2) The term "EPA" means the Administrator of the Environmental Protection Agency.

(b) (1) In order to afford present and future relief and protection to the public health and welfare from aircraft noise and sonic boom, the FAA, after consultation with the Secretary of Transportaion and with EPA, shall prescribe and amend standards for the measurement of aircraft noise and sonic boom and shall prescribe and amend such regulations as the FAA may find necessary to provide for the control and abatement of aircraft noise and sonic boom, including the application of such standards and regulations in the issuance, amendment, modification, suspension, or revocation of any certificate authorized by this subchapter. . . .

(2) The FAA shall not issue an original type certificate under section 1423(a) of this title for any aircraft for which substantial noise abatement can be achieved by prescribing standards and regulations in accordance with this section, unless he shall have prescribed standards

and regulations in accordance with this section which apply to such aircraft and which protect the public from aircraft noise and sonic boom, consistent with the considerations listed in subsection (d) of this section. . . .

## STATES

CONNECTICUT HIGHWAY NOISE CONTROL
(1971, as amended)
14 Conn. Gen. Stat. Sec. 80 et seq.

§ 14-80. Mechanical equipment. . . .

(d) Every motor vehicle when operated upon a highway shall be equipped with a horn in good working order and capable of emitting sound audible under normal conditions from a distance of not less than two hundred feet, but no horn or other warning device shall emit an unreasonably loud or harsh sound or a whistle. No vehicle shall be equipped with, nor shall any person use upon a vehicle, any siren, whistle or bell as a warning signal device, except as otherwise permitted in this section. . . .

(e) Each motor vehicle and the devices thereon shall be so operated, equipped, constructed and adjusted as to prevent unnecessary or unusual noise. No article, device, sticker or ornament shall be attached to, affixed to or hung on or in any motor vehicle in such a manner or location as to interfere with an unobstructed view of the highway upon which any person is operating such motor vehicle or to distract the attention of the operator.

§ 14-80a. Maximum noise levels.

(a) For the purposes of this section, "vehicle" means any vehicle, as defined in subdivision (56) of section 14-1 and "dB(A)" means decibels measured with a calibrated sound level meter weighted to the "A" scale.

(b) No person shall operate, on or after January 1, 1973, a vehicle or combination of vehicles, nor shall the owner of any vehicle allow such vehicle to be operated, at any time or under any condition of grade, surface, speed, load, acceleration, deceleration or weather condition in such a manner as to exceed the decibel levels established under subsection (d). This subsection applies to the total noise generated by a vehicle and shall not be construed as limiting or precluding the enforcement of any other motor vehicle noise provisions of this title.

(c) No person shall sell or offer for sale after January 1, 1975, a new vehicle which produces a maximum decibel level which exceeds the decibel levels established under subsection (d).

(d) The commissioner of motor vehicles shall, with the advice of the commissioner of environmental protection, establish by regulation the maximum decibel levels, which shall not exceed

(1) 90 dB (A), in 1973 and 1974; 88 dB (A) in 1975 and 1976, and 86 dB (A) in 1977 and thereafter, for noise emitted by vehicles operated in the state and

(2) 85 dB (A) in 1975 and thereafter for vehicles sold or offered for sale in the state.

The commissioner of motor vehicles shall establish the procedure for checking such decibel levels. Said decibel level shall be measured fifty feet from the centerline of the vehicle. The commissioner of motor vehicles may provide for measuring at distances closer than fifty feet from the centerline of the vehicle. In such a case, the measuring devices shall be so calibrated as to provide for measurements equivalent to the noise limit established by this section measured at fifty feet.

(e) Any person who violates the provisions of this section shall be fined not less than twenty-five dollars nor more than one hundred dollars.

### MARYLAND ENVIRONMENTAL NOISE CONTROL (1974)
### Md. Code Art. 43, Sec. 822 et seq.

§ 822. Legislative findings and declarations.

The General Assembly of Maryland finds and declares that:

(a) The people of this State have a right to an environment free from noise that may jeopardize their health, general welfare, and property, or that degrades their quality of life;

(b) A substantial body of knowledge exists concerning the adverse effects of excessive noise on the public health, general welfare, and property;

(c) This knowledge should be used to establish environmental noise standards which will protect the public health and general welfare with an adequate margin of safety;

(d) Coordination and statewide leadership of the noise control and abatement activities of many State agencies, county and local governments is essential.

§ 823. Definitions.

(a) In this subtitle, the following words have the meanings indicated.
. . .

(c) "Noise" means the intensity, frequency, duration, and character of sound. Noise includes sound and vibration of subaudible frequencies.

(d) "Environmental noise" means the noise that exists at any location from all sources.

(e) "Environmental noise standards" means the goals for environmental noise, the attainment and maintenance of which, in defined areas and under specified conditions are necessary to protect the public health and general welfare.

§ 824. Responsibility of Department.

The department has the responsibility for the establishment of State ambient noise standards, the coordination of State efforts in the control of noise, the development of a plan for the achievement of the ambient noise standards, and the promulgation of regulations controlling noise emanating from activities on private real property, except as otherwise provided for in the Code.

§ 828. Environmental noise standards; sound level limits and regulations.

(a) Establishment of standards.

The Department shall prepare and submit environmental noise standards to the noise council for comment not later than January 1, 1975, and shall, after receipt of the council's action and comments, promptly adopt such standards, giving due consideration to the council's action and comments.

In establishing environmental noise standards, the Department shall take into consideration scientific information concerning the volume, frequency, duration and other characteristics of noise which may adversely affect public health, safety, or general welfare. Such effects shall include temporary or permanent hearing loss, interference with sleep, speech communication, work or other human activities, adverse physiological responses or psychological distress, adverse effects on animal life, devaluation or damage of property, and unreasonable interference with the enjoyment of life or property. The Department shall also take into consideration information published by the Administrator of the U.S. Environmental Protection Agency pursuant to § 5 (a) (2) of the Noise Control Act of 1972.

(b) Adoption of sound level limits and regulations.

(1) The Department shall adopt, not later than January 1, 1976, sound level limits for various categories of land use to control noise emanating from activities on private real property, not otherwise specifically provided for in the Code. Such limits shall be applied at the boundary of a property or a land use category, as determined by the Department. They shall be consistent with the environmental noise standards established pursuant to subsection (a) of this section.

(2) The Department shall then promulgate regulations for the administration and enforcement of such limits taking into account accepted scientific and professional methods for measurement of sound levels.

(3) In preparing limits and regulations, the Department shall consider, among other things, the residential, commercial or industrial nature of the area affected, zoning, the nature and source of various kinds of environmental noise, the degree of noise reduction achievable through the application of the best available technology, and the cost of compliance.

(c) Hearing.

No standard, limit, or regulation shall be adopted by the Department except after public hearings. . . .

§ 829.  Identification of sound level limits on zoning maps, etc.

The political subdivisions shall identify on all zoning maps, comprehensive plans, and other appropriate documents the sound level limits established pursuant to § 828 (b) of the subtitle.

§ 832.  County or municipal ordinances.

Nothing in this subtitle shall preclude the right of any county or municipality to adopt ordinances or regulations providing for noise control for noise emanating from activities on private real property, provided that said ordinances or regulations are not less stringent than those embodied in State regulations promulgated pursuant to this subtitle. . . .

CHAPTER

# 8

**OCEANS**

A number of treaties and international conventions govern activities on the high seas. Such an international agreement is binding only on those nations that have ratified it and is effective to the extent those nations' domestic laws enforce treaty obligations. Among such agreements to which the United States is a party are the Convention on the Continental Shelf of 1958, enforced by 43 U.S.C. 1331 et seq.; the International Convention for Safety of Life at Sea and the International Regulations for Preventing Collissions at Sea of 1948, enforced by 33 U.S.C. 1051 et seq.; the Convention on the Prevention of Marine Pollution by Dumping from Ships of 1972, enforced by 33 U.S.C. 1401 et seq.; the International Convention for the Prevention of Pollution of the Sea by Oil of 1954, enforced by 33 U.S.C. 1001 et seq.; the International Convention Relating to Intervention on the High Seas in Cases of Oil Pollution Casualties of 1969, enforced by 33 U.S.C. 1471 et seq.; and the Whaling Convention of 1949, enforced by 16 U.S.C. 916 et seq.

While nations have thus obligated themselves to some extent to regulating pollution, collisions, and safety on the high seas, they have at the same time progressively extended their own definitions of territorial waters. The three-mile limit was the accepted standards in an age of simpler technology. It is giving way to pressures arising from the development of super tankers and fishing fleets that double as sea-going processing plants and from discovery of valuable resources in the sea and its floor. None of the international agreements now in effect even partially offers controls for the conservation of mineral resources.

Several conferences have been convened under the auspices of the United Nations for the purpose of arriving at an International Law of the Sea Convention. Such efforts so far have proved unsuccessful.

In fact, Congress, just weeks before the March 1976 Law of the Sea conference took place on U.S. soil, extended U.S. controls over fishing rights 200 miles from the coast to ban foreign nationals from waters traditionally fished by American fleets.

This chapter includes two treaties ratified by the United States and enacted into domestic law and other legislation dealing with ocean waters and the ocean floor. They define the jurisdiction of the United States and the states and subject certain activities in ocean waters to permit procedures while entirely prohibiting others.

Jurisdiction over U.S. waters is divided between the nation and the states. The federal government, in the Submerged Lands Act of 1953 (p. 272), gave up title to "lands beneath navigable waters" within the boundaries of each state. Such lands are to extend from "the line of mean high tide and seaward to a line three geographical miles distant from the coastline" and include "all filled in, made or reclaimed lands which formerly were lands beneath navigable waters" (Sec. 1301[a]). The Coastal Zone Management Act authorizes state management programs "in the national interest" within this zone (Sec. 1455[c][8], p. 180). Lands of the outer continental shelf, that is, "all submerged lands lying seaward and outside of the area of lands beneath navigable waters" (43 U.S.C. 1331[a], p. 275), remain under federal control.

Coastal zone and tidal wetlands legislation, including state laws and constitutional provisions governing beach access, is considered in Chapter 5.

The Oil Pollution Act of 1961 (p. 276) enforces the provisions of the International Convention for the Prevention of the Pollution of the Sea by Oil and prohibits oil discharges within 50 nautical miles from the nearest land. The Marine Protection, Research, and Sanctuaries Act of 1972 (p. 278) requires federal permits for ocean dumping and is known as the "Ocean Dumping Act." It in part parallels the International Convention on Prevention of Marine Pollution. The Federal Water Pollution Control Act governs ocean discharges in Section 1343 and oil and hazardous substances in Section 1321 (pp. 484, 481), supplementing these two acts.

Interest in off-shore oil drilling and the growth of supertankers in recent years spurred enactment of the Ports and Waterways Safety Act of 1973 (p. 283). It directs the Coast Guard to prescribe rules and regulations for oil tankers, among others, in order to protect the marine environment. The Deepwater Port Act of 1974 (p. 285) directs licensing of construction and operation of deepwater ports beyond the three-mile limit.

Several coastal states have responded to the same problem, including Louisiana, which has a public authority with the function of developing deepwater ports in the state's coastal waters, subject to an environmental plan (p. 292).

Ocean dumping is the object of state as well as federal legislation. A Massachusetts statute of 1972 prohibits thermal and toxic as
well as oil discharges into coastal waters (p. 297). New Jersey's
Clean Ocean Act of 1971 (p. 298) extends controls over the dumping of
sewage, industrial wastes, dredged spoils, and other materials.
Florida's Air and Water Pollution Control Act extends specifically to
"brackish, saline, tidal" waters (Sec. 403.031[3], p. 492) and has
been upheld, as has Maine's Oil Discharge Prevention and Pollution
Control Act of 1970 (38 Maine Rev. Stat. 541 et seq.).

California's state park system permits state parks in the "underwater environment" of the state. One of our national parks, the Virgin Islands National Park, includes submerged lands (16 U.S.C. 398c).


## FEDERAL


## SUBMERGED AND OUTER CONTINENTAL SHELF
## LANDS ACTS (1953)
## 43 U.S.C. 1301 et seq.

Section 1301. Definitions
       1302. Resources seaward of the Continental Shelf
       1303. Amendment, modification, or repeal of other laws.
Subchapter II—Lands Beneath Navigable Waters within State Boundaries
Section 1311. Rights of the States
       1312. Seaward boundaries of States
       1313. Exceptions from confirmation and establishment of
             States' title, power and rights
       1314. Rights and powers retained by the United States; pur-
             chase of natural resources; condemnation of lands
       1315. Rights acquired under laws of the United States unaf-
             fected
Subchapter III—Outer Continental Shelf Lands
Section 1331. Definitions
       1332. Congressional declaration of policy; jurisdiction;
             construction
       1333. Laws and regulations governing lands
       1334. Administration of leasing
       1335. Validation and maintenance of prior leases
       1336. Controversies over jurisdiction; agreements; pay-
             ments; final settlement or adjudication; approval of
             notice concerning oil and gas operations in Gulf of
             Mexico
       1337. Grant of leases by Secretary

§ 1301. Definitions.

When used in this chapter—

(a) The term "lands beneath navigable waters" means—

(1) all lands within the boundaries of each of the respective States which are covered by non-tidal waters that were navigable under the laws of the United States at the time such State became a member of the Union, or acquired sovereignty over such lands and waters thereafter, up to the ordinary high water mark as heretofore or hereafter modified by accretion, erosion, and reliction;

(2) all lands permanently or periodically covered by tidal waters up to but not above the line of mean high tide and seaward to a line three geographical miles distant from the coast line of each such State and to the boundary line of each such State where in any case such boundary as it existed at the time such State became a member of the Union, or as heretofore approved by Congress, extends seaward (or into the Gulf of Mexico) beyond three geographical miles, and

(3) all filled in, made, or reclaimed lands which formerly were lands beneath navigable waters, as hereinabove defined;

(b) The term "boundaries" includes the seaward boundaries of a State or its boundaries in the Gulf of Mexico or any of the Great Lakes as they existed at the time such State became a member of the Union, or as heretofore approved by the Congress, or as extended or confirmed pursuant to section 1312 of this title but in no event shall the term "boundaries" or the term "lands beneath navigable waters" be interpreted as extending from the coast line more than three geographical miles into the Atlantic Ocean or the Pacific Ocean, or more than three marine leagues into the Gulf of Mexico;

§ 1302. Resources seaward of the Continental Shelf.

Nothing in this chapter shall be deemed to affect in any wise the rights of the United States to the natural resources of that portion of the subsoil and seabed of the Continental Shelf lying seaward and outside of the area of lands beneath navigable waters, as defined in section 1301 of this title, all of which natural resources appertain to the United States, and the jurisdiction and control of which by the United States is confirmed.

§ 1311.  Rights of the States.

(a) Confirmation and establishment of title and ownership of lands and resources; management, administration, leasing, development, and use.

It is determined and declared to be in the public interest that
(1) title to and ownership of the lands beneath navigable waters within the boundaries of the respective States, and the natural resources within such lands and waters, and
(2) the right and power to manage, administer, lease, develop, and use the said lands and natural resources all in accordance with applicable State law be, and they are, subject to the provisions hereof, recognized, confirmed, established, and vested in and assigned to the respective States or the persons who were on June 5, 1950, entitled thereto under the law of the respective States in which the land is located, and the respective grantees, lessees, or successers in interest thereof. . . .

§ 1312.  Seaward boundaries of States.

The seaward boundary of each original coastal State is approved and confirmed as a line three geographical miles distant from its coast line or, in the case of the Great Lakes, to the international boundary. Any State admitted subsequent to the formation of the Union which has not already done so may extend its seaward boundaries to a line three geographical miles distant from its coast line, or to the international boundaries of the United States in the Great Lakes or any other body of water traversed by such boundaries. Any claim heretofore or hereafter asserted either by constitutional provision, statute, or otherwise, indicating the intent of a State so to extend its boundaries is approved and confirmed, without prejudice to its claim, if any it has, that its boundaries extend beyond that line. Nothing in this section is to be construed as questioning or in any manner prejudicing the existence of any State's seaward boundary beyond three geographical miles if it was so provided by its constitution or laws prior to or at the time such State became a member of the Union, or if it has been heretofore approved by Congress.

§ 1313.  Exceptions from confirmation and establishment of States' title, power and rights.

There is excepted from the operation of section 1311 of this title—

(a) all tracts or parcels of land together with all accretions thereto, resources therein, or improvements thereon, title to which has been lawfully and expressly acquired by the United States from any State or from any person in whom title had vested under the law of the State or of the United States, and all lands which the United States lawfully holds under the law of the State; all lands expressly retained by or ceded to the United States when the State entered the Union (otherwise than by a general retention or cession of lands underlying the marginal sea); all lands acquired by the United States by eminent domain proceedings, purchase, cession, gift, or otherwise in a proprietary capacity; all lands filled in, built up, or otherwise reclaimed by the United States for its own use; and any rights the United States has in lands presently and actually occupied by the United States under claim of right;

(b) such lands beneath navigable waters held, or any interest in which is held by the United States for the benefit of any tribe, band, or group of Indians or for individual Indians; . . .

§ 1331. Definitions.

When used in this subchapter—

(a) The term "outer Continental Shelf" means all submerged lands lying seaward and outside of the area of lands beneath navigable waters as defined in section 1301 of this title, and of which the subsoil and seabed appertain to the United States and are subject to its jurisdiction and control; . . .

§ 1333. Laws and regulations governing lands.

(a) Constitution and United States laws; laws of adjacent States; publication of projected State lines; restriction on State taxation and jurisdiction.

(1) The Constitution and laws and civil and political jurisdiction of the United States are extended to the subsoil and seabed of the outer Continental Shelf and to all artificial islands and fixed structures which may be erected thereon for the purpose of exploring for, developing, removing, and transporting resources therefrom, to the same extent as if the outer Continental Shelf were an area of exclusive Federal jurisdiction located within a State: Provided, however, That mineral leases on the outer Continental Shelf shall be maintained or issued only under the provisions of this subchapter.

§ 1337. Grant of leases by Secretary

(a) Oil and gas leases; award to highest bidder; method of bidding.

In order to meet the urgent need for further exploration and development of the oil and gas deposits of the submerged lands of the outer Continental Shelf, the Secretary is authorized to grant to the highest responsible qualified bidder by competitive bidding under regulations promulgated in advance, oil and gas leases on submerged lands of the outer Continental Shelf which are not covered by leases meeting the requirements of section 1335 (a) of this title. The bidding shall be

(1) by sealed bids, and

(2) at the discretion of the Secretary, on the basis of a cash bonus with a royalty fixed by the Secretary at not less than 12½ per centum in amount or value of the production saved, removed or sold. . . .

(b) Terms and provisions of oil and gas leases.

An oil and gas lease issued by the Secretary pursuant to this section shall

(1) cover a compact area not exceeding five thousand seven hundred and sixty acres, as the Secretary may determine,

(2) be for a period of five years and as long thereafter as oil or gas may be produced from the area in paying quantities, or drilling or well reworking operations as approved by the Secretary are conducted thereon,

(3) require the payment of a royalty of not less than 12½ per centum, in the amount or value of the production saved, removed, or sold from the lease, and

(4) contain such rental provisions and such other terms and provisions as the Secretary may prescribe at the time of offering the area for lease. . . .

(e) Other mineral leases; award to highest bidder; terms and conditions.

The Secretary is authorized to grant to the qualified persons offering the highest cash bonuses on a basis of competitive bidding leases of any mineral other than oil, gas, and sulphur in any area of the outer Continental Shelf not then under lease for such mineral upon such royalty, rental, and other terms and conditions as the Secretary may prescribe at the time of offering the area for lease.

§ 1340. Geological and geophysical explorations.

Any agency of the United States and any person authorized by the Secretary may conduct geological and geophysical explorations in the outer Continental Shelf, which do not interfere with or endanger actual operations under any lease maintained or granted pursuant to this subchapter, and which are not unduly harmful to aquatic life in such area.

OIL POLLUTION ACT (1961, as amended)<br>33 U.S.C. 1001 et seq.

Section 1001. Definitions

        1002. Prohibition against discharge of oil or oily mixtures; permissible discharges; regulations

§ 1001.  Definitions.

As used in this chapter, unless the context otherwise requires—

(a) The term "convention" means the International Convention for the
Prevention of the Pollution of the Sea by Oil, 1954, as amended; . . .

§ 1002.  Prohibition against discharge of oil or oily mixtures; permissible discharges; regulations.

Subject to the provisions of sections 1003 and 1004 of this title, it
shall be unlawful for any person to discharge oil or oily mixture from:

(a) a tanker within any of the prohibited zones.

(b) a ship, other than a tanker, within any of the prohibited zones, except when the ship is proceeding to a port not provided with facilities
adequate for the reception, without causing undue delay, it may discharge
such residues and oily mixture as would remain for disposal if the bulk
of the water had been separated from the mixture: Provided, such
discharge is made as far as practicable from land.

(c) a ship of twenty thousand tons gross tonnage or more, including a
tanker, for which the building contract is placed on or after the effective date of this chapter. However, if in the opinion of the master,
special circumstances make it neither reasonable nor practicable to
retain the oil or oily mixture on board, it may be discharged outside
the prohibited zones. The reasons for such discharge shall be reported
in accordance with the regulations prescribed by the Secretary.

§ 1003. Excepted discharges; securing safety of ship; prevention of damage to ship or cargo; saving life; damaged ship or unavoidable leakage; residue from purification or clarification.

Section 1002 of this title shall not apply to—

(a) the discharge of oil or oily mixture from a ship for the purpose of securing the safety of a ship, preventing damage to a ship or cargo, or saving life at sea; or

(b) the escape of oil, or of oily mixture, resulting from damage to a ship or unavoidable leakage, if all reasonable precautions have been taken after the occurrence of the damage or discovery of the leakage for the purpose of preventing or minimizing the escape;

(c) the discharge of residue arising from the purification or clarification of fuel oil or lubricating oil: Provided, That such discharge is made as far from land as practicable.

§ 1005. Penalties for violations; liability of vessel.

Any person who violates any provision of this chapter, except sections 1007(b) and 1008 of this title, or any regulation prescribed in pursuance thereof, is guilty of a misdemeanor, and upon conviction shall be punished by a fine not exceeding $2,500 nor less than $500, or by imprisonment not exceeding one year, or by both such fine and imprisonment, for each offense. And any ship (other than a ship owned and operated by the United States) from which oil is discharged in violation of this chapter, or any regulation prescribed in pursuance thereof, shall be liable for the pecuniary penalty specified in this section, and clearance of such ship from a port of the United States may be withheld until the penalty is paid, and said penalty shall constitute a lien on such ship which may be recovered in proceedings by libel in rem in the district court of the United States for any district within which the ship may be.

§ 1011. Prohibited zones; publication of reduction or extension of zones.

(a) All sea areas within fifty miles from the nearest land shall be prohibited zones, subject to extensions or reduction effectuated in accordance with the terms of the Convention. . . .

MARINE PROTECTION, RESEARCH, AND SANCTUARIES
ACT (1972, as amended)
33 U.S.C. 1401 et seq.

Section 1401. Finding, policy and purpose
       1402. Definitions

§ 1401. Congressional finding, policy and declaration of purpose.

(a) Unregulated dumping of material into ocean waters endangers human health, welfare, and amenities, and the marine environment, ecological systems, and economic potentialities.

(b) The Congress declares that it is the policy of the United States to regulate the dumping of all types of materials into ocean waters and to prevent or strictly limit the dumping into ocean waters of any material which would adversely affect human health, welfare, or amenities, or the marine environment, ecological systems, or economic potentialities.

(c) It is the purpose of this chapter to regulate
(1) the transportation by any person of material from the United States and, in the case of United States vessels, aircraft, or agencies, the transportation of material from a location outside the United States, when in either case the transportation is for the purpose of dumping the material into ocean waters, and
(2) the dumping of material transported by any person from a location outside the United States, if the dumping occurs in the territorial sea or the contiguous zone of the United States.

§ 1402. Definitions.

(c) "Material" means matter of any kind or description, including, but not limited to, dredged material, solid waste, incinerator residue, garbage, sewage, sewage sludge, munitions, radiological, chemical, and biological warfare agents, radioactive materials, chemicals, biological and laboratory waste, wreck or discarded equipment, rock, sand, excavation debris, and industrial, municipal, agricultural, and

other waste; but such term does not mean oil within the meaning of
section 11 of the Federal Water Pollution Control Act, as amended,
and does not mean sewage from vessels within the meaning of section
13 of such Act.

§ 1411. Prohibited acts.

(a) No person shall transport from the United States any radiological,
chemical, or biological warfare agent or any high-level radioactive
waste, except as may be authorized in a permit issued under this subchapter, and subject to regulations issued under section 1418 of this
title by the Secretary of the Department in which the Coast Guard is
operating, any other material for the purpose of dumping it into ocean
waters.

(b) No person shall dump any radiological, chemical, or biological
warfare agent or any high-level radioactive waste, or, except as may
be authorized in a permit issued under this subchapter, any other material, transported from any location outside the United States,
    (1) into the territorial sea of the United States, or
    (2) into a zone contiguous to the territorial sea of the United States,
extending to a line twelve nautical miles seaward from the base line
from which the breadth of the territorial sea is measured, to the extent that it may affect the territorial sea or the territory of the United
States.

(c) No officer, employee, agent, department, agency, or instrumentality of the United States shall transport from any location outside the
United States any radiological, chemical, or biological warfare agent
or any high-level radioactive waste, or, except as may be authorized
in a permit issued under this subchapter, any other material for the
purpose of dumping it into ocean waters.

§ 1412. Dumping permit program.

(a) Environmental Protection Agency permits.

    Except in relation to dredged material, as provided for in section
1413 of this title, and in relation to radiological, chemical, and biological warfare agents and high-level radioactive waste, as provided
for in section 1411 of this title, the Administrator may issue permits,
after notice and opportunity for public hearings, for the transportation
from the United States or, in the case of an agency or instrumentality
of the United States, for the transportation from a location outside the
United States, of material for the purpose of dumping it into ocean
waters, or for the dumping of material into the waters described in
section 1411(b) of this title, where the Administrator determines that
such dumping will not unreasonably degrade or endanger human health,

welfare, or amenities, or the marine environment, ecological systems, or economic potentalities. The Administrator shall establish and apply criteria for reviewing and evaluating such permit applications, and, in establishing or revising such criteria, shall consider, but not be limited in his consideration to, the following:

(A) The need for the proposed dumping.

(B) The effect of such dumping on human health and welfare, including economic, esthetic, and recreational values.

(C) The effect of such dumping on fisheries resources, plankton, fish, shellfish, wildlife, shore lines and beaches.

(D) The effect of such dumping on marine ecosystems, particularly with respect to—

(i) the transfer, concentration, and dispersion of such material and its byproducts through biological, physical, and chemical processes,

(ii) potential changes in marine ecosystem diversity, productivity, and stability, and

(iii) species and community population dynamics.

(E) The persistence and permanence of the effects of the dumping.

(F) The effect of dumping particular volumes and concentrations of such materials.

(G) Appropriate locations and methods of disposal or recycling, including land-based alternatives and the probable impact of requiring use of such alternate locations or methods upon considerations affecting the public interest.

(H) The effect on alternate uses of oceans, such as scientific study, fishing, and other living resource exploitation, and non-living resource exploitation.

(I) In designating recommended sites, the Administrator shall utilize wherever feasible locations beyond the edge of the Continental Shelf.

In establishing or revising such criteria, the Administrator shall consult with Federal, State, and local officials, and interested members of the general public, as may appear appropriate to the Administrator. With respect to such criteria as may affect the civil works program of the Department of the Army, the Administrator shall also consult with the Secretary. In reviewing applications for permits, the Administrator shall make such provision for consultation with interested Federal and State agencies as he deems useful or necessary. No permit shall be issued for a dumping of material which will violate applicable water quality standards.

§ 1413. Dumping permit program for dredged material.

(a) Issuance by Secretary of the Army.

Subject to the provisions of subsections (b), (c), and (d) of this section, the Secretary may issue permits, after notice and opportunity for public hearings, for the transportation of dredged material for the purpose of dumping it into ocean waters, where the Secretary determines that the dumping will not unreasonably degrade or endanger human health, welfare, or amenities, or the marine environment, ecological systems, or economic potentialities.

## § 1414.  Permit conditions.

(a) Designated and included conditions.

Permits issued under this subchapter shall designate and include
(1) the type of material authorized to be transported for dumping or to be dumped;
(2) the amount of material authorized to be transported for dumping or to be dumped;
(3) the location where such transport for dumping will be terminated or where such dumping will occur;
(4) the length of time for which the permits are valid and their expiration date;
(5) any special provisions deemed necessary by the Administrator or the Secretary, as the case may be, after consultation with the Secretary of the Department in which the Coast Guard is operating, for the monitoring and surveillance of the tranportation or dumping; and
(6) such other matters as the Administrator or the Secretary, as the case may be, deems appropriate.

## § 1415.  Penalties.

(a) Assessment of civil penalty by Administrator; remission or mitigation; court action for appropriate relief.

Any person who violates any provision of this subchapter, or of the regulations promulgated under this subchapter, or a permit issued under this subchapter shall be liable to a civil penalty of not more than $50,000 for each violation to be assessed by the Administrator. No penalty shall be assessed until the person charged shall have been given notice and an opportunity for a hearing of such violation. In determining the amount of the penalty, the gravity of the violation, prior violations, and the demonstrated good faith of the person charged in attempting to achieve rapid compliance after notification of a violation shall be considered by said Administrator. . . .

PORTS AND WATERWAYS SAFETY ACT
(1973, as amended)
46 U.S.C. 391a et seq.

## § 391a. Vessels carrying certain cargoes in bulk.

(1) Statement of Policy.—The Congress hereby finds and declares—

That the carriage by vessels of certain cargoes in bulk creates substantial hazards to life, property, the navigable waters of the United States (including the quality thereof) and the resources contained therein and of the adjoining land, including but not limited to fish, shellfish, and wildlife, marine and coastal ecosystems and recreational and scenic values, which waters and resources are hereafter in this section referred to as the "marine environment".

That existing standards for the design, construction, alteration, repair, maintenance and operation of such vessels must be improved for the adequate protection of the marine environment.

That it is necessary that there be established for all such vessels documented under the laws of the United States or entering the navigable waters of the United States comprehensive minimum standards of design, construction, alteration, repair, maintenance, and operation to prevent or mitigate the hazards to life, property, and the marine environment.

(2) Vessels included.—All vessels, regardless of tonnage size, or manner of propulsion, and whether self-propelled or not, and whether carrying freight or passengers for hire or not, which are documented under the laws of the United States or enter the navigable waters of the United States, except public vessels other than those engaged in commercial service, that shall have on board liquid cargo in bulk which is—

(A) inflammable or combustible, or

(B) oil, of any kind or in any form, including but not limited to petroleum, fuel oil, sludge, oil refuse, and oil mixed with wastes other than dredged spoil, or

(C) designated as a hazardous polluting substance under section 1162(a) of Title 33;

shall be considered steam vessels for the purposes of title 52 of the Revised Statutes of the United States and shall be subject to the provisions thereof.

(3) Rules and regulations.—In order to secure effective provision

(A) for vessel safety, and

(B) for protection of the marine environment,

the Secretary of the department in which the Coast Guard is operating (hereafter referred to in this section as the "Secretary") shall estab-

lish for the vessels to which this section applies such additional rules
and regulations as may be necessary with respect to the design and
construction, alteration, repair, and maintenance of such vessels,
including, but not limited to, the superstructures, hulls, places for
stowing and carrying such cargo, fittings, equipment, appliances,
propulsive machinery, auxiliary machinery, and boilers thereof; and
with respect to all materials used in such construction, alteration,
or repair; and with respect to the handling and stowage of such cargo,
the manner of such handling or stowage, and the machinery and appliances used in such handling and stowage; and with respect to equipment
and appliances for life saving, fire protection, and the prevention and
mitigation of damage to the marine environment; and with respect to
the operation of such vessels; and with respect to the requirements of
the manning of such vessels and the duties and qualifications of the officers and crew thereof; and with respect to the inspection of all the foregoing. . . .

(5) Rules and regulations for safety; inspection; permits; foreign vessels.—No vessel subject to the provisions of this section shall, after
the effective date of the rules and regulations for vessel safety established hereunder, have on board such cargo, until a certificate of inspection has been issued to such vessel in accordance with the provisions of title 52 of the Revised Statutes of the United States and until a
permit has been endorsed on such certificate of inspection by the Secretary, indicating that such vessel is in compliance with the provisions
of this section and the rules and regulations for vessel safety established hereunder, and showing the kinds and grades of such cargo that
such vessel may have on board or transport. Such permit shall not be
endorsed by the Secretary on such certificate of inspection until such
vessel has been inspected by the Secretary and found to be in compliance with the provisions of this section and the rules and regulations
for vessel safety established hereunder. . . .

(6) Rules and regulations for protection of the marine environment;
inspection; certification.—No vessel subject to the provisions of this
section shall, after the effective date of rules and regulations for protection of the marine environment, have on board such cargo, until a
certificate of compliance, or an endorsement on the certificate of inspection for domestic vessels, has been issued by the Secretary indicating that such vessel is in compliance with such rules and regulations.
Such certificate of compliance or endorsement shall not be issued by
the Secretary until such vessel has been inspected by the Secretary and
found to be in compliance with the rules and regulations for protection
of the marine environment established hereunder. . . .

(7) Rules and regulations for protection of the marine environment relating to vessel design and construction, alteration, and repair; international agreement.

(A) The Secretary shall begin publication as soon as practicable of proposed rules and regulations setting forth minimum standards of design, construction, alteration, and repair of the vessels to which this section applies for the purpose of protecting the marine environment. Such rules and regulations shall, to the extent possible, include but not be limited to standards to improve vessel maneuvering and stopping ability and otherwise reduce the possibility of collision, grounding, or other accident, to reduce cargo loss following collision, grounding, or other accident, and to reduce damage to the marine environment by normal vessel operations such as ballasting and deballasting, cargo handling, and other activities. . . .

## DEEPWATER PORT ACT (1974)
### 33 U.S.C. 1501 et seq.

§ 1501.  Congressional declaration of policy.

(a) It is declared to be the purposes of the Congress in this chapter to—

(1) authorize and regulate the location, ownership, construction, and operation of deepwater ports in waters beyond the territorial limits of the United States;

(2) provide for the protection of the marine and coastal environment to prevent or minimize any adverse impact which might occur as a consequence of the development of such ports;

(3) protect the interests of the United States and those of adjacent coastal States in the location, construction, and operation of deepwater ports; and

(4) protect the rights and responsibilities of States and communities to regulate growth, determine land use and otherwise protect the environment in accordance with law. . . .

§ 1502.  Definitions.

As used in this chapter, unless the context otherwise requires, the term—

(1) "adjacent coastal State" means any coastal State which

(A) would be directly connected by pipeline to a deepwater port, as proposed in an application;

(B) would be located within 15 miles of any such proposed deepwater port; or

(C) is designated by the Secretary in accordance with section 1508 (a)(2) of this title; . . .

(6) "coastal environment" means the navigable waters (including the lands therein and thereunder) and the adjacent shorelines including waters therein and thereunder).  The term includes transitional and intertidal areas, bays, lagoons, salt marshes, estuaries, and beaches; the fish, wildlife and other living resources thereof; and the recreational and scenic values of such lands, waters and resources; . . .

(10) "deepwater port" means any fixed or floating manmade structures other than a vessel, or any group of such structures, located beyond the territorial sea and off the coast of the United States and which are used or intended for use as a port or terminal for the loading or unloading and further handling of oil for transportation to any State, except as otherwise provided in section 1522 of this title.  The term includes all associated components and equipment, including pipelines, pumping stations, service platforms, mooring buoys, and similar appurtenances to the extent they are located seaward of the high water mark.  A deepwater port shall be considered a "new source" for purposes of the Clean Air Act, as amended, and the Federal Water Pollution Control Act, as amended; . . .

(13) "marine environment" includes the coastal environment, waters of the contiguous zone, and waters of the high seas; the fish, wildlife, and other living resources of such waters; and the recreational and scenic values of such waters and resources; . . .

§ 1503. License for ownership, construction, and operation of deepwater port—requirement; restrictions on utilization of deepwater port.

(a) No person may engage in the ownership, construction, or operation of a deepwater port except in accordance with a license issued pursuant to this chapter. No person may transport or otherwise transfer any oil between a deepwater port and the United States unless such port has been so licensed and the license is in force. . . .

(b) The Secretary is authorized, upon application and in accordance with the provisions of this chapter, to issue, transfer, amend, or renew a license for the ownership, construction, and operation of a deepwater port.

(c) The Secretary may issue a license in accordance with the provisions of this chapter if— . . .
    (5) he determines, in accordance with the environmental review criteria established pursuant to section 1505 of this title, that the applicant has demonstrated that the deepwater port will be constructed and operated using best available technology, so as to prevent or minimize adverse impact on the marine environment; . . .

(d) If an application is made under this chapter for a license to construct a deepwater port facility off the coast of a State, and a port of the State which will be directly connected by pipeline with such deepwater port, on the date of such application—
    (1) has existing plans for construction of a deep draft channel and harbor; and
    (2) has either
        (A) an active study by the Secretary of the Army relating to the construction of a deep draft channel and harbor, or
        (B) a pending application for a permit under section 403 of this title, for such construction; and
    (3) applies to the Secretary for a determination under this section within 30 days of the date of the license application;
the Secretary shall not issue a license under this chapter until he has examined and compared the economic, social, and environmental effects of the construction and operation of the deepwater port with the economic, social and environmental effects of the construction, expansion, deepening, and operation of such State port, and has determined which project best serves the national interest or that both developments are warranted. The Secretary's determination shall be discretionary and nonreviewable. . . .

§ 1504. Procedure—regulations. . . .

(d)(1) At the time notice of an application is published pursuant to subsection (c) of this section, the Secretary shall publish a description
in the Federal Register of an application area encompassing the deepwater port site proposed by such application and within which construction of the proposed deepwater port would eliminate, at the time such
application was submitted, the need for any other deepwater port
within that application area.

(2) As used in this section, "application area" means any reasonable
geographical area within which a deepwater port may be constructed
and operated. Such application area shall not exceed a circular zone,
the center of which is the principal point of loading and unloading at
the port, and the radius of which is the distance from such point to
the high water mark of the nearest adjacent coastal State.

(3) The Secretary shall accompany such publication with a call for
submission of any other applications for licenses for the ownership,
construction, and operation of a deepwater port within the designated
application area. . . .

(f) For all timely applications covering a single application area, the
Secretary, in cooperation with other involved Federal agencies and
departments, shall, pursuant to section 4332(2)(C) of Title 42, prepare
a single, detailed environmental impact statement, which shall fulfill
the requirement of all Federal agencies in carrying out their responsibilities pursuant to this chapter to prepare an environmental impact
statement. In preparing such statement the Secretary shall consider
the criteria established under section 1505 of this title.

(g) A license may be issued, transferred, or renewed only after public notice and public hearings in accordance with this subsection. At
least one such public hearing shall be held in each adjacent coastal
State. . . .

(h()1) Each person applying for a license pursuant to this chapter shall
remit to the Secretary at the time the application is filed a non-refund-
able application fee established by regulation by the Secretary. In addition, an applicant shall also reimburse the United States and the appropriate adjacent coastal State for any additional costs incurred in
processing an application.

(2) Notwithstanding any other provision of this chapter, an adjacent
coastal State may fix reasonable fees for the use of a deepwater port
facility, and such State and any other State in which land-based facilities directly related to a deepwater port facility are located may set
reasonable fees for the use of such land-based facilities. Fees may
be fixed under authority of this paragraph as compensation for any economic cost attributable to the construction and operation of such deep-

water port and such land-based facilities, which cannot be recovered under other authority of such State or political subdivision thereof, including, but not limited to, ad valorem taxes, and for environmental and administrative costs attributable to the construction and operation of such deepwater port and such land-based facilities. Fees under this paragraph shall not exceed such economic, environmental, and administrative costs of such State. Such fees shall be subject to the approval of the Secretary. As used in this paragraph, the term "land-based facilities directly related to a deepwater port facility" means the onshore tank farm and pipelines connecting such tank farm to the deepwater port facility.

(3) A licensee shall pay annually in advance the fair market rental value (as determined by the Secretary of the Interior) of the subsoil and seabed of the outer Continental Shelf of the United States to be utilized by the deepwater port, including the fair market rental value of the right-of-way necessary for the pipeline segment of the port located on such subsoil and seabed. . . .

(i)(3) In determining whether any one proposed deepwater port clearly best serves the national interest, the Secretary shall consider the following factors:

(A) the degree to which the proposed deepwater ports affect the environment, as determined under criteria established pursuant to section 1505 of this title;

(B) any significant differences between anticipated completion dates for the proposed deepwater ports; and

(C) any differences in costs of construction and operation of the proposed deepwater ports, to the extent that such differential may significantly affect the ultimate cost of oil to the consumer.

§ 1505.  Environmental review criteria—establishment; evaluation of proposed deepwater ports.

(a) The Secretary, in accordance with the recommendations of the Administrator of the Environmental Protection Agency and the Administrator of the National Oceanic and Atmospheric Administration and after consultation with any other Federal departments and agencies having jurisdiction over any aspect of the construction or operation of a deepwater port, shall establish, as soon as practicable after January 3, 1975, environmental review criteria consistent with the National Environmental Policy Act. Such criteria shall be used to evaluate a deepwater port as proposed in an application, including—

(1) the effect on the marine environment;

(2) the effect on oceanographic currents and wave patterns;

(3) the effect on alternate uses of the oceans and navigable waters, such as scientific study, fishing, and exploitation of other living and nonliving resources;

(4) the potential dangers to a deepwater port from waves, winds, weather, and geological conditions, and the steps which can be taken to protect against or minimize such dangers;

(5) effects of land-based developments related to deepwater port development;

(6) the effect on human health and welfare; and

(7) such other considerations as the Secretary deems necessary or appropriate. . . .

§ 1508. Adjacent coastal States—designation; direct pipeline connections; mileage; risk of damage to coastal environment, time for designation.

(a)(1) The Secretary, in issuing notice of application pursuant to section 1504(c) of this title, shall designate as an "adjacent coastal State" any coastal State which

(A) would be directly connected by pipeline to a deepwater port as proposed in an application, or

(B) would be located within 15 miles of any such proposed deepwater port.

(2) The Secretary shall, upon request of a State, and after having received the recommendations of the Administrator of the National Oceanic and Atmospheric Administration, designate such State as an "adjacent coastal State" if he determines that there is a risk of damage to the coastal environment of such State equal to or greater than the risk posed to a State directly connected by pipeline to the proposed deepwater port. . . .

(b)(1) Not later than 10 days after the designation of adjacent coastal States pursuant to this chapter, the Secretary shall transmit a complete copy of the application to the Governor of each adjacent coastal State. The Secretary shall not issue a license without the approval of the Governor of each adjacent coastal State. If the Governor fails to transmit his approval or disapproval to the Secretary not later than 45 days after the last public hearing on applications for a particular application area, such approval shall be conclusively presumed. If the Governor notifies the Secretary that an application, which would otherwise be approved pursuant to this paragraph, is inconsistent with State programs relating to environmental protection, land and water use, and coastal zone management, the Secretary shall condition the license granted so as to make it consistent with such State programs.

(2) Any other interested State shall have the opportunity to make its views known to, and shall be given full consideration by, the Secretary regarding the location, construction, and operation of a deepwater port.

(c) The Secretary shall not issue a license unless the adjacent coastal State to which the deepwater port is to be directly connected by pipeline has developed, or is making, at the time the application is submitted, reasonable progress toward developing an approved coastal zone management program pursuant to the Coastal Zone Management Act of 1972 in the area to be directly and primarily impacted by land and water development in the coastal zone resulting from such deepwater port. For the purposes of this chapter, a State shall be considered to be making reasonable progress if it is receiving a planning grant pursuant to section 305 of the Coastal Zone Management Act . . . .

§ 1515. Citizen civil action—equitable relief; case or controversy; district court jurisdiction.

(a) Except as provided in subsection (b) of this section, any person may commence a civil action for equitable relief on his own behalf, whenever such action constitutes a case or controversy—

(1) against any person (including

(A) the United States, and

(B) any other governmental instrumentality or agency to the extent permitted by the eleventh amendment to the Constitution)
who is alleged to be in violation of any provision of this chapter or any condition of a license issued pursuant to this chapter; or

(2) against the Secretary where there is alleged a failure of the Secretary to perform any act or duty under this chapter which is not discretionary with the Secretary. Any action brought against the Secretary under this paragraph shall be brought in the district court for the District of Columbia or the district of the appropriate adjacent coastal State. . . .

§ 1517. Liability—oil discharge; prohibition; penalty; notice and hearing; separate offense; vessel clearance: withholding, bond or surety.

(a)(1) The discharge of oil into the marine environment from a vessel within any safety zone, from a vessel which has received oil from another vessel at a deepwater port, or from a deepwater port is prohibited.

(2) The owner or operator of a vessel or the licensee of a deepwater port from which oil is discharged in violation of this subsection shall be assessed a civil penalty of not more than $10,000 for each violation.
. . .

(d) Notwithstanding any other provision of law, except as provided in subsection (g) of this section, the owner and operator of a vessel shall be jointly and severally liable, without regard to fault, for cleanup costs and for damages that result from a discharge of oil from such vessel within any safety zone, or from a vessel which has received oil

from another vessel at a deepwater port, except when such vessel is
moored at a deepwater port. Such liability shall not exceed $150 per
gross ton or $20,000,000, whichever is lesser, except that if it can
be shown that such discharge was the result of gross negligence or
willful misconduct within the privity and knowledge of the owner or
operator, such owner and operator shall be jointly and severally liable
for the full amount of all cleanup costs and damages. . . .

(l) The Secretary shall require that any owner or operator of a vessel
using any deepwater port, or any licensee of a deepwater port, shall
carry insurance or give evidence of other financial responsibility in
an amount sufficient to meet the liabilities imposed by this section.

(m) As used in this section the term—
     (1) "cleanup costs" means all actual costs, including but not limited
to costs of the Federal Government, of any State or local government,
of other nations or of their contractors or subcontractors incurred in
the
          (A) removing or attempting to remove, or
          (B) taking other measures to reduce or mitigate damages from,
any oil discharged into the marine environment in violation of subsection (a)(1) of this section;
     (2) "damages" means all damages (except cleanup costs) suffered
by any person, or involving real or personal property, the natural
resources of the marine environment, or the coastal environment of
any nation, including damages claimed without regard to ownership of
any affected lands, structures, fish, wildlife, or biotic or natural resources; . . .

(n)(1) The Attorney General, in cooperation with the Secretary, the
Secretary of State, the Secretary of the Interior, the Administrator
of the Environmental Protection Agency, the Council on Environmental
Quality, and the Administrative Conference of the United States, is
authorized and directed to study methods and procedures for implementing a uniform law providing liability for cleanup costs and damages from
oil spills from Outer Continental Shelf operations, deepwater ports,
vessels, and other ocean-related sources. The study shall give particular attention to methods of adjudicating and settling claims as rapidly,
economically, and equitably as possible. . . .


                              STATES


           LOUISIANA OFFSHORE TERMINAL AUTHORITY (1972)
                    34 La. Rev. Stat. 3101 et seq.

Section 3101.  Object; purpose of chapter
        3102.  Definitions

## § 3101. Object; purpose of chapter.

A. It is the object and purpose of this chapter to provide for the creation of a political subdivision of the state of Louisiana, possessing full corporate powers, known as the Offshore Terminal Authority, hereinafter referred to as the "authority", to promote, plan, finance, develop, construct, control, license, regulate, supervise, operate, manage, maintain and/or modify offshore terminal facilities within the jurisdiction of said authority in order to promote the economic welfare of its citizens. It is hereby declared to be in the public interest that this offshore terminal authority be created as a political subdivision of the state of Louisiana.

B. It is further the object and purpose of this chapter:

(1) To promote the economic and industrial well-being of the state of Louisiana and international trade for the state of Louisiana, its subdivisions and the area served by the Mississippi River and its tributaries;

(2) To promote the industrial and petrochemical base of the Mississippi Valley region of the United States by providing adequate deep draft port facilities for the handling of the cargoes of deep draft vessels;

(3) To promote, in addition to port operations, scientific and all other uses directly related to the offshore terminal facilities which shall be in the public interest;

(4) To accommodate and plan for the technological innovations occurring in the worldwide and domestic shipping industry to increase

efficiency and the flow of commerce through the offshore terminal facilities;

(5) To protect environmental values and Louisiana's unique coastal
marshland ecosystem through the adoption of an environmental protection plan;

(6) To assert and protect Louisiana's economic, social and environmental interests in the development of any offshore terminal facilities
outside the state of Louisiana where such development may have an
impact upon the state of Louisiana;

(7) To create a political subdivision of the state of Louisiana. The
functions exercised by the board empowered herein shall be deemed
to be governmental functions of the state of Louisiana;

(8) To assure that the authority shall not be required to pay any
taxes or assessments on any property acquired or used by it under
the provisions of this chapter or upon the income therefrom. Any
bonds issued hereunder shall be serviced from the income of said facility and shall be exempt from taxation by the state of Louisiana, and
by any municipal or political subdivision of the state.

§ 3102. Definitions.

For the purposes of this chapter, the following definitions shall apply:

(1) "Offshore terminal facilities" means a structure, a series of structures, or facility of any type emplaced within the coastal waters of
Louisiana or seaward thereof and designed to accommodate the cargoes
or passengers of deep draft vessels whose draft is greater than the
depths of typical inland harbors and waterways, commonly used by
ocean going traffic during the first half of the twentieth century, including all pipelines, structures, and facilities directly related thereto
and necessary or useful to the operation thereof whether landward or
seaward of the main structure or facility itself.

(2) "Authority development program" means all the phases of growth
and development through which the concept of offshore terminal facilities may go, . . .

§ 3103. Jurisdiction; domicile.

A. The authority shall have exclusive jurisdiction over the authority
development program within the coastal waters of Louisiana, the areas
of the state extending seaward thereof to the extent of the state's rights
thereto, and over such other waters, water bottoms, wetlands and
lands within the territorial boundaries of the state necessary to effectuate the purposes of this chapter. The jurisdiction of the authority
shall not include or extend to the taking, control, regulation, licensing
or operation of existing, proposed or future facilities of existing port

authorities or port harbor and terminal districts except by mutual
agreement.

B.   The authority shall have the right to acquire by permit, lease, sublease, license, grant, purchase, or otherwise, water bottoms, wetlands, and lands, inside and outside of the territorial limits of the
state of Louisiana, for the construction, operation and maintenance of
the facilities functionally required, related, necessary or useful to the
authority development program.

C.   The authority shall have exclusive power to own, operate, license
or otherwise regulate all offshore terminal facilities within its jurisdiction. . . .

§ 3108.   Acquisition of sites; lease of state owned lands and water bottoms.

A.   To enable the authority to perform the work herein provided, the
state of Louisiana, acting by and through the register of state lands,
is hereby authorized, empowered and directed to grant to the authority
a lease on state owned lands and water bottoms which are selected by
the authority as sites for offshore terminal facilities; provided, however, that the mineral rights on any and all state lands shall be reserved to the state of Louisiana.
   Upon receipt of a request from the governing body of the authority
describing the lands to be leased by the authority, it is hereby made
the mandatory duty of the register of state lands to issue a certificate
of title evidencing the lease of the land to the authority as described
in the request. . . .

§ 3109.   Powers.

A.   The authority shall be empowered to do any and all things necessary
or proper to carry out the purposes of this chapter, including but not
limited to the following: . . .

B.   To assert Louisiana's interest in any offshore terminal facilities
development in proximity to the Louisiana coast, the authority is empowered to negotiate with and enter into contracts, compacts or other
agreements with agencies, bureaus or other divisions of the federal
government or other states of the United States concerning the authority development program, including jurisdictional aspects of the location of the offshore terminal facility, sharing of revenues derived from
the operation of the offshore terminal facilities, and promulgation and
enforcement of regulations governing authority operations. . . .

D.   The authority is hereby empowered to take all necessary steps to
protect Louisiana's unique coastal environment from any short-term

or long-term damage or harm which might occur from any aspect of the authority development program. . . .

§ 3113. Environmental protection plan.

A. Throughout all aspects of the authority development program there shall be in existence an environmental protection plan, the details of which shall be followed in all respects by the executive director in carrying out any aspect of the authority development program. The environmental protection plan shall be applicable to all offshore terminal facilities within the jurisdiction of the authority. . . .

J. The environmental protection plan shall:

(1) Summarize the salient feature of an inventory of all potential and actual stresses on the natural and human environment which can be reasonably expected to occur in pursuing the authority development program. Consideration shall be given to stresses which have occurred in other parts of the country and the world where similar functional operations were being performed. Consideration shall be given to the peculiarities of Louisiana's coastal environment. The inventory of potential and actual stresses shall include a prediction of the stress on the coastal environment of major accidents which could logically be expected to occur throughout the authority development program, even though all precautions against such accidents have been taken.

(2) Describe the essential features of existing environmental data upon which the selection of a site for a deep draft harbor and terminal may be based. Indicate how this data has been analyzed in the above paragraph so that the site selected will result in the least total stress on the environment. Indicate how economic considerations are compared with the assessed total stress on the environment to arrive at the best economic-ecologic formula for determination of a site for the deep draft harbor and terminal. State the location and availability of the environmental data upon which these determinations are based.

(3) State how the deep draft harbor and terminal facility design minimizes potential environmental damage, considers environmental factors as a positive part of the design, and controls long-term development so that growth and additions to the deep draft harbor and terminal do not result in random growth or in gradual environmental deterioration.

(4) Present details of how the operational aspects of the authority development program will be conducted so as to minimize environmental problems, including but not limited to a monitoring program by appropriate public or private persons selected by the board of commissioners; establishment of constructional and operational guidelines for environmental protection; strong enforcement provisions and mechanisms to insure cleanup of accidental spills by technical means, with evidence

of financial responsibility to insure performance of the cleanup, and compliance with the enforcement provisions of the environmental protection plan. The plan shall consider the circumstances which may justify the temporary cessation of the port activities.

(5) Provide procedures for the funding of projects to be paid for by the authority to the Louisiana Wild Life and Fisheries Commission or any agency designated by the governor which shall compensate the coastal environment for loss that may be sustained through the stresses on the environment created by the authority development program.

(6) Analyze ongoing programs of the federal, state and local governments designed to protect the coastal environment, so as to insure that there is no unnecessary duplication of effort and to insure that cooperation and coordination of environmental protection measures are achieved. The opinion of all agencies with a responsibility for monitoring the coastal environment shall be sought with regard to this environmental protection plan prior to its promulgation, to determine if there are incompatibilities between specific provisions of this measure and the requirements of other rules and regulations.

K. Nothing in this section is intended to diminish in any way the authority of the Louisiana Wild Life and Fisheries Commission.

L. The legislature finds that the environmental protection plan as adopted by this authority on January 15, 1974, complies in all respects with the requirements of R.S. 34:3113, and was promulgated as required by law.

§ 3114. Issuance and transfer of licenses.

A. No person shall construct or operate, or cause to be constructed or operated, offshore terminal facilities within the jurisdiction of the authority without first obtaining a license, the transfer of any license granted to the authority, or other appropriate authorization from the authority. . . .

MASSACHUSETTS POLLUTION OF COASTAL
WATERS (1972)
Mass. Ann. Laws, Ch. 130

§ 23. Penalty for discharge of oil or other poisonous substances or heated effluent into coastal waters; use of explosives.

Except in the case of emergency imperilling life or property or an unavoidable accident or except in accordance with the terms of a permit issued pursuant to state or federal water pollution control laws, whoever from any source puts, throws, discharges or suffers or permits to be discharged or to escape into any coastal waters, any oil, poisonous or other injurious substance, including but not limited to, sawdust, shavings, garbage, ashes, acids, sewage and dye-stuffs, whether simple, mixed or compound, or heated effluent, which directly or indirectly materially injure fish, fishspawn or seed therein, or takes any such fish by such means, or whoever kills or destroys fish in such waters by the use of dynamite or other explosives, or takes any such fish in such waters by such means, or explodes dynamite or other explosive in such waters, shall be punished by a fine of not less than one hundred and fifty nor more than five thousand dollars or by imprisonment for not more than one year or both.

§ 25. Discharge into coastal waters of sewage, heated effluent, or other substance injurious to health.

The entrance or discharge into the coastal waters, or the tributaries of such waters, of sewage, heated effluent, or any other substance which might be injurious to the public health or might tend to contaminate any shellfish areas or shellfish therein which may be determined by the director to be of commercial value, or injuriously affect the finfish therein, is hereby prohibited; provided, that this section shall not be deemed to interfere with. . . .

NEW JERSEY CLEAN OCEAN ACT (1971)
58 N.J. Rev. Stat. 10-23.25 et seq.

Section 58:10-23.25.  Short title
        58:10-23.26.  Legislative findings
        58:10-23.27.  Definitions
        58:10-23.28.  Loading of vessels with materials disposable at sea
        58:10-23.29.  Loading of vessels or handling of materials for disposition at sea
        58:10-23.30.  Violations
        58:10-23.31.  Powers, duties, and functions under other laws
        58:10-23.32.  Severability
        58:10-23.33.  Construction of act

§ 58:10-23.26.  Legislative findings.

The Legislature finds and determines that the ocean off the coast of the State is being used increasingly for the disposal of wastes, including sewage sludge, industrial wastes and dredged spoils; that ocean-dumped wastes contain materials which may have adverse effects on the public health, safety, and welfare; that many of these materials are toxic to human and marine life, and are damaging to the fish population and the food chain supporting all life including man, as well as to other valuable natural and economic resources; and that therefore the State must regulate and control this practice and encourage the development and utilization of advanced methods of waste disposal which do not utilize the ocean as the repository for harmful materials.

§ 58:10-23.28.  Loading of vessels with materials disposable at sea; rules and regulations.

The commissioner shall have the power to formulate and promulgate, amend and repeal rules and regulations preventing, conditioning and controlling the loading of a vessel within the State with materials of any composition whatsoever and the handling of such materials which if disposed of at sea cause, or may tend to cause, adverse effects on the waters of the State.

§ 58:10-23.29.  Loading of vessels or handling of materials for disposition at sea; permit; fees for services.

a.  The commissioner may by rule or regulation require that the person responsible for the loading of a vessel or the handling of materials of any composition whatsoever which are to be disposed of at sea first obtain a permit.

The department may, in accordance with a fee schedule adopted as a rule or regulation, establish and charge fees for any of the services it perform in connection with this act, including the issuance of permits, which fees shall be annual or periodical as the department shall deem. The fees charged by the department pursuant to this section shall not be less than $100.00 nor more than $1,500.00 based on criteria contained in the fee schedule. . . .

# 9

On a finite planet the conservation of land for continued production of renewable resources and for continued use after extraction of nonrenewable resources is a clear necessity. The National Environmental Policy Act sets a "balance between population and resource use" and "enhanc[ing] the quality of renewable resources" as national goals (Sec. 4331). Resource conservation may be achieved by laws that spell out permitted uses of publicly owned land and impose royalties on the extraction of natural resources therefrom. They also may seek to encourage individuals to adopt soil and other conservation measures on private land, offer private landowners preferential taxation in return for keeping their lands in agricultural use, or mandate reclamation after mining. Examples of such laws are excerpted in this chapter in two categories: (1) forest and agricultural crop lands and (2) reclamation of mined lands. Preservation of natural, park, and recreation areas is the topic of Chapter 6; general land use legislation, that of Chapter 5.

## CROP LANDS

Forest conservation to ensure improved timber quality and repeated harvests was one of the earliest forms of resource protection. It was instituted in Wisconsin state forests as early as the 1870s. The establishment of national forests "to improve and protect the forest" was authorized in 1897. Only "designated . . . dead, matured, or large growth of trees . . . as may be compatible with the utilization of the forests" may be cut and sold from the national forests (Sec. 476). Clear cutting of timber in the Monangahela National Forest was held in violation of this section in Izaak Walton League v. Butz (522

F. 2d 945 [1975]).  As a result of this decision amendments intended
to clarify permitted timber harvest practices are before the 94th Congress at the time of this writing.  The Forest and Rangeland Renewable Resources Planning Act of 1974 (16 U.S.C. 1601 et seq.) charged
the National Forest Service with undertaking and periodically updating
a Renewable Resources Assessment consisting of analysis of present
and anticipated uses, inventory, and formulation of policy alternatives
for forest management.

   The National Forests for many years served recreational purposes
as well as supplying timber and rangeland.  The Multiple-Use Sustained
Yield Act of 1960 (p. 306) gave congressional approval to what was
administrative practice and mandated "outdoor recreation, range, timber, watershed, and wildlife and fish" as the purposes of the national
forests.

   The National Park and National Forest Services administer national parks and forests, respectively.  All federal lands not dedicated
to these or other specific purposes are under the aegis of the Bureau
of Land Management.  These lands are in government ownership only
"pending final disposal."  They are under no protection as to maintenance of sustained yield or of natural, scenic, or ecological values.
The Taylor Grazing Act (p. 307) authorizes the bureau to issue permits
for grazing by domestic livestock.  The conditions under which these
lands may be mined for various resources are stated in laws considered
on pp. 322 ff. and others.

   Soil conservation on privately owned land has been a concern of
the federal government since the dustbowl years of the 1930s.  The
Soil Conservation Act of 1935 (p. 308) authorizes government grants to
agricultural producers performing prescribed soil conservation practices.

   Approximately two-thirds of the states have instituted preferential or deferred taxation of agricultural, forest, and other open-space
lands for the purpose of preserving such lands in their current state.
In rapid growth areas the market value of land reflects its potential
for residential, commercial, or industrial development even though
it may be used for farming or lie vacant.  Taxes calculated on assessments reflecting such inflated market values force land sales to specu-
lators and result in the loss of prime agricultural land.  Preferential
assessment values land according to its current use and exacts no
penalty when it is later converted to another use.  Deferred taxation
values land similarly but levies a penalty tax when land use changes.
Landowners and local governments or a state agency may also enter
into agreements to restrict land use in return for lower assessments
(see p. 220).

   A close definition of agricultural land eligible for current-use
valuation is found in Ohio's statute (p. 309), which also requires on-

site inspection. New York and other states require farms to be placed
in agricultural districts to obtain tax considerations. Wisconsin's
forest tax law (p. 311) extends tax benefits to owners of forest crop
lands who contract with the state to follow prescribed forestry and
harvesting practices and who permit public hunting and fishing. New
Hampshire, as part of its deferred taxation scheme for forest lands
(New Hampshire Current Use Taxation [1973], Ch. 79), requires a
permit and bonding before owners may cut timber. It offers a combination of deferred taxation and easements to preserve open space,
including farm and forest land (p. 243). Michigan's Farmland and Open
Space Preservation Act of 1974 (Mich. Comp. Laws Ann. 554.701 et
seq.) authorizes development rights agreements or easements for such
lands for terms of not less than ten years. Under such contracts landowners agree not to build or make other "improvements" in return for
tax credit or exemption.

    Other forms of protection for farms and forests are found in New
York's "environmental bill of rights," which calls for "encouraging
the development and improvement of its agricultural lands for the production of food and other agricultural products" (p. 238). The state's
municipalities may acquire agricultural lands "for preservation . . .
as open space land" (General Municipal Law, Sec. 247, p. 246), and
the Adirondack Park Agency Act sets aside agricultural and forest
lands as "resource management areas" where only limited development
is permitted. Hawaii extends protection to forestry and agricultural
lands by placing them in agricultural and conservation districts (pp.
141ff.). Montana specifies how topsoil is to be handled in mine reclamation (Sec. 50-1044[3]), and industrial siting permits in Delaware's
coastal zone require that effect on agriculture and soil be considered
(Sec. 7004[b]).

    Forest practice acts, in force in many states, are designed to in-
duce private woodland owners to observe reforestation and sustained-
yield practices on their lands. Some seek to achieve this by voluntary
agreement. Nevada's act is mandatory, requiring logging permits and
restricting tractor logging on slopes over a certain degree and near
streams (p. 317). Washington, besides having a forceful forest practice statute, also restricts timber cutting on its shorelands under its
Shoreline Management Act Sec. 90.58.150, 188). Snowmobiles are
excluded from forestry plantations by Michigan's snowmobile registration law (Sec. 257.1515[d], p. 457).

## MINING LANDS

    Strip-mining legislation passed both the 93rd and 94th Congresses
but was vetoed both times. NEPA does apply, however, and a program

environmental impact statement must be filed "when the federal government, through exercise of its power to approve leases, mining
plans, rights of way, and water option contracts . . . is engaged in a
regional program," according to the holding in Sierra Club v. Morton
(395 F. Supp. 1187 [1975]).

Use of the public lands for mining is governed by, among others,
the 1872 Mining Law, which gives the discoverer of a resource full
title to the land (p. 321). Its provisions still apply to the exploration
of uranium. Under the Mineral Leasing Act of 1920 (p. 323) rents
and royalties are charged for oil and gas exploitation. The Omnibus
Tribal Leasing Act of 1938 governs leases on Indian lands in similar
fashion. The Geothermal Steam Act's (p. 324) competitive bidding
and application requirements are similar to those of the Mineral
Leasing Act. Oil and gas leases on the Outer Continental Shelf are
governed by the Outer Continental Shelf Act (p. 272) and other laws
governing mining on public land.

The Mining and Minerals Policy Act of 1970 (30 U.S.C. 21a)
stated disposal and reclamation of mineral waste products and the
reclamation of mined land to be the policy of the federal government
along with development of mineral resources and industries. Its only
requirement, however, is an annual report by the Secretary of the Interior "on the state of the domestic mining, minerals, and mineral
reclamation industries . . . with recommendations for legislative
programs."

Several western states have done more to protect the land on
which their mineral wealth is located than has the federal government.
Thus Idaho's two companion acts (pp. 329 ff.) require a permit before
a geothermal resource well may be constructed. Measures to safeguard "subsurface, surface, and atmospheric resources" are required
as a condition of granting a permit (Sec. 4004), and no permit may be
issued if "operation of any well . . . will unreasonably decrease ground
water" (Sec. 4005). State land may be leased for the construction of
geothermal resource wells with rentals and royalties fixed by competitive bidding.

Montana has effectuated a constitutional reclamation mandate
by a group of laws that call for submission of extensive environmental
data, stringent reclamation plans, and bonding before permits are issued (pp. 337 ff.). Related laws include the Strip and Underground
Mine Siting Act (Rev. Code Mont. Sec. 50-1601 et seq.), Open Cut
Mining Act (Sec. 50-1501 et seq.), Conservation of Oil and Gas Act
(Sec. 60-126 et seq.), Control of Uranium Solution Extraction Act
(Sec. 50-1701 et seq.), Reclamation of Mining Lands Act (Sec. 50-
1216), and others. The state imposes a tax on mineral production,
the proceeds of which "shall be used and expended to improve the
total environment and rectify damage thereto" (Resource Indemnity

Trust Fund, Sec. 84-7001 et seq.). Its license tax on strip coal mines
is earmarked for highways and schools needed as a result of coal development (Sec. 50-1801 et seq.).

The proceeds of Wyoming's severance tax on the mining of coal
and other minerals in part pay for water, sewer, and road costs in impacted areas (p. 210). Land quality is a major section of the state's
Environmental Quality Act (WCS 35-502.1 et seq.).

Minnesota, North Dakota, and Illinois are other states noted for
strict mining permit or reclamation laws. Corresponding laws in
eastern states frequently are less effective. Under Colorado's comprehensive land use law mineral resource areas may be designated
areas of state interest, potentially subject to state land use controls
(Sec. 106-7-201 and 202[1]).

# FEDERAL

## Crop Lands

### NATIONAL FOREST SERVICE ORGANIC ACT
### (1897, as amended)
### 16 U.S.C. 471 et seq.

Section 471.   National forests; establishment
      472.   Secretary of Agriculture responsible for National
              Forests
      473.   Clarification of presidential authority
      474.   Surveys
      475.   Purposes of National Forests
      476.   Sale of timber
      477.   Use of timber and stone by settlers
      478.   Egress or ingress of actual settlers
      479.   Sites for school and churches
      480.   Civil and criminal jurisdiction
      481.   Use of waters
      482.   Mineral lands; restoration to public domain; location
              and entry

§ 471.   National forests; establishment; limitation on additions in certain States; lands suitable for production of timber.

The President of the United States may, from time to time, set apart
and reserve, in any State or Territory having public land bearing forests, in any part of the public lands wholly or in part covered with timber or undergrowth, whether of commercial value or not, as national

forests, and the President shall, by public proclamation, declare the establishment of such forests and the limits thereof.

§ 475.  Purposes for which national forests may be established and administered.

All public lands designated and reserved prior to June 4, 1897, by the President of the United States under the provisions of section 471 of this title, the orders for which shall be and remain in full force and effect, unsuspended and unrevoked, and all public lands that may hereafter be set aside and reserved as national forests under said section, shall be as far as practicable controlled and administered in accordance with the following provisions. No national forest shall be established, except to improve and protect the forest within the boundaries, or for the purpose of securing favorable conditions of water flows, and to furnish a continuous supply of timber for the use and necessities of citizens of the United States; but it is not the purpose or intent of these provisions, or of said section, to authorize the inclusion therein of lands more valuable for the mineral therein, or for agricultural purposes, than for forest purposes.

§ 476.  Sale of timber.

For the purpose of preserving the living and growing timber and promoting the younger growth on national forests, the Secretary of Agriculture, under such rules and regulations as he shall prescribe, may cause to be designated and appraised so much of the dead, matured, or large growth of trees found upon such national forests as may be compatible with the utilization of the forests thereon, and may sell the same for not less than the appraised value in such quantities to each purchaser as he shall prescribe, to be used in the State or Territory in which such timber reservation may be situated, respectively, but not for export therefrom. . . .

§ 482.  Mineral lands; restoration to public domain; location and entry.

Upon the recommendation of the Secretary of the Interior, with the approval of the President, after sixty days' notice thereof, published in two papers of general circulation in the State or Territory wherein any national forest is situated, and near the said national forest, any public lands embraced within the limits of any such forest which, after due examination by personal inspection of a competent person appointed for that purpose by the Secretary of the Interior, shall be found better adapted for mining or for agricultural purposes than for forest usage, may be restored to the public domain.  And any mineral lands in any national forest which have been or which may be shown to be such, and subject to entry under the existing mining laws of the United States and

the rules and regulations applying thereto, shall continue to be subject
to such location and entry, notwithstanding any provisions contained in
sections 473 to 478, 479 to 482 and 551 of this title.

MULTIPLE-USE SUSTAINED YIELD ACT (1960)
16 U.S.C. 528 et seq.

Section 528.   Development and administration of renewable surface
                 resources for multiple use and sustained yield of prod-
                 ucts and services; Congressional declaration of policy
                 and purpose
       529.   Same; authorization; consideration to relative values
                 of resources; areas of wilderness
       530    Same; cooperation with State and local governmental
                 agencies and others
       531.   Same; definitions

§ 528.  Development and administration of renewable surface resources for multiple use and sustained yield of products and services;
Congressional declaration of policy and purpose.

It is the policy of the Congress that the national forests are established and shall be administered for outdoor recreation, range, timber, watershed, and wildlife and fish purposes.  The purposes of sections 528 to 531 of this title are declared to be supplemental to, but
not in derogation of, the purposes for which the national forests were
established as set forth in section 475 of this title.  Nothing herein
shall be construed as affecting the jurisdiction or responsibilities of the
several States with respect to wildlife and fish on the national forests.
Nothing herein shall be construed so as to affect the use or administration of the mineral resources of national forest lands or to affect the
use or administration of Federal lands not within national forests.

§ 529.  Same; authorization; consideration to relative values of resources; areas of wilderness.

The Secretary of Agriculture is authorized and directed to develop
and administer the renewable surface resources of the national forests
for multiple use and sustained yield of the several products and services obtained therefrom.  In the administration of the national forests
due consideration shall be given to the relative values of the various
resources in particular areas.  The establishment and maintenance of
areas of wilderness are consistent with the purposes and provisions
of sections 528 to 531 of this title.

§ 530. Same; cooperation with State and local governmental agencies and others.

In the effectuation of sections 528 to 531 of this title the Secretary of Agriculture is authorized to cooperate with interested State and local governmental agencies and others in the development and management of the national forests.

§ 531. Same; definitions.

As used in sections 528 to 531 of this title the following terms shall have the following meanings:

(a) "Multiple use" means: The management of all the various renewable surface resources of the national forests so that they are utilized in the combination that will best meet the needs of the American people; making the most judicious use of the land for some or all of these resources or related services over areas large enough to provide sufficient latitude for periodic adjustments in use to conform to changing needs and conditions; that some land will be used for less than all of the resources; and harmonious and coordinated management of the various resources, each with the other, without impairment of the productivity of the land, with consideration being given to the relative values of the various resources, and not necessarily the combination of uses that will give the greatest dollar return or the greatest unit output.

(b) "Sustained yield of the several products and services" means the achievement and maintenance in perpetuity of a high-level annual or regular periodic output of the various renewable resources of the national forests without impairment of the productivity of the land.

TAYLOR GRAZING ACT (1934)
43 U.S.C. 315 et seq.

§ 315. Grazing districts; establishment; restrictions; prior rights; rights-of-way; hearing and notice; hunting or fishing rights.

In order to promote the highest use of public lands pending its final disposal, the Secretary of the Interior is authorized, in his discretion, by order to establish grazing districts or additions thereto and/or to modify the boundaries thereof of vacant, unappropriated, and unreserved lands from any part of the public domain of the United States (exclusive of Alaska), which are not in national forests, national parks and monuments, Indian reservations, revested Oregon and California Railroad grant lands, or revested Coos Bay Wagon Road grant lands, and which in his opinion are chiefly valuable for grazing and raising forage crops:

Nothing in this Act shall be construed as in any way altering or restricting the right to hunt or fish within a grazing district in accordance
with the laws of the United States or of any State, or as vesting in any
permittee any right whatsoever to interfere with hunting or fishing
within a grazing district.

§ 315a. Protection, administration, regulation, and improvement of
districts.

The Secretary of the Interior shall make provision for the protection,
administration, regulation, and improvement of such grazing districts
as may be created under the authority of the foregoing section, and he
shall make such rules and regulations and establish such service, enter into such cooperative agreements, and do any and all things necessary to accomplish the purposes of this Act and to insure the objects of
such grazing districts, namely to regulate their occupancy and use,
to preserve the land and its resources from destruction or unnecessary
injury, to provide for the orderly use, improvement, and development
of the range; and the Secretary of the Interior is authorized to continue
the study of erosion and flood control. . . .

SOIL CONSERVATION ACT (1935, as amended)<br>16 U.S. 590a et seq.

§ 590a. Prevention of soil erosion; surveys and investigations; preventive measures; cooperation with agencies and persons; acquisition
of land.

It is recognized that the wastage of soil and moisture resources on
farm, grazing, and forest lands of the Nation, resulting from soil
erosion, is a menace to the national welfare and that it is declared to
be the policy of Congress to provide permanently for the control and
prevention of soil erosion and thereby to preserve natural resources,
control floods, prevent impairment of reservoirs, and maintain the
navigability of rivers and harbors, protect public health, public lands
and relieve unemployment, and the Secretary of Agriculture, from now
on, shall coordinate and direct all activities with relation to soil erosion and in order to effectuate this policy is authorized, from time to
time—

(1) To conduct surveys, investigations, and research relating to the
character of soil erosion and the preventive measures needed, to publish the results of any such surveys, investigations, or research, to
disseminate information concerning such methods, and to conduct
demonstrational projects in areas subject to erosion by wind or water;

(2) To carry out preventive measures, including, but not limited to, engineering operations, methods of cultivation, the growing of vegetation, and changes in use of land;

(3) To cooperate or enter into agreements with, or to furnish financial or other aid to, any agency, governmental or otherwise, or any person, subject to such conditions as he may deem necessary, for the purposes of this chapter; and

(4) To acquire lands, or rights or interests therein, by purchase, gift, condemnation, or otherwise, whenever necessary for the purposes of this chapter.

§ 590g. Additional policies and purposes of chapter.

(a) Purposes enumerated.

It is declared to be the policy of this chapter also to secure, and the purposes of this chapter shall also include,
  (1) preservation and improvement of soil fertility;
  (2) promotion of the economic use and conservation of land;
  (3) diminution of exploitation and wasteful and unscientific use of national soil resources;
  (4) the protection of rivers and harbors against the results of soil erosion in aid of maintaining the navigability of waters and water courses and in aid of flood control;
  (5) reestablishment, at the maintenance of such ratio; and
  (6) prevention and abatement of agricultural-related pollution. . . .

§ 590h. Payments and grants of aid. . . .

(b) Payments and grants of aid; local, county, State committees; rules and regulations; rural environmental protection contracts: terms and conditions, period, modification or termination.

The Secretary shall have power to carry out the purposes specified in clauses (1), (2), (3), (4), (5), and (6) of section 590g(a) of this title by making payments or grants of other aid to agricultural producers, including tenants and sharecroppers, in amounts determined by the Secretary to be fair and reasonable. . . .


STATES


Crop Lands


OHIO AGRICULTURAL LAND (1974)
Ohio Rev. Code Sec. 5713.30 et seq.


Section 5713.30.    Definitions
        5713.31.    Valuation of agricultural land; application fee

§ 5713.30.   Definitions.

(A) "Land devoted exclusively to agricultural use" means:

(1) Tracts, lots, or parcels of land totaling not less than thirty
acres which, during the three calendar years prior to the year in which
application is filed . . . were devoted exclusively to commercial animal or poultry husbandry, the production for a commercial purpose of
field crops, tobacco, fruits, vegetables, timber, nursery stock, ornamental trees, sod, or flowers or that were devoted to and qualified
for payments or other compensation under a land retirement or conservation program under an agreement with an agency of the federal
government;

(2) Tracts, lots, or parcels of land totaling less than thirty acres
that, during the three calendar years prior to the year in which application is filed . . . were devoted exclusively to commercial animal or
poultry husbandry, the production for a commercial purpose of field
crops, tobacco, fruits, vegetables, timber, nursery stock, ornamental
trees, sod or flowers where such activities produced an average yearly
gross income of at least twenty-five hundred dollars during such three
year period or where there is evidence of an anticipated gross income
of such amount from such activities during the tax year in which application is made, or that were devoted to and qualified for payments or
other compensation under a land retirement or conservation program
under an agreement with an agency of the federal government. . . .

§ 5713.31.   Valuation of agricultural land application fee.

At any time after the first Monday in January and prior to the first
Monday in March of any year, an owner of agricultural land may file
an application, on a form prescribed by the board of tax appeals, with
the county auditor of the county in which such land is located, request-
ing the auditor to value the land for real property tax purposes at the
current value such land has for agricultural use, in accordance with
rules adopted by the board of tax appeals for the valuation of such
land. . . .

If the auditor determines the application or amended application is
complete and the information therein is correct, he shall, prior to

the first Monday in June, view or cause to be viewed the land described in the application and determine whether the land is land devoted exclusively to agricultural use. . . .

§ 5713.33. Agricultural land tax list.

The county auditor shall make and maintain an "agricultural land tax list," on forms prescribed the board of tax appeals, listing each tract, lot or parcel of land which has been valued for tax purposes as land devoted exclusively to agricultural use under section 5713.31 of the Revised Code, showing:

(A) The name of the owner;

(B) A description of the land;

(C) The current agricultural use value and taxable value of the land as land devoted exclusively to agricultural use, . . .

(D) The true value, and taxable value, of the land as determined in accordance with . . . the Ohio Constitution. . . .

§ 5713.34. Tax savings upon converted land.

Upon the conversion of all or any portion of a tract, lot, or parcel of land devoted exclusively to agricultural use, a portion of the tax savings upon such converted land shall be recouped as provided for by Section 36, Article II, Ohio Constitution by levying a charge on such land in an amount equal to the amount of the tax savings on the converted land during the four tax years immediately preceding the year in which the conversion occurs. The charge shall constitute a lien of the state upon such converted land as of the first day of January of the tax year in which the charge is levied and shall continue until discharged as provided by law.

§ 5713.35. Conversion of land on agricultural land tax list.

On or before the second Monday in September the county auditor shall examine the agricultural land tax list maintained under section 5713.33 of the Revised Code and determine if there has been a conversion of land devoted exclusively to agricultural use of any tract, lot or parcel of land on such list. . . .

WISCONSIN TAXATION OF FOREST CROP LANDS (1971)
Wis. Stat. 77.01 et seq.

Section 77.01.    Purposes
        77.015.    Lands in villages included

§ 77.01.  Purposes.

It is the intent of this chapter to encourage a policy of protecting from destructive or premature cutting the forest growth in this state, and of reproducing and growing for the future adequate crops through sound forestry practices of forest products on lands not more useful for other purposes, so that such lands shall continue to furnish recurring forest crops for commercial use with public hunting and fishing as extra public benefits, all in a manner which shall not hamper the towns in which such lands lie from receiving their just tax revenue from such lands.

§ 77.02.  Forest crop lands.

(I) Petition
    (1) The owner of an entire quarter quarter section, fractional lot or government lot as determined by U.S. government survey plat, excluding public roads and railroad rights-of-way that may have been sold, may file with the department of natural resources a petition stating that he believes the lands therein described are more useful for growing timber and other forest crops than for any other purposes, that he intends to practice forestry thereon, that all persons holding encumbrances thereon have joined such petition and requesting that such lands be approved as "Forest croplands" under this chapter. . . .
    (3) After receiving all the evidence offered at any hearing held on the petition and after making such independent investigation as it sees fit the department shall make its findings of fact and make and enter an order accordingly. If it finds that the facts give reasonable assurance that a stand of merchantable timber will be developed on such de-

scriptions within a reasonable time, and that such descriptions are
then held permanently for the growing of timber under sound forestry
practices, rather than for agricultural, mineral, shoreland development of navigable waters, recreational, residential or other purposes,
and that all persons holding encumbrances against such descriptions
have in writing agreed to the petition, the order entered shall grant
the request of the petitioner on condition that all unpaid taxes against
said descriptions be paid within 30 days thereafter. . . .

### § 77.03. Taxation of forest croplands.

After the filing of the order with the officers under §. 77.02(3) the
lands described therein shall be "Forest Croplands", on which taxes
shall thereafter be payable only as provided under this subchapter.
The passage of this act, petition by the owner and the making of the
order under §. 77.02(3) shall constitute a contract between the state
and the owner, running with said lands, for a period of 25 or 50 years
at the election of the applicant at the time the petition is filed, unless
terminated as hereinafter provided, with privilege of renewal by mutual
agreement between the owner and the state, whereby the state as an
inducement to owners and prospective purchasers of forest croplands
to come under this chapter agrees that until terminated as hereinafter
provided, no change in or repeal of this chapter shall apply to any land
then accepted as forest croplands, except as the department of natural
resources and the owner may expressly agree in writing. If at the
end of the contract period the contract is not renewed by mutual consent,
then the merchantable timber on the land shall be estimated by an es-
timator jointly agreed upon by the department of natural resources
and the owner, . . . and the cost thereof shall be borne jointly by the
department of natural resources and the owner; and the 10% severance
tax paid on the stumpage thereon in the same manner as if said stumpage had been cut. The owners by such contract consent that the public
may hunt and fish on the lands, subject to such rules as the department
of natural resources prescribes regulating hunting and fishing.

### § 77.04. Taxation.

No tax shall be levied on forest croplands except the specific annual
taxes as provided, except that any building located on forest cropland
shall be assessed as personal property, subject to all laws and regulations for the assessment and taxation of general property.

(2) Tax per acre; payment penalty.

(2) Any owner shall be liable for and pay to the town treasurer on
or before the last day of February of each year on each such description a sum herein called the "acreage share" computed at the rate of
10 cents per acre on all lands entered prior to 1972. On all lands en-

tered after December 31, 1971, the "acreage share" shall be computed
every 10 years to the nearest cent by the department of revenue at
the rate of 20 cents per acre multiplied by a ratio using. . . .

### § 77.05. State contribution.

(1) On or before April 20 the county treasurer of each county containing
forest croplands shall certify to the department of natural resources
for each owner the legal description in each town on which the owner
has paid the acreage share pursuant to §. 77.04(2), and also on acreage
share previously returned delinquent and subsequently paid, except
on lands on which an order of cancellation has been issued by the department of natural resources pursuant to §. 77.10(1).

(2) Payment.

As soon after April 20 of each year as feasible, the department of
natural resources shall pay to each town treasurer on each description
as above certified, from the appropriation under §. 20.370(2) (b), the
sum of 20 cents per acre.

### § 77.06. Forestation.

(1) Cutting timber regulated.

(1) No person shall cut any merchantable wood products on any forest croplands where the forest crop taxes are delinquent nor until 30
days after the owner has filed with the department of natural resources
a notice of intention to cut, specifying by descriptions and the estimated
amount of wood products to be removed and the proportion of present
volume to be left as growing stock in the area to be cut. The department
of natural resources may require a bond executed by some surety company licensed in this state or other surety for such amount as may reasonably be required for the payment to the department of natural resources of the severance tax hereinafter provided. The department,
after examination of the lands specified, may prescribe the amount of
forest products to be removed. Cutting in excess of the amount prescribed shall render the owner liable to double the severance tax prescribed in §. 77.06(5) and subject to cancellation under §. 77.10.
Merchantable wood products include all wood products except wood used
for fuel by the owner.

(2) Appraisal of timber, zones.

During the month of July in each year the department of natural resources, at such time and place as it shall fix, and after such public
notice thereof as it deems reasonable, shall hold a public hearing, and
not later than September first thereafter shall make and file, open to
public inspection, a determination of the reasonable stumpage values

of the wood products usually grown in the several towns in which any
forest crop lands lie. If the department of natural resources finds
there is a material variance in such stumpage values in the different
localities, it may fix separate zones and determine such values for
each zone. . . .

(4) Within 30 days after completion of cutting on any land description,
but not more than one year after filing of the notice of intention to cut,
the owner shall transmit to the department of natural resources on
forms provided by the department a written statement of the products
so cut, specifying the variety of wood, kind of product, and quantity of
each variety and kind as shown by the scale or measurement thereof
made on the ground as cut, skidded, loaded, delivered, or by tree scale
certified by a qualified forester when stumpage is sold by tree measurement.

(5) The department of natural resources shall assess and levy
against such owner a severance tax on the right to cut and remove wood
products covered by reports under this section, at the rate of 10 per
cent of the value of such wood products based upon the stumpage value
then in force. . . .

§ 77.10. Withdrawal of forest croplands.

(I) Investigations, refunds, forfeitures.

(1) (a) The department of natural resources shall on the application
of the department of revenue or the owner of any forest croplands or
the town board of the town in which said lands lie and may on its own
motion at any time cause an investigation to be made and hearing to be
had as to whether any forest croplands shall continue under this chapter.
If on such hearing after due notice to and opportunity to be heard by
the department of revenue, the town and the owner, the department of
natural resources finds that any such lands are not meeting the requirements set forth in §. 77. 02 or that the owner has made use of the land
for anything other than forestry or has failed to practice sound forestry
on the land, the department of natural resources shall cancel the entry
of such description and issue an order of withdrawal, and the owner
shall be liable for the tax and penalty under sub. (2). . . .

(2) (a) Any owner of forest croplands may elect to withdraw all or
any of such lands from under this chapter, by filing with the department
of natural resources a declaration withdrawing from this chapter any
description owned by him which he specified, and by payment by such
owner to the department of natural resources within 60 days the amount
of tax due as determined by the department of revenue under §. 77. 04(1)
with simple interest thereon at 5% per annum, less any severance tax
and supplemental severance tax or acreage share paid thereon, with
interest computed according to the rule of partial payments at the
rate of 5% per annum. . . .

§ 77.16. Woodland tax law.

(1) The owner of any tract of land of less than 40 acres may file with the department of natural resources an application setting forth a description of the property which he desires to place under the woodland tax law and on which land he will practice forestry.

(2) Upon filing of such application the department of natural resources shall examine the land, and if it finds that the facts give reasonable assurance that the woodland is more suitable for the growing of timber and other forest products and that such lands are not more useful for any other purpose the department of natural resources shall enter an order approving the application. A copy of such order shall be forwarded to the owner of the land, to the supervisor of property assessments of the district wherein the land is located, to the clerk of the town, to the assessor of the town and to the county clerk of the county wherein the land is located.

(3) The application of the owner of the land and the filing of the order by the department of natural resources shall constitute a contract, running with the land, for a period of 10 years, unless terminated as hereinafter provided. . . .

(5) The owner shall be liable and shall pay to the town treasurer at the same time he pays the taxes on the remaining acreage of his land a tax computed at the rate of 20 cents per acre on the land approved for entry under this section. Such acreage tax shall be part of the total taxes on the land of the owner and subject to the collection of taxes provided for in ch. 74.

(6) The owner of the land shall promote the growth of trees and shall prohibit grazing and burning on lands entered under the woodland tax law. At the request of the owner the department of natural resources shall assist in preparing and carrying out planting and forest management plans. The department of natural resources shall make an annual written report as to the forest practices of each owner of the lands under this section. If the department finds that the owner has not complied with the law, or if the land is no longer used for forestry purposes, it shall issue an order removing the land from the woodland tax law classification. Any declassification order issued on or before March 20 of any year shall take effect in such year. A copy of the declassification order shall be sent to the owner of the land, to the supervisor of property assessments of the district wherein the land is located, to the clerk and to the assessor of the town, and to the county clerk of the county wherein the land is located. Any order issued under this subsection shall be final unless set aside by the department of natural resources.

NEVADA FOREST PRACTICE ACT
(1971, as amended)
Nev. Rev. Stat. Ch. 528

§ 528.030. Statement of purposes.

1. NRS 528.010 to 528.090, inclusive, are adopted:
(a) To establish minimum standards of forest practice and to require compliance therewith by every timber owner or operator.
(b) To promote the sustained productivity of the forests of the Sierra Nevada Mountains in Nevada.
(c) To preserve the natural water supply of the state in the interests of the economic welfare of the state.

2. The provisions of NRS 528.011 to 528.090, inclusive, shall not be construed in any way to condone any activity which causes significant degradation of water quality.

§ 528.042. Logging permit: Requirement; application.

1. Prior to any logging or cutting operation, any timber owner or his agent shall secure a logging permit from the state forester firewarden. . . .

§ 528.043. Logging permit: Logging plan; performance bond.

An application for a logging permit shall be accompanied by:

1. A logging plan including, but not limited to, the following information:
(a) An accurate topographical map showing exterior boundaries of the areas to be logged and the roads, structures and landings, existing and proposed.
(b) The volume of timber to be removed.
(c) The time required for removal of such volume.
(d) The specification as to the percentage of merchantable volume to be removed and the composition of any residual stand.
(e) The revegetation plan, if applicable.
(f) The slash-disposal and cleanup plans.
(g) The road construction specifications and erosion control measures.
(h) An outline of the fire prevention and protection plans and procedures.
(i) A description of tools and equipment suitable and available for firefighting, and the number of men normally available for firefighting.

2. If a variance is requested pursuant to NRS 528.048, the applicant shall also furnish the state forester firewarden with information and data regarding:

(a) Soil characteristics;

(b) Reproduction capability of the area;

(c) Ground and litter cover;

(d) Soil erosion hazards;

(e) Natural drainage features;

(f) Percent of gradient and aspect of slopes;

(g) Description of the method of logging and equipment to be used; and

(h) Such other information as the state forester firewarden may require.

3. A performance bond in an amount set by the state forester firewarden and based upon the contract price or value of the timber to be cut, which shall be conditioned upon compliance with all provisions of the logging permit, and shall be approved as to form and sufficiency by the state forester firewarden.

§ 528.044. Logging permit: Issuance; denial; hearing after denial; return of performance bond.

1. Within 45 days after the receipt of an application for a logging permit, the state forester firewarden shall either:

(a) Issue an original logging permit subject to such conditions or recommendations as he may deem necessary; or

(b) Deny such permit for any of the following reasons: . . .

(4) The logging operation as planned will cause significant soil erosion and siltation.

(5) Failure to correct a violation of a previously issued permit within a period of 3 years prior to the current application.

§ 528.047. Logging permit: Suspension, revocation.

Any logging permit may be suspended or revoked for any of the following reasons:

1. Failure to comply with:

(a) The forest practice rules or regulations;

(b) The conditions of the permit;

(c) The original logging plan; or

(d) Any accepted alternate logging plan.

2. Refusal to allow any inspection by the state forester firewarden or his agent.

3. Inadequate performance bond.

§ 528.048. Variance required for tractor logging on certain slopes.

1. No person may engage in tractor logging on a slope whose gradient is 30 percent or more without first obtaining a variance from the state forester firewarden.

2. The state forester firewarden shall act on a request for a variance within 45 days after receipt of a proper application, which shall include the information required by subsection 2 of NRS 528.043. If a variance is granted, it is subject to such conditions and requirements as the state forester firewarden may prescribe.

3. In acting on a request for a variance, the state forester firewarden shall consider the following factors:
(a) The extent to which tractor logging may destroy advanced regeneration and litter cover;
(b) The extent to which tractor logging may cause soils to be displaced or erode; and
(c) The extent to which tractor logging may cause siltation and eroded soils to infiltrate the 200-foot stream buffer.

4. An applicant may request a hearing before the state forester firewarden within 10 days after the denial of a request for a variance.

5. Upon any final denial, any performance bond shall be returned to the applicant.

§ 528.050. Cutting practices.

The cutting practices of every timber owner or operator conducting logging operations within this state shall conform to the following:

1. Areas of old-growth timber shall have reserved and left uncut for future crops all sound, immature trees 18 inches d.b.h. or less, with an average of not less than 10 satisfactorily located seed trees 18 inches d.b.h. or larger to be left per acre, and no area will be more than one-eighth mile from seed source unless the area is adequately stocked. Seed trees shall be approved by the state forester firewarden.

2. Areas of young-growth and prior-cut timber harvested for saw logs and veneer logs shall have reserved and left uncut for future crops all sound, immature trees of 18 inches d.b.h. or less, with an average of not less than 10 satisfactorily located seed trees 18 inches d.b.h. or larger to be left per acre, and no area will be more than one-eighth mile from the seed source unless the area is adequately stocked. Seed trees shall be approved by the state forester firewarden.

3. On areas of young-growth and prior-cut timber where forest products other than saw logs and veneer logs are being harvested an adequately stocked stand shall be left.

4. The following may be cut regardless of size:

(a) Trees with dead tops.

(b) Trees with butt burns, with over half of the circumference burned and exposed wood showing decay.

(c) Trees with bad lightning scars.

(d) Trees infested with insects or disease.

(e) Trees injured or broken during operations.

(f) Trees to be removed for purpose of clearing of rights-of-way, landings, campsites or firebreaks.

(g) Excessively crooked trees.

(h) Suppressed trees with less than 25 percent crown.

5. No tractor logging shall be conducted on saturated soils.

The provisions of this section do not apply if trees are being removed to change the use of the land from forest production to another use, but the timber owner or his agent shall obtain a timberland conversion certificate as provided in this chapter.

§ 528.053. Certain activities prohibited near water bodies; exceptions.

1. No felling of trees, skidding, rigging or construction of tractor or truck roads or landings, or the operation of vehicles, shall take place within 200 feet, measured on the slope, of the high water mark of any lake, reservoir, stream or other body of water unless a variance is first obtained from a committee composed of the state forester firewarden, the director of the Nevada department of fish and game and the state engineer. . . .

§ 528.055. Erosion controls; Location, construction of skid trails, landings, roads and firebreaks.

1. Tractor skid trails, landings, logging truck roads and firebreaks shall be so located, constructed, used and left after timber harvesting that erosion caused by waterflow therefrom and waterflow in natural watercourses shall be limited to a reasonable minimum that will not impair the productivity of the soil or appreciably diminish the quality of the water.

2. Roadside berms shall be constructed where necessary to guide surface waterflow to the point of planned diversion required by NRS 528.0551 and 528.0552, and to prevent unnecessary erosion of fills and side cast material.

§ 528.0551. Erosion controls: Waterbreaks, culverts required.

1. Except as provided in NRS 528.0552 to 528.0554, inclusive, waterbreaks or culverts, or both, shall be constructed for all logging truck

roads, tractor skid trails and firebreaks no later than November 15 of each year. Waterbreaks or culverts, or both, shall:

(a) Be located in minimal fill areas;

(b) Be effective in diverting surface water from logging truck roads, tractor skid trails and firebreaks;

(c) Provide unrestricted discharge into an area having sufficient filter capacity to effectively remove waterborne sediment to prevent a serious risk of causing significant degradation of water quality; and

(d) Be installed at such intervals as are necessary to reasonably prevent surface water on or from such logging truck roads, tractor skid trails and firebreaks from accumulating in sufficient volume or accelerating to sufficient velocity to cause excessive erosion. The following guidelines shall be considered in determining reasonable waterbreak or culvert intervals:

(1) On grades of 10 percent or less, intervals of 100 to 200 feet;

(2) On grades of 11 to 25 percent, intervals of 75 to 150 feet;

(3) On grades of 26 to 49 percent, intervals of 50 to 100 feet; and

(4) On grades of 50 percent or more, intervals of 30 to 75 feet.

2. Advance flagging of waterbreak or culvert locations shall be provided wherever necessary to insure that the location and spacing of the waterbreaks or culverts, or both, is adequate to prevent water-flow from creating a serious risk of causing significant degradation of water quality.

2. Advance flagging of waterbreak of culvert locations shall be provided wherever necessary to insure that the location and spacing of the waterbreaks or culverts, or both, is adequate to prevent waterflow from creating a serious risk of causing significant degradation of water quality.

3. On permanent truck roads, waterbreaks or culverts, or both, shall be cut a minimum of 12 inches into the firm road surface and shall be constructed so that they will not be rendered ineffective by the passage of motorized vehicles.


FEDERAL


Mining Lands


MINING LAW (1872)
30 U.S.C. 21, et seq.

Section 21.    Mineral lands reserved
        22.    Lands open to purchase by citizens

§ 22.  Lands open to purchase by citizens.

Except as otherwise provided, all valuable mineral deposits in lands belonging to the United States, both surveyed and unsurveyed, shall be free and open to exploration and purchase, and the lands in which they are found to occupation and purchase, by citizens of the United States and those who have declared their intention to become such, under regulations prescribed by law, and according to the local customs or rules of miners in the several mining districts, so far as the same are applicable and not inconsistent with the laws of the United States.

§ 26.  Locators' rights of possession and enjoyment.

The locators of all mining locations made on any mineral vein, lode, or ledge, situated on the public domain, their heirs and assigns, where no adverse claim existed on the 10th day of May 1872 so long as they comply with the laws of the United States, and with State, territorial, and local regulations not in conflict with the laws of the United States governing their possessory title, shall have the exclusive right of possession and enjoyment of all the surface included within the lines of their locations, and of all veins, lodes, and ledges throughout their entire depth, the top or apex of which lies inside of such surface lines extended downward vertically, although such veins, lodes, or ledges may so far depart from a perpendicular in their course downward as to extend outside the vertical side lines of such surface locations. But their right of possession to such outside parts of such veins or ledges shall be confined to such portions thereof as lie between vertical planes drawn downward as above described, through the end lines of their locations, so continued in their own direction that such planes will intersect such exterior parts of such veins or ledges. Nothing in this section shall authorize the locator or possessor of a vein or lode which extends in its downward course beyond the vertical lines of his claim to enter upon the surface of a claim owned or possessed by another.

MINERAL LEASING ACT (1920)
30 U.S.C. 181 et seq.

## § 226. Lease of oil and gas lands—authority of Secretary.

All lands subject to disposition under this chapter which are known or believed to contain oil or gas deposits may be leased by the Secretary.

If the lands to be leased are within any known geological structure of a producing oil or gas field, they shall be leased to the highest responsible qualified bidder by competitive bidding under general regulations in units of not more than six hundred and forty acres, which shall be as nearly compact in form as possible, upon the payment by the lessee of such bonus as may be accepted by the Secretary and of such royalty as may be fixed in the lease, which shall be not less than 12½ per centum in amount or value of the section removed or sold from the lease.

If the lands to be leased are not within any known geological structure of a producing oil or gas field, the person first making application for the lease who is qualified to hold a lease under this chapter shall be entitled to a lease of such lands without competitive bidding. Such leases shall be conditioned upon the payment by the lessee of a royalty of 12½ per centum in amount or value of the section removed or sold from the lease.

All leases issued under this section shall be conditioned upon payment by the lessee of a rental of not less than 50 cents per acre for each year of the lease. Each year's lease rental shall be paid in advance. A minimum royalty of $1 per acre in lieu of rental shall be payable at the expiration of each lease year beginning on or after a discovery of oil or gas in paying quantities on the lands leased. . . .

(g) Whenever it appears to the Secretary that lands owned by the United States are being drained of oil or gas by wells drilled on adjacent lands, he may negotiate agreements whereby the United States, or the United States and its lessees, shall be compensated for such drainage. . . .

(j) For the purpose of more properly conserving the natural resources of any oil or gas pool, field, or like area, or any part thereof (whether or not any part of said oil or gas pool, field, or like area, is then subject to any cooperative or unit plan of development or operation), lessees thereof and their representatives may unite with each other, or jointly or separately with others, in collectively adopting and operating under a cooperative or unit plan of development or operation of such pool, field, or like area, or any part thereof, whenever determined and certified by the Secretary of the Interior to be necessary or advisable in the public interest. The Secretary is thereunto authorized, in

his discretion, with the consent of the holders of leases involved, to
establish, alter, change, or revoke drilling, producing, rental, minimum royalty, and royalty requirements of such leases and to make such
regulations with reference to such leases, with like consent on the part
of the lessees, in connection with the institution and operation of any
such cooperative or unit plan as he may deem necessary or proper to
secure the proper protection of the public interest. . . .

GEOTHERMAL STEAM ACT (1970)
30 U.S.C. 1001 et seq.

§ 1001. Definitions.

As used in this chapter, the term— . . .

(c) "geothermal steam and associated geothermal resources" means
(i) all products of geothermal processes, embracing indigenous steam, hot water and hot brines;
(ii) steam and other gases, hot water and hot brines resulting from water, gas, or other fluids artificially introduced into geothermal formations;
(iii) heat or other associated energy found in geothermal formations; and
(iv) any byproduct derived from them;

(d) "by-product" means any mineral or minerals (exclusive of oil, hydrocarbon gas, and helium) which are found in solution or in association with geothermal steam and which have a value of less than 75 per centum of the value of the geothermal steam or are not, because of quantity, quality, or technical difficulties in extraction and production, of sufficient value to warrant extraction and production by themselves;

(e) "known geothermal resources area" means an area in which the geology, nearby discoveries, competitive interests, or other indicia would, in the opinion of the Secretary, engender a belief in men who are experienced in the subject matter that the prospects for extraction of geothermal steam or associated geothermal resources are good enough to warrant expenditures of money for that purpose.

§ 1002. Lands subject to geothermal leasing.

Subject to the provisions of section 1014 of this title, the Secretary of the Interior may issue leases for the development and utilization of geothermal steam and associated geothermal resources
(1) in lands administered by him, including public, withdrawn, and acquired lands,
(2) in any national forest or other lands administered by the Department of Agriculture through the Forest Service, including public, withdrawn, and acquired lands, and
(3) in lands which have been conveyed by the United States subject to a reservation to the United States of the geothermal steam and associated geothermal resources therein.

§ 1003. Bids; competitive bidding; first application for qualified person without competitive bidding.

If lands to be leased under this chapter are within any known geothermal resources area, they shall be leased to the highest responsible qualified bidder by competitive bidding under regulations formulated by the Secretary. If the lands to be leased are not within any known geothermal resources area, the qualified person first making application for the lease shall be entitled to a lease of such lands without competitive bidding. Notwithstanding the foregoing, at any time within one hundred and eighty days following December 24, 1970.

(a) with respect to all lands which were on September 7, 1965, subject to valid leases or permits issued under the Mineral Leasing Act of February 25, 1920, as amended (section 181 et seq. of this title), or under the Mineral Leasing Act of Acquired Lands, as amended (sections 351, 358 of this title), or to existing miining claims located on or prior to September 7, 1965, the lessees or permittees or claimants or their successors in interest who are qualified to hold geothermal leases shall have the right to convert such leases or permits or claims to geothermal leases covering the same lands; . . .

(f) with respect to lands within any known geothermal resources area and which are subject to a right to conversion to a geothermal lease, such lands shall be leased by competitive bidding: Provided, That, the competitive geothermal lease shall be issued to the person owning the right to conversion to a geothermal lease if he makes payment of an amount equal to the highest bona fide bid for the competitive geothermal lease, plus the rental for the first year, within thirty days after he receives written notice from the Secretary of the amount of the highest bid.

§ 1005. Duration of leases—Primary and continuation terms.

(a) Geothermal leases shall be for a primary term of ten years. If geothermal steam is produced or utilized in commercial quantities within this term, such lease shall continue for so long thereafter as geothermal steam is produced or utilized in commercial quantities, but such continuation shall not exceed an additional forty years.

(b) If, at the end of such forty years, steam is produced or utilized in commercial quantities and the lands are not needed for other purposes, the lessee shall have a preferential right to a renewal of such lease for a second forty-year term in accordance with such terms and conditions as the Secretary deems appropriate.

(c) Any lease for land on which or for which under an approved cooperative or unit plan of development or operation, actual drilling operations were commenced prior to the end of its primary term and are being diligently prosecuted at that time shall be extended for five years and so long thereafter, but not more than thirty-five years, as geothermal steam is produced or utilized in commercial quantities. If, at the end of such extended term, steam is being produced or utilized in commercial quantities and the lands are not needed for other purposes, the lessee shall have a preferential right to a renewal of such lease for a second term in accordance with such terms and conditions as the Secretary deems appropriate. . . .

(e) Leases which have extended by reasons of production, or which have produced geothermal steam, and have been determined by the Secretary to be incapable of further commercial production and utilization of geothermal steam may be further extended for a period of not more than five years from the date of such determination but only for so long as one or more valuable byproducts are produced in commercial quantities. . . .

(f) Minerals locatable under the mining laws of the United States in lands subject to a geothermal lease issued under the provisions of this chapter which are not associated with the geothermal steam and associated geothermal resources of such lands as defined in section 1001(c) of this title shall be locatable under said mining laws in accordance with the principles of the Multiple Mineral Development Act (found in section 521 et seq. of this title).

§ 1006.  Acreage of geothermal lease; irregular subdivisions; State limitation; increase.

A geothermal lease shall embrace a reasonably compact area of not more than two thousand five hundred and sixty acres, except where a departure therefrom is occasioned by an irregular subdivision or subdivisions.  No person, association, or corporation, except as otherwise provided in this chapter, shall take, hold, own, or control at one time, whether acquired directly from the Secretary under this chapter or otherwise, any direct or indirect interest in Federal geothermal leases in any one State exceeding twenty thousand four hundred and eighty acres, including leases acquired under the provisions of section 1003 of this title.

At any time after fifteen years from December 24, 1970, the Secretary, after public hearings, may increase this maximum holding in any one State by regulation, not to exceed fifty-one thousand two hundred acres. . . .

§ 1008.  Byproducts; production or use; water for beneficial uses under State water laws; substantial beneficial production or use; modification of waiver; preexisting rights of lease, claim, or permit holders.

If the production, use, or conversion of geothermal steam is susceptible of producing a valuable byproduct or byproducts, including commercially demineralized water for beneficial uses in accordance with applicable State water laws, the Secretary shall require substantial beneficial production or use thereof unless, in individual circumstances he modifies or waives this requirement in the interest of conservation of natural resources or for other reasons satisfactory to him. However, the production or use of such byproducts shall be subject to the rights of the holders of preexisting leases, claims, or permits covering the same land or the same minerals, if any. . . .

§ 1014. Lands subject to geothermal leasing—terms and conditions for lands withdrawn or acquired for Department of Interior.

(a) Geothermal leases for lands withdrawn or acquired in aid of functions of the Department of the Interior may be issued only under such terms and conditions as the Secretary may prescribe to insure adequate utilization of the lands for the purposes for which they were withdrawn or acquired.

(b) Geothermal leases for lands withdrawn or acquired in aid of functions of the Department of Agriculture may be issued only with the consent of, and subject to such terms and conditions as may be prescribed by the head of that Department to insure adequate utilization of the lands for the purposes for which they were withdrawn or acquired. Geothermal leases for lands to which section 818 of Title 16 is applicable, may be issued only with the consent of and subject to, such terms and conditions as the Federal Power Commission may prescribe to insure adequate utilization of such lands for power and related purposes.

(c) Geothermal leases under this chapter shall not be issued for lands administered in accordance with
     (1) the Act of August 25, 1916 (39 Stat. 535), as amended or supplemented,
     (2) for lands within a national recreation area,
     (3) for lands in a fish hatchery administered by the Secretary, wildlife refuge, wildlife range, game range, wildlife management area, waterfowl production area, or for lands acquired or reserved for the protection and conservation of fish and wildlife that are threatened with extinction,
     (4) for tribally or individually owned Indian trust or restricted lands, within or without the boundaries of Indian reservations.

§ 1017. Cooperative or unit plan of development or operation of geothermal pool, field, or like area; public interest; determination and certification; regulations; protection of parties in interest; authority respecting rate of prospecting, development, and production; leases excepted from control for purposes of State acreage limitation.

For the purpose of properly conserving the natural resources of any geothermal pool, field, or like area, or any part thereof, lessees thereof and their representatives may unite with each other, or jointly

or separately with others, in collectively adopting and operating under
a cooperative or unit plan of development or operation of such pool,
field, or like area, or any part thereof, whenever this is determined
and certified by the Secretary to be necessary or advisable in the public
interest. . . .

§ 1020.  Publication in Federal Register of known geothermal resource
area lands; Federal transfer of surface rights and retention of mineral
rights; necessity of geothermal leases for development or production;
quiet title proceedings; venue; injunction; judicial determination of inclusion of geothermal resources within Federal mineral reservation;
cessation of duty to report and institute proceedings.

(a) Within one hundred and twenty days after December 24, 1970, the
Secretary shall cause to be published in the Federal Register a determination of all lands which were included within any known geothermal
resources area on December 24, 1970.  He shall likewise publish in
the Federal Register from time to time his determination of other known
geothermal resources areas specifying in each case the date the lands
were included in such area; and

(b) Geothermal resources in lands the surface of which has passed from
Federal ownership but in which the minerals have been reserved to the
United States shall not be developed or produced except under geothermal leases made pursuant to this chapter.  If the Secretary of the Interior finds that such development is imminent, or that production from
a well heretofore drilled on such lands is imminent, he shall so report
to the Attorney General, and the Attorney General is authorized and
directed to institute an appropriate proceeding in the United States
district court of the district in which such lands are located, to quiet
the title of the United States in such resources, and if the court determines that the reservation of minerals to the United States in the lands
involved included the geothermal resources, to enjoin their production
otherwise than under the terms of this chapter. . . .


                              STATES


                           Mining Lands

               IDAHO GEOTHERMAL RESOURCES ACT (1972)
                     42 Idaho Code 4001 et seq.

Section 42-4001.    Short title
        42-4002.    Definitions

§ 42-4001.  Short title.—This act may be known and cited as the Idaho
Geothermal Resources Act.

Compiler's notes.  Section 1 of S. L. 1972, ch. 301 read:

> It is hereby declared that the state of Idaho claims the right
> to regulate the development and use of all of the geothermal
> resources within this state and that geothermal resources are
> natural resources of limited quantity and of a unique value
> to all of the people of the state.
>    The legislature of the state of Idaho further declares that
> the geothermal resources of this state may provide an out-
> standing opportunity for enhancement of our economy and
> quality of life with a minimum of environmental degradation
> through a utilization of this energy source.  It is also recog-
> nized that the process of utilization and development of our ge-
> thermal resources on a large scale may be associated with
> risks to the maximum sustained yield from these resources,
> risks to our valuable groundwater resources, and risks to the
> environment in the immediate locality of and around the in-
> stallations at which such utilization is done.
>    The legislature further finds that there is presently sub-
> stantial interest in the geothermal resources of this state,
> that regulation in the public interest is imperative, and that
> regulation must take effect at an early date.
>    The legislature does therefore declare that it is the policy
> and purpose of this state to maximize the benefits to the en-
> tire state which may be derived from the utilization of our geo-
> thermal resources, while minimizing the detriments and costs
> of all kinds which could result from their utilization.  This

policy and purpose is embodied in this act which provides
for the immediate regulation of geothermal resource exploration and development in the public interest.

§ 42-4002.  Definitions. . . .

(c) "Geothermal resource" means the natural heat energy of the earth,
the energy, in whatever form, which may be found in any position and
at any depth below the surface of the earth present in, resulting from,
or created by, or which may be extracted from such natural heat, and
all minerals in solution or other products obtained from the material
medium of any geothermal resource.  Geothermal resources are found
and hereby declared to be sui generis, being neither a mineral resource
nor a water resource, but they are also found and hereby declared to
be closely related to and possibly affecting and affected by water and
mineral resources in many instances.

(d) "Geothermal area" means the same general land area which, in
its subsurface, is underlaid or reasonably appears to be underlaid by
geothermal resources from or in a single reservoir, pool, or other
source or interrelated sources, as such area or areas may be from
time to time designated by the director.

(e) "Material medium" means any substance, including, but not limited
to, naturally heated fluids, brines, associated gases, and steam, in
whatever form, found at any depth and in any position below the surface
of the earth, which contains or transmits the natural heat energy of
the earth, but excluding petroleum, oil, hydrocarbon gas, or other
hydrocarbon substances.

(h) "Waste" means any physical waste including, but not limited to:
    (1) Underground waste resulting from the inefficient, excessive or
improper use or dissipation of geothermal energy in or of any geothermal resource pool, reservoir, or other source; or the locating, spacing, construction, equipping, operating, or producing of any well in
a manner which results, or tends to result, in reducing the quantity
of geothermal energy to be recovered from any geothermal area in this
state;
    (2) The inefficient above-ground transporting and storage of geo-
thermal energy; and the locating, spacing, equipping, operating, or
producing of any well or injection well in a manner causing, or tending
to cause, unnecessary or excessive surface loss or destruction of
geothermal energy;
    (3) The escape into the open air, from a well, of steam or hot water
in excess of what is reasonably necessary in the efficient development
or production of a well.

(i) "Well" means any excavation or other alteration in the earth's surface or crust by means of which the energy of any geothermal resource
and/or its material medium is sought or obtained.

(j) "Injection well" means any special well, converted producing well
or reactivated or converted abandoned well employed for injecting
material into a geothermal area to maintain pressures in a geothermal
reservoir, pool, or other source, or to provide new material or to
serve as a material medium therein, or for reinjecting any material
medium or the residue thereof or any by-product of geothermal resource exploration or development into the earth.

§ 42-4003.  Permits—application—fee—exceptions.

(a) Any person who, as owner or operator, proposes to construct a
well or to alter a well or to construct or to alter an injection well shall
first apply to the director for a geothermal resource well permit.  Such
application shall  set out the following information on a form or forms
prescribed by the department: . . .

(f) The director shall have the authority to and may designate any area
of the state a "geothermal area" when the director finds or has reason
to believe that such designation is necessary to protect the geothermal
resource from waste and to protect other resources of the state from
contamination or waste.

(g) No person shall drill a well for any purpose to a depth of three
thousand (3,000) feet or more below land surface in a designated "geothermal area" without first obtaining a permit under the provisions of
this section.  Such permit shall be in addition to any permit required
by other provisions of law.

(h) The owner of any well constructed or being constructed pursuant
to section 47-320, Idaho Code, which encounters a geothermal resource,
and who intends or desires to utilize such resource, shall make application for a geothermal permit as required under this section, provided
however, that no additional filing fee shall be required.

§ 42.4004.  Processing of applications—investigations—hearings. . . .

(b) Upon receipt and acceptance of a proper application, the director
shall undertake such investigations as necessary to determine that
the construction or alteration of the proposed well or injection well
will be in the public interest.  The director may consider, but is not
limited in his consideration to:
    (1) The financial resources of the applicant, his principal, or other
person who may be legally responsible for the subject well or injection
well, and the probability that such person will be financially able to

bear all costs for which he might be responsible which may be incident to the construction, operation, and maintenance of the well or injection well proposed to be constructed or altered.

(2) The adequacy of measures proposed to safeguard subsurface, surface, and atmospheric resources from unreasonable degradation, and especially to protect ground-water aquifers and surface-water sources from contamination which would render such water of lesser quality than it would have had but for the contamination.

(3) The possibility that the construction and maintenance of the proposed well will cause waste or will damage any geothermal resource, reservoir, or other source, by unreasonable reduction of pressures or unreasonable reduction of any geothermal resource material medium or in any other manner, so as to render any geothermal resource of unreasonably less value.

(4) The adequacy of measures proposed to safeguard the environment of the area around the site of the proposed well from unreasonable contamination or pollution.

(5) Any possible interdependence between any geothermal resource reservoir, pool, or other source expected to be affected under the permit and any aquifers or other sources of ground waters used for beneficial uses other than uses as a material medium or a mineral source, and the probability that such interdependence may cause such groundwater sources to be inadequate to meet demands on them under existing water rights. . . .

§ 42-4005.  Permit—issuance—bond—review—appeal.

(a) If the director does not find that the well or the injection well as it is proposed to be constructed or altered will be against the public interest, he shall issue a permit therefor.  The director may issue a permit substantially in accordance with the specifications on the application, or the director may limit the scope of the permit granted or may issue a permit subject to conditions.

(b) If the director finds that the well or injection well as it is proposed to be constructed or altered in the application will not be in the public interest he shall refuse to issue a permit.  In no case shall the director issue a permit to construct or alter a well or injection well if he finds that use of the proposed well or injection well may be expected to unreasonably reduce the quality of any surface or ground waters below the quality which such waters would have had but for the proposed well. . . .

(e) The director shall not issue a permit if he finds that the operation of any well under a proposed permit will unreasonably decrease ground water available for prior water rights in any aquifer or other groundwater source for water for beneficial uses, other than uses as a mineral source, an energy source, or otherwise as a material medium, unless and until the applicant has also obtained a permit for the appropriation of ground waters under chapter 2, title 42, Idaho Code.

(f) The director shall require, as a condition of every permit, every person who engages in the construction, alteration, testing, or operation of a well to file with the director, on a form prescribed by the director, a bond indemnifying the state of Idaho providing good and sufficient security, conditioned upon the performance of the duties required by this act and the proper abandonment of any well covered by such permit. Such bond shall be in an amount to be determined by the director, but in no case may the bond be in an amount which is less than ten thousand dollars ($10,000) for each individual well.

§ 42.4010. Powers and duties—penalties.

(c) The director may enter onto private land at any time to inspect any well or geothermal resource development project to determine if such well or project is being constructed, operated, or maintained according to any applicable permits or to determine if the construction, operation, or maintenance of such well or project may involve a threat to life or property or an unreasonable risk to subsurface, surface, or atmospheric resources.

(d) If the director finds that any person is constructing, operating or maintaining any well or injection well not in accordance with any applicable permit or in a fashion so as to involve an unreasonable risk of, or so as to cause, damage to life or property or subsurface, surface, or atmospheric resources, the director may issue an order to such person to correct or to stop such practices as are found to be improper and to mitigate any injury of any sort caused by such practices. . . .

(f) Any willful violation of or failure to comply with any provision of this act or, if such order or regulation has been served on such person or is otherwise known to him, any valid order or regulation issued or adopted hereto shall be a misdemeanor punishable by a fine of up to five thousand dollars ($5,000) for each offense or a sentence of up to six (6) months in a county jail or both; each day of a continuing violation shall be a separate offense under this subdivision. A responsible or principal executive officer of any corporate person may be liable under this subdivision if such corporate person is not in compliance with any provision of this act or with any valid order or regulation adopted pursuant hereto.

§ 42-4013. Cooperative unit agreements—voluntary—involuntary.

(a) Whenever the director finds that it is in the public interest and especially in the interest of the conservation of natural resources and of the protection of the geothermal resources of this state from waste, the lessors, lessees, operators, owners, or other persons holding or controlling royalty or other interests in the separate properties of the same geothermal area may, with the approval of the board, enter into an agreement for the purpose of bringing about the cooperative development, operation, and maintenance of all or a portion of the geothermal resources of the geothermal area as a unit; or for the purpose of fixing the time, location, and manner of drilling, operating, and maintaining of wells and of injection wells. . . .

(b) Whenever the director finds that a geothermal resource area should be cooperatively operated as a unit to avoid waste, and the persons owning tracts or interests in such area refuse to enter into a cooperative agreement pursuant to subdivision (a) of this section, the board, after notice and hearing, may issue an order that such area shall be operated as a unit. Such order shall provide an equitable sharing of proceeds and liabilities from the geothermal resource area among the several owners of tracts and interests therein.

IDAHO GEOTHERMAL RESOURCES LAND ACT (1972)
47 Idaho Code 1601 et seq.

§ 47-1601.  Geothermal resources—land leases—authorization.

The state board of land commissioners is hereby authorized and empowered to lease for a term of ten (10) years, and as long thereafter as geothermal resources are produced in paying quantities, or as much longer thereafter as the lessee in good faith shall conduct geothermal resource well drilling or construction operations, thereon, or for such lesser term as it finds to be in the public interest, any state or school lands which may contain geothermal resources, together with the right to use and occupy so much of the surface of said land as may be required for all purposes reasonably incident to the prospecting for,

exploration for, drilling or other well construction for, and production
of geothermal resources.

§ 47-1604. Leases restricted.

No single geothermal resource lease issued under this chapter shall
be for an area exceeding one (1) section, provided that any one (1) person may hold more than one (1) lease.

§ 47-1605. Leases—rental or royalty.

Geothermal resources leases shall be issued at an annual rental of
not less than twenty-five cents (25¢) per acre, payable in advance and/or
a royalty which shall not be less than ten per centum (10%) of the geothermal resources produced from the lands under lease or the value
thereof. The rentals and/or the royalties specified in geothermal leases
shall be fixed in any manner, including but not limited to competitive
bidding. . . .

§ 47-1606. Leases—purposes for which land used.

The state board of land commissioners shall have the right to lease
state or school lands for grazing, agricultural, or other purposes, as
may be otherwise provided by law, and to issue geothermal resource
leases covering lands leased for grazing, agricultural, or other purposes, provided however, that the lessee under a geothermal resource
lease issued under the provisions of this chapter shall have paramount
right to the use of so much of the surface of the land as shall be necessary for the purposes of his lease and shall have the right to ingress
and egress at all times during the term of such lease.

§ 47-1611. Cooperative agreements and modification of leases authorization.

The state board of land commissioners is a person authorized to
join on behalf of the state of Idaho in agreements for cooperative or
unit plans of development or operation of the geothermal resources of
geothermal resource areas involving state or school lands and to do all
things necessary to make operative such plan or plans subject to any
and all provisions of state and federal law; . . .

MONTANA CONSTITUTION (1972, as amended)
Art. IX, Sec. 2

§ 2. Reclamation.

All lands disturbed by the taking of natural resources shall be reclaimed. The legislature shall provide effective requirements and
standards for the reclamation of lands disturbed. . . .

MONTANA STRIP AND UNDERGROUND MINE
RECLAMATION ACT (1974, as amended)
50 Rev. Code Mont. 1034 et seq.

§ 50-1035.  Policy of state—findings.

It being the declared policy of this state and its people

—to maintain and improve the state's clean and healthful environment for present and future generations,

—to protect its environmental life-support system from degradation,

—to prevent unreasonable degradation of its natural resources,

—to restore, enhance, and preserve its scenic, historic, archeologic, scientific, cultural, and recreational sites,

—to demand effective reclamation of all lands disturbed by the taking of natural resources, and

—to require the legislature to provide for proper administration and enforcement, create adequate remedies, and set effective requirements and standards (especially as to reclamation of distrubed lands) in order to achieve the aforementioned objectives,

the legislature hereby finds and declares:

(1) That, in order to achieve the aforementioned policy objectives, promote the health and welfare of the people, control erosion and pollution, protect domestic stock and wildlife, preserve agricultural and recreational productivity, save cultural, historic, and aesthetic values, and assure a long-range dependable tax base, it is reasonably necessary to require, after the effective date of this act, that all strip mining and underground mining operations be limited to those for which annual permits are granted, that no permit be issued until the operator presents a comprehensive plan for reclamation and restoration, together with an adequate performance bond, and the plan is approved, that certain other things must be done, that certain remedies are available, and that certain lands because of their unique or unusual characteristics may not be strip mined or underground mined under any circumstances, all as more particularly appears in the remaining provisions of this act. . . .

§ 50-1039. Permit required to engage in strip mining or underground mining—application for permit—contents—fee—bond—agencies exempt.

(1) An operator may not engage in strip or underground mining without having first obtained from the department a permit designating the area of land affected by the operation. . . .

(2) An operator desiring a permit shall file an application which shall contain a complete and detailed plan for the mining, reclamation, revegatation, and rehabilitation of the land and water to be affected by the operation. Such plan shall reflect thorough advance investigation and study by the operator and shall include all known or readily discoverable past and present uses of the land and water to be affected and the approximate periods of such use and shall state: . . .

(i) the annual rainfall and the direction and average velocity of the prevailing winds in the area where the applicant has requested a permit;

(j) the results of any test borings or core samplings which the applicant or his agent has conducted on the land to be affected, including the nature and the depth of the various strata or overburden and topsoil, the quantities and location of subsurface water and its quality, the thickness of any mineral seam, an analysis of the chemical properties of such minerals, including the acidity, sulphur content, and trace mineral elements of any coal seam, as well as the British thermal unit (B.T.U.) content of such seam, and an analysis of the overburden, including topsoil. If test borings or core samplings are submitted, each permit application shall contain two (2) copies each of two (2) sets of geologic cross-sections accurately depicting the known geologic makeup beneath the surface of the affected land. . . .

(3) The application for a permit shall be accompanied by two (2) copies of all maps meeting the requirements of the subsections below. The maps shall:
(a) identify the area to correspond with the application;
(b) show any adjacent deep mining or surface mining and the boundaries of surface properties and names of owners of record of the affected area and within one thousand (1,000) feet of any part of the affected area;
(c) show the names and locations of all streams, creeks, or other bodies of water, roads, buildings, cemeteries, oil and gas wells, and utility lines on the area of land affected and within one thousand (1,000) feet of such area; . . .
(f) show the final surface and underground water drainage plan on and away from the area of land affected. This plan shall indicate the directional and volume flow of water, constructed drainways, natural waterways used for drainage, and the streams of tributaries receiving the discharge;
(g) show the proposed location of waste or refuse area;
(h) show the proposed location of temporary subsoil and topsoil storage area; . . .
(k) show a listing of plan varieties encountered in the area to be affected and their relative dominance in the area, together with an enumeration of tree varieties and the approximate number of each variety occurring per acre on the area to be affected, and the locations generally of the various kinds and varieties of plants, including but not limited to grasses, shrubs, legumes, forbs and trees; . . .

(4) In addition to the information and maps required above, each application for a permit shall be accompanied by detailed plans or proposals showing the method of operation, the manner, time or distance, and estimated cost for backfilling, subsidence stabilization, water control, grading work, highwall reduction, topsoiling, planting, revegetating, and a reclamation plan for the area affected by the operation, which proposals shall meet the requirements of this act and rules adopted under this act.

(5) An application fee of fifty dollars ($50) shall be paid before the permit required in this section shall be issued. The operator shall file with the department a bond payable to the state of Montana with surety satisfactory to the department in the penal sum to be determined by the board (on the recommendation of the commissioner) of not less than two hundred dollars ($200) nor more than twenty-five hundred dollars

($2,500) for each acre or fraction thereof of the area of land affected, with a minimum bond of two thousand dollars ($2,000), conditioned upon the faithful performance of the requirements set forth in this act and of the rules of the board. A political subdivision or agency of the state need not file a bond unless required to do so by the board. The board may require the filing of the bond prior to permit issuance or at any time thereafter.

In determining the amount of the bond within the above limits, the board shall take into consideration the character and nature of the overburden, the future suitable use of the land involved and the cost of backfilling, grading, highwall reduction, subsidence stabilization, water control, topsoiling, and reclamation to be required; but in no event shall the bond be less than the total estimated cost to the state of completing the work described in the reclamation plan.

### § 50-1039.1. Protection of the surface owner.

In those instances in which the surface owner is not the owner of the mineral estate proposed to be mined by strip mining operations, the application for a permit shall include the written consent, or a waiver by, the owner or owners of the surface lands involved to enter and commence strip mining operations on such land, except that nothing in this section applies when the mineral estate is owned by the federal government in fee or in trust for an Indian tribe.

### § 50-1041. Prospecting permit—application—contents—reclamation plan—fee—bond.

(1) On and after the effective date of this act prospecting by any person on land not included in a valid strip mining or underground mining permit shall be unlawful without possessing a valid prospecting permit issued by the department as provided in this section. No prospecting permit shall be issued until the operator submits an application, the application is examined, amended if necessary, and approved by the department, and adequate reclamation performance bond is posted, all of which prerequisites must be done in conformity with the requirements of this act. . . .

### § 50-1042. Refusal of permit—grounds.

(1) An application for a prospecting, strip mining or underground mining permit shall not be approved by the department if there is found on the basis of the information set forth in the application, an on-site inspection, and an evaluation of the operation by the department that the requirements of the act or rules will not be observed or that the proposed method of operation, backfilling, grading, subsidence stabilization, water control, highwall reduction, topsoiling, revegetation, or

reclamation of the affected area cannot be carried out consistent with the purpose of this act.

(2) The department shall not approve the application for a prospecting, strip mining or underground mining permit where the area of land described in the application includes land having special, exceptional, critical, or unique characteristics, or that mining or prospecting on that area would adversely affect the use, enjoyment, or fundamental character of neighboring land having special, exceptional, critical, or unique characteristics. For the purposes of this act, land is defined as having such characteristics if it possesses special, exceptional, critical or unique:

(a) biological productivity, the loss of which would jeopardize certain species of wildlife or domestic stock; or

(b) ecological fragility, in the sense that the land, once adversely affected, could not return to its former ecological role in the reasonably foreseeable future; or

(c) ecological importance, in the sense that the particular land has such a strong influence on the total ecosystem of which it is a part that even temporary effects felt by it could precipitate a system-wide reaction of unpredictable scope or dimensions; or

(d) scenic, historic, archaeologic, topographic, geologic, ethnologic, scientific, cultural, or recreational significance. In applying this subsection particular attention should be paid to the inadequate preservation previously accorded Plains Indian history and culture.

(3) If the department finds that the overburden on any part of the area of land described in the application for a prospecting, strip mining or underground mining permit is such that experience in the state with a similar type of operation upon land with similar overburden shows that substantial deposition of sediment in streambeds, subsidence, landslides, or water pollution cannot feasibly be prevented, the department shall delete that part of the land described in the application upon which the overburden exists.

(4) If the department finds that the operation will constitute a hazard to a dwelling house, public building, school, church, cemetery, commercial or institutional building, public road, stream, lake, or other public property, the department shall delete those areas from the prospecting, strip mining or underground mining permit application before it can be approved.

§ 50-1043. Reclamation operations—submission and action on plan.

(1) As rapidly, completely, and effectively as the most modern technology and the most advanced state of the art will allow, each operator granted a permit under this act, shall reclaim and revegetate the land

affected by his operation, except that underground tunnels, shafts, or other subsurface excavations need not be revegetated. . . .

(2) In addition to the method of operation, grading, backfilling, subsidence stabilization, water control, highwall reduction, topsoiling and reclamation requirements of this act and rules adopted under this act, the operator, consistent with the directives of subsection (1) of this section shall:

(a) bury under adequate fill all toxic materials, shale, mineral, or any other material determined by the department to be acid producing, toxic, undesirable, or creating a hazard;

(b) seal off, as directed by rules, tunnels, shafts, or other openings or any breakthrough of water creating a hazard;

(c) impound, drain, or treat all runoff or underground mine waters so as to reduce soil erosion, damage to grazing and agricultural lands, and pollution of surface and subsurface waters;

(d) remove or bury all metal, lumber, and other refuse resulting from the operation;

(e) use explosives in connection with the operation only in accordance with department regulations designed to minimize noise, damage to adjacent lands and water pollution, ensure public safety, and for other purposes;

(f) adopt measures to prevent land subsidence unless the board approves a plan for inducing subsidence into an abandoned operation in a predictable and controlled manner with measures for grading, topsoiling, and revegetating the subsided land surface. In order for a controlled plan to be approved the applicant must show that subsidence will not cause a direct or indirect hazard to any public or private buildings, roads, facilities, or use areas; constitute a hazard to human life or health; constitute a hazard to domestic livestock or to a viable agricultural operation; or any other restrictions the board may consider necessary;

(g) stockpile and protect from erosion all mining and processing wastes until such wastes can be disposed of according to the provisions of this act;

(h) deposit as much stockpiled waste material as possible back into the mine voids upon abandonment in such manner as to prevent or minimize land subsidence. The remaining waste material shall be disposed of as provided by this act and the rules of the board;

(i) seal all portals, entryways, drifts, shafts or other openings between the surface and underground mine workings upon abandonment.

(3) An operator may not throw, dump, pile or permit the dumping, piling, or throwing or otherwise placing any overburden, stones, rocks, mineral, earth, soil, dirt, debris, trees, wood, logs or any other materials or substances of any kind or nature beyond or outside

of the area of land which is under permit and for which a bond has been posted under section 50-1039, or place the materials described in this section in such a way that normal erosion or slides brought about by natural physical causes will permit the materials to go beyond or outside of the area of land which is under permit and for which a bond has been posted under section 50-1039.

§ 50-1044. Area mining required—grading and revegetation—release of bond—alternative plan.

(1) Area strip mining, a method of operation which does not produce a bench or fill bench, is required where strip mining is proposed. All highwalls must be reduced and the steepest slope of the reduced highwall shall be no greater than twenty (20) degrees from the horizontal. Highwall reduction shall be commenced at or beyond the top of the highwall and sloped to the graded spoil bank. Reduction, backfilling, and grading shall eliminate all highwalls and spoil peaks. The area of land affected shall be restored to the approximate original contour of the land. When directed by the department, the operator shall construct in the final grading, such diversion ditches, depressions, or terraces as will accumulate or control the water runoff. Additional restoration work may be required by the department according to rules adopted by the board. . . .

(3) All available topsoil shall be removed in a separate layer, guarded from erosion and pollution, kept in such a condition that it can sustain vegetation of at least the quality and variety it sustained prior to removal. . . .

(6) An operator may propose alternative plans other than backfilling, grading, highwall reduction, or topsoiling if the restoration will be consistent with the purpose of this act. . . .

§ 50-1045. Planting of vegetation following grading of disturbed area.

(1) After the operation has been backfilled, graded, topsoiled, and approved by the department, the operator shall prepare the soil and plant such legumes, grasses, shrubs, and trees upon the area of land affected as are necessary to provide a suitable permanent diverse vegetative cover capable of:
    (a) feeding and withstanding grazing pressure from a quantity and mixture of wildlife and livestock at least comparable to that which the land could have sustained prior to the operation;
    (b) regenerating under the natural conditions prevailing at the site, including occasional drought, heavy snowfalls, and strong winds; and
    (c) preventing soil erosion to the extent achieved prior to the operation.

The seed or plant mixtures, quantities, method of planting, type and amount of lime or fertilizer, mulching, irrigation, fencing, and any other measures necessary to provide a suitable permanent diverse vegetative cover shall be defined by rules of the board. . . .

§ 50-1046. Time of commencement of reclamation.

The operator shall commence the reclamation of the area of land affected by his operation as soon as possible after the beginning of strip mining or underground mining of that area in accordance with plans previously approved by the department. Those grading, backfilling, subsidence stabilization, topsoiling, and water management practices that are approved in the plans shall be kept current with the operation as defined by rules of the board and a permit or supplement to a permit may not be issued, if in the discretion of the department, these practices are not current.

§ 50-1052. Receipts paid into special fund—use of fund.

(1) All fees, forfeit funds, and other moneys available or paid to the department under the provisions of this act shall be placed in the state treasury and credited to a special agency account to be designated as the mining and reclamation fund. This fund shall be available to the department by appropriation and shall be expended for the administration and enforcement of this act and for the reclamation and revegetation of land and the rehabilitation of water affected by any mining operations. . . .

§ 50-1055. Mandamus to compel enforcement of law—action for damage to water supply—damage from surface water—other remedies.

(1) A resident of this state, with knowledge that a requirement of this act or a rule adopted under this act, is not being enforced by a public officer or employee whose duty it is to enforce the requirement or rule may bring the failure to enforce to the attention of the public officer or employee by a written statement under oath that shall state the specific facts of the failure to enforce the requirement or rule. Knowingly making false statements or charges in the affidavit subjects the affiant to penalties prescribed under the law of perjury.

(2) If the public officer or employee neglects or refuses for an unreasonable time after receipt of the statement to enforce the requirement or rule the resident may bring an action of mandamus. . . .

(3) An owner of an interest in real property who obtains all or part of his supply of water for domestic, agricultural, industrial, or other legitimate use from an underground source other than a subterranean stream having a permanent, distinct, and known channel, may

sue an operator to recover damages for contamination, diminution, or interruption of the water supply, proximately resulting from strip mining or underground mining. . . .

(b) An owner of water rights adversely affected may file a complaint, detailing the loss in quality, and quantity of his water, with the department. . . .

(4) A servient tract of land is not bound to receive water contaminated by strip mining or underground mining on a dominant tract of land, and the owner of the servient tract may sue an operator to recover the damages proximately resulting from the natural drainage from the dominant tract of waters contaminated by strip mining or underground mining on the dominant tract. . . .

WYOMING SEVERANCE TAX (1969, as amended)<br>39 WCS 227.1 et seq.

§ 39-227.1.  Severance tax on extraction or production of coal; extent of tax. . . .

(f) in addition to the other taxes provided by law, there shall be a severance tax upon the privilege of extracting or producing coal in the state of Wyoming of a percentage of the value of the coal produced according to the following. . . .

(f) The tax levied in subsection (f) of this section shall expire on January 1 next following the year in which the taxes collected pursuant to subsection (f) total one hundred twenty million dollars ($120,000,000.00).

§ 39-227.1:1.  Excise tax on extraction of minerals; amount generally; value of gross product.

(a) There is hereby levied an excise tax payable to the department of revenue and taxation, in an amount equal to two percent (2%) of the value of the gross product extracted, upon the privilege of extracting any gold, silver or other precious metals, soda, saline, uranium, bentonite, or other valuable deposit, except trona, coal, petroleum, natural gas, oil shale, or any other fossil fuel minerals.

(b) There is hereby levied an excise tax on the privilege of severing or extracting trona, coal, petroleum, natural gas, oil shale, or any other fossil fuel, of two percent (2%) of the value of the gross product extracted.  The proceeds from the tax are payable to the department of revenue and taxation and shall be deposited in the permanent Wyoming mineral trust fund.

(c) In addition to the excise tax provided for in subsection (b) of this section, there is hereby levied upon the privilege of extracting trona, coal, petroleum, natural gas, oil shale or any other fossil fuel minerals, an excise tax of two percent (2%) of the value of the gross product extracted. . . .

§ 39-227.6.  Fixing value of production when statement of gross production not filed; examination of books, etc.; requiring attendance of officers, employees, etc.; testimony and proof.

If any person shall fail or refuse to file a statement of gross production with the department of revenue and taxation as above provided, the department of revenue and taxation shall fix the value of production from the best information or knowledge it can obtain.  The department of revenue and taxation, for the purpose of ascertaining the correctness of any return or for the purpose of ascertaining the value that should be fixed when a return has not been filed, shall have power to examine or cause to be examined by any agent or representative designated by it for that purpose, any books, papers, records or memoranda bearing upon the matter required by it therefor, and may require the attendance of any officer or employee of any corporation, person required by this act [§§ 39-227.1 to 39-227.11] to make a return, or the attendance of any other person having knowledge of any pertinent fact, and may take testimony and require proof material to the required information.

§ 39-227.10.  Same; disposition of money received and collected.

(a) All revenue received and collected under the provisions of W.S. 39-227.1 through 39-227.11 shall be transferred to the state treasurer. . . .

(c) All revenue received under the provisions of W.S. 39-227.1 (f)
shall be deposited in the Wyoming coal tax revenue account within the
earmarked revenue fund. Any unexpended balance in the coal tax
revenue account may be invested by the state treasurer and interest
earned shall be credited to the Wyoming coal tax revenue account.

(d) The monies in the Wyoming coal tax revenue account shall be administered by the Wyoming farm loan board and disbursed by the board
for use in areas which are directly or indirectly impacted by the production of coal, to assist in financing public water, sewer, highway,
road or street projects. Not less than sixty (60%) of the revenues to
the coal tax revenue account shall be used to finance state highway,
county road or city street projects.

(e) For the purposes set forth in subsection (d) above, the Wyoming
farm loan board may make grants, or may pledge or otherwise contract with, any county, city, town, sewer district, water district or
other political subdivision of the state, or the state highway department,
with respect to the use of the revenues derived or to be derived from
the excise tax levied pursuant to W.S. 39-277.1 (f). Any recipient
of such revenues or a pledge of future revenues, may, with the approval
of the Wyoming farm loan board, pledge wholly or in part, for the
payment of any obligation to the Wyoming community development
authority, or other obligee, the monies derived or to be derived from
the excise tax, subject to any existing pledges or other contractual
limitations theretofore imposed.

(f) All applications for project assistance shall be made directly to the
Wyoming farm loan board, in whatever form the board may prescribe.
The board may submit any application to the state highway department,
the department of economic planning and development or any other
state agency for review and recommendation before approving or dis-
approving the application. Before any application is approved, the farm
loan board shall determine by proper investigation:
   (i) That the applicant has fully utilized or will fully utilize all local
revenue sources reasonably available for financing the project for which
application is made;
   (ii) That such local revenue sources are insufficient to finance the
project; and
   (iii) That the project applied for is necessary.

The amount of solid waste generated per person has been increasing at a rate that is filling up space available for disposal. Much of what is discarded as waste by both private households and industrial and commercial establishments is still usable or contains usable raw materials. Thanks to federally sponsored research under the Resource Recovery Act technology is no longer a barrier to recovering both materials and energy from solid waste. Such would seem to be the indicated course in a world of limited natural resources. Economic and political factors, however, determine to what extent recovery technology is employed. To "approach the maximum attainable recycling of depletable resources" is one of the goals set by the National Environmental Policy Act (Sec. 4331). Full enforcement of air and water pollution control measures and of the Safe Drinking Water Act may help create the economic necessity for recycling and reuse. In the meantime, disposal remains the practice and the oceans continue to serve as the ultimate dumping ground, albeit subject to the Ocean Dumping Act.

Laws take several approaches to the solid waste problem: they prohibit dumping or require screening of aesthetically offensive disposal sites, aim at reducing the amount of waste, fund research and development in resource recovery, and provide incentives for recovery projects. Examples of each approach are quoted in this chapter, except for laws relating to junkyards, which are found in Chapter 12. Laws dealing with the disposal of hazardous wastes are considered in Chapter 11; and state laws regulating disposal of waste from mining operations, in Chapter 9.

The Resource Recovery Act of 1970 (p. 349, amending the 1965 Solid Waste Disposal Act, provides for research and development, planning, and operational grants to state and local agencies and re-

quires federal agency compliance with environmentally sound waste
disposal practices. Title II, known as the Materials Policy Act, established the National Materials Policy Commission (see Appendix D
for listing of its report). More recently, the Non-Nuclear Research
and Development Act of 1974 calls for comprehensive plans that, among
other purposes, would promote "productive use of waste" and "reuse
and recycling of materials and consumer products" (Sec. 5905,
[b] [3] [A], p. 53).

Waste management is primarily a local function and the states
have adopted various ways to promote recovery practices. Ohio's
Water Development Authority is empowered to make grants and to construct and operate solid waste projects (p. 355). Tennessee encourages construction of municipal energy and resource recovery facilities
by state loans (p. 357). Authorities or public corporations charged
with the responsibility to make long-range plans, fund pilot projects,
and otherwise promote the objectives of using waste as a resource
are in existence in several states.

New Jersey's Waste Control Act, prohibiting importation of out-
of-state waste, was upheld by its State Supreme Court. The case is
on appeal to the United States Supreme Court at the time of writing.

Oregon's "bottle bill" (p. 360) has reduced the total amount of
waste in that state by outlawing nonreturnable containers. It has survived a court test. South Dakota requires reusable or biodegradable
containers (p. 362). California and Minnesota also have container
legislation, as do a number of municipalities.

Solid waste disposal sites and major refuse operations are can-
didates for state and regional land use controls in Colorado (Sec.
106-7-2-3[1] [b] and 204[2]) and Florida (Sec. 380.04[2] [g]). In
Massachusetts citizens may sue to prevent damage to the environment
consisting of "improper operation of dumping grounds" (Sec. 214-7A).

Abandoned vehicles represent a special problem of determining
ownership and value. South Carolina's statute (p. 363) sets minimum
periods after which vehicles left on private or public property are considered abandoned and become property of the state. Similar laws are
in effect elsewhere.


                              FEDERAL


                   RESOURCE RECOVERY ACT (1970)
                        42 USC 3251 et seq.


Section 3251.    Congressional findings and declaration of purpose
        3252.    Definitions

§ 3251.  Congressional findings and declaration of purpose.

(a) The Congress finds—

(1) that the continuing technological progress and improvement in methods of manufacture, packaging, and marketing of consumer products has resulted in an ever-mounting increase, and in a change in the characteristics, of the mass of material discarded by the purchaser of such products;

(2) that the economic and population growth of our Nation, and the improvements in the standard of living enjoyed by our population, have required increased industrial production to meet our needs, and have made necessary the demolition of old buildings, the construction of new buildings, and the provision of highways and other avenues of transportation, which, together with related industrial, commercial, and agricultural operations, have resulted in a rising tide of scrap, discarded, and waste materials;

(3) that the continuing concentration of our population in expanding metropolitan and other urban areas has presented these communities with serious financial, management, intergovernmental, and technical problems in the disposal of solid wastes resulting from the industrial, commercial, domestic, and other activities carried on in such areas;

(4) that inefficient and improper methods of disposal of solid wastes result in scenic blights, create serious hazards to the public health,

including pollution of air and water resources, accident hazards, and increase in rodent and insect vectors of disease, have an adverse effect on land values, create public nuisances, otherwise interfere with community life and development;

(5) that the failure or inability to salvage and reuse such materials economically results in the unnecessary waste and depletion of our natural resources; and

(6) that while the collection and disposal of solid wastes should continue to be primarily the function of State, regional, and local agencies, the problems of waste disposal as set forth above have become a matter national in scope and in concern and necessitate Federal action through financial and technical assistance and leadership in the development, demonstration, and application of new and improved methods and processes to reduce the amount of waste and unsalvageable materials and to provide for proper and economical solid-waste disposal practices.

(b) The purposes of this chapter therefore are—

(1) to promote the demonstration, construction, and application of solid waste management and resource recovery systems which preserve and enhance the quality of air, water, and land resources;

(2) to provide technical and financial assistance to States and local governments and interstate agencies in the planning and development of resource recovery and solid waste disposal programs;

(3) to promote a national research and development program for improved management techniques, more effective organizational arrangements, and new and improved methods of collection, separation, recovery, and recycling of solid wastes, and the environmentally safe disposal of nonrecoverable residues;

(4) to provide for the promulgation of guidelines for solid waste collection, transport, separation, recovery, and disposal systems; and

(5) to provide for training grants in occupations involving the design, operation, and maintenance of solid waste disposal systems.

§ 3253.   Research, demonstrations, training and other activities.

(a) The Secretary shall conduct, and encourage, cooperate with, and render financial and other assistance to appropriate public (whether Federal, State, interstate, or local) authorities, agencies, and institutions, private agencies and institutions, and individuals in the conduct of, and promote the coordination of, research, investigations, experiments, training, demonstrations, surveys, and studies relating to—

(1) any adverse health and welfare effects of the release into the environment of material present in solid waste, and methods to eliminate such effects;

(2) the operation and financing of solid waste disposal programs;

(3) the reduction of the amount of such waste and unsalvageable waste materials;

(4) the development and application of new and improved methods of collecting and disposing of solid waste and processing and recovering materials and energy from solid wastes; and

(5) the identification of solid waste components and potential materials and energy recoverable from such waste components.

(b) In carrying out the provisions of the preceding subsection, the Secretary is authorized to—

(1) collect and make available, through publications and other appropriate means, the results of, and other information pertaining to, such research and other activities, including appropriate recommendations in connection therewith;

(2) cooperate with public and private agencies, institutions, and organizations, and with any industries involved, in the preparation and the conduct of such research and other activities; and

(3) make grants-in-aid to public or private agencies and institutions and to individuals for research, training projects, surveys, and demonstrations (including construction of facilities), and provide for the conduct of research, training, surveys, and demonstrations by contract with public or private agencies and institutions and with individuals.

. . .

(c) Any grant, agreement, or contract made or entered into under this section shall contain provisions effective to insure that all information, uses, processes, patents and other developments resulting from any activity undertaken pursuant to such grant, agreement, or contract will be made readily available on fair and equitable terms to industries utilizing methods of solid-waste disposal and industries engaging in furnishing devices, facilities, equipment, and supplies to be used in connection with solid-waste disposal. . . .

§ 3253a. Recovery of useful energy and materials.

(a) The Secretary shall carry out an investigation and study to determine—

(1) means of recovering materials and energy from solid waste, recommended uses of such materials and energy for national or international welfare, including identification of potential markets for such recovered resources, and the impact of distribution of such resources on existing markets;

(2) Changes in current product characteristics and production and packaging practices which would reduce the amount of solid waste;

(3) methods of collection, separation, and containerization which will encourage efficient utilization of facilities and contribute to more effective programs of reduction, reuse, or disposal of wastes;

(4) the use of Federal procurement to develop market demand for recovered resources;

(5) recommended incentives (including Federal grants, loans, and other assistance) and disincentives to accelerate the reclamation or recycling of materials from solid wastes, with special emphasis on motor vehicle hulks;

(6) the effect of existing public policies, including subsidies and economic incentives and disincentives, percentage depletion allowances, capital gains treatment and other tax incentives and disincentives, upon the recycling and reuse of materials, and the likely effect of the modification or elimination of such incentives and disincentives upon the reuse, recycling and conservation of such materials; and

(7) the necessity and method of imposing disposal or other charges on packaging, containers, vehicles, and other manufactured goods, which charges would reflect the cost of final disposal, the value of recoverable components of the item, and any social costs associated with nonrecycling or uncontrolled disposal of such items.

The Secretary shall from time to time, but not less frequently than annually, report the results of such investigation and study to the President and the Congress.

§ 3254a.  Grants for State, interstate, and local planning.

(a) The Secretary may from time to time, upon such terms and conditions consistent with this section as he finds appropriate to carry out the purposes of this Act, make grants to State, interstate, municipal, and intermunicipal agencies, and organizations composed of public officials which are eligible for assistance under section 701(g) of the Housing Act of 1954, of not to exceed 66 2/3 per centum of the cost in the case of an application with respect to an area including only one municipality, and not to exceed 75 per centum of the cost in any other case, of—

(1) making surveys of solid waste disposal practices and problems within the jurisdictional areas of such agencies and

(2) developing and revising solid waste disposal plans as part of regional environmental protection systems for such areas, providing for recycling or recovery of materials from wastes whenever possible and including planning for the reuse of solid waste disposal areas and studies of the effect and relationship of solid waste disposal practices on areas adjacent to waste disposal sites,

(3) developing proposals for projects to be carried out pursuant to section 208 of this Act, or

(4) planning programs for the removal and processing of abandoned motor vehicle hulks. . . .

§ 3254e. Applicability of solid waste disposal guidelines to Executive agencies.

(a)(1) If—

(A) an Executive agency (as defined in section 105 of title 5, United States Code) has jurisdiction over any real property or facility the operation or administration of which involves such agency in solid waste disposal activities, or

(B) such an agency enters into a contract with any person for the operation by such person of any Federal property or facility, and the performance of such contract involves such person in solid waste disposal activities,

then such agency shall insure compliance with the guidelines recommended under section 209 and the purposes of this Act in the operation or administration of such property or facility, or the performance of such contract, as the case may be.

(2) Each Executive agency which conducts any activity—

(A) which generates solid waste, and

(B) which, if conducted by a person other than such agency, would require a permit or license from such agency in order to dispose of such solid waste, shall insure compliance with such guidelines and the purposes of this Act in conducting such activity.

(3) Each Executive agency which permits the use of Federal property for purposes of disposal of solid waste shall insure compliance with such guidelines and the purposes of this Act in the disposal of such waste.

(4) The President shall prescribe regulations to carry out this subsection.

(b) Each Executive agency which issues any license or permit for disposal of solid waste shall, prior to the issuance of such license or permit, consult with the Secretary to insure compliance with guidelines recommended under section 209 and the purposes of this Act.

§ 3254f. National disposal sites study for the storage and disposal of hazardous wastes.

The Secretary shall submit to the Congress no later than two years after October 26, 1970, a comprehensive report and plan for the creation of a system of national disposal sites for the storage and disposal of hazardous wastes, including radioactive, toxic chemical, biological, and other wastes which may endanger public health or welfare. Such report shall include:

(1) a list of materials which should be subject to disposal in any such site;

(2) current methods of disposal of such materials;

(3) recommended methods of reduction, neutralization, recovery, or disposal of such materials;

(4) an inventory of possible sites including existing land or water disposal sites operated or licensed by Federal agencies;

(5) an estimate of the cost of developing and maintaining sites including consideration of means for distributing the short- and long-term costs of operating such sites among the users thereof; and

(6) such other information as may be appropriate.


STATES

OHIO SOLID WASTE PROJECTS (1970)
Ohio Rev. Code Ch. 6123

§ 6123.03. Purposes

It is hereby declared to be the public policy of the state through the establishment, operation, and maintenance of solid waste projects as provided in Chapter 6123. of the Revised Code to provide for the comfort, health, safety and general welfare of all employees and other inhabitants of the state and for the conservation of the land, air and water resources of the state through efficient and proper methods of disposal, salvage and reuse of solid wastes thereby eliminating or decreasing accident and health hazards including rodent and insect vectors of disease, public nuisance and the adverse effect on land values caused thereby and the scenic blight marring the landscape and to promote the improvement of the economic welfare and employment opportunities of and the creation of jobs for the people of the state, and to assist and cooperate with governmental agencies in achieving such purposes. In furtherance of such public policy, the Ohio water development authority may initiate, acquire, construct, maintain, repair and operate solid waste projects or cause the same to be operated pursuant to a lease, sublease, or agreement with any person or governmental agency; may make loans and grants to governmental agencies for the acquisition or construction of solid waste facilities by such governmental agencies; and may issue solid waste revenue bonds of this state payable solely from revenues, to pay the cost of such projects. Any solid waste project shall be determined by the authority to be in compliance with Chapter 3734. of the Revised Code and with the regulations adopted by the public health council under section 3734.02 of the Revised Code. Any resolution of the authority providing for acquiring or constructing such projects or for making a loan or grant for such projects shall include a finding by the authority that such determination has been made.

§ 6123.04. Powers and duties.

For the purposes of Chapter 6123. of the Revised Code of Ohio the Ohio water development authority may: . . .

(C) Make loans and grants to governmental agencies for the acquisition or construction of solid waste projects by any such governmental agency and adopt rules, regulations and procedures for making such loans and grants;

(D) Acquire, construct, reconstruct, enlarge, improve, furnish, equip, maintain, repair, operate, lease or rent to, or contract for operation by, a person or governmental agency, solid waste projects, and establish rules and regulations for the use of such projects; . . .

(F) Issue solid waste revenue bonds and notes and solid waste revenue refunding bonds of the state, payable solely from revenues as provided

in section 6123. 06 of the Revised Code, unless the bonds be refunded
by refunding bonds, for the purpose of paying any part of the cost of
one or more solid waste projects or parts thereof: . . .

(N) Charge, alter, and collect rentals and other charges for the use or
services of any solid waste project as provided in section 6123.13 of
the Revised Code; . . .

TENNESSEE SOLID WASTE DISPOSAL ACT
53 Tenn. Code Ann. Ch. 43

§ 53-4302.  Public policy.

In order to protect the public health, safety and welfare, prevent the spread of disease and creation of nuisances, conserve our natural resources, enhance the beauty and quality of our environment and provide a coordinated state-wide solid waste disposal program, it is declared to be the public policy of the state of Tennessee to regulate solid waste disposal to:

(1) Provide for safe and sanitary processing and disposal of solid wastes.

(2) Develop long-range plans for adequate solid waste disposal systems to meet future demands.

(3) Provide a coordinated state-wide program of control of solid waste processing and disposal in cooperation with federal, state, and local agencies responsible for the prevention, control, or abatement of air, water, and land pollution.

(4) Encourage efficient and economical solid waste disposal systems.

§ 53-4322.  Resource and energy recovery facility loans—Definitions.

As used in §§ 53-4322—53-4337, unless the context requires otherwise:

(1) "Solid waste" means garbage, refuse, and other discarded solid materials, including waste materials of a solid nature resulting from industrial, commercial, and agricultural operations, and from community activities.

(2) "Energy recovery facility" means a facility for the recovery of energy or energy producing materials from the controlled processing of solid waste.

(3) "Resource recovery facility" means a facility for the systematic separation and recovery of recyclable materials from solid waste. . . .

§ 53-4323.  Loans for recovery facilities authorized.

The state of Tennessee is hereby authorized to make loans to any
municipal corporation or county for the construction of energy recovery
facilities and/or solid waste resource recovery facilities.  Such loans
shall be made from the proceeds of state bond sales authorized pursuant
to implementing acts of the state of Tennessee.

§ 53-4338.  Municipal energy and resource recovery facilities—Definitions.

As used in §§ 53-4338—53-4342, unless the context requires otherwise:

(1) "Solid waste" means garbage, refuse, and other discarded solid
waste materials, including waste materials of a solid nature resulting
from industrial, commercial, and agricultural operations, and from
community activities.

(2) "Energy recovery facility" means a facility for the recovery of
energy or energy producing materials from the controlled processing
of solid waste and the production of energy from said solid waste and
other materials for a heating and cooling system.

(3) "Resource recovery facility" means a facility for the systematic
separation and recovery of recyclable materials from solid waste and
a processing of solid waste, sewage sludge, and other solids for fuel
mixtures or fuel supplements.

§ 53-4339.  Powers of municipality.

A municipality shall have the power to construct, purchase, improve,
operate, and maintain within its corporate limits or within the limits
of the county wherein it is located, an energy recovery facility or facilities and/or resource recovery facility or facilities for the production
of energy from said energy recovery facility for heating or cooling
and/or the production of fuel mixtures or fuel supplements and recovery
of recyclable materials from solid waste and the sale of said fuel
supplements and recyclable materials.  The construction of said
facility shall include all necessary land, right-of-way, easements,
buildings and all other appurtenances usual to such plants as well as
the building of all necessary means of transportation including pipelines for energy or fuel supplements including obtaining all necessary
rights-of-way or easements necessary thereto.

§ 53-4340.  Rates charged by municipality—right to enter into agreements.

The municipality for the production of any energy shall charge the
usual rates for such heating or cooling and may combine it with any

other energy source produced. The municipality shall also have the right to enter into any agreements necessary for the sale of recyclable materials and sale of fuel mixtures. . . .

OREGON MINIMUM DEPOSIT ACT (1971)
Ore. Rev. Stat. 459.810 et seq.

Section 459.810.    Definitions
   459.820.    Refund value required
   459.830.    Practices required of dealers and distributors
   459.840.    When dealer or distributor authorized to refuse to accept or pay refund in certain cases
   459.850.    Indication of refund value required
   459.860.    Certification of containers as reusable by more than one manufacturer
   459.870.    Decision upon certification applications
   459.880.    Redemption centers
   459.890.    Certification and withdrawal procedures

§ 459.810.  Definitions for ORS 459.810 to 459.890.

As used in ORS 459.810 to 459.890 and subsections (5) and (6) of ORS 459.992, unless the context requires otherwise:

(1) "Beverage" means beer or other malt beverages and mineral waters, soda water and similar carbonated soft drinks in liquid form and intended for human consumption.

(2) "Beverage container" means the individual, separate, sealed glass, metal or plastic bottle, can, jar or carton containing a beverage.

§ 459.820.  Refund value required.

(1) Except as provided in subsection (2) of this section, every beverage container sold or offered for sale in this state, shall have a refund value of not less than five cents.

(2) Every beverage container certified as provided in ORS 459.860, sold or offered for sale in this state, shall have a refund value of not less than two cents.

§ 459.830.  Practices required of dealers and distributors.

Except as provided in ORS 459.840:

(1) A dealer shall not refuse to accept from a consumer any empty beverage containers of the kind, size and brand sold by the dealer, or refuse to pay to the consumer the refund value of a beverage container as established by ORS 459.820.

(2) A distributor shall not refuse to accept from a dealer any empty beverage containers of the kind, size and brand sold by the distributor, or refuse to pay the dealer the refund value of a beverage container as established by ORS 459.820.

§ 459.840. When dealer or distributor authorized to refuse to accept or pay refund in certain cases.

(1) A dealer may refuse to accept from a consumer, and a distributor may refuse to accept from a dealer any empty beverage container which does not state thereon a refund value as established by ORS 459.820.

(2) A dealer may refuse to accept and to pay the refund value of empty beverage containers if the place of business of the dealer and the kind and brand of empty beverage containers are included in an order of the commission approving a redemption center under ORS 459.880.

§ 459.850. Indication of refund value required; exception; certain metal containers prohibited.

(1) Every beverage container sold or offered for sale in this state by a dealer shall clearly indicate by embossing or by a stamp, or by a label or other method securely affixed to the beverage container, the refund value of the container.

(2) Subsection (1) of this section shall not apply to glass beverage containers designed for beverages having a brand name permanently marked thereon which, on October 1, 1972, had a refund value of not less than five cents.

(3) No person shall sell or offer for sale at retail in this state any metal beverage container so designed and constructed that a part of the container is detachable in opening the container without the aid of a can opener.

§ 459.860. Certification of containers as reusable by more than one manufacturer.

(1) To promote the use in this state of reusable beverage containers of uniform design, and to facilitate the return of containers to manufacturers for reuse as a beverage container, the commission shall certify beverage containers which satisfy the requirements of this section.

(2) A beverage container shall be certified if:
    (a) It is reusable as a beverage container by more than one manufacturer in the ordinary course of business; and
    (b) More than one manufacturer will in the ordinary course of business accept the beverage container for reuse as a beverage container and pay the refund value of the container.

(3) A beverage container shall not be certified under this section if by reason of its shape or design, or by reason of words or symbols permanently inscribed thereon, whether by engraving, embossing, painting or other permanent method, it is reusable as a beverage container in the ordinary course of business only by a manufacturer of a beverage sold under a specific brand name.

SOUTH DAKOTA LITTER DISPOSAL AND CONTROL (1974)
S. Dak. Public Health & Safety Code Ch. 34-16C

§ 34-16C-9. Reusable or biodegradable beverage containers required.

Every beverage container sold or offered for sale in this state, subsequent to July 1, 1976, shall be either a reusable container or a container which is biodegradable according to standards to be established by the secretary.

SOUTH CAROLINA DISPOSITION OF ABANDONED
AND DERELICT VEHICLES (1974)
Code of Laws of S. Car.
Sec. 46-490.21 et seq.

§ 46-490.21.  Declaration of public interest.

Abandoned and derelict motor vehicles constitute a hazard to the health
and welfare of the people in the State in that such motor vehicles can
harbor noxious diseases, furnish shelter and breeding places for ver-
min, and present physical dangers to the safety and well being of children and other citizens.  It is therefore in the public interest that the
present accumulation of abandoned and derelict motor vehicles be
eliminated and that the future abandonment of such motor vehicles be
prevented.  (1974(58) 2103.)

§ 46-490.22.  Definitions.

For the purposes of this article: . . .

(c) "Abandoned vehicle" means a motor vehicle that is inoperable or is
left unattended on public property for more than seventy-two hours,
or a motor vehicle that has remained illegally on private or public

property for a period of more than seven days without the consent of the owner or person in control of the property.

(d) "Derelict vehicle" means a motor vehicle:

(1) Whose certificate of registration has expired and the registered and legal owner no longer resides at the address listed on the last certificate of registration on record with the Department, or

(2) Whose major parts have been removed so as to render the motor vehicle inoperable and incapable of passing inspection as required under existing standards; or

(3) Manufacturer's serial plates, motor vehicle identification numbers, license number plates and any other means of identification have been removed so as to nullify efforts to locate or identify the registered and legal owner; or

(4) Whose registered and legal owner of record disclaims ownership or releases his rights thereto; or

(5) Which is more than seven years old and does not bear a current license as required by the Department. . . .

§ 46-490.24. Abandoned and derelict motor vehicles subject to removal.

All abandoned and derelict motor vehicles shall be subject to removal from public or private property and disposed of in accordance with the provisions of this article; provided, that all abandoned motor vehicles left on any right-of-way of any road, street or highway for a period of over forty-eight hours shall be removed and disposed of as provided for in Act No. 1263 of 1972 [§§ 46-490.11 to 46-490.18]. (1974 (58) 2103.)

§ 46-490.25. Colored tags to be attached to vehicles; notice to owners; sale of vehicles.

(a) When any motor vehicle is derelict or abandoned, the Commissioner shall cause a colored tag to be placed on the motor vehicle which shall be notice to the owner, the person in possession of the motor vehicle or any lien holder that it is considered to be derelict or abandoned and is subject to forfeiture to the State.

(b) If the motor vehicle is determined to be valued at less than one hundred dollars, the tag shall so state and shall serve as the only legal notice that unless the motor vehicle is removed within seven days from the date of the tag, it shall become property of the State, . . .

(c) If the value of the motor vehicle is determined to be more than one hundred dollars, the colored tag shall so state and shall serve as the only legal notice that if the vehicle is not removed within seven days from the date of the tag that it will be removed to a designated place to be sold. After the motor vehicle is removed the Commissioner shall notify in writing by registered or certified mail, return receipt requested, the person in whose name the motor vehicle was last registered at the last address reflected in the Department's records and to any lienholder of record, by registered or certified mail, return receipt requested, that the motor vehicle is being held, designating the place where it is being held and that if it is not redeemed within thirty days from the date of the notice by paying all cost of removal and storage it shall be sold for recycling purposes or for such other purposes as the Commissioner deems advisable to insure obtaining the highest possible return from the sale. The proceeds of the sale shall be deposited in the highway fund established for the purposes of administering the provisions of this article.

(d) If the value of the motor vehicle is determined to be more than one hundred dollars and if the identity of the last registered owner cannot be determined or if the registration contains no address for the owner, or if it is impossible to determine with reasonable certainty the identification and addresses of any lien holders, notice by one publication in a newspaper of general circulation in the area where the motor vehicle was located shall be sufficient to meet all requirements of notice pursuant to this article. The notice of publication may contain multiple listings of motor vehicles. Twenty days after date of publication the advertised motor vehicle may be sold. The proceeds of such sale shall be deposited in the highway fund established for the purpose of administering the provisions of this article. . . .

(f) All officers defined in this article may appraise or determine the value of derelict or abandoned motor vehicles for the purposes of this article. (1974 (58) 2103.)

§ 46-490.26. Titles to vest in State; identification numbers and records to be destroyed; oath required of demolisher.

Title to all motor vehicles sold or disposed of in accordance with this article shall vest in the State. . . .

§ 46-490.27. Commissioner may contract for collection, etc., of vehicles; collecting areas; sale or recycling.

The Commissioner may contract with any Federal, other state, county or municipal authority or private enterprise for tagging, collection, storage, transportation or any other services necessary to prepare derelict or abandoned motor vehicles for recycling or other methods of disposal. Publicly owned properties, when available, shall be provided as temporary collecting areas for the motor vehicles defined herein. The Commissioner may sell derelict or abandoned motor vehicles or if he deems it more advisable, may contract with private enterprises for the purchase of such motor vehicles for recycling.

§ 46-490.28. Right of entry on private property to enforce article.

All officers, agents and employees of the Department and employees or agents of any person under contract with the Department, are authorized to go on public or private property for the purposes of enforcing this article. . . .

# 11

## TOXIC
## AND HAZARDOUS
## SUBSTANCES

To "attain the widest range of beneficial uses of the environment without degradation, risk to health or safety" is one of the lofty aims of the National Environmental Policy Act (Sec. 4331). A number of statutes address themselves to reaching this goal by seeking to control toxic and hazardous substances and hazardous conditions. They operate by licensing, requiring labeling, and restricting use. In a few cases there are total bans on offending substances. State and federal laws in this area are considered in this chapter in three categories: (1) occupational health and toxic materials generally, (2) pesticides, and (3) nuclear safety.

All substances can be toxic if misused. The problem lies in the definition of "toxic" and of determining permissible levels of use. The Clean Air Act defines a "hazardous air pollutant" as one "to which no ambient air quality standards is applicable and which . . . may cause, or contribute to, an increase in mortality or an increase in serious irreversible, or incapacitating reversible illness" (Sec. 1857c-7[a][1]). EPA emission standards are applicable to stationary sources. The Federal Water Pollution Control Act defines toxic pollutants as substances that "cause death, disease, behavioral abnormalities, cancer, genetic mutations, physiological malfunctions (including malfunctions in reproduction) or physical deformations" (Sec. 1362[13]). Special effluent standards apply, including in some cases total prohibition of discharge (Sec. 1317 and 1321 [b][2][A]). The Resource Recovery Act mandates national disposal sites for storage and disposal of hazardous wastes "which may endanger public health or welfare" (Sec. 3254f).

A comprehensive Toxic Substances Control Act has been introduced in the 94th Congress. It would require extensive testing before specified substances may be manufactured, and, in some cases, prohibit their manufacture.

Toxicity of materials often manifests itself in work place situations before affecting the general public. The Occupational Health and Safety Act of 1970 (p. 370) directs the setting of mandatory occupational health and safety standards, including standards for toxic materials. Earlier, the Coal Mines Health and Safety Act (30 U.S.C. 801 et seq.) and the Metal and Non-Metallic Mine Safety Act (30 U.S.C. 721 et seq.) had provided for mandatory health and safety standards in the mining industry. Pennsylvania is noted for its mine safety laws.

The Food, Drug and Cosmetic Act of 1938 (p. 373) regulates tolerances for poisonous substances and pesticide residues in food and food additives, among other provisions. It bans any additive "found to induce cancer when ingested by man or animal" (Sec. 348[b] [3] [A]).

Among federal laws with more general application the Consumer Product Safety Act of 1972 (p. 376) applies to products not regulated by Food and Drug, pesticide, motor vehicle, and other legislation. It authorizes the setting of safety standards and banning of hazardous products, that is, products that "present an unreasonable risk of injury" for which "no feasible consumer product safety standard . . . would adequately protect the public" (Sec. 2057). Its private enforcement provisions are to be noted (Sec. 2059, 2073). The text of 1976 amendments was not available at the time of this writing. This law was preceded by the more specialized Flammable Fabric Act of 1967 (15 U.S.C. 1191 et seq.), Special Packaging of Household Substances for the Protection of Children Act of 1970 (15 U.S.C. 1471 et seq.), and others. The Radiation Control for Health and Safety Act of 1968 (p. 382) requires performance standards for electronic products. Lead-based paint is thought to represent a serious health hazard to children who may chew on surfaces covered with such paint. Its use is restricted in federally aided housing (p. 384).

The Safe Drinking Water Act (p. 386) was passed in 1974 after studies demonstrated the presence of known carcinogens in drinking water supplies. The act's potential is as yet unknown but may be wide-ranging. It directs the setting of primary and secondary drinking water regulations including maximum contaminant levels and treatment techniques for substances in public water supply systems that may have an adverse effect on health. Secondary standards are to govern qualities such as odor and color. All standards must be upgraded when improved technology and treatment techniques permit greater protection and periodically reviewed.

Minnesota has mandated a statewide plan for control of hazardous wastes (p. 395). California also has hazardous waste control legislation. In 1975 a large number of persons in Virginia were found to have become seriously ill after exposure to kepone, a pesticide manufactured there. In 1976 the Virginia legislature passed four bills that would require registration and labeling of toxic substances and im-

pose controls on their disposal. Massachusetts prohibits discharges
of poisonous substances into its coastal waters (Sec. 130-23, 130-25,
p. 297). Illinois defines degrees of hazardous and toxic substances
and outlaws the manufacture, distribution, and sale of hazardous toys
and other goods (p. 396). The state's Lead Poisoning Prevention Act
of 1973 (Ill. Ann. Stat. Ch. 111½, Sec. 1301 et seq.) prohibits use of
lead-bearing substances and requires reports of the occurrence of
lead poisoning.

The first state legislative efforts to ban polychlorinated biphenyls
(PCBs) may be those of Indiana and Michigan, passed in March and April of 1976, respectively. PCB is a highly toxic chemical, used to
fireproof industrial machinery, that has contaminated the water supply
and halted the fishing industry in several places.


## PESTICIDES

The Federal Environmental Pesticide Control Act (p. 401),
amending the Federal Insecticide, Fungicide, Rodenticide Act of 1947,
requires labeling and registration of pesticides and classifies them for
general and restricted use. Pesticides that have an "unreasonable adverse effect on the environment" may not be registered or used. The
provisions of the Food, Drug and Cosmetic Act regarding pesticide
residues in food appear in Section 346a (p. 373). Chemical run-off
from agricultural lands is controlled as a "non-point source" under
the Federal Water Pollution Control Act (see Chapter 13). That chapter also excerpts state laws prohibiting sale of phosphate products.

Pesticide legislation in many states supplements the federal law.
Kentucky, for instance, subjects pesticide applicators, operators,
consultants, and dealers to strict licensing procedures (p. 406).


## NUCLEAR MATERIALS

The Atomic Energy Act of 1954 envisioned wide use of "the peac-
ful atom" and set up what were then considered appropriate controls
for the development of nucelar technology, including safety controls.
Since that time increasing concern with the dangers that result from
the generation of nuclear energy and from the disposal of nuclear
waste materials and with the possibility of accidents in nuclear generating plants has become a political issue. How we deal with such fears
may determine to what extent earlier hopes for nuclear energy will be
realized. The Nuclear Regulatory Commission, established in 1974,
is charged with administering the licensing and related functions of
the 1954 act. Safety and security are among the new functions added

by the act establishing it (p. 411). Opponents of nuclear energy do not consider them sufficient.

Other federal laws dealing with nuclear materials include the Ocean Dumping Act (Sec. 1403[c], 1411), which establishes permit procedures for the transportation of "radiological, chemical, or biological warfare agent or any high-level radioactive waste" from the United States for the purpose of dumping into the ocean and for such dumping into U.S. territorial waters. The Resource Recovery Act calls for "national disposal sites for the storage of hazardous wastes, including radioactive, toxic chemical, biological" (Sec. 3254f). The Safe Drinking Water Act includes "radiological substance or matter" in its definition of "contaminant" (Sec. 300[6]), and "radioactive materials" are pollutants within the meaning of the Federal Water Pollution Control Act (Sec. 1362).

Arkansas' radiation control act (p. 415) provides for state acquisition of disposal sites for radioactive by-products and licensing of special nuclear material and equipment using same. Radiation control laws are in effect also in Delaware, Maryland, Nebraska, New York, Oregon, South Dakota, among other states.

Vermont's General Assembly in 1975 voted to reserve to itself approval of the construction of new nuclear fission plants (p. 419). Initiatives that would effect a similar legislative veto over future nuclear power plants were before the voters in California and other states in 1976. No court has as yet adjudged the validity of such statutes.

Colorado's Land Use Act terms nuclear detonations and their effects "geologic hazards," thus potentially subjecting them to land use controls by the state (Sec. 106-7-103[8] and [16], 202 [2][a][III], 203[1][i]).

FEDERAL


OCCUPATIONAL SAFETY AND HEALTH ACT (1970)
29 U.S.C. 651 et seq.

Section 651.    Congressional statement of findings and declaration of purpose and policy
       652.    Definitions
       653.    Geographic applicability
       654.    Duties of employers and employees
       655.    Standards
       656.    Administration
       657.    Inspections, investigations, and recordkeeping
       658.    Citations

§ 651.  Congressional statement of findings and declaration of purpose and policy.

The Congress finds that personal injuries and illnesses arising out of work situations impose a substantial burden upon, and are a hindrance to, interstate commerce in terms of lost production, wage loss, medical expenses, and disability compensation payments.

The Congress declares it to be its purpose and policy, through the exercise of its powers to regulate commerce among the several States and with foreign nations and to provide for the general welfare, to assure so far as possible every working man and woman in the Nation safe and healthful working conditions and to preserve our human resources—

(1) by encouraging employers and employees in their efforts to reduce the number of occupational safety and health hazards at their places of employment, and to stimulate employers and employees to institute new and to perfect existing programs for providing safe and healthful working conditions;

(2) by providing that employers and employees have separate but dependent responsibilities and rights with respect to achieving safe and healthful working conditions;

(3) by authorizing the Secretary of Labor to set mandatory occupational safety and health standards applicable to businesses affecting interstate commerce, and by creating an Occupational Safety and Health Review Commission for carrying out adjudicatory functions under this chapter;

(4) by building upon advances already made through employer and employee initiative for providing safe and healthful working conditions;

(5) by providing for research in the field of occupational safety and health, including the psychological factors involved, and by developing innovative methods, techniques, and approaches for dealing with occupational safety and health problems;

(6) by exploring ways to discover latent diseases, establishing causal connections between diseases and work in environmental conditions, and conducting other research relating to health problems, in recognition of the fact that occupational health standards present problems often different from those involved in occupational safety;

(7) by providing medical criteria which will assure insofar as practicable that no employee will suffer diminished health, functional capacity, or life expectancy as a result of his work experience;

(8) by providing for training programs to increase the number and competence of personnel engaged in the field of occupational safety and health;

(9) by providing for the development and promulgation of occupational safety and health standards;

(10) by providing an effective enforcement program which shall include a prohibition against giving advance notice of any inspection and sanctions for any individual violating this prohibition;

(11) by encouraging the States to assume the fullest responsibility for the administration and enforcement of their occupational safety and health laws by providing grants to the States to assist in identifying their needs and responsibilities in the area of occupational safety and health, to develop plans in accordance with the provisions of this chapter, to improve the administration and enforcement of State occupational safety and health laws, and to conduct experimental and demonstration projects in connection therewith;

(12) by providing for appropriate reporting procedures with respect to occupational safety and health which procedures will help achieve the objectives of this chapter and accurately describe the nature of the occupational safety and health problem;

(13) by encouraging joint labor-management efforts to reduce injuries and disease arising out of employment.

§ 655. Standards. . . .

(b) Procedure for promulgation, modification, or revocation of standards. . . .

(5) The Secretary, in promulgating standards dealing with toxic materials or harmful physical agents under this subsection, shall set the standard which most adequately assures, to the extent feasible, on the basis of the best available evidence, that no employee will suffer material impairment of health or functional capacity even if such employee has regular exposure to the hazard dealt with by such standard for the period of his working life. Development of standards under this subsection shall be based upon research, demonstrations, experiments, and such other information as may be appropriate. In addition to the attainment of the highest degree of health and safety protection for the employee, other considerations shall be the latest available scientific data in the field, the feasibility of the standards, and experience gained under this and other health and safety laws. Whenever practicable, the standard promulgated shall be expressed in terms of objective criteria and of the performance desired.

FOOD, DRUG, AND COSMETIC ACT
(1938, as amended)
21 U.S.C. 301 et seq.

## § 321. Definitions; generally.

For the purposes of this chapter—

(q) The term "pesticide chemical" means any substance which, alone, in chemical combination or in formulation with one or more other substances, is "a pesticide" within the meaning of the Federal Insecticide, Fungicide, and Rodenticide Act as now in force or as hereafter amended, and which is used in the production, storage, or transportation of raw agricultural commodities.

(r) The term "raw agricultural commodity" means any food in its raw or natural state, including all fruits that are washed, colored, or otherwise treated in their unpeeled natural form prior to marketing.

(s) The term "food additive" means any substance the intended use of which results or may reasonably be expected to result, directly or indirectly, in its becoming a component or otherwise affecting the characteristics of any food (including any substance intended for use in producing, manufacturing, packing, processing, preparing, treating, packaging, transporting, or holding food; and including any source of radiation intended for any such use), if such substance is not generally recognized, among experts qualified by scientific training and experience to evaluate its safety, as having been adequately shown through scientific procedures (or, in the case of a substance used in food prior to January 1, 1958, through either scientific procedures or experience based on common use in food) to be safe under the conditions of its intended use; except that such term does not include—

(1) a pesticide chemical in or on a raw agricultural commodity; or

(2) a pesticide chemical to the extent that it is intended for use or is used in the production, storage, or transportation or any raw agricultural commodity; or

(3) a color additive; or

(4) any substance used in accordance with a sanction or approval granted prior to September 6, 1958 pursuant to this chapter, the Poultry Products Inspection Act (21 U.S.C. 451 and the following) or the Meat Inspection Act of March 4, 1907, as amended and extended; or

(5) a new animal drug.

(t)(1) The term "color additive" means a material which—

(A) is a dye, pigment, or other substance made by a process of synthesis or similar artifice, or extracted, isolated, or otherwise rived, with or without intermediate or final change of identity, from a vegetable, animal, mineral, or other source, and

(B) when added or applied to a food, drug, or cosmetic, or to the human body or any part thereof, is capable (alone or through reaction with other substance) of imparting color thereto;
except that such term does not include any material which the Secretary, by regulation, determines is used (or intended to be used) solely for a purpose or purposes other than coloring.

(2) The term "color" includes black, white, and intermediate grays.

(3) Nothing in subparagraph (1) of this paragraph shall be construed to apply to any pesticide chemical, soil or plant nutrient, or other agricultural chemical solely because of its effect in aiding, retarding, or otherwise affecting, directly or indirectly, the growth or other natural physiological processes of produce of the soil and thereby affecting its color, whether before or after harvest.

§ 346. Tolerances for poisonous or deleterious substances in food; regulations.

Any poisonojs or deleterious substance added to any food, except where such substance is required in the production thereof or cannot be avoided by good manufacturing practice shall be deemed to be unsafe for purposes of the application of clause (2)(A) of section 342(a) of this title; but when such substance is so required or cannot be avoided, the Secretary shall promulgate regulations limiting the quantity therein or thereon. . . .

§ 346a. Tolerances for pesticide chemicals in or on raw agricultural commodities.

(a) Any poisonous or deleterious pesticide chemical, or any pesticide chemical which is not generally recognized, among experts qualified by scientific training and experience to evaluate the safety of pesticide chemicals, as safe for use, added to a raw agricultural commodity, shall be deemed unsafe for the purposes of the application of clause (2) of section 342(a) of this title unless—

(1) a tolerance for such pesticide chemical in or on the raw agricultural commodity has been prescribed by the Administrator of the Environmental Protection Agency under this section and the quantity of such pesticide chemical in or on the raw agricultural commodity is within the limits of the tolerance so prescribed; or

(2) with respect to use in or on such raw agricultural commodity, the pesticide chemical has been exempted from the requirement of a tolerance by the Administrator under this section . . . .

(e) The Administrator may at any time, upon his own initiative or upon the request of any interested person, propose the issuance of a regulation establishing a tolerance for a pesticide chemical or exempting it from the necessity of a tolerance. . . .

§ 348.  Food additives—unsafe food additives; exception for conformity with exemption or regulation.

(a) A food additive shall, with respect to any particular use or intended use of such additives, be deemed to be unsafe for the purposes of the application of clause (2) (C) of section 342(a) of this title, unless—

(1) it and its use or intended use conform to the terms of an exemption which is in effect pursuant to subsection (i) of this section; or

(2) there is in effect, and it and its use or intended use are in conformity with, a regulation issued under this section prescribing the conditions under which such additive may be safely used.

(b) (1) Any person may, with respect to any intended use of a food additive, file with the Secretary a petition proposing the issuance of a regulation prescribing the conditions under which such additive may be safely used. . . .

(3) No such regulation shall issue if a fair evaluation of the data before the Secretary—

(A) fails to establish that the proposed use of the food additive, under the conditions of use to be specified in the regulation, will be safe: Provided, That no additive shall be deemed to be safe it it is found to induce cancer when ingested by man or animal, or if it is found, after tests which are appropriate for the evaluation of the safety of food additives, to induce cancer in man or animal, except that this proviso shall not apply with respect to the use of a substance as an ingredient of feed for animals which are raised for food production, if the Secretary finds

(i) that, under the conditions of use and feeding specified in proposed labeling and reasonably certain to be followed in practice, such additive will not adversely affect the animals for which such feed is intended, and

(ii) that no residue of the additive will be found (by methods of examination prescribed or approved by the Secretary by regulations, which regulations shall not be subject to subsections (f) and (g) of this section) in any edible portion of such animal after slaughter or in any food yielded by or derived from the living animal; . . .

CONSUMER PRODUCT SAFETY ACT (1972)<br>15 U.S.C. 2051 et seq.

§ 2051. Congressional findings and declaration of purpose.

(a) The Congress finds that—

(1) an unacceptable number of consumer products which present unreasonable risks of injury are distributed in commerce;

(2) complexities of consumer products and the diverse nature and abilities of consumers using them frequently result in an inability of users to anticipate risks and to safeguard themselves adequately;

(3) the public should be protected against unreasonable risks of injury associated with consumer products;

(4) control by State and local governments of unreasonable risks of injury associated with consumer products is inadequate and may be burdensome to manufacturers;

(5) existing Federal authority to protect consumers from exposure to consumer products presenting unreasonable risks of injury is inadequate; and

(6) regulation of consumer products the distribution or use of which affects interstate or foreign commerce is necessary to carry out this chapter.

(b) The purposes of this chapter are—

(1) to protect the public against unreasonable risks of injury associated with consumer products;

(2) to assist consumers in evaluating the comparative safety of consumer products;

(3) to develop uniform safety standards for consumer products and to minimize conflicting State and local regulations; and

(4) to promote research and investigation into the causes and prevention of product-related deaths, illnesses, and injuries.

§ 2056. Consumer product safety standards—types of requirements.

(a) The Commission may by rule, in accordance with this section and section 2058 of this title, promulgate consumer product safety standards. A consumer product safety standard shall consist of one or more of any of the following types of requirements:

(1) Requirements as to performance, composition, contents, design, construction, finish, or packaging of a consumer product.

(2) Requirements that a consumer product be marked with or accompanied by clear and adequate warnings or instructions, or requirements respecting the form of warnings or instructions. . . .

§ 2057. Banned hazardous products.

Whenever the Commission finds that—

(1) a consumer product is being, or will be, distributed in commerce and such consumer product presents an unreasonable risk of injury; and

(2) no feasible consumer product safety standard under this chapter would adequately protect the public from the unreasonable risk of injury associated with such product,

the Commission may propose and, in accordance with section 2058 of this title, promulgate a rule declaring such product a banned hazardous product.

§ 2058. Administrative procedure governing promulgation of consumer product safety rules—promulgation; withdrawal of notice of proceeding.
. . .

(b) A consumer product safety rule shall express in the rule itself the risk of injury which the standard is designed to eliminate or reduce. In promulgating such a rule the Commission shall consider relevant available product data including the results of research, development, testing, and investigation activities conducted generally and pursuant to this chapter.

(c)(1) Prior to promulgating a consumer product safety rule, the Commission shall consider, and shall make appropriate findings for inclusion in such rule with respect to—
(A) the degree and nature of the risk of injury the rule is designed to eliminate or reduce;
(B) the approximate number of consumer products, or types or classes thereof, subject to such rule;
(C) the need of the public for the consumer products subject to such rule, and the probable effect of such rule upon the utility, cost, or availability of such products to meet such need; and
(D) any means of achieving the objective of the order while minimizing adverse effects on competition or disruption or dislocation of manufacturing and other commercial practices consistent with the public health and safety.
(2) The Commission shall not promulgate a consumer product safety rule unless it finds (and includes such finding in the rule)—
(A) that the rule (including its effective date) is reasonably necessary to eliminate or reduce an unreasonable risk of injury associated with such product;
(B) that the promulgation of the rule is in the public interest; and
(C) in the case of a rule declaring the product a banned hazardous product, that no feasible consumer product safety standard under this chapter would adequately protect the public from the unreasonable risk of injury associated with such product. . . .

§ 2059. Petition for consumer product safety rule—filing by interested persons.

(a) Any interested person, including a consumer or consumer organization, may petition the Commission to commence a proceeding for the issuance, amendment, or revocation of a consumer product safety rule. . . .

§ 2062. New consumer products.

(a) The Commission may, by rule, prescribe procedures for the purpose of insuring that the manufacturer of any new consumer product furnish notice and a description of such product to the Commission before its distribution in commerce.

(b) For purposes of this section, the term "new consumer product" means a consumer product which incorporates a design, material, or form of energy exchange which

(1) has not previously been used substantially in consumer products and

(2) as to which there exists a lack of information adequate to determine the safety of such product in use by consumers.

§ 2063. Product certification and labeling.

(a)(1) Every manufacturer of a product which is subject to a consumer product safety standard under this chapter and which is distributed in commerce (and the private labeler of such product if it bears a private label) shall issue a certificate which shall certify that such product conforms to all applicable consumer product safety standards, and shall specify any standard which is applicable. . . .

§ 2064. Substantial product hazards—definition.

(a) For purposes of this section, the term "substantial product hazard" means—

(1) a failure to comply with an applicable consumer product safety rule which creates a substantial risk of injury to the public, or

(2) a product defect which (because of the pattern of defect, the number of defective products distributed in commerce, the severity of the risk, or otherwise) creates a substantial risk of injury to the public. . . .

(c) If the Commission determines (after affording interested persons, including consumers and consumer organizations, an opportunity for a hearing in accordance with subsection (f) of this section) that a product distributed in commerce presents a substantial product hazard and that notification is required in order to adequately protect the public from such substantial product hazard, the Commission may order the manufacturer or any distributor or retailer of the product to take any one or more of the following actions:

(1) To give public notice of the defect or failure to comply.

(2) To mail notice to each person who is a manufacturer, distributor, or retailer of such product.

(3) To mail notice to every person to whom the person required to give notice knows such product was delivered or sold.

Any such order shall specify the form and content of any notice required to be given under such order.

(d) If the Commission determines (after affording interested parties, including consumers and consumer organizations, an opportunity for a hearing in accordance with subsection (f) of this section) that a prod-

uct distributed in commerce presents a substantial product hazard and
that action under this subsection is in the public interest, it may order
the manufacturer or any distributor or retailer of such product to take
whichever of the following actions the person to whom the order is directed elects:

(1) To bring such product into conformity with the requirements of
the applicable consumer product safety rule or to repair the defect in
such product.

(2) To replace such product with a like or equivalent product which
complies with the applicable consumer product safety rule or which
does not contain the defect.

(3) To refund the purchase price of such product (less a reasonable
allowance for use, if such product has been in the possession of a consumer for one year or more

(A) at the time of public notice under subsection (c) of this section, or

(B) at the time the consumer receives actual notice of the defect
or noncompliance, whichever first occurs). . . .

§ 2068. Prohibited acts.

(a) It shall be unlawful for any person to—

(1) manufacture for sale, offer for sale, distribute in commerce,
or import into the United States any consumer product which is not in
conformity with an applicable consumer product safety standard under
this chapter;

(2) manufacture for sale, offer for sale, distribute in commerce,
or import into the United States any consumer product which has been
declared a banned hazardous product by a rule under this chapter;

(3) fail or refuse to permit access to or copying of records, or fail
or refuse to make reports or provide information, or fail or refuse to
permit entry or inspection, as required under this chapter or rule
thereunder. . . .

§ 2069. Civil penalties.

(a)(1) Any person who knowingly violates section 2068 of this title
shall be subject to a civil penalty not to exceed $2,000 for each such
violation . . . except that the maximum civil penalty shall not exceed
$500,000 for any related series of violations. A violation of section
2068(a)(3) of this title shall constitute a separate violation with respect
to each failure or refusal to allow or perform an act required thereby;
and, if such violation is a continuing one, each day of such violation
shall constitute a separate offense, except that the maximum civil
penalty shall not exceed $500,000 for any related series of violations.
. . .

§ 2073.  Private enforcement.

Any interested person may bring an action in any United States district court for the district in which the defendant is found or transacts business to enforce a consumer product safety rule or an order under section 2064 of this title, and to obtain appropriate injunctive relief. . . .

RADIATION CONTROL FOR HEALTH AND SAFETY
ACT (1968)
42 U.S.C. 263b et seq.

§ 263b.  Congressional declaration of purpose.

The Congress hereby declares that the public health and safety must be protected from the dangers of electronic product radiation. Thus, it is the purpose of this subpart to provide for the establishment by the Secretary of an electronic product radiation control program which shall include the development and administration of performance standards to control the emission of electronic product radiation from electronic products and the undertaking by public and private organizations of research and investigation into the effects and control of such radiation emissions.

§ 263c.  Definitions.

As used in this subpart—

(1) the term "electronic product radiation" means
(A) any ionizing or non-ionizing electromagnetic or particulate radiation, or

(B) any sonic, infrasonic, or ultrasonic wave, which is emitted from an electronic product as the result of the operation of an electronic circuit in such product;

(2) the term "electronic product" means
(A) any manufactured or assembled product which, when in operation,
(i) contains or acts as part of an electronic circuit and
(ii) emits (or in the absence of effective shielding or other controls would emit) electronic product radiation, or
(B) any manufactured or assembled article which is intended for use as a component, part, or accessory of a product described in clause (A) and which when in operation emits (or in the absence of effective shielding or other controls would emit) such radiation. . . .

§ 263f. Performance standards for electronic products—promulgation of regulations.

(a)(1) The Secretary shall by regulation prescribe performance standards for electronic products to control the emission of electronic product radiation from such products if he determines that such standards are necessary for the protection of the public health and safety. Such standards may include provisions for the testing of such products and the measurement of their electronic product radiation emissions, may require the attachment of warning signs and labels, and may require the provision of instructions for the installation, operation, and use of such products. Such standards may be prescribed from time to time whenever such determinations are made, but the first of such standards shall be prescribed prior to January 1, 1970. In the development of such standards, the Secretary shall consult with Federal and State departments and agencies having related responsibilities or interests and with appropriate professional organizations and interested persons, including representatives of industries and labor organizations which would be affected by such standards, and shall give consideration to—
(A) the latest available scientific and medical data in the field of electronic product radiation;
(B) the standards currently recommended by
(i) other Federal agencies having responsibilities relating to the control and measurement of electronic product radiation, and
(ii) public or private groups having an expertise in the field of electronic product radiation;
(C) the reasonableness and technical feasibility of such standards as applied to a particular electronic product; . . .

LEAD-BASED PAINT POISONING PREVENTION
ACT (1971, as amended)
42 U.S.C. 4801 et seq.

§ 4801.  Development of local programs—assistance of Secretary.

(a) The Secretary of Health, Education, and Welfare (hereafter referred to in this subchapter as the "Secretary") is authorized to make
grants to public agencies of units of general local government in any
State and to private nonprofit organizations in any State for the purpose of assisting such units in developing and carrying out local programs to detect and treat incidents of lead-based paint poisoning.

§ 4811.  Development of local programs; assistance of Secretary; required provisions; consistency of assisted programs; employment opportunities for local residents; audit and examination of books, documents, papers and records.

  The Secretary of Health, Education, and Welfare is authorized to
make grants to public agencies of units of general local government
in any State and to private nonprofit organizations in any State for the
purpose of assisting such units in developing and carrying out programs that identify those areas that present a high risk to the health
of residents because of the presence of lead-based paints on interior
surfaces, and then to develop and carry out programs to eliminate the
hazards of lead-based paint poisoning.

(a) A local program should include:

(1) development and carrying out of comprehensive testing programs to detect the presence of lead-based paints on surfaces of residential housing;

(2) the development and carrying out of procedures to remove from exposure to young children all interior surfaces of residential housing, porches, and exterior surfaces of such housing to which children may be commonly exposed, in those areas that present a high risk for the health of residents because of the presence of lead based paints. Such programs should include those surfaces on which non-lead-based paints have been used to cover surfaces to which lead-based paints were previously applied; and

(3) any other actions which will reduce or eliminate lead-based paint poisoning.

§ 4822. Federal Housing Administration procedure requirements for elimination of hazards.

The Secretary of Housing and Urban Development . . . shall establish procedures to eliminate as far as practicable the hazards of lead-based paint poisoning with respect to any existing housing which may present such hazards and which is covered by an application for mortgage insurance or housing assistance payments under a program administered by the Secretary. Such procedures shall apply to all such housing constructed prior to 1950 and shall as a minimum provide for

(1) appropriate measures to eliminate as far as practicable immediate hazards due to the presence of paint which may contain lead and to which children may be exposed, and

(2) assured notification to purchasers and tenants of such housing of the hazards of lead-based paint, of the symptoms and treatment of lead-based paint poisoning, and of the importance and availability of maintenance and removal techniques for eliminating such hazards.

Such procedures may apply to housing constructed during or after 1950 if the Secretary determines, in his discretion, that such housing presents hazards of lead-based paint. The Secretary may establish such other procedures as may be appropriate to carry out the purposes of this section. Further, the Secretary shall establish and implement procedures to eliminate the hazards of lead-based paint poisoning in all federally owned properties prior to the sale of such properties when their use is intended for residential habitation.

§ 4831. Use of lead-based paint in residential structures constructed or rehabilitated by Federal government or with Federal assistance and on certain manufactured toys and utensils; consultation.

The Secretary of Health, Education, and Welfare, in consultation with the Secretary of Housing and Urban Development, shall take such steps and impose such conditions as may be necessary or appropriate—

(1) to prohibit the use of lead-based paint in residential structures constructed or rehabilitated by the Federal Government, or with Federal assistance in any form after the date of enactment of this Act, and

(2) to prohibit the application of lead-based paint to any toy, furniture, cooking utensil, drinking utensil, or eating utensil manufactured and distributed after the date of enactment of this Act.

## SAFE DRINKING WATER ACT (1974)
### 42 U.S.C. 300f et seq.

Section 300j-6.   Federal agencies—compliance with national primary
                  drinking water regulations
       300j-7.    Judicial review
       300j-8.    Citizen's civil action—persons subject to civil action;
                  jurisdiction of enforcement proceedings
       300j-9.    General provisions—regulations

§ 300f.  Definitions.

For purposes of this subchapter:

(1) The term "primary drinking water regulation" means a regulation
which—
    (A) applies to public water systems;
    (B) specifies contaminants which, in the judgment of the Adminis-
trator, may have any adverse effect on the health of persons;
    (C) specifies for each such contaminant either—
        (i) a maximum contaminant level, if, in the judgment of the Ad-
ministrator, it is economically and technologically feasible to ascertain the level of such contaminant in water in public water systems, or
        (ii) if, in the judgment of the Administrator, it is not economi-
cally or technologically feasible to so ascertain the level of such
contaminant, each treatment technique known to the Administrator
which leads to a reduction in the level of such contaminant sufficient
to satisfy the requirements of section 300g-1 of this title; and
    (D) contains criteria and procedures to assure a supply of drinking
water which dependably complies with such maximum contaminant
levels; including quality control and testing procedures to insure compliance with such levels and to insure proper operation and maintenance of the system, and requirements as to
        (i) the minimum quality of water which may be taken into the
system and
        (ii) siting for new facilities for public water systems.

(2) The term "secondary drinking water regulation" means a regulation which applies to public water systems and which specifies the maximum contaminant levels which, in the judgment of the Administrator, are
requisite to protect the public welfare.  Such regulations may apply to
any contaminant in drinking water
    (A) which may adversely affect the odor or appearance of such
water and consequently may cause a substantial number of the persons
served by the public water system providing such water to discontinue
its use, or
    (B) which may otherwise adversely affect the public welfare.

Such regulations may vary according to geographic and other circumstances.

(3) The term "maximum contaminant level" means the maximum permissible level of a contaminant in water which is delivered to any user of a public water system. . . .

(6) The term "contaminant" means any physical, chemical, biological, or radiological substance or matter in water. . . .

§ 300g-1. National drinking water regulations—interim primary regulations; publication of proposed regulations; promulgation; effective date; amendments.

(a)(1) The Administrator shall publish proposed national interim primary drinking water regulations within 90 days after December 16, 1974. Within 180 days after December 16, 1974, he shall promulgate such regulations with such modifications as he deems appropriate. Regulations under this paragraph may be amended from time to time.

(2) National interim primary drinking water regulations promulgated under paragraph (1) shall protect health to the extent feasible, using technology, treatment techniques, and other means, which the Administrator determines are generally available (taking costs into consideration) on the date of enactment of this title.

(3) The interim primary regulations first promulgated under paragraph (1) shall take effect eighteen months after the date of their promulgation.

(b)(1)(A) Within 10 days of the date the report on the study conducted pursuant to subsection (e) of this section is submitted to Congress, the Administrator shall publish in the Federal Register, and provide opportunity for comment on, the—

(i) proposals in the report for recommended maximum contaminant levels for national primary drinking water regulations, and

(ii) list in the report of contaminants the levels of which in drinking water cannot be determined but which may have an adverse effect on the health of persons.

(B) Within 90 days after the date the Administrator makes the publication required by subparagraph (A), he shall be rule establish recommended maximum contaminant levels for each contaminant which, in his judgment based on the report on the study conducted pursuant to subsection (e) of this section, may have any adverse effect on the health of persons. Each such recommended maximum contaminant level shall be set at a level at which, in the Administrator's judgment based on such report, no known or anticipated adverse effects on the health of persons occur and which allows an adequate margin of safety. In addition, he shall, on the basis of the report on the study conducted pursuant to subsection (e) of this section, list in the rules under this subparagraph any contaminant the level of which cannot be accurately enough measured in drinking water to establish a recommended maximum contaminant level and which may have any adverse effect on the health of persons. Based on information available to him, the Administrator may by rule change recommended levels established under this subparagraph or change such list. . . .

(3) Revised national primary drinking water regulations . . . shall be primary drinking water regulations which specify a maximum contaminant level or require the use of treatment techniques for each contaminant for which a recommended maximum contaminant level is established or which is listed in a rule under paragraph (1)(B). The maximum contaminant level specified in a revised national primary drinking water regulation for a contaminant shall be as close to the recommended maximum contaminant level established under paragraph (1)(B) for such contaminant as is feasible. A required treatment technique for a contaminant for which a recommended maximum contaminant level has been established under paragraph (1)(B) shall reduce such contaminant to a level which is as close to the recommended maximum contaminant level for such contaminant as is feasible. A required treatment technique for a contaminant which is listed under paragraph (1)(B) shall require treatment necessary in the Administrator's judgment to prevent known or anticipated adverse effects on the health of persons to the extent feasible. For purposes of this paragraph, the term "feasible" means feasible with the use of the best technology, treatment techniques, and other means, which the Administrator finds are generally available (taking cost into consideration).

(4) Revised national primary drinking water regulations shall be amended whenever changes in technology, treatment techniques, and other means permit greater protection of the health of persons, but in any event such regulations shall be reviewed at least once every 3 years.

(5) Revised national primary drinking water regulations promulgated under this subsection (and amendments thereto) shall take effect eighteen months after the date of their promulgation. Regulations under subsection (a) of this section shall be superseded by regulations under this subsection to the extent provided by the regulations under this subsection.

(6) No national primary drinking water regulation may require the addition of any substance for preventive health care purposes unrelated to contamination of drinking water.

(c) The Administrator shall publish proposed national secondary drinking water regulations within 270 days after December 16, 1974. Within 90 days after publication of any such regulation, he shall promulgate such regulation with such modifications as he deems appropriate. Regulations under this subsection may be amended from time to time. . . .

§ 300g-2. State primary enforcement responsibility; regulations; notice and hearing; publication in Federal Register; applications.

(a) For purposes of this subchapter, a State has primary enforcement responsibility for public water systems during any period for which the Administrator determines (pursuant to regulations prescribed under subsection (b) of this section) that such State—
    (1) has adopted drinking water regulations which
        (A) in the case of the period beginning on the date the national interim primary drinking water regulations are promulgated under section 300g-1 of this title and ending on the date such regulations take effect are no less stringent than such regulations, and
        (B) in the case of the period after such effective date are no less stringent than the interim and revised national primary drinking water regulations in effect under such section;
    (2) has adopted and is implementing adequate procedures for the enforcement of such State regulations, including conducting such monitoring and making such inspections as the Administrator may require by regulation;
    (3) will keep such records and make such reports with respect to its activities under paragraphs (1) and (2) as the Administrator may require by regulation;
    (4) if it permits variances or exemptions, or both, from the requirements of its drinking water regulations which meet the requirements of paragraph (1), permits such variances and exemptions under conditions and in a manner which is not less stringent than the conditions under, and the manner in, which variances and exemptions may be granted under sections 300g-4 and 300g-5 of this title; and
    (5) has adopted and can implement an adequate plan for the provision of safe drinking water under emergency circumstances. . . .

§ 300h. Regulations for State programs—publication of proposed regulations; promulgation; amendments; public hearings; administrative consultations.

(a)(1) The Administrator shall publish proposed regulations for State underground injection control programs within 180 days after December 16, 1974. Within 180 days after publication of such proposed regulations, he shall promulgate such regulations with such modifications as he deems appropriate. Any regulation under this subsection may be amended from time to time.
    (2) Any regulation under this section shall be proposed and promulgated in accordance with section 553 of Title 5 (relating to rulemaking), except that the Administrator shall provide opportunity for public hearing prior to promulgation of such regulations. . . .

(b)(1) Regulations under subsection (a) of this section for State underground injection programs shall contain minimum requirements for effective programs to prevent underground injection which endangers drinking water sources within the meaning of subsection (d)(2) of this section. Such regulations shall require that a State program, in order to be approved under section 330h-1 of this title—

(A) shall prohibit, effective three years after December 16, 1974, any underground injection in such State which is not authorized by a permit issued by the State (except that the regulations may permit a State to authorize underground injection by rule); . . .

(C) shall include inspection, monitoring, recordkeeping, and reporting requirements; and

(D) shall apply

(i) as prescribed by section 300j-6(b) of this title, to underground injections by Federal agencies, and

(ii) to underground injections by any other person whether or not occurring on property owned or leased by the United States.

(2) Regulations of the Administrator under this section for State underground injection control programs may not prescribe requirements which interfere with or impede—

(A) the underground injection of brine or other fluids which are brought to the surface in connection with oil or natural gas production, or

(B) any underground injection for the secondary or tertiary recovery of oil or natural gas. . . .

§ 300h-1. State primary enforcement responsibility—list of States in need of a control program; amendment of list.

(a) Within 180 days after December 16, 1974, the Administrator shall list in the Federal Register each State for which in his judgment a State underground injection control program may be necessary to assure that underground injections will not endanger drinking water sources. Such list may be amended from time to time.

(b)(1)(A) Each State listed under subsection (a) of this section shall within 270 days after the date of promulgation of any regulation under section 300h of this title (or, if later, within 270 days after such State is first listed under subsection (a) of this section) submit to the Administrator an application which contains a showing satisfactory to the Administrator that the State—

(i) has adopted after reasonable notice and public hearings, and will implement, an underground injection control program which meets the requirements of regulations in effect under section 330h of this title; and

(ii) will keep such records and make such reports with respect to its activities under its underground injection control program as the Administrator may require by regulation.

(B) Within 270 days of any amendment of a regulation under section 300h of this title revising or adding any requirement respecting State underground injection control programs, each State listed under subsection (a) of this section shall submit (in such form and manner as the Administrator may require) a notice to the Administrator containing a showing satisfactory to him that the State underground injection control program meets the revised or added requirement.

(2) Within ninety days after the State's application under paragraph (1)(A) or notice under paragraph (1)(B) and after reasonable opportunity for presentation of views, the Administrator shall by rule either approve, disapprove, or approve in part and disapprove in part, the State's underground injection control program. . . .

§ 300h-3. Interim regulation of underground injections—necessity for well operation permit; designation of one aquifer areas.

(a)(1) Any person may petition the Administrator to have an area of a State (or States) designated as an area in which no new underground injection well may be operated during the period beginning on the date of the designation and ending on the date on which the applicable underground injection control program covering such area takes effect unless a permit for the operation of such well has been issued by the Administrator under subsection (b) of this section. The Administrator may so designate an area within a State if he finds that the area has one aquifer which is the sole or principal drinking water source for the area and which, if contaminated, would create a significant hazard to public health. . . .

§ 300i. Emergency powers—actions authorized against imminent and substantial endangerment to health.

(a) Notwithstanding any other provision of this subchapter, the Administrator, upon receipt of information that a contaminant which is present in or is likely to enter a public water system may present an imminent and substantial endangerment to the health of persons, and that appropriate State and local authorities have not acted to protect the health of such persons, may take such actions as he may deem necessary in order to protect the health of such persons. To the extent he determines it to be practicable in light of such imminent endangerment, he shall consult with the State and local authorities in order to confirm the correctness of the information on which action proposed to be taken under this subsection is based and to ascertain the action which such authorities are or will be taking. The action which the Administrator may take may include (but shall not be limited to)

(1) issuing such orders as may be necessary to protect the health of persons who are or may be users of such system (including travelers), and

(2) commencing a civil action for appropriate relief, including a restraining order or permanent or temporary injunction. . . .

§ 300j-1. Research, technical assistance, information, training of personnel—specific powers and duties of Administrator.

(a)(1) The Administrator may conduct research, studies, and demonstrations relating to the causes, diagnosis, treatment, control, and prevention of physical and mental diseases and other impairments of man resulting directly or indirectly from contaminants in water, or to the provision of a dependably safe supply of drinking water, including—

(A) improved methods

(i) to identify and measure the existence of contaminants in drinking water (including methods which may be used by State and local health and water officials), and

(ii) to identify the source of such contaminants;

(B) improved methods to identify and measure the health effects of contaminants in drinking water;

(C) new methods of treating raw water to prepare it for drinking, so as to improve the efficiency of water treatment, and to remove contaminants from water;

(D) improved methods for providing a dependably safe supply of drinking water, including improvements in water purification and distribution, and methods of assessing the health related hazards of drinking water; and

(E) improved methods of protecting underground water sources of public water systems from contamination.

(2) The Administrator shall, to the maximum extent feasible, provide technical assistance to the States and municipalities in the establishment and administration of public water system supervision programs (as defined in section 300j-2[c][1] of this title).

(3) The Administrator shall conduct studies, and make periodic reports to Congress, on the costs of carrying out regulations prescribed under section 300g-1 of this title.

(4) The Administrator shall conduct a survey and study of—

(A) disposal of waste (including residential waste) which may endanger underground water which supplies, or can reasonably be expected to supply, any public water systems, and

(B) means of control of such waste disposal.

Not later than one year after December 16, 1974, he shall transmit to the Congress the results of such survey and study, together with such recommendations as he deems appropriate.

(5) The Administrator shall carry out a study of methods of underground injection which do not result in the degradation of underground drinking water sources.

(6) The Administrator shall carry out a study of methods of preventing, detecting, and dealing with surface spills of contaminants which may degrade underground water sources for public water systems.

(7) The Administrator shall carry out a study of virus contamination of drinking water sources and means of control of such contamination.

(8) The Administrator shall carry out a study of the nature and extent of the impact on underground water which supplies or can reasonably be expected to supply public water systems of

(A) abandoned injection or extraction wells;

(B) intensive application of pesticides and fertilizers in underground water recharge areas; and

(C) ponds, pools, lagoons, pits, or other surface disposal of contaminants in underground water recharge areas.

(9) The Administrator shall conduct a comprehensive study of public water supplies and drinking water sources to determine the nature, extent, sources of and means of control of contamination by chemicals or other substances suspected of being carcinogenic. Not later than six months after December 16, 1974, he shall transmit to the Congress the initial results of such study, together with such recommendations for further review and corrective action as he deems appropriate. . . .

§ 300j-8.  Citizen's civil action—persons subject to civil action; jurisdiction of enforcement proceedings.

(a) Except as provided in subsection (b) of this section, any person may commence a civil action on his own behalf—

(1) against any person (including

(A) the United States, and

(B) any other governmental instrumentality or agency to the extent permitted by the eleventh amendment to the Constitution) who is alleged to be in violation of any requirement prescribed by or under this subchapter, or

(2) against the Administrator where there is alleged a failure of the Administrator to perform any act or duty under this subchapter which is not discretionary with the Administrator. . . .

(d) The court, in issuing any final order in any action brought under subsection (a) of this section, may award costs of litigation (including reasonable attorney and expert witness fees) to any party whenever the court determines such an award is appropriate.

STATES

MINNESOTA HAZARDOUS WASTE CONTROL (1974)
Minn. Stat. Ch. 116 (portions)

§ 116.06.

Subd. 13. Pollution Control; Hazardous Waste.

"Hazardous waste" means any refuse or discarded material or combinations of refuse or discarded materials in solid, semi-solid,
liquid, or gaseous form which cannot be handled by routine waste management techniques because they pose a substantial present or potential hazard to human health or other living organisms because of their
chemical, biological, or physical properties. Categories of hazardous waste materials include, but are not limited to: explosives, flam-
mables, oxidizers, poisons, irritants, and corrosives.

§ 116.07.

Subdivision 2. . . . The pollution control agency shall adopt standards
for the identification of hazardous waste and for the labeling, classification, storage, collection, transportation and disposal of hazardous
waste, recognizing that due to variable factors, no single standard
of hazardous waste control is applicable to all areas of the state. In
adopting standards, the pollution control agency shall recognize that
elements of control which may be reasonable and proper in densely
populated areas of the state may be unreasonable and improper in
sparesely populated or remote areas of the state. The agency shall
consider existing physical conditions, topography, soils, and geology,
climate, transportation and land use. Standards of hazardous waste
control shall be premised on technical knowledge, and commonly accepted practices. No local government unit shall set standards of
hazardous waste control which are in conflict or inconsistent with those
set by the pollution control agency.

§ 116.101. Hazardous Waste Control and Spill Contingency Plan.

The pollution control agency shall study and investigate the problems
of hazardous waste control and shall develop a statewide hazardous
waste management plan detailing the location of hazardous waste disposal facilities and storage sites throughout the state and the needs
relative to the interstate transportation of hazardous waste.
Elements of the statewide hazardous spill contingency plan which
relate to hazardous wastes, shall be incorporated into the statewide
hazardous waste management plan. The pollution control agency shall
develop an informational reporting system of hazardous waste quantities generated and disposed of in the state.

ILLINOIS UNIFORM HAZARDOUS SUBSTANCES ACT
(1969, as amended)
Ill. Ann Stat. Ch. 111½, Sec. 251 et seq.

§ 252-4. Hazardous substance.

"Hazardous substance" means any substance or mixture of substances
which is toxic, corrosive, an irritant, strong sensitizer, flammable,
combustible or which generates pressure through decomposition, heat
or other means and which may cause substantial personal injury or illness during or as a proximate result of any customary or reasonably
anticipated handling or use including reasonably forseeable ingestion by
children and also means any radioactive substance, if, with respect
to such substance as used in a particular class of article or as pack-

aged, the Director determines by regulation that the substance is sufficiently hazardous to require labeling in accordance with this Act in order to protect the public health.

### § 252-5. Toxic.

"Toxic" means any substance (other than a radioactive substance) which has the capacity to produce bodily injury or illness to man through ingestion, inhalation, or absorption through any body surface.

### § 252-6. Highly toxic.

"Highly toxic" means any substance which produces death within 14 days in at least half of a group of 10 or more laboratory white rats each weighing between 200 and 300 grams, when a single dose of 50 milligrams or less per kilogram of body weight, is orally administered or when inhaled continuously for a period of one hour or less at an atmospheric concentration of 200 parts per million by volume or less of gas or vapor or two milligrans per liter by volume or less of mist or dust, provided such concentration is likely to be encountered by man when the substance is used in any reasonably forseeable manner, or which produces death within 14 days in at least half of a group of 10 or more rabbits tested in a dosage of 200 milligrams or less per kilogram of body weight, when administered by continous contact with the bare skin for 24 hours or less.

If the Director finds that available data on human experience with any substance indicate results different from those obtained on animals in the above named dosages or concentrations, the human data shall take precedence.

### § 252-10. Flammable—combustible.

"Flammable" means any substance which has a flashpoint of above 20 degrees to and including 80 degrees Fahrenheit as determined by the Tagliabue Open Cup Tester, and "extremely flammable" means any substance which has a flashpoint at or below 20 degrees Fahrenheit as determined by the Tagliabue Open Cup Tester, and "combustible" means any substance which has a flashpoint above 80 degrees Fahrenheit to and including 150 degrees, as determined by the Tagliabue Open Cup Tester; except that the flammability or combustibility of solids and of the contents of self-pressurized containers shall be determined by methods found by the Director to be generally applicable to such materials or containers, respectively, and established by regulations issued by him, which regulations shall also define the terms "flammable", "combustible", and "extremely flammable" in accord with such methods.

§ 252-15. Misbranded hazardous substance.

"Misbranded hazardous substance" means:

A. A hazardous substance (including a toy, or other article intended for use by children, which is a hazardous substance, or which bears or contains a hazardous substance in such manner as to be susceptible of access by a child to whom such toy or other article is entrusted) intended, or packaged in a form suitable, for use in the household or by children, if the packaging or labelling of such substance is in violation of an applicable regulation issued pursuant to Sections 3, 4 or 5 of the Illinois Poison Prevention Packaging Act, enacted by the 77th General Assembly, or if such substance except as otherwise provided by or pursuant to the provisions of this Act, fails to bear a label,

(1) which states conspicuously:

(a) The name and place of business of the manufacturer, packer, distributor, or seller;

(b) The common or usual name or the chemical name (if there be no common or usual name) of the hazardous substance or of each component which contributes substantially to its hazard, unless the Director by regulation permits or requires the use of a recognized generic name;

(c) The signal word "DANGER" on substances which are extremely flammable, corrosive, or highly toxic;

(d) The signal word "WARNING" or "CAUTION" on all other hazardous substances;

(e) An affirmative statement of the principal hazard or hazards, such as "Flammable", "Combustible", "Vapor Harmful", "Causes Burns", "Absorbed through skin", or similar working descriptive of the hazard;

(f) Precautionary measures describing the action to be followed or avoided, except when modified by regulation of the Director pursuant to Section 11 of this Act;

(g) Instruction, when necessary or appropriate, for first-aid treatment;

(h) The word "Poison" for any hazardous substance which is highly toxic;

(i) Instructions for handling and storage of packages which require special care in handling or storage; and

(j) The statement "Keep out of the reach of children" or its practical equivalent, or, if the article is intended for use by children and is not a banned hazardous substance, adequate directions for the protection of children from the hazard, and

(2) on which any statements required under subparagraph (1) of this paragraph are located prominently and are in the English language in conspicuous and legible type in contrast by typography, layout, or color with other printed matter on the label. . . .

C. A hazardous substance in a reused food, drug or cosmetic container or in a container which, though not a reused container is identifiable as a food, drug, or cosmetic container by its labeling or other identification. . . .

§ 252-16. Banned hazardous substance.

"Banned hazardous substance" means:

A. Any toy, or other article intended for use by children, which is a hazardous substance, or which bears or contains a hazardous substance in such manner as to be susceptible of access by a child to whom such toy or other article is entrusted. . . .

C. Any glue, plastic cement or similar adhesive product, packaged in a container containing 4 ounces or less by volume, and containing a solvent which has the property of releasing toxic vapors or fumes which does not include a noxious additive in such form and proportions as required by the Director. The term "noxious additive" shall mean any element or compound designated and approved by the Director for use as a safe and effective ingredient of glue, plastic cement or similar adhesive product containing a solvent having the property of releasing toxic vapors or fumes for the purpose of discouraging the intentional smelling or inhaling of the fumes of such glue, plastic cement or similar adhesive product.

Containers of such glue, plastic cement or similar adhesive product shall have indicated on the label the fact that the glue, plastic cement or similar adhesive product contains such required additive.

§ 252-20. Thermal hazard.

An article may be determined to present a thermal hazard if, in normal use or when subjected to reasonably foreseeable damage or abuse, its design or manufacture presents an unreasonable risk of personal injury or illness because of heat as from heated parts, substances, or surfaces.

§ 253a. Submission of names and amounts of hazardous ingredients—power of director.

The Director, when he deems it necessary in the administration of this Act, may require the submission of the names and amounts of any hazardous ingredients in any hazardous substance.

§ 254. Examinations, inspections and investigations—samples.

The Director is authorized to conduct examinations, inspections, and investigations for the purposes of this Act through officers and employees of the Department.

For purposes of enforcement of this Act, officers or employees duly designated by the Director, upon presenting appropriate credentials and a written notice to the owner, operator, or agent in charge are authorized: to enter, at reasonable times, any factory, warehouse, or establishment in which hazardous substances are manufactured, processed, packed, or held for introduction into commerce or are held after such introduction, or to enter any vehicle being used to transport or hold such hazardous substances in commerce; to inspect, at reasonable times and within reasonable limits and in a reasonable manner, such factory, warehouse, establishment, or vehicle, and all pertinent equipment, finished and unfinished materials, and labeling therein; and to obtain samples of such materials or packages thereof, or of such labeling. . . .

§ 255.  Detention or embargo of misbranded or banned substances— condemnation—destruction—exports exempted.

A.  When the Director or an authorized agent of the Director finds or has probable cause to believe that any substance is a misbranded hazardous substance or banned hazardous substance within the meaning of this Act, he shall affix to such article a tag or other appropriate marking giving notice that the article is or is suspected of being such a substance and has been detained or embargoed and warning all persons not to remove or dispose of such article by sale or otherwise until permission for removal or disposal is given by such agent or the court. . . .

§ 262.  Prohibited acts.

The following acts and the causing thereof are prohibited:

(1) The manufacture, distribution, sale, or offer for sale within this State, or the delivery for introduction or introduction into commerce, or the delivery for transportation or transportation in intrastate commerce or between points within this State through any point outside this State, or the receipt in commerce and subsequent delivery or proffered delivery for pay or otherwise, of a misbranded hazardous substance or a banned hazardous substance.

(2) The alteration, mutilation, destruction, obliteration or removal of the whole or any part of the label of, or the doing of any other act with respect to, a hazardous substance, if such act is done while the substance is in commerce or is being held for sale and results in the substance being a misbranded hazardous substance or a banned hazardous substance.

(3) The use by any person to his own advantage, or revealing other than to the Director or officers or employees of the Department, or

officers or employees of agencies of this state or any other state, or of any federal agency when such information is required in carrying out their statutory duties, or to the courts when relevant in any judicial proceeding under this Act, or to physicians and in emergencies to pharmacists and other qualified persons for use in the preparation of antidotes, in accordance with such directions as the Director may prescribe, of any information acquired under authority of this Act concerning any product formula or any method or process which as a trade secret is entitled to protection.

(4) The opposing or interfering in any way with the Director or his duly authorized agents in carrying out the duties imposed by this Act.

(5) The giving of a guarantee or undertaking referred to in Section 16 which is false, except by a person who relied upon a guarantee or undertaking to the same effect signed by and containing the name and address of the person residing in the State of Illinois from whom he received the hazardous substance in good faith.


## FEDERAL


### Pesticides


ENVIRONMENTAL PESTICIDE CONTROL ACT (1972)
7 U.S.C. 136 et seq.

§ 136. Definitions. . . .

(e) Certified applicator, etc.—

(1) Certified applicator.—The term "certified applicator" means any individual who is certified under section 136b of this title as authorized to use or supervise the use of any pesticide which is classified for restricted use.

(2) Private applicator.—The term "private applicator" means a certified applicator who uses or supervises the use of any pesticide which is classified for restricted use for purposes of producing any agricultural commodity on property owned or rented by him or his employer or (if applied without compensation other than trading of personal services between producers of agricultural commodities) on the property of another person.

(3) Commercial applicator.—The term "commercial applicator" means a certified applicator (whether or not he is a private applicator with respect to some uses) who uses or supervises the use of any pesticide which is classified for restricted use for any purpose or on any property other than as provided by paragraph (2).

(4) Under the direct supervision of a certified applicator.—Unless otherwise prescribed by its labeling, a pesticide shall be considered to be applied under the direct supervision of a certified applicator if it is applied by a competent person acting under the instructions and control of a certified applicator who is available if and when needed, even though such certified applicator is not physically present at the time and place the pesticide is applied. . . .

(j) Environment.—The term "environment" includes water, air, land, and all plants and man and other animals living therein, and the interrelationships which exist among these. . . .

(l) Imminent hazard.—The term "imminent hazard" means a situation which exists when the continued use of a pesticide during the time required for cancellation proceeding would be likely to result in unreasonable adverse effects on the environment or will involve unreasonable hazard to the survival of a species declared endangered or threatened by the Secretary pursuant to the Endangered Species Act of 1973.

§ 136a.  Registration of pesticides.

(a) Requirement. —Except as otherwise provided by this subchapter, no person in any State may distribute, sell, offer for sale, hold for sale, ship, deliver for shipment, or receive and (having so received) deliver or offer to deliver, to any person any pesticide which is not registered with the Administrator. . . .

(c) Procedure for registration. —
    (1) Statement required. —Each applicant for registration of a pesticide shall file with the Administrator a statement which includes . . .
        (C) a complete copy of the labeling of the pesticide, a statement of all claims to be made for it, and any directions for its use;
        (D) if requested by the Administrator, a full description of the tests made and the results thereof upon which the claims are based, except. . . .
    (5) Approval of registration— . . .
        (C) it will perform its intended function without unreasonable adverse effects on the environment; and
        (D) when used in accordance with widespread and commonly recognized practice it will not generally cause unreasonable adverse effects on the environment. . . .

(d) Classification of pesticides. —
    (1) Classification for general use, restricted use, or both. —
        (A) As a part of the registration of a pesticide the Administrator shall classify it as being for general use or for restricted use, provided that if the Administrator determines that some of the uses for which the pesticide is registered should be for general use and that other uses for which it is registered should be for restricted use, he shall classify it for both general use and restricted use. . . .
        (B) If the Administrator determines that the pesticide, when applied in accordance with its directions for use, warnings and cautions and for the uses for which it is registered, or for one or more of such uses, or in accordance with a widespread and commonly recognized practice, will not generally cause unreasonable adverse effects on the environment, he will classify the pesticide, or the particular use or uses of the pesticide to which the determination applies, for general use.
        (C) If the Administrator determines that the pesticide, when applied in accordance with its directions for use, warnings and cautions and for the uses for which it is registered, or for one or more of such uses, or in accordance with a wide-spread and commonly recognized practice, may generally cause, without additional regulatory restrictions, unreasonable adverse effects on the environment, including injury to the applicator, he shall classify the pesticide, or the particular use or uses to which the determination applies, for restricted use: . . .

§ 136b.  Use of restricted use pesticides; certified applicators.

(a) Certification procedure,—

(1) Federal certification.—Subject to paragraph (2), the Administrator shall prescribe standards for the certification of applicators of pesticides.  Such standards shall provide that to be certified, an individual must be determined to be competent with respect to the use and handling of pesticides, or to the use and handling of the pesticide or class of pesticides covered by such individual's certification.

(2) State certification.—If any State, at any time, desires to certify applicators of pesticides, the Governor of such State shall submit a State plan for such purpose.  The Administrator shall approve the plan submitted by any State, or any modification thereof. . . .

§ 136d.  Administrative review; suspension.

(a) Cancellation after five years. . . .
(2) Information.

If at any time after the registration of a pesticide the registrant has additional factual information regarding unreasonable adverse effects on the environment of the pesticide, he shall submit such information to the Administrator.

(b) Cancellation and charge in classification.

If it appears to the Administrator that a pesticide or its labeling or other material required to be submitted does not comply with the provisions of this subchapter or, when used in accordance with widespread and commonly recognized practice, generally causes unreasonable adverse effects on the environment, the Administrator may issue a notice of his intent either—

(1) to cancel its registration or to change its classification together with the reasons (including the factual basis) for his action, or

(2) to hold a hearing to determine whether or not its registration should be canceled or its classification changed.

§ 136e.  Registration of establishments.

(a) Requirement.

No person shall produce any pesticide subject to this subchapter in any State unless the establishment in which it is produced is registered with the Administrator.  The application for registration of any establishment shall include the name and address of the establishment and of the producer who operates such establishment.

## § 136f.  Books and records.

(a) Requirements.

The Administrator may prescribe regulations requiring producers to maintain such records with respect to their operations and the pesticides and devices produced as he determines are necessary for the effective enforcement of this subchapter. . . .

## § 136j.  Unlawful acts.

(a) In general.—
   (1) Except as provided by subsection (b) of this section, it shall be unlawful for any person in any State to distribute, sell, offer for sale, hold for sale, ship, deliver for shipment, or receive and (having so received) deliver or offer to deliver, to any person—
      (A) any pesticide which is not registered under section 136a of this title, except as provided by section 136d(a) (1) of this title;
      (B) any registered pesticide if any claims made for it as a part of its distribution or sale substantially differ from any claims made for it as a part of the statement required in connection with its registration under section 136a of this title;
      (C) any registered pesticide the composition of which differs at the time of its distribution or sale from its composition as described in the statement required in connection with its registration under section 136a of this title;
      (D) any pesticide which has not been colored or discolored pursuant to the provisions of section 136w(c) (5) of this title;
      (E) any pesticide which is adulterated or misbranded; or
      (F) any device which is misbranded. . . .
      (P) to use any pesticide in tests on human beings unless such human beings
         (i) are fully informed of the nature and purposes of the test and of any physical and mental health consequences which are reasonably foreseeable therefrom, and
         (ii) freely volunteer to participate in the test.

## § 136m.  Indemnities.

(a) Requirement.—If—
   (1) the Administrator notifies a registrant that he has suspended the registration of a pesticide because such action is necessary to prevent an imminent hazard;
   (2) the registration of the pesticide is canceled as a result of a final determination that the use of such pesticide will create an imminent hazard; and

(3) any person who owned any quantity of such pesticide immediately before the notice to the registrant under paragraph (1) suffered losses by reason of suspension or cancellation of the registration,

the Administrator shall make an indemnity payment to such person. . . .

STATES

Pesticides

KENTUCKY PESTICIDE USE AND APPLICATION
ACT (1972, as amended)
Ky. Rev. Stat. Ch. 217B

Section 217B.260.   Pesticide advisory board
    217B.990.   Penalties

## § 217B.030.  Purpose.

The purpose of this chapter is to regulate in the public interest, the use and application of insecticides, fungicides, herbicides, defoliants, desiccants, plant growth regulators, nematocides, rodenticides, and any other pesticides designated by the department by regulation.

## § 217B.050.  Regulations.

(1) The department shall administer and enforce the provisions of this chapter and shall have authority to issue regulations after a public hearing, conducted pursuant to KRS 224.-045, to carry out the provisions of this chapter and in such regulations may prescribe methods to be used in the application of pesticides. Where the department finds that such regulations are necessary to carry out the purpose and intent of this chapter such regulations may relate to the time, place, manner, and method of application of the pesticides, may restrict or prohibit use of pesticides in designated areas during specified periods of time and shall encompass all reasonable factors which the department deems necessary to prevent damage or injury by drift or misapplication to:

(a) Plants, including forage plants, on adjacent or nearby lands;
(b) Wildlife in the adjoining or nearby areas;
(c) Fish and other aquatic life in waters in reasonable proximity to the area to be treated;
(d) Pollinating insects, animals, or persons. . . .

(3) The department may by regulation adopt a list of "restricted use pesticides" for the state or for designated areas within the state. . . .

## § 217B.070.  Applicator's license—fees—inspection—application—examination.

(1) No person shall engage in the business of applying pesticides to the lands of another within this state at any time without a pesticide applicator's license issued by the department. The department shall require an annual fee of $25.00 for each pesticide applicator's license issued and, in addition, an inspection fee of $10.00 for each aircraft to be licensed and $10.00 for each piece of equipment to be licensed. Should any equipment fail to pass inspection under KRS 217B.160, making it necessary for a second inspection to be made, the department shall require an added inspection fee of $5.00. In addition to the required inspection, unannounced inspections may be made without charge to determine if equipment is properly calibrated and maintained in conformance with laws and regulations. . . .

(3) The department shall require an applicant for a license to show upon examination that he possesses adequate knowledge concerning the proper use and application of pesticides in the classifications he has applied for, manually or with the various equipment that he may have applied for a license to operate. The examination shall require a working knowledge of:

(a) The proper use of the equipment.

(b) The hazards that may be involved in applying pesticides, including:

  1. The effect of drift of the pesticides on adjacent and nearby lands and other nontarget organisms;

  2. The proper meteorological conditions for the application of pesticides and the precautions to be taken therewith;

  3. The effect of the pesticides on plants or animals in the area, including the possibility of damage to plants or animals or the possibility of illegal pesticide residues resulting on them;

  4. The effect of the application of pesticides to wildlife in the area, including aquatic life;

  5. The identity and classification of pesticides used and the effects of their application in particular circumstances;

  6. The likelihood of contamination of water or injury to persons, plants, livestock, pollinating insects, and vegetation.

(c) Calculating the concentration of pesticides to be used in particular circumstances.

(d) Identification of pests to be controlled by common name only and the damages caused by such pests.

(e) Protective clothing and respiratory equipment required during the handling and application of pesticides.

(f) General precautions to be followed in the disposal of containers as well as the cleaning and decontamination of the equipment which the applicant proposes to use.

(g) Applicable state and federal pesticide laws and regulations. . . .

§ 217B.080.  Operator's license—fees—aerial applications.

It shall be unlawful for any person to act as an employe of a pesticide applicator and apply pesticides manually or as the operator directly in charge of any equipment which is licensed or should be licensed under the provisions of this chapter for the application of any pesticide, without having obtained an operator's license from the department. Such an operator's license shall be in addition to any other license or permit required by law for the operation or use of any such equipment. Any person applying for such an operator's license shall file an application on a form prescribed by the department on or before January 1 of each year. Application for a license to apply pesticides shall be accompanied by a license fee of $10.00. The provisions of this section shall not apply to any individual who has passed the examination provided for in subsection (3) of KRS 217B.070, and is a licensed pesticide applicator. . . .

§ 217B.100. Consultant's license—fee—qualifications.

(1) No person shall perform services as a pest control consultant without first procuring from the department a license. . . .

§ 217B.103. Suspension, revocation, or modification of consultant's license—grounds—application for new license.

(1) The department may suspend for not longer than ten (10) days, pending inquiry, and, after opportunity for a hearing, the department may deny, suspend, revoke, or modify the provision of any license issued under KRS 217B.-100 if it finds that the applicant or licensee or his employe has committed any of the following acts, each of which is declared to be a violation of this section:

(a) Made false or fraudulent claims through any media, misrepresenting the effect of materials or methods to be utilized or sold;

(b) Made a pesticide recommendation not in accordance with the label registered pursuant to KRS 217.540 to 217.640;

(c) Violated any provision of this chapter or any rule or regulation adopted by the department or of any lawful order of the department;

(d) Failed to pay the original or renewal license fee when due, and continue to sell restricted use pesticides without paying the license fee, or sold restricted use pesticides without a license;

(e) Was guilty of gross negligence, incompetency or misconduct in acting as a pesticide dealer;

(f) Refused or neglected to keep and maintain the records required by this chapter, or to make reports when and as required; or

(g) Made false or fraudulent records, invoices, or reports;

(h) Used fraud or misrepresentation in making an application for a license or renewal of a license, or in selling or offering to sell restricted use pesticides;

(i) Refused or neglected to comply with any limitations or restrictions on or in a duly issued license;

(j) Aided or abetted a licensed or an unlicensed person to evade the provisions of this chapter, combined or conspired with such a licensed or unlicensed person to evade the provisions of this chapter, or allowed one's license to be used by an unlicensed person;

(k) Impersonated any state, county, or city inspector or official;

(l) Stored or disposed of containers or pesticides by means other than those prescribed on the label or adopted regulations.

§ 217B.105.  Pesticide dealer's license—fees—records required.

(1) No person shall act in the capacity of a pesticide dealer, or shall engage or offer to engage in the business of, advertise as, or assume to act as a restricted use pesticide dealer unless he is licensed annually as provided in this section. . . .

§ 217B.130.  Financial responsibility.

(1) The director shall not issue a pesticide applicator's license until the applicant has furnished evidence of financial responsibility with the director consisting either of a surety bond or a liability insurance policy or certification thereof, protecting persons who may suffer legal damages as a result of the operations of the applicant.

(2) The amount of the surety bond or liability insurance as provided for in this section shall be not less than $100,000 for public liability and not less than $25,000 for property damage, including loss or damage arising out of the actual use of any pesticide. . . .

(3) Should the surety furnished become unsatisfactory, said applicant shall upon notice execute a new bond or insurance and shall he fail to do so, the department shall cancel his license and it shall be unlawful thereafter for such person to engage in said business of applying pesticides until the bond or insurance is brought into compliance with the requirements of subsection (2) of this section and his license is reinstated by the department.

(4) Nothing in this chapter shall be construed to relieve any person from liability for any damage to the person or lands of another caused by the use of pesticides even though such use conforms to the rules and regulations of the department.

§ 217B.140.  Claim of damage—when filed—effect—inspection of damaged property.

(1) The person claiming damages from pesticide application shall have filed with the department a written statement claiming that he has been damaged, on a form prescribed by the department within sixty (60) days after the date that damages occurred, or prior to the time that twenty-five per cent (25%) of a crop damaged shall have been harvested. Such statement shall contain, but shall not be limited thereto, the name of the person responsible for the application of said pesticide, the name of the owner or lessee of the land on which the crop is grown and for which damages are claimed and the date on which it is alleged that the damage occurred.  The department shall prepare a form to be furnished to persons to be used in such cases and such form shall contain such other requirements as the department may deem proper.

The department shall, upon receipt of such statement, notify the licensee and the owner or lessee of the land or other person who may be
charged with the responsibility, for the damages claimed, and furnish
copies of such statements as may be requested. . . .


FEDERAL


Nuclear Materials

NUCLEAR REGULATORY COMMISSION (1974)
42 U.S.C. 5841 et seq.

§ 5842. Licensing and related regulatory functions respecting selected
Administration facilities.

   Notwithstanding the exclusions provided for in section 2140(a) of this
title or any other provisions of the Atomic Energy Act of 1954, as
amended, the Nuclear Regulatory Commission shall, except as otherwise specifically provided by section 2140(b) of this title, or other
law, have licensing and related regulatory authority pursuant to chapters 6, 7, 8, and 10 of the Atomic Energy Act of 1954, as amended, as
to the following facilities of the Administration:
   (1) Demonstration Liquid Metal Fast Breeder reactors when operated as part of the power generation facilities of an electric utility system, or when operated in any other manner for the purpose of demonstrating the suitability for commercial application of such a reactor.
   (2) Other demonstration nuclear reactors—except those in existence
on the effective date of this chapter—when operated as part of the power
generation facilities of an electric utility system, or when operated
in any other manner for the purpose of demonstrating the suitability
for commercial application of such a reactor.
   (3) Facilities used primarily for the receipt and storage of high-
level radioactive wastes resulting from activities licensed under such
Act.

(4) Retrievable Surface Storage Facilities and other facilities authorized for the express purpose of subsequent long-term storage of high-level radioactive waste generated by the Administration, which are not used for, or are part of, research and development activities.

§ 5843. Office of Nuclear Reactor Regulation—establishment; appointment of Director.

(b) Subject to the provisions of this chapter, the Director of Nuclear Reactor Regulation shall perform such functions as the Commission shall delegate including:

(1) Principal licensing and regulation involving all facilities, and materials licensed under the Atomic Energy Act of 1954, as amended, associated with the construction and operation of nuclear reactors licensed under the Atomic Energy Act of 1954, as amended;

(2) Review the safety and safeguards of all such facilities, materials, and activities, and such review functions shall include, but not be limited to—

(A) monitoring, testing and recommending upgrading of systems designed to prevent substantial health or safety hazards; and

(B) evaluating methods of transporting special nuclear and other nuclear materials and of transporting and storing high-level radioactive wastes to prevent radiation hazards to employees and the general public. . . .

§ 5844. Office of Nuclear Safety and Safeguards—establishment; appointment of Director. . . .

(b) Subject to the provisions of this chapter, the Director of Nuclear Material Safety and Safeguards shall perform such functions as the Commission shall delegate including:

(1) Principal licensing and regulation involving all facilities and materials, licensed under the Atomic Energy Act of 1954, as amended, associated with the processing, transport, and handling of nuclear materials, including the provision and maintenance of safeguards against threats, thefts, and sabotage of such licensed facilities, and materials.

(2) Review safety and safeguards of all such facilities and materials licensed under the Atomic Energy Act of 1954, as amended, and such review shall include, but not be limited to—

(A) monitoring, testing, and recommending upgrading of internal accounting systems for special nuclear and other nuclear materials licensed under the Atomic Energy Act of 1954, as amended;

(B) developing, in consultation and coordination with the Administration, contingency plans for dealing with threats, thefts, and sabotage relating to special nuclear materials, high-level radioactive wastes and nuclear facilities resulting from all activities licensed under the Atomic Energy Act of 1954, as amended;

(C) assessing the need for, and the feasibility of, establishing a security agency within the office for the performance of the safeguards functions, and a report with recommendations on this matter shall be prepared within one year of the effective date of this chapter and promptly transmitted to the Congress by the Commission. . . .

§ 5846. Compliance with safety regulations—notification to the Commission of noncompliance.

(a) Any individual director, or responsible officer of a firm constructing, owning, operating, or supplying the components of any facility or activity which is licensed or otherwise regulated pursuant to the Atomic Energy Act of 1954 as amended, or pursuant to this chapter, who obtains information reasonably indicating that such facility or activity or basic components supplied to such facility or activity—

(1) fails to comply with the Atomic Energy Act of 1954, as amended, or any applicable rule, regulation, order, or license of the Commission relating to substantial safety hazards, or

(2) contains a defect which could create a substantial safety hazard, as defined by regulations which the Commission shall promulgate,

shall immediately notify the Commission of such failure to comply, or of such defect. . . .

§ 5847. Nuclear energy center site survey.

(a)(1) The Commission is authorized and directed to make or cause to be made under its direction, a national survey, which shall include consideration of each of the existing or future electric reliability regions, or other appropriate regional areas, to locate and identify possible nuclear energy center sites. This survey shall be conducted in cooperation with other interested Federal, State, and local agencies, and the views of interested persons, including electric utilities, citizens' groups, and others, shall be solicited and considered.

(2) For purposes of this section, the term "nuclear energy center site" means any site, including a site not restricted to land, large enough to support utility operations or other elements of the total nuclear fuel cycle, or both including, if appropriate, nuclear fuel reprocessing facilities, nuclear fuel fabrication plants, retrievable nuclear waste storage facilities, and uranium enrichment facilities.

(3) The survey shall include—

(a) a regional evaluation of natural resources, including land, air, and water resources, available for use in connection with nuclear energy center sites; estimates of future electric power requirements that can be served by each nuclear energy center site; an assessment of the economic impact of each nuclear energy site; and consideration of any other relevant factors, including but not limited to population distribution, proximity to electric load centers and to other elements of the fuel cycle, transmission line rights-of-way, and the availability of other fuel resources;

(b) an evaluation of the environmental impact likely to result from construction and operation of such nuclear energy centers, including an evaluation whether such nuclear energy centers will result in greater or lesser environmental impact than separate siting of the reactors and/or fuel cycle facilities; and

(c) consideration of the use of federally owned property and other property designated for public use, but excluding national parks, national forests, national wilderness areas, and national historic monuments.

(4) A report of the results of the survey shall be published and transmitted to the Congress and the Council on Environmental Quality not later than one year from October 11, 1974 and shall be made available to the public, and shall be updated from time to time thereafter as the Commission, in its discretion, deems advisable. The report shall include the Commission's evaluation of the results of the survey and any conclusions and recommendations, including recommendations for legislation, which the Commission may have concerning the feasibility and practicality of locating nuclear power reactors and/or other elements of the nuclear fuel cycle on nuclear energy center sites. The Commission is authorized to adopt policies which will encourage the location of nuclear power reactors and related fuel cycle facilities on nuclear energy center sites insofar as practicable.

§ 5848. Abnormal occurrence reports.

The Commission shall submit to the Congress each quarter a report listing for that period any abnormal occurrences at or associated with any facility which is licensed or otherwise regulated pursuant to the Atomic Energy Act of 1954 as amended, or pursuant to this chapter. For the purposes of this section an abnormal occurrence is an unscheduled incident or event which the Commission determines is significant from the standpoint of public health or safety. Nothing in the preceding sentence shall limit the authority of a court to review the determination of the Commission. Each such report shall contain—

(1) the date and place of each occurrence;

(2) the nature and probable consequence of each occurrence;

(3) the cause or causes of each; and

(4) any action taken to prevent reoccurrence;

the Commission shall also provide as wide dissemination to the public of the information specified in clauses (1) and (2) of this section as reasonably possible within fifteen days of its receiving information of each abnormal occurrence and shall provide as wide dissemination to the public as reasonably possible of the information specified in clauses (3) and (4) as soon as such information becomes available to it.

STATES

Nuclear Materials

ARKANSAS RADIATION PROTECTION (1961)
Ark. Stat. Ti. 82, Ch. 15

§ 82.1512.  Ionizing radiation—declaration of policy.

It is the policy of the State of Arkansas in furtherance of its responsibility to protect the public health and safety and in furtherance of
the industrial and economic growth of the State:

(1) to institute and maintain a regulatory program for sources of
ionizing radiation so as to provide for
     (a) compatibility with the standards and regulatory programs of
the federal government,
     (b) an effective system of regulation within the state, and
     (c) a system consonant insofar as possible with those of other
states; and

(2) to institute and maintain a program to permit and encourage development and utilization of sources of ionizing radiation for peaceful
purposes consistent with the health and safety of the public.

§ 82-1513.  Ionizing radiation—purpose.

It is the purpose of this Act to effectuate the policies set forth in
Section 1 [§ 82-1512] by providing for:

(1) a program of effective regulation of sources of ionizing radiation
for the protection of the occupational and public health and safety;

(2) a program to promote an orderly regulatory pattern within the
state, among the states and between the federal government and the
state and to facilitate intergovernmental cooperation with respect to
use and regulation of sources of ionizing radiation to the end that
duplication of regulation may be minimized;

(3) a program to establish procedures for assumption and performance of certain regulatory responsibilities with respect to byproduct,
source and special nuclear materials; and

(4) a program to permit maximum utilization of sources of ionizing
radiation consistent with the health and safety of the public.

§ 82-1514.  Definitions.

(a) "Byproduct material" means any radioactive material (except special nuclear material) yielded in or made radioactive by exposure to

the radiation incident to the process of producing or utilizing special nuclear material.

(b) "Ionizing radiation" means gamma rays and X-rays; alpha and beta particles, high-speed electrons, neutrons, protons, and other nuclear particles; but not sound or radio waves or visible, infrared, or ultraviolet light.

(c)(1) "General license" means a license effective pursuant to regulations promulgated by the State Board of Health without the filing of an application to transfer, acquire, own, process or use quantities of, or devices or equipment utilizing byproduct, source, special nuclear materials, or other radio-active materials occurring naturally or produced artificially.

(2) "Specific license" means a license issued, after application to use, manufacture, produce, transfer, receive, acquire, own, or possess quantities of, or devices or equipment utilizing byproduct, source, special nuclear materials, or other radio-active materials occurring naturally or produced artificially. . . .

(e) "Source material" means

(1) uranium, thorium, or any other material which the Governor declares by order to be source material after the United States Atomic Energy Commission, or any successor thereto, has determined the material to be such; or

(2) ores containing one or more of the foregoing materials, in such concentration as the Governor declares by order to be source material after the United States Atomic Energy Commission, or any successor thereto, has determined the material in such concentration to be source material.

(f) "Special nuclear material" means

(1) plutonium, uranium 233, uranium enriched in the isotope 233 or in the isotope 235, and any other material which the Governor declares by order to be special nuclear material after the United States Atomic Energy Commission, or any successor thereto, has determined the material to be such, but does not include source material; or

(2) any material artificially enriched by any of the foregoing, but does not include source material.

§ 82-1515.  State Radiation Control Board—powers and duties.

(a) The State Board of Health is hereby designated as the State Radiation Control Agency, hereinafter referred to as the Agency. . . .

§ 82-1516.  Licensing and registration of sources of ionizing radiation
—rules and regulations.

(a) The Agency shall provide by rule or regulation for general or
specific licensing of by-product, source, special nuclear materials,
or devices or equipment utilizing such materials.  Such rule or regulation shall provide for amendment, suspension or revocation of licenses.

§ 82-1532.  Licensing and registration—recognition of foreign and
federal licenses.

(1) The agency is authorized to:
    (a) Require registration or licensing for the manufacture, distribu-
tion, installation, repair, and use of electronic products or component
parts of such products as defined in Section 3 [§ 82-1530] and for which
regulations have been promulgated as specified in Section 4 [§ 82-1531]
paragraph (4)(b).
    (b) Exempt certain electronic products from the licensing or regis-
tration requirements set forth in this section when the agency makes
a determination that the exemption of such electronic products or kinds
of uses or users of the products will not constitute a significant risk
to the health and safety of the public. . . .

§ 82-1533.  Inspection.

The agency or its duly authorized representatives shall have the
power to enter at all reasonable times upon any private or public property on or in which electronic products are being manufactured, distributed, used or repaired for the purpose of determining whether or
not there is compliance with, or violation of, the provisions of this
Act [§§ 82-1528—82-1540] and rules and regulations issued thereunder. . . .

§ 82-1538.  Prohibited uses.

It shall be unlawful for any person to use, manufacture, distribute,
install, repair, acquire, own, or possess an electronic product, as
defined in this Act [§§ 82-1528—82-1540] , except in conformance
with regulations for licensing or registration for that product, if any,
promulgated in accordance with the provisions of this Act.

§ 82-1539.  Impounding.

The agency shall have the authority in the event of an emergency to
impound or order the impounding of electronic products in the possession of any person who is not equipped to observe or fails to observe

the provisions of this Act [§§ 82-1528—82-1540] or any rules or regulations issued thereunder.

VERMONT NUCLEAR PLANT CONSTRUCTION (1975)
30 Vt. Stat. Ann. Sec. 248(c)

(c) Before a certificate of public good is issued for the construction of a nuclear fission plant the public service board shall obtain the approval of the general assembly and the assembly's determination that the construction of the proposed facility will promote the general welfare.  The public service board shall advise the general assembly of any petition submitted under this section for the construction of a nuclear fission plant, by written notice delivered to the speaker of the house of representatives and to the president of the senate.  The public service board may submit recommendations relating to the proposed plant, and shall make available all relevant material.  The requirements of this subsection shall be in addition to the findings set forth in subsection (b) of this section.

# 12

## PLANNING AND DESIGN

"Natural beauty" protection and restrictions on billboards in highway authorization statutes were an outgrowth of the awakening conservation conscience of the 1960s. Thus federal-aid highways must be constructed "in the best overall public interest" and with a view to minimizing pollution and destruction of natural resources and preserving natural beauty. Billboards and junkyards near the interstate system are restricted (p. 423 ff.). The natural beauty provision is also part of the act setting up the Department of Transportation (p. 427). There must be a finding of "no feasible or prudent alternative" to the use of land from a park, recreational area, wildlife refuge, or historic site, as well as "all possible planning to minimize harm" to such area. This requirement anticipated the Section 102 environmental impact statement process of the National Environmental Policy Act. The public hearing provisions found in the several federal statutes quoted below have been important vehicles for public scrutiny of the alleged necessity of specific construction projects.

"Construction activity related sources of pollution," which could include construction of transportation facilities, are subject to Section 1288(b)(2) of FWPCA. This section requires the preparation of plans to "regulate the location, modification, and construction of any facilities . . . which may result in any discharge." The Clean Air Act also has potential impact on highway construction, which may be deemed an indirect source of air pollution. Amendments to more closely define "indirect" sources are, as previously mentioned, being considered by the 94th Congress.

Transportation is a major source of noise pollution. The Noise Control Act of 1972, excerpted in Chapter 7, looks toward imposing

emission standards for transportation equipment, including motor
vehicles, railroad and motor carriers, and recreational vehicles.
Also in that chapter are found state statutes dealing with highway
noise.

Similar to the federal law, in Pennsylvania a finding that there
is "no feasible and prudent alternative" to "adverse environmental
effect" and that "all reasonable steps have been taken to minimize such
effect" must precede designation of transportation routes (p. 429).

Vermont permits few except official signs along all of its roads
(p. 430). Washington prohibits junkyards adjacent to federal-aid roads
(p. 433) and billboards on designated roads in its Scenic Vistas Act.

Highway construction near bodies of water is subject to state
regulation as a "land disturbing activity" in North Carolina (Gen.
Stat. N. Car. Sec. 113A-52[f]). Transportation facilities are classified as "key facilities" and subject to appropriate review criteria in
the Land Use Act of Colorado (Sec. 106-7-104[7], 106-7-202 to 204).
An "existing or proposed major public facility or other area of major
public investment" can turn an area into one of critical state concern
in Florida (Sec. 380.05[2][b], p. 492). Minnesota limits highway and
street lighting and mandates wide-ranging studies of traffic redesign
in order to effect energy conservation (Sec. 116H.12, p. 60).


## PUBLIC TRANSPORTATION

Since a quarter of our energy use is accounted for by transportation, effecting changes in traditional transportation modes may
well offer a key to reducing energy shortages. Mass transit saves
fuel and recent years have seen some efforts at a return to public
transportation. Air travel remains the prevailing public transportation mode.

The Airport and Airway Development Act of 1970 (p. 435) requires coordinated planning for "all modes of transportation," and a
finding that "no feasible and prudent alternative" to adverse environmental effects of proposed airport development exists. The Noise
Control Act of 1972 has potential impact on airport site selection
and operation, and airports may be deemed indirect sources of air
pollution. The Clean Air Act also mandated a study of pollutants from
aircraft (Sec. 1857f-9).

Special funding for construction of rail, bus, and other forms
of public ground transportation has been the general pattern for
stimulating an increase in such facilities. Federal legislation since
1964 has sought to foster urban mass transportation, and 1974 amendments make available federal loans and grants (p. 438). Comprehensive planning and findings of "no feasible and prudent alternative" to

422                                         ENVIRONMENTAL LEGISLATION

"adverse environmental effect" are again required. Michigan sets
aside a portion of its gasoline tax to finance public transportation services (p. 441).

The Environmental Protection Agency's requirement that states
submit transportation plans for certain metropolitan areas showing
sharply reduced use of the private automobile has been referred to
above (p. 3).

Minnesota subjected the location of a major metropolitan airport
to regional planning (p. 446).


## NONMOTORIZED TRANSPORTATION

A minimum of 1 percent of Oregon highway funds must be spent
for foot and bicycle path construction (p. 450). Washington authorizes
state aid for establishment of bicycle routes by its municipalities (p.
450). The state also directs that bicycle, pedestrian, and equestrian
facilities be included in certain new highway construction (Rev. Code
Wash. Sec. 47.30.010 et seq.). Michigan directs the expenditure of
"reasonable amounts" of highway funds for nonmotorized transportation
(Sec. 247.660k, p. 442), and the Oklahoma trails system seeks to encourage bicycle routes along highways (Sec. 3455F.1). This and
other laws dealing with recreational trails are found in Chapter 6.


## OFF-ROAD VEHICLES

Off-road vehicles (ORVs), chiefly used for recreational purposes,
frequently are incompatible with other recreational pursuits. They
also may cause damage to the terrain and to wildlife. Thus laws in
the various states prohibit their use in certain areas, require their
registration, and set operator qualifications. Separate trails for ORVs
are often the answer to resolving conflicts with competing recreational
values. Such trails are projected as a part of Kentucky's recreational
trails system (Sec. 148.630[2], p. 249), for example.

Federal agencies are under presidential order to control the use
of ORVs on federal lands (p. 452). Some lands under Bureau of Land
Management jurisdiction have suffered severely from ORV abuse, and
the bureau, in early 1976, denied a permit for a trail bike race in the
California desert.

Utah requires registration of snowmobiles and all-terrain vehicles (p. 454). Michigan's law (p. 457) applies to snowmobiles only
but restricts youthful operators, provides for issuing of snowmobile
safety certificates, and earmarks registration receipts for trail construction. The majority of states with sufficient snowfall require at

least registration of snowmobiles. Others require conformance with
motor vehicle laws for snowmobile use on public roads.

In California maximum noise levels for snowmobiles are a part
of the motor vehicle noise limits law (Vehicle Code Sec. 27160).


FEDERAL


FEDERAL-AID HIGHWAY ACT (1958, as amended)
23 U.S.C. 101 et seq.

§ 109. Standards. . . .

(g) The Secretary shall issue within 30 days after the day of enactment of the Federal-Aid Highway Act of 1970 guidelines for minimizing possible soil erosion from highway construction. Such guidelines
shall apply to all proposed projects with respect to which plans, specifications, and estimates are approved by the Secretary after the issuance of such guidelines.

(h) Not later than July 1, 1972, the Secretary, after consultation with
appropriate Federal and State officials, shall submit to Congress,
and not later than 90 days after such submission, promulgate guidelines
designed to assure that possible adverse economic, social, and environmental effects relating to any proposed project on any Federal-aid
system have been fully considered in developing such project, and that
the final decisions on the project are made in the best overall public
interest, taking into consideration the need for fast safe and efficient
transportation, public services, and the costs of eliminating or minimizing such adverse effects and the following:
   (1) air, noise, and water pollution;
   (2) destruction or disruption of man-made and natural resources,
aesthetic values, community cohesion and the availability of public
facilities and services;
   (3) adverse employment effects, and tax and property value losses;
   (4) injurious displacement of people, businesses and farms; and
   (5) disruption of desirable community and regional growth.
Such guidelines shall apply to all proposed projects with respect to
which plans, specifications, and estimates are approved by the Secretary after the issuance of such guidelines.

(i) The Secretary, after consultation with appropriate Federal, State,
and local officials, shall develop and promulgate standards for highway noise levels compatible with different land uses and after July 1,
1972, shall not approve plans and specifications for any proposed
project on any Federal-aid system for which location approval has

not yet been secured unless he determines that such plans and specifications include adequate measures to implement the appropriate
noise level standards. . . .

(j) The Secretary, after consultation with the Administrator of the Environmental Protection Agency, shall develop and promulgate guidelines to assure that highways constructed pursuant to this title are
consistent with any approved plan for the implementation of any ambient air quality standard for any air quality control region designated
pursuant to the Clean Air Act, as amended. . . .

§ 128. Public hearings.

(a) Any State highway department which submits plans for a Federal-
aid highway project involving the bypassing of, or going through, any
city, town, or village, either incorporated or unincorporated, shall
certify to the Secretary that it has had public hearings, or has afforded the opportunity for such hearings, and has considered the economic and social effects of such a location, its impact on the environment, and its consistency with the goals and objectives of such urban
planning as has been promulgated by the community. Any State highway department which submits plans for an Interstate System project
shall certify to the Secretary that it has had public hearings at a convenient location, or has afforded the opportunity for such hearings, for
the purpose of enabling persons in rural areas through or contiguous
to whose property the highway will pass to express any objections they
may have to the proposed locations of such highway. Such certification
shall be accompanied by a report which indicates the consideration
given to the economic, social, environmental, and other effects of
the plan or highway location or design and various alternatives which
were raised during the hearing or which were otherwise considered.

(b) When hearings have been held under subsection (a), the State highway department shall submit a copy of the transcript of said hearings
to the Secretary, together with the certification and report.

§ 131. Control of outdoor advertising.

(a) The Congress hereby finds and declares that the erection and maintenance of outdoor advertising signs, displays, and devices in areas
adjacent to the Interstate System and the primary system should be
controlled in order to protect the public investment in such highways,
to promote the safety and recreational value of public travel, and to
preserve natural beauty.

(b) Federal-aid highway funds apportioned on or after January 1, 1968,
to any State which the Secretary determines has not made provision
for effective control of the erection and maintenance along the Inter-

state System and the primary system of outdoor advertising signs,
displays, and devices which are within six hundred and sixty feet of
the nearest edge of the right-of-way and visible from the main traveled
way of the system, and Federal-aid highway funds apportioned on or
after January 1, 1975, or after the expiration of the next regular session of the State legislature, whichever is later, to any State which
the Secretary determines has not made provision for effective control
of the erection and maintenance along the Interstate System and the
primary system of those additional outdoor advertising signs, displays,
and devices which are more than six hundred and sixty feet off the
nearest edge of the right-of-way, located outside of urban areas, visible from the main traveled way of the system, and erected with the
purpose of their message being read from such main traveled way, shall
be reduced by amounts equal to 10 per centum of the amounts which
would otherwise be apportioned to such State under section 104 of this
title, until such time as such State shall provide for such effective
control.  Any amount which is withheld from apportionment to any
State hereunder shall be reapportioned to the other States.  Whenever
he determines it to be in the public interest, the Secretary may suspend,
for such periods as he deems necessary, the application of this subsection to a State.

(c) Effective control means that such signs, displays, or devices after
January 1, 1968, if located within six hundred and sixty feet of the right-
of-way and, on or after July 1, 1975, or after the expiration of the
next regular session of the State legislature, whichever is later, if
located beyond six hundred and sixty feet of the right-of-way, located
outside of urban areas, visible from the main traveled way of the
system, and erected with the purpose of their message being read
from such main traveled way, shall, pursuant to this section, be limited
to (1) directional and official signs and notices, which signs and notices
shall include, but not be limited to, signs and notices pertaining to
natural wonders, scenic and historical attractions. . . .

(d) In order to promote the reasonable, orderly and effective display
of outdoor advertising while remaining consistent with the purposes of
this section, signs, displays, and devices whose size, lighting and
spacing, consistent with customary use is to be determined by agreement between the several States and the Secretary, may be erected and
maintained within six hundred and sixty feet of the nearest edge of the
right-of-way within areas adjacent to the Interstate and primary systems which are zoned industrial or commercial under authority of
State law, or in unzoned commercial or industrial areas as may be determined by agreement between the several States and the Secretary.

§ 134.  Transportation planning in certain urban areas.

(a) It is declared to be in the national interest to encourage and promote
the development of transportation systems, embracing various modes
of transport in a manner that will serve the States and local communities efficiently and effectively.  To accomplish this objective the Secretary shall cooperate with the States, as authorized in this title, in
the development of long-range highway plans and programs which are
probably coordinated with plans for improvements in other affected
forms of transportation and which are formulated with due consideration to their probable effect on the future development of urban areas
of more than fifty thousand population.  After July 1, 1965, the Secretary shall not approve, under section 105 of this title any program for
projects in any urban area of more than fifty thousand population unless he finds that such projects are based on a continuing comprehensive
transportation planning process carried on cooperatively by States and
local communities in conformance with the objectives stated in this
section.  No highway project may be constructed in any urban area of
fifty thousand population or more unless the responsible public officials
of such urban area in which the project is located have been consulted
and their views considered with respect to the corridor, the location
and the design of the project.

(b) The Secretary may define those contiguous interstate areas of the
Nation in which the movement of persons and goods between principal
metropolitan areas, cities, and industrial centers has reached, or is
expected to reach, a critical volume in relation to the capacity of
existing and planned transportation systems to efficiently accommodate
present transportation demands and future growth.  After consultation
with the Governors and responsible local officials of affected States,
the Secretary may by regulation designate, for administrative and
planning purposes, as a critical transportation region or a critical
transportation corridor each of those areas which he determines most
urgently require the accelerated development of transportation systems
embracing various modes of transport, in accordance with purposes
of this section.  The Secretary shall immediately notify such Governors
and local officials of such designation.  The Secretary may, after consultation with the Governors and responsible local officials of the affected States, provide by regulation for the establishment of planning
bodies to assist in the development of coordinated transportation planning, including highway planning, to meet the needs of such regions or
corridors, composed of representatives of the affected States and
metropolitan areas, and may provide assistance including financial
assistance to such bodies. . . .

§ 136. Control of junkyards.

(a) The Congress hereby finds and declares that the establishment and use and maintenance of junkyards in areas adjacent to the Interstate System and the primary system should be controlled in order to protect the public investment in such highways, to promote the safety and recreational value of public travel, and to preserve natural beauty.

§ 138. Preservation of parklands.

It is hereby declared to be the national policy that special effort should be made to preserve the natural beauty of the countryside and public park and recreation lands, wildlife and waterfowl refuges, and historic sites. The Secretary of Transportation shall cooperate and consult with the Secretaries of the Interior, Housing and Urban Development, and Agriculture, and with the States in developing transportation plans and programs that include measures to maintain or enhance the natural beauty of the lands traversed. After the effective date of the Federal-Aid Highway Act of 1968, the Secretary shall not approve any program or project which requires the use of any publicly owned land from a public park, recreation area, or wildlife and waterfowl refuge of national, State, or local significance as determined by the Federal, State, or local officials having jurisdiction thereof, or any land from an historic site of national, State, or local significance as so determined by such officials unless

(1) there is no feasible and prudent alternative to the use of such land, and

(2) such program includes all possible planning to minimize harm to such park, recreational area, wildlife and waterfowl refuge, or historic site resulting from such use.

§ 319. Landscaping and scenic enhancement.

(a) The Secretary may approve as a part of the construction of Federal-aid highways the costs of landscape and roadside development, including acquisition and development of publicly owned and controlled rest and recreation areas and sanitary and other facilities reasonably necessary to accommodate the traveling public.

DEPARTMENT OF TRANSPORTATION ACT (1966)
49 U.S.C. 1651 et seq.

Section 1651. Congressional declaration of purpose
1652. Establishment of Department
1653. General provisions
1654. National Tranportation Safety Board
1655. Transfer of functions

Section 1656.  Transportation investment standards
         1657.  Administrative provisions

§ 1651.  Congressional declaration of purpose.

(a) The Congress hereby declares that the general welfare, the economic growth and stability of the Nation and its security require the
development of national transportation policies and programs condu-
cive to the provision of fast, safe, efficient, and convenient transportation at the lowest cost consistent therewith and with other national
objectives, including the efficient utilization and conservation of the
Nation's resources.

(b)(1) The Congress therefore finds that the establishment of a Department of Transportation is necessary in the public interest and to assure the coordinated, effective administration of the transportation
programs of the Federal Government; to facilitate the development
and improvement of coordinated transportation service, to be provided by private enterprise to the maximum extent feasible; to encourage cooperation of Federal, State, and local governments, carriers, labor, and other interested parties toward the achievement of
national transportation objectives; to stimulate technological advances
in transportation; to provide general leadership in the identification
and solution of transportation problems; and to develop and recommend
to the President and the Congress for approval national transportation
policies and programs to accomplish these objectives with full and
appropriate consideration of the needs of the public, users, carriers,
industry, labor, and the national defense.

    (2) It is hereby declared to be the national policy that special ef-
fort should be made to preserve the natural beauty of the countryside
and public park and recreation lands, wildlife and waterfowl refuges,
and historic sites.

§ 1653.  General provisions. . . .

(f) Maintenance and enhancement of natural beauty of land traversed
by transportation lines.

 It is hereby declared to be the national policy that special effort should
be made to preserve the natural beauty of the countryside and public
park and recreation lands, wildlife and waterfowl refuges, and historic
sites.  The Secretary of Transportation shall cooperate and consult
with the Secretaries of the Interior, Housing and Urban Development,
and Agriculture, and with the States in developing transportation plans
and programs that include measures to maintain or enhance the natural beauty of the lands traversed.  After August 23, 1968, the Secretary shall not approve any program or project which requires the use

of any publicly owned land from a public park, recreation area, or
wildlife and waterfowl refuge of national, State, or local significance
as determined by the Federal, State, or local officials having jurisdiction thereof, or any land from an historic site of national, State, or
local significance as so determined by such officials unless

(1) there is no feasible and product alternative to the use of such
land, and

(2) such program includes all possible planning to minimize harm
to such park, recreational area, wildlife and waterfowl refuge, or
historic site resulting from such use.


STATES

PENNSYLVANIA DEPARTMENT OF TRANSPORTATION
(1970)
71 Penn. Stat. Art. XX, Sec. 511 et seq.

§ 512.  Powers and duties of the Department.

(The Department) . . . shall consider the following effects of the
transportation route or program:

(1) Residential and neighborhood character and location;

(2) Conservation including air, erosion, sedimentation, wildlife and
general ecology of the area;

(3) Noise, and air and water pollution; . . .

(6) Displacement of families and businesses;

(7) Recreation and parks;

(8) Aesthetics; . . .

(18) Natural and historic landmarks. . . .

At the hearings required by this section, the public officials named
in clause (15) of subsection (a) of this section shall make a report indicating the environmental effects of the proposed transportation route
or program.  The Department of Transportation shall not construct
or reconstruct any portion of the transportation route or program unless the Secretary of Transportation makes a written finding published in the Pennsylvania Bulletin that:

(1) No adverse environmental effect is likely to result from such transportation route or program; or

(2) There exists no feasible and product alternative to such effect and
all reasonable steps have been taken to minimize such effect.  For

the purpose of this subsection environmental effect shall refer to the effects enumerated in this subsection. . . .

(a) The Department of Transportation . . . shall have the power and its duty shall be. . . .

(b) Upon the submission of the preliminary plan or design to the Department of Transportation for any transportation route or program requiring the acquisition of new or additional right-of-way, the Department of Transportation . . . shall have the power and its duty shall be to follow the hearing procedures now or hereafter required by the Federal Government for Federal aid to programs pursuant to Titles 23 and 49 of the U.S. Code. . . . At the hearings required by this subsection the Department of Transportation shall consider the following effects of the transportation project or programs. . . .

VERMONT TOURIST INFORMATION SERVICES<br>
(1967, as amended)<br>
10 Vt. Stat. Ann., Ch. 21

§ 482.  Legislative findings.

The general assembly of the state of Vermont makes the following findings of fact:

(1) A large and increasing number of tourists has been coming to Vermont, and as a result of the tourist industry is one of the largest sources of income for Vermonters, with an increasing number of persons directly or indirectly dependent upon the tourist industry for their livelihood.

(2) Very few convenient facilities exist in the state to provide information on available public accommodations, commercial services for the travelling public and other lawful businesses and points of scenic, historic, cultural, educational and religious interest.  Provision of those facilities can be a major factor in encouraging the development of the tourist industry in Vermont.

(3) Scenic resources of great value are distributed throughout the state, and have contributed greatly to its economic development, by attracting tourists, permanent and part-time residents, and new industries and cultural facilities.

(4) The scattering of outdoor advertising throughout the state is detrimental to the preservation of those scenic resources, and so to the economic base of the state, and is also not an effective method of providing information to tourists about available facilities.

(5) The proliferation of outdoor advertising is hazardous to highway users.

§ 483.  Purposes and policy.

In order to promote the public health, safety and other aspects of the general welfare, it is in the public interest to provide information about and help guide travellers to public accommodations and services, other businesses and points of scenic, historic, cultural, educational and religious interest.  To provide that information, it is the policy of the state and the purpose of this chapter:

(1) To establish official information centers and official business directional signs (including sign plazas in appropriate locations for the convenient arrangement of those signs).

(2) To provide for publication and distribution of official guidebooks and other publications.

(3) To prohibit the indiscriminate use of other outdoor advertising.

§ 486. Official directional signs.

(a) The highway department, under the direction of the travel information council shall furnish, erect and maintain official business directional signs licensed under this chapter at locations specified in the license. . . .

(c) The travel information council may enter into such contractual or other arrangements as it may consider appropriate under all the circumstances with any town or city of this state, providing for the erection and maintenance of official business directional signs and the fees charged therefor, within that town or city, which may be distinctive to that town or city, or providing for the administration of such official business directional signs, or for any other matter arising under this chapter which the council considers appropriate to be administered by that town or city, provided, however, that any such arrangement or agreement, and all actions taken thereto, shall comply with this chapter and with the regulations adopted hereto.

§ 488. Prohibition of other outdoor advertising.

No person may erect or maintain outdoor advertising visible to the travelling public except as provided in this chapter.

§ 491. Number of signs.

Notwithstanding the provisions of section 499 of this title, the council shall not issue more than four licenses for official business directional signs for any one place of business eligible therefor under section 490 of this title, not more than one of which is visible to traffic moving in any one direction on any one highway leading to the place, unless the travel information council finds that enforcement of this subsection will be unreasonable and will result in unnecessary hardship to the applicant.

§ 495. Other regulations applying to permitted signs.

(a) No official business directional sign, on-premise sign, residential directional sign, or exempt sign may be erected or maintained, along a highway and visible from the highway, which:

(1) Interferes with, imitates or resembles any official traffic control sign, signal or device, or attempts or appears to attempt to direct the movement of traffic.

(2) Prevents the driver of a motor vehicle from having a clear and unobstructed view of official traffic control signs and approaching or merging traffic.

(3) Contains, includes or is illuminated by any flashing intermittent or moving lights, or moves or has any animated or moving parts, ex-

cept that this restriction shall not apply to a traffic control sign, or signs of a public service nature as determined by the travel information council.

(4) Has any lighting, unless such lighting is so effectively shielded as to prevent beams or rays of light from being directed at any portion of the main travelled way of a highway, or is of such low intensity or brilliance as not to cause glare or to impair the vision of the driver of any motor vehicle or otherwise to interfere with the operation thereof.

(5) Is located upon a tree, or painted or drawn upon a rock or other natural feature, except that this restriction shall not apply to residential directional signs.

(6) Advertises or calls attention to a business or other activity, or a profession, commodity, product, service or entertainment not carried on, produced, sold, or offered in this state, or to an activity of any kind which has already occurred or has otherwise terminated.

(7) Is in violation of or at variance with any federal law or regulation, including one containing or providing for conditions to or affecting the allocation of federal highway or other funds to or for the benefit of this state or any subdivision thereof.

(b) No on-premise sign may be erected if it is so located as to be readable primarily from a limited access facility.

(c) No on-premise sign or residential directional sign may be erected or maintained which:

(1) Advertises activities which are illegal under any state or federal law applicable at the location of the sign or of the activities.

(2) Is not clean or in good repair.

(3) Is not securely affixed to a substantial structure.

(4) Is not consistent with the standards in this chapter or regulations of the travel information council.

WASHINGTON JUNKYARDS ADJACENT TO INTERSTATE
AND PRIMARY HIGHWAYS (1971)
47 Rev. Code Wash. 41.040 et seq.

§ 47.41.010.  Legislative declaration—purpose.

For the purpose of promoting the public safety, health, welfare, convenience, and enjoyment of public travel, to protect the public investment in public highways and to preserve and enhance the scenic beauty
of lands bordering public highways, it is hereby declared to be in the
public interest to regulate and restrict the establishment, operation,
and maintenance of junkyards in areas adjacent to the interstate and
federal-aid primary systems within this state.  The legislature hereby
finds and declares that junkyards which do not conform to the requirements of this act are public nuisances.

§ 47.41.020.  Definitions. . . .

(1) "Junk" shall mean old or scrap copper, brass, rope, rags, bat-
teries, paper, trash, rubber debris, waste, or junked, dismantled,
or wrecked automobiles, or parts thereof, iron, steel, and other old
or scrap ferrous or nonferrous material.

(2) "Automobile graveyard" shall mean any establishment or place
of business which is maintained, used, or operated by storing, keeping,
buying, or selling wrecked, scrapped, ruined, or dismantled motor
vehicles or motor vehicle parts.

(3) "Junkyard" shall mean an establishment or place of business which
is maintained, operated, or used for storing, keeping, buying, or
selling junk or for the maintenance or operation of an automobile
graveyard and the term shall include garbage dumps and sanitary fills.
. . .

§ 47.41.030.  Junkyards adjacent to highways prohibited—exceptions.

No person shall establish, operate, or maintain a junkyard any portion of which is within one thousand feet of the nearest edge of the
right of way of any interstate or federal-aid primary highway, except
the following:

(1) Those which are screened by natural objects, plantings, fences,
or other appropriate means so as not to be visible from the main-
traveled way of the system or otherwise removed from sight.

(2) Those located within areas which are zoned for industrial use under authority of law.

(3) Those located within unzoned industrial areas, which areas shall
be determined from actual land uses and defined by regulations to be
promulgated by the commission and approved by the secretary of transportation.

(4) Those which are not visible from the main-traveled way of the system.


FEDERAL


Public Transportation

### AIRPORT AND AIRWAY DEVELOPMENT ACT
(1970, as amended)
49 U.S.C. 1701 et seq.

### § 1701. Congressional declaration of policy.

The Congress hereby finds and declares—

That the Nation's airport and airway system is inadequate to meet the current and projected growth in aviation.

That substantial expansion and improvement of the airport and airway system is required to meet the demands of interstate commerce, the postal service, and the national defense. . . .

§ 1702. National transportation policy—formulation.

(a) Within one year after May 21, 1970, the Secretary of Transportation shall formulate and recommend to the Congress for approval a national transportation policy. In the formulation of such policy, the Secretary shall take into consideration, among other things—

(1) the coordinated development and improvement of all modes of transportation, together with the priority which shall be assigned to the development and improvement of each mode of transportation; and

(2) the coordination of recommendations made under this chapter relating to airport and airway development with all other recommendations to the Congress for the development and improvement of our national transportation system.

§ 1703. Cost allocation study.

The Secretary of Transportation shall conduct a study respecting the appropriate method for allocating the cost of the airport and airway system among the various users, and shall identify the cost to the Federal Government that should appropriately be charged to the system and the value to be assigned to any general public benefit, including military, which may be determined to exist. In conducting the study the Secretary shall consult fully with and give careful consideration to the views of the users of the system. The Secretary shall report the results of the study to Congress within two years from May 21, 1970.

§ 1712. National airport system plan—formulation.

(a) The Secretary is directed to prepare and publish, within three years after May 21, 1970, and thereafter to review and revise as necessary, a national airport system plan for the development of public airports in the United States. The plan shall set forth, for at least a ten-year period, the type and estimated cost of airport development considered by the Secretary to be necessary to provide a system of public airports adequate to anticipate and meet the needs of civil aeronautics, to meet requirements in support of the national defense as determined by the Secretary of Defense, and to meet the special needs of the postal service. . . .

(b) In formulating and revising the plan, the Secretary shall take into consideration, among other things, the relationship of each airport to the rest of the transportation system in the particular area, to the forecasted technological developments in aeronautics, and to developments forecasted in other modes of intercity transportation.

(c) Approval.

(1) All airport development projects shall be subject to the approval of the Secretary, which approval may be given only if he is satisfied that—

(A) the project is reasonably consistent with plans (existing at the time of approval of the project) of planning agencies for the development of the area in which the airport is located and will contribute to the accomplishment of the purposes of this subchapter; . . .

(3) No airport development project may be approved by the Secretary unless he is satisfied that fair consideration has been given to the interest of communities in or near which the project may be located.

(4) It is declared to be national policy that airport development projects authorized pursuant to this subchapter shall provide for the protection and enhancement of the natural resources and the quality of environment of the Nation. In implementing this policy, the Secretary shall consult with the Secretaries of the Interior and Health, Education, and Welfare with regard to the effect that any project involving airport location, a major runway extension, or runway location may have on natural resources including, but not limited to, fish and wildlife, natural, scenic, and recreation assets, water and air quality, and other factors affecting the environment, and shall authorize no such project found to have adverse effect unless the Secretary shall render a finding, in writing, following a full and complete review, which shall be a matter of public record, that no feasible and prudent alternative exists and that all possible steps have been taken to minimize such adverse effect.

(d) Hearings.

(1) No airport development project involving the location of an airport, an airport runway, or a runway extension may be approved by the Secretary unless the public agency sponsoring the project certifies to the Secretary that there has been afforded the opportunity for public hearings for the purpose of considering the economic, social, and environmental effects of the airport location and its consistency with the goals and objectives of such urban planning as has been carried out by the community. . . .

(e) Air and water quality.

(1) The Secretary shall not approve any project application for a project involving airport location, a major runway extension, or runway location unless the Governor of the State in which such project may be located certifies in writing to the Secretary that there is reasonable assurance that the project will be located, designed, constructed, and operated so as to comply with applicable air and water quality standards. . . .

URBAN MASS TRANSPORTATION ACT
(1964, as amended)
49 U.S.C. 1601 et seq.

§ 1601b.  Same; additional findings.

The Congress finds that—

(1) over 70 per centum of the Nation's population lives in urban areas;

(2) transportation is the lifeblood of an urbanized society and the health and welfare of that society depends upon the provision of efficient, economical and convenient transportation within and between its urban area;

(3) for many years the mass transportation industry satisfied the transportation needs of the urban areas of the country capably and profitably;

(4) in recent years the maintenance of even minimal mass transportation service in urban areas has become so financially burdensome as to threaten the continuation of this essential public service;

(5) the termination of such service or the continued increase in its cost to the user is undesirable, and may have a particularly serious adverse effect upon the welfare of a substantial number of lower income persons;

(6) some urban areas are now engaged in developing preliminary plans for, or are actually carrying out, comprehensive projects to revitalize their mass transportation operations; and

(7) immediate substantial Federal assistance is needed to enable many mass transportation systems to continue to provide vital service.

§ 1602. Federal financial assistance—grants or loans to States and local public agencies; uses of funds; eligible facilities and equipment; eligibility of applicant; real property acquisition; prohibitions on uses of grant or loan funds; development of plans and programs of transportation systems for urbanized areas; scope and implementation of projects; cutoff date for approval of projects.

(a)(1) The Secretary is authorized, in accordance with the provisions of this chapter and on such terms and conditions as he may prescribe, to make grants or loans (directly, through the purchase of securities or equipment trust certificates, or otherwise) to assist States and local public bodies and agencies thereof in financing (1) the acquisition, construction, reconstruction, and improvement of facilities and equipment for use, by operation or lease or otherwise, in mass transportation service in urban areas and in coordinating such service with highway and other transportation in such areas, and (2) the establishment and organization of public or quasi-public transit corridor development corporations or entities. Eligible facilities and equipment may include personal property including buses and other rolling stock and real property including land (but not public highways) within, the entire zone affected by the construction and operation of transit improvements, including station sites, needed for an efficient and coordinated mass transportation system which is compatible with socially, economically, and environmentally sound patterns of land use. . . .

(2) It is declared to be in the national interest to encourage and promote the development of transportation systems, embracing various modes of transport in a manner that will serve the States and local communities efficiently and effectively. To accomplish this objective the Secretary shall cooperate with the States in the development of long-range plans and programs which are properly coordinated with plans for improvements in other affected forms of transportation and which are formulated with due consideration to their probable effect on the future development of urban areas of more than fifty thousand population. The development of projects in urbanized areas under this section shall be based upon a continuing, cooperative, and

comprehensive planning process covering all modes of surface transportation and carried on by the States and the governing bodies of local communities in accordance with this paragraph. The Secretary
shall not approve any project in an urbanized area after July 1, 1976,
under this section unless he finds that such project is based on a continuing comprehensive transportation planning process carried out
in conformance with the objectives stated in this paragraph. . . .

(d) Any application for a grant or loan under this chapter to finance
the acquisition, construction, reconstruction, or improvement of
facilities or equipment which will substantially affect a community or
its mass transportation service shall include a certification that the
applicant—

(1) has afforded an adequate opportunity for public hearings pursuant to adequate prior notice, and has held such hearings unless no
one with a significant economic, social, or environmental interest in
the matter requests a hearing;

(2) has considered the economic and social effects of the project
and its impact on the environment; and

(3) has found that the project is consistent with official plans for
the comprehensive development of the urban area. . . .

§ 1603. Long-range program—terms and conditions; planning requirements; "net project cost" defined; Federal grant for two-thirds and
non-Federal funds for one-third of net project cost; refunds.

(a) No Federal financial assistance shall be provided pursuant to subsection (a) of section 1602 of this title unless the Secretary determines
that the facilities and equipment for which the assistance is sought are
needed for carrying out a program, meeting criteria established by
him, for a unified or officially coordinated urban transportation system as a part of the comprehensively planned development of the urban area, and are necessary for the sound, economic, and desirable
development of such area. Such program shall encourage to the maximum extent feasible the participation of private enterprise. . . .

§ 1604. Urban mass transit grant program—definitions. . . .

(h)(2) In approving any project under this section, the Secretary shall
assure that possible adverse economic, social, and environmental effects relating to the proposed project have been fully considered in
developing the project, and that the final decisions on the project are
made in the best overall public interest, taking into consideration the
need for fast, safe, and efficient transportation, public services,
and conservation of environment and natural resources, and the costs
of eliminating or minimizing any such adverse effects, including—

(A) air, noise, and water pollution;

(B) destruction or disruption of manmade and natural resources, esthetic values, community cohesion, and the availability of public facilities and services;

(C) adverse employment effects, and tax and property value losses;

(D) injurious displacement of people, businesses, and farms; and

(E) disruption of desirable community and regional growth.

(i) Upon submission for approval of a proposed project under this section, the Governor or the designated recipient of the urbanized area shall certify to the Secretary that he or it has conducted public hearings (or has afforded the opportunity for such hearings) and that these hearings included (or were scheduled to include) consideration of the economic and social effects of such project, its impact on the environment, including requirements under the Clean Air Act, the Federal Water Pollution Control Act, and other applicable Federal environmental statutes, and its consistency with the goals and objectives of such urban planning as has been promulgated by the community. Such certification shall be accompanied by

(1) a report which indicates the consideration given to the economic, social, environmental, and other effects of the proposed project, including, for construction projects, the effects of its location or design, and the consideration given to the various alternatives which were raised during the hearing or which were otherwise considered, and

(2) upon the Secretary's request, a copy of the transcript of the hearings. . . .

§ 1610. Environmental protection.

(a) It is hereby declared to be the national policy that special effort shall be made to preserve the natural beauty of the countryside, public park and recreation lands, wildlife and waterfowl refuges, and important historical and cultural assets, in the planning, designing, and construction of urban mass transportation porjects for which Federal assistance is provided pursuant to section 1602 of this title. In implementing this policy the Secretary shall cooperate and consult with the Secretaries of Agriculture, Health, Education, and Welfare, Housing and Urban Development, and Interior, and with the Council on Environmental Quality with regard to each project that may have a substantial impact on the environment.

(b) The Secretary shall review each transcript of hearing submitted pursuant to section 1602(d) of this title to assure that an adequate opportunity was afforded for the presentation of views by all parties with

a significant economic, social, or environmental interest, and that
the project application includes a detailed statement on—

(1) the environmental impact of the proposed project,

(2) any adverse environmental effects which cannot be avoided
should the proposal be implemented,

(3) alternatives to the proposed project, and

(4) any irreversible and irretrievable impact on the environment
which may be involved in the proposed project should it be implemented.

(c) The Secretary shall not approve any application for assistance under section 1602 of this title unless he finds in writing, after a full
and complete review of the application and of any hearings held before
the State or local public agency pursuant to section 1602(d) of this
title, that

(1) adequate opportunity was afforded for the presentation of views
by all parties with a significant economic, social, or environmental
interest, and fair consideration has been given to the preservation and
enhancement of the environment and to the interest of the community
in which the project is located, and

(2) either no adverse environmental effect is likely to result from
such project, or there exists no feasible and prudent alternative to
such effect and all reasonable steps have been taken to minimize such
effect.

In any case in which a hearing has not been held before the State or
local agency pursuant to section 1602(d) of this title, or in which the
Secretary determines that the record of hearings before, the State
or local public agency is inadequate to permit him to make the findings
required under the preceding sentence, he shall conduct hearings,
after giving adequate notice to interested persons, on any environmental issues raised by such application.  Findings of the Secretary under
this subsection shall be made a matter of public record.

STATES

Public Transportation

MICHIGAN GENERAL TRANSPORTATION FUND (1972)
Comp. Laws Mich. 247.660b et seq.

§ 247.660b. General transportation fund, creation, appropriation, administration; department of state highways, general functions.

Sec. 10b.

(1) The general transportation fund is created within the motor vehicle highway fund. There is appropriated each fiscal year from the motor vehicle highway fund to the general transportation fund an amount equal to the net revenues, after deducting a proportionate share of refunds and collection costs authorized by law, from ½ cent per gallon of the tax on gasoline and liquefied petroleum gas imposed by Act No. 150 of the Public Acts of 1927, as amended, deposited in the motor vehicle highway fund after January 31, 1973. . . .

(4) The general functions of the department of state highways under the direct supervision of the state highway commission shall include but are not limited to the following:

(a) Establish those urban and public transportation procedures and administrative practices for which there is a clear requirement for uniformity statewide.

(b) Plan for the current and long-range development of a system of public transportation in urban areas for which no eligible authority or eligible governmental agency exists.

(c) Investigate urban transportation conditions and make recommendations for improvement to the state highway commission for forwarding to the legislature.

(d) Review and comment upon policies and programs of local and other state agencies which directly affect urban transportation.

(e) Encourage, coordinate and administer grants for research and demonstration projects to develop the application of new ideas and concepts in urban transportation facilities and services as applied to state as opposed to nationwide problems. . . .

§ 247.660c.  Definitions.

Sec. 10c.

(1) "Urban area" means
    (a) any contiguous developed area in which at least 50,000 people
reside, including the immediate surrounding area where transportation services should reasonably be provided presently or in the future
or
    (b), the area within the jurisdiction of an eligible authority or
    (c) for the purpose of receiving funds for public transportation,
any contiguous developed area of less than 50,000 population that has
an urban public transportation plan accepted by the department of
state highways and the state highway commission determines that public transportation services should reasonably be provided presently
or in the future.

§ 247.660d.  Use and objective of general transportation fund.

Sec. 10d.

(1) The general transportation fund shall be used to make grants for
public transportation purposes to eligible authorities, to make grants
or direct expenditures for public transportation purposes to eligible
governmental agencies which are not within the jurisdiction of an eligible authority and to make grants to eligible governmental agencies
for construction of roads or for direct expenditures by the department
of state highways for construction of state trunk line highways. . . .

§ 247.660e.  Priorities in use of general transportation fund.

Sec. 10e.

(1) The general transportation fund shall be used in the following order of priority:
    (a) To pay debt service on notes and bonds sold by the state, eligi-
ble authorities or eligible governmental agencies to finance the construction or acquisition of public transportation facilities. . . .
    (b) To pay the costs of administration of the general transportation
fund as appropriated by the legislature. . . .
    (c) To pay current administrative, operating, and maintenance costs
including cost of replacement of equipment and acquisition of existing
public transportation facilities, of existing or new urban public transportation systems, where needed to cover operating costs which achiev
the objectives in section 10d(2).  Operating and maintenance costs
shall include maintenance and repair costs and sufficient funds shall
be used for this purpose in order to maintain rolling equipment in
mechanically sound condition. . . .

(d) To make grants for demonstration projects designed to demonstrate improved efficiency of systems or concepts for public transportation in urban areas. An amount not to exceed 10% of the amount appropriated to the general transportation fund in a state fiscal year or not to exceed 15% of the amount in the fund at any one time, may be allocated under this subdivision.

(e) Funds remaining in the fund in each year after meeting the purposes described in subdivisions (a), (b), (c), and (d) shall be disbursed as grants to eligible authorities and eligible governmental agencies for acquisition of public transportation facilities for consolidation, for capital improvements and for equipment replacements, for public transportation systems in accordance with the accepted urban public transportation plans of eligible authorities and eligible governmental agencies, or as grants to eligible government agencies for construction of roads or for direct expenditures by the department of state highways for public transportation purposes on request of eligible governmental agencies and authorities or for construction of state trunk line highways where construction of urban roads or urban sections of state trunk line highways is found by the state highway commission to achieve the objectives stated in section 10d(2) at the lowest economic and social cost. . . .

§ 247.660f.  Urban public transportation plans; development, review, acceptance, notice, comments.

Sec. 10f.

(1) In urban areas where an eligible authority is in existence, the annual urban public transportation plan for that urban area shall be developed by the transportation authority, reviewed by the agency having overall responsibility for land use and urban planning in the urban area and submitted to the department of state highways. In other urban areas the annual urban public transportation plan for the urban area shall be developed by the appropriate eligible governmental agency, reviewed by the agency having overall responsibility for land use and urban planning in the area and shall be submitted to the department of state highways. The department shall accept the annual urban public transportation plan upon the determination that there is a present or projected demand for transportation in accordance with the objectives stated in subsection (2) of section 10d that the proposed public transportation program will meet this demand, and that there is a responsible agency which agrees to provide the public transportation. . . .

§ 247.660k.  Facilities for nonmotorized transportation.

Sec. 10k.

(1) Highway purposes as provided in this act include provisions for facilities for nonmotorized transportation including bicycling.

(2) The department of state highways, the counties, cities and villages receiving funds from the motor vehicle highway fund shall expend reasonable amounts of such funds for establishment and maintenance of lanes, paths, and roads for nonmotorized transportation.

(3) Facilities for nonmotorized transportation may be established in conjunction with already existing highways, roads and streets and shall be established when a highway, road or street is being con-structed, reconstructed or relocated, unless:

    (a) The cost of establishing the facilities would be disproportionate to the need or probable use.

    (b) The establishment of the facilities would be contrary to public safety.

    (c) Adequate facilities for nonmotorized transportation already exist in the area.

    (d) Matching funds are not available through the department of natural resources or other state, local or federal government sources.

    (e) The previous expenditures and projected expenditures for non-motorized transportation facilities for the fiscal year exceed ½ of 1% of that unit's share of the motor vehicle highway fund in which case additional expenditures shall be discretionary.

MINNESOTA DEVELOPMENT OF MAJOR AIRPORT
(1969, as amended)
Minn. Stat. Ann. 360.74 et seq.

§ 360-74.  New major airport; airport development area.

Subdivision 1.  Metropolitan council; land use criteria and guidelines. Within 120 days after the selection by the commission of a site in the metropolitan area for a new major airport to serve as a terminal for regular, scheduled air passenger service and the approval thereof by

the metropolitan council, the council shall adopt criteria and guidelines
for the regulation of use and development of all or a portion of the
property in the metropolitan area extending out three miles from the
proposed boundaries of the site, or out five miles from the boundaries
in any direction the council determines is necessary to protect natural
resources of the metropolitan area, which property shall be known as
an airport development area. The criteria and guidelines shall establish
the boundaries of the airport development area and shall include a
statement of goals and policies to be accomplished by regulation of
the use and development of property in the area. They may relate to
all types of land use and development control measures, including zoning
ordinances, building codes, subdivision regulations, and official maps.
The criteria and guidelines shall encourage controls for the use and
development of property and the planning of public facilities for the
purposes of protecting inhabitants of the airport development area
from aircraft noise and preserving natural underground water reservoirs and other natural resources of the metropolitan area, and such
purposes are hereby declared to be public purposes upon which land
use and development control measures adopted by any government
unit pursuant to law may be based. The criteria and guidelines shall
be a part of the metropolitan development guide when it is adopted,
and a copy of the criteria and guidelines and any amendment thereto
shall be mailed to the governing body of each government unit having
authority to adopt land use and development control measures applicable to the airport development area. . . .

Subd. 2. Local zoning and land use and development controls. Upon
the selection and approval of a site for a new major airport in the
metropolitan area, all land within its airport development area which
is not then zoned for other use is zoned for use exclusively for agricultural purposes, except that a prior nonconforming use established with
reference to any lot or parcel of land may be continued and all land
zoned by this subdivision for agricultural purposes may be rezoned by
the appropriate government unit upon compliance with this subdivision.
Thereafter the governing body of each government unit proposing to
adopt a land use and development control measure applicable to the
airport development area, or any amendment thereto, shall submit
it to the metropolitan council for review, and within 120 days after
receipt of the council's criteria and guidelines shall make and submit
to the council for review such changes in its existing land use and development control measures as it deems necessary to make them consistent with the criteria and guidelines. . . .

Subd. 3. Enforcement of local measures. After the selection and approval of a site for a new major airport in the metropolitan area, no
public or private use contrary to subdivision 2 or any land use and de-

velopment control measure then in effect shall be made of the property
to which it applies within an airport development area, and no government unit shall issue a permit for the use, construction, alteration
or planting of any property, building, structure or tree not in accordance with its general provisions, except for minor footage variances,
until the council has approved changes or variances in such control
measure pursuant to subdivision 2. After the council has approved a
land use and development control measure pursuant to subdivision 2,
no public or private use contrary to its provisions shall be made of
the property to which it applies, and no government unit shall issue
a permit for the use, construction, alteration or planting of any property, building, structure or tree not in accordance with its general
provisions; and no special use permit or variance may be granted which
authorizes a use or development which is contrary to the council's
criteria and guidelines.

§ 360.75.  Aircraft noise zones.

Within 120 days after the selection and approval of a site for a new
major airport in the metropolitan area, the metropolitan council shall
determine the probable levels of noise which will result in various
parts of the metropolitan area from the operation of aircraft using the
site, shall establish aircraft noise zones based thereon applicable to
property affected by such noise, and shall establish acceptable levels
of perceived noise decibels for each land use, using the composite
noise rating method and tables or the noise exposure forecast method
and tables. Each government unit having power to adopt land use and
development control measures applicable to property included in any
aircraft noise zone, shall adopt or incorporate in existing land use and
development control measures the applicable acceptable level of perceived noise decibels established by the council, and shall adopt such
other control measures as may be necessary to prevent the use, construction or improvement of property and buildings under its jurisdiction so that persons using the property and buildings are subjected to
a level of perceived noise decibels in excess of the acceptable level
established for that land use. . . . Each government unit having power
to adopt land use and development control measures applicable to property included in any aircraft noise zone, shall adopt or incorporate in
existing land use and development control measures the applicable
acceptable level of perceived noise decibels established by the council,
and shall adopt such other control measures as may be necessary to
prevent the use, construction or improvement of property and buildings under its jurisdiction so that persons using the property and buildings are subjected to a level of perceived noise decibels in excess of
the acceptable level established for that land use. . . . No property
shall be used, and no building or other structure shall be constructed

or improved, within any aircraft noise zone, so that persons using the property and buildings are subjected to a level of perceived noise decibels in excess of the acceptable level established by the council for that land use.

§ 360.76. Control measure involving taking; condemnation by commission.

Subdivision 1. If either the provisions or the application of section 360.74, subdivision 2, or any land use and development control measure applicable to public or private property in an airport development area is determined by a court of competent jurisdiction to constitute a taking, the commission in the exercise of its power to acquire lands for the airport shall have the power to acquire the property or any similar property or to acquire an interest therein to the extent needed for the application of such measure, by eminent domain exercised in accordance with Minnesota Statutes, Chapter 117. The right of eminent domain shall be exercised if the commission has or will have funds to pay the condemnation award and the council determines that it is necessary to protect the airport from encroachment or hazards, or to protect residents in the area, or to encourage the most appropriate use of property in the airport development area, or to protect and conserve the natural resources of the metropolitan area. . . .

§ 360.78. Government units in airport development area; tax sharing.

The legislature determines that the location of a new major airport in the metropolitan area will increase the value and rate of development of land in the airport development area; that the airport development area may comprise property located in several government units; that the exercise of the powers and duties conferred on government units by sections 360.74 to 360.76 to control development of land in an airport development area may result in greater development of such land within one government unit than another; that the control of such development will be of benefit to the entire airport development area; and that the assessed value of taxable property and the tax resources in the government unit where the most development takes place may be significantly greater than in other government units in the area. Therefore, to encourage the protection of inhabitants of the area and natural resources of the metropolitan area, to increase the likelihood of orderly development in an airport development area, and to provide a way for all government units in the area to share in the tax resources generated by growth of the area, the governing bodies of all government units located wholly or partly in an airport development area shall jointly study and decide upon a plan for the sharing of property tax revenues derived from property located in an airport development area. . . .

Nonmotorized Transportation

OREGON USE OF HIGHWAY FUND FOR FOOTPATHS
AND BICYCLE TRAILS (1971)
Ore. Rev. Stat. 336.514

§ 366.514.   Use of highway fund for footpaths and bicycle trails.

(1) Out of the funds received by the commission or by any county or
city from the State Highway Fund reasonable amounts shall be expended
as necessary for the establishment of footpaths and bicycle trails.
Footpaths and bicycle trails shall be established wherever a highway,
road or street is being constructed, reconstructed or relocated. Funds
received from the State Highway Fund may also be expended to maintain
such footpaths and trails and to establish footpaths and trails along
other highways, roads and streets and in parks and recreation areas.
. . .

(3) The amount expended by the commission or by a city or county as
required or permitted by this section shall never in any one fiscal year
be less than one percent of the total amount of the funds received from
the highway fund. However:

    (a) This subsection does not apply to a city in any year in which
the one percent equals $250 or less, or to a county in any year in
which the one percent equals $1500 or less.

    (b) A city or county in lieu of expending the funds each year may
credit the funds to a financial reserve or special fund in accordance
with ORS 280.100, to be held for not more than 10 years, and to be
expended for the purposes required or permitted by this section.

(4) The commission and cities and counties may restrict the use of
footpaths and bicycle trails under their respective jurisdictions to
pedestrians and nonmotorized vehicles.

WASHINGTON BICYCLE ROUTES (1974)
Rev. Code Wash. 47.26.300 et seq.

§ 47.26.300. Bicycle routes—legislative declaration.

The state of Washington is confronted with emergency shortages of energy sources utilized for the transportation of its citizens and must seek alternative methods of providing public mobility.

Bicycles are suitable for many transportation purposes, and are pollution-free in addition to using a minimal amount of resources and energy. However, the increased use of bicycles for both transportation and recreation has led to an increase in both fatal and nonfatal injuries to bicyclists.

The legislature therefore finds that the establishment, improvement, and upgrading of bicycle routes is necessary to promote public mobility, conserve energy, and provide for the safety of the bicycling and motoring public.

§ 47.26.305. Bicycle routes—establishment of system authorized and directed—use of urban arterial trust funds.

Each city and county eligible for receipt of urban arterial trust funds is hereby authorized and directed to establish a system of bicycle routes throughout its jurisdiction. Such routes shall, when established in accordance with standards adopted by the urban arterial board, be eligible for establishment, improvement, and upgrading with urban arterial trust funds when accomplished in connection with an arterial project.

§ 47.26.310. Bicycle routes—standards for designation of bicycle route systems.

Prior to July 1, 1974, the urban arterial board shall adopt:

(1) Standards for the designation of a bicycle route system which shall include, but need not be limited to, consideration of:

(a) Existing and potential bicycle traffic generating activities, including but not limited to places of employment, schools, colleges, shopping areas, and recreational areas;

(b) Directness of travel and distance between potential bicycle traffic generating activities; and

(c) Safety for bicyclists and avoidance of conflict with vehicular traffic which shall include, wherever feasible, designation of bicycle routes on streets parallel but adjacent to existing designated urban arterial routes. . . .

FEDERAL

## Off-Road Vehicles

### USE OF OFF-ROAD VEHICLES ON THE PUBLIC LANDS (1972)
### Exec. Order 11644, 37 F. Reg. 2877

An estimated 5 million off-road recreational vehicles—motorcycles, minibikes, trail bikes, snowmobiles, dune-buggies, all-terrain vehicles, and others—are in use in the United States today, and their popularity continues to increase rapidly. The widespread use of such vehicles on the public lands—often for legitimate purposes but also in frequent conflict with wise land and resource management practices, environmental values, and other types of recreational activitiy—has demonstrated the need for a unified Federal policy toward the use of such vehicles on the public lands. . . .

§ 1. Purpose.

It is the purpose of this order to establish policies and provide for procedures that will ensure that the use of off-road vehicles on public lands will be controlled and directed so as to protect the resources of those lands, to promote the safety of all users of those lands, and to minimize conflicts among the various uses of those lands.

§ 2. Definitions.

As used in this order, the term:

(1) "public lands" means
(A) all lands under the custody and control of the Secretary of the Interior and the Secretary of Agriculture, except Indian lands,
(B) lands under the custody and control of the Tennessee Valley Authority that are situated in western Kentucky and Tennessee and are designated as "Land Between the Lakes," and
(C) lands under the custody and control of the Secretary of Defense;
. . .

(3) "off-road vehicle" means any motorized vehicle designed for or capable of cross-country travel on or immediately over land, water, sand, snow, ice, marsh, swampland, or other natural terrain; except that such term excludes
(A) any registered motorboat,
(B) any military, fire, emergency, or law enforcement vehicle when used for emergency purposes, and

(C) any vehicle whose use is expressly authorized by the respective agency head under a permit, lease, license, or contract; . . .

## § 3. Zones of use.

(a) Each respective agency head shall develop and issue regulations and administrative instructions, within six months of the date of this order, to provide for administrative designation of the specific areas and trails on public lands on which the use of off-road vehicles may be permitted, and areas in which the use of off-road vehicles may not be permitted, and set a date by which such designation of all public lands shall be completed. Those regulations shall direct that the designation of such areas and trails will be based upon the protection of the resources of the public lands, promotion of the safety of all users of those lands, and minimization of conflicts among the various uses of those lands. The regulations shall further require that the designation of such areas and trails shall be in accordance with the following—

(1) Areas and trails shall be located to minimize damage to soil, watershed, vegetation, or other resources of the public lands.

(2) Areas and trails shall be located to minimize harassment of wildlife or significant disruption of wildlife habitats.

(3) Areas and trails shall be located to minimize conflicts between off-road vehicle use and other existing or proposed recreational uses of the same or neighboring public lands, and to ensure the compatibility of such uses with existing conditions in populated areas, taking into account noise and other factors.

(4) Areas and trails shall not be located in officially designated Wilderness Areas or Primitive Areas. Areas and trails shall be located in areas of the National Park system, Natural Areas, or National Wildlife Refuges and Game Ranges only if the respective agency head determines that off-road vehicle use in such locations will not adversely affect their natural, aesthetic, or scenic values.

(b) The respective agency head shall ensure adequate opportunity for public participation in the promulgation of such regulations and in the designation of areas and trails under this section.

(c) The limitations on off-road vehicle use imposed under this section shall not apply to official use. . . .

STATES

Off-Road Vehicles

UTAH SNOWMOBILES AND ALL-TERRAIN
VEHICLES (1971)
Utah Code Ann. 41-22-1 et seq.

§ 41-22-1. Policy declaration.

It is the policy of this state to promote safety and protection for
persons, property, and the environment connected with the use,
operation and equipment of snowmobiles, all-terrain and other recreation vehicles and to promote uniformity of laws and to adopt and
pursue an educational program and develop trails and other facilities
for the use of these vehicles.

§ 41-22-2. Definitions.

As used in this act: . . .

(3) The words "recreation vehicle" mean any snowmobile or all-terrain vehicle engaged in off-highway, recreational use.

(17) The words "public land" mean:
    (a) Land owned or administered by any federal or state agency or
any political subdivision of the state;
    (b) Any private land which is open to public recreation vehicle use;
and
    (c) Any road or highway closed to motor vehicle traffic.
This definition does not include any portion of the right of way or
surface of any public street, road or highway open to motor vehicles
which are required to be registered with the division of motor vehicles.

§ 41-22-3. Registration of vehicles—application—issuance of stickers
and certificate—proof of property tax payment.

(1) Unless exempted by this act, no person shall operate and no owner
shall give another person permission to operate any snowmobile after
June 30, 1971, or any all-terrain vehicle after December 31, 1971,
on any public land in this state unless the recreation vehicle has been
registered under this act for the current year. . . .

§ 41-22-12. Restrictions on use of public lands.

(1) All federal agencies are encouraged and agencies of the state
and its subdivisions are directed to refrain from closing any public

land to responsible recreation vehicle use except where just and reasonable cuase can be demonstrated such as protection of watersheds, and plant and animal life, but

(2) No person shall operate and no owner of a recreation vehicle shall give another permission to operate a recreation vehicle on any public land which has been closed to recreation vehicles.

§ 41-22-13. Prohibited uses.

No person shall operate a recreation vehicle in connection with acts of vandalism, harassment of wildlife or domestic animals, burglaries or other crimes, or damage to the environment which includes pollution of air, water or land, abuse of the watershed, impairment of plant or animal life or excessive mechanical noise. . . .

§ 41-22-18. Ordinances or local laws relating to operation and equipment of vehicles.

The provisions of this act and other applicable laws of this state shall govern the operation, equipment, registration and all other matters relating to the use of recreation vehicles on public land; but nothing in this act shall be construed to prevent the adoption of any ordinance or local law relating to the operation and equipment of recreation vehicles in which the provisions are identical to the provisions of this act, amendments to this act, or the regulations, but these ordinances or local laws shall be operative only as long as and to the extent that they continue to be identical to the provisions of this act, amendments thereto, or the regulations. . . .

§ 41-22-20. Public land administrating agencies to develop facilities and programs.

All public land administering agencies are hereby encouraged to develop and maintain trials, parking areas, rest rooms, and other related facilities appropriate to recreation vehicle use when a need can be demonstrated and to pursue and adopt educational and other programs designed to promote the safety enjoyment, and responsible use of all forms of this recreational activity. . . .

§ 41-22-23. Operation of snowmobile on street or highway prohibited —exceptions.

No person shall operate a snowmobile upon any street, highway, or public right of way except in the following instances:

(1) When crossing a public street or highway and the driver comes to a complete stop before crossing, proceeds only after yielding the right of way to oncoming traffic, and crosses at right angles.

(2) When loading or unloading a snowmobile from a vehicle or trailer, which must be done with due regard for safety, and at the nearest practical point of operation.

(3) When a street or highway has been officially closed to motor vehicle traffic by the public authority having jurisdiction.

(4) When an emergency exists or during any period of time and at those locations where snow upon the roadway renders travel by motor vehicle impractical, or when the operation is directed by law enforcement officers or other public authorities.

(5) When the snowmobile is being operated on a highway right of way solely for the purpose of gaining access to or from a lawful area of operation.

## MICHIGAN REGISTRATION AND REGULATION OF SNOWMOBILES (1968, as amended)
### Mich. Comp. Laws 257.1501 et seq.

Section 257.1517b.    Failure to stop snowmobile upon signal
        257.1518.    Effective date

§ 257.1504a.  Disposition of revenue; trail programs.

Sec. 4a.  The revenue received under this act shall be deposited in
the general fund of the state.  From the revenues obtained pursuant
to section 1504 the legislature shall make an annual appropriation to
the department for administration of the registration provisions of
this act, and to the department of natural resources for purposes of
constructing and maintaining trails and areas on lands under its control, acquisition and leasing of lands, easements and rights of way to
provide for additional trails and areas.  The department and department of natural resources shall include in their annual budget requests
information detailing the programs.

§ 257.1504c.  Snowmobile information, safety education, and training
program.

Sec. 4c.

(1) The department may implement a comprehensive snowmobile information, safety education and training program which shall include
the preparation and dissemination of snowmobile information and
safety advice to the public and training of operators.  The program
shall provide for the training of youthful operators and for the issuance
of snowmobile safety certificates to those who successfully complete
the training provided under the program. . . .

§ 257.1505.  Registration and identification number; display; decal;
term; awarding certificate; records.

Sec. 5.

(1) The owner of any snowmobile having been issued a certificate of
registration for the snowmobile shall paint on or attach in a permanent
manner to each side of the forward half of the snowmobile the identification number in block characters of good proportion, not less than
3 inches in height, reading from left to right.  The numbers shall contrast so as to be distinctly visible and legible.  No number other than
the number awarded to a snowmobile under this act, or granted recip-
rocity under this act, shall be attached or otherwise displayed on the
snowmobile. . . .

§ 257.1509.  Dealers. . . .

(a) Any dealer renting, leasing or furnishing any snowmobile shall
carry a policy of liability insurance subject to limits exclusive of inter-

ests and costs, with respect to such snowmobile, as follows: $20,000.00 because of bodily injury to or death of 1 person in any 1 accident and subject to said limit for 1 person, $40,000.00 because of bodily injury to or death of 2 or more persons in any 1 accident, and $10,000.00 because of injury to or destruction of property of others in any 1 accident, or in the alternative, demand and be shown proof that the person renting, leasing or being furnished a snowmobile carries liability policy of at least the type and coverage as specified above. . . .

§ 257.1512. Regulation of snowmobile operations.

Sec. 12. A person shall not operate a snowmobile upon a public highway, land used as an airport or street, or on a public or private parking lot not specifically designated for the use of snowmobiles except under the following conditions and circumstances:

(a) A snowmobile may be operated on the right of way of a public highway, except a limited access highway, if it is operated at the extreme right of the open portion of the right of way and with the flow of traffic on the highway.

(b) A snowmobile may be operated on the roadway or shoulder when necessary to cross a bridge or culvert if the snowmobile is brought to a complete stop before entering onto the roadway or shoulder and the driver yields the right of way to any approaching vehicle on the highway.

(c) In any court action in this state where competent evidence demonstrates that a vehicle which is permitted to be operated on a highway pursuant to Act No. 300 of the Public Acts of 1949, as amended, being sections 257.1 to 257.923 of the Michigan Compiled Laws, is in a collision with a snowmobile on a roadway, the driver of the snowmobile involved in the collision shall be considered prima facie negligent. . . .

(g) A snowmobile may be operated on a street or highway for a special event of limited duration conducted according to a prearranged schedule only under permit from the governmental unit having jurisdiction. The event may be conducted on the frozen surface of public waters only under permit from the department of natural resources.

§ 257.1512a. Age restrictions, operators, violations.

Sec. 12a.

(1) A parent or legal guardian shall not permit his child who is under the age of 12 to operate a snowmobile without the direct supervision of an adult except on land owned or under the control of the parent or legal guardian.

(2) Beginning January 1, 1974, a person who is at least 12 but less than 16 years of age may operate a snowmobile if:

(a) he is under the direct supervision of a person who is 18 years of age or older; or if

(b) he has in his immediate possession a snowmobile safety certificate issued pursuant to section 1504b; or

(c) he is on land owned or under the control of his parent or legal guardian.

A person who is operating a snowmobile pursuant to subdivision (b) shall present the snowmobile safety certificate to any peace officer upon demand.

(3) Notwithstanding section 1512, an operator who is under 12 years of age shall not cross a highway or street. Beginning January 1, 1974, an operator who is at least 12 years of age but less than 16 years of age, may cross a highway or street only if he has a valid snowmobile safety certificate in his immediate possession.

(4) The owner of a snowmobile shall not permit his snowmobile to be operated contrary to this section.

(5) When the judge of a juvenile court determines that a person who is less than 16 years of age has violated this act, the judge shall immediately report the determination to the department of natural resources. The director of natural resources upon receiving a notice of a determination pursuant to this subsection may suspend the certificate without a hearing.

§ 257.1512b.  Hunting or pursuing birds or animals, prohibition.

Sec. 12b.  A snowmobile shall not be used to hunt, pursue, worry or kill a wild bird or animal.

§ 257.1514.  Ordinances regulating operations.

Sec. 14.  Any city village or township may pass an ordinance regulating the operation of snowmobiles if the ordinance meets substantially the minimum requirements of this act.  A city, village, township or county may not adopt an ordinance which:

(a) Imposes a fee for a license.

(b) Specifies accessory equipment to be carried on the snowmobile.

(c) Requires a snowmobile operator to possess a motor vehicle driver's license.

(d) Restricts operation of a snowmobile on the frozen surface of public waters or on lands owned by or under the control of the state except pursuant to section 14a. . . .

(3) The department of natural resources on its own initiative, or upon receipt of a certified resolution of the governing body of a political subdivision, may initiate investigations into the need for special rules to govern the operation of snowmobiles on the frozen surface of public waters. . . .

§ 257.1515. Prohibited operations.

Sec. 15. A person shall not operate a snowmobile:

(a) At a rate of speed greater than is reasonable and proper having due regard for conditions then existing.

(b) While under the influence of intoxicating liquor or narcotic drugs, barbital or any derivative of barbital.

(c) During the hours from ½ hour after sunset to ½ hour before sunrise without displaying a lighted headlight and a lighted taillight.

(d) In any forest nursery, planting area, or public lands posted or reasonably identifiable as an area of forest reproduction when growing stock may be damaged or as a natural dedicated area which is in zone 2 or zone 3.

(e) On the frozen surface of public waters within 100 feet of a person, including but not limited to a skater, not in or upon a snowmobile or within 100 feet of a fishing shanty or shelter except at the minimum speed required to maintain forward movement of the snowmobile or on an area which has been cleared of snow for skating purposes unless the area is necessary for access to the public water.

(f) Unless it is equipped with a muffler in good working order and in constant operation from which noise emission at 50 feet at right angles from vehicle path under full throttle does not exceed 86 DBA (decibels on the "a" scale) on a sound meter having characteristics defined by American standards association S1, 4-1966 "general purpose sound meter". All snowmobiles manufactured after February 1, 1972 and sold or offered for sale in this state shall not exceed 82 DBA of the 1970 society of automotive engineers code J-192.

(g) Within 100 feet of a dwelling between 12 midnight and 6 a.m., at a speed greater than minimum required to maintain forward movement of the snowmobile.

(h) In or upon or remain unlawfully on premises which are fenced, otherwise enclosed in a manner to exclude intruders, posted in a conspicuous manner or when notice against trespass is personally communicated to him by the owner or an authorized person. A person shall not operate a snowmobile in or upon farmlands, farm woodlots or platted property in zone 3 without permission of the landowner.

(i) In an area on which public hunting is permitted during the season open to the taking of deer with firearms from 7 a.m. to 11 a.m. and from 2 p.m. to 5 p.m., except during an emergency, for law enforcement purposes, to go to and from a permanent residence or a hunting camp otherwise inaccessible by a conventional wheeled vehicle or for the conduct of necessary work functions involving land and timber survey, communication and transmission line patrol and timber harvest operations, or on his own property or property under his control or as an invited guest.

(j) While transporting thereon a bow unless unstrung or a firearm unless securely encased or equipped with and made inoperative by a manufactured keylocked trigger housing mechanism.

(k) On or across a cemetery or burial ground.

(l) Within 100 feet of a slide, ski or skating area. A snowmobile may enter such an area for the purpose of servicing the area or for medical emergencies.

(m) On a railroad or railroad right of way, except railroad, public utility or law enforcement personnel while in the performance of their duties.

# 13

Federal "clean waters" laws of the 1950s and 1960s were ineffective in stemming the steady deterioration of rivers, lakes, and streams and the loss of both swimming places and fishing grounds. The eutrophication of Lake Erie was perhaps the most noted example. Fishermen and other conservation groups dusted off the 60-year-old Refuse Act and went to court to enforce its prohibitions against discharges into navigable waters. It was only with the passage of the Federal Water Pollution Control Act (FWPCA) in 1972 that the quality of all U.S. waters became a federal responsibility, to be attained by joint federal-state-local mechanisms. For the first time it provided for uniform nationwide standards, enforceable regulations, and a permit program geared to specific goals.

Water resources and their quality also are an aspect of the conservation of land and soil resources (Chapter 9). While the FWPCA extends to ocean waters within territorial limits, ocean pollution is considered primarily in Chapter 8. Chapter 5 excerpts wetlands and shorelands legislation, Chapter 6 deals with scenic river protection, and Chapter 11 quotes portions of the Safe Drinking Water Act.

The provisions of FWPCA are summarized in the Fourth Annual Report of the Council on Environmental Quality (pp. 169-71):

> The law's basic regulatory requirement is that "point source" discharges—industries, municipal treatment plants, feedlots, and other discrete sources—must obtain a permit specifying allowable amounts and constituents of effluent and a schedule for achieving compliance. States meeting requirements specified by the Administrator of EPA are to administer the national permit program, with individual permits subject to EPA review. EPA will

issue the permits in states that fail to submit or carry out
an approved permit program and for Federal facilities.

Permits must be consistent with applicable effluent
guidelines to be issued by EPA for major classes and categories of industrial facilities or with EPA requirements
for publicly owned waste treatment works. The technology-
based effluent limitations and the water quality standards
that may dictate more stringent effluent limitations are to
be applied in two phases. By 1977, municipal plants must
provide "secondary treatment"—a common level of treatment for organic wastes, usually based on bacterial decomposition and stabilization. Also by 1977, industrial facilities must comply with EPA's effluent guidelines prescribing "best practicable control technology currently available." Stricter effluent limitations for both industry and
municipalities will be required in individual cases if best
practicable technology or secondary treatment is inadequate to meet ambient water quality standards which are
set on the basis of water uses, such as propagation of fish
and wildlife and recreation.

By 1983, municipalities must provide "best practicable
waste treatment technology," and industries must comply
with effluent guidelines prescribing best "available technology economically achievable" which will result in "reasonable further progress" toward the goal of eliminating
the discharge of pollutants. More stringent effluent limitations may be imposed for individual industries or municipalities when necessary to "contribute" to water quality
needed to "assure protection of public water supplies, agricultural and industrial uses, and the protection and propagation of a balanced population of shellfish, fish and wildlife,
and allow recreational activities in and on the water." The
more stringent limitation will not apply, however, if the
discharger demonstrates that there is "no reasonable relationship" between the economic and social costs and benefits to be obtained.

In addition to issuing effluent guidelines for existing
point sources, EPA must set special effluent standards
for new industrial point sources, based on best available
demonstrated control technology. These will apply to at
least 27 categories of sources listed in the Act.

The Administrator must also publish a list of toxic
pollutants and effluent limitations or prohibitions for
them. Toxic pollutants are defined as those which, when
assimilated either directly from the environment or in-

directly by ingestion through food chains, will cause death,
disease, behavioral abnormalities, cancer, genetic mutations, physiological malfunctions, or physical deformities
in any organism or its offspring.  Spills of toxic or other
hazardous materials are now subject to the same regulatory
framework—for prevention and Federal cleanup costs—
that previously existed only for oil spills.

    The Administrator must also issue pretreatment stan-
dards requiring an industrial facility discharging into a municipal sewage treatment plant to pretreat its effluent so
that it does not interfere with the operation of or pass
through the plant without adequate treatment.  Because
roughly one-half of all industrial facilities discharge their
wastes into municipal systems, pretreatment standards are
essential to achieving control over industrial effluents

    The Act requires states to develop a comprehensive and
continuing planning process for water quality management.
Plans must include not only the point source controls described above but also controls for diffuse land runoff and
other nonpoint sources.  Beginning in 1975, the states
must submit annual reports to EPA that inventory all point
sources of pollution, assess existing and anticipated water
quality, and propose programs for nonpoint source control.

    EPA has authority to enforce the law through both admin-
istrative and judicial channels.  When the Administrator
discovers a violation of a permit condition or other provision of the law, he must notify the polluter and then either
issue an administrative order prohibiting further violation
or request the Attorney General to seek appropriate relief
in Federal court.  The discharge of pollutants from point
sources except in compliance with a permit is unlawful. . . .

    Private citizens may seek judicial relief, against any
polluter for violating an effluent limitation or an administrative order.  Citizens may also institute proceedings
against the Administrator if he fails to perform a nondis-
cretionary act required by the law. . . .

    The Federal share of these projects is 75 percent, com-
pared to the prior maximum of 55 percent.  The remainder
is borne by the municipalities, which sometimes also receive state aid.  Industrial users must reimburse the Federal and local governments for the share of project costs
attributable to them.

    While previous federal laws had emphasized ambient water
quality and river basin planning, the 1972 act attacked the problem at

its source. It set 1985 as the target date for achieving zero pollutant discharge, and the intermediate dates of 1977 and 1983 for achievement of more limited goals. The year 1977 is the target date for achieving "best practicable" treatment for industrial wastes and secondary treatment for municipal wastes, while the "best available" treatment for industrial and "best practicable" treatment for municipal wastes is to be achieved by 1983. Such municipal waste treatment may involve disposal of wastes on land rather than into water. Amendments that could affect the municipal treatment plant deadlines and other provisions are before the 94th Congress at the time of this writing.

The FWPCA provides federal grants for the construction of sewage treatment plants and requires pretreatment of industrial discharges entering municipal systems.

States may be permitted to administer National Pollutant Discharge Elimination programs with EPA approval, and approximately one-half the states had such approval in early 1976. "Point source" polluters apply for and receive permits for discharge into the surface waters that specify the kind and amount of pollutants that may be discharged and, if necessary, the type of equipment to be installed. No permits may be issued for discharge of radiological or radioactive materials. States may restrict and prohibit additional activities of potential damage to their water resources, such as discharge into groundwater supplies.

The FWPCA instructs the EPA to formulate standards applicable to new sources that "reflect the greatest degree of effluent reduction . . . achievable through application of the best available demonstrated control technology" (Sec. 1316). These standards govern all major industrial categories. The Corps of Engineers is charged with administering a permit program for dredge and fill operations.

Areas of urban-industrial concentration are required to make plans for areawide waste treatment management (Sec. 1288). Such plans may come close to governing the use of land. They must identify and control "nonpoint sources of pollution, including runoff from manure disposal areas, and from land used for livestock and crop production," "construction activity related sources of pollution" and others, and regulate "the location, modification, and construction of any facilities . . . which may result in any discharge."

Belated enforcement of the Refuse Act (Sec. 13[407] of the Rivers and Harbors Act of 1899 [p. 488]), brought about by innovative litigation in the 1960s, was a factor in producing the 1972 legislation.

The Corps of Engineers has been the target of criticism for inundating valuable bottom land, homes and communities, and historic, archaeological, and scenic sites in the process of building dams for flood control. In 1974 the corps was directed to consider "non-structural alternatives" in its flood control work (p. 489).

Water quality and water resources are the concern of other acts of Congress. Power projects licensed by the Federal Power Commission must be adapted to "a comprehensive plan for improving or developing a waterway" (16 U.S.C. 803). Federally aided airports and mass transportation projects must be planned to comply with water quality standards (49 U.S.C. 1604[i], 49 U.S.C. 1716[e]). The Safe Drinking Water Act requires minimum standards for state underground injection control programs (Sec. 300h-1).

States in the arid portion of the West have long had complex regulations governing the use of their scarce water resources. Eastern states, as well, require permits for certain water uses, such as dredging or filling. North Carolina's Sedimentation Pollution Control Act of 1973 (p. 489) controls "land disturbing activities" near bodies of water. Oregon has one of the more comprehensive pieces of legislation, requiring permits for removal and filling on both natural and man-made, freshwater and tidal, navigable and nonnavigable waters of no minimum size. All state laws must be consistent with and comply with the FWPCA.

Florida's Air and Water Pollution Control Act (p. 492) in part incorporates the requirements of the FWPCA and is noted for its strong liability provisions, upheld by the United States Supreme Court. It prohibits the sale of certain detergents. The state's land-use law was passed to "reverse the deterioration of water quality and provide optimum utilization of our limited water resources" (Sec. 380.021, p. 151). Indiana, Maine, and New York, among other states, are banning the sale of phosphate products. Indiana's statute (13 Ind. Stat. Ann. 1-5.5-1 et seq.) has been upheld in court and efforts to repeal it have failed.

Indiana also requires permits for the construction and operation of feedlots (p. 502), a major source of water pollution and "point sources" under the FWPCA (Sec. 1362[14]). A 1975 New York law mandates soil and water conservation plans for all agricultural and forestry lands over a certain size and for all feedlots. Wyoming's Environmental Quality Act of 1973 (p. 501) requires permits for activities affecting both quantity and quality of its waters. Michigan has moved to eliminate waste discharges from boats into its waters (p. 503). Montana's mining laws permit suits for damage to water supply (Sec. 50-1055). Eutrophication is a "damage to the environment" that Massachusetts citizens may sue to enjoin (Sec. 214-7A).

FEDERAL

## FEDERAL WATER POLLUTION CONTROL
ACT (1972)
33 U.S.C. 1251 et seq.

§ 1251. Congressional declaration of goals and policy.

(a) The objective of this chapter is to restore and maintain the chemical, physical, and biological integrity of the Nation's waters. In order to achieve this objective it is hereby declared that, consistent with the provisions of this chapter—

(1) it is the national goal that the discharge of pollutants into the navigable waters be eliminated by 1985;

(2) it is the national goal that wherever attainable, an interim goal of water quality which provides for the protection and propagation of fish, shellfish, and wildlife and provides for recreation in and on the water be achieved by July 1, 1983;

(3) it is the national policy that the discharge of toxic pollutants in toxic amounts be prohibited;

(4) it is the national policy that Federal financial assistance be provided to construct publicly owned waste treatment works;

(5) it is the national policy that areawide waste treatment management planning processes be developed and implemented to assure adequate control of sources of pollutants in each State; and

(6) it is the national policy that a major research and demonstration effort be made to develop technology necessary to eliminate the discharge of pollutants into the navigable waters, waters of the contiguous zone, and the oceans.

(b) It is the policy of the Congress to recognize, preserve, and protect the primary responsibilities and rights of States to prevent, reduce, and eliminate pollution, to plan the development and use (including restoration, preservation, and enhancement) of land and water resources, and to consult with the Administrator in the exercise of his authority under this chapter. It is further the policy of the Congress to support and aid research relating to the prevention, reduction, and elimination of pollution and to provide Federal technical services and financial aid to State and interstate agencies and municipalities in connection with the prevention, reduction, and elimination of pollution.

(c) It is further the policy of Congress that the President, acting through the Secretary of State and such national and international organizations as he determines appropriate, shall take such action as may be necessary to insure that to the fullest extent possible all foreign countries shall take meaningful action for the prevention, reduction, and elimination of pollution in their waters and in international waters and for the achievement of goals regarding the elimination of discharge of pollutants and the improvement of water quality to at least the same extent as the United States does under its laws.

(d) Except as otherwise expressly provided in this chapter, the Administrator of the Environmental Protection Agency (hereinafter in this chapter called "Administrator") shall administer this chapter.

(e) Public participation in the development, revision, and enforcement of any regulation, standard, effluent limitation, plan, or program established by the Administrator or any State under this chapter shall be provided for, encouraged, and assisted by the Administrator and the States. The Administrator, in cooperation with the States, shall

develop and publish regulations specifying minimum guidelines for
public participation in such processes.

(f) It is the national policy that to the maximum extent possible the
procedures utilized for implementing this chapter shall encourage the
drastic minimization of paperwork and interagency decision procedures,
and the best use of available manpower and funds, so as to prevent
needless duplication and unnecessary delays at all levels of government.

## § 1254. Research, investigations, training, and information.

(a) Establishment of national programs; cooperation; investigations;
water quality surveillance system; reports.

The Administrator shall establish national programs for the prevention, reduction, and elimination of pollution and as part of such programs shall— . . .
    (5) in cooperation with the States, and their political subdivisions,
and other Federal agencies establish, equip, and maintain a water
quality surveillance system for the purpose of monitoring the quality
of the navigable waters and ground waters and the contiguous zone and
the oceans. . . .

## § 1281. Congressional declaration of purposes.

(a) It is the purpose of this subchapter to require and to assist the development and implementation of waste treatment management plans
and practices which will achieve the goals of this chapter.

(b) Waste treatment management plans and practices shall provide for
the application of the best practicable waste treatment technology before any discharge into receiving waters, including reclaiming and recycling of water, and confined disposal of pollutants so they will not
migrate to cause water or other environmental pollution and shall provide for consideration of advanced waste treatment techniques.

(c) To the extent practicable, waste treatment management shall be on
an areawide basis and provide control or treatment of all point and
nonpoint sources of pollution, including in place or accumulated pollution sources.

(d) The Administrator shall encourage waste treatment management
which results in the construction of revenue producing facilities providing for—
    (1) the recycling of potential sewage pollutants through the produc-
tion of agriculture, silviculture, or aquaculture products, or any combination thereof;
    (2) the confined and contained disposal of pollutants not recycled;

(3) the reclamation of wastewater; and

(4) the ultimate disposal of sludge in a manner that will not result in environmental hazards.

(e) The Administrator shall encourage waste treatment management which results in integrating facilities for sewage treatment and recycling with facilities to treat, dispose of, or utilize other industrial and municipal wastes, including but not limited to solid waste and waste heat and thermal discharges. Such integrated facilities shall be designed and operated to produce revenues in excess of capital and operation and maintenance costs and such revenues shall be used by the designated regional management agency to aid in financing other environmental improvement programs.

(f) The Administrator shall encourage waste treatment management which combines "open space" and recreational considerations with such management.

(g)(1) The Administrator is authorized to make grants to any State, municipality, or intermunicipal or interstate agency for the construction of publicly owned treatment works. . . .

§ 1284.  Limitations and conditions. . . .

(b)(1) Notwithstanding any other provision of this subchapter, the Administrator shall not approve any grant for any treatment works under section 1281(g)(1) of this title after March 1, 1973, unless he shall first have determined that the applicant

(A) has adopted or will adopt a system of charges to assure that each recipient of waste treatment services within the applicant's jurisdiction, as determined by the Administrator, will pay its proportionate share of the costs of operation and maintenance (including replacement) of any waste treatment services provided by the applicant;

(B) has made provision for the payment to such applicant by the industrial users of the treatment works, of that portion of the cost of construction of such treatment works (as determined by the Administrator) which is allocable to the treatment of such industrial wastes to the extent attributable to the Federal share of the cost of construction; and

(C) has legal, institutional, managerial, and financial capability to insure adequate construction, operation, and maintenance of treatment works throughout the applicant's jurisdiction, as determined by the Administrator.

§ 1288.  Areawide waste treatment management.

(a) Identification and designation of areas having substantial water quality control problems.

For the purpose of encouraging and facilitating the development and implementation of areawide waste treatment management plans—

(1) The Administrator, within ninety days after October 18, 1972, and after consultation with appropriate Federal, State, and local authorities, shall by regulation publish guidelines for the identification of those areas which, as a result of urban-industrial concentrations or other factors, have substantial water quality control problems.

(2) The Governor of each State, within sixty days after publication of the guidelines issued pursuant to paragraph (1) of this subsection, shall identify each area within the State which, as a result of urban-industrial concentrations or other factors, has substantial water quality control problems. . . .

(b) Planning process.

(1) Not later than one year after the date of designation of any organization under subsection (a) of this section such organization shall have in operation a continuing areawide waste treatment management planning process consistent with section 1281 of this title. Plans prepared in accordance with this process shall contain alternatives for waste treatment management and be applicable to all wastes generated within the area involved.

(2) Any plan prepared under such process shall include, but not be limited to— . . .

(C) the establishment of a regulatory program to—

(i) implement the waste treatment management requirements of section 1281(c) of this title,

(ii) regulate the location, modification, and construction of any facilities within such area which may result in any discharge in such area, and

(iii) assure that any industrial or commercial wastes discharged into any treatment works in such area meet applicable pretreatment requirements; . . .

(F) a process to

(i) identify, if appropriate, agriculturally and silviculturally related nonpoint sources of pollution, including runoff from manure disposal areas, and from land used for livestock and crop production, and

(ii) set forth procedures and methods (including land use requirements) to control to the extent feasible such sources;

(G) a process to

(i) identify, if appropriate, mine-related sources of pollution including new, current, and abandoned surface and underground mine runoff, and

(ii) set forth procedures and methods (including land use requirements) to control to the extent feasible such sources;

ENVIRONMENTAL LEGISLATION

(H) a process to

(i) identify construction activity related sources of pollution, and

(ii) set forth procedures and methods (including land use requirements) to control to the extent feasible such sources; . . .

## § 1311.  Effluent limitations.

(a) Illegality of pollutant discharges except in compliance with law.

Except as in compliance with this section and sections 1312, 1316, 1317, 1328, 1342, and 1344 of this title, the discharge of any pollutant by any person shall be unlawful.

(b) Timetable for achievement of objectives.

In order to carry out the objective of this chapter there shall be achieved—

(1)(A) not later than July 1, 1977, effluent limitations for point sources, other than publicly owned treatment works,

(i) which shall require the application of the best practicable control technology currently available as defined by the Administrator pursuant to section 1314(b) of this title, or

(ii) in the case of a discharge into a publicly owned treatment works which meets the requirements of subparagraph (B) of this paragraph, which shall require compliance with any applicable pretreatment requirements and any requirements under section 1317 of this title; and

(B) for publicly owned treatment works in existence on July 1, 1977, or approved pursuant to section 1283 of this title prior to June 30, 1974 (for which construction must be completed within four years of approval), effluent limitations based upon secondary treatment as defined by the Administrator pursuant to section 1314(d)(1) of this title; . . .

(2)(A) not later than July 1, 1983, effluent limitations for categories and classes of point sources, other than publicly owned treatment works, which

(i) shall require application of the best available technology economically achievable for such category or class, which will result in reasonable further progress toward the national goal of eliminating the discharge of all pollutants, as determined in accordance with regulations issued by the Administrator pursuant to section 1314(b)(2) of this title, which such effluent limitations shall require the elimination of discharges of all pollutants if the Administrator finds, on the basis of information available to him (including information developed pursuant to section 1325 of this title), that such elimination is technologically and economically achievable for a category or class of point sources as determined in accordance with regulations issued by the Administrator pursuant to section 1314(b)(2) of this title, or

(ii) in the case of the introduction of a pollutant into a publicly owned treatment works which meets the requirements of subparagraph (B) of this paragraph, shall require compliance with any applicable pretreatment requirements and any other requirement under section 1317 of this title; and

(B) not later than July 1, 1983, compliance by all publicly owned treatment works with the requirements set forth in section 1281(g)(2)(A) of this title.

(c) Modification of timetable.

The Administrator may modify the requirements of subsection (b)(2)(A) of this section with respect to any point source for which a permit application is filed after July 1, 1977, upon a showing by the owner or operator of such point source satisfactory to the Administrator that such modified requirements

(1) will represent the maximum use of technology within the economic capability of the owner or operator; and

(2) will result in reasonable further progress toward the elimination of the discharge of pollutants. . . .

(f) Illegality of discharge of radiological, chemical, or biological warfare agents or high-level radioactive waste.

Notwithstanding any other provisions of this chapter it shall be unlawful to discharge any radiological, chemical, or biological warfare agent or high-level radioactive waste into the navigable waters.

§ 1313. Water quality standards and implementation plans.

(a) Existing water quality standards.

(1) In order to carry out the purpose of this chapter, any water quality standard applicable to interstate waters which was adopted by any State and submitted to, and approved by, or is a waiting approval by, the Administrator pursuant to this Act as in effect immediately prior to the date of enactment of the Federal Water Pollution Control Act Amendments of 1972, shall remain in effect unless the Administrator determined that such standard is not consistent with the applicable requirements of this Act as in effect immediately prior to the date of enactment of the Federal Water Pollution Control Act Amendments of 1972. . . .

(3)(A) Any State which prior to October 18, 1972, has not adopted pursuant to its own laws water quality standards applicable to intrastate waters shall, not later than one hundred and eighty days after October 18, 1972, adopt and submit such standards to the Administrator. . . .

(b) Proposed regulations.

(1) The Administrator shall promptly prepare and publish proposed regulations setting forth water quality standards for a State in accordance with the applicable requirements of this Act as in effect immediately prior to the date of enactment of the Federal Water Pollution Control Act Amendments of 1972, if—

(A) the State fails to submit water quality standards within the times prescribed in subsection (a) of this section

(B) a water quality standard submitted by such State under subsection (a) of this section is determined by the Administrator not to be consistent with the applicable requirements of subsection (a) of this section. . . .

(c) Review; revised standards; publication.

(1) The Governor of a State or the State water pollution control agency of such State shall from time to time (but at least once each three year period beginning with October 18, 1972) hold public hearings for the purpose of reviewing applicable water quality standards and, as appropriate, modifying and adopting standards. Results of such review shall be made available to the Administrator.

(2) Whenever the State revises or adopts a new standard, such revised or new standard shall be submitted to the Administrator. Such revised or new water quality standard shall consist of the designated uses of the navigable waters involved and the water quality criteria for such waters based upon such uses. Such standards shall be such as to protect the public health or welfare, enhance the quality of water and serve the purposes of this chapter. Such standards shall be established taking into consideration their use and value for public water supplies, propagation of fish and wildlife, recreational purposes, and agricultural, industrial, and other purposes, and also taking into consideration their use and value for navigation. . . .

(d) Identification of areas with insufficient controls; maximum daily load.

(1)(A) Each State shall identify those waters within its boundaries for which the effluent limitations required by section 1311(b)(1)(A) and section 1311(b)(1)(B) of this title are not stringent enough to implement any water quality standard applicable to such waters. The State shall establish a priority ranking for such waters, taking into account the severity of the pollution and the uses to be made of such waters.

(B) Each State shall identify those waters or parts thereof within its boundaries for which controls on thermal discharges under section 1311 of this title are not stringent enough to assure protection and propagation of a balanced indigenous population of shellfish, fish, and wildlife.

(C) Each State shall estimate for the waters identified in paragraph (1)(A) of this subsection, and in accordance with the priority ranking, the total maximum daily load, for those pollutants which the Administrator identifies under section 1314(a)(2) of this title as suitable for such calculation. Such load shall be established at a level necessary to implement the applicable water quality standards with seasonal variations and a margin of safety which takes into account any lack of knowledge concerning the relationship between effluent limitations and water quality.

(D) Each State shall estimate for the waters identified in paragraph (1)(B) of this subsection the total maximum daily thermal load required to assure protection and propagation of a balanced, indigenous population of shellfish, fish and wildlife. . . .

(3) For the specific purpose of developing information, each State shall identify all waters within its boundaries, which it has not identified under paragraph (1)(A) and (1)(B) of this subsection and estimate for such waters the total maximum daily load with seasonal variations and margins of safety, for those pollutants which the Administrator identifies under section 1314(a)92) of this title as suitable for such calculation and for thermal discharges, at a level that would assure protection and propagation of a balanced indigenous population of fish, shellfish and wildlife.

(e) Continuing planning process.

(1) Each State shall have a continuing planning process approved under paragraph (2) of this subsection which is consistent with this chapter. . . .

(2) The Administrator shall not approve any State permit program under subchapter IV of this chapter for any State which does not have an approved continuing planning process under this section.

§ 1314. Information and guidelines.

(a) Criteria development and publication.

(1) The Administrator, after consultation with appropriate Federal and State agencies and other interested persons, shall develop and publish, within one year after October 18, 1972 (and from time to time thereafter revise) criteria for water quality accurately reflecting the latest scientific knowledge

(A) on the kind and extent of all identifiable effects on health and welfare including, but not limited to, plankton, fish, shellfish, wildlife, plant life, shorelines, beaches, esthetics, and recreation which may be expected from the presence of pollutants in any body of water, including ground water;

(B) on the concentration and dispersal of pollutants, or their byproducts, through biological, physical, and chemical processes; and

(C) on the effects of pollutants on biological community diversity, productivity, and stability, including information on the factors affecting rates of eutrophication and rates of organic and inorganic sedimentation for varying types of receiving waters.

(2) The Administrator, after consultation with appropriate Federal and State agencies and other interested persons, shall develop and publish, within one year after October 18, 1972 (and from time to time thereafter revise) information

(A) on the factors necessary to restore and maintain the chemical, physical, and biological integrity of all navigable waters, ground waters, waters of the contiguous zone, and the oceans;

(B) on the factors necessary for the protection and propagation of shellfish, fish, and wildlife for classes and categories of receiving waters and to allow recreational activities in and on the water; and

(C) on the measurement and classification of water quality; and

(D) for the purpose of section 1313 of this title, on and the identification of pollutants suitable for maximum daily load measurement correlated with the achievement of water quality objectives. . . .

(b) Effluent limitation guidelines.

For the purpose of adopting or revising effluent limitations under this chapter the Administrator shall, after consultation with appropriate Federal and State agencies and other interested persons, publish within one year of October 18, 1972, regulations, providing guidelines for effluent limitations, and, at least annually thereafter, revise, if appropriate, such regulations. Such regulations shall—

(1)(A) identify, in terms of amounts of consistuents and chemical, physical, and biological characteristics of pollutants, the degree of effluent reduction attainable through the application of the best practicable control technology currently available for classes and categories of point sources (other than publicly owned treatment works); and

(B) specify factors to be taken into account in determining the control measures and practices to be applicable to point sources (other than publicly owned treatment works) within such categories or classes. Factors relating to the assessment of best practicable control technology currently available to comply with subsection (b)(1) of section 1311 of this title shall include consideration of the total cost of application of technology in relation to the effluent reduction benefits to be achieved from such application, and shall also take into account the age of equipment and facilities involved, the process employed, the engineering aspects of the application of various types of control techniques, process changes, non–water quality environmental impact (including energy requirements), and such other factors as the Administrator deems appropriate;

(2)(A) identify, in terms of amounts of constituents and chemical,
physical, and biological characteristics of pollutants, the degree of
effluent reduction attainable through the application of the best control
measures and practices achievable including treatment techniques,
process and procedure innovations, operating methods, and other
alternatives for classes and categories of point sources (other than
publicly owned treatment works); and

(B) specify factors to be taken into account in determining the
best measures and practices available to comply with subsection
(b)(2) of section 1311 of this title to be applicable to any point
source (other than publicly owned treatment works) within such categories or classes. Factors relating to the assessment of best
available technology shall take into account the age of equipment
and facilities involved, the process employed, the engineering aspects of the application of various types of control techniques, process changes, the cost of achieving such effluent reduction, non-
water quality environmental impact (including energy requirements),
and such other factors as the Administrator deems appropriate;
and

(3) identify control measures and practices available to eliminate
the discharge of pollutants from categories and classes of point sources,
taking into account the cost of achieving such elimination of the discharge of pollutants.

(c) Pollution discharge elimination procedures.

The Administrator, after consultation, with appropriate Federal and
State agencies and other interested persons, shall issue to the States
and appropriate water pollution control agencies within 270 days after
October 18, 1972 (and from time to time thereafter) information on
the processes, procedures, or operating methods which result in the
elimination or reduction of the discharge of pollutants to implement
standards of performance under Section 306 of this Act (33 U.S.C.
1316). Such information shall include technical and other data, including costs, as are available on alternative methods of elimination
or reduction of the discharge of pollutants. . . .

§ 1316. National standards of performance.

(a) Definitions.

For purposes of this section:
(1) The term "standard of performance"means a standard for the
control of the discharge of pollutants which reflect the greatest degree
of effluent reduction which the Administrator determines to be
achievable through application of the best available demonstrated control technology, processes, operating methods, or other alternatives,

including, where practicable, a standard permitting no discharge of pollutants.

(2) The term "new source" means any source, the construction of which is commenced after the publication of proposed regulations prescribing a standard of performance under this section which will be applicable to such source, if such standard is thereafter promulgated in accordance with this section.

(b) Categories of sources; Federal standards of performance for new sources.

(1)(A) The Administrator shall, within ninety days after October 18, 1972, publish (and from time to time thereafter shall revise) a list of categories of sources, which shall, at the minimum, include:
. . .

(B) As soon as practicable, but in no case more than one year, after a category of sources is included in a list under subparagraph (A) of this paragraph, the Administrator shall propose and publish regulations establishing Federal standards of performance for new sources within such category. The Administrator shall afford interested persons an opportunity for written comment on such proposed regulations. . . .

§ 1317. Toxic and pretreatment effluent standards; establishment; revision; illegaility of source operation in violation of standards.

(a)(1) The Administrator shall, within ninety days after October 18, 1972, publish (and from time to time thereafter revise) a list which includes any toxic pollutant or combination of such pollutants for which an effluent standard (which may include a prohibition of the discharge of such pollutants or combination of such pollutants) will be established under this section. The Administrator in publishing such list shall take into account the toxicity of the pollutant, its persistence, degradability, the usual or potential presence of the affected organisms in any waters, the importance of the affected organisms and the nature and extent of the effect of the toxic pollutant on such organisms. . . .

(4) Any effluent standard promulgated under this section shall be at that level which the Administrator determines provides an ample margin of safety. . . .

(b)(1) The Administrator shall, within one hundred and eighty days after October 18, 1972, and from time to time thereafter, publish proposed regulations establishing pretreatment standards for introduction of pollutants into treatment works (as defined in section 1292 of this title) which are publicly owned for those pollutants which are determined not to be susceptible to treatment by such treatment works or which would interfere with the operation of such treatment works. . . .

§ 1321. Oil and hazardous substance liability. . . .

(b) Congressional declaration of policy against discharges of oil or hazardous substances; designation of hazardous substances; determination of removability; liability; penalties.

(1) The Congress hereby declares that it is the policy of the United States that there should be no discharges of oil or hazardous substances into or upon the navigable waters of the United States, adjoining shorelines, or into or upon the waters of the contiguous zone.

(2)(A) The Administrator shall develop, promulgate, and revise as may be appropriate, regulations designating as hazardous substances, other than oil as defined in this section, such elements and compounds which, when discharged in any quantity into or upon the navigable waters of the United States or adjoining shorelines or the waters of the contiguous zone, present an imminent and substantial danger to the public health or welfare, including, but not limited to, fish, shellfish, wildlife, shorelines, and beaches.

(b)(i) The Administrator shall include in any designation under subparagraph (A) of this subsection a determination whether any such designated hazardous substance can actually be removed.

(ii) The owner or operator of any vessel, onshore facility, or offshore facility from which there is discharged during the two-year period beginning on October 18, 1972, any hazardous substance determined not removable under clause (i) of this subparagraph shall be liable, subject to the defenses to liability provided under subsection (f) of this section, as appropriate, to the United States for a civil penalty per discharge established by the Administrator based on toxicity, degradability, and dispersal characteristics of such substance, in an amount not to exceed $50,000, except that where the United States can show that such discharge was a result of willful negligence or willful misconduct within the privity and knowledge of the owner, such owner or operator shall be liable to the United States for a civil penalty in such amount as the Administrator shall establish, based upon the toxicity, degradability, and dispersal characteristics of such substance.

(iii) After the expiration of the two-year period referred to in clause (ii) of this subparagraph, the owner or operator of any vessel, onshore facility, or offshore facility, from which there is discharged any hazardous substance determined not removable under clause (i) of this subparagraph shall be liable, subject to the defenses to liability provided in subsection (f) of this section, to the United States. . . .

(f) Liability for actual costs of removal.

(1) Except where an owner or operator can prove that a discharge was caused solely by

(A) an act of God,

(B) an act of war,

(C) negligence on the part of the United States Government, or

(D) an act or omission of a third party without regard to whether any such act or omission was or was not negligent,

or any combination of the foregoing clauses, such owner or operator of any vessel from which oil or a hazardous substance is discharged in violation of subsection (b)(2) of this section shall, notwithstanding any other provision of law, be liable to the United States Government for the actual costs incurred under subsection (c) of this section for the removal of such oil or substance by the United States Government in an amount not to exceed $100 per gross ton of such vessel or $14,000,000 whichever is lesser, except that where the United States can show that such discharge was the result of willful negligence or willful misconduct within the privity and knowledge of the owner, such owner or operator shall be liable to the United States Government for the full amount of such costs. Such costs shall constitute a maritime lien on such vessel which may be recovered in an action in rem in the district court of the United States for any district within which any vessel may be found. The United States may also bring an action against the owner or operator of such vessel in any court of competent jurisdiction to recover such costs. . . .

§ 1323. Federal facilities pollution control.

Each department, agency, or instrumentality of the executive, legislative, and judicial branches of the Federal Government

(1) having jurisdiction over any property or facility, or

(2) engaged in any activity resulting, or which may result, in the discharge or runoff of pollutants shall comply with Federal, State, interstate, and local requirements respecting control and abatement of pollution to the same extent that any person is subject to such requirements, including the payment of reasonable service charges. . . .

§ 1326. Thermal discharges.

(a) Effluent limitations that will assure protection and propagation of balanced, indigenous population of shellfish, fish, and wildlife.

With respect to any point source otherwise subject to the provisions of section 1311 of this title or section 1316 of this title, whenever the owner or operator of any such source, after opportunity for public hearing, can demonstrate to the satisfaction of the Administrator (or, if appropriate, the State) that any effluent limitation proposed for the control of the thermal component of any discharge from such source will require effluent limitations more stringent than necessary to assure the projection and propagation of a balanced, indigenous population of shellfish, fish, and wildlife in and on the body of water into which the discharge is to be made, the Administrator (or, if appropriate, the State) may impose an effluent limitation under such sections for such plant, with respect to the thermal component of such discharge (taking into account the interaction of such thermal component with other pollutants), that will assure the protection and propagation of a balanced, indigenous population of shellfish, fish, and wildlife in and on that body of water. . . .

§ 1342. National pollutant discharge elimination system.

(a) Permits for discharge of pollutants.

(1) Except as provided in sections 1328 and 1344 of this title, the Administrator may, after opportunity for public hearing issue a permit for the discharge of any pollutant, or combination of pollutants, notwithstanding section 1311(a) of this title, upon condition that such discharge will meet either all applicable requirements under sections 1311, 1312, 1316, 1317, 1318, and 1343 of this title, or prior to the taking of necessary implementing actions relating to all such requirements, such conditions as the Administrator determines are necessary to carry out the provisions of this chapter.

(2) The Administrator shall prescribe conditions for such permits to assure compliance with the requirements of paragraph (1) of this subsection, including conditions on data and information collection, reporting, and such other requirements as he deems appropriate.

(3) The permit program of the Administrator under paragraph (1) of this subsection, and permits issued thereunder, shall be subject to the same terms, conditions, and requirements as apply to a State permit program and permits issued thereunder under subsection (b) of this section. . . .

(b) State permit programs.

At any time after the promulgation of the guidelines required by subsection (h)(2) of section 1314 of this title, the Governor of each State desiring to administer its own permit program for discharges into navigable waters within its jurisdiction may submit to the Administration a full and complete description of the program it proposes to establish and administer under State law or under an interstate compact. . . . The Administrator shall approve each submitted program unless he determines that adequate authority does not exist. . . .

(3) To insure that the public, and any other State the waters of which may be affected, receive notice of each application for a permit and to provide an opportunity for public hearing before a ruling on each such application; . . .

(7) To abate violations of the permit or the permit program, including civil and criminal penalties and other ways and means of enforcement;

(8) To insure that any permit for a discharge from a publicly owned treatment works includes conditions to require adequate notice to the permitting agency of

(A) new introductions into such works of pollutants from any source which would be a new source as defined in section 1316 of this title if such source were discharging pollutants,

(B) new introductions of pollutants into such works from a source which would be subject to section 1311 of this title if it were discharging such pollutants, or

(C) a substantial change in volume or character of pollutants being introduced into such works by a source introducing pollutants into such works at the time of issuance of the permit.

Such notice shall include information on the quality and quantity of effluent to be introduced into such treatment works and any anticipated impact of such change in the quantity or quality of effluent to be discharged from such publicly owned treatment works; and

(9) To insure that any industrial user of any publicly owned treatment works will comply with sections 1284(b), 1317, and 1318 of this title. . . .

(j) Public information.

A copy of each permit application and each permit issued under this section shall be available to the public. Such permit application or permit, or portion thereof, shall further be available on request for the purpose of reproduction. . . .

§ 1343. Ocean discharge criteria.

(a) No permit under section 1342 of this title for a discharge into the territorial sea, the waters of the contiguous zone, or the oceans shall be issued, after promulgation of guidelines established under subsection (c) of this section, except in compliance with such guidelines. Prior to the promulgation of such guidelines, a permit may be issued under such section. . . .

§ 1344. Permits for dredged or fill material.

(a) The Secretary of the Army, acting through the Chief of Engineers, may issue permits, after notice and opportunity for public hearings for the discharge of dredged or fill material into the navigable waters at specified disposal sites.

(b) Subject to subsection (c) of this section, each such disposal site shall be specified for each such permit by the Secretary of the Army

(1) through the application of guidelines developed by the Administrator, in conjunction with the Secretary of the Army, which guidelines shall be based upon criteria comparable to the criteria applicable to the territorial seas, the contiguous zone, and the ocean under section 403(c) [33 USCS § 1343(c)], and

(2) in any case where such guidelines under clause (1) alone would prohibit the specification of a site, through the application additionally of the economic impact of the site on navigation and anchorage.

(c) The Administrator is authorized to prohibit the specification (in cluding the withdrawal of specification) of any defined area as a disposal site, and he is authorized to deny or restrict the use of any defined area for specification (including the withdrawal of specification) as a disposal site, whenever he determines, after notice and opportunity for public hearings, that the discharge of such materials into such area will have an unacceptable adverse effect on municipal water supplies, shellfish beds and fishery areas (including spawning and breeding areas), wildlife, or recreational areas. Before making such determination, the Administrator shall consult with the Secretary of the Army. The Administrator shall set forth in writing and make public his findings and his reasons for making any determination under this subsection.

§ 1362. Definitions.

Except as otherwise specifically provided, when used in this chapter:
. . .

(6) The term "pollutant" means dredged soil, solid waste, incinerator residue, sewage, garbage, sewage sludge, munitions, chemical wastes, biological materials, radioactive materials, heat, wrecked or discarded equipment, rock, sand, cellar dirt and industrial, municipal, and agricultural waste discharged into water. This term does not mean

(A) "sewage from vessels" within the meaning of section 1322 of this title; or

(B) water, gas, or other material which is injected into a well to facilitate production of oil or gas, or water derived in association with oil or gas production and disposed of in a well, if the well used either to facilitate production or for disposal purposes is approved by authority of the State in which the well is located, and if such State determines that such injection or disposal will not result in the degradation of ground or surface water resources.

(7) The term "navigable waters" means the waters of the United States, including the territorial seas. . . . .

(11) The term "effluent limitation" means any restriction established by a State or the Administrator on quantities, rates, and concentrations of chemical, physical, biological, and other constituents which are discharged from point sources into navigable waters, the waters of the contiguous zone, or the ocean, including schedules of compliance.

(12) The term "discharge of a pollutant" and the term "discharge of pollutants" each means
(A) any addition of any pollutant to navigable waters from any point source,
(B) any addition of any pollutant to the waters of the contiguous zone or the ocean from any point source other than a vessel or other floating craft.

(13) The term "toxic pollutant" means those pollutants, or combinations of pollutants, including disease-causing agents, which after discharge and upon exposure, ingestion, inhalation or assimilation into any organism, either directly from the environment or indirectly by ingestion through food chains, will, on the basis of information available to the Administrator, cause death, disease, behavioral abnormalities, cancer, genetic mutations, physiological malfunctions (including malfunctions in reproduction), or physical deformations, in such organisms or their offspring.

(14) The term "point source" means any discernible, confined and discrete conveyance, including but not limited to any pipe, ditch, channel, tunnel, conduit, well, discrete fissure, container, rolling stock, concentrated animal feeding operation, or vessel or other floating craft, from which pollutants are or may be discharged.

(15) The term "biological monitoring" shall mean the determination of the effects on aquatic life, including accumulation of pollutants in tissue, in receiving waters due to the discharge of pollutants
(A) by techniques and procedures, including sampling of organisms representative of appropriate levels of the food chain appropriate to the volume and the physical, chemical, and biological characteristics of the effluent, and
(B) at appropriate frequencies and locations.

(16) The term "discharge" when used without qualification includes a discharge of a pollutant, and a discharge of pollutants.

(17) The term "schedule of compliance" means a schedule of remedial measures including an enforceable sequence of actions or operations leading to compliance with an effluent limitation, other limitation, prohibition, or standard.

(18) The term "industrial user" means those industries identified in the Standard Industrial Classification Manual, Bureau of the Budget,

1967, as amended and supplemented, under the category of "Division D—Manufacturing" and such other classes of significant waste producers as, by regulation, the Administrator deems appropriate.

(19) The term "pollution" means the man-made or man-induced alteration of the chemical, physical, biological, and radiological integrity of water.

§ 1365. Citizen suits.

(a) Authorization; jurisdiction.

Except as provided in subsection (b) of this section, any citizen may commence a civil action on his own behalf—
   (1) against any person (including
      (i) the United States, and
      (ii) any other governmental instrumentality or agency to the extent permitted by the eleventh amendment to the Constitution) who is alleged to be in violation of
        (A) an effluent standard or limitation under this chapter or
        (B) an order issued by the Administrator or a State with respect to such a standard or limitation, or
   (2) against the Administrator where there is alleged a failure of the Administrator to perform any act or duty under this chapter which is not discretionary with the Administrator. . . .

(d) Litigation costs.

The court, in issuing any final order in any action brought pursuant to this section, may award costs of litigation (including reasonable attorney and expert witness fees) to any party, whenever the court determines such award is appropriate. The court may, if a temporary restraining order or preliminary injunction is sought, require the filing of a bond or equivalent security in accordance with the Federal Rules of Civil Procedure.

§ 1368. Federal procurement.

(a) Contracts with violators prohibited.

No Federal agency may enter into any contract with any person, who has been convicted of any offense under section 1319(c) of this title, for the procurement of goods, materials, and services if such contract is to be performed at any facility at which the violation which gave rise to such conviction occurred, and if such facility is owned, leased, or supervised by such person. The prohibition in the preceding sentence shall continue until the Administrator certifies that the condition giving rise to such conviction has been corrected. . . .

RIVERS AND HARBORS ACT (1899)
33 U.S.C. 403 et seq.

§ 403. Obstruction of navigable waters generally; wharves; piers, etc.; excavations and filling in.

The creation of any obstruction not affirmatively authorized by Congress, to the navigable capacity of any of the waters of the United States is prohibited; and it shall not be lawful to build or commence the building of any wharf, pier, dolphin, boom, weir, breakwater, bulkhead, jetty, or other structures in any port, roadstead, haven harbor, canal, navigable river, or other water of the United States, outside established harbor lines, or where no harbor lines have been established, except on plans recommended by the Chief of Engineers and authorized by the Secretary of the Army; and it shall not be lawful to excavate or fill, or in any manner to alter or modify the course, location, condition, or capacity of, any port, roadstead, haven, harbor, canal, lake, harbor of refuge, or inclosure within the limits of any breakwater, or of the channel of any navigable water of the United States, unless the work has been recommended by the Chief of Engineers and authorized by the Secretary of the Army prior to beginning the same.

§ 407. Deposit of refuse in navigable waters generally.

It shall not be lawful to throw, discharge, or deposit, or cause, suffer, or procure to be thrown, discharged, or deposited either from or out of any ship, barge, or other floating craft of any kind, or from the shore, wharf, manufacturing establishment, or mill of any kind, any refuse matter of any kind or description whatever other than that flowing from streets and sewers and passing therefrom in a liquid state, into any navigable water of the United States, or into any tributary of any navigable water from which the same shall float or be washed into such navigable water; and it shall not be lawful to deposit, or cause, suffer, or procure to be deposited material of any kind in any place on the bank of any navigable water, or on the bank of any tributary of any navigable water, where the same shall be liable to be washed into such navigable water, either by ordinary or high tides, or by storms or floods, or otherwise, whereby navigation shall or may be impeded or obstructed: Provided, That nothing herein contained shall extend to, apply to, or prohibit the operations in connection with the improvement of navigable waters or construction of public works, considered necessary and proper by the United States officers supervising such improvement or public work: And provided further, That the Secretary of the Army, whenever in the judgment of the Chief of Engineers anchorage and navigation will not be injured thereby,

may permit the deposit of any material above mentioned in navigable
waters, within limits to be defined and under conditions to be prescribed by him, provided application is made to him prior to depositing
such material; and whenever any permit is so granted the conditions
thereof shall be strictly complied with, and any violation thereof shall
be unlawful.

## FLOOD PROTECTION PROJECTS (1974)
## 33. U.S.C. 701b-11

§ 701b-11.  Flood protection projects—general considerations; non-
structural alternatives.

(a) In the survey, planning, or design by any Federal agency of any
project involving flood protection, consideration shall be given to non-
structural alternatives to prevent or reduce flood damages including,
but not limited to, floodproofing of structures; flood plain regulation;
acquisition of flood plain lands for recreational, fish and wildlife,
and other public purposes; and relocation with a view toward formulating the most economically, socially, and environmentally acceptable
means of reducing or preventing flood damages.

## STATES

## NORTH CAROLINA SEDIMENTATION POLLUTION
## CONTROL ACT (1973)
## Gen. Stat. N. Car. 113A-50 et seq.

§ 113A-51. Preamble.

The sedimentation of streams, lakes and other waters of this State constitutes a major pollution problem. Sedimentation occurs from the erosion or depositing of soil and other materials into the waters, principally from construction sites and road maintenance. The continued development of this State will result in an intensification of pollution through sedimentation unless timely and appropriate action is taken. Control of erosion and sedimentation is deemed vital to the public interest and necessary to the public health and welfare, and expenditures of funds for erosion and sedimentation control programs shall be deemed for a public purpose. It is the purpose of this act to provide for the creation, administration, and enforcement of a program and for the adoption of minimal mandatory standards which will permit development of this State to continue with the least detrimental effects from pollution by sedimentation.

§ 113A-52. Definitions.

As used in this act, unless the context otherwise requires:

(a) "Angle of repose for saturated soil conditions" means the angle of maximum slope at which a heap of any loose soil, thoroughly soaked with moisture, will stand without sliding. . . .

(f) "Land disturbing activity" means any use of the land by man in residential, industrial, or commercial development, and highway and road construction and maintenance that results in a change in the natural cover or topography and that may cause or contribute to sedimentation. This act shall not apply to the following land disturbing activities:

1. Those undertaken on agricultural land for the production of plants and animals useful to man, including but not limited to: forages and sod crops, grains and feed crops, tobacco, cotton, and peanuts; dairy animals and dairy products; poultry and poultry products; livestock, including beef cattle, sheep, swine, horses, ponies, mules or goats, including the breeding and grazing of any or all such animals; bees and apiary products; fur animals; and

2. Those undertaken on forest land for the production and harvesting of timber and timber products.

3. Activities undertaken by persons as defined in Section 3(h) who are otherwise regulated by the provisions of G.S. 74-46 through G.S. 74-68, The Mining Act of 1971. . . .

(j) "Sediment" means solid particulate matter, both mineral and organic, that has been moved from its site of origin and is in suspension in water.

§ 113A-54. Powers and duties of the Commission.

(a) The Commission shall, in consultation with the Secretary of the Department of Transportation and Highway Safety and other appropriate State and federal agencies, develop, promulgate, publicize, and administer a comprehensive State erosion and sedimentation control program. . . .

(c) The rules and regulations adopted pursuant to subdivision 5(b) for carrying out the erosion and sedimentation control program shall:

1. be based upon relevant physical and development information concerning the watershed and drainage basins of the State, including, but not limited to, data relating to land use, soils, hydrology, geology, grading, ground cover, size of land area being disturbed, proximate water bodies and their characteristics, transportation, and public facilities and services;

2. include such survey of lands and waters as may be deemed appropriate by the Commission or required by any applicable laws to identify those areas, including multi-jurisdictional and watershed areas, with critical erosion and sedimentation problems; and

3. contain conservation standards for various types of soils and land uses, which standards shall include criteria and alternative techniques and methods for the control of erosion and sediments resulting from land disturbing activities.

(d) In implementing the erosion and sedimentation control program, the Commission is authorized and directed to:

1. Assist and encourage local governments in developing erosion and sediment control programs and as part of such assistance to develop a model local erosion control ordinance, and approve, approve as modified, or disapprove local plans submitted to it pursuant to . . . this act;

2. Assist and encourage other State agencies in developing erosion and sedimentation control programs to be administered in their jurisdictions, and to approve, approve as modified, or disapprove such programs submitted . . . and from time to time review such programs for compliance with regulations issued by the Commission and for adequate enforcement; and to require at its discretion, submission of erosion control plans by those responsible for initiating land disturbing activities for approval prior to commencement of said activities;

3. Develop recommended methods of control of sedimentation and prepare and make availabl e for distribution publications and other materials dealing with sedimentation control techniques appropriate for use by persons engaged in land disturbing activities, general educational materials on erosion and sedimentation control, and instructional materials for persons involved in the enforcement of erosion control regulations, ordinances, and plans.

**§ 113A-57.** Mandatory standards for land disturbing activity.

No land disturbing activity subject to this act shall be undertaken except in accordance with the following mandatory requirements:

(1) No land disturbing activity shall be permitted in proximity to a lake or natural watercourse unless a buffer zone is provided along the margin of the watercourse of sufficient width to confine visible siltation withinthe twenty-five percent (25%) of the buffer zone nearer the land disturbing activity, provided that this subsection shall not apply to a land disturbing activity in connection with the construction of facilities to be located on, over, or under a lake or natural watercourse.

(2) No slope may be graded to an angle greater than the angle of repose for saturated soil conditions applicable for the type of soil involved; unless the soil on such slope is retained by some adequate erosion controlling structure or device. In any event, soil left exposed will, within 30 working days of completion of any phase of grading, be planted or otherwise provided with a groundcover sufficient to restrain erosion.

(3) Whenever land disturbing activity is undertaken on a tract comprising more than one acre, if more than one contiguous acre is uncovered, a groundcover sufficient to restrain erosion must be planted or otherwise provided within 30 working days on that portion of the tract upon which further active construction is not being undertaken, provided, that this subsection shall not apply to cleared land forming the basin of a reservoir later to be inundated.

FLORIDA AIR AND WATER POLLUTION CONTROL
ACT (1971, as amended)
Fla. Stat. Ch. 403

§ 403.021.   Legislative declaration; public policy.

(1) The pollution of the air and waters of this state constitutes a menace to public health and welfare, creates public nuisances, is harmful to wildlife, fish, and other aquatic life, and impairs domestic agricultural, industrial, recreational, and other beneficial uses of air and water.

(2) It is declared to be the public policy of this state to conserve the waters of the state and to protect, maintain, and improve the quality thereof for public water supplies, for the propagation of wildlife, fish and other aquatic life, and for domestic, agricultural, industrial, recreational, and other beneficial uses, and to provide that no wastes be discharged into any waters of the state without first being given the degree of treatment necessary to protect the beneficial uses of such water.

(3) It is declared to be the public policy of this state and the purpose of this act to achieve and maintain such levels or air quality as will protect human health and safety, and to the greatest degree practicable, prevent injury to plant and animal life and property, foster the comfort and convenience of the people, promote the economic and social development of this state and facilitate the enjoyment of the natural attractions of this state.

(4) It is declared that local and regional air and water pollution control programs are to be supported to the extent practicable as essential instruments to provide for a coordinated statewide program of air and water pollution prevention, abatement, and control for the securing and maintenance of appropriate levels of air and water quality.

(5) It is hereby declared that the prevention, abatement, and control of the pollution of the air and waters of this state are affected with a public interest, and the provisions of this act are enacted in the exercise of the police powers of this state for the purpose of protecting the health, peace, and safety, and general welfare of the people of this state.

(6) The legislature finds and declares that control, regulation, and abatement of the activities which are causing or may cause pollution of the air or water resources in the state and which are or may be detrimental to human, animal, aquatic, or plant life, or to property, or unreasonably interfere with the comfortable enjoyment of life or property be increased to insure conservation of natural resources, to insure a continued safe environment, to insure purity of air and water, to insure domestic water supplies, to insure protection and preservation of the public health, safety, welfare, and economic well-being, to insure and provide for recreational and wildlife needs as the population increases and the economy expands, to insure a continuing growth of the economy and industrial development.

(7) The legislature further finds and declares that:

(a) Compliance with this law will require capital outlays of hundreds of millions of dollars for the installation of machinery, equipment, and facilities for the treatment of industrial wastes which are not productive assets and increased operating expenses to owners without any financial return and should be separately classified for assessment purposes;

(b) Industry should be encouraged to install new machinery, equipment, and facilities as technology in environmental matters advances, thereby improving the quality of the air and waters of the state and benefiting the citizens of the state without pecuniary benefit to the owners of industries, and the legislature should prescribe methods whereby just valuation may be secured to such owners and exemptions from certain excise taxes should be offered with respect to such installations;

(c) Facilities as herein defined should be classified separately from other real and personal property of any manufacturing or processing plant or installation, as such facilities contribute only to general welfare and health and are assets producing no profit return to owners; and

(d) In existing manufacturing or processing plants it is more difficult to obtain satisfactory results in treating industrial wastes than in new plants being now planned or constructed and that with respect to existing plants in many instances it will be necessary to demolish and remove substantial portions thereof and replace the same with new and more modern equipment in order to more effectively treat, eliminate or reduce the objectional characteristics of any industrial wastes and that such replacements should be classified and assessed differently from replacements made in the ordinary course of business.

§ 403.031.  Definitions. . . .

(2) "Pollution" is the presence in the outdoor atmosphere or waters of the state of any substances, contaminants, noise, or man-made or man-induced alteration of the chemical, physical, biological, or radiological integrity of air or water in quantities or [at] levels which are or may be potentially harmful or injurious to human health or welfare, animal or plant life, or property, or unreasonably interfere with the enjoyment of life or property, including outdoor recreation.

(3) "Waters" shall include, but not be limited to rivers, lakes, streams, springs, impoundments, and all other waters or bodies of water, including fresh, brackish, saline, tidal, surface, or underground. Waters owned entirely by one person other than the state are included only in regard to possible discharge on other property or water. Underground waters include, but are not limited to, all underground waters passing through pores of rock or soils or flowing through in channels, whether man-made or natural.

§ 403.061.  Department; powers and duties.

The department shall have the power and the duty to control and prohibit pollution of air and water in accordance with the law and rules and regulations adopted and promulgated by it, and for this purpose to: . . .

(11) Adopt a comprehensive program for the prevention, control, and abatement of pollution of the air and waters of the state, and from time to time review and modify such program as necessary.

(12) In order to develop a comprehensive program for the prevention, abatement, and control of the pollution of the waters of the state, a grouping of the waters into classes may be made in accordance with the present and future most beneficial uses, such classifications may from time to time be altered or modified; provided, however, before any such classification is made, or any modifications made thereto, public hearings shall be held by the department.

(13) Establish ambient air quality and water quality standards for the state as a whole or for any part thereof, and also standards for the abatement of excessive and unnecessary noise. The department shall cooperate with the department of highway safety and motor vehicles in the development of regulations required by § 316.272(1).

(14)(a) Cause field studies to be made and samples to be taken out of the air and from the waters of the state periodically and in a logical geographic manner so as to determine the levels of air quality of the air and water quality of the waters of the state. . . .

(18) Require that notice be given to it prior to the undertaking of the construction or installation or expansion of any new air or water contaminant sources. Within thirty days of its receipt of such notice, the department shall require, as a condition precedent to the construction or installation or expansion of such sources, the submission of plans, specifications, and such other information as it deems necessary in order to determine whether the proposed construction or installation will be in accord with applicable laws, rules and regulations. If within sixty days of the receipt of plans, specifications, or other information required pursuant to this chapter, the department determines that the proposed construction or installation will not be in accord with the requirements of this act or applicable rules and regulations, it shall issue an order prohibiting the construction or installation. Failure of such an order to issue within the time prescribed herein shall be deemed a determination that the construction or installation may proceed; provided, that it is in accordance with plans, specifications, or other information, if any, required to be submitted. In regard to any application for a federal National Pollutant Discharge Elimination System (NPDES) permit, the department shall have 100 days to grant or deny the requested NPDES permit and associated state permit, if any. . . .

(22) Make a continuing study of the effects of the emission of air contaminants from motor vehicles on the quality of the outdoor atmosphere of this state and the several parts thereof, and make recommendations to appropriate public and private bodies with respect thereto. . . .

(26) Adopt rules and regulations to insure that no detergents are sold in Florida after December 31, 1972, which are reasonably found to have a harmful or deleterious effect on human health or on the environment. Any regulations adopted pursuant to this subsection shall apply statewide. Subsequent to the promulgation of such rules and regulations, no county, municipality, or other local political subdivision shall adopt or enforce any local ordinance, special law, or local regulation governing detergents which are less stringent than state law or regulation. Regulations, ordinances, or special acts adopted by a county or municipality governing detergents shall be subject to approval by the board of the department of pollution control, except that regulations, ordinances, or special acts adopted by any county or municipality with a local pollution control program approved pursuant to § 403.182 shall be approved as an element of the local pollution control program.

§ 403.085. Sanitary sewage disposal units; advanced and secondary waste treatment; industrial waste, ocean outfall, inland outfall or disposal well waste treatment.

(1) Neither the division of health of the department of health and re-
habilitative services nor any other state agency, county, special district, or municipality shall approve construction of any ocean outfall
or disposal well for sanitary sewage disposal which does not provide
for secondary waste treatment and, in addition thereto, advanced
waste treatment as deemed necessary and ordered by the department
of air and water pollution control.

(2) Sanitary sewage disposal treatment plants which discharge effluent
through ocean outfalls or disposal wells on July 1, 1970, shall provide
for secondary waste treatment and, in addition thereto, advanced waste
treatment as deemed necessary and ordered by the department of air
and water pollution control by January 3, 1974. Failure to conform by
said date shall be punishable by a fine of $500 for each twenty-four
hour day or fraction thereof that such failure is allowed to continue
thereafter.

(3) Neither the division of health of the department of health and re-
habilitative services nor any other state agency, county, special district, or municipality shall approve construction of any ocean outfall,
inland outfall, or disposal well for the discharge of industrial waste
of any kind which does not provide for secondary waste treatment or
such other treatment as is deemed necessary and ordered by the department of pollution control.

(4) Industrial plants or facilities which discharge industrial waste of
any kind through ocean outfalls, inland outfalls, or disposal wells on
July 1, 1971 shall provide for secondary waste treatment or such other
waste treatment as deemed necessary and ordered by January 1, 1973,
by the department of pollution control. Failure to conform by said
date shall be punishable as provided in § 403.161(2).

§ 403.086. Sewage disposal facilities; advanced and secondary waste
treatment.

(1)(a) Neither the division of health of the department of health and re-
habilitative services nor any other state agency, county, special district, or municipality shall approve construction of any facilities for
sanitary sewage disposal which do not provide for secondary waste
treatment and, in addition thereto, advanced waste treatment as
deemed necessary and ordered by the department of pollution control.
. . .

(2) Any facilities for sanitary sewage disposal existing on July 1, 1971
shall provide for secondary waste treatment by January 1, 1973, and,
in addition thereto, advanced waste treatment as deemed necessary
and ordered by the department of pollution control. Failure to conform
by said date shall be punishable by a civil penalty of $500 for each

twenty-four hour day or fraction thereof that such failure is allowed
to continue thereafter. . . .

§ 403.087. Permits; general issuance; denial; revocation; prohibition;
penalty.

(1) No stationary installation which will reasonably be expected to be
a source of air or water pollution shall be operated, maintained, constructed, expanded, or modified without an appropriate and currently
valid permit issued by the department, unless exempted by department
rule. In no event shall a permit for a water pollution source be valid
for more than five years. However, upon expiration, a new permit may
be issued by the department in accordance with this act and the rules
and regulations of the department. . . .

§ 403.088. Water pollution operation permits; temporary permits;
conditions.

(1) No person, without written authorization of the department, shall
discharge into waters within the state any waste which, by itself or in
combination with the wastes of other sources, reduces the quality of
the receiving waters below the classification established for them. . . .

(3)(a) Any person intending to discharge wastes into the waters of the
state shall make application to the department for an operation permit. . . .

 (c) If the department finds that the proposed discharge will reduce
the quality of the receiving waters below the classification established
for them, it shall deny the application and refuse to issue a permit.
If the department finds that the proposed discharge will not reduce
the quality of the receiving waters below the classification established
for them, it may issue an operation permit if it finds that such degradation is necessary or desirable under federal standards and under
circumstances which are clearly in the public interest.

 (d) A permit shall:
  1. Specify the manner, nature, volume, and frequency of the
discharge permitted;
  2. Require proper operation and maintenance of any pollution
abatement facility by qualified personnel in accordance with standards established by the department;
  3. Contain such additional conditions, requirements, and restrictions as the department deems necessary to preserve and
protect the quality of the receiving waters; and
  4. Be valid for the period of time specified therein.

 (e) An operation permit may be renewed upon application to the
department. No renewal permit shall be issued if the department
finds that the proposed discharge will reduce the quality of the receiving waters below the classification established for them.

(4)(a) A person who does not qualify for an operation permit or has
been denied an operation permit under paragraph (c) of subsection (3)
may apply to the department for a temporary operation permit. . . .

§ 403.091. Inspections.

Any duly authorized representative of the department may enter and
inspect any property, premises or place, except a building which is
used exclusively for a private residence, on or at which an air or
water contaminant source is located or is being constructed or installed
at any reasonable time for the purpose of ascertaining the state of compliance with the law, or rules and regulations of the department. . . .

§ 403.141. Civil liability; joint and several liability.

(1) Whoever commits a violation specified in § 403.161(1) is liable to
the state for any damage caused to the air, waters, or property, including animal, plant, or aquatic life, of the state and for reasonable
costs and expenses of the state in tracing the source of the discharge,
in controlling and abating the source and the pollutants, and in restoring the air, waters, and property, including animal, plant, and aquatic
life, of the state to their former condition, and furthermore is subject
to the judicial imposition of a civil penalty for each offense in an amount
of not more than $10,000 per offense. However, the court may receive
evidence in mitigation. Each day during any portion of which such
violation occurs constitutes a separate offense. Nothing herein shall
give the department the right to bring an action on behalf of any private
person. . . .

§ 403.161. Prohibitions, violation, penalty, intent.

(1) It shall be a violation of this chapter, and it shall be prohibited:
     (a) To cause pollution, except as otherwise provided in this chap-
ter, so as to harm or injure human health or welfare, animal, plant,
or aquatic life or property.
     (b) To fail to obtain any permit required by this chapter or by rule
or regulation, or to violate or fail to comply with any rule, regulation,
order, permit, or certification adopted or issued by the department
pursuant to its lawful authority.
     (c) To knowingly make any false statement, representation, or cer--
tification in any application, record, report, plan, or other document t
filed or required to be maintained under this chapter, or to falsify,
tamper with, or knowingly render inactive any monitoring device or
method required to be maintained under this chapter or by any permit, rule, regulation, or order issued under this chapter.

(2) Whoever commits a violation specified in subsection (1) is liable to the state for any damage caused and for civil penalties as provided in § 403.141.

(3) Any person who willfully or negligently commits a violation specified in subsections (1)(a) and (b) shall be guilty of a misdemeanor of the first degree punishable as provided in [§§ 775.082(4)(a) and 775.083(7)] by a fine of not less than $2,500 or more than $25,000. . . .

§ 403.165.   Use of pollution awards; pollution recovery fund.

(1) Any moneys recovered by the state in an action against any person who has polluted the air, soil, or water of the state in violation of this chapter shall be used to restore the polluted area which was the subject of suit to its former condition.

(2) There is hereby created a pollution recovery fund which is to be supervised and used by the department to restore polluted areas of the state, as defined by the department, to the condition they were in before pollution occurred.  The fund shall consist of all moneys specified in subsection (1). . . .

§ 403.182.   Local pollution control programs.

(1) Each county and municipality or any combination thereof may establish and administer a local pollution control program if it complies with this act.  Local pollution control programs in existence on the effective date of this act shall not be ousted of jurisdiction if such local program complies with this act.  All local pollution control programs, whether established before or after the effective date of this act, must:
   (a) Be approved by the department as adequate to meet the requirements of this act and any applicable rules and regulations pursuant thereto.
   (b) Provide by ordinance, regulation, or local law for requirements compatible with, or stricter or more extensive than those imposed by this act and regulations issued thereunder.
   (c) Provide for the enforcement of such requirements by appropriate administrative and judicial process.
   (d) Provide for administrative organization, staff, financial and other resources necessary to effectively and efficiently carry out its program. . . .

(3) If the department finds that the location, character or extent of particular concentrations of population, contaminant sources, the geographic, topographic or meteorological considerations, or any combinations thereof, are such as to make impracticable the maintenance of appropriate levels of air and water quality without an areawide pol-

lution control program, the department may determine the boundaries within which such program is necessary and require it as the only acceptable alternative to direct state administration. . . .

WYOMING ENVIRONMENTAL QUALITY ACT (1973)
35 Wyo. Stat. 502.1 et seq.

§ 35-502.18.  Prohibited acts.

(a) No person, except when authorized by a permit issued pursuant to the provisions of this act [§§ 35-502.1 to 35-502.56], shall:

(i) Cause, threaten or allow the discharge of any pollution or wastes into the waters of the state;

(ii) Alter the physical, chemical, radiological, biological or bacteriological properties of any waters of the state;

(iii) Construct, install, modify or operate any sewerage system, treatment works, disposal system or other facility, capable of causing or contributing to pollution;

(iv) Increase the quantity or strength of any discharge;

(v) Construct, install, modify or operate any public water supply.

§ 35-502.19.  Administrator's authority to recommend rules, regulations, etc.

(a) The administrator, after consultation with the advisory board, shall recommend to the director rules, regulations, standards and permit systems to promote the purposes of this act [§§ 35-502.1 to 35-502.56]. Such rules, regulations, standards and permit systems shall prescribe:

(i) Water quality standards specifying the maximum short-term and long-term concentrations of pollution, the minimum permissible concentrations of dissolved oxygen and other matter, and the permissible temperatures of the waters of the state;

(ii) Effluent standards and limitations specifying the maximum amounts or concentrations of pollution and wastes which may be discharged into the waters of the state;

(iii) Standards for the issuance of permits for construction, installation, modification or operation of any public water supply and sewerage system, treatment works, disposal system or other facility, capable of causing or contributing to pollution;

(iv) Standards for the definition of technical competency and the certification of operating personnel for public water supply and sewerage systems, treatment works and disposal systems and for determining that the operation shall be under the supervision of certified personnel;

(v) Standards for the issuance of permits as authorized pursuant to section 1342(b) of the Federal Water Pollution Control Act as amended in 1972, and as may be hereafter amended;

(vi) In recommending any standards, rules, regulations, or permits, the administrator and advisory board shall consider all the facts and circumstances bearing on the reasonableness of the pollution involved including:

(A) The character and degree of injury to or interference with the health and well-being of the people, animals, wildlife, aquatic life and plant life affected;

(B) The social and economic value of the source of pollution;

(C) The priority of location in the area involved;

(D) The technical practicability and economic reasonableness of reducing or eliminating the source of pollution; and

(E) The effect upon the environment;

(vii) Such reasonable time as may be necessary for owners and operators of pollution sources to comply with rules, regulations, standards or permits.

INDIANA CONFINED FEEDING CONTROL LAW (1971)
13 Ind. Stat. Ann. 1-5.7-1 et seq.

§ 13-1-5.7-1 [16-2701]. Definitions.— . . .

(c) The term "confined feeding" means the confined feeding of animals for food, fur or pleasure purposes in lots, pens, ponds, sheds, or buildings where food is supplied to the animals only by means other than grazing.

(d) The term "confined feeding operation" means

(1) any confined feeding of three hundred [300] or more cattle, six hundred [600] or more swine or sheep and thirty thousand [30,000] or more fowl; or

(2) any animal feeding operation electing to come under this chapter; or

(3) any animal feeding operation that is causing a violation of IC 1971, 13-1-3 [13-1-3-1—13-1-3-18] or any regulations of the board.

§ 13-1-5.7-2 [16-2702]. Application for board approval required.

(a) On and after the effective date of this law [April 2, 1971], no person shall start construction of a confined feeding operation without obtaining the prior approval of the board.

(b) All confined feeding operations existing prior to, and all confined feeding operations in the state of construction prior to the effective date of this chapter shall submit an application and pertinent information as may be required by the board as outlined in IC 1971, 13-1-5.7-5 [13-1-5.7-3], on or before July 1, 1973; Provided, however, That nothing in this section shall prohibit the board from holding hearings and taking action.

§ 13-1-5.7-3 [16-2703]. Plans and specifications for waste treatment and control facilities submitted with application.

(a) Application for approval shall be made on a form provided by the board. Applicants shall submit the completed application form to the board together with plans for waste treatment and control facilities and supplemental information as the board may require, regarding, but not limited to, general features of topography, soil types, drainage course, and identification of nearest receiving stream.

(b) Plans and specifications for waste treatment and/or control facilities for a confined feeding operation must secure the approval of the board. The board shall give its approval to construct or operate the confined feeding operation if the water pollution control proposal is satisfactory.

§ 13-1-5.7-4 [16-2704]. Disallowing continued operation because of certain violations.

The board may disallow continued operation by any operator following a hearing before the board or designated member of the board when it is found that the confined feeding operation is causing a violation of IC 1971, 13-1-3 [13-1-3-1--13-1-3-18] and any regulations of the board. . . .

MICHIGAN WATERCRAFT POLLUTION CONTROL ACT
(1970, as amended)
Mich. Comp. Laws 323.331 et seq.

§ 323.333.  Litter, sewage, oil, garbage, or other materials render-
ing water unsightly, noxious, or unwholesome; prohibition.

Sec. 3.

(1) A person shall not place, throw, deposit, discharge or cause to be
discharged into or onto the waters of this state, any litter, sewage,
oil or other liquid or solid materials which render the water unsightly,
noxious or otherwise unwholesome so as to be detrimental to the public health or welfare or to the enjoyment of the water for recreational
purposes.

(2) It is unlawful to discharge, dump, throw or deposit garbage, litter,
sewage or oil from a recreational, domestic or foreign watercraft
used for pleasure or for the purpose of carrying passengers, cargo
or otherwise engaged in commerce on the waters of this state.

§ 323.334.  Watercraft, moored or registered in another jurisdiction,
pollution control device approved by other jurisdiction; marine toilets,
requirements.

Sec. 4.

(1) Any pleasure or recreational watercraft operated on the waters of this state which is moored or registered in another state or jurisdiction, if equipped with a pollution control device approved by that jurisdiction, may be approved by the commission to operate on the waters of this state.

(2) A person owning, operating or otherwise concerned in the operation, navigation or management of a watercraft having a marine toilet shall not own, use or permit the use of such toilet on the waters of this state unless the toilet is equipped with 1 of the following pollution control devices:

(a) A holding tank or self-contained marine toilet which will retain all sewage produced on the watercraft for subsequent disposal at approved dockside or onshore collection and treatment facilities.

(b) An incinerating device which will reduce to ash all sewage produced on the watercraft. The ash shall be disposed of onshore in a manner which will preclude pollution.

§ 323.335. Pump-out facilities for marine toilet holding tanks.

Sec. 5.

All public, private, and commercial marinas, yacht clubs, docks, and wharves used for mooring, serving, or otherwise handling watercraft of the size capable of being equipped with marine toilet facilities, shall provide pump-out facilities approved by the department of public health for marine toilet holding tanks on the watercraft. An installation that would otherwise be required by this section to have pump-out facilities, is not required to have those facilities if it has a contract to use, and does use, the pump-out facilities of an adjacent installation. The contract must be approved by the department of natural resources.

§ 323.337. Oil or oily wastes, discharge, prohibition; removal; duty; cost of removal by state, persons liable, actions.

Sec. 7.

(1) A person owning, operating or otherwise concerned in the operation, navigation or management of a watercraft operating on the waters of this state shall not discharge or permit the discharge of oil or oily wastes from the watercraft into or onto the waters of this state if the oil or oily wastes threaten to pollute or contribute to the pollution of the waters or adjoining shorelines or beaches.

(2) The owner or operator of any watercraft who, whether directly or through any person concerned in the operation, navigation or manage-

ment of the watercraft, discharges or permits or causes or contributes
to the discharge of oil or oily wastes into or onto the waters of this
state or adjoining shorelines or beaches shall immediately remove
the oil or oily wastes from the waters, shorelines or beaches. If the
state removes the oil or oily wastes which were discharged by an owner
or operator, the watercraft and the owner or operator are liable to
the state for the full amount of the costs reasonably incurred for its
removal. The state may bring action against the owner or operator
to recover such costs in any court of competent jurisdiction.

Endangered and threatened species of wildlife are protected in sanctuaries, by closed seasons, and by restrictions on trade in products derived from them. Chapter 6 should be consulted for legislation setting aside land for wildlife refuges and Chapter 11 for pesticide legislation, in part enacted because of its damaging effect on wildlife.

The Endangered Species Act of 1973 (p. 508) prohibits trade in designated species or parts thereof, including plants, and offers emphatic habitat protection in Section 1536. Congressional acts affording protection to specific species include the Marine Mammal Protection (p. 515) and Bald and Golden Eagle Protection Act (p. 518). Other acts enforce the Convention on the Conservation of North Pacific Fur Seals of 1957 (16 U.S.C. 1151 et seq.), protect Wild Horses and Burros from capture and killing (16 U.S.C. 1331 et seq.), prohibit commerce in black bass and other fish taken in violation of laws of a state or foreign country (16 U.S.C. 851 et seq.), and prohibit importation of specified animals injurious to humans, domestic animals, or wildlife (18 U.S.C. 42).

The Fish and Wildlife Service enforces the nation's wildlife laws, including that prohibiting hunting from airplanes (p. 519). The Migratory Bird Treaty Act (p. 520) enforces obligations of treaties with Canada and Mexico. Wildlife protection is a mandated consideration of all federal water resource projects (p. 522).

Corps of Engineers rivers and harbors projects "shall include a due regard for wildlife conservation" (33 U.S.C. 540). Action "for the improvement of feeding and spawning conditions, for the protection of fishery resources, and for facilitating the free migration of the fish" in connection with water resources developments is authorized by the Anadromous and Great Lakes Fisheries Act of 1965,

as amended (16 U.S.C. 757a et seq.). Fishways must be provided
at power projects licensed by the Federal Power Commission (16
U.S.C. 811) and at river and harbor projects (33 U.S.C. 680). Fish
and wildlife conservation is authorized on military reservations (16
U.S.C. 670a).

The Coastal Zone Management Act encourages the establishment
of estuarine sanctuaries (Sec. 1461). National forests are to be "administered . . . for fish and wildlife purposes" along with others
(16 U.S.C. 528). The Ocean Dumping Act requires consideration of
effects of dumping on "fisheries resources, plankton, fish, shellfish,
wildlife" and "marine ecosystems" before permits may be granted
(Sec. 1412[a][C] and [D]). Fisheries protection is also a purpose
of many other laws concerning oceans, as well as of scenic river and
wetlands laws.

"Special effort" to preserve "wildlife and waterfowl refuges"
is required in the construction of federal-aid highways (23 U.S.C.
138) and other federal transportation projects (49 U.S.C. 1651[b][2]
1653[f], 1610[a]). Effect of airport development projects on fish
and wildlife must be determined before authorization and a finding
made that no "feasible and prudent alternative" exists (49 U.S.C.
1716[c][4]). Off-road vehicle trails on public lands "shall be located
to minimize harassment of wildlife or significant disruption of wildlife habitats" (Exec. Order 11644, Sec. 3[2]).

State endangered species protection may extend to species not
protected by federal law, as in New York (p. 523).

In Utah "no person shall operate a recreation vehicle in connection with . . . harassment of wildlife" (Sec. 41-22-13), and in Michigan "a snowmobile shall not be used to hunt, pursue, worry or kill a
wild bird or animal" (Sec. 257.1512b).

"Minimum adverse environmental impact" on fish and wildlife
are among the standards to be met by power plants seeking licensing
in New York (Sec. 146). "Destruction of . . . flora and fauna" are a
consideration in granting industrial permits in Delaware's Coastal
Zone (Sec. 7004[b][1]).

FEDERAL

ENDANGERED SPECIES ACT (1973)
16 U.S.C. 1531 et seq.

Section 1531. Congressional findings and declaration of purposes and
policy
1532. Definitions
1533. Determination of endangered species and threatened
species

§ 1531.  Congressional findings and declaration of purposes and policy.

The Congress finds and declares that—

(1) various species of fish, wildlife, and plants in the United States have been rendered extinct as a consequence of economic growth and development untempered by adequate concern and conservation;

(2) other species of fish, wildlife, and plants have been so depleted in numbers that they are in danger of or threatened with extinction;

(3) these species of fish, wildlife, and plants are of esthetic, ecological, educational, historical, recreational, and scientific value to the Nation and its people;

(4) the United States has pledged itself as a sovereign state in the international community to conserve to the extent practicable the various species of fish or wildlife and plants facing extinction, pursuant to—

(A) migratory bird treaties with Canada and Mexico;

(B) the Migratory and Endangered Bird Treaty with Japan;

(C) the Convention on Nature Protection and Wildlife Preservation in the Western Hemisphere;

(D) the International Convention for the Northwest Atlantic Fisheries;

(E) the International Convention for the High Seas Fisheries of the North Pacific Ocean;

(F) the Convention on International Trade in Endangered Species of Wild Fauna and Flora; and

(G) other international agreements.

(5) encouraging the States and other interested parties, through Federal financial assistance and a system of incentives, to develop and maintain conservation programs which meet national and international standards is a key to meeting the Nation's international commitments and to better safeguarding, for the benefit of all citizens, the Nation's heritage in fish and wildlife.

(b) The purposes of this chapter are to provide a means whereby the ecosystems upon which endangered species and threatened species depend may be conserved, to provide a program for the conservation of such endangered species and threatened species, and to take such steps as may be appropriate to achieve the purposes of the treaties and conventions set forth in subsection (a) of this section.

(c) It is further declared to be the policy of Congress that all Federal departments and agencies shall seek to conserve endangered species and threatened species and shall utilize their authorities in furtherance of the purposes of this chapter.

§ 1532. Definitions.

For the purposes of this chapter— . . .

(4) The term "endangered species" means any species which is in danger of extinction throughout all or a significant portion of its range other than a species of the Class Insecta determined by the Secretary to constitute a pest whose protection under the provisions of this chapter would present an overwhelming and overriding risk to man.

(5) The term "fish or wildlife" means any member of the animal kingdom, including without limitation any mammal, fish, bird (including any migratory, nonmigratory, or endangered bird for which protection is also afforded by treaty or other international agreement), amphibian, reptile, mollusk, crustacean, arthropod or other invertebrate, and includes any part, product, egg, or offspring thereof, or the dead body or parts thereof. . . .

(9) The term "plant" means any member of the plant kingdom, including seeds, roots and other parts thereof. . . .

(14) The term "take" means to harass, harm  pursue, hunt, shoot, wound, kill, trap, capture, or collect, or to attempt to engage in any such conduct.

(15) The term "threatened species" means any species which is likely to become an endangered species within the foreseeable future throughout all or a significant portion of its range.

§ 1533. Determination of endangered species and threatened species —generally.

(a)(1) The Secretary shall by regulation determine whether any species is an endangered species or a threatened species because of any of the following factors:

(1) the present or threatened destruction, modification, or curtailment of its habitat or range;

(2) overutilization for commercial, sporting, scientific, or educational purposes;

(3) disease or predation;

(4) the inadequacy of existing regulatory mechanisms; or

(5) other natural or man-made factors affecting its continued existence; . . .

(b)(1) The Secretary shall make determinations required by subsection (a) of this section on the basis of the best scientific and commercial data available to him and after consultation, as appropriate, with the affected States, interested persons and organizations, other interested Federal agencies, and, in cooperation with the Secretary of State, with the country or countries in which the species concerned is normally found or whose citizens harvest such species on the high seas. . . .

(e) The Secretary may, by regulation, and to the extent he deems advisable, treat any species as an endangered species or threatened species even though it is not listed pursuant to this section if he finds that—

(A) such species so closely resembles in appearance, at the point in question, a species which has been listed pursuant to such section that enforcement personnel would have substantial difficulty in attempting to differentiate between the listed and unlisted species;

(B) the effect of this substantial difficulty is an additional threat to an endangered or threatened species; and

(C) such treatment of an unlisted species will substantially facilitate the enforcement and further the policy of this chapter.

§ 1534. Land acquisition.

(a) The Secretary of the Interior shall establish and implement a program to conserve

(A) fish or wildlife which are listed as endangered species or threatened species pursuant to section 1533 of this title; or

(B) plants which are concluded in Appendices to the Convention. To carry out such program, he—

(1) shall utilize the land acquisition and other authority under the Fish and Wildlife Act of 1956, as amended, the Fish and Wildlife Coordination Act, as amended, and the Migratory Bird Conservation Act, as appropriate; and

(2) is authorized to acquire by purchase, donation, or otherwise, lands, waters, or interest therein, and such authority shall be in addition to any other land acquisition authority vested in him. . . .

§ 1536.  Interagency cooperation.

The Secretary shall review other programs administered by him and
utilize such programs in furtherance of the purposes of this chapter.
All other Federal departments and agencies shall, in consultation
with and with the assistance of the Secretary, utilize their authorities
in furtherance of the purposes of this chapter by carrying out programs for the conservation of endangered species and threatened
species listed pursuant to section 1533 of this title and by taking such
action necessary to insure that actions authorized, funded, or carried
out by them do not jeopardize the continued existence of such endangered species and threatened species or result in the destruction or
modification of habitat of such species which is determined by the Secretary, after consultation as appropriate with the affected States, to
be critical.

§ 1538.  Prohibited acts—generally.

(a)(1) Except as provided in sections 1535(g)(2) and 1539 of this title
with respect to any endangered species of fish or wildlife listed pursuant to section 1533 of this title it is unlawful for any person subject
to the jurisdiction of the United States to—
 (A) import any such species into, or export any such species
from, the United States;
 (B) take any such species within the United States or the territorial sea of the United States;
 (C) take any such species upon the high seas;
 (D) possess, sell, deliver, carry, transport, or ship, by any
means whatsoever, any such species taken in violation of subpara-
graphs (B) and (C);
 (E) deliver, receive, carry, transport, or ship in interstate or
foreign commerce, by any means whatsoever and in the course of
a commercial activity, any such species;
 (F) sell or offer for sale in interstate or foreign commerce any
such species; or
 (G) violate any regulation pertaining to such species or to any
threatened species of fish or wildlife listed pursuant to section
1533 of this title and promulgated by the Secretary pursuant to
authority provided by this chapter.
(2) Except as provided in sections 1535(g)(2) and 1539 of this title,
with respect to any endangered species of plants listed pursuant to
section 1533 of this title, it is unlawful for any person subject to the
jurisdiction of the United States to—
 (A) import any such species into, or export any such species
from, the United States;

(B) deliver, receive, carry, transport, or ship in interstate or foreign commerce, by any means whatsoever and in the course of a commercial activity, any such species;

(C) sell or offer for sale in interstate or foreign commerce any such species; or

(D) violate any regulation pertaining to such species or to any threatened species of plants listed pursuant to section 1533 of this title and promulgated by the Secretary pursuant to authority provided by this chapter. . . .

(c)(1) It is unlawful for any person subject to the jurisdiction of the United States to engage in any trade in any specimens contrary to the provisions of the Convention, or to possess any specimens traded contrary to the provisions of the Convention, including the definitions of terms in article I thereof. . . .

(d)(1) It is unlawful for any person to engage in business as an importer or exporter of fish or wildlife (other than shellfish and fishery products which

(A) are not listed pursuant to section 1533 of this title as endangered species or threatened species, and

(B) are imported for purposes of human or animal consumption or taken in waters under the jurisdiction of the United States or on the high seas for recreational purposes) or plants without first having obtained permission from the Secretary. . . .

§ 1539.  Exceptions—permits.

(a) The Secretary may permit, under such terms and conditions as he may prescribe, any act otherwise prohibited by section 1538 of this title for scientific purposes or to enhance the propagation or survival of the affected species. . . .

(e)(1) Except as provided in paragraph (4) of this subsection the provisions of this chapter shall not apply with respect to the taking of any endangered species or threatened species, or the importation of any such species taken pursuant to this section, by

(A) any Indian, Aleut, or Eskimo who is an Alaskan Native who resides in Alaska; or

(B) any non-native permanent resident of an Alaskan native village;

if such taking is primarily for subsistence purposes. . . .

(4) Notwithstanding the provisions of paragraph (1) of this subsection, whenever the Secretary determines that any species of fish or wildlife which is subject to taking under the provisions of this subsection is an endangered species or threatened species, and that such taking materially and negatively affects the threatened or endangered

species, he may prescribe regulations upon the taking of such species by any such Indian, Aleut, Eskimo, or non-Native Alaskan resident of an Alaskan native village. . . .

§ 1540.  Penalties and enforcement—civil penalties.

(a)(1) Any person who knowingly violates, or who knowingly commits an act in the course of a commercial activity which violates, any provision of this chapter, or any provision of any permit or certificate issued hereunder, . . . may be assessed a civil penalty by the Secretary of not more than $10,000 for each violation.  Any person who knowingly violates, or who knowingly commits an act in the course of a commercial activity which violates, any provision of any other regulation issued under this chapter may be assessed a civil penalty by the Secretary of not more than $5,000 for each such violation. . . .

(b)(1) Any person who willfully commits an act which violates any provision of this chapter . . . shall, upon conviction, be fined not more than $20,000 or imprisoned for not more than one year, or both. Any person who willfully commits an act which violates any provision of any other regulation issued under this chapter shall, upon conviction, be fined not more than $10,000 or imprisoned for not more than six months, or both. . . .

(d) Upon the recommendation of the Secretary, the Secretary of the Treasury is authorized to pay an amount equal to one-half of the civil penalty or fine paid, but not to exceed $2,500, to any person who furnishes information which leads to a finding of civil violation or a conviction of a criminal violation of any provision of this chapter or any regulation or permit issued thereunder.  Any officer or employee of the United States or of any State or local government who furnishes information or renders service in the performance of his official duties shall not be eligible for payment under this section. . . .

(g)(1) Except as provided in paragraph (2) of this subsection any person may commence a civil suit on his own behalf
    (A) to enjoin any person, including the United States and any other governmental instrumentality or agency (to the extent permitted by the eleventh amendment to the Constitution), who is alleged to be in violation of any provision of this chapter or regulation issued under the authority thereof; or
    (B) to compel the Secretary to apply, pursuant to section 1535(g)(2)(B)(ii) of this title, the prohibitions set forth in or authorized pursuant to section 1533(d) or 1538(a)(1)(B) of this title with respect to the taking of any resident endangered species or threatened species within any State. . . .

§ 1541.  Endangered plants.

The Secretary of the Smithsonian Institution, in conjunction with
other affected agencies, is authorized and directed to review

(1) species of plants which are now or may become endangered or
threatened and

(2) methods of adequately conserving such species, and to report
to Congress, within one year after December 28, 1973, the results
of such review including recommendations for new legislation or the
amendment of existing legislation.

§ 1543.  Construction with Marine Mammal Protection Act of 1972.

Except as otherwise provided in this chapter, no provision of this
chapter shall take precedence over any more restrictive conflicting
provision of the Marine Mammal Protection Act of 1972.

MARINE MAMMAL PROTECTION ACT (1972)
16 U.S.C. 1361 et seq.

§ 1361.  Congressional findings and declaration of policy.

The Congress finds that—

(1) certain species and population stocks of marine mammals are,
or may be, in danger of extinction or depletion as a result of man's
activities;

(2) such species and population stocks should not be permitted to diminish beyond the point at which they cease to be a significant functioning element in the ecosystem of which they are a part, and, consistent with this major objective, they should not be permitted to diminish below their optimum sustainable population. Further measures should be immediately taken to replenish any species or population stock which has already diminished below that population. In particular, efforts should be made to protect the rookeries, mating grounds, and areas of similar significance for each species of marine mammal from the adverse effect of man's actions;

(3) there is inadequate knowledge of the ecology and population dynamics of such marine mammals and of the factors which bear upon their ability to reproduce themselves successfully;

(4) negotiations should be undertaken immediately to encourage the development of international arrangements for research on, and conservation of, all marine mammals; . . .

(6) marine mammals have proven themselves to be resources of great international significance, esthetic and recreational as well as economic, and it is the sense of the Congress that they should be protected and encouraged to develop to the greatest extent feasible commensurate with sound policies of resource management and that the primary objective of their management should be to maintain the health and stability of the marine ecosystem. Whenever consistent with this primary objective, it should be the goal to obtain an optimum sustainable population keeping in mind the optimum carrying capacity of the habitat.

§ 1371. Moratorium on taking and importing marine mammals and marine mammal products.

(a) Imposition; exceptions.

There shall be a moratorium on the taking and importation of marine mammals and marine mammal products, commencing on the effective date of this Act, during which time no permit may be issued for the taking of any marine mammal and no marine mammal or marine mammal product may be imported into the United States except in the following cases: . . .

§ 1372. Prohibitions.

(a) Taking.

Except as provided in sections 1371, 1373, 1374, 1381, and 1388 of this title, it is unlawful—

(1) for any person subject to the jurisdiction of the United States or any vessel or other conveyance subject to the jurisdiction of the United States to take any marine mammal on the high seas;

(2) except as expressly provided for by an international treaty, convention, or agreement to which the United States is a party and which was entered into before the effective date of this subchapter or by any statute implementing any such treaty, convention, or agreement—

(A) for any person or vessel or other conveyance to take any marine mammal in waters or on lands under the jurisdiction of the United States; or

(B) for any person to use any port, harbor, or other place under the jurisdiction of the United States for any purpose in any way connected with the taking or importation of marine mammals or marine mammal products; and

(3) for any person, with respect to any marine mammal taken in violation of this subchapter—

(A) to possess any such mammal; or

(B) to transport, sell, or offer for sale any such mammal or any marine mammal product made from any such mammal; and

(4) for any person to use, in a commercial fishery, any means or methods of fishing in contravention of any regulations or limitations, issued by the Secretary for that fishery to achieve the purposes of this chapter.

(b) Importation of pregnant or nursing mammals; depleted species or stock; inhumane taking.

Except pursuant to a permit for scientific research issued under section 1374(c) of this title, it is unlawful to import into the United States any marine mammal if such mammal was—

(1) pregnant at the time of taking;

(2) nursing at the time of taking, or less than eight months old, whichever occurs later;

(3) taken from a species or population stock which the Secretary has, by regulation published in the Federal Register, designated as a depleted species or stock or which has been listed as endangered under the Endangered Species Conservation Act of 1969; or

(4) taken in a manner deemed inhumane by the Secretary.

(c) Importation of illegally taken mammals.

It is unlawful to import into the United States any of the following:

(1) Any marine mammal which was—

(A) taken in violation of this subchapter; or

(B) taken in another country in violation of the law of that country;

(2) Any marine mammal product if—

(A) the importation into the United States of the marine mammal from which such product is made is unlawful under paragraph (1) of this subsection; or

(B) the sale in commerce of such product in the country of origin
of the product is illegal;

(3) Any fish, whether fresh, frozen, or otherwise prepared, if
such fish was caught in a manner which the Secretary has prescribed
for persons subject to the jurisdiction of the United States, whether
or not any marine mammals were in fact taken incident to the catching
of the fish.

## § 1374. Permits.

(a) Issuance.

The Secretary may issue permits which authorize the taking or importation of any marine mammal.

PROTECTION OF BALD AND GOLDEN EAGLES
(1940, as amended)
16 U.S.C. 668 et seq.

Section 668.   Bald and golden eagles
    668a.   Same; taking and using for scientific, exhibition and
           religious purposes
    668b.   Same; enforcement
    668c.   Same; definitions
    668d.   Same; availability of appropriations for Migratory
    Bird Treaty Act

## § 668. Bald and golden eagles.

(a) Prohibited acts; criminal penalties.

Whoever, within the United States or any place subject to the jurisdiction thereof, without being permitted to do so as provided in sections 668 to 668d of this title, shall knowingly, or with wanton disre-
gard for the consequences of his act take, possess, sell, purchase,
barter, offer to sell, purchase or barter, transport, export or import, at any time or in any manner any bald eagle commonly known
as the American eagle or any golden eagle, alive or dead, or any
part, nest, or egg thereof of the foregoing eagles, or whoever violates any permit or regulation issued pursuant to sections 668 to 668d
of this title, shall be fined not more than $5,000 or imprisoned not
more than one year or both. . . .

(c) Cancellation of grazing agreements.

The head of any Federal agency who has issued a lease, license,
permit, or other agreement authorizing the grazing of domestic livestock on Federal lands to any person who is convicted of a violation

of sections 668 to 668d of this title or of any permit or regulation
issued hereunder may immediately cancel each such lease, license,
permit, or other agreement. The United States shall not be liable for
the payment of any compensation, reimbursement, or damages in connection with the cancellation of any lease, license, permit, or other
agreement pursuant to this section.

FISH AND WILDLIFE SERVICE (1956, as amended)
16 U.S.C. 742a et seq.

## § 742a. Declaration of policy.

The Congress declares that the fish, shellfish, and wildlife resources
of the Nation make a material contribution to our national economy
and food supply, as well as a material contribution to the health, recreation, and well-being of our citizens; that such resources are a living,
renewable form of national wealth that is capable of being maintained
and greatly increased with proper management, but equally capable
of destruction if neglected or unwisely exploited; that such resources
afford outdoor recreation throughout the Nation and provide employment, directly or indirectly, to a substantial number of citizens; that
the fishing industries strengthen the defense of the United States
through the provision of a trained seafaring citizenry and action-ready
fleets of seaworthy vessels; that the training and sport afforded by
fish and wildlife resources strengthen the national defense by contributing to the general health and physical fitness of millions of citizens; and that properly developed, such fish and wildlife resources
are capable of steadily increasing these valuable contributions to the
life of the Nation. . . .

## § 742j-1. Airborne hunting.

(a) Prohibition; penalty.

Any person who—
   (1) while airborne in an aircraft shoots or attempts to shoot for
the purpose of capturing or killing any bird, fish, or other animal;
or
   (2) uses an aircraft to harass any bird, fish, or other animal; or
   (3) knowingly participates in using an aircraft for any purpose referred to in paragraph (1) or (2);
shall be fined not more than $5,000 or imprisoned not more than one
year, or both.

(b) Exception; report of State to Secretary.
   (1) This section shall not apply to any person if such person is
employed by, or is an authorized agent of or is operating under a

license or permit of, any State or the United States to administer or
protect or aid in the administration or protection of land, water,
wildlife, livestock, domesticated animals, human life, or crops, and
each such person so operating under a license or permit shall report
to the applicable issuing authority each calendar quarter the number
and type of animals so taken. . . .

MIGRATORY BIRD TREATY ACT
(1918, as amended)
16 U.S.C. 703 et seq.

§ 703.  Taking, killing, or possessing migratory birds unlawful.

Unless and except as permitted by regulations made as hereinafter
provided in sections 703 to 711 of this title, it shall be unlawful at
any time, by any means or in any manner, to pursue, hunt, take,
capture, kill, attempt to take, capture, or kill, possess, offer for
sale, sell, offer to barter, barter, offer to purchase, purchase,
deliver for shipment, ship export, import, cause to be shipped, ex-
ported, or imported, deliver for transportation, transport or cause
to be transported, carry or cause to be carried, or receive for shipment, transportation, carriage, or export, any migratory bird, or
any part, nest, or egg of any such birds, included in the terms of the
conventions between the United States and Great Britain for the protection of migratory birds concluded August 16, 1916 (39 Stat. 1702),
and the United States and the United Mexican States for the protection
of migratory birds and game mammals concluded February 7, 1936.

§ 704. Determination as to when and how migratory birds may be taken, killed, or possessed.

Subject to the provisions and in order to carry out the purposes of the conventions, referred to in section 703 of this title, the Secretary of the Interior is authorized and directed, from time to time, having due regard to the zones of temperature and to the distribution, abundance, economic value, breeding habits, and times and lines of migratory flight of such birds, to determine when, to what extent, if at all, and by what means, it is compatible with the terms of the conventions to allow hunting, taking, capture, killing, possession, sale, purchase, shipment, transportation, carriage, or export of any such bird, or any part, nest, or egg thereof, and to adopt suitable regulations permitting and governing the same, in accordance with such determinations, which regulations shall become effective when approved by the President.

§ 715a. Migratory Bird Conservation Commission; creation; composition; duties; approval of areas of land and water recommended for purchase or rental.

A commission to be known as the Migratory Bird Conservation Commission, consisting of the Secretary of the Interior, as chairman, the Secretary of Transportation, the Secretary of Agriculture and two Members of the Senate, to be selected by the President of the Senate, and two Members of the House of Representatives to be selected by the Speaker, is created and authorized to consider and pass upon any area of land, water, or land and water that may be recommended by the Secretary of the Interior for purchase or rental under sections 715 to 715d, 715e, 715f to 715k and 715l to 715r of this title, and to fix the price or prices at which such area may be purchased or rented. . . .

§ 715d. Purchase or rental of approved areas; gifts and devises; United States lands.

The Secretary of the Interior is authorized to purchase or rent such areas as have been approved for purchase or rental by the commission, at the price or prices fixed by said commission, and to acquire by gift or devise, for use as inviolate sanctuaries for migratory birds, areas which he shall determine to be suitable for such purposes, and to pay the purchase or rental price and expenses incident to the location, examination, and survey of such areas and the acquisition of title thereto, including options when deemed necessary by the Secretary of the Interior from moneys to be appropriated hereunder by Congress from time to time: . . .

PROTECTION AND CONSERVATION OF WILDLIFE
(1934, as amended)
16 U.S.C. 661 et seq.

Section 661.    Declaration of purpose
       662.    Impounding, diverting, or controlling of waters

§ 662. Impounding, diverting, or controlling of waters—consultations
between agencies.

(a) Except as hereafter stated in subsection (h) of this section, whenever the waters of any stream or other body of water are proposed
or authorized to be impounded, diverted, the channel deepened, or
the stream or other body of water otherwise controlled or modified
for any purpose whatever, including navigation and drainage, by any
department or agency of the United States, or by any public or private
agency under Federal permit or license, such department or agency
first shall consult with the United States Fish and Wildlife Service,
Department of the Interior, and with the head of the agency exercising
administration over the wildlife resources of the particular State
wherein the impoundment, diversion, or other control facility is to be
constructed, with a view to the conservation of wildlife resources by
preventing loss of and damage to such resources as well as providing
for the development and improvement thereof in connection with such
water-resource development.

(b) In furtherance of such purposes, the reports and recommendations
of the Secretary of the Interior on the wildlife aspects of such projects, and any report of the head of the State agency exercising administration over the wildlife resources of the State, based on surveys
and investigations conducted by the United States Fish and Wildlife
Service and such State agency for the purpose of determining the possible damage to wildlife resources and for the purpose of determining
means and measures that should be adopted to prevent the loss of or
damage to such wildlife resources, as well as to provide concurrently
for the development and improvement of such resources, shall be
made an integral part of any report. . . . Recommendations of the
Secretary of the Interior shall be as specific as is practicable with
respect to features recommended for wildlife conservation and development, lands to be utilized or acquired for such purposes, the results expected, and shall describe the damage to wildlife attributable
to the project and the measures proposed for mitigating or compensat-
ing for these damages. The reporting officers in project reports of
the Federal agencies shall give full consideration to the report and
recommendations of the Secretary of the Interior and to any report
of the State agency on the wildlife aspects of such projects, and the

project plan shall include such justifiable means and measures for wildlife purposes as the reporting agency finds should be adopted to obtain maximum overall project benefits. . . .

§ 663. Same—conservation, maintenance, and management of wildlife resources; development and improvement.

(a) Subject to the exceptions prescribed in section 662(h) of this title, whenever the waters of any stream or other body of water are impounded, diverted, the channel deepened, or the stream or other body of water otherwise controlled or modified for any purpose whatever, including navigation and drainage, by any department or agency of the United States, adequate provision, consistent with the primary purposes of such impoundment, diversion, or other control, shall be made for the use thereof, together with any areas of land, water, or interests therein, acquired or administered by a Federal agency in connection therewith, for the conservation, maintenance, and management of wildlife resources thereof, and its habitat thereon, including the development and improvement of such wildlife resources pursuant to the provisions of section 662 of this title. . . .


STATES

NEW YORK ENDANGERED SPECIES ACT (1972)
N.Y. Environmental Conservation Law Sec. 11-0535

§ 11-0535. Endangered species.

1. For the purposes of this section, "endangered species" shall mean those species of fish and wildlife designated by the department . . . as seriously threatened with extinction. Such order shall include, but not be limited to, endangered species as so designated by the Secretary of the Interior. . . .

2. Notwithstanding any other provision of this chapter, the importation, transportation, possession or sale of any endangered species of fish or wildlife, or hides or other parts thereof, or the sale or possession with intent to sell any article made in whole or in part from the skin, hide or other parts of any endangered species of fish or wildlife is prohibited except under license or permit from the department.

# APPENDIX A:
# ORGANIZATIONS;
# GOVERNMENT AGENCIES;
# PUBLIC INTEREST
# LAW FIRMS

## ORGANIZATIONS

The Conservation Directory supplies annually revised, extensive listings of citizens' groups, both national and state-by-state. Similar lists appear in the Directory of Consumer Protection and Environmental Agencies, and briefer ones in Environment U.S.A. and Environmental Information Sources Handbook.

## GOVERNMENT AGENCIES

### Federal

A Clear View, Washington Information Directory, and Working on the System are the most useful guides to agencies of the federal government and committees of Congress. There are also listings in Conservation Directory, Directory of Consumer Protection and Environmental Agencies, Environmental Information Sources Handbook, and Environment U.S.A. The Federal Laws section of Environment Reporter lists membership of congressional committees and subcommittees and federal agencies.

### States

State-by-state listings appear in the Conservation Directory and Directory of Consumer Protection and Environmental Agencies, and briefer ones in Environment U.S.A.

## PUBLIC INTEREST LAW FIRMS

Public interest law firms provide legal representation to groups and interests that otherwise are unable to obtain such representation, including groups with noneconomic interests. The pattern was set by the successful work of the Legal Defense Fund of the National Association for the Advancement of Colored People in its battles over civil rights. Public interest law firms in the environmental field

524

act as watchdogs over the implementation of environmental laws.
Frequently staffed with scientists and other technical experts in addition to lawyers, they bring actions and intervene in court and administrative agency proceedings arising out of governmental action or inac-
tion. Many of these are concerned simply with holding the EPA and
other agencies to timetables spelled out in various laws. These cases
have broadened the scope and efficacy of environmental legislation.
Largely because of the public interest bar's efforts, federal agencies
now routinely fulfill NEPA requirements instead of trying to routinely
ignore them. Following is a list of some of these agencies:

Businessmen for the Public Interest
109 N. Dearborn
Chicago, Ill. 60602

Center for Law and Social Policy
1751 N Street N.W.
Washington, D.C. 20036

Center for Law in the Public Interest
10203 Santa Monica
Los Angeles, Calif. 90067

Environmental Defense Fund, Inc.
1525 18th Street N.W.                    2728 Durant Ave.
Washington, D.C. 20036                   Berkeley, Calif. 94704

                                         162 Old Town Road
                                         East Setauket, N.Y. 11733

Institute for Public Interest Representation
Prof. Victor H. Kramer
Georgetown University
Washington, D.C. 20001

Natural Resources Defense Council, Inc.
15 West 44th Street                      664 Hamilton Ave.
New York, N.Y. 10036                     Palo Alto, Calif. 94301

                                         917 15th Street N.W.
                                         Washington, D.C. 20005

Public Advocates, Inc.
433 Turk Street
San Francisco, Calif. 94102

Public Citizen Litigation Group
2000 P Street N.W.
Washington, D.C. 20036

Public Interest Research Groups
1025 15th Street N.W.
Washington, D.C. 20005

Sierra Club Legal Defense Fund, Inc.
311 California Street                  Majestic Building
San Francisco, Calif. 94104            Denver, Colo. 80202

What is the law on . . .

The "law" consists of two elements   1) Statutory law, including constitutions, statutes, municipal ordinances, rules of courts, regulations of administrative bodies, etc.:  2) Case law (decisions of courts and administrative bodies).

A fundamental doctrine of our legal system is stare decisis. Simply, this is the theory that similar cases should be decided in similar ways.  The precedent set by similar cases must be taken into account, particularly cases decided in the same jurisdiction.

To know the law on a given problem, you must therefore find all the constitutional provisions, federal and state statutes, ordinances, agency regulations, etc., that pertain to your case (agency regulations are often overlooked, e.g., no statute says you must use form 1040 to file your income tax but since it is required by IRS regulations, it is law and must be obeyed).

Then you must know the circumstances and findings of all the relevant court decisions on all levels.

All of this must be brought up to date, meaning today!

After you have found all of this and understand it all, you can then pit your new knowledge of the "law" against someone else who did exactly what you did but who came up with a different interpretation.

To make matters worse, stare decisis is by no means a guarantee, since no two cases are ever exactly alike in law and in the circumstances involved in the case.  Times change and law changes with them.  Law is therefore never a cut-and-dried matter and even those who are brilliant and who have devoted their entire lives to its study honestly disagree when the question arises, "What is the law on . . . ?"

Needless to say, not all lawyers (or judges) are brilliant.  This adds the element of chance to any court decision.  Juries add to the confusion.  Fortunately, our legal system usually allows for appeals to higher courts.

---

Portions reprinted from Research and Reference Guide #21 of Connecticut College Library, New London, Conn.

## Legal Citation

When doing legal research you will quickly come across some
odd citations such as 10 USC 971 or 71 Stat 343. Translated these
mean respectively; title 10 of the U.S. Code, section 971 and volume
71 of Statutes at Large, page 343 (a brief list and explanation of abbreviations is appended to this guide). Such citations are invariably used
in law when citing standard works familiar to lawyers.

## Federal Law

Federal laws, as soon as they are passed, are printed individually as "slip laws." These are cumulated periodically in Statutes
at Large in chronological order. Those laws which are of a permanent nature are then compiled in subject arrangement in the U.S.
Code (and U.S. Code Service).

Each agency of the government responsible for carrying out the
law issues regulations defining the specific means by which a law
will be carried out. These regulations are also binding and are part
of the "law." They are compiled in the Code of Federal Regulations,
supplemented daily by the Federal Register.

## U.S. Code
sample citation: 21 USC 97 = Title 21 section 97

Statutes at Large is a running account of the laws passed each
year. U.S. Code is the full text of federal law, in subject arrangement, as it stands right now regardless of when the individual laws
were passed. Only certain portions of the U.S. Code, however,
legally supersede the statutes at large upon which they are based.
These sections are listed in the first pages of the Code. It does not
contain acts which were temporary in nature, even if they are in effect right now.

## State laws

Each state has a code similar to the U.S. Code. These codes
go by various names, some being named after the compiler or publisher (see Table of Abbreviations), and follow various numbering and
subject classification schemes. The practice of placing the volume
or title number ahead of the name of the work is followed here as
well. Thus 47 Rev. Code Wash. Ch. 27 is the Revised Code of Wash-

ington, Title 47, Chapter 27.  Some state codes are in loose-leaf
format but most follow the pocket part arrangement common in legal
publishing: cumulative pamphlet supplements are issued each year
and placed in a specially designed pocket in the back of each volume.


## How to read laws

Our laws are written in English and are intelligible to laymen.
It may be necessary to look behind some of the "legalese" to pinpoint
the basic provisions, as we have tried to do here.  Moreover, both
the U.S. Code and state codes are well-indexed.  A half-hour spent
getting acquainted with the organization of one's own state code can be
fruitful.
It is essential not to overlook pocket parts.  These contain new
laws and amendments passed since the last printing of the full volume
and may replace text printed in the hard-cover volume.  To be completely up-to-date, these are supplemented with the session laws of
the current or most recent legislative session.


## Where to find law books

College and larger public libraries generally carry the U.S.
Code (annotated or unannotated edition) and compilations of laws of
their own state.  County courthouses generally have law libraries.
Laws and other legal materials of other states can be found in libraries
of law schools and major bar associations.

STATUTES AND ENACTMENTS

Federal

## AREAS OF CONCERN

citizen participation            71-74, 103-04, vi
citizen suits                    vi, 73, 105-08
coastal zone                     139-40, 176-203
conservation easements           220, 240-43
conservation of natural
  resources                      Chap. 9
constitutional rights            70, 97-100
critical areas                   131, 137-38, 150-62

detergents                       467, 496, 503
development rights transfer      109-10, 122-25
drinking water                   368, 385-94

easements                        220, 240-42
electric power plants            140-41, 203-17
endangered species               Chap. 14
energy                           viii, Chap. 2
environmental impact state-
  ments                          vi, 69, 77, 81-86, 96-100
environmental policy             Chap. 3
environmental rights             70-71, 97-100

feed lots                        502-03
fish and wildlife                68, Chap. 14
flood plains                     139-40, 181-87, 489
food additives                   368, 373-75
forestry                         300-03, 304-07, 312-20

hazardous substances             Chap. 11
highways                         266, 420-21, 423-35
historic preservation            Chap. 4

industry, heavy                  197-98, 210-17

land use                         Chap. 5
lead                             384-86

mass transportation              3, 421-22, 438-45
mining                           302-04, 305-07, 321-47
motor vehicles                   1-3, 11-21, 31, 260-64, 266-67,
                                 362-64

natural resources                Chap. 9
nature preserves                 Chap. 6
noise                            137-38, Chap. 7
nuclear energy                   viii, 30, 35-39, 368-70, 452-63

MONOGRAPHS

America's Land and Its Uses. Marion Clawson. Johns Hopkins, 1972.
166 pp. $8.50.

The Automobile and the Regulation of Its Impact on the Environment.
Frank P. Grad and A. Rosenthal. University of Oklahoma Press,
1975. 481 pp. $19.95.

Battle for the Wilderness. Michael Frome. Praeger, 1974. 246 pp.
$8.95.

The philosophical foundations and the politics of the Wilderness
Act of 1964.

Beyond the Energy Crisis. John Maddox. McGraw-Hill, 1975. 208
pp. $8.95.

Calls for reduced oil consumption and development of new energy
sources, primarily nuclear. The author's Doomsday Syndrome
(1972) is a reasoned critique of environmentalist positions.

A Citizen's Action Guide to the Federal Flood Insurance Program.
American Rivers Conservation Council, 324 C Street S.E.,
Washington, D.C. 20003, 1974. 8 pp. Contribution.

A Citizen's Guide to Clean Water. Izaak Walton League of America,
1800 N. Kent Street, Arlington, Va. 22209, 1973. 93 pp. Free.

Detailed explanation of the FWPCA, with emphasis on citizen action.

A Clear View: Guide to Industrial Pollution Control. James S. Can-
non. Rodale, 1976. 246 pp. $6.95; $3.95 paperback.

A step-by-step guide for laymen to enforcement of air and water
acts and to information sources for economic and technical data.
Lists of state air and water pollution control agencies, EPA and
OSHA regional offices. Tables showing ambient air quality
standards, new source standards (air and water), effluent limitation guidelines, toxic substances standards, others.

Coastal Zone Management. U.S. Senate, Committee on Commerce.
    Superintendent of Documents, Washington, D.C. 20402, 1974.
    196 pp. $2.10.

    Proceedings of the Second Annual Coastal Zone Management
    Conference, 1974.

Congress and the Nation's Environment. U.S. Senate, Committee on
    Interior and Insular Affairs. Superintendent of Documents,
    Washington, D.C. 20402, 1975. 940 pp.

    Summary of actions of the 93rd Congress, prepared by the Con-
    gressional Research Service of the Library of Congress.

The Cost of Clean Air. U.S. Environmental Protection Agency.
    Senate Document Room, Washington, D.C. 20510, 1973. 104
    pp. Free.

    Annual report to Congress.

The Costs of Sprawl. U.S. Council on Environmental Quality. Super-
    intendent of Documents, Washington, D.C. 20402, 1974. Execu-
    tive summary: 55¢ paperback. S/N 4111-00023; Detailed cost
    analysis: S/N 4111-00021; Literature review and bibliography:
    $3.25 paperback. S/N 4111-00022.

Defending the Environment. Joseph L. Sax. Knopf, 1971. 252 pp.
    $6.95.

    Account of leading environmental litigation of the 1960s by the
    author of Michigan's Environmental Protection Act.

Don't Leave It All to the Experts: The Citizen's Role in Environmental
    Decision Making. U.S. Environmental Protection Agency. Super-
    intendent of Documents, Washington, D.C. 20402, 1972. 20 pp.
    55¢. EP 1.2:D71.

The Economics of Airborne Emission: The Case for an Air Rights
    Market. Douglas R. MacKintosh. Praeger, 1973. 121 pp.
    $13.50.

The Economics of Clean Water. U.S. Environmental Protection Agen-
    cy. Agency of U.S. Senate, Public Works Committee, 1973.
    120 pp.

    Annual report to Congress.

The Economics of Environmental Improvement. Donald Savage.
    Houghton-Mifflin, 1974. $5.25 paperback.

    "The environmental problem is a special case of the general
    concept of market failure." A superior text.

Energy and the Environment—Electric Power. U.S. Council on En-
    vironmental Quality. Superintendent of Documents, Washington,
    D.C. 20402, 1973. 58 pp. 85¢ paperback. S/N 4111-00019.

Energy Conservation in Building Design. AIA Research Corp. Amer-
    ican Institute of Architects, 1974. $5.00 paperback.

Energy, Ecology, Economy. Gerald Garvey. Norton, 1972. 235 pp.
    $8.95; $3.75 paperback.

    The concept and application of effluent charges. Under custo-
    mary practice, costs of resource extraction are charged to the
    public rather than reflected in the cost of the product.

Energy, Economic Growth and the Environment. Sam Schurr, ed.
    Johns Hopkins, 1972. 232 pp. $10.00; $2.95 paperback.

    Papers read at a 1971 Resources for the Future symposium, of
    continuing significance and supplying excellent references.

Energy from Geothermal Resources. U.S. House, Committee on
    Science and Astronautics, Subcommittee on Energy. Superin-
    tendent of Documents, Washington, D.C. 20402, 1974. 88 pp.

Energy Policy and Resource Management. U.S. House, Committee
    on Science and Astronautics, Subcommittee on Energy. Super-
    intendent of Documents, Washington, D.C. 20402, 1974. 100
    pp.

Energy: The New Era. S. David Freeman. Walker, 1974. 386 pp.
    $14.50. Also Vintage Books, $2.45 paperback.

    Analysis of energy crisis and proposed solutions by the director
    of the Ford Foundation's Energy Policy Project.

Environment and the Law. Irving J. Sloan. Oceana, 1971. 120 pp.
    $4.00.

    Includes chapters on procedural aspects of environmental law
    and international aspects.

Environmental Economics. Joseph J. Seneca and Michael K. Taussig.
Prentice-Hall, 1974. 354 pp. $11.95.

Discussion of environmental control tools—such as effluent
charges, regulation, prohibition, government environmental
services—and of relation of population to economic growth and
environmental quality.

Environmental Impact Handbook. Robert Burchell and David Listokin.
Center for Urban Policy Research, Rutgers University, New
Brunswick, N.J. 08903, 1975. $8.95 paperback.

Environmental Impact Requirements in the States: NEPA's Offspring.
Thaddeus C. Trzyna. Center for California Public Affairs,
226 W. Foothill Blvd., Claremont, Calif. 91711, 1974. 83 pp.
$6.50.

Environmental Issues; Population, Pollution and Economics. Lawrence
G. Hines. Norton, 1973. 339 pp. $9.75; $3.95 paperback.

The Environmental Law Handbook. Norman J. Landau and Paul D.
Rheingold. Ballantine, 1971. Out of print.

Environmental Legislation. William D. Hurley. Charles C. Thomas,
Springfield, Ill., 1971. 81 pp. $6.50.

Environmental Policy and Administration. Daniel H. Henning. American Elsevier, 1974. 205 pp. $12.50.

Environmental Policy: Concepts and International Implications. Al-
bert E. Utton and Daniel H. Henning. Praeger, 1973. 266 pp.
$15.00.

Reprints of July 1971 and April 1972 issues of Natural Resources
Journal.

Environmental Politics. Stuart S. Nagel. Praeger, 1974. 342 pp.
$20.00.

Papers read at a 1973 symposium.

Environmental Quality and Society. Richard A. Tybout. Ohio State
University Press, 1975. $7.50 paperback.

Environmental Quality and Water Development. Charles R. Goldman.
Freeman, 1973. 510 pp. $17.50.

Papers for a study sponsored by the National Water Commission, covering political, legal, and technical aspects of water resources controls in the United States, the states, and abroad. Note "The American Public's Concern with the Environment" (pp. 135-56), a good summary of environmental activism with bibliography, and "Decision-Making at Local, State, Federal and International Levels" (pp. 398-412).

The Forest Service: A Study in Public Land Management. Glen O. Robinson. Johns Hopkins, 1975. 368 pp. $16.95; $4.95 paperback.

Broad retrospective survey.

Forests for Whom and for What? Marion Clawson. Johns Hopkins, 1975. 175 pp. $11.95; $3.65 paperback.

Future forest policies for private and public lands.

Future Land Use: Energy, Environmental, and Legal Constraints. Robert W. Burchell and David Listokin. Center for Urban Policy Research, Rutgers University, New Brunswick, N.J. 08903, 1975. 369 pp. $17.95.

Papers on growth controls by various authors.

The Good Earth of America: Planning Our Land Use. C. L. Harriss. Prentice-Hall, 1974. 179 pp. $7.95; $2.95 paperback.

The Grass Roots Primer. James Robertson and John Lewallen. Sierra Club Books, 1975. 224 pp. $7.95 paperback.

A Guide to Federal Programs for Historic Preservation. National Trust for Historic Preservation, 1974. 400 pp. $8.00 paperback.

Historic Preservation: A Guide to State Programs. National Trust for Historic Preservation, 1976. 542 pp. $9.00 paperback; Supplement 1976, $3.00.

Historic Preservation in California—A Legal Handbook. Stanford Environmental Law Society. National Trust for Historic Preservation, 1975. 146 pp. $3.95 paperback.

Impact of Federal Legislation and Programs on Private Land in Urban and Metropolitan Development. Joseph Stevens. Praeger, 1973. 266 pp. $16.50; $7.95 paperback.

In Defense of People. Richard Neuhaus. Macmillan, 1971. 315 pp. $6.95.

Environmentalists are charged with overlooking urban problems.

Issues and Recommendations—State Critical Areas Programs. Council of State Governments, Lexington, Ky. 40511, 1974. 45 pp. $2.00 paperback.

Issues for Consideration: Review of National Breeder Reactor Program. U.S. Congress, Joint Committee on Atomic Energy. Superintendent of Documents, Washington, D.C. 20402, 1975. 677 pp. $5.55 paperback. S/N 052-070-03043-7.

Comments by concerned groups and individuals, with bibliography of literature published 1973-May 1975.

The Land No One Knows: America and the Public Domain. T. H. Watkins and Charles S. Watson. Sierra Club Books, 1975. 256 pp. $9.95.

Land: Private Property, Public Control. R. W. G. Bryant. Harvest House, Montreal, 1972. $12.50.

Though the emphasis is Canadian, the discussion of site value, current use, and other forms of land taxation is valuable.

Land Use Controls in New York State; A Handbook on the Legal Rights of Citizens. Natural Resources Defense Council, Inc. Dial, 1975. 368 pp. $12.95.

Chapters dealing with federal legislation and "property tax myths and realities" are applicable to other states as well.

Land Use Controls: Present Problems and Future Reforms. David Listokin. Center for Urban Policy Research, Rutgers University, New Brunswick, N.J. 08903, 1974. 398 pp. $8.95.

Reprints of previously published materials.

Land Use Management and Regulation in Hazardous Areas. Earl J. Baker and Joe G. McPhee. U.S. Senate, Committee on Interior and Insular Affairs, 1975. 129 pp. Free.

Assessment of research on natural hazards by staff at Institute of Behavioral Science, University of Colorado.

Land Use, Urban Form and Environmental Quality. University of Chicago Press, 1974. 440 pp. $5.00 paperback.

Study by the University's Department of Geography for the U.S. Environmental Protection Agency, investigating the relation between patterns of urban development and air and water quality.

Law and the Environment. Malcolm Baldwin. Walker, 1970. 432 pp. $15.00.

Proceedings of a conference sponsored by the Conservation Foundation in September 1969, the first assembly of the new environmental law profession.

Legal Foundations of Land Use Planning. Jerome Rose. Center for Urban Policy Research, Rutgers University, New Brunswick, N.J. 08903, 1974. 319 pp. $10.00.

The Legislation of Product Safety. Samuel S. Epstein. Massachusetts Institute of Technology Press, 1974. 2 volumes. $15.00.

Covers chemicals, electronic products, radiation, drugs and cosmetics, pesticides, food additives.

The Logarithmic Century. Ralph E. Lapp. Prentice-Hall, 1973. 228 pp. $6.95.

Attempt at a balanced view of energy and environmental needs by a physicist.

Man and His Environment: Law. Earl Finbar Murphy. Harper, 1971. 168 pp. $5.50 paperback.

Basic concepts and principles of legal control of environmental usage, measurement of environmental costs and values.

Material Needs and the Environment Today and Tomorrow. National Commission on Materials Policy. Superintendent of Documents, Washington, D.C. 20402, 1973. 312 pp. $3.20. S/N 5203-00005.

The commission's final report.

The Mirage of Safety: Food Additives and Federal Policy. Beatrice Trim Hunter. Scribner's, 1975. $8.95.

Documented critique of FDA.

Motorcycle Park Planning and Management. Motorcycle Industry Council, 1001 Connecticut Avenue N.W., Washington, D.C. 20036, 1973. 2d ed. 24 pp. Free.

NEPA in the Courts. Frederick R. Anderson. Johns Hopkins, 1973.
   324 pp.  $15.00; $6.95 paperback.

   The case law under the National Environmental Policy Act.

New Directions in United States Water Policy. National Water Commission. Superintendent of Documents, Washington, D.C.
   20402, 1973.  197 pp.  $2.50.  Y3.N 21/24:2P75.

   Summary, conclusions, and recommendations from commission's
   final report.

The New Oregon Trail. Conservation Foundation, 1717 Massachusetts
   Avenue N.W., Washington, D.C.  20036, 1974.  $2.00 paper-
   back.

   Accounts by Conservation Foundation staff members of the
   drafting, passage, and implementation of state land-use legislation in Oregon.

OCS Oil and Gas—An Environmental Assessment. U.S. Council on Environmental Quality. Superintendent of Documents, Washington,
   D.C.  20402, 1974.  5 volumes.  $31.00.  S/N 4000-00322-6.

   Volume 1 (214 pp., $2.90) contains summary and findings.

The Off-Road Vehicle and Environmental Quality. Malcolm Baldwin
   and Dan H. Stoddard, Jr. Conservation Foundation, 1973.  2d
   ed.  61 pp.  $4.00 paperback.

   Documented study of ORV's, their effects on vegetation and wildlife, safety, and other aspects. Includes chart of state regulations.

One Third of the Nation's Land; A Report to the President and to the
   Congress. U.S. Public Land Law Review Commission. Superintendent of Documents, Washington, D.C.  20402, 1970.  342
   pp.  $4.50.  Y3.P96/7:20n2.

Our Land and Water Resources; Current and Prospective Supplies
   and Uses. U.S. Department of Agriculture, Economic Research
   Service. Superintendent of Documents, Washington, D.C.  20402,
   1974.  54 pp.  $1.00 paperback.  S/N 0100-03250.

People or Penguins. William Baxter. Columbia University Press,
   1974.  110 pp.  $1.95 paperback.

   Argues that there is a level of "optimal pollution."

The Politics of Environmental Concern. Walter A. Rosenbaum.
Praeger, 1973. 304 pp. $9.00.

Explores the genesis of the environmental political movement in
the 1960s and the process of shaping public policy.

The Politics of Pollution in a Comparative Perspective. Cynthia H.
Enloe. McKay, 1975. 342 pp. $12.50; $4.95 paperback.

The Politics of the Ocean. Edward Wenk, Jr. University of Washington Press, 1974. 590 pp. $14.95.

Pollution, Prices, and Public Policy. Allen V. Kneese and Charles
L. Schultze. Brookings Institution, 1775 Massachusetts Avenue
N.W., Washington, D.C. 20036, 1975. 125 pp. $2.95.

A critique of federal pollution control approaches. Marketplace
mechanisms are said to be preferable.

Pollution, Resources and the Environment. Alain C. Enthoven and A.
Myrick Freeman. Norton, 1974. 3rd ed. 285 pp. $10.00;
$2.95 paperback.

Anthology of previously published articles.

The Quiet Revolution in Land Use Control. U.S. Council on Environmental Quality. Superintendent of Documents, Washington, D.C.
20402, 1971. 327 pp. $2.75 paperback. S/N 4111-0006; Sum-
mary report: 34 pp. 45¢ paperback. PrEx 14.2:L22/Sum.

Seminal study of early state and regional land use controls.

Readings on Land Use Policy. U.S. Senate, Committee on Interior
and Insular Affairs. Superintendent of Documents, Washington,
D.C. 20402, 1975. 642 pp. $5.30. S/N 051-070-02983-8.

Reprints of reports (or portions of reports) published by the
American Bar Association, Bureau of National Affairs, Conservation Foundation, Council on Environmental Quality, Council
of State Governments, and others.

Regional Environmental Management. L. Edwin Coate, ed. Wiley,
1976. 348 pp. $19.95.

Proceedings of 1973 conference.

Regulation of Flood Hazard Areas. U.S. Water Resources Council,
2120 L Street N.W., Washington, D.C. 20037. Superintendent

of Documents, Washington, D.C. 20402, 1972-73. 2 volumes.
$5.00.

Report on Aircraft/Airport Noise. U.S. Environmental Protection
Agency. Superintendent of Documents, Washington, D.C. 20402,
1973. 116 pp. $1.25 paperback. S/N 5270-01936.

Report to the People. Hawaii State Land Use Commission, P.O. Box
2359, Honolulu, Hawaii 96804, 1975. 36 pp. Free.

Representative Government and Environmental Management. Edwin
T. Haefele. Johns Hopkins, 1973. 188 pp. $8.95.

Analysis of regional planning in river basins and the San Francisco Bay area.

The Restoration of the Earth. Theodore Taylor. Harper & Row, 1973.
166 pp. $7.95.

Argues containment of environmental effects of human activity
within areas dedicated to such activity.

Slow Start in Paradise. Conservation Foundation, 1717 Massachusetts
Avenue N.W., Washington, D.C. 20036, 1974. $2.00 paper-
back.

Accounts by Conservation Foundation staff members of the drafting, passage, and implementation of state land-use legislation
in Florida.

So Goes Vermont. Conservation Foundation, 1717 Massachusetts
Avenue N.W., Washington, D.C. 20036, 1974. $2.00 paper-
back.

Accounts by Conservation Foundation staff members of the drafting, passage, and implementation of state land-use legislation in
Vermont.

Space Adrift: Landmark Preservation and the Market Place. John J.
Costonis. University of Illinois Press, 1974. 207 pp. $10.00.

Costonis originated the "transfer of development rights" concept
used for historic and natural resource preservation.

State Environmental Management: Case Studies of Nine States. Eliza-
beth H. Haskell. Praeger, 1973. 283 pp. $16.50.

Illinois, Maine (land use), Maryland (solid waste), Michigan
(citizen suits), Minnesota, New York, Vermont (land use),
Washington, Wisconsin are the states studied.

State Land Use Programs. U.S. Senate, Committee on Interior and
Insular Affairs. Superintendent of Documents, Washington,
D.C. 20402, 1974. 95 pp. $1.10 paperback. Y 4.In 8/13:L22/
11.

Summaries of land use regulation in eight states (California,
Colorado, Connecticut, Maryland, Nevada, New York, Oregon,
Washington) prepared by a committee of the American Bar Association in 1973. Also includes fifty-state survey of state land
use controls.

State Programs for the Differential Assessment of Farm and Open
Space Land. U.S. Department of Agriculture, Economic Research Service. Agricultural Economic Report No. 256. 1974.
65 pp. Free.

Analysis of preferential assessment, deferred taxation, restrictive agreements, and summaries of laws in 31 states.

Status of Environmental Economics. U.S. Senate, Committee on Public Works. Superintendent of Documents, Washington, D.C.
20402, 1975. 203 pp. $2.00. Y 4.P96/10:94-6.

Excerpts from macro- and microeconomic studies commissioned
by the Council on Environmental Quality and reprints of journal
articles published 1974-75, compiled by the Congressional Research Service.

The Taking Issue. U.S. Council on Environmental Quality. Superintendent of Documents, Washington, D.C. 20402, 1973. 329 pp.
$2.35. S/N 4111-00017.

The case law on the taking of property.

Technology and Growth; The Price We Pay. Ezra J. Mishan. Praeger,
1969. 193 pp. $7.95; $2.95 paperback.

Argues that amenities such as quiet and clean air should not be
treated as free goods, but as property with compensation for
their loss.

A Time to Choose: America's Energy Future. Ford Foundation Energy Policy Project. Ballinger, 1974. 512 pp. $12.95; $4.95
paperback.

The project's final report projects three possible scenarios for future energy use: historical growth, technical fix, and zero growth.

To Preserve a Heritage: Conservation Easements. Maryland Environmental Trust, Baltimore, Md., 1974. 24 pp. $1.50 paperback.

Legal foundation, potential use, and tax consequences of easement donations, based on Maryland law.

Toward a Steady-State Economy. Herman Daly. Freeman, 1973. 332 pp. $8.95; $3.95 paperback.

Anthology of previously published work examining the measures required to reach the "stationary state" of constant capital and constant population projected by John Stuart Mill.

Urban Mass Transportation: A Dozen Years of Federal Policy. George M. Smerk. Indiana University Press, 1974. 448 pp. $14.95.

Comprehensive work providing useful references.

The Use of Land. William K. Reilly. Crowell, 1973. 318 pp. $3.95 paperback.

The influential report of the Rockefeller-funded Task Force on Land Use and Urban Growth.

Water Policies for the Future. National Water Commission. Water Information Center, Inc., Port Washington, N.Y. 11050, 1973. 579 pp. $17.50. Also Superintendent of Documents, Washington, D.C. 20402, 1973. $9.30 paperback. S/N 5248-00006.

The commission's final report.


ENVIRONMENTAL LAW TEXTS AND TREATISES

Cases and Materials on Environmental Law. Oscar Gray. Bureau of National Affairs, 1973. 1420 pp. $19.50.

Cases and Materials on Environmental Law and Policy. John Hanks, Eva Hanks, Dan Tarlock. West Publishing Co., 1974. 1150 pp. $20.00.

Cases and Materials on Legislation: An Environmental Perspective. Gilbert T. Venable. College of Law, Arizona State University, Tempe, Ariz. 85281, 1972. 170 pp. $3.00. Mimeographed.

Environmental Control: Priorities, Policies and the Law. Frank P.
    Grad. Columbia University Press, 1971. 311 pp. $12.50.

Environmental Planning: Law of Land and Resources. Arnold W.
    Reitze. North American International, Washington, D.C.
    20005, 1974. $25.00.

Federal Environmental Law. Environmental Law Institute. West
    Publishing Co., 1974. 1600 pp. $22.50.

    Contributions by authorities in government, academia, private
    practice, public interest law firms, and other environmental
    organizations.

Treatise on Environmental Law. Frank P. Grad. Matthew Bender,
    1973-  . 3 volumes. $150.00.


## REFERENCE BOOKS AND ANNUALS

Annual Report. U.S. Council on Environmental Quality. Superinten-
    dent of Documents, Washington, D.C. 20402, 1970-  . $5.20.
    S/N 4000-00327 (1974 report).

    Each volume contains summaries of the year's events, tables,
    charts, reprints of important documents, and notes providing
    citations to important laws, government reports, and other pub-
    lications. The prime entry point to environmental information.

Conservation Directory. National Wildlife Federation, 1412 16th
    Street N.W., Washington, D.C. 20036. 220 pp. $2.50 paper-
    back (1975 issue).

    Federal, state, regional, Canadian, and international agencies
    and organizations.

Directory of Consumer Protection and Environmental Agencies. Aca-
    demic Media, 1973. 627 pp. $44.50.

    Private and public agencies.

Encyclopedia of Environmental Science. McGraw-Hill, 1974. 754
    pp. $24.50.

    Approximately 300 articles selected from the multivolume Mc-
    Graw-Hill Encyclopedia of Science and Technology.

Energy Directory. Environment Information Center, 124 East 39th
     Street, New York, N.Y. 10016, 1974. 418 pp. $50.00.

     State, regional, federal, and international agencies, including
     congressional committees, names and telephone numbers of
     contact individuals, professional and trade associations.

Energy Information Resources: An Inventory of Energy Research and
     Development Information Resources in the Continental United
     States, Hawaii and Alaska. American Society for Information
     Science, 1155 Sixteenth Street, Washington, D.C. 20036, 1975.
     207 pp. $18.50.

     Federal and state agencies, professional and trade associations,
     publications and publishers.

The Environment Committees. Ralph Nader, Congress Project.
     Grossman, 1975. 340 pp. $16.50.

Environment Index. Environment Information Center, 1970–
     $75.00 each year.

     Annual index to monthly Environment Abstracts, with review of
     congressional action during the year.

Environment Law Review. H. Floyd Sherrod, ed. Clark Boardman
     Co., 1970–     $32.50 each year.

     Reprints of selected law review articles published in the previous
     year, with an introductory survey by the editor.

Environment U.S.A. Bowker, 1974. 451 pp. $15.95.

     Lists of organizations, agencies, books (pre-1972), films, and
     so on. Note chapter "The Environment and the Law" (pp. 258–
     74), an introduction by a staff attorney of the Natural Resources
     Defense Council.

Environmental Information Sources Handbook. Garwood R. Wolff, ed.
     Simon & Schuster, 1974. 568 pp. $25.00.

     Organizations, federal, state, and interstate agencies, journals,
     other publications, films, curriculum sources, and directories
     are listed and annotated.

Finding the Law, a Guide to Legal Research. David Lloyd. Oceana,
     1974. 119 pp. $4.00.

Easy-to-understand guide, including "Researching Environmental Law" (pp. 51-56).

Land Use Controls Annual. American Society of Planning Officials, 1313 East 60th Street, Chicago, Ill. 60637. $7.00 each year.

Survey articles.

Legal Secretary's Complete Handbook. Besse May Miller. Prentice-Hall, 1970. 684 pp. $8.95.

Part V includes "The Law Library and How to Use It," "Latin Words and Phrases," "Law Terms," tables of abbreviations.

Suggested State Legislation. Council of State Governments, Lexington, Ky. 40511, 1941- . $6.50 paperback.

Annual compilation of model statutes and uniform acts. Volumes for 1973 and 1974 contain proposals of the National Symposium on State Environmental Legislation (April 1973).

Washington Information Directory 1975-76. Congressional Quarterly, 1414 22nd Street N.W., Washington, D.C. 20037, 1974. 864 pp. $18.00. Also Quadrangle, $7.95 paperback.

Executive agencies, offices within agencies, congressional committees and subcommittees, nongovernmental groups (including unions), listed by subject and with names, addresses, and telephone numbers. Pertinent subjects include area and regional development (pp. 61-63), energy (chap. 6), natural resources, environment, and agriculture (chap. 15), transportation (pp. 579-611).

Working on the System. James R. Michael. Basic Books, 1974. 950 pp. $15.00.

Introductory chapters on relations between federal agencies and citizens are followed by chapters dealing separately with the Freedom of Information Act, the Administrative Procedure Act, and a number of agencies, including EPA, OSHA, Consumer Products Safety Commission, many others. A Nader Organization publication.

## COMPILATIONS OF LAWS

Atomic Energy Legislation Through 93rd Congress, 2d Session. U.S.
Congress, Joint Committee on Atomic Energy. 1975. 497 pp.
$4.25 paperback.

Annually updated compilation of federal laws and treaties and
sundry other materials.

Citizens' Handbook on Environmental Legislation. Bill Williamson.
Northwestern School of Law, Portland, Oreg. 97219, 1972. 23
pp. $3.00.

A Compilation of Federal Laws Relating to Conservation and Development of Our Nation's Fish and Wildlife Resources, Environmental
Quality, and Oceanography. U.S. House, Committee on Merchant
Marine and Fisheries. Superintendent of Documents, Washington, D.C. 20402, 1975. 844 pp. $10.20. S/N 052-070-02971-4.

Federal Power Commission Laws and Hydro-Electric Power Development Laws. U.S. Congress. 1975. 433 pp. $3.85.

Covers 66th through 93rd Congress.

Laws of the United States Relating to Water Pollution Control and Environmental Quality. U.S. House, Committee on Public Works.
Superintendent of Documents, Washington, D.C. 20402, 1973.
55 pp. $3.10. S/N 5270-01765.

Laws Relating to Forestry, Game Conservation, Flood Control and
Related Subjects. U.S. Congress. 1975. 705 pp. $5.80.

Noise Source Regulation in State and Local Noise Ordinances. U.S.
Environmental Protection Agency. Superintendent of Documents,
Washington, D.C. 20402, 1973. 15 pp. 35¢ paperback. Ep
1.2:N69/22.

Preservation Law Bibliography. National Trust for Historic Preservation. 1976. 125 pp. $4.00 paperback.

Summary-Digest of State Water Laws. National Water Commission.
Superintendent of Documents, Washington, D.C. 20402, 1973.
826 pp. $4.55 paperback. Y 3N21/24:2L44/2.

Summary-Digest of the Federal Water Laws and Programs. National
Water Commission. Superintendent of Documents, Washington,
D.C. 20402, 1973. 205 pp. Free.

## BIBLIOGRAPHIES

Chicorel Index to Environment and Ecology; Index to Environmental
and Urban Design. Chicorel Library Publishing Corp., 275
Central Park West, New York, NY 10024, 1975. 3 volumes.
$60.00 each.

Listing of trade and other books under more than 200 topics.

ECOL. American Library Association, 1974. 201 pp. $6.95 paper-
back.

The catalog of the Environmental Conservation Library of the
Minneapolis Public Library.

Environmental Awareness Reading List. U.S. Department of the Interior. National Technical Information Service, Springfield,
Va. 22151.

Semimonthly list of books and periodicals.

An Environmental Bibliography. U.S. Environmental Protection Agency.
Superintendent of Documents, Washington, D.C. 20402, 1974.
28 pp. 30¢. EP 1.21:En 8/974.

Annotated list of some ninety titles published through 1973.

Exchange Bibliographies. Council of Planning Librarians, Box 229,
Monticello, Ill. 61856. About $2.00 each.

Bibliographies are published at irregular intervals on topics
such as development rights transfer, environmental mangement,
many other related topics.

Senate National Fuels and Energy Policy Study. U.S. Senate, Committee on Interior and Insular Affairs. 1975. 10 pp. Free.

List of publications of the study, periodically revised.


## PERIODICALS

Audubon. National Audubon Society, 950 Third Avenue, New York,
N.Y. 10022. $13.00 a year. Bimonthly.

The magazine is known for its outstanding photography, but
"The Audubon Cause" at the back carries news of legislation
and other public policy issues.

Bulletin of the Atomic Scientists. 1020–24 East 58th Street, Chicago,
Ill. 60637. $15.00 a year. Monthly.

The leading forum for the nuclear power debate.

Catalyst for Environmental Quality. 333 East 46th Street, New York,
N.Y. 10016. $7.00 a year. Quarterly.

"Government News" column.

Coastal Zone Management Journal. 347 Madison Avenue, New York,
N.Y. 10016. $32.00 a year. Quarterly.

Columbia Journal of Environmental Law. Columbia University School
of Law, 435 West 116th Street, New York, N.Y. 10027. $15.00
a year. Semiannual.

Congressional Information Service (CIS). 600 Montgomery Building,
Washington, D.C. 20014. Rates vary. Monthly.

Congressional publications, abstracted and indexed, and available
from the publisher on microfiche, often prior to dissemination
through official channels. Annual cumulations.

Conservation Foundation Letter. 1717 Massachusetts Avenue N.W.,
Washington, D.C. 20036. $10.00 a year. Monthly.

Each issue focuses on one topic (transportation, solid waste,
wetlands, and so on).

Conservation Report. National Wildlife Federation, 1412 16th Street
N.W., Washington, D.C. 20036. Free.

Reports status of federal legislation.

Design and Environment. R.C. Publications, 355 Lexington Avenue,
New York, N.Y. 10017. $11.00 a year. Quarterly.

"Man-Environment News" column.

Digest of Public General Bills and Resolutions. Congressional Research Service, Library of Congress, Washington, D.C. 20540.
$90.00 a year. LC 14.6. Five or more cumulative issues dur-
ing each session, plus supplements. Summaries of provisions
of bills, committee and floor action, enactments, listed numeri-
cally with subject and other indexes.

Ecology Law Quarterly. University of California Law School, Berkeley,
    Calif. 94720. $10.50 a year.

Environment. Scientists' Institute for Public Information, 1438 N.
    Skinker Blvd., St. Louis, Mo. 63130. $10.00 a year. Monthly.

    "Environmental Law" column.

Environment Abstracts. Environment Information Center, 124 East
    39th Street, New York, N.Y. 10006. $200.00 a year. Monthly.

    Comprehensive indexing, abstracting, and retrieval service and
    listing of publications.

Environment Reporter. Bureau of National Affairs, 1231 25th Street
    N.W., Washington, D.C. 20037. $420.00 a year.

    Comprehensive service including weekly "Current Develop-
    ments," reprints of federal and state laws and administrative
    regulations, monographs.

Environmental Action. 1346 Connecticut Avenue N.W., Washington,
    D.C. 20036. $10.00 a year. Biweekly.

    "Government Environment" and "Legislative Roundup" occasional
    columns.

Environmental Affairs. Boston College Law School, Brighton, Mass.
    02135. $18.00 a year.

Environmental Law. Northwestern School of Law, Portland, Oreg.
    97219. $8.00 a year. 3 times a year.

Environmental Law Reporter. Environmental Law Institute, 1346
    Connecticut Avenue N.W., Washington, D.C. 20036. $2.50 a
    year. Monthly.

    Feature articles on legislation, litigation, reprints of decisions,
    federal and state laws, and citations to law review articles.

Environmental Quality Abstracts. Data Courier, Inc., 620 South Fifth
    Street, Louisville, Ky. 40202. $25.00 a year. Quarterly.

    Selections from Pollution Abstracts.

Environmental Science and Technology. American Chemical Society,
    1155 16th Street N.W., Washington, D.C. 20036. $10.00 a
    year. Monthly.

EPA Citizens' Bulletin. U.S. Environmental Protection Agency,
  Room W239, Waterside Mall, Washington, D.C. 20460. Free.
  Irregular.

FDA Consumer. U.S. Food and Drug Administration, Superintendent
  of Documents, Washington, D.C. 20402. $8.55 a year. Monthly.
  HE 20.4010.

Land Use Law and Zoning Digest. American Society of Planning Officials, 1313 East 60th Street, Chicago, Ill. 60637. Monthly.

  Among other features, each issue summarizes new state and
  federal legislation (giving citations), with annual index to new
  legislation in December issue. Copies of the laws mentioned
  are available from the publisher.

The Living Wilderness. Wilderness Society, 1901 Pennsylvania
  Avenue N.W., Washington, D.C. 20006. $10.00 a year. Quar-
  terly.

  "Capitol Watch" and "Letter from Washington" report congressional happenings.

National Parks and Conservation. National Parks and Conservation
  Association, 1701 18th Street N.W., Washington, D.C. 20009.
  $6.00 a year. Monthly.

  "Conservation Docket" reports congressional action, with annual
  wrap-up in March issue supplying citations of passed laws.

National Wildlife. National Wildlife Federation, 1412 16th Street
  N.W., Washington, D.C. 20036. Membership. Bimonthly.

  February-March issue each year includes an Environmental
  Quality Index that takes into account progress on air and water
  clean-up efforts, among other factors.

Natural Resources Journal. University of New Mexico School of Law,
  1117 Stanford, Albuquerque, N. Mex. 87131. $12.00 a year.

Not Man Apart. Friends of the Earth, 529 Commercial, San Francisco, Calif. 94111. $10.00 a year. Semimonthly.

102 Monitor. U.S. Council on Environmental Quality. Superintendent
  of Documents, Washington, D.C. 20402. $21.50 a year. Monthly.
  PrEx 14.10.

ORV Monitor. Environmental Defense Fund, 2728 Durant Avenue,
    Berkeley, Calif. 94704. $6.00 a year. Bimonthly.

Planning. American Society of Planning Officials. Membership.
    Monthly.

Pollution Abstracts. 620 S. Fifth Street, Louisville, Ky. 40202.
    $94.00 a year. Bimonthly.

Preservation News. National Trust for Historic Preservation, 740-
    748 Jackson Place N.W., Washington, D.C. 20006. $1.20 a
    year. Monthly.

    Feature articles on legislation and litigation. Status report on
    federal legislation a regular feature.

Science. American Association for the Advancement of Science, 1515
    Massachusetts Avenue, Washington, D.C. 20005. $40.00 a
    year. Weekly.

    Columns occasionally deal with environmental topics.

Sierra Club Bulletin. Sierra Club, 530 Bush Street, San Francisco,
    Calif. 94108. $8.00 a year. Monthly.

Soil Conservation. U.S. Department of Agriculture, Soil Conservation
    Service. Superintendent of Documents, Washington, D.C. 20402.
    $6.85 a year. Monthly. A 57.9.

State Government. Council of State Government Lexington, Ky. 40505.
    $7.00 a year. Quarterly.

Urban Land. Urban Land Institute, 1200 18th Street N.W., Washing-
    ton, D.C. 20036. $25.00 a year. Monthly.

    "Legal Notes" column; "Land Use Abstracts," a quarterly sup-
    plement, gives brief summaries of new publications.

Water Spectrum. U.S. Corps of Engineers, Superintendent of Docu-
    ments, Washington, D.C. 20402. $6.20 a year. Quarterly.

ARTICLES ON ADMINISTRATIVE DECISION MAKING

"Information Channels and Environmental Decision Making." Helen
    M. Ingram. Natural Resources Journal, January 1973, pp. 150-
    69.

"NEPA and the Freedom of Information Act: A Prospect for Disclosure." Gilda M. Tuoni. Environmental Affairs, Winter 1975, pp. 179-201.

"Private Influence on Environmental Policy: The Case of the National Industrial Pollution Control Council." Henry J. Steck. Environmental Law, Winter 1975, pp. 241-81.

## ABOUT THE AUTHOR

MARY ROBINSON SIVE is an information specialist and author
of Educators Guide to Media Lists (Libraries Unlimited, Inc., 1975).
A former librarian, she served as director of the Education and Library Department, Environment Information Center, New York City,
as environmental education consultant to school districts, and contributes frequently to professional journals.

Ms. Sive received her Master of Library Service degree from
Rutgers University. She is married to David Sive, well-known environmental lawyer.

ENVIRONMENTAL MANAGEMENT IN
LOCAL GOVERNMENT: A Study of Local
Response to Federal Mandate
Alan H. Magazine

ENVIRONMENTAL MODELING AND
DECISION MAKING: The U.S. Experience
Holcomb Research Institute

ENVIRONMENTAL REGULATION AND
THE ALLOCATION OF COAL: A Regional
Analysis
Alan M. Schlottmann

MANAGING ENVIRONMENTAL CHANGE:
A Legal and Behavioral Perspective
Joseph F. DiMento

PERSPECTIVES ON U.S. ENERGY POLICY:
A Critique of Regulation
edited by<br>Edward J. Mitchell

WATER POLLUTION CONTROL: Assessing
the Impacts and Costs of Environmental Standards
Ralph A. Luken<br>Edward H. Pechan